THOSE OLD SCHOOL RECORDS

1,000 Selected R&B, Rock 'n' Roll, and Soul 45 RPM Singles

1946-1987

Stephen C. Propes

Genius Music Books

Milwaukee Wisconsin USA

Originally published by Apropropes Publishing, Long Beach, California, 2018

Contact the author: writerguy@live.com

Cover design: Sylvia Propes and Stephen Propes

Published by:
Genius Music Books, an imprint of Genius Book Publishing
PO Box 250380
Milwaukee, Wisconsin 53225 USA
GeniusBookPublishing.com

ISBN: 978-1-958727-05-8

230111 Letter

Also by Stephen C. Propes

Those Oldies But Goodies, 1973

Golden Oldies: A guide to 60's record collecting, 1974

Golden Goodies: A Guide To 50's & 60's Popular Rock & Roll Record Collecting, 1975

What Was the First Rock 'N' Roll Record? (with Jim Dawson), 1992, 2022

Merry Christmas, Baby: Holiday Music from Bing to Sting (with Dave Marsh)—Hardcover 1993

L.A. R&B Vocal Groups, 1945-1965 (with Galen Gart), 2001

45 RPM: The History, Heroes, and Villains of a Pop Music Revolution (with Jim Dawson), 2003

Old School 77 Years of Southern California R&B & Vocal Group Harmony Records, 1934-2011 2013

Table of Contents

Blues, Rhythm and Blues, Rock 'n' Roll, Garage, Soul, Surf, and Rock: 1960s..... 177

Those Old School Records

To Sylvia

Introduction

Since the 1970s, and probably before, researching different genres of music meant finding out who invented what, who popularized what, when certain classic songs originated, migrated, were pirated, influenced other songs and basically set the table for what we now consider classic rock 'n' roll/rockabilly/rhythm and blues/soul and all the other forms that added texture and richness to the entire landscape. Setting tables? Rich landscape? Mixed metaphors anyone? Now you can mix your own metaphors, add a dash of rhythm, avoid having the blues and come up with an easy to use listening plan. And with YouTube available, no more record pulling, no more intense research.

From the early days of the post-war single, the idea was to sell the song and perhaps the artist, so that he, she or they could repeat and success and profits would follow. That was the idea throughout the '50s and most of the '60s until the "concept album" by the likes of the Beach Boys, The Beatles, The Doors, Carole King, Elton John and later, Aerosmith, Michael Jackson as well as dozens of other high-profile acts changed the assumption. Slowly but surely, the 45 stopped being the prime goal of recording. Instead of taking a dozen or so hit singles and making an album, an album was released and 45s were pulled from that multi-track LP. Post 1970s was no longer the era of the free-standing single, though many were released. Those fewer free-standing 45s are among those described in this work.

These are the author's choice of the best, most recognizable, highly influential and easy to hum songs and instrumentals, with a few wild cards thrown in. Except for a few influential ballads, doo wop and the like, most of the songs on this list are, well… rock or rhythm and blues. Influential pop records (Herb Alpert, etc.) are also included. History or unexpected twists on the record along with other records that either influenced or were influenced, most usually sound-a-likes, are identified as suggested pairings.

Records in this tome are in more or less chronological order; only a few are based on a speculative release date.

Sources consulted:

45cat.com
Discogs.com
http://www.las-solanas.com/arsa/index.php
http://www.originalsproject.us/
Songfacts.com
Very rarely: Wikipedia

Blues, Boogie, and Race Music

1940s

Arthur Big Boy Crudup "That's All Right" Victor/RCA 1946

Style: Blues
Where from: Omaha, NE
Where recorded: Chicago, IL
Suggested pairings: Blind Lemon Jefferson "Right Of Way Blues" 1927; Tampa Kid "Keep On Trying" 1936; Son House "My Black Mamma" 1930; Jimmy Rushing "Boogie Woogie" 1938; Arthur Big Boy Crudup "Keep Your Arms Around Me" 1944; Arthur Big Boy Crudup "If I Get Lucky" 1941

This blues combo—with Arthur Big Boy Crudup, guitar and vocal; Ransom Knowling, bass; and Judge Davis, drums—was recorded in September 1946. "I wasn't making money off those records to amount to nothing," Crudup told an interviewer as he was paid a flat sum for each song during recording sessions. Between sessions, he sharecropped or moonshined to support his family.

In March 1949, record technology radically changed with the marketing of the 45 RPM record by RCA/Victor when a reissue of Arthur Big Boy Crudup's original of "That's All Right" was the first blues 45 issued by RCA/Victor.

Remakes: Elvis Presley 1954; Marty Robbins 1955

It's said that Presley financed a Crudup session he made for Bobby Robinson's Fire Records in about 1959 which resulted in a later remake of "That's All Right," though Robinson claimed Presley had nothing to do with the record.

—

Peggy Lee "Manana" Capitol 1948

Style: Samba
Where from: North Dakota
Where recorded: Hollywood, CA

Peggy Lee (real name: Norman Jean Egstrom) arrived in Los Angeles three times: about 1937, in 1940 and about 1943. Though she also recorded for ARA, she signed with the Capitol label in 1943. Peggy Lee's "Manana" backed with "All Dressed Up With A Broken Heart" with Dave Barbour & the Brazilians, which was really Carmen Miranda's band, was her first chart topper in January 1948.

Recorded just prior to the recording ban, when "Manana" hit big, Lee recalled, litigation was begun against her and her husband Dave Barbour by songwriter Haps McKay over the song. According to Lee, the suit was thrown out when sheet music entered into evidence by McKay described the composition as a "samba," but was dated prior to the introduction of the term. Lee never recorded during the AFM recording ban, which began on January 1, 1948.

—

Wynonie Harris "Good Rockin' Tonight" King 1948

Style: Rhythm and blues
Where from: Omaha, NE
Where recorded: Cincinnati, OH
Original version: Roy Brown 1947
Suggested pairings: Lucky Millinder "There's Good News Tonight" 1946

"Good Rockin' Tonight" was a Roy Brown original recorded in 1947. It was covered by Wynonie Harris and went to #1 R&B, after Brown failed in getting the song to him. Wynonie Harris then recorded "Good

Rockin' Tonight" to cover Brown's version and created one of rock 'n' roll's most enduring hits—reissued several times in the 1950s and 1960s.

Remakes: Elvis Presley 1955; The Treniers 1956; Pat Boone 1958; James Brown 1967

—

Paul Williams & His Hucklebuckers "The Hucklebuck" Savoy 1948

Style: Rhythm and blues
Where from: Detroit, MI
Where recorded: New York City, NY
Suggested pairings: Charlie Parker "Now's the Time" 1945; Lucky Millinder "D'Natural Blues" 1949

"The Hucklebuck" by Paul Williams and His Hucklebuckers—Phil Guilbeau, trumpet; Miller Sam, tenor sax; Paul Williams, baritone and alto sax; Floyd Taylor, piano; Herman Hopkins, bass and Reetham Mallett, drums—was a major instrumental hit based on the eponymous dance craze, mainly in Newark NJ. Williams' concerts were riotous, leading some municipalities to ban the record and the dance. Williams was "kicking as he played, bending and dipping, getting down on the floor while blowing that saxophone," said Savoy producer Teddy Reig, who claimed that he taught Williams to perform vigorously.

"The Hucklebuck" became a wildly successful dance craze, partly due to its sexual connotations. The basic dance has been described as having "a double point with the feet to the side on each side (four counts) then a lift and twist of the leg and a small kick, then a shimmy, hip gyration. The dance could get very sexual in nature when done as a couple dance with the male dancing behind the female, one hand on her waist or hip and the other on her shoulder, gyrating the hips in unison or with shocking variations such as when the female dancers would lay down on their backs and the male dancers would stand over the center of her, slowly doing hip gyrations, hip rolling, wiggling dance movements, slowly working their way over and past the female's head" [streetswing.com]

Though Williams had several earlier R&B hits, "The Hucklebuck" established his popularity, and he was billed as Paul "Hucklebuck" Williams for the remainder of his career.

Covers: Roy Milton (with vocals); Lucky Millinder; Frank Sinatra; Lionel Hampton; Tito Burns; Pearl Bailey with Hot Lips Page; Louis Armstrong; Tommy Dorsey Orch with vocals by Charlie Shavers
Remake: Chubby Checker 1960

—

John Lee Hooker "Boogie Chillen" Modern 1949

Style: Blues
Where from: Clarksdale, MS
Where recorded: Detroit, MI
Suggested pairings: Blind Blake's "Hastings Street Boogie" 1939; Little Junior's Blue Flames "Feelin' Good" 1954; Lightning Slim "Just Made 21" 1956

Taken from the theme, if not the beat, of the pre-war blues legend, Blind Blake's 1939 original, "Hastings Street Boogie," refers to a club district that John Lee Hooker also sings about in "Boogie Chillen," his very first known release in 1949. Hooker's session was simple, a guitar with a microphone planted inside for echo and Hooker's tapping footsteps to keep the beat.

According to Wikipedia, Detroit label owner Bernie Besman recalled, "We amplified his guitar. He had an old Stella and no amp. We put a mike onto his guitar, and we put a speaker. This was a tiny two room studio. We put it in a toilet bowl next door, actually in a toilet bowl. Then we put a mike under that so the sound would bounce off the water, I wanted an echo effect. Then the sound went back into a speaker in the studio, came out of that, and got picked up along with his voice. I put a board under his feet to make his tapping louder, and put a mike down there."

Joe Bihari of Modern recalled, "One record that broke nationally overnight was John Lee Hooker's 'Boogie Chillen.' Saul was in Detroit, I was in New York, he picked it up from our record distributor in Detroit. Bernie Besman had the acetate, said, 'Joe, what do you think of this?' The distributor asked him to take it, see if he wanted to release it. I said, 'Saul, I think it's a hit record, I'm going to the studio, make some dubs, first thing, I'm going to Nashville, Tennessee. Gene Nobles, 50,000 watt clear channel station, they sold an awful lot of records off that station, mail order Randy's Record Shop where they sold mail order around the country.' I took it to Gene with a bottle of bourbon, I said, 'Gene, I just got this record in Detroit, I think it's a hit record. Tell me what you think.' He put it on, he played it 12 times in a row. In a day's time, when I called the office in a day or two, hey we have a smash hit in 'Boogie Chillen.' We haven't got the thing out yet. Saul got back to Los Angeles, we processed it, made the master off the acetate, went with the thing, pressed it, pressed it, pressed it, it was an overnight smash across the country. Bernie had the Sensation label at the time, but he didn't have the distribution," though he did release an alternate take as "Boogie Chillen #2" on Sensation in 1949. "I think Bernie didn't have... either you're in distribution or recording business."

Much of Hooker's bass line showed up in Little Junior's Blue Flames on "Feelin' Good" on Sun in 1954.

Answer: John Lee Hooker "Mambo Chillun" 1955
Remakes: John Lee Hooker 1959; John Fred & the Playboys 1964; The Chambers Brothers 1973

—

Big Jay McNeely "The Deacon's Hop" Savoy 1949

Style: Rhythm and blues
From and recorded in: Los Angeles, CA
Suggested pairing: Lester Young "Broadway" 1944

Having just graduated from Jordan High School in Watts, honking tenor sax player Big Jay McNeely recorded "The Deacon's Hop" in January 1949, a variation on Lester Young's "Broadway." McNeely said, "I let myself go. Fellow I'll never forget named Prince Stansill was with Ralph Bass and Savoy. He said, 'Jay I'd like you to cut a record. Fellow who owned a record shop in Watts played me a record for me by Glenn Miller, with the drum going 'da da da da.' I went home and wrote 'Deacon's Hop.'" The Deacon reference probably derived from Louis Jordan's "Deacon Jones" from 1944 as well as the Lucky Millinder hit, "Fare Thee Well Deacon Jones" from 1946. Big Jay was dubbed Deacon McNeely on his next "California Hop," a blatant slice of advertising for the popular California Club in Los Angeles. Everything became deacon with his name change for the flipside of the February 1949 hit, "Wild Wig."

"Benson's Groove," designed to tempt Chicago DJ Al Benson into playing the release, was changed to "Deacon's Groove" when all other Windy City DJs resisted a title naming the competition. McNeely's "Deac's Blowout" in 1950, "The Deacon Blows For Ray" and "The Deacon Rides Again" in 1951 ultimately wore out the deacon reference.

—

Ray Charles and the Maxim Trio "Confession Blues" Swing Time 1949

Style: Blues
Where from: Florida by way of Seattle, WA
Where recorded: Los Angeles, CA

Members of the Maxim Trio were Gosady McKee, bass; Milton S. Garret, guitar and Ray Charles, piano. This was a Johnny Moore's Three Blazers-influenced act from Seattle, formed during the heyday of that city's vibrant Jackson Street jazz era. The Maxim Trio were soon billed as the Maxim Trio with Ray Charles, and finally as Ray Charles with the Maxim Trio. According to Harold Jackson of the Jackson Brothers Orchestra, Modern Records had originally sent for Charles to audition for their label. "I came down here to cut some records," Charles told Jackson at the time. "I cut eight or 10 songs. The guys at Modern didn't like my voice, but they won't send me back home." Jackson added, "I said, 'Come out stay with us' on 69th Street."

After Charles' first hit on Down Beat, later known as Swing Time, "Modern Records searched for his tape, but couldn't find it. They had erased it and recorded someone else over it." Probably unaware their session with Charles had been erased, Modern's budget Crown label made deals with Down Beat/Swing Time to reissue much of his earlier work at the peak of Charles' popularity in the early 1960s.

Hite and Dorinda Morgan started in the music business "in the late 1920s in New York. My mother was a writer and they recorded some of her songs. They were demos. My dad published her songs himself. This was during the time Irving Berlin was buying up songs for $5 during the Depression. The Morgans came to L.A. in 1941 or 1942. They were always in the music business, but weren't making a living at it. They recorded Ray Charles' first record at Crystal Records, owned by organ player Henry Shelb, who had a recording studio and a pressing plant by the L.A. River. He recorded more or less extensively during the recording ban. He had presses there in the back of his studio, didn't have electroplating though, but put his records out there. My folks used his studio to record Ray in 1948 after they heard him sing or heard about him."

Hite and Dorinda had several labels and went on the discover and record The Beach Boys in 1961.

—

Fats Domino "The Fat Man" Imperial 1949

Style: Rhythm and blues
From and recorded in: New Orleans, LA
Suggested pairings: Jack Dupree "Junker's Blues" 1941; Lloyd Price "Lawdy Miss Clawdy" 1952; Billy Tate "Single Life" 1952; Smiley Lewis "I Hear You Knocking" 1955

Possibly inspired by the radio private eye show, "The Fat Man," as a launching pad for Fats Domino, who introduced himself in this boogie backed vocal "The Fat Man" with plenty of "wah wha's" on Imperial in 1949. This song very much borrowed from Champion Jack Dupree's tale of drug addiction, "Junker's Blues" from 1941. Recorded at the Cosimo Matassa studio at Rampart and Canal, mentioned in the rollicking lyrics, "The Fat Man" was nearly the earliest #1 R&B hit from New Orleans and set the style for various major New Orleans hits like Lloyd Price's "Lawdy Miss Clawdy" in 1952 and Smiley Lewis' "I Hear You Knocking" in 1955. There was no cover or remake of "The Fat Man," as who could?

—

Clarence Garlow "Bon Ton Roula" Macy's 1949

Style: Zydeco
Where from: ??
Where recorded: Houston, TX
Suggested pairings: Shirley & Lee "Let the Good Times Roll" 1956; Larry Williams "Bony Maronie" 1957

Louisiana Creole French for "good times roll" as in "Laissez les bons temps rouler" or "Let the good times roll," this song was a regional invitation to join in a festive celebration. Said Garlow, "I happened to be coming through the town of Houston and stopped at the Coconut Grove. They had a band and I asked the guy if I could sit in. I did and they must have liked it. They called Macy Henry and Steve Poncio to come listen and they came over. I didn't think I was good enough but they thought differently. 'Bon Ton Roula' was born in the studio when we was trying to find something to record. It caught like a shot in the arm and the crowds got bigger."

Remakes: Clarence Garlow "New Bon Ton Roulet" 1951; Emma Dell Lee 1953; "New Bon Ton Roula" by Clarence Garlow on Aladdin 1953; Goldband 1958

Blues, Rhythm and Blues, Rock 'n' Roll, and Rockabilly

1950s

Professor Longhair & His New Orleans Boys "Mardi Gras In New Orleans" Atlantic 1950

Style: Rhythm and blues
From and recorded in: New Orleans, LA

Roy Byrd as Professor Longhair was the earliest, but not the only quirky entertainer produced by the colorful New Orleans scene. "Everybody wanted a Mardi Gras song," he said. "So I wrote one." And in late 1949, he recorded the original poorly reproduced "Mardi Gras In New Orleans" by Professor Longhair & His Shufflin' Hungarians at the Hi-Hat Club for the Dallas-based Star Talent label, which quickly went out of business. As with their other pickup, "Drinkin' Wine Spo Dee O Dee," by Stick McGhee, the Atlantic label, desperate for their next big hit, went to New Orleans and brought Longhair into Cosimo's studio to record a professional version produced by Ahmet Ertugun and Herb Abramson.

Described by Billboard as "wonderfully spirited side with a strange three-beat rhythm should be great in Delta territory, and could catch in other locales." As to the "She Walks Right In" B-side: Billboard called it "hypnotic, medium tempo boogie blues swings a storm. The title phrase repeated over and over, has curiously compelling effect. Group has distinctive sound."

Remake: Fats Domino 1953

—

Johnny Otis and the Robins "Double Crossin' Blues" Savoy 1950

Style: Rhythm and blues
Where from: Vallejo, CA
Where recorded: Los Angeles, CA

In the late 1940s, there was effectively no vocal group scene in Los Angeles. Whatever records came close were the products of the combos, which generally used a single vocalist to front their generally relaxed sound. The first pairing of a vocal group act was the product of a talent show put on by Johnny Otis at his Barrelhouse Club at 11713 Wilmington Ave. in Watts. At first called the Four Bluebirds, they soon became the Robins. Recalled Robins tenor Ty Terrell, who arrived in California in 1944, "I was a church boy. White families paid my mother to have me play with their children. The three of us," Terrell and twins, Roy and Billy Richards, "started hanging out together.

Terrell continued, "In the Bay Area, after we saw Duke Ellington's Band with 'Ooh Looka There' with Sammy Davis & Will Mastin Trio on the bill doing three part harmony at the RKO Theater in Oakland, that's when we decided to come down here. We were the A-Sharp Trio in 1946, but we did not know we were dis-unified as a people. We went to work to try to sign up at all the talent shows. At the Barrelhouse run by Bardu Ali, we won $5 apiece first prize, three of us singing 'Satchelmouth Baby' and 'Ooh, Looka There Ain't She Pretty.' We were told, 'If you can sing with Bobby Nunn in here, you can sing like The Ink Spots.' We started making records for Savoy. Everywhere went in Hollywood, white people heard us singing. The guys were afraid to go up to them. I'd just go up there. 'Oh here's the King Cole Trio, you guys are the King Cole Trio.' 'No, we are A Sharp Trio.' Johnny Otis wanted us to put Bobby Nunn in the group, and said, 'You guys sing like birds, you oughta called yourself the

Robins. You'd hear the Mills Brothers on the radio, 'up a lazy river, where the Robins sing.'"

Their breakthrough release, "Double Crossing Blues," was credited to Little Esther & the Robins on Savoy and hit #10 R&B in January, 1950. It was known to record buyers of the day as "Lady Bears," because of the lyrical interplay between Little Esther and Bobby Nunn, who effectively calls her a "lady bear." Written by L.A. songwriter Jessie Mae Robinson, Johnny Otis added the lady bears dialog which he took from Apus and Estrelita, a black comedy act. At first, Savoy owner Herman Lubinsky didn't like the dub, but when WAAT DJ Bill Cook (who recorded for Savoy in 1951) out of Newark, NJ heard it, he played it on his show that evening, and the response was positive. As Lubinsky only had that song, he had to find an instrumental filler for the B-side. The first pressings used an instrumental credited to the Beale Street Gang, one of several flip sides over the years.

"Double Crossing Blues" became the first 45rpm record pressed by Savoy, a Newark, NJ-based race and jazz label dating back to 1939. "When we made 'Lady Bears' with Johnny Otis, we learned four songs, put the music to it, got a date from Ralph Bass, went to the studio for four hours," said Terrell. "When they released that stuff, it sold 300,000 copies in New York City alone in several days." When the record listed Otis as composer, songwriter Jessie Mae Robinson sued. "Johnny Otis had asked her to write a song for a recording session," said Jessie Mae Robinson's daughter June Lynch. "Some of the stuff about the bear out in the jungle was added in the studio. The song was 'Double Crossin' Blues.'" According to the L.A. Sentinel of March 30, 1950, Robinson was awarded an out-of-court settlement because her song had been appropriated and recorded by "a local drummer." "We always had some time left over, you could tell they liked the way we did it, put a bottle of wine," said Terrell. "'Double Crossin' Blues' was the tag record."

—

Baby Face Leroy Trio "Rollin' and Tumblin'" Parkway 1950/Herald 1953

Style: Blues
Where from: Mississippi
Where recorded: Chicago, IL
Suggested pairings: Gus Cannon's Jug Stompers "Minglewood Blues" 1928; Hambone Willie Newbern "Roll and Tumble Blues" 1929

With Muddy Waters on guitar and Little Walter on harmonica, the Baby Face Leroy Trio with Leroy Foster on drums recorded this chaotic, cranking original of the blues classic "Rollin' and Tumblin'" for the Parkway label of Chicago. When Muddy's label got wind of this contract no-no, they had Muddy record a more subdued version of "Rollin' and Tumblin' Part 1 & 2" on Aristocrat in April 1950, pretty much the end of that label, out of which the Chess label was born. In 1953, after Little Walter hit #1 R&B with "Juke" in 1952, "Rollin' and Tumblin'" was reissued as "Rollin'Blues" by Little Walter on the newly formed Herald label.

Cover: Muddy Waters "Rollin' and Tumblin'" 1950
Remakes: Elmore James & His Broomdusters 1960; Canned Heat 1967; Johnny Winter 1969
Many variations on "Rollin' and Tumblin'" with many titles exist

—

Muddy Waters "Rollin' Stone" Chess June 1950

Style: Blues
Where from: Mississippi
Where recorded: Chicago, IL
Original version: Robert Petway "Catfish Blues" 1941

For Chess Records' second 78, Waters turned Mississippi bluesman Robert Petway's "Catfish Blues" into a spare track he named "Rollin' Stone." "We wouldn't do it exactly like those older fellows," Waters said. "We put the beat with it, put a little drive to it." The Rolling Stones took their name from it, as well as the magazine.

—

Lowell Fulson "Every Day I Have the Blues" Swing Time/Hollywood 1950

Style: Blues
Where from: Oklahoma
Where recorded: Los Angeles, CA
Suggested pairings: Pine Top "Every Day I Have the Blues" 1935; Memphis Slim "Nobody Loves Me" 1949

As "Every Day I Have the Blues" was a reworking of Memphis Slim's "Nobody Loves Me," which itself was a rework. Fulson observed, "All you gotta do is hang around the night club circuit. Them guys come up with these songs and if you hear one you like, cut it. If you don't cut it, copyright it. I know guys, they remember a couple of lines from songs, they finish the song on out. I tried to do that to Memphis Slim. He had 'Nobody Loves Me,' the pattern was mostly the same. I changed some of the lyrics and the title. I didn't call myself stealing the song, but preparing it for myself to get it a little better for my way of singing it. I put my name on it. He hit the ceiling."

Remakes: Irene Reid 1964; B. B. King 1965; Billy Stewart 1967; Howard Tate 1968; Jimmy McGriff 1973

Memphis Slim's composer royalties from the later hits by other artists "were sufficient to buy a Rolls Royce with which to squire himself around Paris," said writer Colin Escott.

—

Ruth Brown "Teardrops From My Eyes" Atlantic October 1950

Style: Rhythm and blues
Where from: Virginia
Where recorded: New York

Ruth Brown recalled, "When Atlantic signed me they really weren't too sure whether I could fit into that pocket or not and it wasn't until they brought a writer around named Rudy Toombs who came up with the first rhythm and blues thing I did. They weren't really sure what direction I was going in. They were searching. Until that point, Ruth Brown [I] was considered just a good ballad singer, show tunes, Ethel Waters' 'Happiness Is A Thing Called Joe,' 'Good For Nothing Joe,' the Yiddish thing, 'Be A Little Boy Of Mine,' 'Tell Me Where Can I Go,' 'I Can Dream Can't I,' Andrews Sisters songs. It was when we did 'Teardrops From My Eyes,' which I was very skeptical about, that they realized they had hit on the chemistry there, that's when they started recording with the backbeat, that's when they really started. Atlantic moved into position when that record came out. I was skeptical because prior to that I had been dealing with standards, the ballad type thing. This was very possibly the first thing they gave me that dealt with a change of tempo, 4/4 was the backbeat. It was really a change of pace for me. I fought it tooth and nail, but of course Ahmet Ertegun and Herb Abramson won out and I'm glad they did, because 'Teardrops From My Eyes' was the tune that turned it around for me and for Atlantic Records too."

—

Arkie Shibley "Hot Rod Race" Mountain Dew (supposedly)/Gilt-Edge 1950

Style: Country
Where from: Arkansas
Where recorded: Hollywood, CA

Arkie Shibley recorded the original "Hot Rod Race," which pioneered racing hot rods onto the charts. This country boogie-style talking blues song was about a race between a Ford and a Mercury from San Pedro "late at night" to the Grapevine, which connected L.A. north to Bakersfield, where both cars were overtaken by a Model A. Shibley was turned down by 4-Star Records—about which he sang in "Archie's Talkin' Blues." Undeterred, "Hot Rod Race" by Arkie Shibley and his Mountain Dew Boys—Shibley, rhythm guitar; Leon Kelley, lead guitar; Jackie Hayes, bass and banjo and Phil Fregon, fiddle—recorded it on Shibley's own Mountain Dew label.

Once it began to sell, Shibley's "Hot Rod Race" was acquired by the 4-Star subsidiary, Gilt Edge, and hit the country charts in January 1951. When the song hit big, various labels issued cover versions. Lyrical references to "like white folks might" were changed in later cover versions: Tiny Hill on Mercury referenced "rich folks," Red Foley on Decca referenced "poor folks" and Ramblin' Jimmy Dolan on Capitol referenced "plain folks."

Covers: Tiny Hill; Red Foley; Ramblin' Jimmy Dolan
Sequels: Arkie Shibley "Hot Rod Race # 2" 1951; Arkie Shibley "Arkie Meets the Judge (Hot Rod Race # 3)" 1951; Arkie Shibley "The Guy in the Mercury (Hot Rod Race # 4)" 1951; Arkie Shibley "The Kid in the Model A (Hot Rod Race # 5)" 1951
Answers: Charlie Ryan "Hot Rod Lincoln" 1959; Johnny Bond 1960; Commander Cody 1972; Asleep at the Wheel

—

B.B. King "Three O'Clock Blues" RPM 1951

Style: Blues
Where from: Mississippi
Where recorded: Memphis, TN
Original version: Lowell Fulson "Three O'Clock Blues" 1948

B.B. King's recorded version of Lowell Fulson's "Three O'Clock Blues" for the newly established RPM subsidiary of Modern in 1951 was almost inevitable. As the song was original to Fulson for Bob Geddins in Oakland in 1948, no doubt RPM wanted a shot at that song. However Geddins leased it to Swing Time well before RPM was able to get to Geddins for their share of that historic 1948 Fulson session. But what RPM got out of the deal was much more than they could imagine. Though no one knew it at the time, the first RPM label release by B.B. King set the course for the Modern label, and at a much greater level, for post-World War II, or truly modern blues as we know it to this very day.

Gifted with an exceptionally clear tenor voice, King played guitar in an emotional Delta style. His debut releases on RPM (after two singles on the Bullet label out of Nashville) were "B.B. Boogie" backed with "Mistreated Woman," followed by "The Other Night Blues" backed with "Walkin' and Cryin.'" Joe Bihari said of this all-star session, "I did that in Memphis," I knew right from the start he had the talent, I think he was recorded improperly. The first thing I look for is the tune, then the artist and the arrangement, I used pretty much the same backing on 'Three O'Clock Blues,' Calvin Newborn was the guitar player, Phineas, his father. Newborn was the drummer, the piano player was Phineas Newborn, but it just wasn't coming off. Phineas played jazz while others were playing R&B. During a break in the recording, Ike Turner just came in, started playing piano and I said that's exactly what I want. I paid Phineas, Ike came in on the session and after that I hired Ike. It was at the black YMCA at Memphis... Bobby Bland, Johnny Ace, Little Junior Parker, Earl Forrest, they just happened to be there. I think I did one or two sides on each one of them. I held some of it back, maybe I felt it wasn't good enough or else it got smothered some place."

According to Joe Bihari, he and brother Saul were payola pioneers. "Saul and I made it possible, we were the first to pay disc jockeys. We paid them all cash, whenever we went in to see a disc jockey, we carried cash with us. It was never asked for, it was just a shake of the hand, $50 or $100, whatever you could afford in those days in appreciation for playing our records. In the '50s, in the early '50s, it could have been right after 'Three O'Clock Blues,' it was mostly black DJs around the country, I don't recall paying anybody in the city of L.A. What we did is we paid them cash, there was an investigation of payola in the '50s; our books were investigated, but they found no payola. We paid everybody in cash, there was no record of a check or anything, what happened after that, we quit paying, after the investigation."

—

The Dominoes "Sixty Minute Man" Federal 1951

Style: Rhythm and blues vocal group harmony
Where from: New York City, NY
Where recorded: Cincinnati, OH
Suggested pairing: Georgia White "Dan, the Backdoor Man" 1937

Talent scout Rene Hall recalled, "I was working for Syd Nathan who owned King Records who told me if I saw any talent around New York City to give him a call, he'd okay permission to audition them, send him a copy, eventually he'd offer them a contract. I heard The Dominoes showcased on the Arthur Godfrey Talent Show, also noticed the audience reaction to their presentation. I gave Syd a call. He had Ralph Bass come up to New York. They listened to the group in person, discovered they were so fabulous, he didn't want to put them on King Records, he created a label for them which he called Federal.

"We went into the old National Studios on 48th St. in New York and cut four tunes, their record was so sensational their record immediately went to #1 rhythm n blues, that was 'Do Something For Me.' He had us come to their studios in Cincinnati, that's where we recorded the famous 'Sixty Minute Man,' which also went to #1 despite the fact it was banned from radio broadcast, they said it was too suggestive, today it would be too tame."

Though not singing lead on this hit, tenor lead singer Clyde McPhatter, who had several hits with The Dominoes, was the original lead singer with The Drifters and had a distinguished career as a single artist into the 1960s. "The record was banned because it was considered suggestive by the puritanical people in charge at the time with the FCC," said Rene Hall. "It got plays everywhere, then it got pulled off which made it a hit."

The Dominoes' "Sixty Minute Man" was reissued on King in 1959, but with horribly dubbed-in female voices ruining the song in an effort to update the sound as was the custom in that period. According to collector Billy Vera, "Alternate takes of The Dominoes' 'Sixty Minute Man' without the female voices were exclusively pressed on a few Federal reissues for Times Square Records in New York in a 1961 oldies revival."

Covers: The York Brothers 1951; The Elliott Lawrence Orch. vocals by Melvin Moore 1951; Roberta Lee and Hardrock Gunter 1951
Answers: The Dudroppers "Can't Do Sixty No More" 1952; The Four Jacks "Last Of the Good Rockin' Men" 1952; The Checkers "Don't Stop Dan" 1954; The Imperials "Life Of Ease" 1954; Billy Ward & The Dominoes "Can't Do Sixty No More" 1955; The Robins "The Hatchet Man" 1955; The Cadets "Dancin' Dan" 1956; Bob Markley "Summer's Comin' On" 1960; Bobby Nunn "Sixty Minute Man Is Back" 1962
Remakes: The Jive Bombers 1952; The Untouchables 1960; The Four Sportsmen 1961

—

Jackie Brenston "Rocket 88" Chess 1951

Style: Blues
Where from: Mississippi
Where recorded: Memphis
Suggested pairings: Jimmy Liggins "Cadillac Boogie" 1947; Jesse Allen "What A Party" 1954; Little Richard "Good Golly Miss Molly" 1958

This was the session that created the competition between RPM/Modern out of Los Angeles and Chess out of Chicago for the next big blues sound out of Sam Phillips' Memphis Recording Service studio. In this case, in the March 5, 1951 session, piano player and talent scout Ike Turner showed up with his Kings of Rhythm and recorded enough material for two records. The first was credited to Jackie Brenston & his Delta Cats—Ike Turner, piano; Raymond Hill and Jackie Brenston, tenor saxes; Willie Kizart, electric guitar and Willie Sims, drums—who recorded the very influential raucous vocal, "Rocket 88," to which blues harmonica specialist James Cotton claims to have contributed. "Ike Turner was the original writer of it, but by him playing with Howlin' Wolf and I was playing with Howlin' Wolf also, before the song come out, I put a few lines in it, 'V-8 motor is smart in design.'" Cotton also said of Memphis Recording Service, "They had a small studio, but they didn't do any record pressing. Most of the Memphis people who recorded hadn't had the chance before and were ready to jump on it. Living in the south, you play two days a week if you're lucky, Friday and Saturday."

Kizart's loud and accidentally fuzz-toned guitar (legend has it that his amplifier fell off the roof of the band's car, somewhere along Highway 61, inflicting irreversible damage on its speaker) pushes into rock 'n' roll territory. Nowadays "Rocket 88" is often billed as the first rock 'n' roll record, but rock 'n' roll was the product of a gradual evolution and there are earlier competitors for this notional honor. In 1951, no one thought to call it rock 'n' roll, but it's fair to infer that a lot of record buyers sensed something different about it and liked it. The record was a big hit, and in 1954 the company even gave it a belated release on 45 rpm, most likely to compete with Bill Haley's cover on Holiday. That Chess label reissue 45 now commands a price in the four to five figure range. The 45s have been bootlegged on colored vinyl.

Cover: Bill Haley & the Saddlemen 1951

—

Peppermint Harris "I Got Loaded" Aladdin 1951

Style: Blues
Where from: Texas
Where recorded: Los Angeles, CA
Suggested pairing: Ray Charles "Roll With My Baby" 1952; Amos Milburn "Let Me Go Home Whiskey" 1953

In 1951, Peppermint Harris arrived in L.A. from Texas, where he recorded for Sittin' In With before recording a real life drinking classic, "I Got Loaded," backed with "It's You, Yes It's You" with the Maxwell Davis combo on Aladdin (3097), which went to R&B #1 on September 15, 1951. In short order, Amos Milburn replaced Harris as its designated drinking star.

Covers: Earl Bostic 1951; Zeb Turner 1951
Remake: The Cadets 1956

—

Elmore James "I Believe My Time Ain't Long" Trumpet/Ace/Jewel August 1951

Style: Blues
Where from: Canton, MS
Where recorded: Jackson, MS
Suggested pairings: Robert Johnson "I Believe I'll Dust My Blues" 1938; Arthur Crudup "Dust My Broom" 1950; Robert Jr. Lockwood "Dust My Broom" 1951; Elmore James and His Broomdusters "Dust My Blues" 1955; Ike & Tina Turner "Dust My Broom" 1966; Ike Turner "Dust My Broom" 1972

When musician Leon Holston was growing up in Canton, MS, he recalled knowing Elmore James. "Elmore just had that musical bug; he'd take a piece of wire and broomstick and pluck at it, play it. Elmore did have a great voice. Kinda did it on his own, his style was pretty much his own. Elmore was a friend of Robert Johnson. I do know him and Elmore knew each other. I would imagine, if you hear somebody do something, you inspire to do it the way they were doing that. Most memorable was 'Dust My Broom,' everybody wanted to hear about 'Dust My Broom.' Elmore James worked in my dad's radio and TV shop. I can remember as far back as six years old sitting in his shop. He'd check in radios and TVs people were bringing in, and in the meantime, he was learning stuff from my dad about electronics, my dad was quite an electronics man. He was a clerk at the time, he'd give you a ticket, take your item, he and my dad would fix it and people would pick it up. When I was a small kid, I remember listening to them play. He would practice in the shop when nobody was there. The knife on the keyboard is something I never seen before. As

I remember him as a kid I remember he used to play his guitar with a knife sitting on his lap. When I was a kid he used to sit it on his lap and slide a knife up and down the keyboard, that's how he played it. Him and my dad playing together in the old juke joints they used to call them. I should remember that, I was about 9 or 10. I started playing the guitar they way Elmore played it, my dad didn't want me to play it that way. He made me tune my guitar the proper way; Elmore James didn't tune the guitar the proper way to play it. He could slide a knife up and down the keyboard, and played the chords it that way. You can't do that if you tune the guitar they way you're supposed to have it tuned."

Elmore James recorded the original Robert Johnson blues, "I Believe I'll Dust My Blues," as "I Believe My Time Ain't Long," which resulted in a conflict between Trumpet Records of Jackson, MI and Joe Bihari of Modern Records. Trumpet owner Lillian McMurray said Sonny Boy Williamson brought James to her. As she told Almost Slim, "He couldn't get any original material together. I didn't know he didn't write 'Dust My Blues.' We even lent him money against his royalties. All those records he cut after he left us sounded like 'Dust My Blues.'" Legend has it, when McMurray first asked Elmore to record "Dust My Blues," a shy Elmore James said no. Suggesting he rehearse with Sonny Boy Williamson, McMurray surreptitiously recorded the rehearsal. It became a hit.

—

Howlin' Wolf "Moanin' At Midnight" Chess 1951; Howlin' Wolf "Morning At Midnight" RPM 1951

Style: Blues
Where from: Mississippi
Where recorded: Memphis, TN

In 1951, the Bihari-owned Modern/RPM label out of L.A. and the Chess label out of Chicago continued their red hot competition for the next blues star out of Sam Phillips' Memphis Recording Service studio. That was the debut of harp playing vocalist Howlin' Wolf on this evocative blues song, "Moanin' At Midnight," with Ike Turner on piano. Recorded in May 1951, it was immediately sent to Chess. According to Joe Bihari, "Leonard Chess happened to be in Memphis at the time. Sam was getting ready to send it, Leonard bought it right there." Bihari went to West Memphis, AR in September 1951 to record Howlin' Wolf on the amazingly similar "Morning At Midnight" for his RPM label. Said Bihari, "Chess bootlegged it, we had a run in with Leonard, we had Wolf at that time." Not quite true. Chess had the first release, Bihari came out with the similar sound. Eventually, said Bihari, "We gave them Howlin' Wolf, we kept Roscoe Gordon."

—

Roscoe Gordon "Booted" Chess 1951/RPM 1951

Style: Blues
From and recorded in: Memphis, TN

Gordon dubbed his piano style "the Rosco rhythm," with the emphasis on the off-beat. This rhythm was an influence on the Jamaican pianist Theophilus Beckford and hence on reggae music as a whole. Sam Phillips, who recorded Gordon on "Booted," sold the master to RPM and Chess Records at the same time and both labels released the track as a single. The RPM release prevailed, reaching # 1 on the R&B record charts. The Chess release B-side was "Love You 'Til the Day I Die," an uncredited duet with the recently discovered Bobby Bland. Gordon's next release, "No More Doggin'" kept up the "the Rosco rhythm," hitting well on the charts. Gordon's next move was to sign with the just-established Duke label as its earliest artist, Bland soon joining his one-time duet partner as the dominant Duke artist.

—

Bill Haley & the Saddlemen "Rock the Joint" Essex 1952
Style: Rock 'n' roll
Where from: Chester, PA
Where recorded: Philadelphia, PA
Original version: Jimmy Preston "Rock the Joint" 1949
Suggested pairing: Bill Haley & the Comets "Rock Around the Clock" 1954

This rocking cover of fellow Philly recording artist Jimmy Preston, Bill Haley's "Rock the Joint" had some of the characteristics of Haley's later #1 hit, "Rock Around the Clock" in 1954. Haley's guitarist Danny Cedrone played pretty much the same solo on "Rock Around the Clock" that he did on Haley's 1952 cover of the Jimmy Preston "Rock the Joint." This song was a big break for Haley, selling over 150,000 copies, establishing the style he would use on his more famous hit.

—

The Clovers "One Mint Julep" Atlantic March 1952
Style: Rhythm and blues vocal group harmony
Where from: Washington, DC
Where recorded: New York City, NY
Suggested pairings: Richard Berry & Dreamers "Bye Bye Baby" 1954; The Cheers "Bazoom" 1955; The Coasters "Young Blood" 1957; Booker T & MGs "Jelly Bread" 1962

"One Mint Julep" is about an alcoholic drink associated with the Kentucky Derby. The storyline has to do with picking up a woman, taking her home, getting her drunk and winding up with "three extra children from'a gettin' frisky." Said Clovers' member Buddy Bailey, "Atlantic hired Rudy Toombs to write some things, we agreed it was a good novelty tune, uptempo rhythm and blues, sort of hilarious. We figured the drinking songs, it was the drinking era. The only thing we did was our ideas for the arrangement. It was agreed we would pick it up, we wanted it to be danceable. It got all of us in trouble when we were 17, especially black kids. Only thing, it hits all classes now, equal opportunity. We wanted it humorous, we wanted it true to life. It was sort of hidden, funny, but true to life stuff. Even today, we were very ahead of our time."

Cover: Louis Prima; Buddy Morrow and His Orchestra
Remakes: Chet Atkins 1959; Freddie Hubbard 1960; Ray Charles 1961; Willie Mitchell 1961; Sarah Vaughan 1962; The Ventures 1964; The Stokes 1965

—

The Royals "Every Beat Of My Heart" Federal March 1952
Style: Rhythm and blues
From and recorded in: Detroit, MI
Suggested pairing: The Heartbeats Qt "Tormented" 1955

In 1952, Johnny Otis was judging a Federal label talent search in Detroit. "I picked Jackie Wilson, Little Willie John and The Royals. There were others equally potent who came up during that evening, I knew Federal was not going to like Jackie Wilson because he's going to sing 'Trees' or 'My Buddy.' They're not going to hear what I hear in him, so I better write him something bluesy, he being very gifted, he picked it right up. It was 'Every Beat Of My Heart.' When they got there, they listened. They didn't like him, they liked the song. They didn't like Little Willie John either. They chased their tails. They had The Dominoes, suddenly it was all vocal groups, so they liked The Royals because they were a vocal group. They gave the song to The Royals and they recorded it. Not much of a record. It didn't do much."

Hank Ballard recalled, "The group was already formed when I came on the scene. That was the song Johnny brought to us. He auditioned about 200 groups at the Paradise Theater in Detroit and he dug our sound. One of the members was inducted into the service and they were looking for a replacement. I was working at Ford Motors, I was 16. A guy named Sonny Woods, with the Royals originally, heard me singing up and down the assembly line, humming and try[ing] to emulate everything I heard on the radio. We thought I had a voice, different sound, he called me in for an audition. I went in as a baritone singer." At that point, the group was set as Sonny Woods, Charles Sutton, Henry Booth, Hank Ballard and Alonzo Tucker, guitar. The B-side, the uptempo "All Night Long," featured an uncredited vocal appearance by Wynonie Harris who, when the vocalist with The Royals couldn't make a note, strolled into the studio, grabbed the mike and improvised that vocal part. The producer, Ralph Bass, kept it on the release.

Remakes: The Pips 1961; Gladys Knight & the Pips 1962

—

Lloyd Price "Lawdy Miss Clawdy" Specialty April 1952

Style: Rhythm and blues
From and recorded in: New Orleans, LA
Suggested pairings: Joe Turner "Tri Li Lee" 1953; The Cardinals "Lovie Darling" 1953; Earl King "Have You Gone Crazy" 1953; Billy Gayles "Night Howler" 1954; Earl King "Those Lonely Lonely Nights" 1955; Johnny & Hurricanes "High Voltage" 1961

Specialty owner Art Rupe "never had an operation in New Orleans," said producer Harold Battiste. "Before that, he'd just come to town, set up operations temporarily at Cosimo's Studio. Lloyd Price came in on one of those audition deals, Fats Domino played piano in the group on 'Lawdy Miss Clawdy,'" a title taken from an expression used by WBOK deejay, James "Okey Dokey" Smith, for whom Price, a teenaged employee of the station, wrote music for jingles. Earl King said, "They paid Fats a flat fee, $500, to play piano on that. That's plenty of money in those days." King said the song was "adapted from a slang [expression], like a lot of hit songs over the years. I think Lloyd Price picked up on that and just put it in a song. Huey Smith was great about those things, hearing people say funny little things and put them into songs."

Elvis biographer Malcolm Leo said, "Elvis Presley, after signing with RCA, recorded a rocking version of 'Lawdy Miss Clawdy.' Lloyd Price was a huge Memphis figure in the sense that when he came to town, everybody would go down to Beale Street or to the Chicsa, which was the short name for the Memphis Chicsaw Hotel. Elvis Presley just adored 'Lawdy Miss Clawdy.'"

Remakes: Elvis Presley 1956; Gary Stites 1960; Rocky Matero 1960; The Appalachians 1963; Solomon Burke 1966; The Buckinghams 1967; Sandy Nelson 1967; Ike Turner 1972

—

The Dominoes "Have Mercy Baby" Federal May 1952

Style: Rhythm and blues vocal group harmony
Where from: New York City, NY
Where recorded: Cincinnati, OH
Suggested pairings: Clyde McPhatter & the Drifters "Whatcha Gonna Do" 1954; The Robins "Double Crossin' Baby" 1954; The Cadets "So You Wanna Rock" 1955; Little Richard "True Fine Mama" 1958.

The Dominoes hit with the gospel inspired "Have Mercy Baby" featuring an emotive Clyde McPhatter on lead. About two years after he left, McPhatter led The Drifters on a similar, "Whatcha Gonna Do," in 1954, a song known for similarities to "The Twist."

Remakes: Titus Turner 1957; The Matadors 1957; The Bobbettes 1960; Buddy Lamp 1964; James Brown & The Famous Flames 1964

—

The Clovers "Ting-A-Ling" Atlantic June 1952

Style: Rhythm and blues vocal group harmony
Where from: Washington, DC
Where recorded: New York City NY
Suggested pairings: The Harptones "That's the Way It Goes" 1956; The Moonglows "In My Diary" 1956; Buddy Holly "Ting-A-Ling" 1957

This was the second hit by the Clovers, which quickly became the premier Atlantic label vocal group.

—

Dave Bartholomew "My Ding-A-Ling" King July 1952

Style: Rhythm and blues
From and recorded in: New Orleans, LA

Said Lee Allen of the song "My Ding-A-Ling," "There was a comedian out of Chicago, when I first heard it, he came in to the Dew Drop. He used to do that as part of his act. I distinctly remember that song. He was just a happy little guy, chubby, nothing extraordinary, just the way he put it over was kind of cute."

Remakes: Dave Bartholomew "Little Girl Sing Ting-A-Ling" 1952; The Bees "Toy Bell" 1954; Chuck Berry 1972

—

Johnny Ace "My Song" Duke July 1952

Style: Rhythm and blues
From and recorded in: Memphis, TN

With backing by Johnny Otis' band, Johnny Ace made his recording debut with this mournful vocal, "My Song."

Covers: Dinah Washington; Johnny Moore's Three Blazers; Hadda Brooks 1952; Marie Adams 1952
Remakes: Aretha Franklin 1968; B.B. King 1974

—

Little Willie Littlefield "K.C. Lovin'" Federal November 1952

Style: Blues
Where from: Texas
Where recorded: Los Angeles, CA
Suggested pairings: Wilbert Harrison "That Woman Of Mine" 1952; Wilbert Harrison "Kansas City" 1959

Little Willie Littlefield arrived in L.A. in 1949, recording first for Modern. In '52, Littlefield recorded material by songwriters Leiber-Stoller, whose "K.C. Lovin," though not a chart hit, became one of the most influential and remade examples of that decade's R&B. "We were just writing a song about Kansas City, the birthplace of so many wonderful styles of music," said Mike Stoller. "Jay McShann and Charlie Parker came out of that. We just wanted to do kind of a tribute. It was in a sense of fantasy, because neither Jerry nor I have ever been to Kansas City. We did research, when I say research, we asked somebody what are the streets in Kansas City and we got 12th St. and Vine from people who've been there. We called the song 'Kansas City.' The head of A&R at Federal Records, Ralph Bass, said, 'Kansas City,' that's not going to make it. 'K.C. is the hip thing, K.C., that's hip.' So he retitled it, as apparently he had the right to do, called it 'K.C. Loving.'"

In 1959, Wilbert Harrison remade this blues song into the #1 hit, "Kansas City." However, the story of the song gets really convoluted with a song called "Hey Hey Hey Hey."

Remake: Wilbert Harrison "Kansas City" 1959
Remake, different song: Little Richard "Hey Hey Hey Hey" 1959. The Beatles "Kansas City" 1964

—

Moose Jackson "Big Ten Inch Record" King November 1952

Style: Rhythm and blues
Where from: Cleveland, OH
Where recorded: Cincinnati, OH

Moose Jackson's outrageous lyric and title, "Big Ten Inch Record," got banned quickly in the days when dirty records caused arrests. As a favorite party record, the legendary suggestive lyric was, "I got out my Big Ten Inch... record of the band that plays the blues." Born in 1919, Bernard Jackson was a violin-playing child prodigy who favored the saxophone. He joined the sax section of Lucky Millinder's big band as a teenager. A bandmate famously said Jackson looked like a damn bull moose, and the nickname stuck. Shortly thereafter, Jackson took to the microphone one night in Texas to sing for no-show Wynonie Harris. Jackson brought down the house.

Syd Nathan wanted to expand his King Records empire in Cincinnati, so Millinder suggested Jackson go solo. Good decision. "I Love You Yes I Do" became one of the first R&B singles to sell a million copies. A string of hits followed. Bull Moose Jackson was hot! One of the songs, "Nosey Joe," written by two Jewish teenagers, Mike Leiber and Jerry Stoller, set new standards for pure raunch. Soon, Bull Moose had a reputation for risqué material. It drove crowds crazy, record buyers not. In the top-selling singles of 1952, "Big Ten-Inch (Record of the Blues)" couldn't be found because radio stations wouldn't touch it.

Remake: Aerosmith 1975

—

The "5" Royales "Baby Don't Do It" Apollo December 1952

Style: Rhythm and blues vocal group harmony
Where from: North Carolina
Where recorded: New York
Suggested pairing: The Royals "Get It" 1953

Originally The Royal Sons Quintet, this group signed with the New York-based Apollo Records as The Royals after abandoning gospel for secular music. Because of the existing Royals out of Detroit, they became The "5" Royales, led by Lowman Pauling and his brother Clarence, along with lead singer Johnny Tanner. With The "5" Royales hitting with "Baby Don't Do It," according to members of The "5" Royales, in 1953, the confusion with The Royals peaked when the Royals had a hit with "Get It," which was profoundly influenced by "Baby Don't Do It." A crooked promoter tried to pawn off The Royals as the more popular "5" Royales in Winston-Salem, and gave both groups a bad name. For about two years, whichever group had the bigger hit, the similarly named group would tour on the other group's success.

When The "5" Royales signed with King/Federal in 1954, The Royals had to give way, changing their name to The Midnighters. "I didn't know anything about them when they were doing gospel," said The Royals' Hank Ballard. "The first time I heard about them was when they did 'Baby Don't Do It.'" That's when Ballard and The Royals recorded the knock off "Get It."

—

Johnny Ace "Cross My Heart" Duke January 1953

Style: Rhythm and blues
From and recorded in: Memphis, TN
Suggested pairing: Charles Brown "So Long" 1949

This was Johnny Ace's second major hit.

Remakes: Little Milton 1961; James Booker 1963

—

Amos Milburn "Let Me Go Home Whiskey" Aladdin January 1953

Style: Rhythm and blues
Suggested pairings: Peppermint Harris "I Got Loaded" 1951; Floyd Dixon "Tired, Broke and Busted" 1952

Amos Milburn's golden age of booze songs peaked with "Let Me Go Home Whiskey," one of R&B's great drinking odes. Milburn found himself locked into drinking during live shows to support titles like "Let Me Go Home Whiskey."

Remake: Lee Roy Little 1960

—

Ruth Brown "(Mama) He Treats Your Daughter Mean" Atlantic January 1953

Style: Rhythm and blues
Where from: Virginia
Where recorded: New York
Suggested pairing: Scat Man Crothers "Papa I Don't Treat That Little Girl Mean" 1954

Ruth Brown began a trend that created at least a half decade of answers with this hit uptempo vocal, "(Mama) He Treats Your Daughter Mean" in early 1953, ending, more or less, with The Miracles' "Shop Around" in 1960.

Answers: The Checkers "Mama's Daughter" 1954; Irving, Gloria "Daughter (That's Your Red Wagon)" 1954; J.B. Lenore "Mama Your Daughter Is Going To Miss Me" 1955; J.B. Lenore "Mamma Talk To Your Daughter" 1955; The Delegates "Mother's Son" 1956; J.B. Lenore "Daddy Talk To Your Son" 1958; Harmonica Fats "Mama Mama Talk To Your Daughter" 1963; The Rainbows "Mama Take Your Daughter Back" 1964

—

Fats Domino "Going to the River" Imperial March 1953

Style: Rhythm and blues
Suggested pairings: Roy Milton "RM Blues" 1946; Bill Doggett "Honky Tonk" 1956

There was no doubt what Fats Domino was singing about in "Going To the River," the lyric "gonna jump overboard and drown" making it all clear. The flip, a redo of Roy Byrd's anthemic "Mardi Gras In New Orleans," put the boogie woogie back into the party.

Cover: Chuck Willis 1953
Remakes: Ford Eaglin 1962; Dave Bartholomew 1962

—

Willie Mae Thornton "Hound Dog" Peacock 1953

Style: Rhythm and blues
Where from: Montgomery, AL
Where recorded: Los Angeles, CA

After not exactly setting the record industry on fire with compositions like "Ugly Women" and "Too Much Jelly Roll," the novice songwriting team of Leiber-Stoller with some help by Johnny Otis came up with perhaps the most important release of the 1950s, "Hound Dog." Written expressly for Willie Mae Thornton, whose label, the Houston-based Peacock, was searching for the right material after her debut in 1951, Peacock's Don Robey assigned Johnny Otis to conduct Thornton's next session and Otis went in search of new material, which took him to a young, just-blossoming songwriting team of Jerry Leiber and Mike Stoller.

"We had done some work with Johnny Otis here in L.A., that's where we lived and in fact we were 18—19 years [old] at the time," said Mike Stoller. "We'd written songs for Little Esther, and Johnny asked us to come over to his home where he had converted his garage to a rehearsal room and he said, 'I've got this singer and I've got to produce some sides with her. Willie Mae Thornton.' We caught the rehearsal and Willie Mae was a very formidable character. It appeared to us that she was close to 300 pounds and even in rehearsal, she'd fool around. She'd pick up one of those old microphones with a steel base with one hand and turn it upside down with the base up in the air and sing like that.

"She was a powerful, powerful woman, she had a few scars, looked like a knife scar on her face. She had a very beautiful smile when she smiled, but most of the time, she looked pretty salty. Jerry and I listened and we went back to my house in the West Adams area and I started playing and Jerry started shouting and I think we wrote 'Hound Dog' in about 10 minutes. Got back in my '37 Plymouth and drove back to Johnny's and we sang it to her. She said, 'Aw rite, I can do that' and we went back to the studio about two days later.

"Johnny had been playing drums and he'd tuned the drums in a particular way that had a wonderful kind of tom tom sound. We did two takes and started rehearsing and it wasn't happening. Johnny had a wonderful drummer Laird Bell (Kansas City Bell), but it wasn't the same thing. We said to Johnny, 'You gotta get out there and play or it's not gonna happen.'

"Johnny said, 'Who's gonna produce?' Jerry said, 'We'll produce.' Jerry sat in the booth, I stayed on the floor and Johnny got on his drums and tuned the drums back. Jerry said to Big Mama, 'I want you to growl the words,' and she said, 'Don't be telling me how to sing,' but she tried it and it worked. I'm very happy with that record." Willie Mae "Big Mama" Thornton's "Hound Dog" backed with "Nightmare" was thus issued on Robey's Peacock label. Otis claimed he helped them finish the song, taking out references to razors and knifes and putting in "you're just looking for a home." When the record came out, his name was listed as a third writer, but was removed after Leiber-Stoller disaffirmed the contract on account of them being minors. "Of course it was a problem," said Otis. "It was a legal swindle." After Elvis Presley hit with the song, Peacock reissued Thornton's "Hound Dog" backed with "Rock-A-Bye Baby."

Covers: Eddie Hazelwood; Betsy Gay; Tommy Duncan; Charlie Gore, Little Esther, Jack Turner, Billy Starr and Burl Ives 1953
Answers: Rufus Thomas Jr "Bear Cat" 1953; Chuck Higgins "Real Gone Hound Dog" 1953; Lula Reed "Watch Dog" 1953; Jimmy Wilson "Call Me A Hound Dog" 1953; John Brim "Rattlesnake" 1953; Smiley Lewis "Play Girl" 1953; Roy Brown "Mr. Hound Dog's in Town" 1953; Charlie Gore "(You Ain't Nothin' But A Female) Hound Dog" 1953; Homer & Jethro "How Much Is That Hound Dog In The Winder" 1953; Curley Bridges "New Hound Dog" Big Town 116 1954; Eugene Jackson & Juanita Moore "You Call Me A Hound Dog" 1954; Jesse "Big 'Tiny'" Kennedy "Country Boy" 1955
Remakes: Freddie Bell & the Bell Boys 1955; Elvis Presley 1956

—

Duces of Rhythm and Tempo Toppers, lead Little Richard "Fool at the Wheel" Peacock 1953

Style: Rhythm and blues
Where from: Georgia
Where recorded: Houston, TX
Suggested pairing: The Dominoes "Have Mercy Baby" 1952

The horn part of this song was straight outta The Dominoes' rockin' hit "Have Mercy Baby" from 1952. It's a story of a reckless driver with an energetic background harmony, nothing like the more outrageous lyrics in "Tutti Frutti." About Little Richard's style, "He never did that kind of stuff," said long-time New Orleans musician Earl King. "He did a lot of uptempo stuff, but it had a different kind of texture to it. Richard was more of a balladeer than anything. He changed because when we were putting on a show, he did these fired up things. It's just like you see him now, but always had a different kind of texture to it. When he did his real wild and bizarre stuff, that was another side of Little Richard he was projecting." And the start of his journey to his more successful shouting style two years later.

—

The Crows "Gee" Rama May 1953

Style: Rhythm and blues vocal group
Where from: New York City, NY
Where recorded: Beltone Studios in New York City, NY
Suggested pairings: The Flairs "Love Me Girl" 1954; The Meadowlarks "Love Only You" 1954

After The Orioles, The Ravens and The Robins had hit chart pay dirt, the next in the so-called series of bird groups was The Crows. Historically, groups named after dark birds, like The Four Blackbirds, which was the antecedent to The Robins, were code to alert radio stations, record shops and record buyers that the group was black. The first release by The Crows was the intended A-side, a smooth ballad, "I Love You So," out in early 1953, but deejays soon turned it over to discover "Gee," written by William Davis and Viola Watkins. The record died and was forgotten.

"It was a real great hook. The term they use in pop music, 'doo doo doo doo,'" said George Carlin. "Who can resist that? Especially when you're somewhat mindless in your teens and you need solid things you can lean on. It was something you could easily think you might have invented. I know that's the secret of a lot of those successful riffs. It sounds like something you might have come up with. We sang it in the hallway a lot, we were very bad impersonators of sounds we heard. In the hallways, we sounded fabulous because it was a story and a half and there was a lot of marble. It was the same thing as singing in the bathroom where there was a lot of marble and porcelain and you got the echo effect."

After stopping play on "Gee," L.A. DJ Huggy Boy recalled, "I was dating a girl. I was on the night shift. She liked that song. She found it in the wastepaper basket where we used to throw our box-o-bombs. She said, 'Honey, will you play this record?' We didn't particularly play it a lot. Hunter Hancock had stopped playing the record. It was going to be lost. We had an argument in the studio, she left. I found the record, played 'Gee.' I kept playing it over and over again. The studio was in Los Angeles, she lived in North Hollywood," about 20 miles away. "By the time she got to North Hollywood, she called the studio. 'Gee, Huggy. You've been playing the same record for 10 or 12 minutes. You're going to get fired.' I said, 'I don't care. I'm not going to stop playing the record until you come back here.' She said, 'I don't want you to be fired,' so I took the record off. Two days later, when I went to the distributor, 'Huggy, we got a smash hit, you played a coupla' times in a row.' We owe that record, courtesy of an ex-wife."

Gee charted in April 1954, one year after its release. George Goldner, the owner of the Rama label on which "Gee" was released, was so pleased, he drove to L.A. to thank Huggy Boy, and in a few years, when Huggy Boy began putting out oldies LPs to compete with Art LaBoe, the owner of Rama gladly allowed Huggy to use whatever of his label songs he wanted to include. Goldner began the Gee label, which hit big with "Why Do Fools Fall In Love" by Frankie Lymon & the Teenagers in 1955.

Remakes: The Harmony Grits 1959; Jan & Dean 1960; The Hollywood Flames 1961

—

The Dominoes "These Foolish Things" Federal May 1953

Style: Rhythm and blues group vocal
Where from: New York City, NY
Where recorded: Cincinnati, OH
Original version: Billie Holiday 1936
Suggested pairings: The Penguins "Earth Angel" 1954; Bobby Hendricks "A Thousand Dreams" 1958

The emotive "These Foolish Things Remind Me of You" was recorded by The Dominoes in 1953. When Times Square ordered up a repressing in 1961 during the great oldies revival, an alternate take was sent, creating an instant collector's item. The original version featured Clyde McPhatter's voice; the reissued version was Billy Ward doing the recitation.

Cover: The Five Keys 1953

—

The Royals "Get It" Federal June 1953

Style: Rhythm and blues group vocal
From and recorded in: Detroit, MI
Suggested pairing: The "5" Royales "Baby Don't Do It" 1952

After several fine ballad releases, The Royals took to more aggressive material with the addition of lead singer Hank Ballard, who wrote and sang lead on "Get It," their first chart hit. "That was the first tune I wrote," said Ballard. "That's when I started singing lead with the group. We had a wild hit with that, a regional hit. If you wanna generate some excitement, you gotta be different. That's what I was really singing for. There was only one company that would take a chance, that was King/Federal Records. We had a lot of guts in those days. That song sold approximately 250,000 records, that was enough evidence there was a market out there for this kind of material."

—

The Orioles "Crying in the Chapel" Jubilee July 1953

Style: Rhythm and blues group vocal
From and recorded in: Baltimore, MD
Original version: Darrell Glenn 1953

"Crying in the Chapel" was written by Artie Glenn for his son Darrell Glenn, who recorded it on the Valley label in 1953. The song was rejected by Hill and Range Songs and Acuff-Rose Music. In June 1953, The Orioles recorded Glenn's country original "Crying in the Chapel," amounting to The Orioles' biggest hit, #1 in the R&B charts for five weeks in August and September and #11 on the pop charts.

Covers: The Four Dukes; The Womack Brothers; Buster Smith; June Valli; Rex Allen; Ella Fitzgerald; Wesley Tuttle
Remakes: Sunny Gale 1963; Little Richard 1963; The Velvets 1963; Adam Wade 1964; The Superior Angels 1964; Carol Fran 1965; The Staple Singers 1968; Cleophus Robinson 1968

—

Jimmy Reed "High and Lonesome" Vee Jay July 1953/Chance August 1953

Style: Blues
Where from: Dunleith, MI
Where recorded: Chicago, IL

Famous for his laid-back drawling delivery accompanied by harmonica and rudimentary guitar strumming, Vee-Jay's second signing, Mathis James Reed, was born on a Mississippi plantation on September 6, 1925, In 1943, after serving in the Navy during World War II, Reed settled in Gary, IN. His first session in June 1953 produced no hits, but Reed's blues "High and Lonesome" sold enough to keep the fledgling company high and interested. "Vee Jay was doing business out of [a] garage, 47th Street," said session sax man Red Holloway. "They had just been doing a few things. The Spaniels from Gary and Jimmy Reed. They were doing some fairly good business at the time."

—

The Spaniels "Baby It's You" Vee Jay/Chance July 1953

Style: Rhythm and blues group vocal
From and recorded in: Gary, IN

Pookie Hudson and the Hudsonaires was formed at Roosevelt High School in Gary, Indiana in the last part of 1952. "We graduated in 1953," said lead singer James "Pookie" Hudson. "Gerald Gregory was the bass; Ernest Warren, tenor; Opal Courtney, top tenor; Willis C. Jackson, baritone. They found us, we were in high school singing in talent shows. One of the girls worked at Vivian Bracken's record store and she told Vivian about us. They came and heard us. They asked us to write some songs. We put something together and presented it to them. They liked what we had." Vee Jay "didn't have any distribution, so they leased 'Baby It's You' to Chance. Chance had it for a while, but when Chance went under, Vee Jay got the master back." As Art Sheridan, the owner of Chance Records, was one of the financial backers of Vee Jay, he leased it back to himself as silent partner with Vee Jay founders James Bracken and Vivian Carter.

—

Joe Turner "Honey Hush" Atlantic August 1953

Style: Rhythm and blues
Where from: Kansas City, KS
Where recorded: New York
Original title: "Yakity-Yak"

This was the first of Turner's great rocking hits from the Atlantic label. Its lyrics suggested "yakity-yak," the label thought better of it, changed the title to "Honey Hush" in mid-pressing. "I have a habit of always ad-libbing, putting in different phrases," said Turner. "Things I hear about town, cats wise cracking and everything, I put into 'Honey Hush,' 'shut up baby,' 'yakity yak,' all that stuff." I just throwed in 'hi yo Silver,' thought it would fit in with the song. I just pop something in my head, I'll put this in there, give a little more swing to it."

Answer: Cordelia DeMilo "Ain't Gonna Hush" 1955

—

Joe Turner "Crawdad Hole" Atlantic August 1953

Style: Rhythm and blues
Where from: Kansas City, KS
Where recorded: New York

About the flip side of "Honey Hush," "Crawdad Hole," Joe Turner recalled, "I used to go fishing all the time when I was a kid. Just an idea I had sitting down riding a train one day. I saw some kids fishing in the little pond. They were doing what I used to do, so I wrote a little number on the train, called it 'Crawdad Hole.'" Turner denied any attempt at a double meaning.

—

Clyde McPhatter & the Drifters "Money Honey" Atlantic August 1953

Style: Rhythm and blues vocal group
Where from: North Carolina
Where recorded: New York City, NY
Suggested pairings: Richard Berry "Next Time" 1954; Eugene Fox "Stay At Home" 1954; Jesse Allen "What A Party" 1954; Bobby Charles "One Eyed Jack" 1957

Having left The Dominoes as lead tenor, Clyde McPhatter was signed to a new vocal group, Clyde McPhatter & the Drifters—Bill Pinkney, baritone; Andrew "Bubba" Thrasher, second tenor; Gerhart "Gay" Thrasher, top tenor and Willie Ferbie, bass with Walter Adams and Mickey Baker, guitar; Van Walls or Jesse Stone, piano and Sam "the Man" Taylor, tenor sax. There was a small bit of resistance to the Drifters name as it sounded like a country music outfit, such as The Driftin' Cowboys who backed Hank Williams. McPhatter's idea was that members had drifted in from various groups. The arrangement of "Money Honey" starts with a vocal "va-oom" drone, dubbed "bagpipe harmonies" by Atlantic's Jerry Wexler, then goes into the main shuffle about hard times, a warning from the landlord, "you gotta have money, honey," and the same warning from his girlfriend. McPhatter's voice is clear and bright and in the midst of the sax solo he gives off a monumental scream for the rocking vocal,

"Money Honey." This was a #1 R&B hit for Atlantic. Reportedly, two different takes were used in the 45 rpm and 78 rpm issues.

Cover: Ella Mae Morse 1954
Remakes: Elvis Presley 1956; The Coasters 1965

—

The Flamingos "Golden Teardrops" Chance September 1953/Vee Jay April 1961

Style: Rhythm and blues group vocal
From and recorded in: Chicago, IL

"I liked The Flamingos because they had a vocalist with a real fine voice," said sax man Red Holloway. "His range was like Bill Kenney of The Ink Spots, a four octave range. They definitely had their own style, fantastic group. They had a choreographer for the Sammy Dyer Dancers, doing stuff for the show at the Club D'Lisa, they were young fellows, could do those dances."

One-time Flamingos lead singer Solly McElroy recalled how the group was named: "We were at a Chicago theater, they had a lot of ducks and flamingoes in a pond. At that time, we were searching for a name, and the flamingoes stood out on the pond so much that we decided, 'Look at the long legs on that bird.' We were always teasing each other about our legs, so we said, 'We'll call ourselves the Flamingos. There were four cousins, one outsider," said McElroy. "They were rehearsing, singing all together. [The] group was Jake Carey, bass; Zeke Carey, second tenor; Johnny Carter, first tenor; Paul Wilson, baritone and myself, Solly McElroy, lead singer; and a guy named Earl, he was only with them for a year. We were trying to get away from 'doo wah doo wah,' trying to get something of our own style, our own sound. Zeke was the weakest of the group. The note I could hit, Jake could hit, Paul could hit, Johnny could hit, Zeke couldn't," said McElroy.

"The two tenors sliding and gliding all around just killed me when I was a kid. 'Golden Teardrops' was it," said George Carlin. "'Golden Teardrops was a very difficult sound to put together because it was something new we were trying to do with Johnny on lead tenor. It was singing that was very close harmony, but different from what we'd been hearing in the market. It took us a long time to get the song together, but when we did, we were elated with the way the sound came out and the way the arrangement was done."

Then McElroy formed his own group, The Moroccos. "Nate Nelson was rehearsing at the time, because they didn't know if I was going to leave. I wasn't fired, I left." Holloway reflected on that change. "I'm positive he made a bad mistake. They weren't really making any money, he had a family. They didn't find anyone to replace him."

—

The Checkers "White Cliffs Of Dover" King/Federal October 1953

Style: Rhythm and blues group vocal
Where from: New York
Where recorded: Cincinnati, OH
Original version: Vera Lynn 1942

Popular as a fine melody and a rallying cry during WWII, "(There'll Be Bluebirds Over) The White Cliffs of Dover" was a reference to British RAF and RCAF blue unformed fighter pilots, called "bluebirds," and expresses confidence that they shall prevail during the dark days of the Battle of Britain. The Checkers, an offshoot of the influential Dominoes, whose bass singer, Bill Brown, failed to chart an untypical rocking version of this standard with a booting sax, was a best seller on both King and Federal well into the 1960s.

George Carlin recalled he began picking up records in about 1953. "The rhythm and blues, some of it came from the jukeboxes first. I didn't know about the radio stations yet. By hanging around, you'd go past a bar or you'd go past a candy store or an ice cream parlor with a jukebox, and that's where 'White Cliffs of Dover' was played. I used to go in to the Hillside. I was way too young be served, but I'd go in, put a quarter in and just play it five times and kneel down next to the speaker and listen to that Checkers record, that great tenor and bass and that sax solo, those were my sources. It just sort of grew to where it became important to play those records—at will, not wait for them to come on the radio or spend a quarter, to be able to go home and listen to them, that's when I went out and started buying them."

Covers: The Blue Jays 1953; The Five Willows 1953
Remakes: Lee Andrews & the Hearts 1954; Johnny Rivers 1959; Scott English 1960; The Mystics 1960; Etta Jones 1961; The Robins 1961; The Versatiles 1962; Sir Raleigh and The Cupons 1964; The Epics 1964; The Righteous Brothers 1966

—

Little Junior's Blue Flames "Mystery Train" Sun November 1953

Style: Blues
From and recorded in: Memphis, TN
Suggested pairings: Blind Lemon Jefferson's "Right Of Way Blues" 1927; The Carter Family "Worried Man Blues" 1930

In mid-1953, Little Junior's Blue Flames debuted with the R&B hit rocker "Feelin' Good," which clearly owed a debt to John Lee Hooker's "Boogie Chillen" from 1948. Little Junior's Blue Flames then recorded the classic "Mystery Train," another rocker influenced by both blues and by country. With a guitar riff by Pat Hare considered influential in the start of rockabilly, this first "Mystery Train" didn't chart until it was redone by fellow Sun label artist Elvis Presley in 1955. Little Junior was soon much better known as Little Junior Parker on Duke.

Remake: The Turtles 1955; Elvis Presley 1955; Junior Wells 1968

—

Joe Turner and His Blues Kings "TV Mama" Atlantic December 1953

Style: Rhythm and blues
Where from: Kansas City, KS
Where recorded: Chicago, IL
Suggested pairings: Stan Freberg "Wide Screen Mama Blues" 1954; Chuck Berry "Childhood Sweetheart" 1959

"That was Elmore James on guitar," said Turner. "I was living in Chicago at that time, when Atlantic came there to record. They generally picked out the band, they would go around and listen to the cabaret bands and pick out who they wanted. They asked me about Elmore James. I said, 'Well, that would be nice, he plays pretty good.' So we got him on the session. And we got a few other cats out of Chicago. Things were moving kind of fast. I didn't pay much attention to who they got, because there was always an argument who they were going to get, who they wanted, who they didn't want and all that blah, blah, blah, yakity yak stuff. When they bring me the approval, I said, 'I ain't never heard the cat who is he?' They said, 'We heard him last night. He's good.' I said, 'Okay, it's your money. You want to do it, go ahead and do it. I'm fine as long as he keeps time.' I'd heard of Elmore long before they brought him up. I used to go around to the nightclubs where he played at, we'd sit in together for fun. He was a nice gentleman, nice fellow. He could play a guitar, he could."

—

Johnny Ace "Yes Baby" Duke December 1953

Style: Rhythm and blues
Where from: Memphis, TN
Where recorded: Los Angeles, CA
Suggested pairing: Johnny Otis "Hey Hey Hey Hey" 1957

Produced by Johnny Otis, Johnny Ace dueted with Big Mama Thornton on this rollicking "Yes Baby," the B-side to his hit, "Saving My Love For You." In turn, Otis turned "Yes Baby" into a local L.A. hit, Otis' own "Hey Hey Hey Hey" in 1957, a song purloined by Little Richard who, at the time of "Yes Baby," was recording for the Duke sister label, Peacock. Otis' band was used on most releases by Johnny Ace and several releases by Little Richard and Willie Mae Thornton, who was not credited on the first pressings of "Yes Baby," only on 1960s reissues.

—

Chuck Higgins "Pachuko Hop" Combo 1953

Style: Rhythm and blues instrumental
Where from: Gary, Indiana
Where recorded: Los Angeles, CA
Suggested pairings: Lucky Millinder "Apollo Jump" 1943; Johnny Otis "Barrelhouse Stomp" 1947; Chuck Higgins "Greasy Pig" 1954; Chuck Higgins "Wetback Hop" 1955

Tenor sax player Chuck Higgins arrived in Los Angeles in 1926. Higgins' first song on Combo, "Pachuko Hop," loosely based on Lucky Millinder's "Apollo Jump," was a one-note performance as Higgins had just learned to play the horn. "It was a tune I used to play when we was in school at the L.A. Conservatory. I remembered the hop. I used to live in East L.A., around the Aliso Village," a largely Mexican housing project. "My buddies would all hang around the pad, rehearsing and jamming. They all called it the hop, 'come on man, play the hop.'" The title "goes way back before 'Pachuko Hop' was around," said Higgins of the term pachuco, which was and is a term for a Mexican youth of the streets. It was later expanded to include a definition of gang members. "It was around for years, it caught on [at] just the right time. It came during the era when saxophone players was honking, nobody was singing, just blowing." In a sense, it was a message to the Mexican project "homeboys" that Higgins, a black, had made it with them in mind.

"It was done during the first recording session in 1952," Higgens added. Backing Higgins on "Pachuko Hop" were Eli Toney, bass: Joe Usury, drums and a piano player named Young John Watson, later known as Johnny "Guitar" Watson who sang on the rocking flip side, "Motor Head Baby." "We had recorded a year or so before," said Higgins, "and we took the grand tour around to all the companies to see if anybody wanted it. It was sort of a thing we couldn't let go, because every time we played it, everybody said, 'Ah, the hop.' We kept fighting it, we finally got it."

After leaving Higgins, Watson redid "Motor Head Baby" as a slow guitar blues for Federal. "Pachuko Hop" became a bit of an anthem based on plays on Hunter Hancock's radio show on KFVD. Higgins then recorded "Pachuko Hop" for the Specialty label and for "Memories Of El Monte" on Art LaBoe's Starla from an El Monte Legion Stadium concert. Higgins first LP, "Pachuko Hop," was issued with a scandalously suggestive **cover:** a nude woman, identified as Nyla Hugg, wife of DJ Huggy Boy, photographed laid out on a linoleum floor, a necktie covering her private parts. That cover was quickly pulled from the market, and replaced by a crude drawing of a saxophone.

Cover: Ike Carpenter 1953
Remake: Chuck Higgins "Pachuko Hop Twist" 1962

—

Guitar Slim "The Things That I Used To Do" Specialty December 1953

Style: Blues
From and recorded in: New Orleans, LA
Suggested pairings: Norfolk Jazz Qt. "Great Change" 1938; Lover Boy (aka Ike Turner) "The Way You Treated Me" 1954

When he recorded the historic "Certainly All" as Eddie Jones, just before he became Guitar Slim, Huey Smith was the original piano player with Guitar Slim. According to Earl King, after Slim hooked up with a new road band, the Lloyd Lambert Band, Huey was dropped when they went on tour and Ray Charles became Guitar Slim's piano player on tour and on the recording of the classic guitar blues vocal "The Things That I Used To Do" and about four other compositions.

"That was Ray Charles, he coordinated the music on those," said King.

King added, "Slim was a funny guy, offstage and onstage. When he gets drinking, no telling what he may do. He had just bought this brand new Cadillac, and was going down the street, goes around a curve and runs into a parked bulldozer and smashes up his car," as well as smashing up Slim himself. "They had to put him in a hospital. The agency he was working for that the time had a string of dates booked on him and Charles Brown, who refused to go on the gig. They didn't pay him what he thought he wanted. They sent me in Slim's place and Ray Charles in Charles Brown's place. They got two people on the show that don't belong on the show. Lucky for me, I played places Slim had not been before. The first date I played was Atlanta, the Magnolia Ballroom. It was mobbed."

Later, King was coming out of the Dewdrop, "and who's coming out at one or two in the morning with a hospital gown on, overnight bag and a guitar on his back. He said, 'Earl, I heard you been out there in my place on the road. If you did anything wrong, I'm going to kill you." Then he said, "How did it go? Did you get paid any money?" I said, 'No, about $25 a night." Hearing this, he hit the ceiling.

Remakes: Joe Houston 1957; Earl King 1961; James Brown 1964; Chuck Berry 1964; Junior Parker 1964; Chick Willis 1964; The Salem Travelers 1965; Johnny Walker 1965; Little Johnny Taylor 1966; Earl Gaines 1967; Larry Dale 1969; Jimmy Dawkins 1972

—

The Spaniels "Goodnite, Sweetheart, Goodnite" Vee Jay December 1953

Style: Doo wop vocal group harmony
From and recorded in: Gary, IN

The Spaniels' third record but first hit was this romantic ballad, "Goodnite, Sweetheart, Goodnite," characterized by the distinctive bass voice of Gerald Gregory. "Gregory was very inventive, he was one of those who started to do the 'doo wahs,' the different kind[s] of trick singing," said lead singer James "Pookie" Hudson. "The record company had a thing with Gregory. He was very outspoken, always brought things down to the point where they had to explain things. I really don't think they had too much love for Gregory, so they did not try to push him too much. They had to do it as a group because he was in the group. He was very much the rebel of the group," but also the owner of the trademark bass voice.

"Goodnite, Sweetheart, Goodnite" "was the biggest record we had," said Hudson. "I think it was the second cover record. After Pat Boone covered Fats Domino, I think The McGuire Sisters were the second one to cover and they covered us. We were in a position where they called it race music at the time or R&B and white stations on a whole would not play black records. Covers came in for the simple reason, they could take white acts, knowing they could get played. Even though they wouldn't play our song, it would be the same song, the white stations would play it. So they made big acts out of white people for our songs and we got very little reward for it. I saw one of The McGuire Sisters on TV. Someone asked her if a black person wrote the song, a black person sang the song, and she thought the song was wrote for them. She had no idea anyone else had wrote the same tune. Lot of people think 'Goodnite, Sweetheart, Goodnite' is a Sha Na Na song because of the television thing. People say, 'You sing Sha Na Na songs.'"

Covers: The McGuire Sisters; Ella Mae Morse; Johnnie & Jack; The Tennessee Mountain Boys; Gloria Mann with the Carter Rays
Remake: The Untouchables 1960

—

Clyde McPhatter & the Drifters "Such a Night" Atlantic January 1954

Style: Rhythm and blues group vocal
Where from: North Carolina
Where recorded: New York City, NY

This song was banned by some stations because of lyrics, title and McPhatter's sexually sounding delivery.

Cover: Dinah Washington 1954
Remakes: Bunny Paul 1959; Vince Everett 1962; Elvis Presley 1964

—

The Spiders "I Didn't Want To Do It" Imperial January 1954

Style: Rhythm and blues group vocal
From and recorded in: New Orleans, LA
Suggested pairings: The El Dorados "At My Front Door" 1955; The Flairs "Baby Wants" 1955

This vocal group began as The Consolations, then The Consolators, and "just whatever came to the guys minds is what they wrote down," said Spiders' tenor and lead singer, Chuck Carbo. Members were Carbo's brother Leonard "Chick" Carbo and Oliver Howard, bass; Joe Maxim, first tenor; Matthew West, baritone. "The reason we used two bass singers was when we were singing the gospel songs, I done all the arranging, what I had was an up bass and a deep bass and that way I would have a blend."

At the same early 1954 session, they recorded two gospel songs with "I Didn't Want To Do It" and "You're the One."

"We didn't choose Imperial Records. Cosmo Matassa discovered us and Dave Bartholomew was the A&R guy for Imperial. We were young, we had another record company here, a guy named Blackwell with Specialty. He kept promising and promising he'd call us, but Imperial was more, they wanted us more, that's why they recorded us. The Spiders was my wife's idea. "'I Didn't Want To Do It' was the intended A-side. In certain parts of the country, Detroit, Chicago, Milwaukee, didn't want this song on the radio because they said it was too suggestive and they started playing the flip side, 'You're the One.' So people said, 'Well hell, we're going to buy 'You're the One' just to find out what the other side is really all about. Can't play it on the radio and that's how it got to be a big hit."

New Orleans tenor sax player Lee Allen said, "I think they'd been doing a lot of gospel. Dave Bartholomew heard them do this song. He brought them in there to put a little background to it, push it a little bit."

—

The Spiders "You're the One" Imperial January 1954

Style: Rhythm and blues group vocal
From and recorded in: New Orleans, LA

"From the beginning, I thought 'You're the One' was a better record. 'You're the One' was more like singing a gospel song. I had that feeling then, as if I were singing a gospel song," said Spiders' lead singer, Chuck Carbo, whose first love was always gospel. "Locally, they would play both sides, but when the write-in and call-in requests [came], it was 'You're the One,' hell, this must be the side, I forgot about 'I Didn't Want To Do It.'"

—

The Clovers "Lovey Dovey" Atlantic February 1954

Style: Rhythm and blues group vocal
Where from: Washington, DC
Where recorded: New York City, NY
Suggested pairings: Ray Charles "Kissa Me Baby" 1949; The Cadillacs "Sugar Sugar" 1957; The Drifters "Yodee Yakee" 1957; Steve Miller Band "The Joker" 1973; Steve Miller Band "Rockn Me" 1976

This song is another prime example of a record thought to contain a sexual message, and a hit despite that.

Covers: Ella Mae Morse 1954; Bunny Paul 1954
Remakes: Clyde McPhatter 1959; Buddy Knox; The Coasters 1964

—

The Royals/Midnighters "Work With Me Annie" Federal February 1954

Style: Rhythm and blues group vocal
Where from: Detroit, MI
Where recorded: Cincinnati, OH
Suggested pairing: The Gentlemen "Something To Remember You By" 1954

"I was trying to woo her," said Royals/Midnighters lead singer Hank Ballard of Annie. "She became a challenge. It was just ghetto slang, which meant play, work and play, do you believe that? It aroused a lot of curiosity, man, the sales just skyrocketed." Lead singer Hank Ballard had joined The Royals, which became The Midnighters while their first major hit, "Work With Me Annie," was on The charts.

The group's name was changed because King had signed the better known '5' Royales. Ballard explained, "When I joined the group, the name was The Royals. I don't even think we were aware there was a gospel group called The '5' Royales. But when we recorded 'Work With Me Annie,' it was a national hit. They went out on the road first and made all the money, because the promoters was afraid to book us, because people were so confused, they thought The '5' Royales and The Royals were all the same." The name change to The Midnighters "was my idea," added Ballard. "When 'Work With Me Annie' took off, I knew it was a national hit. I went to the president of King and said, let's change the name of the group right now. Right in the midst of the hit." Incredibly it hit since it was almost uniformly banned from radio play. L.A.'s R&B DJ Hunter Hancock announced on-air that he couldn't play the lyrics, but he could play the instrumental vamp. That just increased sales for those who just had to hear the lyrics.

Answers: The Midnighters "Annie Had A Baby" 1954; Etta James "Roll With Me Henry" 1954; Linda Hayes & the Platters "My Name Ain't Annie" 1954; The El Dorados w/ Hazel McCollum "Annie's Answer" 1954; The Midnighters "Annie's Aunt Fannie" 1954; The Lamplighters "Roll On" 1955; Lena Gordon "Mama Took the Baby" 1954; The Cadets "Annie Met Henry" 1955; The Champions "Annie Met Henry" 1955; The Nu-Tones "Annie Kicked the Bucket" 1955; The Midnights "Annie Pulled A Hum Bug" 1955; Danny Taylor "I'm the Father Of Annie's Baby" 1955; Little Richard "Annie's Back" 1959; Little Junior Parker "Annie Get Your Yo Yo" 1962

"You know, 'Annie Had A Baby' went to #1 in one week of release," said Hank Ballard. "After I did 'Work With Me Annie,' 'Annie Had A Baby' and 'Sexy Ways,' I was through with it, but the company wasn't. They saw dollars, milked it until every drop was gone."

—

Les Elgart "Bandstand Boogie" Columbia March 1, 1954

Style: Big band
Where from: New Haven, CT

Released on March 1, 1954, bandleader Les Elgart's uptempo "Bandstand Boogie" was the world famous opening to ABC-TV's "American Bandstand," first aired nationally in August 1957.

—

Sugar Boy & the Cane Cutters "Jockomo" Checker 1954

Style: Rhythm and blues
From and recorded in: New Orleans, LA
Suggested pairings: Danny Barker & the Creole Cats "Chockomo Fendo Hey" 1949; The Dixie Cups "Iko Iko" 1964

Taken from the obscure Danny Barker & the Creole Cats' "Chockomo Fendo Hey" on Zulu from 1949, this Mardi Gras chant "Jockomo" was turned into a R&B hit by Sugar Boy & the Cane Cutters—James "Sugar Boy" Crawford, vocal and piano with Edgar "Big Boy" Myles trombone; Alfred Bernard and David Lastie sax; Snooks Eaglin guitar; Frank Fields bass; Eric Warner drums and Slim Sanders backing vocal.

"There's a lot of bad news that went down with 'Jockomo'" said Earl King. Checker Records' owner "Leonard Chess and them hadn't copyrighted 'Jockomo' and somebody found that out and he goes to the copyright office and re-copyrights this in his name and somebody else's name. Sugar Boy was such a passive guy and he never did anything about it."

According to Wavelength in 1989, the song has "long been a mystery, masquerading under the name 'Jockomo.' Interpreted to mean anything from Creole French phrase of celebration to a curse. Attempts to ascertain the composition's ownership and find out, who, if anyone is profiting locally have been met with silence."

James "Sugar Boy" Crawford only had three single releases on Checker, but this was by far the most enduring. Based on Mardi Gras Indian chants, this is the tune reworked by The Dixie Cups as "Iko Iko," and Sugar Boy was not credited until years later. The "Cane Cutters" billing was an invention of Leonard Chess.

—

Joe Turner "Shake, Rattle and Roll" Atlantic April 1954

Style: Rhythm and blues
Where from: Kansas City, KS
Where recorded: New York City, NY

This was the biggest early hit by the Boss of the Blues, Joe Turner. Turner told how the Bill Haley version and Elvis' version kept in the most sexual lyrics: "I thought it sounded pretty good the first time the man brought it up to the studio. I went into the back, took the piano player (Jesse Stone), and he said 'I'll play the piano for you. I know how it goes.' He said he's going to give me part of the song, but he never got around to that. We didn't have no singers to back me up, so we had the cats in the studio. Ahmet Ertegun, Jerry Wexler and them, they was backing me up, they was singing. Jesse Stone had left, someplace he had to go, he want to get rid of his other numbers. It turned out to be pretty good.

"Then Bill Haley jumped up and did it, then Elvis Presley did it," added Turner. Everybody was doing 'Shake, Rattle and Roll,' so the cat that wrote that, he got rich. He was from my home town, Kansas City." Asked about Haley's version, Turner said, "I didn't mind it. I'd been out there about a month before he got out there with it. He switched the lyrics around a little bit, he caught himself cleaning it up. There wasn't nothing wrong with the way it did it. 'Get out of that bed.' Everybody sleeps in a bed. The whole world sleeps in beds. About the sun shining through the dresses, well, that's what they do. Sun shines right through, it's still doing it." However, the off-color reference missed by Haley's label was the lyric, "one eyed cat peekin' in a seafood store."

Cover: Edna McGriff
Answers: John Lee Hooker "Shake Holler & Run" 1954; Jesse Knight "Nothing But Money" 1954; Big Walter "Pack Fair & Square" 1955; Conway Twitty "Shake It Up" 1957; Young Jesse "Hit Git & Split" 1957
Remakes: Bill Haley & the Comets 1954; Elvis Presley 1956; Count Basie with Joe Williams 1959; The Swinging Blue Jeans 1964; Burd & the Bombshells 1964; Arthur Conley 1967; Billy Swan 1976; Rod Bernard and Clifton Chenier 1976

—

Frankie Valley & the Travelers "Forgive and Forget" Mercury May 1954

Style: Pop vocal group
Where from: New Jersey
Where recorded: New York City

Frankie Valley & the Travelers on "Forgive and Forget," rendered in a nasally optimistic group sound of the day, was the second known recording by Frankie Valli, who would later achieve massive success with The Four Seasons.

—

The Drifters Featuring Clyde McPhatter "Honey Love" Atlantic May 1954

Style: Rhythm and blues group vocal
Where from: North Carolina
Where recorded: New York City, NY
Suggested pairings: The Larks "Honey From the Bee" 1954; The Marigolds "Rollin' Stone" 1955; Clyde McPhatter "Rock & Cry" 1957

This is an early example of mambo meets R&B with a strong organ backing. It also included McPhatter's squealing vocals, assured of being censored, which it was.

Covers: Bunny Paul With The Harptones; The Carlisles; Vicki Young
Remakes: The Four Lovers 1956; Narvel Felts 1959; Billy Storm 1961; Mac Davis 1963

—

The Eagles "Tryin' To Get To You" Mercury May 1954

Style: Rhythm and blues group vocal
From and recorded in: Washington, DC

Recorded by unknown personnel, possibly with members of The Cues, a prolific session group, "Tryin' To Get To You" by the Eagles was the first version of the Rosemary McCoy/Charlie Singleton composition picked up by several rock and rockabilly acts.

Remakes: Elvis Presley 1956; Johnny Carroll & His Hot Rocks 1956; Roy Orbison as Weldon Rogers 1957; Ricky Nelson 1959; The Astronauts 1961; Ersel Hickey 1967

—

Bill Haley & the Comets "Rock Around the Clock" Decca May 10, 1954

Style: "Fox trot"/rock 'n' roll
Where from: Michigan/Pennsylvania
Where recorded: New York City, NY
Original version: Sonny Dae & the Knights 1954
Suggested pairings: Benny Goodman "How High the Moon" 1940; Charlie Barnet "Victory Walk" 1944; Wynonie Harris "Around the Clock Blues" 1944; Hank Williams "Move It On Over" 1947; Hal Singer "Cornbread" 1948; Leroy Anderson "The Syncopated Clock" 1951; Bill Haley & the Saddlemen "Rock the Joint" 1951; The Robins "Get It Off Your Mind" 19541 Marvin & Johnny "Tick Tock" 1954; Great Gates "Jump Jump Jump" 1955

Bill Haley first recorded western swing with The Downhomers, covering "Rocket 88" in 1951, and had just hit with "Crazy Man Crazy." Songwriter Jimmy Myers claimed "Rock Around the Clock" was recorded as a favor because he had brought Haley to Decca. "The idea came out of my army days and when I sat in my office here in Philadelphia, it crept up on me. I finally needed a melody to go with it, worked on the lyrics quite some time. Finally, an old friend of mine who was pretty good with lyrics just walked into the office one day and said, 'Hey that sounds pretty good. Can I work on the lyrics with you?' I said, 'What the hell do you know about melody, you can't hear anything, you got a deaf ear.' He said, 'I like what I can hear.' We sat down, the late Max Friedman and I. I used my name, Jimmy DeKnight. We knocked out the song. I had written it originally with Haley in mind, but the company Haley was recording for at the time, the guy threw it out of two recording sessions, ripped it up, said it would never sell. Haley came to me and said, 'Look, Jim, my contract's up, the guy's not paying my royalties, can you get me another record company?'

Myers continued, "I went to New York, scouted around, came up with Decca. I brought the contract back to Haley in Philadelphia. He almost did it in his pants, [he was] so amazed, surprised and pleased. When we recorded it for Decca, they only recorded it as a favor to me for bring[ing] them Bill Haley and they put it on the B-side of the record. They didn't know what to call that type of music in 1954."

Haley was late for the session. "He had taken the ferry over from Jersey," Myers explained, "they were an hour or so late. When you call a recording session, the clock starts at the time the session is called. You had three hours to do at least two songs, or four, if you get them in. He set up hurriedly, did the other[s he] said the Decca producer wanted him to do. Finally they had a few minutes left, so we cut 'Rock Around the Clock' once for balance, and the second time was it. It was the only good take. It was that or forget it. I was bouncing up and down in the control room with the producer. They had two gentlemen who looked like the[y] worked for Tom Edison. They had the needle bouncing around and they wouldn't dare go near the red marks. I said 'peak peak' at the top of my voice in the room. Their two heads swiveled, faces of horror, they had never made a record before that was deliberately distorted."

The musicians for this song were Billy Williamson, steel guitar; Johnny Grande, piano; Joey d'Ambrosio, tenor sax; Danny Cedrone, lead guitar and Marshall Lytle, bass with session drummer Billy Gussack. Cedrone was paid $21 for his classic rock solo.

On May 15, 1954, Billboard picked the flip, "Thirteen Women," about what remained after a nuclear blast. About "Rock Around the Clock," they wrote, "Big beat and repetitious blues lyric makes this a good attempt at 'cat music' and one which should grab coin in the right locations." "Rock Around the Clock" first charted mildly in early 1954. "It sold about ten records because Billboard and Cashbox, following Decca's lead, went with the other side," said Myers. "When I found out they were getting off it, I loaded up the truck and went out for six or eight weeks. Every time I saw a radio antennae, I drove off the road into the radio station. In those days it was very unusual for a writer, producer or publisher to walk in to see them. So they immediately gave me a hearing, usually putting the record right on the turntable. By the time I got back to Philadelphia, it was selling.

Myers added, "Then I shot out about 200 records to every name I could get in Hollywood who was producing or directing a movie. I was lucky enough to get "Blackboard Jungle.' At the time, there was a new writer, producer and director working on a screenplay for MGM. When he heard the record, he said he put it on the turntable and played it 24 hours a day as he wrote the screenplay. Then when they started to shoot the picture, if you remember, it opens in a school yard with a bunch of kids dancing and the record blasting out. He'd pick up the dialogue later. He was concentrating on getting the feel and the beat. It sure proved itself." When used in the juvenile delinquency opus, "Blackboard Jungle" shot to #1.

Covers: The MGM Studio Orchestra 1954; Jimmy DeKnight & the Knights of Rhythm aka Jimmy Myers 1954
Remakes: Phil Flowers 1964; Freddie Cannon 1968; Bill Haley & the Comets 1970
Satires: Mickey Katz & his Orchestra "Knock Around the Clock (Rock Around the Clock)" 1957; Bruce Morrow & D Clock "Stop Around the Clock" 1960; Title changes: Clay Cole "Twist Around the Clock" 1962; Bill Haley "Dance Around the Clock" 1964

—

The Chords "Sh Boom" Cat June 1954/Atco (as The Sh Booms) 1961

Style: Rhythm and blues group vocal
Where from: The Bronx, NY
Where recorded: New York City, NY
Suggested pairings: The Five Crowns "You Could Be My Love" 1953; The Four Knights "I Get So Lonely" 1953; The Willows "Church Bells May Ring" 1956

The original hit side, "Cross Over the Bridge," was a cover of a Patti Page hit. The B-side, "Sh Boom," was the hit. Jimmy Keyes said, "We'll never livc it down. Around New York, the slang word was 'boom, dig,' 'Boom, dig man, did you see that beautiful girl? Wow she gave me her number, boom, dig man, c'mon let's go to the pool.' 1954 was the year of the hydrogen bomb. In 1954 when 'Sh Boom' broke big, we were rushed from the Bronx to California. 'Sh Boom' was a happy song, our strong intention was to bust up the racism in the industry—a few black stations, race music that you read about and heard about. The entire group was writers of the song."

When "Sh Boom" hit, "Cross Over the Bridge" was dropped, replaced by "Little Maiden." The Chords had to change their name because of an earlier Chords, so they became The Chord Cats and lost momentum. "Carl Feaster was the original lead singer of The Chords, I myself, Jimmy Keyes, was the original first tenor, Carl Feaster's brother Claude Feaster was the baritone in the group, William Edwards was the bass, Floyd McCrea, the 2nd tenor." Spawning nonsense titles, "'Sh Boom' was one of those records that was part of the changeover to the white mainstream music industry recognizing what was there," George Carlin explained. "'Sh Boom' was covered by The Crew Cuts and everything began to change, that's why it's significant to me."

Cover: The Crew Cuts
Remakes: Sha Na Na 1974; Big Wheelie and the Hubcaps 1978
Satire: Stan Freberg with The Toads 1954

—

The Cadillacs "Gloria" Josie June 1954

Style: Doo wop
From and recorded in: New York City, NY
Original version: Bob Hayward 1946
Earlier versions: Johnny Moore's Three Blazers with Charles Brown 1947; The Four Gabriels 1948; The Mills Brothers 1948; Ray Anthony with Ronnie Deauville 1948

"Gloria" originated with L.A. songwriter Leon Rene and was performed by a variety of artists from 1946 through 1948 including, but not limited to, Charles Brown and The Mills Brothers. "I did 'Gloria.'" recalled Charles Brown. "When we got to Chicago at the Regal Theater, they said, 'Anybody whose name is Gloria can get a kiss.' When I got through the stage, they had so many girls. I said, 'Is your name Gloria?' 'Yes, my name's Gloria.' I had to kiss all these girls." The big hit was by The Mills Brothers, then it was largely forgotten.

"Then came "Gloria" by The Cadillacs, likely the first doo wop vocal group named after a car with the songwriting credit to their manager, Esther Navarro. "Esther Narvarro was not a songwriter," said lead Earl Speedo Carroll of The Cadillacs. "We were young kids in the business. She took credit for the lyrics most of the group wrote. We're very versatile, we can do uptempo things. We enjoy doing ballads, so it's a mixture of the two." Among die-hard fans, The Cadillacs' "Gloria" became known as the doo wop national anthem and remains so to this day.

Hands down, there were more different and unrelated songs with the title "Gloria" (The Five Thrills, Arthur Lee Maye & the Crowns, The Five Chances, Dee Clark, Troy Parrish, Jimi Hendrix, Shadows of Knight, Them, Laura Branigan, U2, etc.) than just about any other title.

Remakes: The Passions 1960; Vito & the Salutations 1962; The Love Notes 1963

—

The Moonglows "I Was Wrong" Chance June 1954

Style: Doo wop vocal group harmony
Where from: Cleveland, OH
Where recorded: Chicago, IL

The Moonglows began their existence as The Crazy Sounds. According to the group's leader, Harvey Fuqua, the Cleveland disc jockey Alan Freed "looked at us and said, 'The Crazy Sounds sounds crazy. Let's change the name.' His nickname was the Moondog. We had just sung for him. He looked at us, we were perspiring. 'You guys are awfully greasy, man. That's it, The Moonglows.' [I] didn't like the greasy comment, but okay." From then on, it was all Freed. The Moonglows' first release, "I Just Can't Tell No Lie," on Champagne gave writer credit to Alan Lance, a Freed pseudo. "It was done in conjunction with Chess and Alan Freed. Phil Chess was at the session."

Then came a deal with Chance. "Chance was owned by Art Sheridan, who was in oil. 'I Was Wrong' was the biggest record we had in Chicago," said Fuqua, who ranked it with their best "because I was singing lead on it. That was me, vying for lead singer. The song was as strong as 'Sincerely.' Background harmony and the bass figure are sort of similar, not the same, but similar. The bass figure is more prevalent than anything else in the song and the background harmony." Red Holloway who backed the Moonglows said, "'I Was Wrong' was very popular in Chicago, but it was hard to get their records played. The stations would take them. People would write in. They'd play it once or twice a day. Al Benson, the most popular disc jockey of the day: 12 to 2 would be the jazz hour, 2 to 3 would be the blues hour." Fuqua added, "Chance was only distributed regionally. It folded right after we signed with Chess. I had called Phil Chess and he said, 'Come over.' They bought the contract from Chance, $500. I had more than that coming in royalties, they were glad to sell it. Chess was distributed nationally and internationally. I'm sure that had a lot to do with it."

—

Young John Watson "Space Guitar" Federal 1954

Style: Blues instrumental
Where from: Houston, TX
Where recorded: Los Angeles, CA

Young John Watson switched from piano to guitar and began to create his own distinctive style with this instrumental single, the ferocious "Space Guitar," which pioneered guitar feedback and reverb, backed with the vocal "Half Pint Of Whiskey," with backing by Bill Gaither, tenor sax; Devonia Williams, piano; Mario Delagarde, bass and Charles Pendagraph, drums. But it was the seemingly psychedelic guitar on the instrumental "Space Guitar" that proved that Watson was way ahead of his time as early as 1954.

—

The Robins "Riot In Cell Block #9" Spark July 10, 1954

Style: Rhythm and blues group vocal
From and recorded in: Los Angeles, CA
Suggested pairing: Richard Berry "The Big Break" 1954

When Leiber-Stoller and Lester Sill began the Spark label, the third record released was "Riot In Cell Block #9" by The Robins. "We were the only group on Spark," recalled tenor lead singer Grady Chapman. Even though the skit was foundational to hits Leiber-Stoller created with The Coasters, the singer on "Riot In Cell Block #9" wasn't even a member of the Robins and never sang with them again. Tenor Carl Gardner said, "Leiber-Stoller wanted us to talk like black people, Bobby Nunn couldn't and I wouldn't," said Gardner. "I told them, 'Don't give me no words like that. He wrote a song called "I Ain't Here,"' which Gardner turned down. "They asked me, 'Is there something wrong with these songs?' Then they gave it to Peggy Lee, who had a hit. It was very 'Negroish.' I was very angry with what happened in the South. They'd come to me, said, 'I want you to hear the song.' I turned it down. There weren't too many. Once they found out what I was, they wouldn't do that any more. I wanted to sing pop, 'Stardust,' things like that. Got to singing the blues, things like that." For this record only, Leiber-Stoller decided not to use Bobby Nunn, opting for Richard Berry, with whom they had worked when The Flairs first recorded. The theme of the song was based on the popular Neville Brand movie "Riot In Cell Block 11," and was growled so convincingly that fans of the song assumed Berry had done hard time. "The bass singer that they had," said Berry, "they didn't want him to do the song, as actually he was a very smooth singer. He had a beautiful bass voice.

"I established a 'rap' thing, one of the first rap records," Berry continued. The song opened with sound effects of a wailing police siren and the tat-a-tat of a machine gun and the lyrics involved references to a date in 1953 and a prison sentence for armed robbery. The sirens, machine guns and the riot theme sent shockwaves through the radio and TV industry. The record was banned by the CBS network on the West Coast, heightening its impact on those who had heard it. Even so, The Robins sang the song on ABC-TV's "Make Believe Ballroom," hosted by Al Jarvis. Berry's voice was so distinctive and as Berry was under contract to the Modern/RPM/Flair family of labels, they had him copy "Riot" with the laughably lame "The Big Break" on Flair. Berry's solo career led to the demise of Berry's first group, The Flairs. "Record companies in those days divided and conquered. They approached me about going out on my own, which was what I would call fascinating. I felt that loyalty to the group. I thought I could do both, but the guys in the group really didn't take to me going out on my own in the first place. To be in the group and on my own just didn't work out."

Cover: Vikki Young 1954
Remakes: by Ron & Joe & the Crew 1959; by Wanda Jackson 1961, by Little Johnny and the Rumblers 1964 and by Commander Cody & his Lost Planet Airmen 1974

Note: Jackson thought the song was written for her and was about a women's prison in Tehachapi.

—

Bill Haley & the Comets "Shake, Rattle and Roll" Decca July 12, 1954

Style: Rock 'n' roll
Where recorded: New York
Original version: Joe Turner 1954

Bill Haley's follow-up to "Rock Around the Clock" was a remake of Joe Turner's recent original R&B hit, "Shake, Rattle and Roll," with some significant lyric changes, taking out references to dresses, the "sun comes shining through." Even this careful cleansing of the lyrics missed the most sexual of all, "one-eyed cat peeking in a seafood store."

—

Elvis Presley, Scotty and Bill "That's All Right" Sun July 19, 1954/RCA December 1955

Style: Rock 'n' roll/rockabilly
Where from: Tupelo, MS
Where recorded: Memphis, TN
Original version: Arthur Crudup 1946

Sun label blues artist Little Milton, who already had two releases under his belt, recalled, "When Elvis came along, he took that same sound" identified with Memphis and Sun label blues. "He started doing things, in fact, he did some of Big Boy Crudup's stuff. He took the same thing that was there, because basically, that's all he really knew and had heard and that's what he liked."

"That's All Right" was Elvis' first commercial release. The Presley B-side was a remake of country material, Bill Monroe's bluegrass classic, "Blue Moon Of Kentucky," from 1947. On August 7, 1954, Billboard reviewed it: "He comes thru with a solid performance on an r&b-type tune and then on the flip side does another fine job with a country ditty. A strong new talent"—to put it mildly.

On August 18, the B-side, "Blue Moon Of Kentucky," hit #3 on the Memphis region Billboard country charts. Someone flipped the record: On August 24, "That's All Right" hit #4 on the Memphis region Billboard country charts.

Malcolm Leo noted, "When Crudup was very ill, Elvis donated some money to him. The two never met. It's amazing to think of the early black Delta blues singers, Elvis covered three Crudup songs, 'So Glad You're Mine,' 'My Baby Left Me' and of course, Elvis' debut on Sun, 'That's All Right.'"

Cover: Marty Robbins 1955

—

The Medallions "The Letter" Dootone August 1954

Style: Rhythm and blues group vocal
Where from: Denver, CO and Los Angeles, CA
Where recorded: Los Angeles, CA
Suggested pairing: Steve Miller "The Joker"

Medallions' lead singer Vernon Green arrived in L.A. in 1948 with his brother Jimmy, who had been taken in by grandparents. "We used to sing in the car in the Watts area, went to school at Jordan High," recalled second tenor Willie Graham. They sang at Will Rogers Park. "Dootsie Williams was staying in the area on Central Ave. and 96th Street. I stayed on 99th Street, right around the corner from him. We used to do house gigs before we had a hit for a couple of years." Impressed with Green, Dootsie asked him to put together a vocal group. The first lineup was Vernon on lead; Randolph Bryant, tenor; Graham, Rudolph Brown, baritone and a bass, recalled Chuck. Graham recalled, "Andrew Blue was the piano player, he played on 'Buick 59' and 'The Letter.' He was just around there, when we was together."

"The Letter," which contained Green's recitation "the pulpitudes of love" was the clear basis of Steve Miller's "pompitudes of love," which he called "jive talk" in the 1990s. Crippled by polio, Green "used to look up to my older brother. He would get on the phone and talk to the ladies." With this skill in mind, Green developed his own language of "sweet words of pismotology." Said Green, "I would make that up and I didn't even know what I was doing. Green later said the lyric actually started as "puppetutes," which was a paper doll he cut out of his dream woman.

"I didn't put any standard on the new creative material that was coming out," said Dootsie Williams. "If I didn't understand it, I'd put it out anyway because I figured the creative surge coming out of American youth was authentic and they were the judge of the standards, so it was their language, it was their feeling, it was their saying. Some of it was against my better judgment. It seemed to be the best judgment."

—

The Medallions "Buick 59" Dootone August 1954

Style: Rhythm and blues group vocal
Where from: Denver, CO and Los Angeles, CA
Where recorded: Los Angeles, CA
Suggested pairing: Todd Rhodes "Rocket 69" 1952

In 1954, there was no such thing as a "Buick 59," except the expectation the record would become popular again in 1959. It was. The inspiration for the song was cruising the snowy streets of Denver in boyhood friend Haskell Sadler's '37 Buick when they ran out of gas. The performance was peppered with Vernon Green's totally improvised imitations of tires and brakes screeching and motors running. While their record was hot, Graham and Bryant got jobs at Minata's Pressing Plant, as did The Penguins.

—

The Penguins "Earth Angel" Dootone August 1954

Style: Rhythm and blues group vocal
From and recorded in: Los Angeles, CA
Suggested pairings: Damita Jo and the Red Caps "I Went To Your Wedding" 1952; Jesse & Marvin "Dream Girl" 1952; The Hollywood Flames "I Know" 1954

After one flop release, the gospel-flavored "No There Ain't No News Today" on Dootone, The Penguins were ready for new material. The group's tenor, Curtis Williams, brought a ballad he had worked on with Jesse Belvin and Gaynel Hodge. Don Julian recalled, "After Jesse went in to the service, other group members forgot a lot of words to that song, so they added some stuff to supplement what they didn't remember." Some of the finished song derived from a demo The Flames had made of Jessie Mae Robinson's hit, "I Went To Your Wedding" about "a vision of loveliness."

Lead singer Cleve Duncan recalled five takes of "Earth Angel," the ballad side were required in "trying to make everything as perfect as possible." Around the third take, the group began to get the needed feeling and tempo, rounding out the song with the descending arpeggio… "you, you, you." "We all thought of that together. We were trying to conclude the song as a group and give each a voice at the end; myself, first; Dexter; Bruce and then Curtis; tenor down to the bass. We went through a few endings and this was the one we felt most comfortable with."

Label owner Dootsie Williams took the metal dub to a few influential distributors and DJs, pushing the rhythmic "Hey Senorita" side. Johnny Otis and Charles Trammell aired the side to positive response, then Dootsie took it to Dolphins of Hollywood where Huggy Boy was on the air with his all night show. "Huggy Boy played 'Earth Angel' and the phones lit up." Dootsie was caught off-guard, not having a record to sell. "I had to go down to the pressing plant, get 200 records in each hand—78s, and they were heavy, too, 100 in each box," said Dootsie. Members of The Penguins worked at the Minata Pressing Plant on Long Beach Ave., thus laboring in pressing the record on which they sang. The plant soon ran out of the glossy red paper Dootsie preferred, so they switched to blue, black and maroon labels to cover the demand. "We were selling so many records, we almost put it on toilet paper," Dootsie joked.

"I was the first one to play this record," said DJ Huggy Boy. "It wasn't even pressed yet. It was an acetate. They liked 'Hey Senorita,' evidentially. Both sides were played. People liked 'Earth Angel.' That's what they wanted. Gaynel Hodge and those kids was about to record for me, they made tunes like 'Emily' and 'I'm A Fool.'"

The Penguins' "Earth Angel" backed with "Hey Senorita" was released on Dootone and hit the Hunter Hancock radio charts at #1 on September 26, 1954, going R&B #1 on December 18, 1954 and #8 pop on December 25, 1954. "Earth Angel" never really went out of print until the purported death of the 45.

Covers: The Crew Cuts; Pat O'Day; Gloria Mann
Remakes: The Penguins 1956; Johnny Tillotson 1960; The Cleftones 1961; Yvonne Carroll 1964; The Viceroys 1964; The Vogues 1970; Richard "Dimples" Fields 1981; New Edition 1986

—

The Diablos (Feat. Nolan Strong) "The Wind" Fortune September 1954

Where from: Scottsboro, AL
Where recorded: Detroit

Lead singer of The Diablos, Nolan Strong, had an appealingly smooth voice, influenced greatly by Clyde McPhatter of The Drifters. In turn, he was a primary influence on Smokey Robinson of The Miracles. "Nolan Strong had some similar sound," said Claudette Robinson. "Smokey's voice was [a] naturally high voice. He sang with first soprano, not a falsetto."

Formed at Central High School in Detroit around 1950, The Diablos were Strong with Juan Guitierrez, lead tenor; Willie Hunter, baritone; Quentin Eubanks, and Bob "Chico" Edwards. The Diablos name is said to have come from a book, *El Nino Diablo* (The Little Devil), that Strong was reading for a high-school book report. In 1954, The Diablos went into Detroit's tiny storefront Fortune Record Studios to cut some demo sides. Fortune owners Jack and Devora Brown signed the group to record for their label. It's said that Devora would take the group to the recording studio in the back of the Fortune Record Shop, turn on the lights and tell the group, "Okay, boys, go ahead and record," which amounted to the extent of her production supervision.

Perhaps apocryphally, it is said they'd cook on a small stove in the back room while recording, thus the sound of sizzling bacon on some sides. Others have observed that the recordings sound like they were made in a closet, with really poor acoustics, which give their recordings a "live" concert sound. According to Lamont Dozier of the Holland-Dozier-Holland songwriting team, the studio had a four track machine. He said, "When I was a kid, I used to knock on their door and ask for an audition, but never did pass it."

Their first Fortune 45 was the Devora Brown-penned cha cha, "Adios My Desert Love." Then came the haunting ballad, "The Wind," with the group chanting "blow wind" in harmony behind Strong's tenor lead, and a unique talking bridge that caught on in vocal group circles in a big way to the extent that Slim of Times Square Records in New York made a deal to re-press "The Wind" in the early 1960s during the first doo wop oldies revival. Dozier also noted how Strong influenced Smokey Robinson. "I didn't know if you would call it quite falsetto singing that Nolan did. Smokey's the best at it. I would venture to say he was somewhat influenced by Nolan in his delivery."

Remake: The Jesters 1960

—

The Jewels "Hearts Of Stone" R&B September 1954/Original Sound 1963

Style: Rhythm and blues group vocal
Where from: San Bernardino, CA
Where recorded: Los Angeles, CA

Johnny Torrence managed the Paradise Record Shop in San Bernardino, where he met Eddie Ray, head buyer for Central Record Sales. Torrence formed The Marbles, a one release group on John Dolphin's Lucky label. Torrence's group had rehearsed "Hearts Made Of Stone," which was based on a song recorded by Torrence's gospel group The Hollywood Rising Stars. They took a dub of the song to Art Rupe of Specialty. "Art Rupe throwed it in the trashcan," said Torrence. "About two months later, we went to another label and Art said, 'I should let you guys kick me for throwing it away.'" Ray then took it to the brand new R and B label, which hired Ernie Freeman to arrange the material. The Jewels with co-leads Torrence and Rudy Jackson, tenor Dee Hawkins and bass James Brown out of San Bernardino debuted with the original A-side "Runnin'" backed with "Hearts Of Stone" on R and B, where it hit the L.A. R&B charts at #7 on September 11, 1954.

From then on, it was downhill. The Jewels' original of "Hearts Of Stone" was frozen out by The Charms' cover on DeLuxe, which hit #1 R&B on October 20, 1954 and #15 pop on November 27, 1954. When The Jewels appeared with The Charms on tour, they were asked not to perform their hit, as only one group was allowed to perform the song live. The promoter "really got on his knees to my fellows and asked us not to do 'Hearts Of Stone.' From then on, I knew something was wrong. They had sold us out," said Torrence.

Covers: The Charms 1954; The Fontane Sisters 1954

—

Elvis Presley "Good Rockin' Tonight" Sun September 22, 1954/RCA

Style: Rock 'n' roll/rockabilly
Where from: Tupelo, MS
Where recorded: Memphis
Suggested pairings: Roy Milton "Hop, Skip & Jump" 1948; The Treniers "Good Rockin' Tonight" 1956; Andy Starr "Rockin' Rollin' Stone" 1956

Elvis' rockabilly remake of "Good Rockin' Tonight" reinforced the R&B/blues hip shaking style of Wynonie Harris and turned the R&B roots song into a rockabilly classic. "Roy Brown recalled playing Tupelo in the mid-40s, and he swears he recognized a young Elvis Presley hanging by the bandstand," said Malcolm Leo. "Roy Brown and Presley remained friends." Presley's remake was not covered. How could it be? The original version by Wynonie Harris on King was reissued twice, Presley's once.

Cover: Sid King & the Five Strings 1956
Remakes: Pat Boone 1959; James Brown 1967; Jerry Lee Lewis 1973

—

The Robins "Framed" Spark October 5, 1954

Style: Rhythm and blues group vocal
From and recorded in: Los Angeles, CA

With Richard Berry out, regular Robins' bass Bobby Nunn took lead on the group's second "talking" vocal, "Framed." According to Robins member Grady Chapman, tenor sax backing was by Plas Johnson and Barney Kessell on guitar with Carl Gardner singing tenor lead on the flipside, the much more popular title in L.A., "Loop De Loop Mambo."

Remakes: Ritchie Valens 1958; Bill Haley & the Comets 1970; Cheech & Chong 1976; Los Lobos 1987

—

The Five Keys "Ling, Ting, Tong" Capitol October 1954

Style: Rhythm and blues group vocal
Where from: Virginia
Where recorded: New York City, NY

The Five Keys were discovered when they won the amateur program at the Apollo Theater in late 1950, according to lead singer Rudy West. "Eddie Mesner, president of Aladdin Records, had been in New York. Most of the record producers and owners usually came to the Apollo Theater on amateur night, so he heard us. I guess he liked what he heard, he offered us a contract a week later."

After recording several rhythm and blues classics like "Glory Of Love" and "My Saddest Hour," The Five Keys were signed by Capitol Records. West said, "We were hooked up through an agency head, his name was Sol Richfield, he and Dave Cavanaugh were good friends, Dave Cavanaugh was a producer at Capitol. I would say there were three, at the most, prominent black groups, The Ink Spots, The Mills Brothers, The Four Knights. We always wanted to be in the category, work the places The Ink Spots and The Mills Brothers [did]. Bill Kenney and The Ink Spots and Nat King Cole were my idols.

"'Ling Ting Tong' was considered like a novelty, it was just a novelty," West continued. "We knew that egg foo young is a Chinese dinner, 'tai samoka boom die ae,' don't ask me what it means," but it didn't mean smoking drugs. "Somebody could've taken it easily for that. Otis Williams & the Charms really pushed our version of it, because their cover was a direct replica from word to word, from harmony to arrangement." Asked if the group was avoiding the rock 'n' roll label, West said, "I wasn't trying to avoid the label. We knew we shouldn't have been branded outright as a rock and roll group. We knew we had the ability to perform in Las Vegas and Hollywood and everywhere. It was a sign of the times."

Cover: The Charms 1954
Remakes: Buddy Knox 1961; The Allisons 1963; Wolfman Jack 1973

—

Arthur Gunter "Baby Let's Play House" Excello November 1954

Style: Blues
Where from: Oglethorpe County, GA
Where recorded: Nashville, TN
Suggested pairing: Johnny Burnette Rock & Roll Trio "Oh, Baby Babe" 1955

This is the original R&B version of the classic rocker "Baby Let's Play House," which Elvis turned into a rockabilly staple, though he did change an important lyric about "you ain't got religion" to "you don't drive a pink Cadillac" so as not to offend his religious mom.

Cover: Elvis Presley 1955

—

The Drifters Featuring Clyde McPhatter "White Christmas" Atlantic November 1954

Style: Rhythm and blues group vocal
Where from: North Carolina
Where recorded: New York City, NY
Original version: Bing Crosby 1942

The first known R&B version of "White Christmas" was this song by The Ravens in 1947. Seven years later, with the appealing tenor lead voice of Clyde McPhatter, The Drifters turned this rocking version of "White Christmas" into an even more enduring Yuletide classic.

—

The Moonglows "Sincerely" Chess November 1954

Style: Rhythm and blues group vocal
Where from: Kentucky
Recorded in: Cincinnati, OH
Suggested pairings: Billy Eckstine "Blue Moon" 1948; The Dominoes "That's What You're Doin' To Me" 1952; Arthur Lee Maye "Truly" 1955; The Isley Brothers "Don't Be Jealous" 1958; Bo Diddley "I'm Sorry" 1959; Freddy Fender "Holy One" 1959; Ruben & the Jets "Fountain Of Love" 1969

After a solitary release for the Champagne label in 1952, and five releases on Chance in 1953/54, The Moonglows finally hit with the emotionally rendered "Sincerely." "It was the biggest record we had in Chicago," said Moonglows' leader Harvey Fuqua about the Chess label. "Chance was only distributed regionally, Chess was distributed nationally and internationally. It sold 700,000. Of course, the McGuire Sisters did double platinum. I believe we would have done more if the pop stations would've played the record. We were limited to a limited amount of stations, none of the pop stations would've played it at all in that era. It sort of threw me in another frame of mind. We'd been struggling for a long time. We might make some money. We all made money, probably didn't make the amount due us, but we all made money."

Moonglows' guitarist Billy Johnson, whose career began with Charles Brown and Sonny Thompson, recalled the downside of having a well-known hit while playing for a live audience. "I had to work the four hours, do the whole number that was revived by Jimi Hendrix. All the guitarists had to do the same things in those days. Had to walk the bar, play behind my head, pick with my teeth, my toes, everything else. $22.50 a night for that. Everybody got $20, I got $22.50. It was traditional that any of R&B bands that worked down south, it was expected. The saxophone player with one hand behind the back, walking the bar, all meant to keep the people stirred up. You couldn't stretch too far. If there was a record on what you were doing, you have to do the record verbatim for your audience, otherwise, they'd swear you were imposters. In those days, there weren't any imposters. If you decided to stretch out on your solos, put anything extra in there, the whole crowd in unison would yell, 'That's not them, they're fakes.' They want[ed] to hear exactly what they heard on jukeboxes, they don't want any deviation at all."

Fuqua also said it opened up new buyers for Chess, previously a blues label. "It sort of opened up more stations to play the blues. It did a lot of things for them DJ-wise. Everybody was looking for a label that was promoting their act at the time."

Cover: The McGuire Sisters 1955; The Bop-A-Loos 1955
Remakes: Roosevelt Grier 1960; The Tokens 1961; Louis Armstrong, The Platters 1964; The Four Seasons 1964; Pat Boone 1964; Paris Sisters 1966; Paul Anka 1969

—

Bobby Lester and the Moonlighters "Shoo Doo-Be Doo (My Loving Baby)" Checker November 1954

Style: Rhythm and blues group vocal
Where from: Kentucky
Where recorded: Cincinnati, OH

One and the same group as The Moonglows, Bobby Lester and the Moonlighters were created for an uptempo sound. In case "Sincerely" didn't hit, "Shoo Doo-Be Doo" might sell. In fact, both "Shoo Doo-Be Doo" and "Sincerely" were recorded at the same session. "The Moonlighters consisted of Bobby Lester and myself," said The Moonglows' Harvey Fuqua. "It was a duet, actually. We did ten songs in two sessions. There was a trend happening with songs like 'Sh Boom.' We did 'Shoo Doo-Be Doo' which was sort of reminiscent of that. We wanted to put that out to capitalize on that sound The Crew Cuts were doing. We couldn't release it like Moonglows number one and number two, so we said, 'How about The Moonlighters?' They were released simultaneously. They were both hits at the same time, which I thought was wonderful. The Chess and Checker labels got a duet out of The Moonglows. Bobby and Harvey. They could book two groups at live shows, charge twice as much, change costumes and The Moonglows would become The Moonlighters."

—

LaVern Baker "Tweedlee Dee" Atlantic November 1954

Style: Rhythm and blues
Where from: Detroit, MI
Where recorded: New York

After dropping the moniker Little Miss Sharecropper, LaVern Baker joined the Todd Rhodes Orchestra, debuting with the soulful ballad, "Trying," later a hit by The Hilltoppers, on King in 1952. It stiffed. After another ballad, "Lost Child," also with the Rhodes Orchestra, Baker signed with the fledgling Atlantic label to record the emotive "Soul On Fire," which also stiffed in 1954. A change in style seemed in order, so in 1954, she pepped things up with this quasi-calypso novelty, "Tweedlee Dee," which became her signature song.

"There was a rumor back then that 'Tweedle Dee' would have gone to me," said Ruth Brown. "I became pregnant with my first child and had to slow down. That's when Lavern came in. We worked together. Promoters tried to get the impression there was a feud between us, but that was not true. For ticket sales, it was good. Ruth Brown versus Lavern Baker. The Blues Against the Blues." However, Baker wasn't happy with another matter altogether. As with the serious hits by black artists, major labels assigned their star of the day to record as cover. So when Georgia Gibbs covered "Tweedlee Dee" on Mercury, taking it to #1 pop, Baker sued, claiming Gibbs had used the very same session players, thus creating the exact same backing and unfairly scored a big hit. Baker lost the suit, and cover versions continued for at least three more years.

Cover: Dorothy Collins 1954; The Lancers 1955; Bonnie Lou 1955; Georgia Gibbs 1955

—

Marvin & Johnny "Cherry Pie" Modern November 1954
Style: Rhythm and blues
From and recorded in: Los Angeles, CA

Marvin Phillips and Emory "Johnny" Perry as Marvin & Johnny recorded this strong double-sided goodie, the syncopated "Tick Tock," backed by the somewhat racy ballad, "Cherry Pie" at the first session held at the sleek new modern Modern building in Culver City. On the drive out, the duo passed L.A.'s Union Station near downtown and were inspired by the clock tower. They began singing, "tick tock, tick tock goes the clock," the melody lifted from Bill Haley's "Rock Around the Clock," and the song "Tick Tock" was born. Though "Cherry Pie" became a doo wop classic, it was "Tick Tock" by Marvin & Johnny on Modern that hit the charts. "I wrote the song, 'Cherry Pie,' said Phillips. "At that time they thought it was dirty." "Tick Tock" was the L.A. hit.

Cover: The Bel Aires
Remakes: The Tri-Lads 1958; Volcanoes 1958; Skip & Flip 1959; Adrian & the Sunsets 1963; Lani & Boni & the Cochrane Twins 1964; Dave Bartholomew & his Orchestra 1964; Tikis & Fabulons 1965
Answer: Marvin Phillips "Patootie Pie" 1960; Marvin & Johnny "Second Helping Of Cherry Pie" 1963

—

Lowell Fulson "Reconsider Baby" Checker November 1954
Style: Blues
Where from: Oklahoma/Los Angeles, CA
Where recorded: Dallas

A big-voiced blues guitarist and songwriter in the West Coast blues tradition. Lowell Fulson was born in Tulsa, Oklahoma. Also recording for business reasons as Lowell Fullsom and Lowell Fulsom, he moved to California, forming a band which soon included a young Ray Charles and tenor saxophone player Stanley Turrentine. "Ray Charles had a change to his style when he was with me. [I told him,] 'Man, you're a genius, forget about Nat Cole and get your own thing. I'm going to have to let you, I can't afford you. You're a million dollar talent.' I couldn't support this man, he was too expensive. They only pay me so much a night for a ten piece band. I had to cut him loose. They picked him up in Texas, took him to New York. Man went on and made hits.

"Reconsider Baby" came from a long term contract with Chess Records in 1954. Recorded in Dallas under Stan Lewis' supervision with a saxophone section that included David "Fathead" Newman on tenor and Leroy Cooper on baritone, it was a major R&B hit.

Remakes: Elvis Presley 1960; Al King 1964

—

Floyd Dixon "Hey Bartender" Cat December 1954
Style: Rhythm and blues
Where from: Texas
Where recorded: New York

The Floyd Dixon vocal "Hey Bartender" was true to life. "I came up with it, I used to drink a lot of Rainier Ale at one time," said Floyd Dixon. "I always used to hang around the bar lot of times, until I refrained. You got to grow up a little bit. I used to think beer was the thing with me. I'd go to have me a few beers, then I stopped and I started to write about beer."

Cover: Red Saunders 1954
Remake: The Blues Brothers 1979—Blues collectors Belushi and Ackroyd displayed their depth by reviving "Hey Bartender" into a hit single.

—

Joe Houston "All Night Long" Money December 1954

Style: Rhythm and blues
Where from: Texas
Where recorded: Los Angeles, CA
Suggested pairings: Lucky Millinder "Let It Roll"; Hal Singer "Cornbread" 1949; Rusty Bryant "All Night Long" 1952

Joe Houston broke "All Night Long" way open. Heard on the release were DJ Huggy Boy, which assured radio play, on vocals and "some friends that used to drink wine and they could dance good. I bought three quarts of wine, took them to the studio with me to clap hands and I said, 'When we get to the part, holler "all night long!"' It was a noisy record and we played for 45 minutes before the engineer said, 'Tell them to stop drinking, they're dropping the wine bottles.'"

"Rusty Bryant had a record called 'All Night Long,'" said Houston. "He was playing 'Night Train' and used a tag of Lucky Millinder's 'let it roll, let it roll, all night long.' I put 'Cornbread' on 'All Night Long,' that's where it started. Mine was the big record." Record shop owner "John Dolphin had 12 hours of radio time and he was the hottest person in Los Angeles. I knew I'd get some play on it. If I didn't get any money, I knew I'd get some gigs. I made four sides, gave him the tapes with 'Way Out,'" Despite Huggy Boy's vocal appearance, "All Night Long" charted on Hunter Hancock's competing "Harlem Matinee" on KFVD on Halloween 1954.

Remakes: Billy Vaughn 1960; Paul Revere & the Raiders 1962; Sandy Nelson 1962

—

Gene & Eunice "Ko Ko Mo" Combo December 1954

Style: Rhythm and blues
From and recorded in: Los Angeles, CA

After recording with The Four Feathers, Gene Forrest and Eunice Levy brought a new song, "Ko Ko Mo," to their label, Aladdin, who had a hit duo, Shirley & Lee, and turned them down flat. Gene & Eunice brought "Ko Ko Mo" backed with "You and Me" to Jake Porter's Combo (64) with Jonsey's Combo, Fletcher Smith on piano, Chuck Hamilton on drums and leader Reginald Jones on bass in very late 1954. As Gene Forrest and his group The Four Feathers with Eunice were still under contract to Aladdin, at the very time the Combo version charted on Hunter Hancock's show, Gene & Eunice were forced to cover both "Ko Ko Mo" backed with "You and Me" on Aladdin (3276) with Johnny's Combo—instead of Jonsey's Combo—a reference to Johnny Otis, who according to Forrest "didn't do a very good job. They tried to duplicate it, just asked him to capitalize on the idea. The only musician used on both sessions was the piano player, Clarence Lively. We felt the piano player would give it the original flavor." Jake Porter claimed Aladdin "took Gene & Eunice to their office and told them if they didn't record the number for Aladdin, they would have me put in jail." That competing version caused some confusion in the market and gave the Aladdin label some sales to which Combo was entitled. The duet was never again heard from on Combo. "After we cut 'Ko Ko Mo,' Jake Porter cut us loose."

Gene & Eunice's "Ko Ko Mo" didn't chart pop, yet attracted a large number of covers.

Covers: Marvin & Johnny; The Charms; The Flamingos; Two Crows & the Diggers; Perry Como; Andy Griffith; The Crew Cuts; The Hutton Sisters; Bill Darnell & Betty Clooney; Gary Crosby with Louis Armstrong; Hawkshaw Hawkins (all in 1954)

—

Etta James & the Peaches "The Wallflower" Modern December 1954

Style: Rhythm and blues group vocal
From and recorded in: Los Angeles, CA
Original title: "Roll With Me Henry"
Suggested pairings: The Royals/Midnighters "Work With Me Annie" 1954; Etta James "Hey! Henry" 1955; The Midnighters "Henry's Got Flat Feet" 1955; Young Jesse "Here Comes Henry" 1957

Etta James reputedly had already put down the first version of "Roll With Me Henry" for the Bay Area-based Rhythm label while she was living with relatives in San Francisco. At the age of 15, she met sisters Jean and Abysinia Mitchell from New Orleans and formed the Creolettes group. After encountering Hank Ballard, James answered his hit "Work With Me Annie" with her own "Roll With Me Henry." Johnny Otis recalled, "We were in San Francisco, somebody called me on the phone, we were asleep, we were to play that night and the little girl said, 'Hey Mr. Otis I want to sing for you.' [I said,] 'Come to the gig tonight, I want to sleep now.' She said, 'No, I want to sing now.' Came up, knocked on the door, had two little girls with her, came in and even though she had that much nerve, still there was an element of shyness because she turned her face away, she faced into the bathroom when she was singing, it sounded so good like an echo chamber. It sounded so good, I said, 'Wow!' We called her mother up and I brought her right to Los Angeles with me. She lived in our home for a while. She had this idea for a song. She had a crush on Hank Ballard at the time and she had this little idea that went 'Roll With Me Henry.'

She then moved in with her mother and attended Jefferson High School. Richard Berry then got the call to record with her in the role of Henry with the group called The Creolettes, with backing by the Otis band. "Johnny Otis brought Etta in," said Joe Bihari of Modern Records. "I was in Atlanta, recording. Jules called me, 'You better come back in. We set up a day for you to record on Thanksgiving night. I got in early. I did all the engineering, producing." On Thanksgiving, Otis was playing the song on his KFOX radio show from the Red Hut in L.A. Not liking the group's name, he created a contest to name the act. "She's got big ol' jaws, a hefty backside and she's only 15. I call her Miss Peaches, but she needs a better name than that." After about a week of this, James' nickname of Peaches became the group; Jamesetta Hawkins became Etta James.

Upon release in early 1955, "Roll With Me Henry," considered lewd, was changed to "The Wallflower" in later pressings on which Otis took writer credit. "My attorney filed an injunction," said Hank Ballard. "It restrained them temporarily." "The Wallflower" hit R&B #1 on February 19, 1955. "Thinking back, I can see why Johnny felt like he deserved a piece of the song; he'd discovered me," James said in her biography. "On the other hand, he didn't write a lick of the lyrics or music." George Gibbs covered and retitled the already retitled song as "Dance With Me Henry" on Mercury, a title Etta's label used for her original in some later pressings.

Covers: "Dance With Me Henry" by Georgia Gibbs 1955; Chet Atkins 1955; Edna McGriff 1955
Remakes: Damita Jo "Dance With Me Henry" 1961

—

Ray Charles "I've Got a Woman" Atlantic December 1954

Style: Rhythm and blues
Where from: Florida
Where recorded: Atlanta, GA
Suggested parings: The Trumpeteers "Milky White Way" 1947; The Bailey Gospel Singers "I've Got a Savior (Across Town)" 1951; The Southern Tones "It Must Be Jesus" 1954; Little Richard on "Ain't That Good News" 1953; Maddox Brothers & Sister Rose "Death Of Rock & Roll" 1955; Ray Charles "Talkin' Bout You" 1957; The Ding Dongs "Early in the Morning" 1958; Sam Cooke "Good News" 1963

Charles had heard the spiritual "It Must Be Jesus" by the gospel quartet the Southern Tones on the radio while Ray Charles and his band were on the road. This secular version of the gospel "My Jesus Is All the World to Me" was the first R&B hit song to use secular lyrics in a gospel style, creating a fusion of R&B, gospel and jazz, or the first soul record. "I was just being myself," Charles said.

Lowell Fulson recalled when Ray Charles began recording gospel-based blues: "They laughed when he was getting himself with The Five Blind Boys. Archie Brownlee went into a room, started to play records and stuff, when he came out, he had that style. I said you don't hear nobody with that style, he may get lucky. They waited too late, laying back to see what would happen." Even so, there was plenty of resistance.

"Of course it created a lot of static from a lot of people," said Charles. "But then, on the other hand, it was a hit. It was a hit in the black community and the white community," partly because of Elvis Presley's remake in 1956, as one of four singles, including "Lawdy Miss Clawdy," released at one time. Malcolm Leo noted, "In England, they were worried about the Presley title, so they changed it to 'I've Got a Sweetie,' but I don't think it did much." Blues singer Big Bill Broonzy criticized Ray Charles' original as "mixing the sacred with the profane."

Remakes: Eddie Bond & the Stompers 1956; Elvis Presley 1956; Bill Haley & His Comets 1959; Sammy Davis Jr. 1960; Bobby Darin 1960; Jimmy Smith 1960; Troy Shondell 1962; Rick Nelson 1963; Freddie Scott 1963; The Everly Brothers 1965; Trini Lopez 1965; Jimmy McGriff 1968; Al Kooper 1970

—

Elvis Presley, Scotty and Bill "Milkcow Blues Boogie" Sun January 8, 1955/RCA December 1955

Style: Rockabilly
Where from: Tupelo, MS
Where recorded: Memphis, TN
Original version: "Milk Cow Blues" by Kokomo Arnold 1934
Earlier version: Johnny Lee Wills & His Boys 1941

By far the poorest selling of the five Elvis Presley singles on the Sun label, likely because it wasn't properly equalized, so the original record sounds dull. This rockabilly take on a "Milkcow Blues Boogie" was quickly dropped from Presley's live shows in the early days.

Remake: Ricky Nelson "Milk Cow Blues" 1960

—

Johnny Ace "Pledging My Love" Duke 1955

Style: Rhythm and blues
Where from: Memphis, TN
Where recorded: Los Angeles, CA
Suggested pairings: The Weavers "Down in the Valley" 1951

Johnny Ace never experienced the benefits of his greatest hit, this classic love ballad, "Pledging My Love," in which the title is never referenced in the lyrics, as he fell victim to a losing round of Russian roulette backstage in Houston, TX on Christmas Eve, 1954 just as the record was being released.

Johnny Alexander was born in Memphis in 1929. His early work was backing B.B. King and Bobby Bland on piano. In fact, the three men, along with Roscoe Gordon were dubbed the Beale Streeters. Also a piano player with the Beale Streeters, Bobby Bland recalled him as "kind of a happy go lucky feller. Everything was fun with him, and a very good singer." He changed his recording surname from Alexander to Ace, based on Johnny Ray and the Four Aces, to not embarrass his family. He immediately recorded hit ballads like "My Song" in 1952. Then came "Cross My Heart" and "The Clock" with dry, emotionless delivery, not employed by any other vocalist at the time.

Working behind Ace was the Johnny Otis Band on a melody derived from "Down in the Valley," which resulted in "Pledging My Love." Ace's well-publicized death, the first documented death of an R&B star, shook music fans worldwide. Word has it that his death and this song prompted "grown women to weep and write suicidal poems to newspapers and magazines."

In 1958, Johnny Ace's "Pledging My Love" was reissued with a new B-side, "Anymore," with an annoying background by The Jordanaires dubbed in. It also sold well.

Tribute records: Frankie Ervin "Johnny Ace's Last Letter" 1955; Linda Hayes "Why, Johnny, Why?" 1955; Varetta Dillard "Johnny Has Gone" 1955; The Five Wings "Johnny Has Gone" 1955; Patti Jerome "Johnny Has Gone" 1955; The Five Wings " Johnny's Still Singing" 1955
Soundalikes: Jimmy Reed "Honest I Do" 1957; Paul Anka "Lonely Boy" 1958; Jimmy Clanton "Letter To An Angel" 1958; John Lennon "Happy Xmas" 1971
Remakes: Roy Hamilton 1958; Jesse Belvin 1958; The Four Coins 1960; Sanford Clark 1960; Johnny Tillotson 1960; Brian Hyland 1964; Don & Juan 1964; Joe Hinton 1965; Lavern Baker 1965; Van McCoy 1966; O.V. Wright 1971; Oscar Weathers 1972; Wilson Pickett 1972; Tom Jones 1975
Covers: Louis Armstrong; Tommy Mara; The Four Lads; Teresa Brewer; Ronnie Gaylord; Cowboy Copas; The Thunderbirds (all 1955)

—

The Hawketts "Mardi Gras Mambo" Chess February 1955

Style: Rhythm and blues group vocal
From and recorded in: New Orleans, LA
Original version: Jody Leviens and His Boys—country styled version—1954
Suggested pairings: The Kings "'Til I Say Well Done" 1955

The Hawketts' "Mardi Gras Mambo" was the first recording date for lead singer and pianist Art Neville, as well as the other teenaged band members, John Boudreaux, drums; Alfred August, guitar; Israel Bell and August Fleuri, trumpet; Carroll Joseph, trombone; George Davis, alto sax and Morris Bechamin, tenor sax. The original version of "Mardi Gras Mambo" was by country singer Jody Leviens and His Boys on Sapphire in 1953. WWEZ DJ, Jack the Cat (Ken Elliott), thought an R&B version of "Mardi Gras Mambo" might sell, so they recorded at the WWEZ radio studios in January 1954.

At the same time, Earl King took the name the Kings for his local release, "'Til I Say Well Done," on Specialty in June 1954. "We heard someone had went in the studio, a group out of New Orleans, and had cut a record similar to "Til I Say Well Done,' and the name of that record was 'Mardi Gras Mambo.' At the time," said King, "Art Rupe said 'hurry up and get this record out on the market' as The Kings." Turned out, "Mardi Gras Mambo" was a local smash and has become a standard of the Mardi Gras genre. Art Neville signed to the Specialty label, and by 1968 formed The Meters, an Allen Toussaint and Marshall Sehorn studio band.

Remake: The Meters 1975

—

The Hearts "Lonely Nights" Baton February 1955

Style: Rhythm and blues vocal group
From and recorded in: New York
Suggested pairings: The Ink Spots "If I Didn't Care" 1939; Jaynettes "Where Are You Tonight" 1958; The Five Satins "She's Gone" 1958

Session piano player Rex Garvin recalled to Brian Lee on KVMR, "I grew up in Harlem at 224 127nd Street, between 7th and 8th. Zell Sanders lived at 222." She was starting The Hearts: Joyce West, lead, Forestine Barnes, Hazel Crutchfield and Louise Harris. Mrs. Sanders was a security guard, very stout. I got to comingle with these girls. At age 13 or 14, I was playing with The Hearts, I remember [I] used to play in the middle of the keyboard, every record had the treble, in the higher keys, you had to get the sound that was radio friendly." On "Lonely Nights" by The Hearts, "that was Louise Harris on the talking bridge," Garvin added. "Miss Sanders had the vision of the female Ink Spots, she wanted the girls to do that too.' It was a nominal hit, enough to get us local gigs in Baltimore, Philly, Chicago, the chittlin' circuit."

Baby Washington joined The Hearts in 1956.

—

Clyde McPhatter and the Drifters "What'cha Gonna Do" Atlantic February 1955

Style: Rhythm and blues group vocal
Where from: North Carolina
Where recorded: New York City, NY
Suggested pairings: The Dominoes "Have Mercy Baby" 1952; The Midnighters "Is Your Love For Real " 1955; Hank Ballard & the Midnighters "The Twist" 1959

Influenced twice by a Clyde McPhatter lead vocal, Hank Ballard noted two records, "Is Your Love For Real" in 1955 and "The Twist" in 1959. "Clyde went into the service," said Ruth Brown. "When he came back, no one hardly wanted to remember. It's all about who's knocking on doors for you."

—

The Clovers "Blue Velvet" Atlantic February 1955

Style: Rhythm and blues group vocal
Where from: Washington, DC
Where recorded: New York City, NY
Original version: Tony Bennett 1951

The Clovers gave the standard "Blue Velvet" a velvety texture with serious ballad-style sax backing under Buddy Bailey's lead vocal.

Remakes: The Moonglows 1958; The Velours 1959; The Statues 1960; The Paragons 1960; Bobby Vinton 1963; Earl Grant 1966

—

Joe Turner and His Blues Kings "Flip, Flop & Fly" Atlantic February 1955

Style: Rhythm and blues
Where from: Kansas City, KS
Where recorded: New York

"I was just fooling around with some music just came up with 'Flip, Flop & Fly,'" said Joe Turner. "I don't write them down. I keep them in my head. I get an idea and run up to the recording studio and they says, 'Where's the songs at?' I say, 'I got it in my head what I'm going to do.' I learned that when I first started out. I used to get up and have all these numbers written down and everything and I didn't know you got paid for writing songs, all that stuff, publishers of music and all that. I woke up to the facts, white boys tipped me to that, getting by real cool there with me. I said, 'From now on, I'll just keep the songs in my head when they ask who wrote it, I'll tell them they'll have to come by me. They don't know what I'm going to do until I get to the studio."

As the writer credit was by Charles Calhoun and Joe Turner by way of Lou Willie Turner, Joe Turner's ex-wife. Big Joe told the story of how he almost didn't get paid for the song. Songwriter "Doc Pomus called me up, talking about how some bunch of boys had done the number and sold a million, so he said, 'You oughta get a nice royalty check.' I found out who they recorded for and we called them just in time after they sold all them records and after the sent the royalty check. I used to live in New Orleans, 4 Marlborough Gate. That's the only address I had at the time. I had all my mail sent down there. My ex-wife was getting them down there and cashing them. She had the check and tried to take it to the bank. She had a brother named Joe Brown, prizefighter, lightweight champion of the world. She tried to palm him off that he was me, they told the bank manager they'd made a mistake in the name, instead of Joe Turner, it should have been Joe Brown. The people said it was too much money to take a chance like that. Joe Turner would have to come in here, get this money himself. Wouldn't touch it any other way. The company told me about it, so I told them to send it to me. I lived in California, so they put a stop to it right away. We got lucky on that one. The other ones been going down there, ain't nothing I could do because a lot of record labels I recorded for, it's been so long ago, they put out the record all over again, the royalties still do down there because they don't have my address."

Covers: Johnnie Ray 1955; The Goofers 1955
Remakes: Billy Riley 1961, Jon Thomas 1961; Bill Haley & His Comets 1961

—

The Four Deuces "W-P-L-J" Music City February 1955

Style: Rhythm and blues vocal group
Where from: Fort Ord, CA
Where recorded: Berkeley, CA
Suggested pairing: The Bel-Aires "White Port and Lemon Juice" 1954

With lead singer Luther McDaniel, The Four Deuces were in the military, stationed at Fort Ord, near Salinas, CA. The group grew from gospel roots, but during their live shows, they showcased a so-called "mystery drink," two parts port, one part lemon juice, obviously under the influence of the L.A. non-hit "White Port and Lemon Juice" by The Bel-Aires, a group destined to become Donald Woods & the Vel-Aires on their major most controversial hit, "Death Of An Angel," on Flip in 1955.

The Four Deuces took their name from the black deuces, for them, representing the devil. They were referred to Music City's Ray Dobard by Oakland label owner Bob Geddins, who was passing through and caught their show. With backing by Johnny Heartsman, bass and piano; Melvin Davis, tenor sax and Ray Cotton, drums, "W-P-L-J" was controversial upon release, but for different reasons. Berkeley-based Music City made deals with Italian Swiss Colony wineries to market the disc with bottles of cheap wine, issuing and reissuing "W-P-L-J" with various flip sides on various colored vinyl 45s. No one got paid any royalties, that was just life with Dobard.

A major New York City FM rock station adapted the WPLJ calls in 1971, no doubt thinking the song was original to R&B record collector Frank Zappa's Mothers Of Invention.

Remake: The Mothers Of Invention 1970

—

Bo Diddley "Bo Diddley" Checker March 1955

Style: Blues
Where from: Mississippi
Where recorded: Chicago, IL
Suggested pairings: Red Saunders & the Hambone Kids "Hambone" 1952

Bo went by Ellis McDaniel, though some contend that Bates was his true father. "The only ones he knew were Robert and Gussie McDaniel. He was born on either December 28 or 29, 1928 and was raised in Chicago by Mama Ethel Christopher," said his ex-wife Kay. "The name Bo Diddley came from Chicago grammar school days. The kids started calling me Bo Diddley," said Diddley. "I still don't know what it means, but it's a catchy name. At one time, I wanted to play like Louis Jordan, but on a stringed instrument. I'm the man who created something different. I don't copy nobody. I'm always searching for that new type of rhythm that identifies Ellis McDaniels, which is better know[n] as Bo Diddley."

The original lyrics of Diddley's "Uncle John" were rejected by the label as "too dirty" for the white American record-buying public. In response, Diddley re-wrote the lyrics as he recorded the new song, which he named after himself. From then on, Diddley often put his name in his songs.

On this song, Diddley was accompanied by maracas player Jerome Green, whose efforts were fed through an echo chamber. "Jerome was with my group. The maracas gave the unique sound, that jungle type rhythm feel. We didn't have no drums at that time and when we first started playing this thing, we later added drums. The drummer didn't have cymbals, so we put the maracas in there to fill it up, to make it sound like we was in the wilderness somewhere and gave that big sound we found out sounded good in each type surrounding."

At song's end, the lyrics sound like "my pretty baby said she was a bird." Diddley responded, "They get the lyrics all screwed up. It's not that at all, but it sounds very much like that. It's really 'my pretty baby said she wasn't for it.'"

Covers: Jean Dinning; Harmonicats; Joe Reisman Orchestra; Bonnemere & Piano (all 1955)
Use of Diddley beat: The Blues Rockers "Calling All Cows" 1955; Billy Bland "Chicken In the Basket" 1956; Screamin' Jay Hawkins "Alligator Wine" 1957; The Crickets "Not Fade Away" 1958; Johnny Otis "Willie & the Hand Jive" 1958; Duane Eddy "Cannonball" 1958; Bill Haley & the Comets "Skinny Minnie" 1958; The Monotones "Tom Foolery" 1959; Dee Clark "Hey Little Girl" 1959; Robert & Johnny "Baby Baby" 1959; The Miracles "Way Over There" 1960; Elvis Presley "His Latest Flame" 1961; Tico & the Triumphs "Wild Flower" 1962; Inez & Charlie Foxx "Mockingbird" 1963; The Supremes "When the Lovelight Starts Shining" 1963; The Raindrops "The Kind Of Boy You Can't Forget" 1963; Freddy Cannon "Abigail Beecher" 1964; Sonny Curtis "Bo Diddley Bach" 1964; The Rolling Stones "Not Fade Away" 1964; The Strangeloves "I Want Candy" 1966; The Seeds "Lose Your Mind" 1966; The Kingsmen "Bo Diddley Bach" 1967; Sly and the Family Stone "Dance To the Music" 1968; The Who "Magic Bus" 1968; Iggy Pop "1969" 1969; Steppenwolf "Magic Carpet Ride" 1969; Guess Who "American Woman" 1970; Bo Diddley "Bo Diddley-Itis" 1972; Shirley & Co "Shame Shame Shame" 1975; George Michael "Faith" 1987; Guns N Roses "Mr. Brownstone" 1987; U2 "Desire" 1988
Answer: Bo Diddley as " Bo Diddley '69" 1969
Remakes: The Carroll Bros 1962; Jimmy Elledge 1962; Ronnie Hawkins 1963; Buddy Holly 1963; Billy Lee Riley 1964; Juveniles 1966; Art Neville 1968

—

Bo Diddley "I'm a Man" Checker March 1955

Style: Blues
Where from: Mississippi
Where recorded: Chicago, IL
Suggested pairings: Muddy Waters "She Moves Me" 1951; The Robins "Riot In Cell Block #9" 1954; Muddy Waters "I'm Your Hoochie Coochie Man" 1954l Muddy Waters "Manish Boy" 1955; Chuck Berry "No Money Down" 1955; Etta James "WOMAN" 1957; The Voxhoppers "The Last Drag" 1957; George Thorogood "Bad to the Bone" 1982

The B-side to "Bo Diddley," "I'm a Man" is a more intense mainly talking statement of prowess, meant to create a potentially ominous feeling. Bo Diddley based "I'm a Man" on the feeling and bass line of Muddy Waters hit, "She Moves Me." Bo Diddley said, "I tried to play blues like Muddy Waters, but I couldn't hang. So I had to back off and go create my own thing, which now turned into what you know as rock and roll."

When Muddy Waters answered with "Manish Boy" in 1955, Diddley said, "That was his, Muddy caught himself telling me you're just a little old mannish kid, go back and sit down somewhere. I thought it was really nice. Muddy and I were very tight. Willie Dixon and Little Walter and others that came through the Chess thing, they were there when I showed up."

—

Fats Domino "Ain't It a Shame" Imperial April 1955

Style: Rhythm and blues
From and recorded in: New Orleans, LA
Suggested pairings: Jimmy Yancey "Yancey's Stomp" 1939; Young Jesse "Don't Happen No More" 1957; Bobby Darin "Don't Call My Name" 1958

When DJ Bill Randle sent the original of Fats Domino's "Ain't It a Shame" to Pat Boone, the cover king considered correcting the title to "Isn't It A Shame." Instead, he retitled the title to the more grammatical "Ain't That A Shame" while taking it to #1.

Cover: Pat Boone 1955; Ella Mae Morse "Ain't That A Shame" 1955
Remake: John Lennon 1975

—

Elvis Presley "Baby Let's Play House" Sun April 25, 1955/RCA December 1955

Style: Rockabilly
Where from: Tupelo, MS
Where recorded: Memphis, TN
Original version: Arthur Gunter "Baby Let's Play House" 1954
Suggested pairing: Sammy Masters "Pink Cadillac" 1955

Presley historical producer Malcolm Leo said, "The song was selected by Sam Phillips of Sun right after his [Elvis'] first several releases on Sun, which Sam thought would bring the talent out of Elvis. They would talk things over, along with Scotty Moore and Bill Black, and Elvis would free himself of any inhibitions and would start talking about blues singers he had heard and said, 'There's the great tune, "Baby Let's Play House," and we could do a good version of it.' However, there was inhibition in that the original by Arthur Gunter on Excello, Gunter sang 'you ain't got religion,' which Elvis changed to 'you don't drive a pink Cadillac' so as not offend his highly religious mother."

—

Donald Woods & the Vel-Aires "Death Of An Angel" Flip June 1955

Style: Rhythm and blues vocal group
From and recorded in: Los Angeles, CA
Suggested pairing: The Dominoes "The Bells" 1952; Donald Woods "Memories Of An Angel" 1958

Donald Woods' vocal group, The Bel-Aires, became Donald Woods & the Vel-Aires for their most controversial release, "Death Of An Angel," because of a pre-existing Bel-Aires group. This song is from the school of records like "The Bells" by The Dominoes, in which the vocalist sobs out lyrics. In the case of "Death Of An Angel," Randolph Bryant cried uncontrollably. Rumors abounded about girls committing suicide over the lyrics and the mood of the performance.

Ray Johnson, whose conga playing helped set the mood, recalled, "I arranged the song so there'd be space for the crying part to be in. I didn't know it would be such a smash hit." Neither did his brother, Plas Johnson, who played the mournful backing sax.

"Max Feirtag was the producer," said Ray Johnson. "It was different from any of the other group was doing at the time, that has become somewhat of a classic, something that's played a lot." Both Al Jarvis and Johnny Otis plugged the song on their respective radio and TV shows, and soon it was a bit of an underground hit. "To some extent, it didn't get as much play as it would've," Woods recalled. "On the Al Jarvis Show, it skyrocketed because of the controversy. It was the most controversial record of the year. The stories were rampant, supposed suicides, all kinds of wretched things. This was unfounded rumor. What we picked up because of the controversy, I don't know that it offset what we might have gained had it been showcased. Bryant did one hell of a job on that crying scene. It moved me, it had to have some effect on the listeners. We did three or four, he really put his heart into it." In live performance, "he was really doing a solo. In some performances, he was so moved, he was hysterical." Then the censors moved in, and the label responded by withdrawing the original title, reissuing it with the alternative title, "My Baby's Gone."

Remakes: The Viceroys 1964; The Kingsmen 1964

—

Bo Diddley "She's Fine, She's Mine" Checker June 1955

Style: Blues
Where from: Mississippi
Where recorded: Chicago, IL

In Bo Diddley's "She's Fine, She's Mine," the title is not heard in the lyrics, instead it's more like "You Don't Love Me." Diddley said, "It's just something I made up, it's a good clean title. It's like saying 'your lady is pretty and you're happy she's part of you.' Today, people might get upset over saying 'she's mine' because it's indicating she's a piece of merchandise or something, you dig. I didn't have that in mind when I wrote the song. A lot of people would frown on that today. That's one of the reasons we've run out of rhyming lyrics."

Remakes: Willie Cobbs as "You Don't Love Me" 1961; Tommy Raye 1964

—

Chuck Berry "Maybellene" Chess July 1955

Style: Rock 'n' roll
Where from: St. Louis, MO
Where recorded: Chicago, IL
Suggested pairings: Bob Wills & His Texas Playboys "Ida Red" 1938; Young Jessie "Mary Lou" 1955

At the first record credited to Chuck Berry, "Maybellene" was inspired by a makeup brand. Influenced by Bob Willis' country standard "Ida Red," at first titled "Ida Mae," Chuck Berry changed the title to "Maybellene" after makeup packaging he found on the studio floor. "Maybellene" was the story of a race between a Ford and a Caddy—with a subtext of a cheating woman named Maybellene—with the Ford winning. It was censored by the BBC for naming auto brands "Ford" and "Cadillac."

Legendary blues songwriter and bass player Willie Dixon recalled when Berry joined Chess, "It was still a blues label. He added more of rock to the situation, he and Bo Diddley too. I was working with Chess when he first came there. I had been working with Chuck Berry ever since he first started with Chess. I did all his first things with him." Bo Diddley said, "Chuck didn't do very much talking to people at that time. Neither did I. Everybody was locked into their own fantasy world they had going for themselves, scared of the next guy. 'Hey man, I don't want him to hear my stuff because he might steal something from me.' Since people has dropped their guard, there's been a lot of that going on. Chuck Berry and myself back in those days was right about not letting nobody hear nothing because they would rip it off."

Covers: Marty Robbins 1955; Jim Lowe 1955; Johnny Long and Orchestra 1955; Ralph Marterie 1955
Soundalikes: Jesse Belvin and the Spacemen "My Satellite" 1957; Eddie Cochran "Twenty Flight Rock" 1957; Evelyn Freeman "Didn't It Rain" 1958
Answers: Rayvon Darnell "Don't Want You Maybellene" 1955; Mercy Dee "Come Back Maybellene" 1955; John Greer "Come Back Maybelline" 1955
Remakes: Matt Lucas 1963; Johnny Rivers 1964; The Challengers; Larry Bright 1964; Bob Luman 1970

—

Elmore James and His Broomdusters "Dust My Blues" Flair July 1955

Style: Blues
Where from: Canton, MS
Where recorded: Jackson, MS
Suggested pairings: Robert Johnson "I Believe I'll Dust My Blues" 1938; Arthur Crudup "Dust My Broom" 1950; Robert Jr. Lockwood "Dust My Broom" 1951; Elmore James "I Believe My Time Ain't Long" 1952; Elmore James and His Broomdusters "I Believe" 1955; Ike & Tina Turner "Dust My Broom" 1966; Ike Turner "Dust My Broom" 1972

The original Robert Johnson blues, also known as ""I Believe I'll Dust My Blues," was first recorded by Elmore James as "I Believe My Time Ain't Long" and became the basis of great conflict between Trumpet

Records of Jackson, MS and Joe Bihari of Modern Records.

Joe Bihari, who was talent scouting and recording local talent at the time, had heard of Elmore James' prowess, and said, "Lillian McMurray came out from Trumpet in Jackson. I went down there to find Elmore. I went with Ike Turner to West Memphis to record Sonny Blair and Boyd Gilmore. Sonny Boy Williamson would play but not sing for me. I started inquiring about Elmore. Found out Elmore was in Canton, MS and had a radio repair shop. Elmore took a liking to me and signed a contract. I recorded him, went into a nightclub, Ike played piano. I sent a contact to McMurray and she sued us, I pulled the record back. He would not record for her again."

McMurray said she and her lawyer caught two Biharis, probably Joe and Lester of Meteor Records, recording an act her Trumpet label had under contract. Regardless, a different version of Elmore James on "I Believe" was issued as the first Meteor release in October 1952. Meteor was the family label run by Lester Bihari out of Memphis, TN. All Joe would say was, "We never got along with Lester, he was our older brother and worked for us in the shipping department." After the release on Meteor flamed out, Joe Bihari re-recorded Elmore James and His Broomdusters' "Dust My Blues" on the Bihari Flair label in July 1955.

—

Bernard Hardison "Too Much" Republic July 1955

Style: Blues
From and recorded in: Nashville, TN

Owner of Republic records, Bill Beasley's wife Joan Norris wrote "Too Much," which was recorded by Bernard Hardison backed by the Louis Brooks Band. The credited writers were Norris-Weinman, which was Bernie Weinman, a financial partner with Beasley. The record stiffed, and the song was forgotten until Bill Beasley heard it on the radio, sung by Elvis. Norris' name was replaced by Lee Rosenberg, most likely Weinman's secretary. Rosenberg had given the Hardison record to Elvis as he left for the West Coast to film his first movie. According to the lawsuit, Weinman and Rosenberg filed for a copyright as the writers of "Too Much" in 1956, having not copyrighted it in 1955 under the actual writers' names. Financing the legal action with the proceeds of a number one Elvis single, Weinman hired the best attorneys and won; Beasley and Norris left with nothing at all. Reportedly, Rosenberg's publishing shares went to Elvis.

Remake: Elvis Presley 1957

—

Little Willie John "All Around the World" King July 1955

Style: Rhythm and blues
Where from: Detroit, MI
Where recorded: Cincinnati, OH
Original version: Titus Turner 1955

"Willie left home and he told me, 'I won't be back until I have a hit record. I'm going on the road with Paul Williams,'" said his sister, Mabel John. "They ended up in Cincinnati, [OH]," home of King Records, which Willie visited. "Titus Turner was in the studio of King Records doing a song called 'All Around the World,' which he wrote. Willie told a fib and said he had an appointment with Mr. Syd Nathan, and he didn't. He'd never met him. Willie wormed his way in, listened to what Titus Turner was doing and the producer was trying to get him to make a run, a run you make on a song, and Titus just couldn't hear that run. So Willie opened the door on a break and said, 'Is this what you're trying to do?' And really, Willie just sang that riff," and recorded the song, got signed by Syd Nathan himself to King, and had his first hit.

Remake: Scotty McKay & His Orch. 1966; as "Grits Ain't Groceries (All Around the World)" Little Milton 1968; Savoy Brown 1969

—

The Platters "Only You" Mercury July 1955

Style: Rhythm and blues group vocal
From and recorded in: Los Angeles, CA

The Platters with Tony Williams, lead tenor; David Lynch, tenor; Paul Robi, baritone; Herb Reed, bass and Zola Taylor as the female foil were signed by Mercury as a throw-in, because the label really wanted The Penguins, which were hot with "Earth Angel." Buck Ram negotiated both groups joining the label. The Penguins never hit again.

When The Platters' ballad "Only You" showed promise for Mercury, an earlier inferior version with a whistling bridge on Federal from 1954 was trotted out to compete against the hit. The Platters and Mercury sued King and Federal Records. A settlement was reached in favor of the defendants as reported on January 14, 1956. In the original action, The Platters sought to have the diskeries enjoined from further issuance of copies of the group's hit disk, "Only You." It was alleged that King was continuing to issue the disk after the group had recut the tune for Mercury Records. In the decision handed down, the court held that the plaintiffs had not sustained their burden of proof. It was also held that by virtue of an agreement between Tony Williams, lead singer of the group, and Federal Records, dated June 2, 1953, "It may well be that the defendants, rather than the plaintiffs, are the aggrieved party."

Zola Taylor recalled, "Prior to that, I had joined the group in 1953, we had recorded 'Only You,' but we canned that one, then recorded it again after Paul Robi came into the group." The hit version of "Only You" hit the L.A. R&B charts at #1 on July 9, 1955; the national R&B charts at #1 on July 30, 1955 and the national pop charts at #5 on October 1, 1955.

Covers: The Platters on Federal; Dorothy Collins 1955; The Cues 1955
Remakes: Frank Pourcel 1959; Little Richard 1964; Wayne Newton 1964; Bobby Hatfield 1969; Ringo Starr 1974

—

Elvis Presley, Scotty and Bill "Mystery Train" Sun August 1, 1955/RCA December 1955

Style: Rockabilly
Where from: Tupelo, MS
Where recorded: Memphis, TN
Original version: Little Junior's Blue Flames 1953

Elvis Presley's final Sun label release and his first on RCA/Victor was a remake of fellow Sun label blues artist Little Junior's Blue Flames' "Mystery Train." Sun label blues vocalist Little Milton recalled, "Elvis did 'Train I Ride,' Junior Parker's tune."

Remakes: The Turtles 1955

—

Earl King "Those Lonely Lonely Nights" Ace August 1955

Style: Rhythm and blues
Where from: New Orleans, LA
Where recorded: Jackson, MS
Suggested pairings: Joe Turner "Chains Of Love" 1951; Smiley Lewis "I Hear You Knocking" 1955; Huey "Piano" Smith "High Blood Pressure" 1958

On the label of Earl King's "Those Lonely, Lonely Nights," the piano player is credited as "Fats," even though Huey Smith filled that role. King explained that Ace label owner "Johnny Vincent would do those things for promotional gimmicks. He figured if you saw the original record, they had it [in] little tiny words and they had 'Fats' in big old letters on piano, everybody would say, 'Is Fats playing on it?' I'd say, 'No, that's Huey Smith, that's not Fats Domino.' I played guitar on all of Huey's session.

"At that session," King continued, "he hadn't even formed the Clowns yet. That was Joe Dyson's band out of Jackson. We recorded it in Lillian McMurray's studio in Jackson. The piano break I did in 'Those Lonely, Lonely Nights' was the same break in 'I Hear You Knocking'" by Smiley Lewis. Same break in 'High Blood Pressure" by Huey Smith. It's been pointed out to me that same break was from Van Walls, who backed Joe Turner on 'Chains Of Love.' Van Walls was Huey's idol. He loved Van Walls, but that break was derived from me. That should have originally been a mandolin, and I said, 'I can't get that out of a guitar.'" Later, Johnny "Guitar" Watson got that very same break on guitar. King added, "Dave Bartholomew heard 'Those Lonely, Lonely Nights' and he told Huey, 'Play that thing you played behind Earl's record' on 'High Blood Pressure.' That's the way Dave does, that's how that came about."

Cover: Johnny "Guitar" Watson

—

The Turbans "When You Dance" Herald August 1955

Style: Rhythm and blues vocal group
From and recorded in: Philadelphia, PA
Suggested pairings: The Gassers "Hum De Hum" 1956; The Drifters "Save the Last Dance For Me" 1959; The Velvets "Tonight" 1961

Noted for its rocking "split tempo" performance and vocal shifts by lead singer Al Banks from tenor to falsetto, The Turbans' "When You Dance" was a tribute to several dance steps, including the "mambo, calypso, or the shag," and a big hit in both the U.S. and Jamaica.

Cover: The Laurie Sisters 1955
Remakes: Billy Storm 1961; The Paramounts 1961; Lou Christie 1964; Glen Madison 1964; Jay and The Americans 1969

—

The El Dorados "At My Front Door" Vee Jay August 1955

Style: Rhythm and blues vocal group
From and recorded in: Chicago, IL
Suggested pairings: Golden Gate Quartet "No Restricted Signs" 1947; The Spiders "I Didn't Want To Do It" 1954

Many fans of the day thought the real title of The El Dorados' major hit, "At My Front Door," was "Crazy Little Mama." According to lead singer Pirkle Lee Moses, "That was the company's decision because originally that's what we called it. It was kind of part of another song the Spiders had out, it wasn't the main part of the tune, this was just a phrase from a line, 'hip shakin' mama come knockin.' I changed it to 'crazy little mama come knockin.' It wasn't in any way suggestive. I had kids at the time, a couple of my songs were centered around my daughter, first born daughter, writing songs about her, about her being a crazy little mama. My daughter's name [is] Raina, at the time she was one year old. She couldn't care less."

Covers: The Modernaires 1955; Pat Boone 1955

Pirkle Lee Moses described the covers as "kind of a hurting thing because I never got paid for the song. It was stolen from me by Vee Jay Records. Not only did Pat Boone cover it, but The Modernaires also. I never got a quarter for it."

—

The Cheers "Black Denim Trousers and Motorcycle Boots" Capitol August 1955

Style: Pop vocal group
From and recorded in: Los Angeles, CA
Suggested pairing: Frankie Laine "Cry Of the Wild Goose" 1950; The Shangri-Las "Leader of the Pack" 1964

"I had gone in the army in September '53," said Perry Botkin Jr. "I got out of the army in 1955 and joined The Cheers." Gil Garfield was one of the founding members with Bert Convy, Sue Allen on recordings, Sally Bremmer on live shows.

Botkin met famed songwriters Jerry Leiber and Mike Stoller, who wrote "Black Denim Trousers And Motorcycle Boots" ("... the terror of Highway 101") as a response to motorcycle gang culture popularized by Brando's "The Wild One," reinforced by other juvenile delinquency movies like 'Blackboard Jungle" with a rather mild intro out of "Cry of the Wild Goose" by Frankie Laine. "Black Denim Trousers And Motorcycle Boots" soon became the subject of great controversy and even censorship. "I believe it was Leiber-Stoller's first crossover hit," said Botkin. "Gil left the group shortly after I got out of the army. Bert asked me, 'Do you wanna be a Cheer?' At its time we were considered a rock 'n' roll group during the time of Bill Haley & the Comets. As the hits began to drop, our money began to drop." Botkin left the group. "Gil and Bert owned the name, so there was no point in waiting for more hits. I wanted to arrange and compose, all the things I wanted to do."

Covers: Ramblin Jimmie Dolan 1955; The Diamonds 1955; Eddie Hill 1955; Vaughn Monroe 1955; Jackie Brooks 1955; Edith Piaf 1956

—

Johnny "Guitar" Watson "Those Lonely Lonely Nights" RPM October 1955

Style: Blues
Where from: Houston, TX
Where recorded: Los Angeles, CA
Original version: Earl King 1955

When he signed with the RPM label, John Watson and RPM co-owner Joe Bihari went to see the Sterling Hayden western "Johnny Guitar," which inspired Watson to adopt the Johnny "Guitar" nickname that would stick with him for his entire performing career. Bihari recalled, "Johnny Guitar was a guitar player who liked to play very loud. I had a lot of problems recording loud. I had to turn him down like they do today."

Watson scored his first hit with a note-perfect cover of New Orleanian Earl King's two-chord swamp ballad "Those Lonely Lonely Nights." Earl King reacted to Watson's **cover:** "I was happy someone had thought of even doing the song." Label owner "Johnny Vincent didn't realize the song was going as well as it was and some of the distributors got word out to Johnny 'Guitar' Watson's people that this was a potential hit song, so they jumped on it on the West Coast. "When Johnny Vincent realized that it was covered, then he went to getting on the move with the record. It helped my sales, but on the West Coast, Johnny 'Guitar' Watson had more sales than I did. I like Johnny's version, I think he did a good version on that. Matter of fact, I like Johnny 'Guitar' Watson, he likes Gatemouth and I used to like Gatemouth, so the relativity's all there."

—

The Spiders "Witchcraft" Imperial October 1955

Style: Rhythm and blues group vocal
From and recorded in: New Orleans, LA

"Dave Bartholomew brought that song to me," said Spiders lead singer Chuck Carbo about this medium tempo blues 'Witchcraft.'" He didn't have any music to it. 'Chuck, see what you can do with this.' I took the music from 'I Didn't Want To Do It.'"

—

The Cadillacs "Speedoo" Josie October 1955

Style: Rhythm and blues vocal group
From and recorded in: New York City, NU
Suggested pairing: The Regals "Got the Water Boiling" 1955; Muddy Waters "Got My Mojo Working" 1956; The Sensations "Kitty Car Love" 1958

"I was about 18 years old," said Earl "Speedo" Carroll. "I have a little pointy head, the guys used to tease me a lot about it. We were working [at] an armory in the Massachusetts area. We were on our way to the car and one of the hams of the group, Bobby Phillips, he sees a big torpedo shell outside the armory and said, 'Hey Speedo, there's your torpedo.' He was referring to my head and the shape of the torpedo and I got a little hot under the collar and I said, 'My name ain't Speedo, it's Mr. Earl.' They used to tease me quite a bit about it. Before we got back to New York in the car, we'd written the tune up, gone in the studio, and recorded it. We took the 'wah wah a doobie doo' from 'Got the Water Boiling' by The Regals and used it in 'Speedoo.'"

Cover: Steve Lawrence

—

The Robins "Smokey Joe's Café" Spark October 22, 1955/Atco December 3, 1955

Style: Rhythm and blues group vocal
From and recorded in: Los Angeles, CA

"Smokey Joe's Café" was written by Leiber-Stoller, who based it on a hot dog stand located in the San Fernando Valley, or at LaCienega Blvd. and San Vincente Blvd., depending on who's telling the story. This tale of an impending fight between a customer and the cook at the café, "Smokey Joe's Café" broke out first on Spark, the final release on that label because Leiber-Stoller left town, closing up shop. It was then picked up by the new Atco subsidiary of Atlantic.

Allegedly, Jerry Leiber's decision to leave L.A. was helped by the LAPD's notorious Hat Squad. According to Huggy Boy, the LAPD was not fond of Leiber-Stoller as the squad disdained interracial relationships. When Jerry Leiber was out with a married black woman in his small sports car and flipped it in the Mulholland Drive area, killing her, the cops gave them an offer they couldn't refuse: avoid prosecution by leaving town for good. About this incident involving Leiber, The Robins' lead singer Carl Gardner recalled, "I knew that he was dating a black girl. He told me something about that."

Shortly after that incident, Leiber-Stoller shuttered their Spark label and took "Smokey Joe's Café" by The Robins, selling Spark to the newly established New York-based Atco label, and were hired as independent producers, a job unique to the business in those days, but would soon become common in the business. With them, they brought two Spark label acts, crooner Frankie Marshall and two members of The Robins, Carl Gardner and Bobby Nunn, whom they teamed with other L.A. singers like Billy Guy as The Coasters. That group's first release, "Down In Mexico," hit the charts in March 1956, so little time was wasted in the process.

—

Tony Allen & the Champs "Nite Owl" Specialty October 1955

Style: Rhythm and blues group vocal
Where from: New Orleans, LA
Where recorded: Los Angeles, CA

Tony Allen's key song was "Nite Owl," Allen's nickname. "My mother gave me that name. I used to go out all the time, come in at 11, 12 o'clock. She'd say, 'Here comes my little nite owl, walking through the front door.' When Jesse Belvin went to Specialty, it stuck with me. I had a little $35 piano, nine keys worked, I went to plunking on that, it became a thing."

At the same time Allen was recording, Jesse Belvin was leaving Specialty. "I went with Jesse to Specialty to relinquish Jesse's contract. I was just plunking with the thing, Bumps Blackwell came down, 'What's that you're singing?' 'I don't know man, some little old "Nite Owl."' 'I like that, would you like to record it?' 'I don't know.' 'I'm serious. Write me another side, we'll have a session.'"

According to Allen, his backing group the Champs were "Horace Wooten, Charles Jackson, David Cobb, Booker Washington and Barbara McNeil." The backing band consisted of William Pyles, guitar; Duke Harris, bass; Hubert "Bumps" Myers, tenor sax; Zebedee Kindred, piano and Roy Porter, drums.

Tony Allen signed a contract with Specialty Records, the label on which he had his greatest success, in August 1955. Tony Allen & the Champs' "Nite Owl" backed with "I" on Specialty was his most major and best-known release. Through a label mispressing committed by Allen himself who was working for the plant pressing "Nite Owl," it was cross-credited with the flipside, "I." "Do you remember a Turks record called 'Emily'?" Allen asked. "If you notice the background on 'I' and the background to 'Emily,' it's identical. I was pressing my record at this time, I was under contract to Specialty so I was at the plant pressing. I had just recorded the session, the record got a good review in Cashbox and Billboard. Art Rupe called me, 'Get up to the office,' I said, 'Wait a minute, I'm working.' I must've messed up 2,000 records, that's how the labels got mixed up, it was on the 78s and a few of the 45s. They was playing 'I,' but they thought it was 'Nite Owl,' but they was playing the wrong side."

On L.A.'s R&B charts, "Nite Owl" was #4 on December 10, 1955. Though "Nite Owl" was very popular in the L.A. area, it did little nationally, possibly because it was overshadowed by the very next Specialty 45, a rockin' ditty by Little Richard called "Tutti Frutti," which not only permanently altered the Specialty business plan but revolutionized pop culture as we knew it at the time. "It came out about a week later I think. Specialty was the big R&B record company on the West Coast. They had spiritual groups like the Soul Stirrers and the Pilgrim Travelers. I came from church, you had that inner sight for people. It was not the company I wanted to be with, it was Johnny Otis and that fast company. "He pre-dated those contracts to where Art Rupe had to give him royalties off of those things. I really liked Art, but I was young and foolish and wanted that prestige being with Johnny Otis. I wouldn't listen to Art. Art wasn't moving fast enough for me, I didn't know he had so many irons in the fire for me. Everyone at this time was with Johnny Otis. Johnny was the big thing. Mel Williams, Jesse Belvin, Rolling Crew, The Penguins, Don and Dewey, Mickey Lynn. Johnny approached me, and Frank Gallo and says, 'Why don't you come on with us?'

Allen continued, "He was putting me on shows with me and said, 'I'll tell you what I'm going to do, will you go [a]long with it?' He says, 'I'm going to give a contract, you pre-date it before you signed with Specialty. I said, 'Well OK.' Me, Johnny and Frank Gallo go out to Art Rupe. He said, 'How can you record Tony, I had Tony a year prior to this.' Art went up in the ceiling, about a week later, he told me, 'Man how could you do this to me, I had to give Johnny half the royalties and Johnny had nothing to do with your session.'" On December 15, 1955, Allen was given his Specialty release, Arthur Lee Maye witnessing his signature. "Johnny had another session with me in less than two weeks."

"Nite Owl" was a popular song at live venues like El Monte Legion Stadium and stayed in print until Specialty sold and stopped issuing singles in the 1990s. Tony Allen's "Nite Owl" was very popular in the L.A. area, getting renewed action on Art LaBoe's popular Oldies But Goodies LP in 1959 and more action in the oldies craze of the 1960s and early 1970s.

Remakes (as "Night Owl"): The Clouds 1964; Bobby Paris 1966; The Bad Habits 1969

—

Chuck Berry and His Combo "Thirty Days (To Come Back Home)" Chess October 1955

Style: Rock 'n' roll
Where from: St. Louis, MO
Where recorded: Chicago, IL
Suggested pairings: Red River Dave "Comin' Round the Mountain" 1944; Sister Rosetta Tharpe "Strange Things Happening" 1945; Eddie Cochran "Summertime Blues" 1958

Chuck Berry's rocking story about having his girl "back home" in "Thirty Days" is rock's earliest plea to the United Nations, three years prior to Eddie Cochran's U.N. reference in "Summertime Blues," with the spirit, feel and irony of Sister Rosetta Tharpe's "Strange Things Happening" from 1945.

"Chuck Berry had a unique talent of getting the best licks from the best players, incorporating it into his playing," said sax man Red Holloway, who occasionally backed Berry on live dates. He played with Berry "all told, about a month. We had lines at the Stage Lounge. You didn't see the crowds like you see today." Holloway didn't see him do the duck walk. "Not during those days, no. He played his guitar, instead of holding it down, he would hold it up like he was playing the bass, straight up. He's run from one side of the stage to the other, but he didn't do the duck walk. Playing the guitar behind his head, laying on his back, that was part of his show."

Remake: as "Forty Days" by Ronnie Hawkins & the Hawks 1959

—

Little Richard "Tutti Frutti" Specialty November 1955

Style: Rhythm and blues
Where from: Macon, GA
Where recorded: J&M studios New Orleans, LA

Dating back to 1951, Little Richard already had an extensive recording history for RCA/Victor, Peacock, when he came out of New Orleans complete with his explosive "Tutti Frutti" recorded at Cosimo Matassa's studio on Rampart Street. Little Richard had sent a tape to Specialty, who instructed, "We've got to get him out of our hair, let's give him a shot." His manager, Brantley said, "He's under contract to Peacock. Don Robey said, "If you give me $600, I'll clear the debt and you can have him." After all, according to New Orleans songwriter Earl King, Don Robey, who owned Peacock, had apparently beaten up Little Richard. He sounded so uninhibited.

Bumps Blackwell went to record him on September 13th and 14th, but he wanted to introduce his band, the Upsetters. "I don't think we have anything. Bring back whatever you've got." It was really blues. Bumps said, "We can't record that." One of his hangers-on, Dorothy Labostrie, was at the session trying to sell songs. She was assigned to clean up "good booty" into "ah rooty," making "Tutti Frutti" radio friendly.

Drummer Earl Palmer said, "On 'Tutti Frutti' you can hear me playing a shuffle. Listening to it now, it's easy to hear I should have been playing that rock beat." In October of that year, Billboard said 'Tutti Frutti' was "a cleverly styled novelty with nonsense words delivered rapid-fire. The singer shows a compelling personality and an attractive vocal style."

"He [Richard] used a lot of the same studio guys, Lee Allen, Red Tyler and Earl Palmer, Frank Fields. Those were the guys who did a lot of New Orleans music for everybody," said old friend Earl King. "When I heard Little Richard on 'Tutti Frutti,' I turned on the radio and they said, 'We got a brand new record by Little Richard.' I said, 'That's not the Little Richard I know.' I was so used to Little Richard singing all those pretty ballads, those Dinah Washington songs. All the gimmicky stuff he can do is one thing, but pound for pound, he can sing.

Little Richard claimed he wrote some of the lyrics while employed as a dishwasher at a Greyhound bus station in his hometown of Macon, saying when the boss brought pots back for him to wash, he exclaimed, "Awap bop a lup bop a wop bam boom, take 'em out!"

"Tutti Frutti" was covered by Pat Boone, one of his first hit R&B covers. A cottage industry emulating Little Richard included Esquerita, James Brown, Dee Clark, Don Covay and fellow Maconite, Otis Redding.

Covers: Pat Boone 1955; Boyd Bennett and His Rockets 1956; Bob Roubian 1956
Remakes: Elvis Presley 1956; The Jesters 1960; The Swinging Blue Jeans 1964; Little Richard 1988

—

Bobby Charles "Later Alligator" Chess November 1955
Style: Rhythm and blues
Where from: Louisiana
Where recorded: New Orleans, LA
Suggested pairings: Guitar Slim "Later For You Baby" 1954; Roy Hall "See You Later Alligator" 1956; Bill Haley & the Comets "See You Later Alligator" 1956

"Bobby Charles is from Abbeyville," said Earl King, comparing his music to that made in New Orleans, LA. "He started doing a series of things down there, they got a totally different flavor, texture as opposed to New Orleans. It lends itself to a bayou kind of music." In fact, Bobby Charles took his most recorded composition, "Later Alligator," from New Orleans based Guitar Slim's "Later For You Baby."

Charles' "Later Alligator" was reworked into Bill Haley & the Comets' "See You Later Alligator" in 1956.

—

Ernie Freeman "Jivin' Around" Cash November 26, 1955
Style: Rhythm and blues instrumental
Where from: Cleveland, OH
Where recorded: Los Angeles, CA

Before there was "Honky Tonk" by Bill Doggett, there was "Jivin' Around," which amounted to long time piano session man Ernie Freeman's first credited effort. "Jivin' Around Pt. 1 & Pt. 2" was not an immediate hit, instead becoming a multi-decade slow and steady seller. As recalled by Huggy Boy, it was created at the end of a Hollywood Flames session that produced "Wagon Wheels," credited to the Turks. "The orchestra was Ernie Freeman. I was in there recording 'Wagon Wheels' and we plugged it big on our program, not a big hit. When the vocal group went home, Ernie said, 'Huggy you want me to do an instrumental for you?' I said, 'Sure.'

"With combo members Irving Ashby on guitar; Joe Comfort, bass and Raymond Martinez, drums," Huggy Boy continued, "he sat down and played the piano, right as the song was going on. We were waiting for John Dolphin to arrive with the money to pay everybody off. When he walked in the room, you can hear the drummer yell 'yeah' at the end of the thing." The drummer was "Raymond Martinez, who created that beat on 'Jivin' Around,'" said Elliott Shavers. "When the engineer was putting away the tape, he wrote 'Huggy Boy Jivin' Around,'" said Huggy Boy. "I was jiving around, waiting for the guy with the money.

After three or four months, we were doing the program, and a big instrumental came out in the top ten. Dolphin said, 'We better make an instrumental.' I said, 'We have an instrumental, there's one in the studio.' I went over to the studio, next day, the engineer pulled down the tape. 'Here it is Huggy. Ernie Freeman, what do you want to call the thing?' I said, 'Call it "Jivin' Around.' It wasn't long enough. We only had part one. 'I need a part two.' He said, 'That's very simple.' We played part one, put a piece of tape like a band aid around it, changed the speed slightly, ran it again and made that part two. Except for the speed, part one and part two were identical."

"Jivin' Around" charted in L.A. on November 26, 1955 and nationally at R&B #5 on January 7, 1956.

—

The Platters "The Great Pretender" Mercury December 1, 1955
Style: Rhythm and blues group vocal
From and recorded in: Los Angeles, CA

The Platters struck twice with this Buck Ram composition, "The Great Pretender," on Mercury, a much bigger hit than "Only You." It was hardly an immediate hit with the group, especially Zola Taylor, who said. "That was me that thought it was like a hillbilly song. I thought it was a cowboy song. I think the whole group didn't particularly go for 'The Great Pretender,' but in two weeks it went to #1. If you had heard the way Buck Ram sang it or the rest of the songs he had wrote, at the piano, listening to it, by me being a teenager [saying] 'What is this?'" It became a #1 hit.

Remakes: Ace Cannon 1960; Tony Bellus 1960; Kathy Young & the Innocents 1961; Rudy Ray Moore & the Fillmore Street Soul Rebellion 1964; Linda Hopkins 1965; Dolly Parton 1984 Freddie Mercury 1987
Satires: Stan Freberg 1955

—

Frankie Lymon & the Teenagers "Why Do Fools Fall In Love" Gee December 1955

Style: Doo wop vocal group harmony
From and recorded in: New York City, NY

In late 1954, a New York teen group, The Premiers, auditioned a song they called "Why Do Birds Sing So Gay?" for George Goldner, owner of Gee Records. Herman Santiago, tenor of the group, had written the song based on a line from some love letters given to the guys by a tenant in bassist Sherman Garnes' apartment building. Tenor Jimmy Merchant sang the group's audition lead voice, but Goldner heard Lymon in the background and told the group he would be the lead singer. It was a high tenor preteen sound record buyers had not heard before and was an instant success.

"Why Do Fools Fall In Love" created a whole new genre of music: "Kiddie lead doo wop harmony," successfully pursued by Lymon's brother, Louis Lymon & the Teen Chords and Jimmy Castor and the Juniors, who often replaced Frankie at out of town concerts. Louis Lymon hated his brother because of what success did to their relationship. Not so for Castor. "Frankie was my neighbor. My mother made [me] go to school, so I worked only weekends, more than I wanted to do. I wanted more, knew my mother would beat my ass. He [Lymon] began to smoke weed, get high." When Lymon couldn't work a date, Castor would fill in and nobody knew the difference.

Castor added, "I would disappear to towns like Hershey, Pennsylvania, Toronto and rest of Canada. We would helicopter straight to Hershey. It was the first super group, period. Goldner was a genius as a producer, Sherman was a great bass, Joe, Herman and Jimmy were perfect. For only 18 months, they were huge. The Teenagers reached the masses." Early vinyl single releases of "Why Do Fools Fall in Love" credit Frankie Lymon, Herman Santiago, and George Goldner as co-writers of the song; however, later releases and cover versions were attributed only to Lymon and record producer George Goldner. In the early 1960s, Goldner's name was later replaced by Morris Levy when Levy bought Goldner's interest in Gee.

After their Mercury label tried them out on that type of material. Diamonds' lead singer David Somerville said he was in an integrated vocal group with two black members while in Canada and was influenced by the approach. "I got a feeling for that kind of singing. It stayed with me."

Covers: The Diamonds, Gale Storm; Gloria Mann; The Cadets (all 1956)
Remakes: The Gallahads 1961; The Fabulous Four 1964; The Beach Boys 1964; The Fuller Brothers 1966; The Happenings 1967; Eddie Holman 1967; Jimmy Briscoe & the Little Beavers 1971; The Chesterfields 1978; Joni Mitchell 1980; Diana Ross 1981

Some Beach Boys labels credit Lymon-Goldner and others credit Lymon-Santiago-Goldner. Diana Ross labels credit Lymon-Levy as writers. After a lengthy court battle, in December 1992, song-writing credits were awarded to original Teenagers Herman Santiago and Jimmy Merchant.

—

Carl Perkins "Blue Suede Shoes" Sun January 1, 1956

Style: Rockabilly
Where from: Jackson, TN
Recorded in Memphis, TN
Suggested pairing: Chuck Berry "Roll Over Beethoven" 1956

Blues artist Little Milton who recorded for Sun before Elvis Presley and Carl Perkins arrived on the scene, recalled, "I just didn't know any better and I really just didn't care, but you had people like Jerry Lee Lewis, Carl Perkins, Charlie Rich and Johnny Cash, all of these people were there. We used to see these guys around the studio when we were there recording. But it just didn't faze us one way or another."

Carl Perkins' "Blue Suede Shoes" was the first hit rockabilly recording that put Sun on the map. Not Perkins first release on Sun, but his first national hit. After hearing the comment at a dance, "I took three Irish potatoes out of a brown paper sack, [used the sack to write on, and] wrote it as it is today at three o'clock in the morning." Both sides were rockers.

The lyric, "Blue Suede Shoes" showed up in Chuck Berry's "Roll Over Beethoven." Some anti-moonshine music listeners objected to the lyric about drinking "[my] liquor in an old fruit jar," though it was never a major issue.

Covers: Sid King & the Five Strings; Roy Hall; Jim Lowe; Boyd Bennett; Sam the Man Taylor; Walter Hayes; Bob Roubian; Elvis Presley (all 1956)
Remakes: Elvis Presley 1956; Johnny Rivers 1973

—

Elvis Presley "Heartbreak Hotel" RCA January 1956

Style: Novelty rock 'n' roll
Where from: Tupelo, MS
Where recorded: Nashville, TN

This song was taken from a newspaper article about a man who had committed suicide with a note in his pocket: "I walk a lonely street." This was spotted by a young songwriter, Tommy Durden, who took the scrap to Mae Axton, whom Elvis Presley told he needed material. Within a short while, they had come up with the song. Rockabilly singer Glenn Reeves sang the demo and was offered part of the song as payment, but he commented, "It's a silly song," damned if he'd allow his name attached to it, so it wasn't. Elvis loved it. His recording contained so much echo, it was a natural for a Stan Freberg spoof.

Covers: Hank Smith & the Nashville Playboys—really George Jones 1956; The Cadets 1956
Remakes: The Bill Smith Combo 1960; Ernie Freeman 1960; The Orlons 1964; Delaney Bramlett 1964; Roger Miller 1966; Frijid Pink 1970; Willie Nelson & Leon Russell 1979
Satire: Stan Freberg 1956

—

Chuck Berry "No Money Down" Chess January 1956

Style: Talking blues
Where from: St. Louis, MO
Where recorded: Chicago, IL
Suggested pairings: Muddy Waters "She Moves Me" 1950; The Robins "Framed" 1954; Bo Diddley "I'm a Man" 1955; The Coasters "Shoppin For Clothes" 1961

Muddy, Berry and Bo's hits had roots in Chess blues from 1950. In this talking blues "No Money Down," Chuck Berry attempts to outwit a used car salesman, coming out with one of the first rap performances.

During his first year in the business, according to Chess label session sax man Red Holloway, the storyline wasn't far from reality for Berry. "He tried to save money" while on the road. "He'd sleep in his car. The first year, he saved $100,000. Uncle Sam was looking for his hotel receipts, eating receipts, they charged him $48,000 in taxes. He went out and bought two Cadillacs and a station wagon. Now he stays in the best hotels."

This form of talking blues was an approach used in records from Muddy to The Coasters and well beyond.

—

The Willows "Church Bells May Ring" Melba January/February 1956

Style: Rhythm and blues vocal group
From and recorded in: New York City, NY
Original title: "Church Bells Are Ringing"
Suggested pairings: The Chords "Sh Boom" 1954; The Revalons "Dreams Are For Fools" 1958; The Fascinators "I Wonder Who" 1958

After releasing a half dozen titles as The Five Willows, three on Allen, one on Pee Dee and two on Herald between 1953 and 1954, the group finally hit as The Willows on "Church Bells Are Ringing," quickly retitled "Church Bells May Ring" when Melba realized the new title matched the actual lyrics. Urban legend has a very young Neil Sedaka, who later recorded with The Tokens on Melba, playing chimes on this session.

Covers: The Cadets; The Diamonds "The Church Bells May Ring" 1957

—

Howlin' Wolf "Smokestack Lightning" Chess February 1956

Style: Blues
Where from: Mississippi
Where recorded: Chicago, IL
Suggested pairings: Tommy Johnson's "Big Road Blues" 1928; The Mississippi Sheiks' "Stop and Listen Blues" 1930; Charley Patton "Moon Going Down" 1930; Howlin' Wolf "Crying at Daybreak" 1951; Sanford Clark "The Fool" 1956

Since the 1930s, while performing with Charley Patton in the Delta, Howlin' Wolf named this "a hypnotic one-chord drone piece," also known as "Smokestack Lightning." Wolf said the song was inspired by watching trains in the night: "We used to sit out in the country and see the trains go by, watch the sparks come out of the smokestack. That was smokestack lightning." Howlin' Wolf"s own "Crying at Daybreak" carries the line, "O-oh smokestack lightnin', shinin', just like gold, oh don't you hear me cryin'," apparently lifted from the Mississippi Sheiks' lyric "A-ah, smokestack lightnin', that bell shine just like gold, now don't you hear me talkin'." Howlin' Wolf's "Smokestack Lightning" was by far his most major and, possibly, most memorable hit.

—

Teen Queens "Eddie My Love" RPM February 18, 1956

Style: Rhythm and blues
Where from: Venice, CA
Where recorded: Culver City, CA
Suggested pairing: The Cadillacs "Betty My Love" 1956

Sisters Betty, 16, and Rose Collins, 14, were The Teen Queens. They came from a musical family, as brother Aaron Collins was a founding member of The Jacks and The Cadets and he arranged for them to record for the same Modern and RPM label family. "My sisters came from our original home in Arkansas and my father bought a house," Collins told Jim Dawson. "They were living in Venice with my dad and going to Venice High School."

According to Collins, who was living in nearby Santa Monica at the time, sister Betty came by and asked, "Why don't you try to get me and Rosie going?" Collins recalled, "They both sang in church, I thought it was a good idea, so I decided to write them a song we could take in to Maxwell Davis at Modern." He wrote the song "Johnny My Love" as a tribute to Johnny Ace who had died about a year previously. "There were a lot of girl singers out there singing about Johnny, 'dear Johnny,' 'why Johnny why?' I came up with this thing about 'Johnny My Love,' and then I changed the name to 'Eddie My Love' because the 'Johnny' thing was going out."

The Teen Queens name was chosen off the recent popularity of Frankie Lymon & the Teenagers. "They had an ear for harmony, but Rosie was the more talented of the two. Betty would just sing the melody and Rosie would harmonize a third above her," said Collins. "That was their sound."

With Davis' velvety horn supplementing the sound of the Teen Queens' plaintive "Eddie My Love" backed with "Just Goofed," the legendary songwriter P.F. Sloan loved it. "It was really influential, a discordant chord in the record, a minor chord and a flat underneath it. It just shocks you how great it is, the sax on there is doing incredible harmony work, Phil Spector picked up on that. It was R&B, had these great harmonies."

"Eddie My Love" hit big in February 1956.

When Aaron Collins' Cadets hit with "Stranded In the Jungle," The Cadets went on tour, freeing The Teen Queens from supervision. That was a bad thing. "I put my wife on the road with the girls, and that's when they really went wild. When they came back home and their record started going down, they got in with their friends and started using dope."

Cover: The Chordettes 1956; The Fontane Sisters 1956
Remake: Jo Ann Campbell 1961; The Sweethearts 1965

—

Little Richard "Long Tall Sally" Specialty March 1956

Style: Rhythm and blues
Where from: Macon, GA
Where recorded: at J&M Studio, New Orleans, LA
Suggested pairing: Dee Clark "24 Boyfriends" 1957; Al Calloway "Uncle John" 1957; Wild Child Gipson "Uncle John" 1958

"Long Tall Sally" was about whiskey drinking Mary, who had an affair with John. Mary also inspired "Short Fat Fanny" by Larry Williams on Specialty in 1957. When John saw Mary approach he would in fact duck back in the alley.

John inspired "Uncle John" by Al Calloway on Cash and by Wild Child Gipson on It's A Hit [record label], both in 1958. Featuring a saxophone solo by Lee Allen, who also played on "Tutti Frutti," Bumps Blackwell, Little Richard's producer, sped up the tempo of "Long Tall Sally" to try to prevent a Pat Boone cover as he had done with "Tutti Frutti."

Covers: Pat Boone 1956; Elvis Presley 1956
Remakes: The Beatles 1964; The Kinks in 1964

—

Little Richard "Slippin' and Slidin'" Specialty March 1956

Style: Rhythm and blues
Where from: Georgia
Where recorded: J&M Studio, New Orleans, LA
Suggested pairings: Al Collins "I Got the Blues For You Baby" 1955; Eddie Bo "I'm Wise" 1956; The Crickets "Oh Boy" 1957; Joe Houston "Shuckin' & Jivin'" 1957

With Lee Allen on sax and Huey Smith on piano, the flip of Little Richard's "Long Tall Sally," "Slippin' and Slidin'," had roots in several New Orleans recordings, including the first release on the Ace label, "I Got the Blues For You Baby" by Al Collins, of whom, Earl King said, "We used to call him Chocolate. One of my favorite writers of all time. Al Collins had tons of stuff he never was able to do anything with, one of the things he had during the times, people said was too suggestive, and not only that, Al wound up having a mental problem, he just went out of it, never got it back together."

Eddie Bo then adapted that song into "I'm Wise," the template for Little Richard's "Slippin' and Slidin'." Pat Boone passed. However, Lee Allen recalled it was "written by Dorothy LaBostrie. She and her secretary wrote a couple of songs. By that time, Little Richard had moved to bigger studios down in the French Quarter. It was still called Cossimo's. At this time, there were several in New Orleans, nice studios. He hung in there, made it big."

Remake: John Lennon 1975

—

James Brown & the Famous Flames "Please Please Please" Federal March 1956

Style: Rhythm and blues
Where from: Macon, GA
Where recorded: Cincinnati, OH
Suggested pairings: Big Joe Williams "Baby Please Don't Go" 1935; Billy Wright "Turn Your Lamps Down Low"; Luther Bond & the Emeralds "He Don't Love You" 1956

When Ralph Bass discovered James Brown and recorded him, Syd Nathan, owner of King/Federal, was displeased, calling this debut release, "Please Please Please," the worst thing he ever heard and a bunch of noise. When "Please Please Please" went to #1 R&B, he changed his mind, allowing Bass to keep him in the studio.

"Please Please Please" was influenced by Big Joe Williams' "Baby Please Don't Go" from 1935 and Billy Wright's "Turn Your Lamps Down Low," both of which also influenced Ray Charles' "Don't You Know."

Hank Ballard recalled, "When I first heard 'Please Please Please,' Ralph Bass was the A&R man for King Records. We heard it on a raggedy tape record[er] and we knew it was a hit. Syd Nathan didn't like it: 'Hank, they're not going to buy that.' But Ralph Bass and I knew it was a hit so we convinced Syd Nathan it was a hit. He put it out. It's still a hit today."

—

Elvis Presley "Blue Suede Shoes" RCA March 1956

Style: Rockabilly
Where from: Tupelo, MS
Where recorded: New York
Original version: Carl Perkins 1955

The day after Elvis Presley made his television debut, on Jimmy and Tommy Dorsey's Stage Show, he kicked off a recording session with "Blue Suede Shoes." According to Carl Perkins, his relationship to fellow Sun rocker Elvis meant Presley held off issuing his "Blue Suede Shoes" until Perkins' original had played out. "He didn't jump on the song right away," said Perkins.

"Chet Atkins was producing Elvis. He said, 'Elvis, there's a hit song out there, it's "Blue Suede Shoes."' He said, 'Yeah, I know it. That's my friend, Carl Perkins.' Atkins said, 'New York wants you to cut it now.' 'Let's do it later. I don't want to jump on the man's song right now.' He waited until it peaked and then he did it."

—

Joe Turner "Corrine Corrina" Atlantic March 1956

Style: Rhythm and blues
Where from: Kansas City, KS
Where recorded: New York City, NY
Suggested pairings: Tampa Red "Corrine Corrina" 1929; Joe Turner "Corrine Corrina" 1941; Charlie Feathers "Get With It" 1955

"I come up with that," said Joe Turner of "Corrine Corrina." "They didn't have nothing to put on one of the sides, so it was my idea. 'I know a song that's older than me. I heard people talking about it when I was a kid.' I made up my own idea, it's been done before. I put my own lyrics to it, and I said, 'We'll do this one up' and that's how 'Corrina' came up."

When Turner's "Corrine Corrina" hit in '56, the Decca label reissued Turner's first attempt at "Corrine Corrina" from 1941.

Remakes: Roy Moss 1956; Johnny Carroll & His Hot Rocks 1956; Bill Haley & the Comets 1958; Ray Peterson 1960; Bobby Vinton 1961; Dean Martin 1963

—

The Coasters "Down In Mexico" Atco March 1956

Style: Rhythm and blues vocal group
Where recorded: Los Angeles, CA

"Smokey Joe's Café" by The Robins was still charting in very late 1955 when Robins member Ty Terrell arrived at Spark on Melrose Avenue in Hollywood to find Lester Sill, manager of both Leiber-Stoller and The Robins, in the office. Sill had worked for Modern Records, urging Hunter Hancock to play R&B in 1947, and had established a reputation in the business when he began working for Spark. According to Terrell, upon learning Terrell had copyrighted The Robins name, an enraged Sill picked up a typewriter on his desk and tossed it at the bass man. That move meant Leiber-Stoller would have to create a new identity for The Robins, in reality a blessing in disguise.

"So we had four guys in the group," said Stoller. At the time, the group was ex-Robins lead singer Carl Gardner, bass singer Bobby Nunn, tenor Leon Hughes from The Hollywood Flames and The Lamplighters and baritone Billy Guy from Bip & Bop, who had a gift for on-stage comic routines. "Lester Sill named them The Coasters because they were from The Coast," ignoring the fact that Gardner, Guy and Hughes came from Texas and Nunn was from Alabama by way of Detroit. Robins lead singer Chapmen recalled. "The reasons The Coasters came about, if I had been married, that's why they moved back to New York. They took Carl and Bobby Nunn, they weren't married, they had no family back here. Young Jessie didn't start with us, Leon Hughes was playing with Bobby Nunn in Watts. The city fathers said they needed to be somewhere else."

Said Grady Chapman about Leiber-Stoller at the time of "Smokey Joe's Café," "They devoted more time to The Coasters than they did to The Robins. Ty Terrell had a lot to do with it; I don't know where he came from. He just messed up everything." As noted in The Robins story, Gardner was about to sing lead on The Robins' "Cherry Lips," when Leiber-Stoller arrived with documents barring him for recording for the label. Instead, he joined The Coasters at Radio Recorders on January 11 and sang on "Down In Mexico," with characters and descriptions borrowed from "Smokey Joe's Café" and the novelty up-tempo "Turtle Dovin'" with Barney Kessell on guitar; Waldo Hamilton, bass; Mike Stoller, piano; Gil Bernal, tenor sax; Jesse Sailes, drums; Frank "Chico" Guerrero, congas. "Jerry and I were always taken with Latin rhythms," said Mike Stoller. "I guess 'Loop De Loop Mambo' may have been the first time we used it with an otherwise rhythm and blues record."

After the first session's worth of hits was exhausted, apparently so was Leon Hughes, who left the group as he and Sill did not get along.

Covers: Ella Mae Morse; Champ Butler
Remakes: The Boston Crabs 1965; Cornel Gunter 1976

—

The Five Satins "In the Still of the Night" Standord April 1956/Ember June 1956

Style: Doo wop vocal group harmony
From and recorded in: New Haven, CT
Interim title: "I'll Remember"

This group was led by tenor Fred Parris, who began as The Scarlets' lead in 1954, which recorded several doo wop comps, most notably "Dear One" for the Harlem-based Red Robin label. Parris' next move was as lead of The Five Satins, who recorded "All Mine" for the Standord label in 1955, a release that went nowhere—possibly because the sound of a passing truck near the church basement/recording studio can be heard at song's finish.

The Five Satins then recorded "In the Still of the Night" for Standord, a release that was quickly picked up by the indie subsidiary of Herald, Ember Records, out of New York City. It was not an instant success. The flipside, "The Jones Girl," reportedly an answer to The Mills Brothers' "The Jones Boy," was chosen as the A-side by some jocks. Ember/Herald label owner Al Silver said he bought the record because his Boston distributor told him "In the Still of the Night" was hot and other labels were sniffing around. Silver bought everything the boys recorded at that New Haven church as well as the group themselves. The first three singles were all purchased at the same time. A few of early promo copies were issued as "I'll Remember" because the label wanted to avoid legal action over the same title, "In the Still of the Night," a different song by Cole Porter.

Lawsuits notwithstanding, The Five Satins' "In the Still of the Night" began hitting on New York's WMGM in August 1956, reaching a high of #13, hardly big hit numbers. Nationally, it hit #24 pop and #3 R&B in September. But that slow start indicated little. It was one of those records that developed market to market instead of hitting all at once nationally. Thus this slice of deep doo wop harmony with an active slow dobie dobie do" background was destined for the long term, selling well through the remainder of the decade and well into the sixties, a big seller for the next half century, or as long as 45s were actively available.

Remakes: The Safaris 1960; The Reflections 1963; Paul Anka 1969; Sha Na Na 1972; The Marcels 1973; Fred Parris & the Restless Hearts 1976; Boyz II Men 1992

—

Roy Orbison and the Teen Kings "Ooby Dooby" Je-Wel April 1956

Style: Rockabilly
From and recorded in: Texas

With Johnny Wilson, guitar; James Morrow, electric mandolin; Jack Kennelly, bass and Billy Parr Ellis, drums, The Teen Kings, who backed Roy Orbison on "Ooby Dooby," credited as Roy Orbison, recorded the first version of his later first hit on the Je-Wel label out of Odessa, Texas. Chester Oliver and his wife had a daughter, Jean, who was going with Weldon Rogers, thus Je-Wel Records. As Jean played with The Wink Westerners, which included Roy Orbison, Chester started Je-Wel records to record him.

After Roy was turned down by Columbia Records, he auditioned for Sam Phillips at Sun in Memphis. To sign with Sun, Roy had to break his contract with Oliver, who had paid for everything, as Roy was underage and the contract wasn't valid.

—

The Six Teens "A Casual Look" Flip May 1956

Style: Rhythm and blues vocal group
From and recorded in: Los Angeles, CA

The Six Teens were lead singer Trudy Williams; alto Louise Williams; first soprano Beverly Pecot; tenor Kenneth Sinclair; baritone Darryl "Cappy" Lewis and songwriter and occasional baritone Ed Wells. The Williams sisters attended Bishop Conaty High School in Los Angeles, while their cousin Lewis as well as Pecot was out of Centennial High School in Compton, and Sinclair was out of Fremont High School in Los Angeles. Ed Wells graduated as class valedictorian from St. Anthony's High School in Long Beach, though he lived in Willowbrook, sandwiched between Watts to the north and Compton to the South.

"We got together in 1956, me and Kenny Sinclair," Wells recalled. "We went to St. Leo's on Imperial and Central, we were in the ninth grade. It was a pretty poor school, so we were janitors, we started singing to get away from cleaning up."

Wells recruited Pecot and her cousin Diane on this just-written a love ballad, "A Casual Look," which the teens immediately began practicing with Diane as lead singer. Diane didn't have the singing skills Wells required, so he reached out to the Williams sisters, Louise and Trudy, who had already began singing as a duo. "When I first put the group together, I wanted one or two girls because they're more dependable than guys and because the Platters had Zola Taylor, whose voice sweetened their music," Wells told this book's author, Jim Dawson.

"When Louise showed up to audition, she brought along her 12-year-old sister, Trudy," Wells continued, "and she changed everything around. All of a sudden, she was the lead singer and we were doing Frankie Lymon songs with Trudy changing the pronouns like on 'I Want You To Be My Boy.' Louise came up with the Six Teens name in line with the six teenaged members. Wells told Dawson. "We came up with our name by adding up our ages and dividing it by six to get an average, which was sixteen."

Wells contacted Max Feirtag, who had success with Donald Woods & the Velaires. "We did a lot of rehearsing," he recalled. "They were counting on the song 'Teen Age Promise' because of the teenage thing, what with Frankie Lymon. 'A Casual Look' wasn't looked at as the A-side."

Ray Johnson, Flip's in-house pianist and arranger recalled, "That was their one and only big hit. We had extensive rehearsals and I tried to mold the musical arrangement behind what the group was singing." Recorded at the studio of Bunny Robyn near Fairfax High School, Wells recalled, "We knew the song so well, the first take was the one they accepted." Max Feirtag asserted that because of the fact members were still in school, "we used to only record them on Saturday."

Basically a duet between Trudy Williams and Sinclair, "A Casual Look" hit big in summer 1956.

Cover: Little Clydie & the Teens
Remake: Chris Darlin 1960

—

Little Willie John "Fever" King May 1956

Style: Rhythm and blues
Where from: Detroit, MI
Where recorded: Cincinnati, OH
Suggested pairings: Otis Blackwell "Daddy Rollin' Stone" 1953; Joe Tex "Pneumonia" 1956; Jack Lewis "Glendora" 1956; Linda Leigh "Beri Beri" 1959; Johnny Love "Chills & Fever" 1960

The first major hit for Little Willie John, "Fever" was written by Otis Blackwell, who had recorded the very similar "Daddy Rollin' Stone" in 1953. Writing credits were disputed by Little Willie John's sister, Mabel John, "Almost everything Willie did was inspired in some way by him. Willie just wanted to sing, he would give you all the lyrics to a song or change all the lyrics you gave him. He'd sing it and do it better than the teacher, he was unique in that way. He'd never care if his name was here, it wasn't important to him. 'Fever' was his own idea, his own mold."

"Willie John lived only a few blocks from me," said Lamont Dozier. "We got together on several occasions and he taught me a lot about singing as far as technique goes, different riffs. I didn't know how they did that, how they slurred words. We call it musical acrobatics. It was fun and the techniques were invaluable."

According to New York singer Freddie Houston, the real writer was Danny 'Run Joe' Taylor. "Run Joe was partially inept, came off the road, being with The Ink Spots, went to Beefsteak Charlie's, a bar where a lot of entertainers hang out, a lot of the girls come in there, I'd hang around there all day, make me two or three hundred dollars just for being there, that's where record companies got their background singers. He wrote a tune, I think he wrote 'Fever,' sold it to Otis Blackwell, I ran into Joe, 'Let's have a drink,' he said, 'No, I already have a drink.' Reached into his overcoat, had a bottle of wine in his overcoat and a suit in a bag, he got that for the song from Otis Blackwell and $30 to $40 dollars. He probably thought it was the best score he made in a long time."

Fellow King/Federal vocalist Hank Ballard said, "During that time, Little Willie was the best singer around: jazz, blues, pop, you name it. He had so much charisma, all he had to do was come out on stage and the house would come down. When he opened his mouth, the house would just burn. He was a cold-blooded professional; Little Willie was a lot of fun. A lot of people couldn't understand his behavior, but I did. He would do a lot of things out of the ordinary, but I got along with him and so did Syd Nathan, president of King, because he was making money. The tolerance level had to be up there sometimes to deal with it, but a lot of artists are like that."

Remakes: Earl Grant 1957; Ray Peterson 1957; Peggy Lee 1958; Elvis Presley 1960; Little Caesar & The Romans 1961; Sonny Ace & the Twisters 1961; Barbara English & the Fashions 1962; Alvin Robinson and Bobby Freeman 1964; The McCoys 1965; Esther Phillips 1966; Little Joe & the Latinaires 1968; The Manhattans 1972; Conway Twitty 1972; James Cotton Blues Band 1975; Esther Phillips 1976; Roy Ayers 1979

—

Sanford Clark "The Fool" MCI/Dot May 1956

Style: Rockabilly
Where from: Tulsa, OK
Where recorded: Phoenix, AZ
Suggested pairings: Howlin' Wolf "Smokestack Lightning" 1956; Al Casey "A Fool's Blues" 1956

Sanford Clark got his first guitar at age 12. When local DJ Lee Hazlewood was looking for somebody to record a song he had just written, fellow guitarist Al Casey suggested Hazelwood listen to Clark. Hazelwood went to Floyd Ramsey's studio with Casey and recorded "The Fool." That's when Hazelwood got in trouble, because as a DJ he wasn't allowed to play or promote his own record, so Hazelwood took what MCI stock he had and scratched off his name as co-writer with his wife, Naomi Ford, short for Shackleford, as a way to get around the conflict of interest.

"The Fool" was issued twice on MCI; Al Casey's guitar is less pronounced than on the second issue. When Dot Records got a hold of the master, they brightened the sound even more. Al Casey then recorded the bassline as "A Fool's Blues" for Dot in late 1956, but it went nowhere. Hazelwood went on to create the Ford label to showcase early Duane Eddy sides.

Cover: The Gallahads 1956; Scat Man Crothers 1956

—

Eddie Cochran "Skinny Jim" Crest 1956

Style: Rockabilly
Where from: Bell Gardens, CA
Where recorded: Los Angeles, CA

After several duets with Hank Cochran on Ekko and Cash, Eddie Cochran's first as a single artist was this stripped down rockabilly vocal full of hiccups and wolf whistles, "Skinny Jim," on Crest. It was also archaic and anachronistic as rock & roll was already moving to newer pop quarters. Recorded in a split session with Gene Davis whose "Let's Coast Awhile" was released as Bo Davis, both records had the same backing: Cochran, guitar; Ray Stanley, piano; Connie 'Guybo' Smith, stand-up bass; Jesse Sailes, drums and Hank Cochran, vocals. It's noted by some that "Skinny Jim" was an answer to Little Richard's "Long Tall Sally."

—

The Four Tops "Could It Be You" Chess May 1956

Style: Rhythm and blues vocal group
Where from: Detroit, MI
Where recorded: Chicago, IL

After a debut release backing Dolores Carroll on "Everybody Knows" in 1955, The Four Tops moved on to the Chicago-based Chess label, for which they recorded this almost word-jazz comp. "Could It Be You" has careful enunciation, uncommon in rhythm and blues record releases of the day.

"They got together in high school," said Lamon Dozier of the group, featuring lead singer Levi Stubbs with Abdul "Duke" Fakir, Renaldo "Obie" Benson and Lawrence Payton. "Lawrence Payton was very good buddies with Little Willie John. They went to school together and they were in the same music class. I often hear Lawrence talk about it. He's somewhat of a genius when it comes to arranging for the group." After poor sales, The Four Tops next recorded for Columbia in 1960 and for Riverside in 1962 with, again, poor results. They then hooked up with Motown in 1964 as an "overnight success."

—

Nervous Norvus "Transfusion" Dot May 1956

Style: Novelty rock 'n' roll
Where from: Memphis, TN
Where recorded: San Francisco, CA (vocal) and Los Angeles, CA (sound effects)

Stockton, CA DJ Jimmy Drake was Nervous Norvous, a name that summed up his deadpan yet nervous delivery. According to the songpoemmusic.com website, Drake told Time Magazine for the "Transfusion" idea, "I was driving, see, cool like down the freeway. A young kid in a twin pipe job come up on me fast on the right. He was a goner. He cockeyed near cooled me, man. So I said, 'Jimmy, let's write a song about this cool cat.' I don't even know the name of the guy. But I got even. Man, I got even!"

Drake sent a "Transfusion" demo to his old pal, DJ Red Blanchard at KPOP, Los Angeles. Blanchard decided it needed a sound effects punch, so "he pulled a 78 from the Standard Sound Effects series from KPOP's record library, cued it to 'Auto Skids and Crashes,' and played the brief track repeatedly to punctuate each mini-tale of reckless driving that form the song's verses. "That was just a natural to add the crashes," said Blanchard. "It's almost like there was a pause there just right for it." He added the effect on the fly, manually cueing and recuing while Drake's demo played from another tape deck. "I did the whole thing in one afternoon."

Blanchard put the pastiched "Transfusion" on the air, where it was an immediate hit with his listeners. Randy Wood, president of Dot Records, called to see if the recording was still available for release. After making the deal, "I gave him the tape I had," says Blanchard, "and that's what they made the record out of, just that demo tape with the sound effects added."

Cover: The Four Jokers—same vocalist, Jimmy Drake; Scatman Crothers 1956

—

Johnny Burnette and the Rock 'n Roll Trio "Tear It Up" Coral May 1956

Style: Rockabilly
Where from: Memphis, TN
Where recorded: Pythian Temple in New York City, NY

Johnny Burnette's first single was the countrified rocker "You're Undecided" backed with "Go Mule Go" on Von, selling fewer than 200 copies making it an extreme current rockabilly rarity. Burnette's family lost their only 78 after a continental rockabilly collector paid them a visit and got the holy grail. Both Paul Burlison and Dorsey Burnette worked for Crown Electric Company, where Elvis Presley had been employed, but were laid off in spring 1956.

Moving to New York, they appeared on TV's Ted Mack Original Amateur Hour, where they won as "The Rock and Roll Boys from Memphis." Signing with Coral Records, they regretted the move. "Capitol Records was after us, ABC Paramount, Chess and Decca. I wanted to go to Capitol but they said it didn't matter, a hit record would make us rich."

Becoming The Rock and Roll Trio, they recorded at the legendary Pythian Temple in New York City, where Bill Haley & His Comets had cut "Rock Around the Clock." At the first session, held on May 7, 1956, they recorded their first single, "Tear It Up," backed with a more rocking version of their "You're Undecided." This was the only release under the name Johnny Burnette and the Rock 'n Roll Trio.

—

Roy Orbison "Ooby Dooby" Sun May 1956

Style: Rockabilly
Where from: Texas
Where recorded: Memphis, TN

Based on this recording, Sun's Sam Phillips offered The Teen Kings a contract. It was a troubled session at Sun, as Orbison was rankled over Phillips dictating what and how the band would play. The record broke big, selling a reported 200,000 copies. After a handful of recordings, Orbison, probably inspired by Elvis Presley's success, switched to the RCA label, but had no hits. He became one of the original artists on the new Nashville start-up, Monument.

—

Gene Vincent & His Blue Caps "Be-Bop-A-Lula" Capitol May 1956

Style: Rock 'n' roll
Where from: Norfolk, VA
Where recorded: Nashville, TN

Gene Vincent and his Blue Caps were signed by Capitol Records in search of someone like Elvis Presley. Gene Vincent and his record company circulated the story that he wrote "Be-Bop-A-Lula" during a six-month stay in Portsmouth Naval Hospital, where he was recovering from a motorcycle accident. He played his guitar and came up with the tune inspired by the newspaper cartoon strip Little Lulu. Dickie Harrell, who was the drummer with The Blue Caps, told Mojo in 2000, "Actually the song was written by a guy from Portsmouth named Donald Graves." Vincent and his first manager, Bill "Sheriff Tex" Davis, bought the song from Graves for $25 bucks. Said Harrell, "It happened a lot in those days. Guys would take the sure money." Vincent and Graves may have written the songs with Graves, buying his writing interest.

Recorded in Nashville on May 4, 1956, "Be-Bop-A-Lula" was released as the B-side of Vincent's first single, a provocative number called "Woman Love."

Radio stations in the United States wanted nothing to do with "Woman Love," and the BBC banned it, so Capitol flipped the sides and put out "Be-Bop-a-Lula" as the A-side and sold 200,000 copies in the first month it was released. Harrell screamed during an early performance of the song, so he screamed every time the group performed the song, including in the studio.

Steve Allen lampooned the lyrics in a recitation on his TV show, earning a deserved reputation as a rock 'n' roll hater.

Cover: Scatman Crothers 1956
Remakes: The Everly Brothers 1960; Five Cards Stud 1966; John Lennon 1975

—

Chuck Berry and His Combo "Roll Over Beethoven" Chess May 1956

Style: Rock 'n' roll
Where from: St. Louis, MO
Where recorded: Chicago, IL
Suggested pairings: The Mills Brothers "Glow Worm" 1952; Carl Perkins "Blue Suede Shoes" 1956; Huey "Piano" Smith "Rockin' Pneumonia & the Boogie Woogie Flu" 1957; Jerry Lee Lewis "High School Confidential" 1958; Buddy Holly "Early in the Morning" 1958; Arthur Alexander "A Shot Of Rhythm and Blues" 1961; The Beatles "Get Back" 1969

Banned by some of the world's most famed broadcasters, the BBC in 1956 and China's pop music service in 1988, Chuck Berry's "Roll Over Beethoven" portrayed a classical music icon with a rock 'n' roll beat. Berry referenced lyrics past, "Glow Worm" by The Mills Brothers, to lyrics future, Arthur Alexander's "A Shot Of Rhythm and Blues" in 1961.

Legendary producer Willie Dixon recalled working on "Roll Over Beethoven" as well as "all the early things he done with the Chess company when he first came there: A&R work, also played bass on them. When I first met him [Berry], I could see he had in his mind to do something different from everybody else, along the musical lines. I tried to assist in any way I could." Sax man Red Holloway said, "When he [Berry] first started off, he'd do a lot of his original material and songs of that day, songs that were popular, quite a bit for his own material."

Remakes: The Velairs 1962; The Beatles 1964; Jerry Lee Lewis 1964.

—

Billy Stewart "Billy's Blues" Chess June 1956/Argo August 1956

Style: Rhythm and blues instrumental
Where from: Washington, DC
Where recorded: Chicago, IL
Suggested pairing: Mickey & Sylvia "Love Is Strange" 1956

This song was an aggressive instrumental that set the pattern for Mickey & Sylvia's "Love Is Strange." The flipside had a stuttering vocal over the instrumental bed. "Billy was a marvelous entertainer. I was the one that was responsible for him recording at Chess Records," said Bo Diddley. "I took him to Chess Records," where Stewart recorded this hit, "Billy's Blues," with a vocal on one side, the instrumental bed on the reverse. "I was on that," Diddley added. "Me and Little Papa Joe, which was known as Joe Williams. Jerome Green was there too. All of us used to help each other."

—

Shirley & Lee "Let the Good Times Roll" Aladdin June 1956

Style: Rhythm and blues
From and recorded in: New Orleans, LA
Suggested pairings: Clarence Garlow "Bon Ton Roulet" 1952; Shirley & Lee "Feel So Good" 1955; Clarence "Frogman" Henry "Ain't Got No Home" 1956

The first half dozen or so records by this duo were about their relationship, beginning with the highly regarded "I'm Gone," dubbing them "the Sweethearts of the Blues." Shirley Goodman said, "Ah baby, let the good times roll. Lee had been drinking a lot, 'come on baby,' it was almost as he sang it. And I said, 'Listen to this man, this song's great.' That night, we sat at the piano, while the band was packing, we sat down, we started picking on the piano, singing 'come on baby, let the good times roll,' which is almost reversed to 'Feel So Good,' because if you hear the beat of it, feel so good, let the good times roll is almost the same thing, same keys. All we did was start playing it, just chopping it, and putting the words in. It went on for a couple of weeks while we were on the road, everywhere we['d] go, we'd sit down and write some, put it on the side, write some, until we got it all together.

"And then we got to New Orleans," Goodman continued, "so we really sat down with it and took some out and put some in, really got it together. It started with a man coming up to the stage, saying, 'come on baby, let the good times roll.' Got to the court room, that's what I had to do was sing it." "Let the Good Times Roll" was perhaps the biggest of the early R&B hits not to be covered when it first hit big. It influenced "Ain't Got No Home" by fellow Crescent City performer Clarence "Frogman" Henry, who could sing like the high-voiced Shirley.

Remakes: The Brown Brothers 1958; Scotty McKay 1960; The Crenshaws—really The Rivingtons 1961; The Velvets 1962; Candy & the Kisses 1963; Dave Myers & his Surftones 1964; Keith Colley & Kathy Stephens 1964; Roy Orbison 1965; Caesar & Cleo—really Sonny & Cher 1965; Bunny Sigler 1967; Bill Medley 1968; The Righteous Bros 1969; Little Joe & the Latinaires 1973; Phoebe Snow 1974; Johnny Winter & Edgar Winter 1976

—

The Cadets "Stranded in the Jungle" Modern 1956

Style: Rhythm and blues vocal group
Where from: Santa Monica, CA
Where recorded: Culver City, CA
Original version: The Jayhawks 1956

While in the studio during a Cadets session, tenor Prentice Moreland was asked to replace Ted Taylor and came up with the "great googly moo, lemme out of here!" shout. "Ted Taylor couldn't show up at the session," Moreland recalled. "The Cadets, Etta James and B.B. King were at Modern Records. We were standing around drinking Scotch, when they said, 'Prentice, you do the tenor part.'" Moreland recalled a Cincinnati DJ whose on-air patter included the "great googly moo, we got a great one for you now."

New member Thomas "Pete" Fox said, "I went with The Jacks in '56, they replaced their baritone, Lloyd McCraw, I went with them. Once I got in the group, Fox found out The Cadets had not heard the original version and were just given the sheet music of "Stranded in the Jungle," a hit in the Big Apple in June 1956. "Stranded in the Jungle" was the only national hit The Cadets or The Jayhawks would have. When Taylor left The Cadets, he recalled, "They had a chance to record me as a single artist, but they passed on it because they felt I was group material." With the departure of Taylor and Moreland, The Cadets were a quartet of Collins, Davis, Fox and Jones.

Cover: The Gadabouts 1956
Remakes: The Vibrations 1961; The Fearsome Foursome 1965; The New York Dolls 1974

—

Little Richard "Rip It Up" Specialty June 1956

Style: Rhythm and blues

Songwriter John Marascalco arrived in L.A. with two new songs. "I wrote 'Ready Teddy' while still in Mississippi and intended to give it to Elvis Presley. I worked at a radio station WNAG (Grenada) as a copyrighter. I had originally presented the song to Elvis at a personal appearance. I went to Charleston, MS, where he was appearing at a high school gym, told them, 'I got a song I'd like to play for Elvis.' I brought my tape recorder, thought he was going to be a giant hit. Bill Black and Scotty were there. They said, 'When you go back home, call Sam Phillips, tell him I like the song.' I played it for him and he said, 'It sounds good, but it has a country feel, I want him to go into more rock and roll,' Well it was Saturday night, they played 'Long Tall Sally' by Little Richard on WLAC, out of Nashville, it blew my mind, I was with a couple of three friends, 'Damn I gotta write a song for that guy.'"

Marascalco continued, "In church I got the idea for the chorus, while driving out here, I wrote the song. I just drove in from Mississippi, walked into Specialty Records, presented it to Bumps, who said, 'It's a hit, got anything else?' First thing I said to Mr. Rupe's wife was 'Do you accept songs?' I went back to the car, got my buddy, sang it to him, got it to him, when I came out, I presented 'Rip It Up' to Bumps who wanted to know where I was staying. When he came back, he said, 'Mr. Rupe liked only one song, 'Ready Teddy.'" In Southern vernacular, "Ready Teddy" was about a girl ready for sex. "We're going down to distributor on a Saturday, call me, we'll give you the decision. On Saturday, he told me, 'They picked both of your sides to be back-to-back smashes.'"

Remakes: Elvis Presley 1956; Bill Haley & the Comets 1956; The Everly Brothers 1958; The Rivieras 1964

—

Bill Doggett "Honky Tonk" King July 1956

Style: Rhythm and blues instrumental

Suggested pairings: Fats Domino "Going to the River" 1953; Jimmy Reed "You Don't Have To Go" 1955; Bill Doggett with Tommy Brown "Honky Tonk" 1957; James Brown "Let's Make It" 1957; Scott Elliott "Fast Freight" 1958; Marvin Gaye "Ain't Nothin' Like the Real Thing" 1968

Bill Doggett had been a jazz organist/arranger, working with Louis Armstrong, Count Basie, Ella Fitzgerald, and Lionel Hampton. He signed with King Records in 1951, but didn't have a major hit until 1956. Considered the black American national anthem, jazz organist Bill Doggett's "Honky Tonk" was a nightclub break instrumental, "We'll be right back after this short intermission."

Doggett co-wrote with guitarist Billy Butler, who was on the session with featured saxophonist Clifford Scott. A previous association with Chicago sax man Red Holloway, who had played on Jimmy Reed sessions, was the basis for the use of Reed's popular riff from "You Don't Have To Go."

Remake: Tommy Brown (Doggett's original session, vocals dubbed in) 1956

—

Bo Diddley "Who Do You Love" Checker July 1956

Style: Blues
Where from: Mississippi
Where recorded: Chicago, IL

Making "who do" sound like "voodoo," Bo Diddley went to the ominous side on "Who Do You Love." "That's a comical tune," said Bo. "It's called comedy in music. There's only one part about 'the house on the roadside, tombstone hand and a graveyard mind.'"

Remake: George Thorogood and the Destroyers 1979

—

Bo Diddley "I'm Bad" Checker July 1956

Style: Blues
Where from: Mississippi
Where recorded: Chicago, IL
Suggested pairing: George Thorogood and the Destroyers "Bad To the Bone" 1981

About his talking blues "I'm Bad," Bo Diddley said, "What runs through my mind about that when I wrote that is I'm the baddest thing you ever wanted to run up to, understand? Like Muddy Waters has a song, 'I've got a .38 pistol built on a .45 frame, a tombstone bullet shoots balls and chains.' That's a bad dude, you don't run into nobody with that hanging on his side."

—

Elvis Presley "Hound Dog" RCA July 13, 1956

Style: Rock 'n' roll
Where from: Tupelo, MS
Where recorded: New York
Original version: Big Mama Thornton 1953
Influential version: Freddie Bell and the Bell Boys 1955

It was "Hound Dog" that hooked up songwriters Leiber-Stoller with Elvis, resulting eventually in "Jailhouse Rock" in 1957. As indicated by the picture sleeve placement, the intended A-side was the syncopated rock composition "Don't Be Cruel," but via TV appearances like that on the Steve Allen Show, Elvis Presley's remake of Willie Mae Thornton's "Hound Dog" from 1953, with additional drumming in a remake by Freddie Bell and the Bell Boys on Mercury, became the hit side.

Said Mike Stoller, "I'm told that 'Hound Dog' was take 39, but they didn't have to look at the clock. He [Elvis] was very relaxed, so it was very easy to work with him." On the UK show Songbook, asked what he thought of the Elvis version when they first heard it, Mike Stoller said, "I thought it was nervous and too fast and they changed the words, some of them, because obviously the original lyric was a woman's song. I don't think they improved upon Jerry's lyrics." Jerry Leiber commented, "I thought it ruined the song. It was a song that had to do with obliterated romance. In effect, she was saying, 'Get out of my house.' And 'you ain't caught a rabbit, and you ain't no friend of mine' is inane. It doesn't mean anything to me."

Cover: Scat Man Crothers 1956
Answers: Vernon Anders "Hound Dog & Alley Cat" 1956
Remakes: Candy Johnson Show 1964; Dirty Blues Band 1966; Chuck Jackson 1967; Ruby Andrews 1971; Jerry Lee Lewis 1980; Charlie Rich 1980; Eric Clapton 1990
Satire: Lalo Guerrero "Pound Dog" 1956

—

Elvis Presley "Don't Be Cruel" RCA July 13, 1956

Style: Rock 'n' roll
Where from: Tupelo, MS
Where recorded: New York

On Christmas Eve 1955, songwriter Otis Blackwell was on the streets in front of the Brill Building in New York City trying to stay warm. Things were going poorly for Blackwell. It was raining and his shoes leaked. A friend, Leroy Kirkland, walked by and asked Otis if he had written any more songs. Otis said yes. Over the next week, he sold six of them to a publishing company for $25 each. Management at The Brill Building liked him so much they offered him a full-time job writing, and Blackwell accepted.

Not long after, Otis got some very good news. An up-and-coming rock star wanted to record one of his songs, but the guy wanted half the writer's fee. Otis said, "No." After friends convinced him that half of something was better than all of nothing, and this new singer just might "make it," and if he did, Otis' royalties would be tremendous, finally, Otis agreed. He found out it wasn't Elvis who wanted half the "writer's fee," but his manager, Colonel Tom Parker. The flipside of "Hound Dog," the syncopated rocker, "Don't Be Cruel," was one of the best sellers of all time, making it the only example of both sides of one record reaching the top position until that time and for several decades after.

Remakes: Bill Black 1960; Barbara Lynn 1963; The Mojo and by the Upsetters 1968; Jerry Lee Lewis 1972; Billy Swan 1979; Cheap Trick 1988

—

Buchanan & Goodman "Flying Saucer" Luniverse 1956

Style: Novelty
Suggested pairings: "Open Up That Door" by Nappy Brown (saxophone intro only)
Record snippets: "The Great Pretender" The Platters ("Too Real" by The Clatters); "I Want You To Be My Girl" Frankie Lymon and the Teenagers; "Long Tall Sally" Little Richard; "Poor Me" by Fats Domino; "Heartbreak Hotel" by Elvis Presley; "Earth Angel" by The Penguins ("Earth" by The Pelicans); "I Hear You Knocking" by Smiley Lewis ("Knocking" by Laughing Lewis); "Tutti Frutti" by Little Richard; "(You've Got) The Magic Touch" by The Platters ("Uh-Oh" by The Clatters); "The Great Pretender" by The Platters
Side Two: "Band of Gold" by Don Cherry; "Ain't That A Shame" by Fats Domino ("That's A Shame" by Skinny Dynamo); "Don't Be Angry" by Nappy Brown; "Blue Suede Shoes" by Carl Perkins ("Shoes" by Pa Gherkins); "Maybellene" by Chuck Berry ("The Motor Cooled Down" by Huckle Berry); "See You Later Alligator" by Bill Haley & His Comets; "My Prayer" by The Platters

"Flying Saucer" amounted to a Martian invasion story line punctuated by snippets of hits of the day. Turned down by local labels, Alan Freed played the record on WINS. Suddenly it became the talk of the Big Apple. Roulette's George Goldner backed Buchanan and Goodman's Universe label. About 2,000 45s and 78s were pressed when a pre-existing Universe got in touch. So Buchanan, Goodman and George had to take out ballpoint pens and add a hand lettered L to the label logo.

"It was so big the bootleggers had to move in," said Henry Stone, a Miami distributor. "Big huge million selling record, man. Just one of those clever records that took a bunch of songs and put em together y'know. He was a character, man. Everybody knew him for doing these great novelty records." Then the Harry Fox Agency informed them of plans to file an infringement suit in the U.S. District Court for use of published songs. When those labels experienced an upswing in sales, the effort to shoot down the "Flying Saucer" halted and Buchanan and Goodman agreed to a fraction of a cent royalty per song excerpt for each disc sold.

Covers: Sid Noel 1956; Dave Barry "Out Of This World With Flying Saucers" 1956
Answer: Alan Freed, Al "Jazzbo" Collins and Steve Allen "The Space Man" 1956

—

The Johnny Burnette Trio "Oh, Baby Babe" Coral July 1956

Style: Rockabilly
Where from: Memphis, TN
Where recorded: Owen Bradley Studio in Nashville, TN
Suggested pairing: Elvis Presley "Baby Let's Play House" 1955

The Johnny Burnette Trio departed New York for the more friendly climes of Owen Bradley's Studio at 804 16th Avenue South, Nashville, Tennessee, where for three days in July they teamed up with Buddy Harman, drums and Grady Martin, guitar for "Oh, Baby Babe."

—

Otis Rush "I Can't Quit You Baby" Cobra USA August 1956
Style: Blues
Where from: Philadelphia, MI
Where recorded: Chicago, IL

As recalled by fellow blues guitarist Buddy Guy, "I went to Chicago, didn't nobody know who I was. I ran into Magic Sam and Otis Rush and other great guitar players. I was kinda shy. I told myself, 'Only way you're gonna get in these doors is to tell 'em you're gonna come out playing and that's the way they say, 'I gotta see this to believe it.' After a few weeks, they said, 'He can play.' Sam took me over to Cobra Records. At that time, Cobra didn't have a talent scout. Otis came to my house and said, 'Eli wants to see you, Buddy.' Then we both were there. I wound up being more like a studio guy than Otis did. The president Eli Toscano would go out and get everything he had engineering himself. I didn't know if that made it better for blues players, but you get ready to record, you go straight to the horse's head. You didn't have to go through anybody else, we had Willie Dixon hanging around then."

In fact, Dixon wrote Otis Rush's first release, "I Can't Quit You Baby," with Rush on guitar and vocals; Big Walter Horton on harmonica; Red Holloway on tenor sax; Lafayette Leake on piano; Wayne Bennett on second guitar; Dixon on bass and Al Duncan on drums. "It was great fun in those days. That guy died; Chess got Otis Rush first." Shortly after this session, Dixon went over to Chess full time. Dixon got credit on "I Can't Quit You Baby" by Led Zeppelin. "We got all that straightened out," said Dixon. "It wasn't much, but we finally got it into a state where we get results from my own songs."

Remakes: Led Zeppelin 1969; Little Milton 1969

—

The Channels "The Closer You Are" Whirlin Disc August 1956
Style: Doo wop vocal group harmony
From and recorded in: New York

Writer and lead singer of "The Closer You Are," Earl Lewis, said the group was named after their style of singing. "The bridge of a song is called a channel. We always had trouble with it. It was an accident. When we recorded it, I was off alone practicing my falsetto. Bobby Robinson of Whirlin' Disc had that put in," thus The Channels. For several releases, the group changed labels to George Goldner's Gone. "We felt had our done our work with Bobby Robinson." But after a pair of releases on Gone, they returned to Robinson's Fury in 1958. Lewis did not care for the term doo wop. "It's a second name of the same music. It was renamed, but it should always be R&B." In 1961, during the doo wop revival, The Channels' "The Closer You Are" hit #28 on KFWB in L.A., meaning it was a true nationwide revival.

—

Elvis Presley "Shake, Rattle and Roll" Sun/RCA August 31, 1956
Style: Rockabilly
Where from: Tupelo, MI
Where recorded: New York
Original version: Joe Turner 1954
Earlier version: Bill Haley 1956

"Elvis put a strong rockabilly feel behind the song," said Malcolm Leo, "losing several of the Turner/Haley lyrical passages, but he kept the one about a "one-eyed cat peeking in a seafood store."

—

Fats Domino "Blueberry Hill" Imperial September 1956

Style: Rhythm and blues
Where from: New Orleans, LA
Where recorded: Hollywood, CA
Original version: Gene Autry 1940
Suggested pairings: The Weavers "On Top of Old Smokey" 1951; Louis Armstrong "Blueberry Hill" 1949; Lavern Baker "Still" 1956; Ricky Nelson "You Are My One and Only Love" 1957
Cover: Louis Armstrong 1956; Scatman Crothers 1956

Written by Vincent Rose, Al Lewis and Larry Stock, "Blueberry Hill" was performed by Gene Autry in the 1940 western "The Singing Hill." When Fats Domino ran out of material, he messed around with different titles. One of them was "Blueberry Hill." His producer Dave Bartholomew objected and Fats forgot the lyrics while he was recording the song. The engineer pieced together the final version from many fragmentary takes. At 1:07, the tape stretched and vocals were distorted at the line "vows we made," which later in the 45 became "vows you made." When Fats' version hit, Louis Armstrong's 1949 version of "Blueberry Hill" was reissued to compete against Fats Domino's patched together hit. Patched together won out.

Note: In the 1970s, the tape stretch was removed.

Remakes: Skeeter Davis 1961; Ramsey Lewis 1962; Jimmy Smith 1963; The Soul Sisters 1963; Hank Crawford 1963; Little Richard 1964; Pat Boone 1965

—

The Heartbeats "A Thousand Miles Away" Hull September 1956/Rama November 1956

Style: Doo wop vocal group harmony
Where from: Queens, NY
Where recorded: New York City, NY
Suggested pairing: The Royals "Every Beat Of My Heart" 1952; The Elegants "Little Star" 1958

The Heartbeats were formed around the tenor lead voice of James "Shep" Sheppard with bass singer Wally Roker. Their first release, as The Heartbeats Quintet, was "Tormented," pretty much a steal of the Royals' "Every Beat Of My Heart" from 1952; thus The Heartbeats.

In 1955, The Heartbeats signed with Hull Records and came out with two fine singles, "Crazy For You" and "People Are Talking," but with paltry sales. Then came their breakthrough hit, this evocative ballad, "A Thousand Miles Away"

As recalled by Wally Roker, "Shep's girlfriend left, went to Texas, that's how 'A Thousand Miles Away' came about. She created the song in his mind, he wrote it, we didn't think that much of it, just his girlfriend going to Texas, but it was very important. Evidently it captured a feeling that went over very well. That was the most important person in his life, Shirley. That was his wife. She came back later from Texas [and they were] husband for wife for many years.

Roker continued, "I thought Bea Kaslin of Hull Records didn't have the ability to take it around the world like it needed to be taken, so I told her we needed to be on a bigger label. She let the record go on a bigger label so we could get the better response. My mistake. We moved it from Hull to Rama, still didn't see any money."

Cover: The Diamonds 1956
Answer: Shep & the Limelites "Daddy's Home" 1961
Remakes: The Day Brothers 1960; Danny and the Juniors 1960; Johnny Nash 1961; Santo & Johnny 1964; The Temprees 1984

—

Lee Allen and His Band "Rockin' At Cosmos" Aladdin September 1956

Style: Rhythm and blues instrumental
From and recorded in: New Orleans, LA

Lee Allen said, "We were doing a lot of work for Aladdin, Shirley & Lee. Eddie Mesner used to say, 'We'd like you to do something.' We were in the studio for most artists who came from out of town, who were sent to us. They seemed to like the New Orleans sound. We just messed around, doing different things that would come out from us at times. You try to give a title to something within the surroundings, right there. Unless it's somebody you want to dedicate it to. It [the title] was in reference to the studio we cut it in named after the young man who used to be the engineer on all those records out of New Orleans, Cosimo Matassa. We just made it up right there, gave it a name, it was befitting him."

—

The Dells "Oh What a Night" Vee Jay September 1956

Style: Doo wop vocal group harmony
From and recorded in: Chicago, IL

"Marvin Junior and Johnny Funches are the two writers on 'Oh What a Night,'" said Dells' bass singer Chuck Barksdale. "We had all been out the night before, partying. The next day at rehearsal, Marvin Junior and Johnny Funches were standing around, talking about 'Oh what a night we had last night, this little chick was fine.' They collaborated at some point, it must have been after this particular night, 'Oh What A Nite,' the lyrics and the melody followed that. The record company was about to kick us off the label because we hadn't sold a lot of records."

Remake: The Dells "Oh What A Night" 1969

—

Chuck Berry "Brown Eyed Handsome Man" Chess September 1956

Style: Rock 'n' roll
Where from: St. Louis, MO
Where recorded: Chicago, IL
Suggested pairings: Duane Eddy "Movin' & Groovin'" 1957; The Blasters "Border Radio" 1979

Amounting to Chuck Berry's first autobiography, two years before his legendary "Johnny B Goode," "Brown Eyed Handsome Man" was an example of a socially conscious message hidden in an adventure style story, with mysteriously dyslexic lyrics "two three the count," a baseball impossibility, and "Milo de Venus." This song influenced Duane Eddy's "Movin' & Groovin'" bass line in 1957 and The Blasters on "Border Radio" in 1979.

Sax man Red Holloway said, "People were in awe of some of the things he'd [Berry] do. Most players would play a T-Bone Walker. He had his own style of playing. That's why a lot of the different guitar players sound like him."

—

Chuck Berry "Too Much Monkey Business" Chess September 1956

Style: Rock 'n' roll
Where from: St. Louis, MO
Where recorded: Chicago, IL
Suggested pairings: Louis Jordan "Ain't That Just Like A Woman" 1946; Bob Dylan "Subterranean Homesick Blues" 1966

In this slice of social protest, this flipside to "Brown Eyed Handsome Man," Berry took aim at his employer, bill collectors, buying on time salesmen, future spouses, school hours, the phone company, the army, and gas station customers, and ended it with another of Berry's coined words—"botheration." Sax man Red Holloway said, "Most of his music was happy-type music. [This] was something in-between. He might have a rock 'n' roll beat and a pop style of playing, it was mixed up. I think his original material went over best."

—

Sonny Knight "Confidential" Vita September 29. 1956/Dot November 1956

Style: Rhythm and blues
From and recorded in: Los Angeles, CA

Vocalist Sonny Knight was a Belmont High School student when he was discovered at Tommy's Burgers in the north downtown L.A. area near his high school. Knight recorded the fine ballad "Confidential" backed with the novelty "Jail Bird," lifted from Fats Domino's "Bo Weevil" for the small Pasadena-based Vita label.

Knight wrote "Confidential" with Dorinda Morgan, who had already recorded him on "Dedicated To You" as Joe Smith for Cal West. "She gave me a set of lyrics and I put the music to them," Knight recalled. "She wasn't very fussy about me taking liberties with lyrics. She thought I had a 'confidential' sounding voice and the lyrics reflect that. It was a very interesting date—Plas Johnson on sax, Adolphus Jacobs on bass, Ray Martinez on drums, Ernie Freeman on piano. It was recorded at the old Master's Studio on Fairfax."

Morgan's son Bruce recalled, "We did 'Confidential' at Radio Recorders and leased it to Randy Wood, who put it out on Dot. We would put out a test record to see if we could generate any interest, take it around to radio stations to see if we could get it played, went to Dot for distribution power, Dot was hot at the time," thus a Big Apple charter.

"Confidential" hit first in L.A., then New York, then on the pop charts in November. "I took Sonny on a cross-country promo tour, it stayed on the charts for 50 weeks," said Morgan. Even though Dot controlled the release, Dewey Terry, who recorded and delivered for Vita, recalled the label kept shipping to stores long after they had sold the record. "They sold the master to Dot and were supposed to stop shipping," said Terry. "Larry Meade only had a couple of presses, but kept on bootlegging records. It showed up on [the] Minneapolis chart for 16 weeks in a row on Vita."

—

Sammy Masters "Pink Cadillac" 4-Star 1956

Style: Rockabilly
Where from: Oklahoma
Where recorded: Hollywood, CA
Suggested pairing: Elvis Presley "Baby Let's Play House" 1955

Sammy Masters recorded demos for Bill McCall's 4-Star label in Pasadena in 1953. Sammy had a day job working as a used car salesman in Los Angeles when he wrote "Pink Cadillac" about one of his customers. Sammy Masters and his Rocking Rhythm—Ralph Roe and Jimmy Bryant on guitar; Jerry Miller, steel and Jimmy Randal, drums—cut one of the few real rockabilly records out of the L.A. scene.

An alternate take of Masters' "Pink Cadillac" was issued under the name Johnny Todd, Masters' real first and middle name, on Modern in late 1956. "I believe they used my tracks when they put the drums on it. It isn't clear how Modern got my tracks," said Masters much later. "Bill Mc Call was very clever."

Cover: Johnny Todd—really Sammy Masters 1956; Rusty Draper 1956

—

The Johnny Burnette Trio "The Train Kept A-Rollin'" Coral 1956

Style: Rockabilly
Where from: Memphis, TN
Where recorded: Owen Bradley Studio in Nashville, TN
Original version: Lucky Millinder 1952

As it employed ground-breaking fuzzed guitar by session player Grady Martin's hard driving guitar with the solos on the bass strings and guitar amplifier used in the studio by the legendary Cliff Gallup on all those great Gene Vincent hits, it gives "The Train Kept A-Rollin'" status as a must-record for rock 'n' roll and heavy metal guitarists with versions by The Yardbirds and by Aerosmith.

The B-side was a rocking redo of Joe Turner's classic, "Honey Hush."

Burnette's "Train Kept A-Rollin'" charted top 10 on WCOP, Boston in late 1956, but nowhere else. Both Johnny and Dorsey Burnette moved to Los Angeles in late 1957 and each had hits on several local labels.

Remakes: Scotty McKay Quintet 1957; The Yardbirds 1965; Aerosmith 1974

—

The Chips "Rubber Biscuit" Josie October 1956

Style: Novelty doo wop
Where from: Bed-Sty section of Brooklyn, NY
Where recorded: New York City, NY
Suggested pairing: The Boulevards "Chop Chop Hole In the Wall" 1959

Barely out of high school, some neighborhood guys came up with a street song they first called "Cow Cow Ooh." The Chips—Sammy Strain, first tenor; Nathaniel Epps, Kinrod Johnson, Shedrick Lincoln and Paul Fulton, bass—came up with a rockaballad, "Oh My Darlin'" backed with this novelty "Rubber Biscuit" for which they found a willing label in Josie. With backing by Ernie Hayes, piano; Panama Francis, drums; Mickey Baker, guitar and King Curtis, sax, The Chips hit big—in New York City, that is. A few years later, another Big Apple group, The Boulevards, came up with the very similar "Chop Chop Hole In the Wall" in 1959. Strain went on to record with The Fantastics, The O'Jays and Little Anthony and The Imperials.

Remake: The Blues Brothers 1978

—

Elvis Presley "Love Me Tender" RCA October 1956

Style: Rock 'n' roll
Where from: Tupelo, MS
Where recorded: Hollywood, CA
Suggested pairing: Shelton Brothers & The Sunshine Boys "Aura Lee" 1938

In 1956 Elvis was contracted into his first role, in a movie to be called Love Me Tender. It was decided that in it he would sing his first-ever non-rock ballad, so a song was needed. The music director on the movie was Ken Darby, who found the 95-year-old melody Aura Lee. The simple tune needed no restructuring, but new words were called for. It is believed that Darby himself was responsible for the revised lyrics, but he gave the credit to his wife Vera Matson—and Presley. So was born the song Love Me Tender. Elvis recorded it in August 1956 on a large sound stage without his usual band and backing singers.

Cover: Dave Burgess 1956; The Toppers 1956
Remakes: Richard Chamberlain 1962; The Platters 1964; Chuck Jackson 1967; Percy Sledge 1967; Engelbert Humperdinck 1978; James Brown 1978; Linda Ronstadt 1979; The Turtles 1980; B.B. King 1982

—

James Brown With the Famous Flames "Chonnie-On-Chon" Federal October 1956

Style: Rhythm and blues
Where from: Macon, GA
Where recorded: Cincinnati, OH

After Little Richard's screaming style was an established way of selling records, many labels tried to have R&B artists to emulate his unique style, Federal being one with this James Brown song. Brown had not hit since "Please Please Please" in early 1956, and this fine rocker, "Chonnie-On-Chon," didn't move the needle.

—

Chuck Berry "You Can't Catch Me" Chess November 1956

Style: Rock 'n' roll
Where from: St. Louis, MO
Where recorded: Chicago, IL
Suggested pairing: The Beatles "Come Together" 1969

In "You Can't Catch Me," Chuck Berry referenced his competition with Bo Diddley, supposedly a taunt to guitar-backed label mate Bo Diddley, whose recording career also began in 1955 on a sister label, Checker. Diddley recalled, "Chuck Berry was an artist at Chess Records, but Chuck didn't do very much talking to people at that time which I didn't either, because everybody was locked into their own fantasy world they had going for themselves, scared of the next guy. 'Hey man, I don't want him to hear my stuff because he might steal something from me.' Since people has dropped their guard, there's been a lot of that going on. Chuck Berry and myself back in those days was right about not letting nobody hear nothing because they would rip it off."

Berry's lyrics, "here come ol' flat top" was lifted by The Beatles in "Come Together" in 1969, prompting a lawsuit, which was settled by John Lennon agreeing to record some classic '50s songs for the label that filed the suit. In turn, when that label released those songs on the John Lennon "Rock and Roll" LP without his permission, Lennon countersued and won.

—

Chuck Berry "Havana Moon" Chess November 1, 1956

Style: Rock 'n' roll
Where from: St. Louis, MO
Where recorded: Chicago, IL
Suggested pairings: Nat "King" Cole "Calypso Blues" 1951; Richard Berry & the Pharaohs "Louie Louie" 1957

This atypical Berry work with an island calypso vibe came at the height of Harry Belafonte's popularity, and of calypso, the flipside to "You Can't Catch Me," Berry's "Havana Moon" was a gentle story about a warm sleepy island beach and lost love, his first over two-and-a-half-minute work, hidden, because, until '58, Chess didn't bother to list playing time on any of their releases. "Havana Moon" was an influence on Richard Berry's original recording of "Louie Louie" in 1957.

—

Jesse Belvin "Goodnight My Love" Modern November 1956

Style: Rhythm and blues
Where from: Texas
Where recorded: Los Angeles, CA
Suggested pairings: Nat "King" Cole "Sentimental Reasons" 1946; Donnie Owens "Need You" 1958; Jesse Belvin "Guess Who" 1959

The legend of the sale of half interest in this song, "Goodnight My Love," involved various local R&B characters. Huggy Boy recalled he was the first to visit George Motola in his office and was offered the song. Huggy left the office to gather up the $400, but when he returned, songwriter John Marascalso had already done the deal. Marascalco recalled, "I met George Motola, I thought I could do something besides write for Little Richard. Jesse Belvin called me up, wanted to sell his share of the song. They had initially started the song, I was there that night. I'm sure they'd been working on it before. Before it was finished, I walked in, I said I liked it. Jesse called me up days later, 'Hey man I need money, want to buy my share?' 'How much?' '$400.' 'Sounds okay to me.' Jesse was one of the nicest guys you'll ever meet." Marascalco added, "I did contribute to the writing of the thing, mainly the bridge."

Crown and Modern label pop producer and choral conductor Don Ralke arranged this song and his singers provided the white-sounding background, anticipating the similar sound in Sam Cooke's "You Send Me" in 1957.

Belvin's "Goodnight My Love" backed with "I Want You With Me Xmas" on Modern hit on the cusp of the holiday season in San Francisco and in New York via Alan Freed. After the holidays, the Christmas side was dropped in favor of "Let Me Love You Tonight."

Covers: The McGuire Sisters 1956; Earl Grant 1956; Eileen Barton 1957
Remakes: Ray Peterson 1959; The Fleetwoods 1963; The Four Seasons 1964; Ben E. King 1964; The Happenings 1966; Lenny Welch 1973; James Brown 1976

—

Screamin' Jay Hawkins "I Put a Spell On You" Okeh November 1956

Style: Rhythm and blues
Where from: Cleveland, OH
Where recorded: New York

Screamin' Jay Hawkins, real name Jalacy Hawkins, wanted to be an opera singer and imagined "I Put aSpell On You" as a love ballad. "I didn't have the best voice for blues and R&B. But I could scream. I called on my opera training. I can scream soprano, like a woman." Supposedly so hammered when he recorded "I Put a Spell On You," Hawkins couldn't remember the session or the song, loaded with primal grunts, howls and moans. Never charting, it became a cult hit, one of R&B greatest primal screams.

Remakes: Nina Simone 1965; The Alan Price Set 1966; Screamin' Jay Hawkins 1967 and 1978; Creedence Clearwater Revival 1968; The Crazy World of Arthur Brown 1968

—

Mickey & Sylvia "Love Is Strange" Groove November 1956

Style: Rhythm and blues
Where from: Kentucky; New York City, NY
Where recorded: New York
Suggested pairings: Billy Stewart "Billy's Blues" 1956; Buddy Holly "Words of Love" 1957; Buddy Holly "Listen To Me" 1958; Bobby Rydell "The Cha Cha Cha" 1962; Dave Cortez "Rinky Dink" 1962; The Rockyfellers "Killer Joe" 1963; Bobby Moore "Try My Love Again" 1966

Bo Diddley was married to "Tootsie" aka Ethel Smith from 1952 to 1964, though they had been separated since the late 1950s. About Bo's song, "Love Is Strange," Bo said, "It came up in Baltimore, Maryland. They heard us singing it in the dressing room and Sylvia wanted the song. When I offered to record the song, my label, Chess, had asked me who do you think I was, Perry Como or someone. Phil and Leonard Chess did not see, if you came in with one style, they wasn't too anxious if you moved to somewhere else until they drained that dry. And me doing ballads and things, there were a lot of things that Chess never knew I knew how to do.

"Chess tried to sue Sylvia to get the song back," Diddley continued. "Chess tried to sue to get the song, but ran into a brick wall when they found out it wasn't in my name. It was in my wife's name. I put it in her name because at the time I was no[t] hip to record contracts and all this kind of stuff. I thought everything I wrote had to go to Chess Records because I was under contract. She didn't have no contract with them, so I put it under Ethel Smith. If you check with the copyright office, you'll find Ethel Smith is a subsidiary of Ellis McDaniel."

Remakes: Caesar and Cleo—really Sonny & Cher 1965

—

Bo Diddley "Cops and Robbers" Checker November 1956

Style: Blues
Where from: Mississippi
Where recorded: Chicago, IL
Original version: Boogaloo and his Gallant Crew "Cops and Robbers" 1956

Bo Diddley covered songwriter Kent Harris, aka Boogaloo and his Gallant Crew, on this early rap style narrative, "Cops and Robbers," which described an amusing encounter by the bad guys with the police. Neither version charted, yet both became classics.

—

The Jive Bombers "Bad Boy" Savoy December 1956

Style: Doo wop vocal group harmony
Where from: Pawtucket, RI
Where recorded: Newark, NJ
Original version: Lil Armstrong "Brown Gal" 1936

Lil Armstrong wrote and recorded Brown Gal for Decca in 1936, with covers by The Ink Spots and Benny Calloway with the Four Steps of Jive. Al Sears and The Sparrows introduced the title "Bad Boy" on Coral in 1950. In 1952, Clarence Palmer & the Jive Bombers recorded their first version of "Bad Boy" on Citation. In 1957, a unique stuttering lead vocal by Clarence Palmer hit on an updated "Bad Boy" by The Jive Bombers on WMGM in New York in January 1957.

—

The Del-Vikings "Come Go With Me" Fee Bee/Dot December 1956

Style: Doo wop vocal group harmony
From and recorded in: Pittsburgh, PA

According to Del-Vikings member Dave Lerchey, "Clarence Quick was out of Brooklyn singing bass; Norman Wright was out of Philadelphia; Kripp Johnson came out of Pittsburgh, lived in Koreopolis; Don Jackson was out of Toledo, Ohio; I was out of California. The cuts we made for Barry Kaye's studio in the basement, the demo tapes, he was going to take around to various labels to try to get us a contract when we signed up with Fee Bee, a tri state little company.

"When Dot put it out nationwide, it kind of worked its way like a wave across the country," Lerchey, continued, "from here it went across the ocean to Europe, it was still #1 a year later. It was like a tidal wave, it picked up and got heavy on the East Coast... the first place it broke was Pittsburgh... went New York, it came back to Pittsburgh where it had never stopped, it was #1 30 weeks in a row."

Lerchey added, "Just before we started breaking up, we started getting shipped out. Gus Backus got shipped to Weisbaden, West Germany and he started a little group over there—the Videls, kind of a takeoff on the same group, when he got discharged he did so well he went back over there. Don and Kripp sang a while after the group broke up, Norm went off with a single, Quick stayed with Kripp."

Remakes: The Chevrons 1960; Dion 1963; Sugar N' Spice 1964; The Reasons 1965; Gloria Jones 1966; The Beach Boys 1981

—

Fats Domino "Blue Monday" Imperial December 1956

Style: Rhythm and blues
From and recorded in: New Orleans, LA
Original version: Smiley Lewis 1954

In New Orleans, the term "Blue Monday" refers to a bar tradition of low-priced drinks and food, something like happy hour. "Blue Monday" is also a reference to beginning a hard-working schedule.

"Blue Monday" was also a minor hit by Smiley Lewis in 1954, so it was a natural for Imperial Records to assign Fats Domino to record "Blue Monday," perhaps his best effort.

—

Little Julian Herrera "Lonely Lonely Nights" Dig 1956

Style: Rhythm and blues
From and recorded in: Los Angeles, CA

Little Julian Herrera, real name, Ronald Wayne Gregory, was taken in by Johnny Otis after growing up in East L.A. To adapt to the pachuco culture of the day he changed his name. According to Don Julian, whose group The Meadowlarks was at the peak of its popularity, "When my record first came out, Dootsie Williams and I went over to the Johnny Otis show on KFOX. Johnny was starting a record company and he wanted an artist like myself, so he got Little Julian. That's how his name came about," from the Julian in Don Julian's name.

"Little Julian Herrera was the first constructed idol," said Ruben Guevara. "Johnny Otis found him, 'Hey kid do you wanna be a star?' Kid looked good, could carry a tune, he became the first singing idol." Sammy Yates of The Premiers said, "Julian Herrera used to be cleaning up around the Dig recording studio. He wanted to sing, Johnny gave him the opportunity to do it. I came up with an arrangement for him. I looked at him as a friend, never looked at him as a singer. We never took him seriously. Hey 'let's back him up. When it hit the radio, it turned into another thing," said Yates. "He was the first Latino to break through on radio and records. A nice guy, kinda a crazy, Julian was cool."

Guevara said, "I was Huggy Boy's gofer, doing shows at the Big Union in Vernon and the Montebello Ballroom at 10th & Whittier." "I picked Little Julian up at Hal Zeigler's office, Eldo Records, 1713 N. Vine," for a[n] El Monte Legion Stadium show. "Half the time he [Herrera] was ripped on wine, got drunk, went to jail. He was always half buzzed."

Buzzed or no, Herrera toured with a major Johnny Otis show with Julie Stevens, Mel Williams, Don and Dewey, Big Mama Thornton, Arthur Lee Maye, The Youngsters, The Premiers and others to San Francisco on February 6, 1957 and Bakersfield on May 25, 1957.

—

Johnny Otis "Hey Hey Hey Hey Hey" Dig 1956

Style: Rhythm and blues
Where from: Vallejo, CA
Where recorded: Los Angeles, CA
Suggested pairings: Count Basie "Don't You Miss Your Baby?" 1937

In 1956, Johnny Otis recorded a whole new song based on Jimmy Rushing's "Boogie Woogie" he called "Hey Hey Hey Hey Hey," using a reference to going back to Kansas City for Otis' own Dig label. "That's Jimmy Rushing and Count Basie, 'don't you miss your baby rolling in your arms.' There's a lot of things in there," said Otis.

"Little Richard did something called 'Goin' To Birmingham,'" Otis added. "He'd been in the studio with me and he'd heard 'Hey Hey Hey Hey Hey,' he'd go run, put it right on his record," said Otis. "It was 'Kansas City.'" Little Richard's "Hey Hey Hey Hey Hey" backed with the giant hit "Good Golly Miss Molly" was issued on Specialty in 1958.

In 1959, Wilbert Harrison's #1 hit "Kansas City" was covered by a dozen singers of all genres, including a reissue of Little Richard's "Hey Hey Hey Hey Hey," retitled "Kansas City" on Specialty.

In 1964, The Beatles redid "Hey Hey Hey Hey Hey" as "Kansas City" because of the title, shifting the writer credit from Johnny Otis to Leiber-Stoller, who had the original writing credit on the different song "K.C. Lovin'," thus depriving Otis of a Beatles best-seller. In 1986, Otis was asked about this songwriting credit gaffe of The Beatles' version in a Cal State Long Beach rock 'n' roll history class. He responded, "What Beatles song?"

Remakes as "Kansas City": Little Richard 1958; The Beatles 1964

—

Buddy Knox "Party Doll" Blue Moon/Triple D/Roulette December 1956

Style: Rock 'n' roll
Where from: Texas
Where recorded: Clovis, NM
Suggested pairing: Elvis Presley "Good Rockin' Tonight" 1956

Buddy Knox wrote the original verses of this song in 1948 behind a haystack on his Texas family farm. Knox got together with some college friends to record this tune several years later at the Clovis, New Mexico studio of Norman Petty.

The drum sound on this was actually made by a cardboard box filled with cotton. The Crickets' stickman Jerry Allison was inspired to also use a cardboard box instead of a drum for "Not Fade Away." Just 1,500 Blue Moon 45s were pressed, but when a DJ in Amarillo began playing the tune in 1956, "Party Doll" soon became a regional hit on Triple D. Picked up by Morris Levy's Roulette in New York and given a national release, "Party Doll" topped radio playlists coast to coast and rose to the top of the Top 100 chart, though it was censored, at least in Chicago.

Covers: Steve Lawrence 1957; Roy Brown 1957

—

Little Richard "The Girl Can't Help It" Specialty December 1956

Style: Rhythm and blues
Where from: Macon, GA
Where recorded: Los Angeles, CA

Backed by the uncredited Robins, this Little Richard rocker, "The Girl Can't Help It," was issued on Specialty. The Robins' lead singer Grady Chapman said, "We sang right behind Little Richard, yeah."

Shortly after that session, Chapman recalled the incident that caused Little Richard renounce rock 'n' roll. "We went down to the Philippines with Little Richard on a Pan Am flight. One of the motors froze up, and when we woke up they'd turned it off so it wouldn't catch fire. Little Richard said, 'If we get there, I won't sing no more. Birds was meant to fly.' He gave up singing, got rid of all his jewelry. He caught a boat coming back." This is one of many stories of Little Richard's defection from rock 'n' roll that have been advanced. Some historians have claimed he spotted the flaming re-entry of Sputnik from the deck of a ship and threw all of his jewelry into the Pacific off the coast of Australia. Rene Hall, who backed Little Richard on bass guitar said, "I heard he was on a ship coming from Australia, claimed he had a visitation from God, went to the rail, threw over his jewelry, all of his money, didn't want any more of his ill-gotten gains from the music he was doing, went into gospel."

Hall continued, "Specialty was very very panicky, Specialty and Art Rupe would try to make all subsequent artists sound like that hit artist [Little Richard] which is why he turned Sam Cooke down when Sam Cooke went into pop music. He [Rupe] had another group that was making it, Little Richard came along, he went into the Little Richard syndrome. He had Larry Williams who sounded like Little Richard."

According to other accounts, after Richard's visitation, Joe Lutcher convinced him to keep away from rock 'n' roll for a little less than a decade, but when The Beatles began having hits, Little Richard caught the first rock 'n' roll flight back.

Cover: Alan Dale
Remakes: The Rockin' Ramrods 1964; The British Walkers 1965; Keith Allison 1965; B. J. Thomas 1967; Delaney 1970; Bonnie and Friends with Eric Clapton 1970

—

Lalo Guerrero "Elvis Perez" L&M 1956

Style: Satirical rock 'n' roll
Where from: Tucson, AZ
Where recorded: Los Angeles, CA

This friendly satire of Elvis Presley's #1 hits "Hound Dog," "Heartbreak Hotel" and "Don't Be Cruel" with the satirical Spanish language "Elvis Perez," included two styles of music, mariachi and rock 'n' roll, with the multi-lingual "Elvis Perez" backed with "Lola" on a label he set up with Manuel Acuna, L&M, L for Lalo; M for Manuel.

Guerrero said, "We did Pound Dog in a garage in South Central, with a bunch of black guys playing on, that that's why it swings so good. The owner of the garage was a black guy who plays piano [with] about four or five guys—I did 'Pancho Claus' with those guys." Guerrero explained that there were two bands at the session, an R&B band for the English lyrics and a mariachi band for the Spanish lyrics. When he switched between languages, one band would stop; the other would play. It was complicated and popular.

—

Elvis Presley "Too Much" RCA January 1957

Style: Rock 'n' roll
Where from: Tupelo, MS
Where recorded: Hollywood, CA
Original version: Bernard Hardison"Too Much" 1954

This song turned a teen catchphrase ("baby, you're too much!"), much like "So Fine" or "Ready Teddy," into a title and key lyric. "Too Much" was blues derived from Republic, a small Tennessee label, and had a whole lotta musical bottom.

The song's co-writer, Lee Rosenberg, heard that Elvis was taking a cross-country train trip in 1955, so he met Presley at a train station with a copy of the Hardison original. Elvis, always equipped with a record player, played during his journey and decided to record it. However it took about two years before it was issued.

—

James Brown With the Famous Flames "Let's Make It" Federal January 1957

Style: Rhythm and blues
Where from: Macon, GA
Where recorded: Cincinnati, OH

James Brown with the Famous Flames recorded this rocking vocal, "Let's Make It" over the bed of Bill Doggett's #1 R&B hit, "Honky Tonk" from 1956.

—

The Gladiolas "Little Darlin'" Excello January 1957

Style: Doo wop vocal group harmony
Where from: Lancaster, SC
Where recorded: Nashville, TN

This was the original version of the major rumba beat hit, "Little Darlin'" by the Atlantic seaboard vocal group The Gladiolas, led by Maurice Williams. "I personally became a snob about the whole thing," said George

Carlin. "When I became a deejay in Shreveport, LA and Ft. Worth, Texas where I had my two good top 40 jobs, I would comment on the air about this stuff that was happening, like when 'Little Darlin" came out by The Diamonds, I played The Gladiolas. I insisted to my radio station, 'I'm not playing that Diamonds' thing.' I would tell the audience, 'This is not real music, this is popular music, this is manufactured, it's artificial. These, The Gladiolas, this is where it's happening."

Cover: The Diamonds

—

The Diamonds "Little Darlin'" Mercury 1957

Style: Rock 'n' roll
Where from: Canada
Where recorded: Chicago, IL
Original version: The Gladiolas
Suggested pairings: Del Vikings "I'm Spinning" 1957; Bobby Rydell "Cherie" 1961; Elton John "Crocodile Rock" 1972

With lead singer David Somerville, The Diamonds took "Little Darlin'" almost to the top of the charts. According to Somerville, "'Little Darlin'" was done in a single take. I learned it in one take in the middle of the night." The Diamonds' next release, "Words Of Love," required 76 takes. Diamonds member Ted Kowalski thought up The Diamonds name. "Little Darlin'" was not a spoof, but sung seriously. "We recorded it as seriously as we could," said Somerville. However, it was spoofed by The Diamonds by request on the Perry Como TV show, thus causing fans to believe it was not intended to be serious.

Remake: The Classics IV 1966

—

Johnnie & Joe "Over the Mountain Across the Sea" J&S/Chess February 1957

Style: Doo wop duet
From and recorded in: New York City, NY
Original title: "Over the Mountain Cross the Sea"

Apparently written with Korea in mind, Johnnie & Joe were an American R&B vocal duo from The Bronx who were best known for their 1957 hit "Over the Mountain, Across the Sea." For the duet the daughter of the label owner, Zelma Zell Sanders, Johnnie Louise Richardson paired with Joe Rivers. Sanders, who had been a touring member of The Hearts, paired the two. Said the song's piano player Rex Garvin to DJ Brian Lee, "Joe Rivers was from South Carolina, we started playing and singing. He sang Dean Martin and Frank Sinatra. Miss Sanders said, 'Bring him by. I'm going to pair Johnnie with Joe.' I was a kid, all I did was play piano. You didn't question Miss Sanders, she called me Maestro. It made me feel like I was accomplishing something. I knew every song that came out, it was a new beginning of the new music R&B. She was very strict and stern, she had a vision. Chess was the distributor."

Garvin explained, "Over the Mountain, Across the Sea' was a love song about a soldier in Korea. That was a soldier remembering his love back home. I hope she's going to be there when I get back. It was a testament to the Korean soldier. Rex Garvin & his Orchestra, that was a misnomer, it looked good there." When first released on J&S, the title was "Over the Mountain, Cross the Sea"; on Chess, the title read "Over the Mountain Across the Sea," which was also the spelling on J&S reissues.

Remakes: Billy & Lillie 1960; Paul Evans 1961; Bobby Vinton 1963

—

Fats Domino "I'm Walkin'" Imperial February 1957

Style: Rhythm and blues
Where from: New Orleans, LA
Where recorded: Hollywood, CA
Cover: Ricky Nelson 1957; Scat Man Crothers 1957

Almost a march with an unusual Dixieland style beat, Fats Domino's "I'm Walkin'" was transferred into teenage cool by Ricky Nelson's deadpan vocal style shortly thereafter. Imperial label's "Lew Chudd thought of that idea of covering Fats Domino, then he signed Ricky Nelson," recalled musician Jimmie Maddin who also recorded for Imperial.

Remake: Rosie Flores 1987

—

Eddie Cochran "Sittin' in the Balcony" Liberty 1957

Style: Rock 'n' roll
Where from: Oklahoma/Bell Gardens, CA
Where recorded: Los Angeles, CA
Original version: Johnny Dee 1957

Eddie Cochran had been featured both as a credited vocalist and frequently-used backing guitarist for a variety of labels, including Liberty. After one release on Crest, Eddie Cochran's manager Jerry Capehart knew most major labels were searching for another Elvis and took some dubs to Liberty's owner Sy Waronker and his partner, Al Bennett.

In late 1956, Liberty attempted to purchase the rights to John D. Loudermilk's pseudonym, Johnny Dee's "Sittin' in the Balcony," from Colonial; however, the label's owner Jack Bentley placed the master with ABC/Paramount, though apparently that label never released it. In response, Waronker had Eddie Cochran record a cover of "Sittin' in the Balcony" with plenty of reverb and hiccups. Capehart recalled when Cochran heard Dee's version, he asked Eddie what he thought of the song. Eddie turned to him and said, "Well dad, I think it's a hit!" But it just didn't rock.

During a 1960 tour to the U.K., NME asked Cochran to describe his biggest disappointment. "Hearing the playbacks after my first recording session. I cut 'Sittin' in the Balcony' and didn't like it at all."

—

Baldemar Huerta the Be Bop Kid "No Seas Cruel" Falcon 1957

Style: Rock 'n' roll
From and recorded in: Texas

In 1957, Elvis Presley's recording of "Don't Be Cruel" was still very much on the radio waves, said Freddy Fender, whose given name was Baldemar Huerta. Huerta said, "Rafael Ramirez was with Falcon Records which later became ARB. He was a great composer himself. He's the one who said, 'I want you to sing like Elvis Presley.' So I would sing in Spanish. 'No no, you gotta sing more expressively.' I recorded the song. He said, 'Go back, I understood a couple of words.'"

At the time, Huerta's look was "the sideburns, the collar up, the white suede shoes. When I was singing and playing, I used to dance to the be bop while I was doing that. Right now, I wouldn't do that for a million dollars. It would be one hell of a video watching me try to do it," Huerra added.

—

The Paragons "Florence" Winley March 1957

Style: Doo wop
From and recorded in: New York City, NY

Label owner Paul Winley described The Paragons as a gang name used by members who carried zip-guns, hoodlums involved in street gang fights, but since Winley had been into such behavior, it made no difference. For Winley, The Paragons recorded the simplistic yet appealing "Florence," led by the high tenor voice of Julius McMichaels, who later joined The Olympics in L.A. after one of their members was killed in the Watts Riots. Ironically, the song and title, "Florence" is revered by the durable, mainly Hispanic, Florencia street gang representing Florence Ave. in South L.A., a flash point of those very Watts Riots.

—

Jerry Lee Lewis "Whole Lotta Shakin' Goin' On" Sun March 1957

Style: Rock 'n' roll/rockabilly
Where from: Ferriday, LA
Where recorded: Memphis, TN
Original version: Big Maybelle 1955
Earlier versions: Roy Hall; The Commodores 1955; Delores Frederick 1955
Suggested pairings: Elvis Presley "Good Rockin' Tonight" 1955; Danny & the Juniors "At the Hop" 1957; Roy Orbison "Mean Woman Blues" 1963

"Whole Lotta Shakin' Goin' On" was Jerry Lee Lewis' second Sun. The first was a countrified "Crazy Arms." Labeled suggestive because "Whole Lotta Shakin' Goin' On" was itself suggestive. Radio found all kinds of reasons not to play it, including the fact that Lewis cursed on it ("We-e-ll-a" sounded like "We-hella") and he sounded black, and most stations didn't play black artists. Some religious leaders thought the piano melody was from the hymn "Abide With Me" at a different rhythm. Jerry Lee Lewis turned it into a lascivious rocker, wildly divergent from the original, with no bass guitar, as Lewis got a lot of low end out of his piano.

Remakes: Chubby Checker 1960; Little Richard 1964 and 1969

—

Ann Cole & the Suburbans "I've Got My Mo-Jo Working" Baton March 1957

Style: Rhythm and blues
From and recorded in: New York
Cover: Muddy Waters "Got My Mo-Jo Working" 1957

"I've Got My Mo-Jo Working" was written by Preston Foster. It was first recorded by Ann Cole & the Suburbans the same week Muddy released his version, which he claimed as his own.

—

Muddy Waters "Got My Mo-Jo Working" Chess March 1957

Style: Blues
Where from: Mississippi
Where recorded: Chicago, IL
Original version: Ann Cole & the Suburbans "I've Got My Mo-Jo Working" 1957

"There were a lot of blues singers who came through Chicago," said session sax man Red Holloway, "but they didn't make the impact Muddy did. He was a roustabout type of person. I remember working with him at the 708 Club in Chicago. A customer wanted a request. He wanted to give him a five. Muddy said, 'Man that ain't nothing but change. Give me that twenty.'"

Muddy Waters claimed to have written "Got My Mojo Working," released the same week as Ann Cole's record was released on Baton. Waters had heard Cole sing the song while they were on tour together and adopted it as his own. Later, a court later ruled the song was written by Foster.

Remake: Larry Bright "Mojo Workout" 1960

—

Chuck Willis "C.C. Rider" Atlantic March 8, 1957

Style: Rhythm and blues
Where from: Atlanta, GA
Where recorded: New York
Suggested pairings: Ma Rainey "See See Rider Blues" 1925; Timmie Rogers "Back To School Again" 1957

After a five-year recording career and with backing by The Cookies, the first major hit by Chuck Willis was the durable vocal "C.C. Rider," played a great deal on "American Bandstand" for dancers who wanted to do the stroll.

After The Diamonds recorded "The Stroll" in 1958, Willis' earlier effort was eclipsed. "He came out of Atlanta, where there was so much talent," said Ruth Brown, for whom Willis wrote "Oh What a Dream." Atlantic label president "Ahmet Ertegun was really searching," she continued. "He could always see a long way down the line. They went ahead and signed Chuck. It was a very successful, a very short career.

Remake: Mitch Ryder and the Detroit Wheels "C.C. Rider"/"Jenny Jenny" 1965

—

The Everly Brothers "Bye Bye Love" Cadence 1957

Style: Rock 'n' roll
Where from: Kentucky
Where recorded: Nashville

Boudleaux and Felice Bryant were a husband-and-wife songwriting team, possibly the first songwriters to come to Nashville and make a living only by writing songs like "Bye Bye Love," written to be recorded by The Everly Brothers. It wasn't The Everly's first release, which was much more in the country vein. The guitar intro was not originally part of the song but was something that Don Everly had come up with that was just tacked on to the beginning. Chet Atkins was lead guitar player on the session; Buddy Harmon was the drummer.

—

Elvis Presley "All Shook Up" RCA March 1957

Style: Rock 'n' roll
Where from: Tupelo, MS
Where recorded: Hollywood, CA
Cover: David Hall, a commercial release of the demo played for Elvis

Songwriter Otis Blackwell was shaking a bottle of Pepsi when fellow writer Al Stanton walked up and challenged him to write a song called "All Shook Up." Presley fell in love with the shook up tune and gave it the freewheeling charm he'd given Blackwell's "Don't Be Cruel," even reprising the guitar-backslapping trick he'd used on that track. It worked. The song went on to sell 2 million copies.

—

Chuck Berry "School Day (Ring! Ring! Goes the Bell)" March 1957

Style: Rock 'n' roll
Where from: St. Louis, MO
Where recorded: Chicago, IL
Suggested pairing: Chuck Berry "No Particular Place To Go" 1964

His first out-and-out attempt at being a teen tunesmith, Chuck Berry's "School Day" was the first linkage of rock 'n' roll lyrics to school. In keeping in the protest nature of his earlier hits, "School Day" is hailed as the first salvo on school-rock rebellion, teaming teen tension with an attitude ("hail, hail, rock and roll"), taking it to the streets and thus influencing school-oriented hits like "Mr. Lee" by The Bobbettes, "Back To School Again" by Timmie Rodger and "Waitin' In School" by Ricky Nelson, all in 1957; Jerry Lee Lewis' "High School Confidential" in 1958; The Coasters' "Charlie Brown"; "Class Cutter" by Dale Hawkins and Tommy Facenda's "High School U.S.A." in 1959, all the way to "Rock and Roll High School" by The Ramones.

Chuck Berry's "Vacation Time" was an attempt to create a summertime counterpart to "School Day," similar to The Jamies' "Summertime Summertime" in 1958. Chuck Berry's "School Day" echoed in the attitude of Martha and the Vandellas "Dancing in the Streets" in 1964.

Remakes: Jan and Dean 1966; The Beach Boys 1980

—

Bo Diddley "Mona" Checker April 1957

Style: Blues
Where from: Mississippi
Where recorded: Chicago, IL
Suggested pairing: The Crickets "Not Fade Away" 1957

"When the Stones did my thing, it didn't bother me that much," said Bo Diddley about The Rolling Stones' remake of "Mona." "I didn't basically like it. I had been schooled in the meaning for the whole thing. I thought if I had enough talent to write my own song, somebody else had the talent to write their own, leave mine alone. Finally, I figured out I had something somebody thought something of, so I said, 'Hey, this ain't so bad after all.'"

Remake: The Rolling Stones 1964

—

Don and Dewey "Jungle Hop" Specialty April 1957

Style: Rhythm and blues
Where from: Pasadena, CA
Where recorded: Hollywood, CA

Don and Dewey were brought to the forefront as dual Little Richards after his dramatic departure from rock 'n' roll. As the Specialty label desperately needed one or several rock 'n' rollers capable of wild-style Little Richard vocalizing, Larry Williams was one, the team of Don and Dewey was another.

Their manager and foster mother, Effie Smith, for whom they had recorded on her Shade label, made their deal with Specialty. Asked if they were brought on to replace Little Richard, Terry responded, "It's in-between. Little Richard was very independent. Art Rupe could not accept Little Richard had the power to move his own destiny. Record companies wanted to control everything you did. Little Richard always has been a religious person; Art Rupe was just a thorn in the side with his 'control this or control that.' Little Richard wouldn't let him. Little Richard played his own dates. They had certain songs they wanted Little Richard to sing, but lot of songs they brought in were junk."

Don Harris recalled, "I think we got a lot of inspiration at the time we started out from Little Richard. He had 'Tutti Frutti' out at the time; I thought a lot about that side. Art Rupe was successful with Little Richard and he wanted to play it safe."

Don and Dewey's "Jungle Hop" was their first on Specialty. Dewey Terry, obviously not a fan of the material, was circumspect: "It was a crazy song. Art Rupe had asked us to do a rock and roll song, looking for a Little Richard sound. He was successful, so we counted as Little Richard. This is what we did."

—

Charlie Gracie "Fabulous" Cameo April 1957

Style: Rock 'n' roll/rockabilly
From and recorded in: Philadelphia, PPA
Suggested pairing: Elvis Presley "Don't Be Cruel" 1956

Charlie Gracie's "Fabulous," similar to Elvis Presley's "Don't Be Cruel" from 1956, may have led to threatened litigation. It is interesting to note how Cameo principals Bernie Lowe and Kal Mann wrote 'Teddy Bear" for the same Elvis Presley. Bernie Lowe was a label guy who, if his kids didn't like a record, wouldn't put it out. Said John Madara, "Bernie was a big force in the business, but was advised by his doctor to get a regular job behind a counter with nuts and bolts to simplify his life. He made a comeback later, kind of under the table."

—

The Crickets "That'll Be the Day" Brunswick 1957

Style: Rock 'n' roll
Where from: Lubbock, TX
Where recorded: Clovis, NM

This song referenced Buddy Holly and the Lubbock/ Clovis connection, and the song title was taken from the John Wayne movie "The Searchers." Crickets leader Buddy Holly had already recorded a noticeably different Nashville version of "That'll Be the Day" with Three Tunes in early 1957.

This hit version was recorded in the Clovis, NM studio owned by Norman Petty. Thinking it was only a demo version, after all the drum came in early in one passage, Petty sent a copy to Roulette, which had released the earlier Petty studio cutting of Buddy Knox's #1 hit, "Party Doll." Roulette did not like the version, wanting the song for Knox, but Holly resisted so Petty then shopped it to Brunswick, a subsidiary of Holly's earlier Decca label, which released the demo version to great success.

As Decca intended to enforce their contract with Holly, they missed this version as they were unaware The Crickets release was actually by Holly. By the time they figured out the problem, The Crickets had a hit and all Decca could do was cover that hit with Holly's version with The Three Tunes backing.

Covers: Buddy Holly; The Three Tunes; The Ravens (all 1957)

The Beatles' first release was "That'll Be the Day" as The Quarrymen. The Beatles then named themselves after The Crickets. Another major UK band, The Searchers, were also inspired by the same John Wayne movie, whereas there was still another UK band The Hollies taken from Holly's name.

Remakes: Bobby Hart 1964; The Crossfires 1965; The Everly Brothers 1965; The Statler Brothers 1966; Kay Adams with The Cliffie Stone Group 1966; Jerry Naylor 1972; Foghat 1974; Pure Prairie League 1976; Linda Ronstadt 1976

—

The Coasters "Young Blood" Atco April 1957

Style: Rhythm and blues vocal group
Where from: Los Angeles, CA
Where recorded: New York
Suggested pairings: The Clovers "One Mint Julep" 1952; The Cheers "Bazoom" 1954; The Royal Teens "Short Shorts" 1957

The Coasters were Leon Hughes, Billy, Carl, and Bobby Nunn, the bass singer. "Billy Guy was sort of a loner; we became close friend[s]," said Coasters' guitarist Adolph Jacobs. "He's the one who got me the job with The Coasters.

The Coasters' first #1, on the R&B charts at least, this intended hit "Young Blood" echoed of another Leiber-Stoller hit, "Bazoom," by The Cheers from '55. "We thought 'Young Blood' was the hit side," recalled Mike Stoller of the session. So did Billboard on May 6: "Both sides are being requested but 'Young Blood' seems to be the top side. After a fair period, sales have began to grow." For a week or so, this was correct, nationally that is, though KOBY was already hot on the flipside, charting early in Baltimore.

—

The Coasters "Searchin'" Atco April 1957

Style: Rhythm and blues vocal group
Where from: Los Angeles, CA
Where recorded: New York
Suggested pairings: Smokey Hogg "Little School Girl" 1949; Mercy Dee "Trailin' My Baby" 1954; Chubby Checker "Private Eyes" 1959; The Marathons "C. Mercy Percy Of Scotland Yard" 1961; Dick Dale "Surfin'" 1964

When it came to a B-side to "Young Blood," part-time Coasters member Obie "Young" Jessie recalled, "The clock was running out, we had five minutes to go," and the group had yet to record a B-side. 'Searchin" was put together by Bobby Day and Prentice Moreland, Earl Nelson and myself. We weren't trying to write anything, just clowning. I think George Motola and Lester Sill opened an office, we used to be there and do different sessions."

Bobby Nunn said, "I heard 'Searchin" over at Bobby Day's house three years before I even knew about Spark Records." Coasters guitarist Adolph Jacobs said, "Before me, Billy Guy played guitar, then Barney Kessell on 'Down In Mexico.' Billy Guy "was a comedy guy; he sang lead on 'Searchin'."

According to Jim Balcom, in 1957, "Adolph Jacobs played guitar for us before The Coasters stole him." Jacobs recalled, "I had a guitar part when Leiber-Stoller took over. We loved that country, 'chanka boon, chanka boon, gonna find her.'"

Then Bobby Nunn got fired, and was replaced by Dub Jones, bass and Cornel Gunter, tenor.

"That was the fourth record, just something to make out the session, and we had about 15 minutes," added Balcom. Leiber-Stoller caught the action on a tape recorder and worked on the lyrics, adding references to various TV and movie sleuths: Sam Spade, Charlie Chan, Boston Blackie, Sgt. Friday and Bulldog Drummond. "They just took the idea and made a story out of it," said Jessie, who replaced Leon Hughes as baritone on this session. "We was really mad doin' it," Nunn told writer Dave Booth. "We didn't like it. So we gave it to Billy Guy. We said, 'Bad as he's going to sing it, ain't nothin' gonna happen.'"

—

Richard Berry and the Pharaohs "Louie Louie" Flip April 1957

Style: Rhythm and blues vocal group
Where from: New Orleans, LA
Where recorded: Los Angeles, CA
Suggested pairings: Chuck Berry "Havana Moon" 1956; Rene Touzet "El Loco Cha Cha" 1957

Richard Berry's and perhaps rock 'n' roll's most famous composition was a result of a live appearance he was making with the Latin band The Rhythm Rockers at the Harmony Park Ballroom, a one-time packinghouse in the middle of orange groves in the appropriately named Orange, CA. "After the first gig we did, we developed a rapport with Berry," said Filipino Rhythm Rockers sax player Barry Rillera. "He came in one night, saying, 'I like that tune you guys do and I wrote a song.'" The song they did was "El Loco Cha Cha" as recorded by Cuban bandleader Rene Touzet for GNP Crescendo, which began with a distinctive "duh duh duh" riff repeated by piano, bass and drums.

"I was honest to god Richard Berry when I did 'Louie Louie," Berry said later, noting storyline influences like "Havana Moon" by Chuck Berry and even "One For My Baby and One More For the Road" as performed by The Rhythm Rockers.

The first pressing of the material was with the A-side "You Are My Sunshine" backed with "Louie Lovie" by Richard Berry and the Pharaohs on Flip, which indicated the staff at the pressing plant believed "Lovie" made more sense and assumed the requested title was a mistake. It wasn't. Less than a dozen copies of "Louie Lovie" are known to exist. The corrected title, "Louie Louie" backed with "You Are My Sunshine," was pressed up at the very plant that employed Berry. "I was pressing records and the radio was playing 'Louie Louie' every hour on the hour. The foreman fired me.

He said I shouldn't be working there since I had a hit record. I said, 'Man, I'm not making any money, yet.' He put me outside breaking returnables," overstock records that couldn't be resold, thus were melted down to repress new records. "I was outside in the cold, breaking up a lot of Chess and Atlantic records. I was glad I was left there in case any 'Louie Louie's' came back."

Only the A-side charted, on April 27, 1957. "That song made me a rock and roll artist," said Berry. As the record sold over 130,000 copies on the West Coast, the original flip side was replaced by "Rock Rock Rock" so that the label would have publishing on both sides, a common technique when a B-side unexpectedly hit—in this case, seven month later. As his next hit proved, Berry was about to travel on.

—

Dale Hawkins "Susie Q" Checker May 1957

Style: Rock 'n' roll
Where from: Louisiana,
Where recorded: KWKH radio studio Shreveport LA
Suggested pairings: The Clovers "I've Got My Eyes On You" 1954; Elvis Presley "Good Rockin' Tonight" 1956; Howlin' Wolf "Smokestack Lightning" 1956; Buddy Knox "Party Doll" 1957

A night club instrumental, Dale Hawkins added lyrics well as cowbell percussion and guitar by 15-year-old virtuoso James Burton. Record shop owner Stan Lewis took partial writer credit and arranged for the recording at radio KWKH of the song he named after his daughter, "Suzie Q." Lewis then called on his connection with Leonard Chess of Chess Records, which signed Hawkins to Checker Records.

By the way, "Suzie Q" was a major hit.

Remakes: Lonnie Mack 1963; Creedence Clearwater Revival 1968; Carmel Covered Popcorn 1968

—

The Five Royales "Think" May 1957

Style: Rhythm and blues vocal group
Where from: North Carolina
Where recorded: Cincinnati, OH

The Five Royales put a strong gospel style into "Think."

Remake: James Brown 1958

—

The Midnighters "Is Your Love For Real" February/May 1955

Style: Rhythm and blues vocal group
Where from: North Carolina
Where recorded: Cincinnati, OH
Suggested pairings: The Dominoes "Have Mercy Baby" 1952; Clyde McPhatter and The Drifters "What'cha Gonna Do" 1955; Hank Ballard & the Midnighters "The Twist" 1959

The Midnighters' "Is Your Love For Real" was influenced twice by a Clyde McPhatter-led vocal, leading The Dominoes on "Have Mercy Baby" from 1952 and as Clyde McPhatter & the Drifters on "What'cha Gonna Do" from 1955. Lead singer Hank Ballard said, "Everything was 'oooh' and real pretty, until Clyde McPhatter came through and had 'Have Mercy Baby,' brought the tempo up. It was all slow ballads, Sonny Til, The Ravens, The Ink Spots. Clyde McPhatter changed the whole trend and when he changed that trend, I knew it was my time." The Midnighters' "Is Your Love For Real" was the prototype for The Midnighters' future hit, "The Twist."

—

The Del-Vikings (Feat. Krips Johnson) "Whispering Bells" Fee Bee/Dot May 1957

Style: Doo wop vocal group harmony
From and recorded in: Pittsburgh, PA
Suggested pairings: The Chiffons "A Love So Fine" 1963; Paul Simon "Graceland" 1986

This song is one of the greatest doo wop offerings, with a strong sax-drenched intro and underpinnings. "The compelling sax was played by experienced session man, Sam the Man Taylor. There's something about the depth of a real bass that's irreplaceable," said group member Dave Lerchey. "We picked up quite a few standards—there's a lot of real good ones. We put our own style to them, more or less. Fee Bee was just a small company, they would lease the tapes through Dot, but we were actually on contract to Fee Bee. Whatever deal Dot had with Fee Bee wasn't our business."

—

The Diamonds "Words Of Love" Mercury May 1957

Style: Rock 'n' roll
Where from: Canada
Where recorded: Chicago, IL

"'Words of Love' became Buddy Holly's first hit as a songwriter when it was submitted by the publisher to Mercury Records for The Diamonds. The group wasted no time in recording Buddy's tune. 'Words of Love' was released on May 20, 1957 and became The Diamonds' seventh hit and their follow-up to 'Little Darlin,'" said David Somerville of The Diamonds. All their songs were selected by the label. "They told us to go into this room and learn the song." The "Love Is Strange"-based guitar break was by Mike Simpson. The performance itself is an exaggerated comedic style vocal, which bears little relation to Holly's cover version a month later.

Cover: Buddy Holly 1957

—

Larry Williams "Short Fat Fannie" Specialty June 4, 1957

Style: Rhythm and blues
Where from: New Orleans, LA
Where recorded: Hollywood, CA

After scoring with a cover of "Just Because" by his former employer, Lloyd Price, on Price's former label, Specialty, Larry Williams' first original hit with backing by Jesse James (J.J.) Jones, tenor sax; Rene Hall, guitar; Ted Brinson, bass and Earl Palmer, drums was the rocking ode to "Short Fat Fannie," with lyrics based on titles of current hits of the day.

—

The Bobbettes "Mr. Lee" Atlantic June 1957

Style: Rock 'n' roll
From and recorded in: New York

The Bobbettes met at glee club at P.S. 109 in New York's Spanish Harlem. Signed by Atlantic Records at ages between 11 and 13 years old, they were first known as The Harlem Queens. Becoming the Bobbettes, based on the name of a members' niece, they debuted with "Mr. Lee," about a fifth grade instructor they called "the ugliest teacher that you ever did see," a song they had been singing in the hallways for at least a year or two. Atlantic had them change the lyric to 'the handsomest sweetie that you ever did see.' Too young to work the club circuit, they sang backup for fellow Atlantic label vocalists Ivory Joe Hunter and Clyde McPhatter.

Answers: Kenny Martin "I'm the Jivin' Mr. Lee" 1957; The Bobbettes "I Shot Mr. Lee" 1960; Kenny Martin "The Last Words of the Jivin' Mr. Lee" 1960

—

Buddy Holly "Words of Love" Coral June 20, 1957

Style: Rock 'n' roll
Where from: Lubbock, TX
Where recorded: Clovis, NM
Original version: The Diamonds 1957
Suggested pairing: Mickey & Sylvia "Love is Strange" 1956

Before Buddy Holly had a chance to record his rockaballad, "Words of Love," his publisher sent out lyrics to several labels, including Mercury for which The Diamonds recorded. That pop group had a hit with a spoof version with over-the-top vocals before Holly had a chance to record the song, which he did with a "Love is Strange" guitar backing. By then it was too late, Holly's cover of The Diamonds' original vanished.

—

Paul Anka "Diana" ABC June 1957

Style: Rock 'n' roll
Where from: Toronto, Canada
Where recorded: New York City, NY
Suggested pairing: Elton John "Crocodile Rock" 1972

This was supposedly written about a girl five years older, named Diana Ayoub, who Paul Anka had a crush on. His first song was "I Confess" in 1956 for the mainly rhythm and blues RPM label out of L.A. It stiffed. "Diana," his second U.S. release, was almost an instant #1 hit.

Answers: Annette "Tall Paul" 1959; Paul Anka "Remember Diana" 1963

—

Huey Piano Smith & the Clowns "Rockin' Pneumonia & the Boogie Woogie Flu" Ace June 1957

Style: Rhythm and blues
From and recorded in: New Orleans, LA
Suggested pairings: Joe Tex "Pneumonia" 1956; Huey Smith & the Clowns "Behind the Wheel" 1961

Huey Piano Smith & the Clowns' "Rockin' Pneumonia & the Boogie Woogie Flu" was derived from the flu epidemic of the late 1950s. According to tenor sax session man Lee Allen, the band was Alvin Tyler, baritone; Earl Palmer, drums; Justin Adams, guitar; Frank Fields on bass and Edward Frank on piano. "We were the studio band for most artists who came from out of town who were sent to us from other cities. They seemed to like the New Orleans sound. We just messed around, doing different things that would come out from us at times. Huey usually had an idea of the way he wanted a song to go and most cases, the horns, we'd help him get the background together if he had an idea of the tempo he wanted the song. Once we got into it, it was a party, it was a lot of fun."

Answer: Paul Perryman "Asiatic Flu" 1957

—

The Charts "Deserie" Everlast June 1957

Style: Doo wop
From and recorded in: New York

Supposedly out of the New York street gang scene, at 17 Joe Grier fronted The Charts on the unique doo wop "Deserie," which featured Leroy Binns, first tenor; Steve Brown, second tenor; Glenmore Jackson, baritone and Ross Bufford, bass, on one set of almost hypnotic lyrics, with the group singing the lyrics, then Grier coming in as both lead and falsetto on another lyric, amounting to a proto-rap performance. It was reissued in about 1961 through a special deal with Times Square Records.

—

Slim Harpo "I'm a King Bee" Excello July 1957
Style: Blues
Where from: Baton Rouge, LA
Where recorded: Crowley, LA

Harmonica player James Moore, aka Slim Harpo, first showed up in Crowley to back a Lightnin' Slim session. Replaced by Lazy Lester, Slim showed up again in 1957 to audition. Studio owner J.D. Miller liked Slim Harpo's "I'm a King Bee," but not his vocal, so he had him sing in a nasal manner, which became his trademark.

Guitar Gable's band backed Harpo on "I'm a King Bee," which was a regional hit, despite some worries about sexual content intent. The flip, Slim Harpo's rumba beat "I Got Love If You Want It" also was a Brit blues band fave.

Remakes: The Rolling Stones 1964; The Coachmen 1965

—

Little Joe & the Thrillers "Peanuts" OKeh July 1957
Style: Doo wop
From and recorded in: Philadelphia, PA

Falsetto vocalist Little Joe Cook, who had sung with several gospel groups, signed with Okeh, created Little Joe & the Thrillers and recorded "Do the Slop" in early 1957, which sold well in Philly. His distinctive high tenor lead vocal on the amusing "Peanuts" created a hit in New York and L.A. radio in August and September 1957, and continued on the charts until 1958. No doubt, the title neatly tied in with the popular Charles Schulz cartoon, though no reference is made in the song's lyrics, at least as is discernible.

—

Joe Bennett and the Sparkletones "Black Slacks" ABC/Paramount July 1957
Style: Rock 'n' roll
Where from: Spartanburg, SC
Where recorded: New York City, NY

A rockin' fashion statement, "Black Slacks" had stuttering vocals by guitar player 16-year-old Joe Bennett; and was backed by 15-year-old Jimmy Denton, drums; 14-year-old Wayne Arthur, bass and 12-year-old Howard "Sparky" Childress, rhythm guitar and vocal harmony. After an audition for ABC-Paramount, they recorded at Bell Sound Studios and came up with "Black Slacks" and "Boppin' Rock Boogie," with rapid-reflex lead guitar by Bennett, which more than sold the songs about the well-dressed hep cat, "a real cool breeze!" The song debuted in Boston, and charted well in San Francisco and Phoenix.

—

The Everly Brothers "Wake Up Little Susie" Cadence 1957
Style: Rock 'n' roll
Where from: Kentucky by way of Iowa
Where recorded: Nashville, TN
Suggested pairing: Tommy James: "I Think We're Alone Now" 1967

Literally banned in Boston, This Everly Brothers' second-in-a-row major hit, "Wake Up Little Suzie," was thought to be advocating two teens of different genders staying out all night, disregarding the lyrics, "we fell asleep." Apparently, their reputation was shot.

Answer: Tom & Jerry "Hey Schoolgirl" 1957

—

Sonny Knight "Dedicated To You" Cal West/Starla 1957

Style: Rhythm and blues
From and recorded in: Los Angeles, CA

Sonny Knight's "Dedicated To You" was first issued as by Joe Smith on Cal-West, then picked up for national distribution by King, of which only DJ copies are known to exist, so it likely was not officially released.

Then Art LaBoe picked up "Dedicated To You" to debut his new Starla label, named after his girlfriend, Starla Kay. LaBoe recalled, "'Dedicated To You' belonged to a guy named Hite Morgan." As Sonny Knight was hot with "Confidential" on Vita, LaBoe saw potential for this release. "Cal West was Art's label when he still lived in Fresno," recalled Knight. "He didn't do anything with it." In 1956, "The Art LaBoe Show" on KPOP radio was the #1 radio program in the Los Angeles area, holding a 33 share, a ratings record which still stands. In doing so, he was able to make a success out of Starla with group harmony, rocking instrumentals by Mexican bands from El Monte Legion Stadium and rockabilly from the Westside. Bruce Morgan recalled, "Cal West was owned by a fellow with a hardware store up in Fresno. Jack Arbuckle and my dad [Hite Morgan] released a couple of things on his label.

"After 'Confidential' became a hit, I asked him if he had any Sonny Knight. We overdubbed Patti Ross and a girlfriend of hers on it," said LaBoe, referring to Aardell label owner Bob Ross' wife. "Years later, Art LaBoe and Hite Morgan made a deal, they overdubbed some schmaltzy chorus on it," Knight recalled. "'Short Walk' was a fun thing with no message behind it. All the people dealing with us were just hustlers, pretty low life things." LaBoe added, "The record hadn't done anything. Timing has a lot to do with it."

—

Ricky Nelson "Be Bop Baby" Imperial 1957

Style: Rock 'n' roll
From and recorded in: Hollywood, CA
Suggested pairing: Jimmy Bowen "I'm Stickin' With You Baby" 1957

With the assistance from the Collins Kids and Eddie Cochran, Ricky Nelson's label switch from Verve to Imperial at once triggered L.A.'s rockabilly ground zero and shaped L.A.'s first ubiquitous teen idol, save Tommy Sands. Everything Nelson recorded between '57 and '62 charted, some on several charts, 15 of them twice and many in the top 10. Sands and Cochran didn't come close. In fact only Elvis outpaced Ricky during the late 1950s. Guitarists Bob Bain and Howard Roberts; Ray Siegel, bass; Earl Palmer, drums; Roger Renner, piano and the Four Preps on vocals backed Nelson on this rockin' boppin' ode to a "Be Bop Baby," which struck first in San Francisco in early September and #3 nationally in October.

—

The Chantels "He's Gone" End August 1957

Style: Rhythm and blues vocal group
Where from: The Bronx, NY
Where recorded: New York

The Chantels were formed when lead singer Arlene Smith was in the third grade. "I started singing at seven or eight in the cherub choir and that's where I met the future Chantels. About the time I was in the seventh grade, I was allowed to go to the community center instead of the boys playing ball at the time. The thing was to get together little groups and sing. Of course, the gym is the perfect place, the schools we[re] open in the evening to allow kids to have recreation. The guys would go off and sing, they wore their slacks and suit jackets and [would] get up and just sing. I think that formed an attitude or direction for musical form, because it was [as] a group and we patterned ourselves after that in terms of structure. Musically, we got it from Sister Marie, the head conductor of St. Anthony of Padua School in the Bronx. But the format was set for the male groups."

The Chantels name was taken from rival school St. Frances de Chantal, and their booming sound from their background in classical music and Latin hymns and not gospel music, as was common with black vocal groups in the day.

About their first release, "I wrote 'He's Gone' and 'The Plea' at the same time," said Chantels' lead singer Smith. "I liked poetry, I saw myself an actress writing a monologue and that's how I approached most of the song. There was a little guy I liked very much and he just couldn't see me. I would just get that all off and write something," said Smith. "'He's Gone' is a tone poem set to music. We were out of St. Anthony of Padua Church Choir, so we were doing Gregorian chants. It was really harmonic. It was rearranged by Richard Barrett at End Records into commercial form.

Smith continued, "I don't think they knew what they wanted on the A-side because we recorded two ballads, which is unheard of in the first place. 'He's Gone' was the stronger of the two. That's not in its original form either, they made it commercial. So they chose 'He's Gone.' In the southern states, they played 'The Plea.' It gets a lot of requests. I was surprised. I was even more surprised when I got no royalty checks."

—

Don and Dewey "Leavin' It All Up To You" Specialty August 1957

Style: Rhythm and blues
Where from: Pasadena, CA
Where recorded: Los Angeles, CA

About the classic "Leavin' It All Up To You" by Don and Dewey, Dewey Terry said, "I wrote it in my mother's kitchen. It was written for the first wife. I had just gotten married, my first big love affair with my childhood sweetheart. We were all fine until the day we got married when things got haywire. We stayed together 30 days. I left at midnight and this song I sketched out for her. We had stormy times, so I wrote, 'do you want my love or are we through?' "It sold all the time, that record has never stopped selling, we sold 100,000 copies down south. It's done quite well. I played the piano and the guitar over the piano track on it."

Remakes: The Heartbreakers "I'm Leaving It All Up To You 1962; The Specials 1963; Dale and Grace "I'm Leaving It Up To You" 1963; Donny and Marie Osmond 1974; Freddy Fender 1978

—

Sam Cooke "You Send Me" Keen August 1957

Style: Rhythm and blues
Where from: Chicago, IL
Where recorded: Los Angeles, CA
Suggested pairing: Buddy Johnson "Since I Fell For You" 1946

On December 5, 1957, the California Eagle reported, "Sam Cooke, who was formerly a member of the Soul Stirrers gospel group, currently has the top selling 'pop' record in the nation. His 'You Send Me' is Number One on all the charts!"

In 1957, Sam Cooke recorded "You Send Me" for Specialty. Arranger and session bass player Rene Hall recalled how Cooke overcame his hesitancy to record secular music as his gospel fan base considered that switch to be sinful. Bumps Blackwell, the A&R in charge of rhythm and blues at Specialty, had already tried to convince Kylo Turner, the lead of the Soul Stirrers, the group that Sam was in, to do this pop thing: 'Why don't you do just one pop thing?' 'I'll have to pray on it.' He did, he prayed on it. His thinking was God didn't want him to do it. "Bumps spoke to Sam. Sam, not being as popular as Kylo at the time, said, 'I'll take a chance; it can't hurt. If it doesn't work, I can always do gospel.' He was trying to do a simple tune. 'Rene, if you could show me a couple of chords on the guitar, I could do this thing.' Every time Sam tried to play the guitar, he'd lose the pick. With the few chords I showed him, 3, 4 actually, he formulated 'You Send Me.' He couldn't think of many lyrics, he repeated over and over sang 'you send me' At that time repetitious lyrics weren't making it. When this came out, this seemed to be a new trend in rhythm and blues records, [and] everybody liked it.

"For the flip side, he decided to do 'Summertime,'" said Hall. "We created a rhythmic version of 'Summertime.' We used the Lee Gotch Singers to put the classical frosting on the cake so to speak," said Hall.

"I had gone to Specialty," said Harold Battiste. "We had an Ornette Coleman record we were trying to push. Specialty A&R man Bumps Blackwell, while I was trying to get him to listen to this, asked me: 'Help me do this record date on Sam Cooke.' "I helped him, the result was 'You Send Me.'"

When Specialty owner Art Rupe arrived at the session, he was disturbed that Cooke was being backed by the white Lee Gotch Singers. Rupe, who had faithfully recorded mainly black acts in the past, gave Cooke's Blackwell and Cooke their release. For compensation, Blackwell was allowed to take "You Send Me" with him, a decision Rupe has regretted over the years. "Art said 'I'm not going to put this crap out'" Rene Hall recalled. "'You do me a decent bunch of tunes, not this bunch of stuff. Incidentally, Bumps, you're fired.' I said, 'Bumps, I think we got good product, we should try to get control. Why don't you trade him what he owes you for these sessions?'" Valiants' member Rip Spencer said, "Bumps left and took the tapes with him. Rupe got mad because he didn't have control of Sam anymore. Rupe wanted him to stay in gospel. Bumps wanted to better Sam's career, make him into a big pop star.

Hall added, "I met Sam at Specialty Records when Bumps was recording him. I met Lou Rawls and I met J.W. Alexander (the Gray Fox), a smart dude who sang with the Pilgrim Travelers. Sam stayed at Bumps' house, we were there all the time to rehearse, Bumps said, 'Why don't you run around with Rip, learn the city.' Sam would be waiting for me after I got out from school in Bumps' new red convertible Chrysler. I showed him where to get his hair processed at Adams and Western, where you go get a do me up, right by the Watkins Hotel. Bumps was in with Bob Keane, that's when it all started."

Bob Keane recalled, "I was approached by Art Foxhall, a black saxophone player and bandleader. He asked, 'Are you going to have a rhythm and blues department?' I said, 'Well, sure, of course.' 'Well I know a fellow who was just released from his label and has a couple of masters if you'd like to hear them.' I had picked 'Summertime' for the hit record. There was a kind of underground throughout the south and when they found out Sam Cooke had a pop record, they were responsible for having it happen. We sold 50,000 to 60,000 records in L.A. before it was played on a white station."

Rene Hall said, "Bob Keane wanted to start a label. When this record came out, Rupe was so furious, he paid disc jockeys not to play the record. The only person who played it was John Dolphin. He was sort of a maverick, 'I'm going to play this boy's record.' He had two disc jockeys, Lonnie Johnson and the Moondog, played it every 15 minutes just to spite Art Rupe. It caught on. At the old Elks Club on Central, John Dolphin had a big promotion, spotlighting Googie Rene's hit. When Sam sung, Googie couldn't come on. People had been brainwashed hearing this record around the clock, he was a star. He and Bumps Blackwell contacted all disc jockeys in black radio, there was no stopping it."

Consequent to the Blackwell sacking, Battiste was brought in as replacement, "Art Rupe didn't like what happened, so he gave the master to Bumps, but he hired me. Maybe he saw my work, saw the kind of cat I was," said Battiste. "He wanted someone from New Orleans, who could go down there and tap some of the talent down there. I came out to do jazz, next thing I know, I'm doing R&B. It was an opportunity to get inside the record studios, which was new to me. I saw it as an opportunity to go to school." As a result, New Orleans acts like The Monitors, The Crystals and Jerry Byrne were signed to Specialty.

—

Bobby Day & the Satellites "Little Bitty Pretty One" Class September 6, 1957

Style: Rhythm and blues
From and recorded in: Los Angeles, LA
Cover: Thurston Harris & the Sharps

"I named Bobby Day," said Googie Rene, the man in charge of the Class label. "At the time there was a guy named Sonny Knight, he was a friend [of] ours, he was good. The time Bobby came to us, there was a group [of] five guys, Earl Nelson, Bobby Relf, Gaynel Hodge, Alex Hodge; Bobby Byrd became Bobby Day."

The first release credited to Bobby Day & the Satellites was "Little Bitty Pretty One," which delivered Day to the national charts at the same time The Hollywood Flames were hitting the same charts with "Buzz Buzz Buzz." Day said, "I wanted a melody that would catch on, that everybody would sing and hum," which explained the humming introduction and outro of "Little Bitty Pretty One."

Remakes: Frankie Lymon 1960; Clyde McPhatter 1962; Jewel Akens 1967; The Jackson Five 1972

—

Jackie Wilson "Reet Petite (The Finest Girl You Ever Want To Meet)" Brunswick September 1957

Style: Rhythm and blues
Where from: Detroit, MI
Where recorded: New York City, NY

The earliest major hit by songwriter Berry Gordy Jr., this song established Gordy as the go-to guy for Wilson's management, with "Lonely Teardrops" becoming the major success in this skein.

—

Little Richard "Keep a Knockin" Specialty September 1957

Style: Rhythm and blues
Where from: Georgia
Where recorded: Los Angeles, CA and Washington, DC
Original version: "**B**oodle It" Wiggins "Keep a Knockin'" 1928
Earlier version: Louis Jordan "Keep a Knockin'" 1939
Suggested pairings: Eddie Cochran "Somethin' Else" 1959; Led Zeppelin "Rock & Roll" 1972

The story of Little Richard's exciting drum-heavy hit "Keep a Knockin'" is the story of an unfinished track, never completed because Little Richard had forsaken rock 'n' roll in his airplane scare. According to drummer Charles Connor, who created that "four bar intro into "Keep a Knockin," "It was really something different for those days and that drive. Whole lotta musicians say it sounds like a choo choo train." Connor said they were looking for a new intro sound. "They tried a piano, they tried a guitar, they tried a sax. It was the first four bar drum intro into a rock 'n' roll record ever.

When Specialty needed a new release from Little Richard, they found an uncompleted track of "Keep a Knockin'," and spliced together the same verses into a completed "Keep a Knockin.'" Connor said, "It was recorded at a radio station in Washington, DC. Richard had all kinds of tricks he'd do with his voice. He was the first entertainer I played behind who didn't need a mike in a small nightclub."

—

Buddy Holly "Peggy Sue" Coral 20 September 1957

Style: Rock 'n' roll
Where from: Lubbock, TX
Where recorded: Clovis, NM
Suggested pairings: Bobby Vee "Suzy Baby" 1959; Tommy Roe "Sheila" 1962; Herman's Hermits "Can't You Hear My Heartbeat" 1965

At first, Buddy Holly was going to call the song "Cindy Lou." Holly's drummer Jerry Allison asked if the name could be changed to "Peggy Sue" for his current girlfriend, Peggy Sue Gerron, a change Holly had no problem with. This was the first hit credited to Holly without his backing band, The Crickets, which did back him on this hit. In the Decca family of labels, Coral Records credited him as a solo artist and Brunswick with the Crickets.

Apparently, Allison had trouble keeping the right beat when they recorded this. The song had been written in cha-cha time. The engineer came on the mike and told Jerry: "If you don't get it right in the next take we're gonna change the name back to Cindy Lou." Jerry thought the guy might not be kidding so he asked for a few more minutes to "go through some exercises." He did just that. As he was going through the "new" warm-up, the beat to the song was changed from cha-cha to Jerry's new beat that was merely a part of his warm-up routine for his high school band. Buddy began to change the guitar licks to fit the beat and the new rhythm developed right there on the spot.

Covers: Rusty York 1957; Jackie Walker 1958; Jack Sheldon 1958
Answers: Buddy Holly "Peggy Sue Got Married" 1959; Ray Campi "Ballad Of Donna and Peggy Sue" 1959
Remakes: The American Express 1969; The Beach Boys 1978

—

Elvis Presley "Jailhouse Rock" RCA September 24, 1957

Style: Rock 'n' roll
Where from: Tupelo, MS
Recorded in Los Angeles, CA

This was a Leiber-Stoller composition by the team that composed "Riot In Cell Block #9" by the Robins on their Spark label in 1954. In those days, Mike Stoller recalled, "When the clock started at the beginning of a session, we were determined to get four sides in three hours, because in those days, I think it was $41.25 for each of the musicians, you just couldn't waste money. You had to pay studio time, we got it all done in three hours. We were conditioned to do that."

"When we started coming to sessions with Elvis," Stoller continued, "I think the first one was 'Jailhouse Rock,' they never watched the clock. They were very relaxed. They sent out for orange sodas and peanut butter sandwiches. If Elvis felt good, he'd do a number in two or three takes.

In this case, the song was custom composed for the Elvis movie, Jailhouse Rock. According to Malcolm Leo, "Jailhouse Rock" was recorded in mid-1957. "Stereo came into big prominence in 1958. RCA did something I objected to, they artificially recreated stereo, but since 'Jailhouse Rock' was the title tune to something he did at MGM, there turned out to be a version recorded in stereo at the MGM vaults, and that is the only true stereo version of 'Jailhouse Rock.'" The line, "You're the cutest jailbird I ever did see," is taken as a sly reference to prison sex but was not offensive enough to be banned.

—

Chuck Berry "Rock and Roll Music" Chess October 1957

Style: Rock 'n' roll
Where from: St. Louis, MO
Where recorded: Chicago, IL
Suggested pairing: The Rivieras "Little Donna" 1964

Chuck Berry attempted to write the national anthem of "Rock and Roll Music," "any ol' way you choose it," something that had been done by Bill Haley in "R-O-C-K" in 1955. Many similar anthems followed, including "Reelin' & Rockin'" by Berry himself, Danny & the Juniors' "Rock and Roll Is Here To Stay" and Chuck Willis' "Hang Up My Rock and Roll Shoes" in 1958; The Coasters' "That Is Rock and Roll" in 1959; The Showmen "It Will Stand" in 1961 and Bob Seger's "Old Time Rock and Roll" in 1979.

Remake: The Beach Boys 1976

—

Larry Williams "Bony Maronie" Specialty October 20, 1957

Style: Rhythm and blues
Where from: New Orleans, LA
Where recorded: Hollywood, CA
Suggested pairing: Clarence Garlow "Bon Ton Roula" 1949

Larry Williams' hit streak continued with another Little Richard-like rocker about a skinny girl, "Bony Maronie," backed with "You Bug Me Baby," with Plas Johnson on booting tenor sax; Jewell Grant, baritone sax; Rene Hall, guitar; Chuck Norris and Howard Roberts, guitar; Ted Brinson, bass; Earl Palmer, drums, and likely Billy Guy of The Coasters doing the ubiquitous whistling part.

"The most successful clone of Little Richard was Larry Williams," said Rene Hall. "I played guitar, did the arrangements, sketched the chords. Larry was a[n] imitator of Little Richard, Richard was his hero, he always tried to sing like Little Richard even before he was signed by Specialty. He believed in Richard. It's a vehicle for getting started, if you imitate something currently popular, it's a good entre, if you're clever enough you can shift to your own style. It's difficult, if you get a hit, the public wants to hear that style."

Remake: The Appalachians 1963; Freddy Fender 1963; Hub Kapp and The Wheels 1964; The Princetons 1965; Jay Bee Bryant 1968; The Upsetters 1985

—

The Hollywood Flames "Buzz Buzz Buzz" Ebb October 25, 1957

Style: Rhythm and blues vocal group
Where from: Los Angeles, CA
Where recorded: Hollywood, CA

Having recorded since 1949, by 1957 The Hollywood Flames were Robert Byrd, Earl Nelson and David Ford. Curtis Williams, formerly of The Penguins, "had a falling out with Buck Ram over royalties," Byrd recalled. Thus, Williams replaced Clyde Tillis, who had taken to drinking.

That was before the group recorded "Buzz Buzz Buzz" for John Dolphin's Cash label. "We recorded things he'd put a name on it. He'd have it fixed up and have Huggy Boy play it. As the Hollywood Flames, we'd get ten or 15 bucks per man and come back the next week. We did everything for John Dolphin. We'd go and write songs, take ten minutes; everything was on short notice—there was nothing planned. He had his own record shop and had Huggy Boy play it; John would press enough copies to sell. All we would do was walk into the shop. We could go in and emulate other singers we were listening to."

Nelson recalled the night in 1957 when the group entered Dolphin's Of Hollywood. "Oh, boy! Here come the hit makers!" Dolphin taunted them: "You guys got any songs?" "The fellows needed a little money, that's how it really happened," Byrd added. "So I told John I had some good songs. I didn't have anything at all." Byrd began singing "Buzz Buzz Buzz... goes the bumble bee…" Nelson said, "We thought it was so stupid. "The song was written in 15 minutes. We turned it over to John Dolphin." Dolphin told the group to come back tomorrow night at 8 o'clock and he'd have a band ready to back them. Byrd completed the song before the session. The following evening, Dolphin and the band were ready at Austin McCoy's backyard studio. "We recognized the band," Byrd recalled. "We could talk to them about what we wanted and how we wanted it played."

There was one tape recorder in the middle of the studio floor and only one microphone for the entire group, so Nelson had to stand on a phone book to be heard, singing the lyrics to a song he disliked. "I had to beg him to sing lead," Byrd said. "But I liked it. I really did." After the session, the guys collected their $25 fee and went home. As the group hadn't recorded as The Hollywood Flames since putting out "Fare Thee Well" for Dolphin in 1954, Dolphin decided to revive that name, which if the song hit, would make his vintage Hollywood Flames material more commercially viable and the word Hollywood would suggest his South L.A. record shop. Dolphin dealt the Hollywood Flames master to Art Rupe's ex, Lee Rupe, who remastered, edited and overdubbed the original recording, masking the crude circumstances of the session into "Buzz Buzz Buzz" from a two-year-old Bobby Byrd session, which Rupe also remastered and released on Ebb.

By the time Rupe decided to send the group to Philadelphia, Byrd was making some noise as Bobby Day. "Bobby didn't want to go, because I was singing lead," said Nelson. "He didn't want anything to do with The Hollywood Flames," so he was replaced by Clyde "Thin Man" Tillis to appear on American Bandstand, which had just gone national. Nelson continued, "We did the Dick Clark Show. After 'Buzz Buzz Buzz,' Bobby got a deal with Leon Rene. The very first song Bobby said Rene wanted us to record was 'Little Bitty Pretty One,' It was always Leon Rene who supervised the session."

By the end of 1958, Bobby Day had scored heavily with "Rock-In Robin" backed with "Over and Over" for Class, but was still performing with The Hollywood Flames on shows where Day would lead the Satellites, Nelson would lead the Flames and both would duet as Bob & Earl, obviously saving promoters a ton of dough on booking extra acts.

—

Thurston Harris & the Sharps "Little Bitty Pretty One" Aladdin/Intro October 29, 1957

Style: Rhythm and blues vocal group
Where from: Los Angeles, CA
Where recorded: Hollywood, CA
Original version: Bobby Day & the Satellites 1957

In 1952, Thurston Harris joined The Lamplighters on Federal, which evolved into The Sharps, which recorded for Aladdin. Harris recalled Aladdin's Eddie Mesner brought him a copy of "Little Bitty Pretty One" by Bobby Day. "He came in the studio one day and said, 'I got a record I want you to hear.' He asked if I liked it. I said, 'I don't.' 'You're going to record it anyway,' "I said 'I don't care.' I did it. I got lucky. I was of a more of a ballad singer I thought, I wasn't off into rock and roll then."

Backed by the same session players like drummer Earl Palmer, who had backed Bobby Day on the same song, Harris cut "Little Bitty Pretty One." The backing group was "my Lamplighters, The Sharps," members of which were lead singer Carl White; John "Sonny" Harris; group founder Al Frazier and Rocky Turner Wilson Jr. III, bass. "We figured The Lamplighters name was used up, so when they went from Federal to Aladdin, they changed the Lamplighters to the Sharps. We were just one group; we believed in singing together. When I could use them, I could use them. When they could use me, they'd use me." As with many originals of the day, the 45 was kept in print well after Aladdin ceased operations in 1960.

—

Ernie Freeman "Raunchy" Imperial October 1957

Style: Rhythm and blues instrumental
Where from: Cleveland, OH
Where recorded: Los Angeles, CA
Original version: Bill Justis 1957

Oft-used session piano player Ernie Freeman signed his first deal with Imperial while still doing session work for John Dolphin and many other local labels under various pseudonyms. For the most part, Freeman's combo was Freeman, piano; Irving Ashby, guitar; Rene Hall, bass; Plas Johnson, sax and Earl Palmer, drums. Ray Johnson, piano; Barney Kessel, guitar and others of that stature filled in from time to time. Freeman's breakthrough was this superior rocking piano-based cover of Bill Justis' more pop based version of "Raunchy."

Covers: Muvva Guitar Hubbard 1957; Billy Vaughn 1957
Remakes: Bill Smith Combo 1961; Gene Moles 1963; Marty Cooper 1963; Bill Black Combo 1964; Eddie Bond 1965; Billy Strange 1965; Jimmy Bowen 1967; Ace Cannon 1974

—

Danny & the Juniors "At the Hop" Singular/ABC November 1957

Style: Rock 'n' roll
From and recorded in: Philadelphia, PA

Original members of Danny & the Juniors were Danny Rapp, Frank Maffei, Joe Terranova and David White. "It starts with John Barcham High School in Philadelphia," said White. "I was impressed with the black vocal groups when rock 'n' roll was emerging, an exciting period of time. These black groups were singing in the boys' room. I used to harmonize with them. I learned harmonies, they let me sing with them. I went to the neighborhood, auditioned all these guys, got the best singers, then John Madara heard about us and discovered us. He took us to his record producer. We wrote 'Let's All Do the Bop' on the elevated train."

John Madara said, "We were talking about the dance, the bop. I made the actual recording. It was Danny & the Juniors, I was singing lead. It was meant to be my next record, I had 'Be My Girl' on Prep. Then we went to record 'Let's All Do the Bop,' played it for Capitol; Capitol hated it. We went back to Philly and played it for Dick Clark. Dick said, the bop isn't really happening. I think you should change the lyrics, write something about the record hops.'" White added, "Then Artie Singer changed some of the lyrics around so it would fit."

Madara recalled, "We really came up with The Juniors name. That was my idea. Then someone said, 'Let's pull one of the names out.' That was Danny."

"At the Hop" was only three instruments: Artie Singer on upright bass; Walt Gates on piano and Joe Kelly on drums. "We definitely were always leaning on the drums, it was definitely a part of our sound. We would always put pauses and breaks before a saxophone solo or whatever kind of solo it was, we'd put a break in there, a drum or bass break usually," said White.

"When the record broke on Singular," said Madara, "it was already a hit in Philadelphia, so there were quite a few companies after the record exploded. Artie Singer got $10,000 from ABC."

—

The Chantels "Maybe" End November 1957

Style: Rhythm and blues vocal group
Where from: The Bronx, NY
Where recorded: New York

The Chantels on "Maybe" was the first major "girl group" release to hit both the rhythm and blues and pop charts. "It was very exciting," said Chantels' lead singer Arlene Smith. "I think it was an attitude I had as a little girl. To be in front of a microphone and something that's going eventually to be in somebody's home across the country meant I had to put all my energy into it. By the time they listened to it, that followed me through. I wanted to make the song live even if the person was several miles away or at a different time. We worked hard on 'Maybe.' We had some minimal success with 'He's Gone.' The label saw us as marketable and having potential, so they got me into singing. The more I sang, the better I got. When the record was finished, I was told I'd be singing the record for the rest of my life. The people who said that knew what they were saying. They got an honest performance, they got that.

"'Maybe' came at a time radio stations opened up," Smith continued. "They were actively playing black artists; their stuff wasn't just covered anymore. There was a time in the early '50s when Lavern Baker and The Chords would record and Georgia Gibbs and the Crew Cuts would cover it, note for note, and you would never hear the black artists. The white artists got the exposure. WINS, the New York station played 'Maybe' on the hour. We had to monitor the stations ourselves to see who was playing it. Jocko played it on WWRL We got good airplay."

Remakes: The Shangri-Las 1964; The Three Degrees 1966; Janis Joplin 1970; The Delights 1978 (for the movie "American Hot Wax")

—

Lee Allen and His Band "Walkin' With Mr. Lee" Ember November 1957

Style: Rhythm and blues instrumental
From and recorded in: New Orleans, LA

"We were on tour with Fats Domino," said Lee Allen. "I would play this line in my head. Paul Hucklebuck Williams' band had joined Fats' band. They would answer me, just what I'm playing on my song, and the fellows kept saying, 'Lee, why don't you record that?' Week or ten days before the tour was over, I send myself a telegram that I had to go back home, that's when I went and recorded it for Al Silver. I'd known him quite a few years, through Paul Gayten. Then [Silver] heard this and liked it. We just kept on going.

Allen continued, "Before my record, they wanted me to do something like 'Flying Home.' I said, 'Flying Home' has been out too many times. So we took our time with Alvin Red Tyler on bass, Edward Frank on piano, Justin Adams on guitar and Earl Palmer on drums. He [Silver] called a week later, said, 'Guess what, we got a hit.' I said, 'Where?' He said, 'Listen to Dick Clark.'" The title was very close to the current hit "Mr. Lee" by The Bobbettes. "I didn't even know nothing about The Bobbettes. Their song was named after a teacher they had. This was named after me. How many people named Lee?"

Answer: Lee Allen and His Band "Strolling with Mr. Lee" 1958

—

Ricky Nelson "Stood Up" Imperial November 1957

Style: Rock 'n' roll
From and recorded in: Hollywood, CA

Ricky Nelson's rocking double sided "Stood Up" backed with "Waitin' In School" set the pace with Joe Maphis on lead guitar; James Burton out of Dale Hawkins' ("Suzie Q") band, who stayed with Nelson for two years and played with Ricky for ten years on rhythm guitar; Richie Frost on drums, and co-produced by Ricky's father—Ozzie Nelson's final hurrah as producer.

"Waitin' In School" broke first, then "Stood Up" broke. Bigger sales were lost with two great songs on one 45. They could have sold twice as well.

While at Imperial, Nelson had 15 such double-sided hits.

—

Tom and Jerry "Hey, Schoolgirl" Big November 1957

Style: Rock 'n' roll
Where from: Queens, NY
Where recorded: New York City
Suggested pairing: The Everly Brothers "Wake Up Little Susie" 1957

At Forest Hills High School in Queens, Paul Simon and Art Garfunkel used high school stage names Tom & Jerry on the hit, "Hey Schoolgirl," an answer to The Everly Brothers' "Wake Up Little Susie" with the key line "let's wait."

Sidney Prosen, owner of Big Records, recorded Simon on two more Tom and Jerry 45s: "Two Teenagers" in March 1958 and "That's My Story" in May 1958 as well as one 45 credited to True Taylor, "True Or False," in March 1958. Simon also put down vinyl as Jerry Landis, his girlfriend's last name, and as Tico and the Triumphs. Simon used a variety of pen names before hitting big with high school pal Art Garfunkel as Simon & Garfunkel in 1965.

—

The Silhouettes "Get a Job" Junior/Ember December 1957

Style: Rhythm and blues group harmony
From and recorded in: Philadelphia, PA

The Silhouettes were first known as The Gospel Tornadoes with lead vocalist William Horton from North Carolina, and gospel singers Earl Beal, Raymond Edwards and Richard Lewis. Unable to compete in the gospel field, they found a rhythm and blues niche using gospel derived vocal gymnastics in the doo wop arena. As The Thunderbirds, they met disc jockey Kae Williams, who chose to record them on his label, Junior Records. At the same time, Billy Ford's Thunderbirds gained sales in late '57 backing Billy and Lillie, so they changed from The Thunderbirds to The Silhouettes, taken from the title of the Rays' hit, "Silhouettes."

Richard Lewis recalled that, after his army discharge, his mom demanded he get out and find a job. Their initial output, "Get a Job," with backing by sax man Rollee McGill, hit big when Dick Clark got a copy of the single and jumped on the uptempo side.

Cover: The Mills Brothers 1958
Answers: The Miracles "Got a Job" 1958; Little Joe Moseley & Sequins "I Found a Job" 1958; The Heartbeats "I Found a Job" 1958; The Chesterfields "I Got Fired" 1958; The Tempos "I Got a Job" 1958; Bennie Bunn & the Cadets "I'm Looking For a Job" 1960
Remake: The Tokens 1969
Note: In the late 1960s, the nonsense backing of "Get a Job" inspired the name of '50s tribute act, Sha Na Na.

—

The Diamonds "The Stroll" Mercury December 2, 1957

Style: Rock 'n' roll
Where from: Canada
Where recorded: Chicago, IL

With the popularity of Chuck Willis' stroll-beat vocal on "C.C. Rider" and Timmie Rodgers on "Back To School Again," there came a need for an actual stroll record, and The Diamonds were recruited to fill that need. "The dance was being done on 'American Bandstand' to 'C.C. Rider,'" said Diamonds' lead singer, David Somerville. "Dick Clark made a comment to our manager that there was no record called the stroll." A week later, The Diamonds recorded the Clyde Otis-Nancy Lee composition, "The Stroll."

Otis' mother had him change one line, from "let's go strolling across the park" to "across the floor," making Nancy Lee possibly his mother. Otis' writing partner, "Brook Benton, told me how to sing the song," said Somerville. "We flew up the Fats Domino band from New Orleans. King Curtis played sax on it," and Somerville himself whistled out the song's finishing notes. The song's tempo later inspired "Rumble" by Link Wray & the Ray Men.

—

Roy Hamilton "Don't Let Go" Epic December 2, 1957

Style: Rhythm and blues
Where from: Georgia
Where recorded: New York City, NY
Cover: Billy Williams 1958
Suggested pairing: Dee Clark "Just Keep It Up" 1959

Perhaps the first pop hit to also be released in stereo, this Jesse Stone composition, "Don't Let Go" by Roy Hamilton with vocal backing by The Cues, was one of the few uptempo sides by this powerful pop vocalist more associated with lushly arranged inspirational ballads like "You'll Never Walk Alone" from 1954.

Remake: Billy Storm 1961

—

The Five Royales "Dedicated To the One I Love" King December 1957

Style: Rhythm and blues
Where from: Winston-Salem, NC
Recorded in: Cincinnati, OH
Suggested pairing: The Casanovas "I Don't Want You To Go" 1957

"Dedicated To the One I Love" by The Five Royales included stunning Lowman Pauling guitar riffs with group chants into call and response on the bridge of the spoken-sung lyrics with a Eugene Tanner lead that was similar to the Casanovas' non-hit "I Don't Want You To Go" on Apollo, The Five Royales' earlier label, from 1955.

Remakes: The Shirelles 1959; The Mamas & the Papas 1966

—

Frankie Avalon "Dee Dee Dinah" Chancellor December 1957

Style: Rock 'n' roll
From and recorded in: Philadelphia, PA

At age 12, Frankie Avalon joined Rocco and the Saints, a dance band that featured drummer Robert Ridarelli, soon called Bobby Rydell. The combo performed at weekend sock hops in school gyms and dances at teen clubs. Rocco and the Saints released a single, "Cupid," that charted well on Boston radio. It was released on the Chancellor label, owned by songwriters and music publishers Peter De Angelis and Robert Marucci, who wanted to get involved with Bandstand artists.

De Angelis often invited Frankie to his home where they rehearsed, Frankie on the trumpet and DeAngelis on the saxophone. Signed to Chancellor, Avalon sang "De De Dinah" while pinching his nose as an indication of how he felt about the material, according to urban legend. It worked well.

This song was released in December 1957. One week before, Avalon made a second performance and sang "De De Dinah" on American Bandstand. In January 1958, "De De Dinah" hit #7 pop, #3 on WMGM New York, #30 on KDAY in L.A., and #25 on L.A.'s KFWB in March.

—

The Monotones "Book Of Love" Mascot/Argo December 1957

Style: Doo wop
Where from: Newark, NJ
Where recorded: New York City, NY

This was based on the Pepsodent jingle, "You'll wonder where the yellow went when you brush your teeth with Pepsodent!" which became "I wonder, wonder, who-who-ba-doo-oo who... who wrote the book of love?"

The seven-member group were named The Monotones as they felt they had one trademark style. Tenors

Warren Davis and George Malone helped lead singer Charles Patrick finish "Book Of Love." Other members were baritone Warren Ryanes; his brother, bass singer John Ryanes and bass Frank Smith. The six sang at the New Hope Baptist Church Choir with teenage sisters Dionne and Dee Dee Warwick, Charles' cousins, and Cissy Houston, later a member of The Sweet Inspirations and mother of Whitney Houston.

Hull Records owner Bea Kaslin brought the six friends to the big city to record the song with only a guitar, drums and vocals at Bell Sound studios that fall. Released on Kaslin's Mascot, it charted only after it was picked up by the much larger Chicago-based Chess subsidiary, Argo, charting in L.A. #3 KDAY on March 7 and #4 KFWB March 22; #4 New York WMGM; and #4 Chicago WJJD on March 24, 1958.

—

Johnny Faire "Bertha Lou" Surf December 1957

Style: Rockabilly
Where from: Texas
Where recorded: Hollywood, CA
Suggested pairings: Pete Roberts "Twinkie Lee" 1960; Ring A Dings/Del Mars "Snacky-Poo" 1962/1964; Larry Bright "Twinkie Lee" 1964

Dorsey Burnette recorded this song, but as he was under contract to Coral Records, his voice was replaced by Johnny Faire, aka Donnie Brooks, who recalled, "Dorsey and Johnny Burnette wrote those songs. John Marascalco produced the record, he got Johnny and Dorsey. Dorsey sold him the song, 'Bertha Lou.'"

Session players were Odell Huff, guitar; Danny Flores, piano and H.B. Barnum, drums. Brooks added, "Surf put this out by Dorsey Burnette and when he got a pick hit of the week, he mentioned he was signed with Coral Records ('by the way I'm on Coral'). Dorsey didn't care, he just wanted money. The label panicked, called me and that's when I first met Johnny and Dorsey. The slap bass was Dorsey, Johnny was rhythm guitar, not sure who was on lead guitar."

Faire was hired to replace Dorsey's voice to avoid a lawsuit by Coral. Faire explained, "'Bertha Lou' was easy, I did two cuts, no problem. Then they said, 'Dorsey's voice is on "Til the Law Says Stop," the flip side. 'We can't take it off. You'll have to do two of your voice to cover it.' Well, he's rockabilly. I didn't know what rockabilly was. I'm a pop singer. Because I was born in Texas, I did a little of everything. Everybody wants you in a bag. I was doing all types of things. And so it must've taken all day to do this over. I had to do this part just before and just after his but... but I can still hear him on it. Dorsey and I are singing together on it."

Note: Original copies of Surf credit Dorsey Burnette, more common later copies credit Faire. Marascalco reissued the original Burnette version of "Bertha Lou" on Cee-Jam in the 1960s after Coral didn't care anymore.

"Bertha Lou" was covered and charted by Clint Miller on ABC in 1957. No one knows what happened to Miller, but Johnny Faire became Donnie Brooks and hit big with "Mission Bell" in 1960. Dorsey Burnette also hit with "Tall Oak Tree" in 1960, both on the Era label. In 1960, Marascalco refashioned "Bertha Lou" into "Twinkie Lee" by Pete Roberts on Highland, reissued as "Snacky Poo" by the Ring-A-Dings on Infinity in 1962 and as Larry Bright on Rendezvous in 1964, then reissued as the Del Mars on Mercury in 1964. The Dorsey Burnette original of "Bertha Lou" was reissued on Cee-Jam in 1966, when the heat was off.

Cover: Clint Miller

—

Dickie Doo and the Don'ts "Click Clack" Swan December 1957

Style: Rock 'n' roll
Where from: Pennsylvania
Where recorded: New York City, NY

With folkish lead vocals by Gerry Granahan over rock 'n' roll backing, the subject of this song is a train meant to reunite lovers.

"Click Clack" was recorded by Granahan, who needed a pseudonym as he was under contract to Atco, for whom he had recorded as Jerry Grant & the Rockabilly Bandits on "Talkin' About Love," which stiffed as the label decided to promote Bobby Darin instead. Granahan took the demo to Dick Clark in Philadelphia who recommended Granahan look up Tony Mammarella, who was just starting his brand new Swan label, the design of which copied the Specialty label, currently hot with Little Richard.

Dickie Doo was a pet name Clark used while talking to his new baby son. "Click Clack" by Dickie Doo and the Don'ts was a major hit.

During the session, Granahan tinkered with an early version of overdubbing, constantly reinforcing the vocals by the Perrone sisters of Paterson, NJ by using two tape recorders and bouncing the vocals off of each machine, losing some sound each time but building up the vocals. He also sped up the tape to make the guitar sound higher and to vary the speed of the drums.

—

Jesse Belvin "Beware" Cash 1957

Style: Rhythm and blues
Where from: Los Angeles, CA
Where recorded: Hollywood, CA

When the Gassers reunited, only Jesse Belvin received label credit for this exceptional ballad, "Beware," with vocal group backing by The Gassers, friends of his who included Eugene Church, who claimed, "I'm one of the writers of 'Beware,' also one of the singers on 'Beware.'"

According to Tony Allen, "'Beware' was written on the spur of the moment by Jesse. That's how he wrote songs. He could write 50,000 songs on one chord. He wrote with his voice. It's the same chord, he could take his voice and restructure it. He had a very unique talent with his voice. A common c chord, you could hear other instruments of his voice. 'Guess Who' and 'Goodnight My Love' were the same basic structure. If you took his voice out you'd hear the same melodic line, but he'd use his voice to trick you. Jessie just stood there, his trick of the trade was his voice. Other guys used tricks—flips, spinning—to get over, he just stood there to get to you."

Allen added, "'Beware' was Jesse Belvin, Gaynel and Alex Hodge, and myself, singing second. Gaynel was tenor, Jesse was baritone, he overdubbed certain parts. Red Callender, who was Dolphin's A&R man, said, 'Don't do those guys.'"

"Beware" with dubbed in voices was reissued by Jesse Belvin & the Capris, really The Hollywood Saxons, on Tender, the result of a deal between John Dolphin's widow Ruth and Tony Hilder, who had replaced George Motola at the Tender label in 1959. According to Hilder, he and Ruth Dolphin agreed to split the royalties on the reissued "Beware" in exchange for Dolphin getting a piece of "Play the Game Fair" by The Shields on Tender.

—

The Valiants "This is the Nite" Keen 1957

Style: Rhythm and blues vocal group
Where from: Los Angeles, CA
Where recorded: Hollywood, CA

The Valiants were high tenor Billy Jones, who also sang as Billy Fortune or Billy Storm; Jordan High student Sheridan "Rip" Spencer (b. Kansas City, KS December 16, 1938) who arrived in L.A. in 1945; his cousin Brice Coefield, who attended L.A. High School, and Chester

Pipkin. They had recorded as the Sabres on Cal-West and as the Chavelles on Vita.

"Billy was a very shy person when he started singing," said Spencer. "Billy changed after singing in front of girls. Brice did fast tunes; Billy did slow tunes."

—

The Valiants "Good Golly Miss Molly" Keen 1957

Style: Rhythm and blues vocal group
Where from: Los Angeles, CA
Where recorded: Hollywood, CA
Cover: Little Richard 1958

When Bumps Blackwell came over to Keen from Specialty with Sam Cooke, he also brought over the song "Good Golly Miss Molly," which Little Richard was about to record. With the Ernie Freeman Combo—Don and Dewey's Don Harris, bass and guitar; Dewey Terry, frantic piano; Adolphus Jacobs and/or Cliff White, guitar; Jackie Kelso. tenor sax and Earl Palmer, drums—The Valiants, who took their name from the Prince Valiant comic strip, recorded their too-fast version of "Good Golly Miss Molly," released just prior to Little Richard's major hit version.

—

The Four Preps "26 Miles (Santa Catalina)" Capitol 1957

Style: Pop group
From and recorded in: Hollywood, CA
Suggested pairing: Sonny James "Young Love" 1957

The first song written by members of The Four Preps was also their biggest and most enduring hit, "26 Miles (Santa Catalina)." Bruce Belland recalled, "It's a song I wrote in five years and fifteen minutes. I wrote the first part of it in junior high school. I'd broken my leg riding my bicycle. I was laid up in my family living room for a couple of weeks with a big cast. One of our friends gave me a ukulele and a book of instructions to pass the time. I used the first four chords I learned. Number one, it's not twenty-six miles away and number two I'd never been to Catalina when I started to write it. I wrote a little verse with that refrain 'romance romance,' but did not touch it for five years. Now we have a recording contract and we're looking for a hit. Glen Larson said to me, 'What about that song you wrote about Catalina?' We took it out, sat down and in about fifteen minutes, we put in a bridge and some extra verses."

Blending an opening guitar figure from Sonny James' "Young Love," the whimsical romp, "26 Miles (Santa Catalina)," used Gwen Johnson's "highest obbligato voice in the business," said her brother Ray Johnson.

—

Little Richard "Good Golly Miss Molly" Specialty January 1958

Style: Rhythm and blues
Where from: Georgia
Where recorded: Los Angeles, CA
Original version: The Valiants 1957
Suggested pairings: Jackie Brenston "Rocket 88" 1951; Creedence Clearwater Revival "Travelin' Band" 1969

Little Richard hit big with "Good Golly Miss Molly" with a piano opening straight out of the 1951 hit "Rocket 88" by Jackie Brenston backed with a cover of Johnny Otis' "Hey Hey Hey Hey."

"Good Golly Miss Molly" quickly got play on KDAY in L.A., ending up #10 pop February 17, 1958.

Though it was written by Richard Penniman, The Valiants got the jump on the release in the label switch when Sam Cooke left Specialty for Keen. "I remember a lady named Miss Molly from Macon, Georgia," said Richard's drummer Charles Connor.

In 1959, to compete with Wilbert Harrison's #1, "Kansas City," Little Richard's "Hey Hey Hey Hey" was reissued as "Kansas City"—with writer credits changed from Penniman to Leiber-Stoller.

Remakes: Jerry Lee Lewis 1962; The Swinging Blue Jeans 1964; Creedence Clearwater Revival 1976
Medley: Mitch Ryder & the Detroit Wheels "Devil With A Blue Dress On/Good Golly Miss Molly" 1966

—

Little Julian Herrera & the Tigers "I Remember Linda" Starla January 1958

Style: Rhythm and blues
Where from: Los Angeles, CA
Where recorded: Hollywood, CA
Suggested pairing: The Romancers "I Still Remember" 1957

Sammy Yates introduced Little Julian Herrera to the Tigers, a Pomona group formed in about 1956 with tenor James Thompson, second tenor Ron Shy and baritone Ernest Prentice. Baritone Ray Collins was also at the Herrera session, making a group out of three black musicians; one white, Collins; and a Mexican musician, Herrera. "The Tigers were acquaintances of mine from Pomona," Collins recalled. "They were performing with Little Julian, so I just kind of went along with them. In the studio, Art LaBoe asked me, 'Can you do a falsetto?' So I jumped up and did it right there. I don't think Little Julian was too thrilled about that."

Collins explained, Herrera's "I Remember Linda" was taken from "I Still Remember" by The Romancers on Dootone "Yeah, at the time, I had heard it. Julian even talked about it. Ron Shy told me that he and James Thompson wrote 'I Remember Linda.' I think Linda was James Thompson's girlfriend."

With Collins' falsetto, Herrera alternated between lead and falsetto tenor. A highlight was the famous "sour" note heading into the song's final chorus. "That's got to be one of the greatest sour notes in history," said Collins. "Coming right out of the bridge, it's a horrible note, but it's a classic. I love it. I sang falsetto on the bridge too, although Julian told me not to. By the way, Art LaBoe paid me $10 for the session."

Jim Balcom's band, which according to Balcom was either Bobby Rey or "Barry Rillera on sax, Ruben Bettancourt out of Wilmington on guitar, my brother on bass and George Gray on drums." Collins recalled, "Julian was a very nice looking man. He seemed to be involved with girls a lot, which I wasn't. I was more into singing with these guys than scoring chicks. I didn't think he was talented too much. But he had the chutzpah to get a record." LaBoe recalled, "We took that one shot with him. He had a rhubarb about a girl named Linda."

—

Little Julian Herrera & the Tigers "True Fine Mama" Starla January 1958

Style: Rhythm and blues
Where from: Los Angeles, CA
Where recorded: Hollywood, CA
Suggested pairing: Joe Fritz "Honey Honey" 1954

About the B-side for Little Julian Herrera & the Tigers, the first release of Little Richard's hit rocker, "True Fine Mama," Starla owner Art LaBoe recalled, "Julian just wanted to do it. I didn't think he could be Little Richard." He wasn't. Soon, Herrera got a new type of record, a police record. He was arrested on January 27, 1958 as reported in the L.A. Examiner of February 1, 1958. "Little Julian Herrera, 19, rock-and-roll recording star and two other youths were booked yesterday at Hollywood Police Station on suspicion of criminal attack."

Collins recalled that as Herrera was appearing with Johnny Otis in San Diego, "the police came and arrested Julian, so we went on without him after that. They were pretty mean, kind of threw him up against the wall and took him away abruptly." The news account stated, "Two teenage girls told police Herrera, whose real name is Ronald Wayne Gregory, David Luan, 20 and Manny Ortiz, 19, of Glendale drove them to a lonely spot near the Griffith Park Observatory Tuesday night. One of the girls said Herrera attempted to molest her and the other two succeeded in attacking her on a hillside slope. Herrera and Ortiz admit being in the park with the girls, but deny the charges made. Herrera of xxxx Verdant St. was scheduled to appear in a rock-and-roll stage show at a downtown theater today and tomorrow."

On February 7, the Times reported "Municipal Judge Vernon W. Hunt said after hearing how the 14-year-old girl was plied with vodka and beer before being outraged, 'This is what led up to these catastrophic results.'" In a third report, "Herrera admitted striking the girl, but denied the morals assault." Hunt "commented that the alleged offense resulted after a 'considerable amount of drinking. It would seem that it's a case of failure of parents to exercise proper supervision over their teenagers.'" It wasn't clear if the judge was referring to Herrera, the teenage girl or both. Eventually, Herrera was sentenced to state prison.

Despite Huggy Boy's advertisement for a Herrera show in the early 1960s, "He's been gone away for a year and a day, but now he's back to stay," the sentence Hererra served was well in excess of 366 days.

Cover: Little Richard 1958

—

Jimmy McCracklin "The Walk" Checker January 1958

Style: Rhythm and blues
Where from: Richmond, CA
Where recorded: Chicago, IL
Suggested pairings: Freddy King "Hideaway" 1961; Lazy Lester "It's Mighty Crazy"; Elliott Shavers "Thin Possum" 1965

Blues giant Jimmy McCracklin's only important hit was "The Walk," a dance supposedly triggered by The Diamonds' late 1957 hit, "The Stroll." When McCracklin spotted a young couple on the dance floor doing a front-and-back walking motion, he thought of the title. "The Walk" also benefited from play on American Bandstand, which was hungry for new and original dance steps.

Born in rural Arkansas, thanks to military service, James David Walker wound up in Long Beach, California, where he recorded the fine blues rocker "Miss Mattie Left Me" in 1945. As Jimmy McCracklin, he moved to Oakland, where he formed his Blues Blasters band, recording for various R&B labels.

"There wasn't but five in the band," McCracklin told Charlie Lange. McCracklin and "Lafayette Thomas, Johnny Parker, drummer called Ray Cotto and Horace Hall. We got stranded in Chicago. We came up with 'The Walk' cause we were off about a week and we had to pay rent, [we were] stranded and hungry. We went by a place called Alfredo's Lounge on the South Side and we played there. He was paying us fo' dollars apiece a night. I took my money and went to the studio. It cost me $12 to record 'The Walk.' Wasn't but $12 backing it up, but it was mine.

"I promised 'em," McCracklin continued, "if we could get a record started, we would go from there and get their money out for playin' the session. So I walk around Chicago with it for three days from record company to record company. There were lots of small record companies back then. No one would accept it, no one would even listen to it. Then I went into Chess and the big boss wouldn't listen to it. He sent me to his brother named Phil. Phil told me, "Yeah, I'll listen to it sometime.' I left it with Phil and a couple days later, befo' I could get back to Phil, Joe Turner called us and we had to leave Chicago to work behind him. And I didn't know for sure if Phil had accepted the record or what had happened. A few days later, we was down in North Carolina and I heard the record on the radio." The lyrics contained various dance references, "Suzy-Q, chicken, cha-cha, Texas hop, fox trot, mambo."

McCracklin followed with various R&B and soul hits well into the 1960s.

—

Huey Piano Smith & the Clowns "Don't You Just Know It" Ace January 1958

Style: Rhythm and blues
From and recorded in: New Orleans, LA
Suggested pairings: Huey Smith & Clowns "Little Liza Jane" 1956; The Impalas "Sorry (I Ran All the Way Home)" 1959; Bobby Rydell "I Wanna Thank You" 1961; Sly and the Family Stone "Dance To the Music" 1968

Sax player Lee Allen first met Huey Smith as a session pianist in the late 1940s. "He was brought in later as a recording artist. He was quite different, a combination of Professor Longhair and Eddie Bocage," and later known as Eddie Bo. "He had a good idea on what he was doing. Things happened to him, his titles would come up from the way he lived."

In the case of Smith's "Don't You Just Know It," it was the result of singer/comedian Rudy Ray Moore, who was hired to drive for the Huey Smith entourage in the Midwest and southern states and would often utter that phrase when confronted by Smith over his driving habits... "don't you just know it."

Bobby Marchan took the playful lead vocals, with Geri Hall vocal rejoinders in this call and response effort, which hit first in Houston in late February 1958, charting in New York in late March and in L.A. in early April 1958. In August and September 1960, Smith's "Don't You Just Know It" charted all over again in Philadelphia and in the Bay Area of California.

—

Huey Piano Smith & the Clowns "High Blood Pressure" Ace January 1958

Style: Rhythm and blues
From and recorded in: New Orleans, LA
Suggested pairings: Earl King "Those Lonely Lonely Nights" 1955; Smiley Lewis "I Hear You Knocking" 1955

As the B-side to "Don't You Just Know It," Huey Piano Smith & the Clowns recorded the frantic vocal "High Blood Pressure" with a debt to Smiley Lewis' "I Hear You Knocking" and Earl King's "Those Lonely Lonely Nights" from 1955.

—

Danny & the Juniors "Rock and Roll Is Here To Stay" ABC January 1858

Style: Rock 'n' roll
From and recorded in: Philadelphia, PA
Suggested pairing: Little Richard "All Around the World" 1956

After playing a stack of 45s, including Little Richard's "All Around the World," which had a lyric with the title, David White recalled that the label told him, "You've gotta write something because we need a follow-up to 'At the Hop.' You're on the road, Johnny's in town. When you come back, we gotta go right into the studio. I just thought of it, 'Rock and Roll Is Here To Stay.' It was such an emphatic feeling at the time. Rock 'n' roll was so exciting. A lot of people were saying it wouldn't last. I and a lot of my peers at the time felt it was going to last, so it was natural title."

Piano backing was by a Philadelphia arranger, Walter Gates. "It was achieved more or less from the Jerry Lee Lewis record, 'Whole Lotta Shakin' Goin' On,' White explained. "But instead of playing a boogie woogie, he played the straight eights, dat dat, dat, dat, dat, dat, like that, which shaped the whole feel so it really didn't sound like 'Whole Lotta Shakin' Goin' On,' but that's what we were going after, that kind of sound." It hit #7 in New York City in early February 1958 and scraped the bottom of the L.A. charts, KFWB and KDAY, at the same time.

—

Chuck Berry "Sweet Little Sixteen" Chess January 1958

Style: Rock 'n' roll
Where from: St. Louis, MO
Where recorded: Chicago, IL
Suggested pairings: T-Bone Walker "Bobby Sox Blues" 1946; Leadbelly "Midnight Special" 1946; Clarence Garlow "Route 90" 1954; The Beach Boys "Surfin' USA" 1962; Jamie Coe "Summertime Symphony" 1958; Freddy Cannon's "Little Autograph Seeker" 1964

Chuck Berry's greatest two-sided hit, "Sweet Little Sixteen," was a breakthrough as it mentioned "rockin' on Bandstand," assuring plays on that national venue. It also listed key locales: Boston, MA; Pittsburgh, PA; deep in the heart of Texas; Frisco Bay, though locals hate that term. It also referred to the average age of a female Berry fan—what else? 16.

Based on this song, Berry eventually collected writer credit and royalties for the Beach Boys' 1962 hit "Surfin' USA."

Remake: Jerry Lee Lewis 1962
Influenced: Bobby Rydell "Kissin' Time" 1959; Tommy Facenda "High School U.S.A." 1959; Marvin Gaye "Hitch Hike" 1963; Martha and the Vandellas "Dancin' in the Streets" 1966

—

Chuck Berry "Reelin' & Rockin'" Chess 1958

Style: Rock 'n' roll
Where from: St. Louis, MO
Where recorded: Chicago, IL
Suggested pairings: T-Bone Walker with Freddie Slack "I Got A Break Baby" 1942; Louis Jordan "Saturday Night Fish Fry" 1949; Wynonie Harris "Around the Clock Blues" 1945; Jimmy Rushing "Around the Clock Blues" 1945

The flipside of "Sweet Little Sixteen," Chuck Berry's "Reelin' & Rockin'" was a direct lift of "Around the Clock Blues" by Wynonie Harris, covered by Jimmy Rushing. Johnny Otis, who was involved in both those early recordings, recalled, "The whole idea of 'the clock struck one, come on baby, let's have some fun,' that's a traditional thing that goes back so far. We always heard those things in the clubs and we played them all the time. It was another version of a traditional black thing we did often. They're all twigs off the main branch. All over the country, it was done in traditional black circles. It goes back to antiquity. I heard it so much, when it was on record or not. None of us could claim that. So we copyrighted it."

Influenced: Rod McKuen as Oliver & Twisters "Mother Goose Twist" 1962

—

The Pips "Ching Chong" Brunswick January 1958

Style: R&B vocal group
Where from: Atlanta, GA

Gladys Knight was born in 1944 in Atlanta, Georgia. At the age of seven in 1952, she won Ted Mack's Original Amateur Hour television show contest. In 1953, Knight and her brother Bubba, sister Brenda, and their cousins William and Eleanor Guest started The Pips, named after another cousin, James "Pip" Woods. The Pips won another talent show, the award for which was a one-release recording contract, thus the muddled novelty title, "Ching Chong," credited to The Pips with nary a mention of Gladys Knight's lead vocal. She may have said, "I'd walk from Hong Kong to China…" but it stiffed, everywhere.

—

Ersel Hickey "Bluebirds Over the Mountain" Epic February 10, 1958

Style: Rock 'n' roll
Where from: Buffalo, NY
Where recorded: New York City, NY

In 1954, Ersel Hickey heard "I Don't Care If The Sun Don't Shine" by Elvis and went crazy over it, telling everyone about Elvis. Ersel was playing a few places in Rochester that his brother booked him, and he was drawing very well. It was around this time that he recorded his first record on Fine Records. One side was "Then I'll Be Happy," an old song, and the other side was called "Baby You're No Good," which Ersel had written.

The single was released locally, not much happened with it. One night Ersel went to a show at the War Memorial in Rochester and was in a restaurant after, and one of the members of the show walked in, Phil Everly. Ersel approached Phil and said, "I want to be a singer, what should I do?" He said, "Well, you got to have a song." That night Ersel went home and wrote "Bluebirds Over the Mountain." Ersel woke his brother up at 2:30 in the morning and asked him what he thought. He said, "It's a hit!" Ersel decided to leave for Buffalo the next morning with $20 his brother gave him. Manager Mike Corda paid for a demo session for the song at National Studio in New York with Jimmy Mitchell, guitar and Corda, bass. When Joe Sherman at Epic Records heard the demo, he didn't believe re-recording it would help. Released January 1958, "Bluebirds Over the Mountain" hit the charts in Buffalo's WBNY on February 1 and went national in March.

—

The Miracles "Got a Job" End February 1958

Style: Rhythm and blues vocal group
Where from: Detroit, MI
Where recorded: New York
Suggested pairing: The Silhouettes "Get a Job" 1957

This very first release by the Detroit-based Miracles was an answer to a #1 hit by the Silhouettes. "'Get a Job' was such a big record that an answer would be a good idea," said Smokey Robinson's wife, Claudette. "As a songwriter, you believe it's going to be a hit for you."

The B-side, "My Mama Done Told Me," has been named as an early version of their first big hit, "Shop Around." To that, Claudette replied, "'My Mama Done Told Me' in some ways, I don't think for him it represented that. The idea is there. His mother was a vital force in his life."

—

The Champs "Train To Nowhere" Challenge February 1958

Style: Rock 'n' roll instrumental
Where from: Long Beach , CA
Where recorded: Los Angeles, CA

Needing a band to back his "Train To Nowhere," Lancaster, CA DJ and Challenge label rhythm guitarist Dave Burgess scouted multi-instrumentalist Danny Flores (aka Chuck Rio), who had most recently been signed to RPM in late '57 and worked with his 3-D Boys at Hollywood On the Pike in Long Beach. "I had a band," said Flores. "Instead of calling one guy here and one guy there, they'd just call me with my guys from Long Beach.

Flores added, "The guys were Buddy Bruce from Oklahoma who played the teardrop guitar, a very good guitar player; Gene Aldin, our drummer, who said, 'I'll never play rock & roll, I'm a jazz drummer, it's below me,' from San Pedro and Cliff Hils, who played upright bass and didn't belong to my band—nobody could hear him, no Fender electric bass until later on; these guys made the whole band. "Dave Burgess from North Hollywood was the rhythm guitar and was a good strummer," said Flores. "We spent a lot of time on 'Train To Nowhere,' it had a lot of background singing. In those days you had to overdub and I had to put the horn first, then the piano and all those voices and it was worth it because that was going to be the side."

Challenge named the band after the label's silent partner, Gene Autry's horse Champion, thus The Champs and the highly produced "Train To Nowhere," which charted first on two L.A. radio outlets, KDAY and the brand new KFWB, before falling victim to "Tequila."

—

The Champs "Tequila" Challenge February 1958

Style: Rock 'n' roll instrumental
Where from: Long Beach, CA
Where recorded: Los Angeles, CA
Suggested pairings: Dizzy Gillespie "Manteca" 1947; Les Baxter "Da Rain" 1957; Boots Brown "Cerveza" 1958; The Pets "Chi Wa Wa" 1958; Eddie Platt "Vodka" 1958

Written by Flores as B-side to "Train To Nowhere," "Tequila" was a nightclub break tune. Flores explained, "I'd been using this as a little riff before we'd take an intermission at the club. We'd have a 'dum dum dum, we'll be right back, we're taking a short break' and that became a song so we decided 'let's use that.' We were going to spell it 'Tekila.' We didn't want to spell it like the alcohol because we thought parents wouldn't let kids buy the record. The parents would say, 'What do you want to buy that record for?' The way I wrote it is the way we used to do in the '40s, we called it mutuno, which means 'jam, get lost, do your own thing.' All stay in the same key and we'll all jam, the trumpet players, the piano player, the sax player all take a solo, all in one key."

When the Eddie Platt cover of "Tequila" on ABC/Paramount began to hit regionally, Challenge told DJs to "turn the record over" and play the hit side. When KDAY switched the pick hit to "Tequila," it then went to #1 in New York and everywhere else. "Tequila" by Eddie Platt hit first and big in Detroit, with Platt and the Champs sharing the chart position in L.A. and NYC.

Les Baxter sued over alleged infringement of the song "Da Rain" in the quickie flick "Bop Girl Goes Calypso" from 1957. Despite being a marginal cause of action, the label settled for $60,000. "I never saw that movie before until they had me on the deposition and asked me had I been in Bakersfield on a certain date, had I been in San Diego when that movie had been shown, but I had no access to the movie," said Flores, who changed his name to Chuck Rio.

As a result of the success of "Tequila" in 1958, at least a dozen releases involved Flores under a range of names like The Champs: Danny Boy and Chuck "Tequila" Rio on Kent, The Contenders and The Originals on Jackpot, every name but Danny Flores. Then came "Tequila" spin-offs: "Corrido Rock" (Jim Balcom); "Chi Hua Hua" (The Pets); "Cerveza" (Boots Brown); "Margarita" (Chuck Rio); "Vodka" (Eddie Platt); "Hot Saki" (Eddie Atwood & the Goodies with Priscilla Lee on vocals, sax solo by Danny Flores and by Mo Klein in 1959) and "La Cucaracha Rock" (Joe Houston). In 1959, "Tequila" won the first Grammy for best rhythm and blues song and kept selling through the decades.

—

Sonny West "Rave On" Atlantic February 17, 1958

Style: Rock 'n' roll
Where from: Texas
Where recorded: Clovis, NM
Cover: Buddy Holly 1958

In November 1957, West cut "Rave On" in a somewhat laid-back style accompanied by the Dallas-based Big Beats, formed by Trini Lopez and which later backed

Gene Vincent and other rock 'n' roll performers. Trini then auditioned for The Crickets, but never recorded with them before launching his highly successful solo career. Atlantic's Jerry Wexler flew to Clovis around the New Year and reached an agreement with Norman Petty to release "Rave On."

Remakes: Waylon Jennings 1963; The Nitty Gritty Dirt Band 1970; Jesse Colin Young 1978; Jerry Naylor 1978; Rick Nelson 1980; John Cougar Mellencamp 1988

—

John Ramistella "Two By Two" Suede February 1958

Style: Rock 'n' roll
Where from: Baton Rouge, LA
Where recorded: New Orleans, LA

The recording career of John Rivers began with this very obscure double-sided second line rocker by John Ramistella entitled "Two By Two," with a Chuck Berry beat and phrasing like Jerry Lee Lewis on a Natchez, MS label Suede in early 1958.

—

John Zacherle "Dinner With Drac" Cameo February 1958

Style: Novelty rock 'n' roll
From and recorded in: Philadelphia, PA
Original title: "Igor"

Philadelphia's channel 10, WCAU, premiered a program titled Shock Theater in fall of 1957. Its host, Roland, played by character actor John Zacherle, recited horror-themed limericks from a mad doctor's lab, which he turned into a successful record, "Dinner With Drac," featuring Dave Appell's guitar and Zacherle's sick limericks ("A dinner was served for three... at Dracula's house by the sea... the hors d'oeuvres were fine... but I choked on my wine... when I learned that the main course was me!")... rock on.

—

Handsome Jim Balcom "Corrido Rock" Starla/Dot February 24, 1958

Style: Latin rock 'n' roll
Where from: Lomita, CA
Where recorded: Willowbrook, CA
Cover: Tortilla Pete

"Corrido Rock Pt. 1 & 2" by Handsome Jim Balcom released on Art LaBoe's Starla, reissued on Dot, was an answer of sorts to The Champs #1 hit, "Tequila." Based on a popular Mexican dance, the corrido involved dancing back and forth in and out in a bowing position. According to Balcom, "My original sax player, Guillermo Burrola, used to play it as a Mexican song. I did the session by myself, then took it to Art and he put it on Starla. The sax player was Bobby Rey from East L.A. He was a great sax player. It was in the middle of the set when people were dancing. It was mainly Art LaBoe and Huggy Boy, they were the emcees on those shows. Huggy Boy and Art Laboe would see us play it and see us dance, both got the idea, 'Why don't you record this?'"

Balcom continued, "For the first session, we went to Austin McCoy's studio, Art LaBoe was there, nothing worked. I went back and did it by myself, the beat was more Hispanic polka tempo and we changed it to more of a rock beat. Since I wrote the rock and roll part, I did get the writer's royalties from the airplay.

For "Corrido Rock," backing was by Barry Rillera, bass, who played with Balcom "most of that year," Balcom said, "Ruben Bettancourt, guitar; my brother Orville played bass; George Gray, drummer, from San Gabriel Valley," said Balcom, who decided to have LaBoe release it instead of Huggy Boy, who still owed him for the previously issued "Bubble Gum" on Caddy and "Strollin' Around" for Norwood, both Huggy Boy labels.

"When I took Art the master, he loved it, started playing it on the air, there was pent-up demand, which caused a sales spike," said Balcom. "Bill Balance was on it. Then Art came up with Handsome to my name, then he added it to the label. Is Jim your middle name?"

As it was on LaBoe's label, LaBoe the DJ promoted it first on the air. Balcom said, "Art played a demo for the first couple of weeks. I was going to school, it got to be too much." Balcom's version competed with a cover by Tortilla Pete, local DJ Sal Chico, on Imperial, which shared the XEAK chart listing. "Imperial also wanted it, I think Huggy Boy had something to do with Tortilla Pete."

Though it never hit the national pop charts, "it did well in Australia as an accordion song," said Balcom. "We were the backup band for a year, 1958, at El Monte Legion Stadium. After I split from Hal Zeigler, it was uncomfortable for Art LaBoe, so he didn't record me again."

As of November 30, 1960, "Corrido Rock" by Jim Balcom was valued in the Starla archives at $1000, the highest value of any Starla master.

—

Eddie L. Davis & the Bureaucrats "I Was a Teenage Brain Surgeon for the FBI" Fable March 1958

Style: Novelty
Where from: Los Angeles, CA
Where recorded: Hollywood, CA
Suggested pairing: Tennessee Ernie Ford "16 Tons" 1955

Eddie Davis recalled, "I was born in West Los Angeles, moved to East Los Angeles at an early age. I wanted to be a singer. Going back a lot of years, any time a little kid is singing the 'Ave Maria' in the movies, that's me. 'Boys Town,' 'Angels With Dirty Faces,' 'Pork Chop Hill,' 'Men of Boys Town.' I was with Bob Mitchell's Boys Choir.

Davis continued, "After graduating from Fairfax High, I went to war as everybody did, when I came back, I was 20 years old and I'd outgrown my soprano voice. I wanted to be a bass singer. No one would give me a deal, so I went into the restaurant business, made a lot of money, decided if no one would record me, I'd record myself. I did the first custom session at the Capitol Records building when they first built the building.

"I Was a Teenage Brain Surgeon for the FBI" was sung to the tune of "Sixteen Tons" backed with the mild Bill Haley-style vocal on the Davis-Corps comp "Tick Tock Rock" by Eddie L. Davis & the Bureaucats on the song poem label Fable in March 1958. Tony Butala, later of The Lettermen, and Conchetta Angolis, later known as Connie Stevens, supplied background vocals.

Davis had his greatest success as owner of the Faro, Rampart, Linda, Gordo and other labels that produced East Side hits in the 1960s by The Premiers, The Blendells, Cannibal & the Headhunters, El Chicano, et al.

—

Robert & Johnny "We Belong Together" Old Town 1958

Style: Doo wop duet
Where from: The Bronx, NY
Where recorded: New York

Robert Carr and Johnny Mitchell were Robert & Johnny, whose unique duet, the lowrider style "We Belong Together" was a major hit.

Remakes: Ritchie Valens 1959; The Belmonts 1960; Johnny and Bob 1960; Dash & Dot 1961; Jimmy Velvet 1963; Tierra 1973

—

Link Wray and His Ray Men "Rumble" Cadence March 1958
Style: Rock 'n' roll instrumental
Where from: North Carolina
Where recorded: Nashville, TN

At a Fredericksburg, VA sock hop, Link Wray & His Ray Men improvised an instrumental based on the Diamonds' hit, "The Stroll." Wray added an extra riff on his Gibson Les Paul that added volume and distortion. The kids liked the riff and The Ray Men recorded it spontaneously at the end of a vocal session by Ray Vernon, Link's brother, who'd been signed by Cameo Records. They called it "Rumble," based on writer Jimmy McDonough's phraseology, "just three chords and a bad attitude."

Credited to Link Wray and the Ray Men, "Rumble" was picked up by Cadence Records which, after the hit ran its course, dropped the act, lest Cadence be accused of favoring juvenile delinquency and/or gang wars. Wray moved on with rumbling-style hits "Rawhide" on Epic in 1959 and "Jack the Ripper" on Swan in 1961, while "Rumble" inspired the name The Rumblers who hit with "Boss" in 1962.

Remake: Jack Nitzsche 1963
Answer: Link Wray and the Wraymen "Rumble Mambo" 1963

—

Larry Williams "Dizzy Miss Lizzy" Specialty March 10, 1958
Style: Rhythm and blues
Where from: New Orleans, LA
Where recorded: Los Angeles, CA

With backing by Rene Hall, guitar; Plas Johnson, sax; Jewell Grant, bass; and Earl Palmer, drums, Larry Williams recorded this two-sided rocker, "Dizzy Miss Lizzy," a big hit in Phoenix, backed with "Slow Down" which tore up Toronto and the Bay Area too.

"This was the Little Richard type syndrome," said Rene Hall. "Everything he did, he wanted to sound as close to Little Richard as he could. It was a strange guitar, the instrument was different, a Gretsch guitar, everybody was using Gibson and Fenders. I wanted to be identified with this guitar, to let this guitar sound be my calling card. I could immediately know if I played on a recording date because of the sound of the guitar. Everything I played on it sounded different from any other guitar. At the end of "You Send Me" and at the end of a lot of dates—it was a penetrating sound that had a certain amount of resonance you couldn't get from the flat sound of the Fender or the resonant sound of the Gibson, it was a cross between the two."

Remakes: The Beatles 1964

—

Chuck Willis "What Am I Living For" Atlantic March 30, 1958
Style: Rhythm and blues
Where from: Atlanta, GA
Where recorded: New York
Suggested pairing: LaVern Baker "I Cried a Tear" 1958

No doubt the biggest success for Chuck Willis was this, his ironic last. Though Willis was an accomplished songwriter, the Willis title "What Am I Living For" was written by Philly jazz composers Art Harris and Fred Jay.

As the B-side, the Willis composition, "Hang Up My Rock and Roll Shoes," also foreshadowed Willis' fate. On April 10, 1958, Willis reportedly died of a perforated ulcer, though others suggest an auto accident. A third theory was advanced by label mate Ruth Brown: "He died rather hard. Angina associated with high blood pressure."

Remakes: Jack Scott 1960; Jimmy Clanton 1961; Carl McVoy 1962; Billy Fury 1964; Millie Small 1964; Dale & Grace 1965; Willie Hightower 1965; Danny & the Velaires 1967; Percy Sledge 1967; Z.Z. Hill

1967; Johnny Tillotson 1969; Solomon Burke 1969; Conway Twitty 1970

Cover: Ernest Tubb

—

Jody Reynolds "Endless Sleep" Demon 1958

Style: Rock 'n' roll
Where from: Denver, CO
Where recorded: Hollywood, CA
Suggested pairing: Eddie Cochran "Summertime Blues" 1958

Jody Reynolds grew up in Oklahoma with his family. About the menacing sounding death rocker "Endless Sleep," Reynolds said, "I actually wrote it in 1956—two years before I recorded it. I was in Yuma, Arizona, playing rockabilly there and that's where I wrote 'Endless Sleep.'" After relocating to San Diego, he sent out demos, he got a record deal only upon agreeing to rewrite a happy resolution.

Reynolds continued, "The guy who played on it was Al Casey," who was also heard on several Duane Eddy hits. "He was from Phoenix, Arizona. Howard Roberts was a jazz-playing friend of mine and he played rhythm guitar on 'Endless Sleep.'" Partial songwriting credit was assigned to Dolores Nance, about whom Reynolds said, "There is no Dolores Nance. It's just a fictitious name that the record people used." In the hit recording of "Endless Sleep," it was death rock in title only as the he saved his baby, which got early San Francisco spins in late March '58 and went pop in mid-May.

Asked if "Endless Sleep" influenced "Summertime Blues" by Eddie Cochran, Reynolds said, "Eddie Cochran carried that song around in his back pocket a year before recording it."

—

Donnie Elbert "My Confession Of Love" DeLuxe 1958

Style: Rhythm and blues
Where from: Buffalo, NY
Where recorded: Cincinnati, OH
Suggested pairings: Edna McGriff "Heavenly Father" 1952; The Crystals "I Do Believe" 1956; Bo Diddley "Dearest Darling" 1957; B.B. King "Please Accept My Love" 1958; The Hi Tones' "Just For You" 1961

Having recorded two great ballads, "What Can I Do" and "Have I Sinned," high tenor balladeer Donnie Elbert tried one more time with the deep and apparently heartfelt "My Confession Of Love," with a famous spoken plea about "if I go to heaven before you do" from Edna McGriff's "Heavenly Father" from 1952.

—

The Everly Brothers "All I Have To Do Is Dream" Cadence 1958

Style: Rock 'n' roll
Where recorded: Nashville, TN

This song was another cleverly veiled sexually charged '50s slab'o rock 'n' roll, clearly referencing sexual fantasizing, an almost impossible-to-stop urge while being a teen. Phil Everly recalled hearing "All I Have To Do Is Dream" on an acetate with co-writer Boudleaux Bryant—who wrote almost all of The Everly's hits—singing, and thought Boudleaux's version could have been a hit. Chet Atkins played tremolo-style guitar chords, providing a solid bed for The Everly Brothers' harmonies.

Remakes: Richard Chamberlain 1963; Glen Campbell 1970; Bobby Gentry 1970; The Nitty Gritty Band 1975; Andy Gibb 1981; Victoria Principal 1981

—

Buddy Holly "Rave On" Coral 20 April 1958

Style: Rock 'n' roll
Where from: Lubbock, TX
Where recorded: Bell Sound Studio, New York
Original version: Sonny West 1958

Buddy Holly's cover version of "Rave On" was intended as an LP track, but enough response led to it being pulled for single release. It barely scraped into the USA Top 40 as an anti-rock'n'roll DJ described it in a testimony to congressional payola hearings as "music to steal hub-caps by."

—

Jan & Arnie "Jennie Lee" Arwin April 1958

Style: Rock 'n' roll
Where from: Bel Air, CA
Where recorded: Hollywood, CA

Jan Berry and Dean Torrence met as students at Emerson Junior High School in West L.A. and began singing together on an informal basis. At University High School in Pacific Palisades, they formed an embryonic group called The Barons, based on the name of their car club with Bruce Johnston and Sandy Nelson, who went with Kip Tyler and the Flips.

A major record collector, Berry printed up cards in his high school print shop for hoax radio station KJAN, which he used to entice record companies to send him promo copies of 45s. Berry also was fascinated by electronics and had set up a home recording studio where he dubbed over voices and echoes of himself, Dean Torrence and Arnie Ginsberg onto a complete recording of "Jennie Lee." Dean Torrence even recalled the stripper's workplace, "a Follies Burlesque the fellows had heard about. We took a carload to see boobs. Free parking," said Torrence. "We recorded the song, I did the percussion using a metronome. It sounded pretty good, so we went to the studio to re-record the song professionally and add extra voices and instrumentation. It was Arwin's first attempt at real rock and roll," but at the same time, keeping that real garage sound.

According to Joe Lubin, the song was not about a stripper, but rather had to do with a girl that Berry knew about. After home recording the catchy lyrics, Berry and gang took the finished tape to a studio in Hollywood to get several records made to give to friends. While the engineer was making the discs, Lubin, who worked at Doris Day's Arwin, was passing by. Upon hearing "Jennie Lee," he talked the duo into commercially releasing the song on Day's Arwin label. "I was in the studio when I heard something in another room. They were playing a demo and I was interested. I spoke with them and we went to Jan's house in Bel Air," said Lubin. "Jan had a studio in his garage. He had made up a fake radio station letterhead and had written to record companies who sent him promo records. He had a very large record collection at that time." Lubin made a deal with the teens, "If you pay for the acetate, I'll let you record two free acetates. I'll make you a big as The Everly Brothers."

As Torrence was about to go into military service, "Jennie Lee" was released as by Jan & Arnie on Arwin so they could work the song in live events. When the record hit, Berry advised Torrence that he should put off going into the National Guard. Torrence said he'd get right on it… about nine months later.

—

Jerry Butler and the Impressions "For Your Precious Love" Vee Jay/Falcon/Abner 1958

Style: Doo wop vocal group harmony
From and recorded in: Chicago, IL

Impressions leader Curtis Mayfield recalled his groups' early experience with label shopping. "We were lined up to go across the street to Chess Records. We're in Chicago, the snow is up to your waist. I guess it's five above. We're standing at the door of Chess. I guess there's nobody there but a secretary who can see us through the window who would not let us in—we had an appointment—we froze. We were standing there looking in the window. Someone turns around, right across the street, there was Vee Jay Records, we didn't even walk to the corner, we caved our way right through and jumped across the street, and as we walked into Vee Jay, the first element we met was a Great Dane. We stood there, he held us toward the door until someone would come downstairs. That was our introduction to the people at Vee Jay.

"We performed 'For Your Precious Love' right downstairs," Mayfield said. "Three more days we were in the studio, just as it came out. It was something a little different, the high-pitched tenor part comes from the church. The basic mood could've been a nice gospel tune. There was one or two things I had written that got lost in the shuffle. I was yet to be discovered. The gentleman who was playing was Guitar Red. He also played the instrument I was just in love with, the Stratocaster Fender guitar which had just come out in those early years. Guitar Red and Lefty Bates played guitar, Johnny Pate played upright bass and Al Duncan played drums.

During those days, there were no charts. We'd go in with Calvin Carter who was [the] A&R man and they were things off the top of your head. You'd come in, group around who was the originator of the song, in ten or fifteen minutes, you got the tune, you got the ending, the middle, everything. Then the group is right there, it all locks in. You go for that, that's life. 'For Your Precious Love' was done the same way, we made no change. The only difference was we had a bunch of musicians to show the tune to. I wasn't even in the union, I was playing with a bunch of professional cats who added music to my ears.

"It was so important to us to move ourselves as a group, the way things happened with Jerry Butler & the Impressions—no intention from Jerry," Mayfield continued. "We began getting things in after 'For Your Precious Love' from bigger writers who had sort of made their mark. During all those years all the labels would take the lead away after one or two hits and try to do that cross-over thing. I guess they felt they could hit another horizon. When it happened the group would just dwindle away. For one of the first times I can recall, The Impressions even surpassed the lead singer as a group. We'd do many shows where Jerry was co-liner and we were headliners and of course it was total fulfillment knowing where we came from."

—

Dickie Doo and the Don'ts "Nee Nee Na Na Na Na Nu Nu" Swan 1958

Style: Rock 'n' roll
Where from: Pennsylvania
Where recorded: New York City, NY

This was one of the era's toughest sax and guitar instrumentals, though not really an instrumental, as the title, "Nee Nee Na Na Na Na Nu Nu," was repeated throughout the performance by Gerry Granahan's Dickie Doo and the Don'ts. In fact, in some circles, the very phrase "Nee Nee Na Na Na Na Nu Nu" had racial connotations.

—

Gerry Granahan "No Chemise, Please" Sunbeam 1958

Style: Rock 'n' roll
Where from: Pennsylvania
Where recorded: New York City, NY

While hotter than a flaming saxophone with Dickie Doo and the Don'ts, group leader Gerry Granahan hit very large with the fashion non-statement vocal, "No Chemise, Please," starting as a slow love song, then increasing the tempo to fail against the current fashion, the chemise, a straight skirt meant to conceal the wearer's curvaceous shape, rendered Bobby Darin style. As with his other singles, the B-side, "Girl Of My Dreams," was a fine doo wop.

—

The Johnny Otis Show "Willie & the Hand Jive" Capitol 1958

Style: Rhythm and blues
Where from: Vallejo, CA
Where recorded: Hollywood, CA
Suggested pairings: Bo Diddley "Bo Diddley" 1955; Don Lang & His Frantic Five "Hand Jive" 1958

The Johnny Otis Show hit big with this Bo Diddley beat from Jimmy Nolan's distinctive guitar based on an earlier record by Otis. Otis said, "We had a hit in England called 'Ma (He's Makin' Eyes At Me),' thinking it would be a hit here, but it didn't make it here. It was a hit in England."

Otis' manager, Hal Zeigler then "went over and set up a tour, and he said, 'I saw the kids in the venues where they couldn't dance, theaters and little concert halls where they had to sit, doing a thing you used to do in black show business, the big bands called 'The Hand Jive.'"

"He said 'make a record on that and we'll probably have a hit in England.' Not only was it a hit in England, but we got real lucky with that one." Otis understood the relationship with the Bo Diddley beat. "It was that beat again. If it were possible we could trace that back to West Africa, but my first experience with that beat was with Count Otis Matthews & the West Oakland House Rockers when I was a kid in the late '30s and we would play in the gymnasium in West Oakland.

"At the end of the evening he'd pick up these cans and fill them up with little rocks and he'd sit them on the piano, call out the cute little girls out of the audience and bring them up and he gave them these things to shake and he'd have them do 'shave and a haircut, six bits.' He'd do 'mama killed a chicken, thought it was a duck.'"

With vocal support by the Planets, Johnny Otis' "Willie & the Hand Jive" broke in Buffalo, then took Tijuana, then went national.

Remakes: Wes Farrell 1961; The Moongooners 1962; Jerry Kennedy 1963; Sonny Burgess 1964; Eric Clapton 1974; The Warriors 1979; George Thorogood & the Destroyers 1985

—

Chuck Berry "Johnny B. Goode" Chess 1958

Style: Rock 'n' roll
Where from: St. Louis, MO
Where recorded: Chicago, IL
Suggested pairings: Louis Jordan "Ain't That Just Like A Woman" 1946; T-Bone Walker "Strollin' With Bones" 1950; George Jones "White Lightnin'" 1959

Chuck Berry lifted some guitar licks for this song: The intro came from the Louis Jordan song "Ain't That Just Like A Woman" from 1946 and the guitar break came from a 1950 T-Bone Walker song, "Strollin' With Bones." Jordan was a very influential R&B singer and a huge influence on Berry; Walker was a famous guitarist in the '40s and early '50s who came up with an electric guitar sound and raucous stage act that Berry shaped into a monumental work.

Chuck Berry joined Johnnie Johnson's group, The Sir John Trio, in 1953, and quickly became the lead singer and centerpiece of the band. After the flop single "Oh Maria" by Joe Alexander & the Cubans, Berry started defining rock 'n' roll with hits like "Maybellene."

The composition and performance of "Johnny B Goode" incorporated all the better descriptions of whence and where rock 'n' roll birthed—"way back upon the woods among the evergreens"—with fine guitar break. Based on Berry's life, "Johnny B Goode" tells the tale of a boy with humble beginnings with a talent for guitar. Some details were altered to protect no one in particular. Berry was from St. Louis, MO, not Louisiana, and knew how to read and write very well. He graduated from beauty school with a degree in hairdressing and cosmetology. Berry got the word "Goode" from xxxx Goode Avenue in St. Louis where he grew up. His grandfather lived in a Louisiana log cabin, back up in the woods in the evergreens. The line, "that little country boy could play" was originally, "that little colored boy can play." Berry knew to change it if he wanted radio play. Berry got the name "Johnny" from piano player Johnnie Johnson, who collaborated with Berry on many songs, including "Maybellene," "Roll Over Beethoven" and "Sweet Little Sixteen." Johnson could write songs on piano; Berry converted them to guitar and wrote lyrics.

Answers: Bobby Hendricks "Molly B. Goode" 1959; Jimmy Clanton "Go Jimmy Go" 1959; Chuck Berry "Bye Bye Johnny" 1960; Mungo Jerry "Johnny B. Badde" 1970; Bruce Springsteen "Bye Bye Johnny" 1985
Remakes: Dion 1964; Johnny Winter 1970; The Grateful Dead; The Jimi Hendrix Experience 1972; Elton John 1979

—

Ed Townsend "For Your Love" Capitol 1958

Style: Rhythm and blues
Where from: Memphis, TN
Where recorded: Los Angeles, CA

Ed Townsend had scant success on Aladdin, Dot and Carlton. "Nat Cole brought me over to Capitol; I met him in Las Vegas when I sang with Horace Heidt," he said.

"For Your Love" was enhanced by "the full sound of the combining of two gospel groups, one white, one black, in the background of this studio session, going pop at #13 in April 1958. Gloria Jones of The Blossoms recalled, "Plas Johnson's sister Gwen Johnson was on that and a girl who went to school with us, Edna Wright of the COGIC Singers. It was not us, period."

Arranger Rene Hall recalled how Townsend was strongly opinionated about how he wanted the session to sound. "That would be an Ed Townsend trademark. He liked background singers that sing in the Broadway production style and violas instead of violins. I only followed his style. He'd say, 'Get me plenty of violas and keep those high screechy things down as much as you can,' that's what he called violins."

—

The Coasters "Yakety Yak" Atco

Style: Rhythm and blues vocal group
Where from: Los Angeles, CA
Where recorded: New York City, NY

The Coasters' greatest year, 1958, began slowly, but with a 50 percent brand new lineup. Carryovers, lead singer Carl Gardner and alternate lead singer, baritone Billy Guy, were joined by tenor Cornel Gunter from The Flairs replacing his former Flairs' singing partner Obie Jesse; and bass Dub Jones from the Jacks/Cadets replacing Bobby Nunn.

After "Searchin'" hit, "Bobby Nunn took off, Lester fired him, everyone was glad," said Coasters' guitar player Adolph Jacobs. "They brought in Dub and Cornel at the same time. That same day, Leon got put in jail, had to get Young Jessie, the day of the studio, he got put in jail. Cornel would take his gay friends in his Caddy." Gunter's sister Shirley recalled, "He just loved singing, putting in harmony bits, getting the sound, he just loved that. He'd sing the high, the first tenor, anything comical. He was just happy." However, Gardner recalled Gunter's aggressive homosexuality caused problems with the group. "Cornel Gunter was strong as hell. He had a 19" neck. He wanted me, but I don't go that way. Everybody refrained. He had to go out in the street to do his thing."

Despite the problems, this new line-up would remain in place until 1961. According to Gardner, "Cornel was not happy being a back-up singer. Actually we were all great together as performers. I just didn't like his underhanded ways and lies he told after he left the group."

The pop breakthrough for The Coasters was the novelty rebel treatise, "Yakety Yak" backed with the Jones-led standard, "Zing Went the Strings Of My Heart," when standards like "Sweet Georgia Brown" had been trotted out for rockin' interpretation. "Yakety Yak" was The Coasters' first example of "unison singing," a style that continued with "Charlie Brown" and "Poison Ivy."

"Yakety Yak" hit #1 on the Mighty 690 in mid-May and pop in early June.

—

Art and Dotty Todd "Chanson D'Amour (Song Of Love)" Era March 1958

Style: Pop
From and recorded in: Los Angeles, CA
Suggested pairing: The Elegants "Little Star" 1958

While performing at the Chapman Park Hotel in Los Angeles, Art (b. Baltimore, MD March 11, 1914) and Dotty (real name: Doris Dabb, b. Elizabeth, New Jersey June 22, 1913) Todd encountered songwriter Wayne Shanklin who promoted the song to the duet, who cut a demo on the ultra sensuous romantic ballad, "Chanson D'Amour (Song Of Love)," backed with "Along The Trail With You" on Era, which released the demo track as a single, breaking in New York and hitting large in L.A. Art Todd recalled, "the airplay was just sensational. This was just at the beginning of rock 'n' roll and the old-time DJs hated rock 'n' roll and they jumped on our song." The "rat-a-tata-tata" lyrical device soon showed up in "Little Star" by the Elegants, a #1 hit in 1958.

Remakes: The Lettermen 1966; Manhattan Transfer 1976

—

Don and Dewey "Justine" Specialty April 28, 1958

Style: Rhythm and blues
Where from: Pasadena, CA
Where recorded: Los Angeles, CA

Don and Dewey's pounding rocker "Justine" was a minor local hit for the duo. "'Justine' was one of my ladies," said Harris. "I have two lovely children by her." Terry added, "Justine was a fine lady we knew. We'd go over to a friend's house and started playing, 'Hey it sounds good.' 'Justine' was a good rockin' thing, a good party rocker."

Frank Zappa said to DJ Les Carter on KPPC, "Don and Dewey worked very hard to put their act together and played many times at El Monte Legion Stadium, thrilling their audience with their zany antics. One of them would play an electric violin and would double on guitar, the other one would play organ and sometimes bass and had this special kind of vocal harmony that was very individualistic and they had these gala costumes, which were sort of Day-Glo rayon with bolero balls hanging all over their chest and they would jump around. They had huge phenomenal processed pompadours going up two and a half feet from the top of their head and they really had it together. Then the Righteous Brothers came along and sort of borrowed their whole number and because they were white became very rich."

Remakes: Ray Sharpe 1960; Adrian & The Sunsets 1963; The Leggeriors 1963; Meep Meep and the Roadrunner 1965; The Righteous Brothers 1966

—

Dick Bush "Hollywood Party" Era April 1958

Style: Rock 'n' roll
Where from: Texas
Where recorded: Hollywood, CA

Donnie Brooks, who recorded as Johnny Faire in 1957, took a new name based on a smutty junior high joke: Dick Bush, on "Hollywood Party." According to Donnie Brooks, who recorded only once as Dick Bush, but had hits for Era about two years later, the name change made sense. "If you recorded a hit as Johnny Faire, there's a mindset. If he thinks it's a hit, he wants to put out the next hit, but he doesn't want to have all these other songs coming out under the same name to kill the second hit, so that was the thinking."

Brooks pointed out the gimmick to "Hollywood Party." The lyrics were "about Fats, Rick, Jerry, Cash, Little Richard, the whole things was built around these recording acts" who attended the same party. "It took off really big in El Paso and never did anything."

—

Dion and the Belmonts "I Wonder Why" Laurie May 1958

Style: Doo-wop
Where from: The Bronx, NY
Where recorded: New York City
Suggested pairings: The Keynotes "I Don't Know Why" 1955; The Legends "Now I'm Telling You" 1957

The Belmonts' name was because two of the four members lived on Belmont Avenue in the Bronx, and the other two lived near Belmont Avenue. After Dion debuted to add vocals to a song by the pop group The Timberlanes, his first hit was under the name Dion & the Belmonts, a staccato-style uptempo doo wop. "I Wonder Why" is a song very similar to "I Don't Know Why" by the Keynotes on Apollo and the Legends' "Now I'm Telling You."

Dion recalled of The Belmonts, "I'd give 'em sounds. I'd give 'em parts and stuff. That's what 'I Wonder Why' was about. We kind of invented this percussive rhythmic sound. If you listen to that song, everybody was doing something different. It was totally amazing. When I listen to it today, oftentimes I think, 'Man, those kids are talented.'" The group followed with other major hits, notably the more pop-oriented "A Teenager In Love" in 1959.

—

The Four Preps "Big Man" Capitol May 1, 1958

Style: Pop
From and recorded in: Hollywood, CA

"We had a big hit with '26 Miles,'" said Four Preps lead singer Bruce Belland. "Our producer said, 'Anyone can get a hit these days. You get a second hit then you're on your way.' Okay. We were in Oklahoma City at an amusement park and we went up to our room, #126. I took that as an omen. Glen got his guitar out said, 'You know what's a big expression now, "big man on campus." If we can think of a big man song about someone who used to be a big man.' We wrote it that night." With the powerful and dramatic piano by Lincoln Mayorga, "Big Man" was big.

—

Bobby Darin "Splish Splash" Atco May 1958

Style: Rock 'n' roll
Where from: The Bronx, NY
Where recorded: New York City
Suggested pairing: Duane Eddy "Moovin' 'N' Groovin'" 1958

In 1956, Bobby Darin recorded a cover of "Rock Island Line." With few sales, he switched to the Atlantic label startup, Atco. Ruth Brown, for whom Darin wrote "This Little Girl's Gone Rockin," said, "Bobby Darin sounded a lot like Ray Charles when he first came in. He wanted to do the Litchman chain of theaters, the Apollo, the Regal in Chicago, the Royale in Baltimore, the Hippodrome in Richmond, VA. It was a little odd, 'I'm going to get booed, everybody thinks I'm doing Ray Charles.' I went down for Bobby's opening, they loved him. That's how we became friends."

Several releases in, Darin's career was going nowhere. That situation soon changed. DJ Murray 'the K' Kaufman's mother, Jean, suggested the title and penned the music while Bobby and Murray wrote the lyrics, inspired by a Central Park softball game. After the game, they were in Murray's apartment soaking their feet in basins of Epsom salts. Somehow, Murray's mother Jean was told by Murray of "the agony of de feet." She turned that term into "Splish, splash, take a bath." The "movin' and a groovin'" lyric was lifted from the Duane Eddy instrumental title, "Moovin' 'N' Groovin.'" And "Splish Splash" took off, thanks to spins by Murray 'the K' who was a WMGM DJ at the time, where "Splish Splash" first charted.

—

The Drifters "Drip Drop" Atlantic 1958

Style: Rhythm and blues vocal group
From and recorded in: New York City, NY
Suggested pairings: Jesse Belvin "Little Darling" 1958; Sam Hawkins "Hurts So Bad" 1965

With new lead singer Bobby Hendricks, The Drifters hit with this Leiber-Stoller composition, "Drip Drop." In 1957, Hendricks had been in The Flyers with Bill Pinkney, one time bass singer of The Drifters. Hendricks explained, "Bill Pinkney fell out of grace with Drifters' management, he was replaced by Tommy Evans, so Bill Pinkney formed a group called The High Flyers. He got me to sing with the group and we did a few records" like "On Bended Knee" by The Flyers on Atco. "You can see there is a correlation. When he got back into their good graces, that's when he came back." And brought Bobby Hendricks with him.

"The Drifters had no lead singer, they were falling apart at the seams," Hendricks continued. I went back that week with Jimmy Oliver as a favor to The Drifters so they could make an Apollo Theater appearance that week. I was really on my own. We set the stage on fire and they were very impressed with our performance. Bill Pinkney told me their lead singer was going in the service, if I wanted a job stay in touch. About six months later, Johnny Moore did go into the service. They called me, I flew down in St. Louis. I stayed with The Drifters about two solid years. The Drifters broke up and another group came out. I didn't have a contract with The Drifters, it made me easy to go to Juggy Murray and Jimmy Oliver. I wrote 'Itchy Twitchy Feeling' and we recorded it on Sue Records."

Remake: Dion 1963

—

The Drifters "Moonlight Bay" Atlantic 1958

Style: Barbershop ensemble singing
From and recorded in: New York City, NY
Suggested pairing: The Mills Brothers 1949

Perhaps the worst record in the history of the label, certainly by The Drifters, was the flip side of "Drip Drop," a Mitch Miller sing-a-long styled remake of The Mills Brothers hit "Moonlight Bay." "It was a double track of The Drifters," said Hendricks. "I think I was the only member of The Drifters actually on that recording. Some of the other fellows were backup guys we used, friends of ours we found in New York, like The Coasters, and another group," the name of which Hendricks couldn't recall. "Tommy Evans and myself were the only Drifters on this record. We really didn't have any foundation for going into that session. Someone suggested it, 'Let's do "Moonlight Bay."' It was something we could harmonize on and we jumped in there and we did it. It was not something I wanted to do, I didn't even like the tune. We had more than a fifth that day, the gin and grapefruit juice was very heavy around there. It was horrible, I hated it. Material was very scarce at the time. There weren't any good songs out and some of us thought, 'We might have a change over.' Not even The Four Aces would do something like that. It was the worst Drifters record ever recorded."

Even so, in May 1958, The Drifters' "Moonlight Bay" charted on Houston, Phoenix, Detroit, Buffalo and Toronto area radio stations, hitting #1 in one Canadian market, while "Drip Drop" hit only in Boston in August.

—

Danleers "One Summer Night" AMP-3/Mercury May 1958

Style: Doo wop
Where from: Brooklyn, NY
Where recorded: New York

One of many street-corner doo-wop groups, Danny Webb became this group's manager and principal songwriter, naming them after himself, first as The Dandleers, then as The Danleers. The group was Jimmy Weston, Johnny Lee, Willie Ephraim, Nat McCune, and Roosevelt Mays. Their major hit was "One Summer Night," written by Webb on the AMP-3 label, owned by Bill Lasley, who signed the group in spring 1958. The song began gaining traction regionally and, unable to handle distribution, the label leased the single to Mercury Records. Mercury helped push the song to become one of that year's biggest summer songs, and to sell over one million copies.

Answer: The Capris "There's a Moon Out Tonight" 1959/60

—

Duane Eddy & His "Twangy" Guitar "Rebel Rouser" Jamie May 28, 1958

Style: Rock 'n' roll
Where from: Phoenix, AZ
Where recorded: Hollywood, CA
Suggested pairings: Don Rondo "White Silver Sands" 1957; Chuck Berry "Johnny B. Goode" 1958; Johnny Preston "Running Bear" 1959; The Knock-Outs "Riot in Room C" 1959

The Sharps were heard in the background of Duane Eddy's uptempo guitar instrumental "Rebel Rouser," said the R&B group's Al Frazier. "We first met Duane at the Paramount Theater in downtown L.A. It was the Roy Hamilton Show and Thurston Harris and the Sharps. We had 'Little Bitty Pretty One' and Duane had a record called 'Movin' N Groovin.' He opened up the show; we kind of became good buddies. He [was] affiliated with Lee Hazelwood and Lester Sil at the time. He was getting ready to go into the studio to do some more recording, so he thought about us."

The dubbed-in sax over Eddy's guitar was by L.A. R&B session sax man Gil Bernal.

—

Dick Dale "Ooh Wee Marie" Deltone May 31, 1958

Style: Rock 'n' roll
Where from: Boston, MA or Beirut, Lebanon
Where recorded: Hollywood, CA

Richard Monsour, better known as Dick Dale, arrived in El Segundo in 1954 and attended Washington High School. In about 1958, Mark Hendrix, father of guitarist Marlow Stewart, who managed the United Artists Theater in Long Beach, held an Elvis sound-a-like contest. First place prize was a live rock 'n' roll tour of the United Artists theaters. "We had three top singers my dad picked, but they couldn't do the tour," said Marlow. "Then he talked to Jim Monsour, father of Dick Monsour, who said, 'Hey he's on vacation.' He came in fourth, was the winner, did a three week tour of my dad's theaters. Turned out that was Dick Dale, renamed by 400-pound country DJ T. Texas Tiny.

"My dad did all that promotional stuff," continued Marlow, "including an interview show on KLFM in Lakewood Village." Dale's earliest record was the energetic vocal on "Ooh Wee Marie" with Mike Deasy on guitar. It hit locally. The Deltone label was first located at Dick Dale's residence on S. Wilton Ave. in L.A., and soon moved to the business address of 145 W. 154th St. in Gardena, the location of Case, Gardena and a few other indie labels associated with John Gus and Mike Gradney. At about the same time, Dale, president of the Sultans Motorcycle Club, went surfing and searched for live action at a local ballroom… and a brand new sound.

—

The Ding Dongs/Rinky Dinks "Early In the Morning" Brunswick/Atco 1958

Style: Rock 'n' roll
From and recorded in: New York City, NY
Suggested pairings: Ray Charles "I've Got a Woman" 1954; Chuck Berry "Roll Over Beethoven" 1956; Lavern Baker "Substitute" 1957; Buddy Knox "Somebody Touched Me" 1958; The Chiffons "One Fine Day" 1963

Aware he was going to be dropped from the Atco label prior to his first hit, "Splish Splash," Bobby Darin recorded two songs, "Early in the Morning" and "Now We're One," for Brunswick, which released them as a single. As he couldn't use his real name, the artist credit went to The Ding Dongs, a fake name takeoff on an early 1958 hit, "Nee Nee Nah Nu Nah" by Dicky Doo & the Don'ts used by Gerry Granahan.

Very shortly after The Ding Dongs release Atco found out that Darin had recorded out of his contract and demanded the master tapes. They then rush released the tracks under the name the Rinky Dinks. It wasn't simultaneous but close.

Cover: Buddy Holly 1958

—

Buddy Holly "Early in the Morning" Coral 1958

Style: Rock 'n' roll
Where from: Lubbock, TX
Where recorded: New York City, NY
Original version: The Ding Dongs/Rinky Dinks 1958

When the Atco label grabbed rights to the song "Early in The Morning" by the Ding Dongs, really Bobby Darin from Brunswick, the Brunswick sister label, Coral, had the song's composer, Buddy Holly, record a very close version of both sides of the release to compete on the charts. Both sides did chart, but neither version was a major hit.

—

The Imperials "Tears On My Pillow" End 1958

Style: Rhythm and blues vocal group
From and recorded in: New York City, NY
Suggested pairings: The Penguins "Earth Angel" 1954; The Duponts "You" 1956

Coming off lead singer roles with The Chesters on Apollo and with The Duponts, with whom Little Anthony Gourdine sang the influential "You" for the Winley label, Little Anthony created The Imperials, which recorded "Tears On My Pillow" as their first release and major hit, surpassed only by the B-side, "Two People In the World."

Supposedly "Tears On My Pillow" was first credited to The Chesters, but no sightings of such a pressing have ever been reported.

Reissue: Little Anthony and the Imperials 1958—when Little Anthony got famous

—

The Elegants "Little Star" Apt 1958

Style: Doo-wop
Where from: Staten Island, NY
Where recorded: New York City, NY
Suggested pairings: The Heartbeats "A Thousand Miles Away" 1956; Art & Dottie Todd "Chanson D'Amour" 1958

The Elegants' "Little Star" was based on the children's song "Twinkle, Twinkle, Little Star." Vito Picone and Carman Romano had recorded with Pat Cordel and the Crescents on "Darling, Come Back" on Club, an uptempo Frankie Lymon soundalike from 1956. Joining three other Staten Island teenagers—tenors Arthur Venosa and Frank Tardogno and bass Jimmy Moscello—they created The Elegants, inspired by an advertising slogan, Schenley Distilleries' "Whiskies of Elegance."

Auditioning for several companies, they signed with Bea Kaslin's Hull Records, which had already hit with "A Thousand Miles Away" by the Heartbeats, before she leased it to Rama for national distribution. The "Little Star" lyric "twinkle, twinkle, little star... how I wonder where you are..." added a doo wop hook, not unlike the hook used in "A Thousand Miles Away," "rat-a-tata-tata-to-ooo..." and another major hit, Art & Dottie Todd's "Chanson D'Amour" from late 1957. Kaslin again leased this appealing doo wop performance to a more major label, a brand new ABC-Paramount subsidiary, Apt Records, for which it was an easy New York and national #1.

Reportedly, The Elegants refused to pay payola to a prominent New York disc jockey, which inhibited airplay of their follow up recordings. There's a lesson in here.

—

The Shields "You Cheated" Tender/Dot 1958

Style: Rhythm and blues vocal group
From and recorded in: Los Angeles, CA
Suggested pairings: The Slades "You Gambled" 1959; Frankie Ervin & the Spears "Why Did You Lie" 1959; The Plaids "Hungry For Your Love" 1959
Original version: The Slades "You Cheated" 1957

Prior to "You Cheated," there were no Shields, vocal group that is. L.A. R&B producer and label entrepreneur George Motola first heard of the song when he was contacted by the Dot label distributor about a Texas group, The Slades, whose "You Cheated" was becoming a regional hit on the Domino label. "Don Burch wrote the song, I guess," Motola recalled. "A record distributor, Mr. Shapiro from Dallas Texas, called me up, said, 'How'd you like to make some money and record a song called "You Cheated"? We've already sold over 15,000 and it's starting to break out in New Orleans and all over. It's going into Billboard,' he said. 'I'll help you break the record, but you've got to give me 5,000 records free. If you agree to the terms, I will get the record all over in the south.' Shapiro called because the woman who owned the Domino label wouldn't make a deal for them to buy records at a certain price. Everything in those days were priced and the royalties were so limited, you couldn't make too much money. The pressings were 10 cents and by the time you got through with everything, they wanted to buy them for 30 cents, you'd be lucky to make a dime. Then you got to pay the artist and everything. She was complaining, so they called me up. I said, 'All right, send me the record.'

"The next day I got the record, two o'clock in the afternoon, I got a hold of a kid called Frankie Ervin, who I never heard," continued Motola. "Frankie Ervin came into the office just by accident. I knew all the people, I just called them. He came over and auditioned, I was pressed for time. I got a hold of Rene Hall, there was no instruments but just guitar on the record, there was no bass, no drums or piano, went in at 8 o'clock at night, we cut the record, it cost $30 to cut it.

"There was no Shields, that's a trade name," Ervin recalled. "I ran into a BMI publisher named Jack Carroll who knew Jack Hoffman so he asked me to sing, so I sung him my song. George Motola called me on the telephone. I was at Kirkwood Ave., barely existing. I came on the bus after they heard me sing, they was really excited, they could see money signs. Motola and Hoffman was excited. He [Motola] says, 'I don't want to tie you up be your manager or anything like that I just want to freelance you—get you to the majors.' I was excited. They said, 'You haven't had a hit since "Dragnet" and that was in 1953. Stick with me, I'll make a star out of you.' Motola gave me a demo and a lead sheet, 'Take this home and learn this and in two or three days,' he mentioned, 'there's a group named The Slades on Domino Records in Texas who had this record out, but we want to beat them. We know you can do a better job than The Slades. We're going to take it to Electrovox Studios on Melrose. I'm going to get Jesse Belvin.' He was handling Jesse at the time before Alan Freed.

"I took the lead sheet," continued Ervin. "I went home. I couldn't sing it in the present form so I started working on the lyrics to fit my style. I don't know about co-writers. I worked it up I got it to fit my style. Jesse Belvin sang first falsetto and bass; Mel Williams sang second tenor; Johnny 'Guitar' Watson sang bass and Buster Williams sang baritone."

Motola said, "When you got Jesse and his group, their ears, everything is trained, he was such a phenomenal manipulator of voices, he could do anything with voices. He was a genius in the business. He'd get the guys, and they'd come down and they'd do it. Didn't take long at all. His ear was a phenomenal ear. All I done was call Jesse and say, 'I'm doing a session tonight.' We were close, we hung out together."

According to Motola, the only instrumental backing was by Rene Hall on guitar, while Ervin recalled, "Ernie Freeman was playing piano; Irving Ashby on bass; Rene Hall on guitar and Davis Williams on drums. We laid it down with four pieces. Three takes on me." Aurally, Motola's version is probably correct, as only the guitar is evident, thus Ervin may have been referring to a later Shields session.

"I cut it at eight o'clock at night in a little studio on Melrose, at ten dollars an hour," Motola recalled. "It cost $30 to cut it. I was there for three hours, we finished it, I had it in vats at 12 o'clock midnight, the next morning, we had labels, got pressings at nine o'clock in the morning. I shipped it out that day, next thing you know the Domino record showed up at Billboard." In reality, The Slades hit first in the label's backyard, Houston, then reached #42 nationally in early August 1958, though The Shields hit the local charts several weeks earlier.

Motola recalled, "The next week, it was off the chart completely because Dick Clark, Tony Mammarella and I called up and told them to pull it off the air completely because mine was a better version, which they did because I had the connections at the time to do it. Even in their own town with the Domino label they couldn't penetrate it. That was the end of the label at the time. I was threatened by Domino; they didn't bother me; I didn't care. I was young and aggressive at the time. I thought it was good, let them threaten me, they didn't do anything, I didn't think they would."

In partnership with Imogene Fadely and Buddy Motola, "You Cheated" hit top ten in L.A. and #12 nationally. Motola recalled how he got radio play. "Jim Randolph was at KNOK in Dallas, Texas. I had told him they were looking for a DJ at KGFJ. Art LaBoe and Jim Randolph were playing it in Los Angeles. Today it's a big payola game. I never gave a dime out for anything. I was the one who told Alan Freed to come out here at KDAY. When Alan Freed came out here with his wife Inga, he didn't have any money. I called all the distributors up and got $500 each from the distributors to get him to stay out here. I got a place for him and everything; they was really rough on him; they broke him in the '50s.

Motola continued, "Randy Wood of Dot came down; he made a deal with Imogene Fadely. She didn't have enough money to meet the pressings demands of 'You Cheated.' They didn't think it was going to be a big hit as it was. Dot Records would cover anything to make a dollar, if they could sell 50,000 copies, fine, or 30, whatever traffic would bear. If they picked up a master for a couple thousand dollars, that was nothing to Randy Wood at the time. He liked the record, so they wound up with 'You Cheated' on Dot."

Ervin recalled, "George Motola and his partner Jack Hoffman was over a meat packing wholesale place. They had an apartment up there. When George Motola copyrighted the trade name, it was supposed to come out as Frankie Ervin. "I was coerced to sign a contract, but I didn't understand the contract. Motola had me believe the record was going to come out under my name. When I signed the contract, paragraph seven said we can use any names when we release the master. I was so angry I went back to Imogene Fadely; I raised holy hell." Ervin's anger about not getting label credit caused the demise of The Shields. "They tried to talk to me before doing the Dick Clark Show and tried to tell me how to act. I didn't want nobody to tell me how to act. So they got mad at me because I did that. They took their feelings, went farther and reconsidered me. They already had their minds made up. They hired Willie McGowen to replace me in The Shields and sent him to the Apollo Theater in New York; they hired Tony Allen and sent him to Hawaii. They started hiring professional groups and started calling them The Shields.

Ervin continued, "Jack Levy, Motola and Jack Hoffman and Imogene Fadely of Tender Records broke up. They started fighting over me, over the success of 'You Cheated.' The woman I was in business with on Tender Records then went behind my back when I didn't know what was going on. We were supposed to have a 50/50 deal. She spent $30 for the record, she turned around, started to usurp, I didn't see any money off of that." Tender went out of business in 1959.

Cover: The Del-Vikings
Remakes: Beverly Noble 1959; Tab Hunter 1961

—

Bobby Hendricks "Itchy Twitchy Feeling" Sue 1958

Style: Rhythm and blues
Where from: Columbus, OH
Suggested pairings: The Clovers "Lovey Dovey" 1954; The Drifters "Yodee Yakee" 1957; The Coasters "Yakety Yak" 1958

One-time short-lived lead singer of the Drifters, Bobby Hendricks debuted as a solo artist on this rocking R&B dance-style vocal, "Itchy Twitchy Feeling," which had evolved from "Lovey Dovey" by the Clovers and "Yodee Yakee" by the Drifters. The flip, the fine doo wop "A Thousand Dreams," was the designated A-side.

Backed by the Coasters on both sides, Hendricks described "Itchy Twitchy Feeling" as a gimmick. "You've got the dog yapping, the hound dog, people wanted to hear things like that. It sounded like The Coasters' "Yakety Yak," it sold, though Juggy Murray of Sue Records didn't come up with royalties. "He was never swift on paying them, we could say none. One of his claims was expenses for getting the records out there. Promotion ate up all the royalties. We had nothing to say about it."

"Itchy Twitchy Feeling" took two months to hit. "It was a disc jockey in New York, Dr. Jive. New York, New Jersey, Ohio," Hendricks added.

Cover: The Swallows. Two years earlier, Hendricks had sung with The Swallows. "I was surprised they did a follow-up."

—

Ricky Nelson "Poor Little Fool" Imperial 1958

Style: Rock 'n' roll
From and recorded in: Hollywood, CA
Suggested pairings: Patience & Prudence "Gonna Get Along Without You Now" 1956; The Dodgers and Johnny Angel "Poor Little Fool"; Glen Glenn "Kathleen" 1957; Dion & the Belmonts' "A Teenager In Love" 1959

The evolution of Ricky Nelson's rockaballad "Poor Little Fool" on Imperial was like none other in the Nelson songbook. In 1957, DJ Huggy Boy rescued songwriter Sharon Sheeley from a bad situation in Hollywood, bringing her to her [to his] Dana Point family home in south Orange County. During the visit, Sheeley showed Huggy her new song, "Poor Little Fool," which had just been recorded by The Dodgers and Johnny Angel as an uptempo jive with writer credits to Shari Shelley.

When Imperial owner Lew Chudd had Ricky Nelson record "Poor Little Fool" in late 1957, he had no idea there was an earlier recording. When Huggy Boy approached Imperial's Lew Chudd, he had two demands, pick up a Johnny Flamingo duet, Jack & Jill's "No One To Talk To (But the Blues)" backed with "Party Time" on Huggy's Caddy for release on Imperial. Done. The other demand was a little more complicated: pull "Poor Little Fool" off Nelson's latest LP, release it as a 45. Chudd agreed and by early June 1958, "Poor Little Fool," was Nelson's first #1 hit and was also the only Nelson 45 on Imperial to not be released with a picture sleeve, because of the rush nature of breaking it out of the LP.

—

The Olympics "Western Movies" Demon 1958

Style: Rhythm and blues vocal group
From and recorded in: Los Angeles, CA

Originally known as Walter Ward & the Challengers, The Olympics were formed in L.A. in 1958, an Olympic year. The success of the Olympics, the group, was predicated on the unique voice of lead singer Walter Ward and the production skills of Cliff Goldsmith and Fred Smith, son of Effie Smith. "The late Jesse Belvin was a very close friend of mine and he introduced me to Smith and Goldsmith," said Ward. "They said, 'Hey I like that voice.' I've never been fond of it myself. They handed me the music that said 'Western Movies.' 'Western Movies?' We went in the studio and did it."

Punctuated by gunshot sound effects and the listing of westerns viewed on the fictitious channel 8 came "Western Movies," which hit first in the Bay Area. Said Ward, "Demon Records gave away a stereo to everybody who could name all the westerns (Maverick, Sugarfoot, Cheyenne, Have Gun Will Travel, Wagon Train, Broken Arrow, Jim Bowie, Wyatt Earp and Boots & Saddles) in the song."

—

The Edsels "Rama Lama Ding Dong" Dub International/Twin June 1958/April 1961

Style: Doo wop
Where from: Youngstown, OH
Where recorded: Little Rock, AR
Earliest title: "Lama Rama Ding Dong"

In the same year Ford introduced the Edsel, The Edsels recorded this doo wop novelty, "Lama Rama Ding Dong"—though the lyrics were clearly "Rama Lama Ding Dong"—for the totally unknown Dub International out of Little Rock, Arkansas.

Hardly a hit when released, a year later, at the very start of the great doo wop revival in 1959, two enterprising New York area record collectors saw opportunity in this so-called "bomb." The owner of Dub International sold them the remaining copies in his stock. Times Square Records in New York took in 100 copies and when the word got out, sales began growing. These collectors became East Coast distributors of the record based on word of mouth and radio play.

In 1961, the Twin label was formed by the owner of Old Town Records, which had acquired certain rights, to fully release the song under the correct title, "Rama Lama Ding Dong," a version that went top 10 in New York and top 40 nationally in April and May. Then the owner of Dub International moved his label to Lawndale, California, pressing up an alternate take as "Rama Lama Ding Dong." On the first Dub pressing, "Lama Rama Ding Dong" became a collector's item. "Rama Lama Ding Dong" was a major hit.

—

The Imperials "Two People in the World" End July 1958

Style: Rhythm and blues vocal group
From and recorded in: New York City, NY
Suggested pairing: The Vocaltones "Three People In the World"

On "Two People in the World," the group sang the main vocal, and Little Anthony sang the high part, over the lead vocals. This was the surprise hit of the pairing, and is still a fave among L.A. lowriders.

—

Ivan "Real Wild Child" Coral July 11, 1958

Style: Rockabilly
Where from: Texas
Where recorded: New York
Original version: Johnny O'Keefe & the Deejays "Wild One" 1958

Ivan was Crickets' drummer, Jerry Allison. An Aussie, Johnny O'Keefe's original U.S. and UK versions of the song were titled "Real Wild Child." Both were a close-but-different take from the Australian original, probably using the same backing track but with a different intro edit. The US & UK versions also eliminated the crowd sounds and added cheers to simulate a "live" recording.

Remakes: The Bell Notes 1960; Iggy Pop 1987

—

Bobby Day "Over and Over" Class July 1958

Style: Rhythm and blues
Where from: Texas
Where recorded: Los Angeles, CA
Cover: Thurston Harris 1958

In a classic instance of picking the wrong side, Bobby Day's "Over and Over" backed with "Rock-In Robin" on Class was covered Thurston Harris who had already swamped Day on his original "Little Bitty Pretty One" in 1957. And it might have worked, had the original A-side had been the hot side. Day's original "Over and Over" on Class shared chart positions with Thurston Harris' cover version on Aladdin as one listing on the Mighty 690 survey. It seemed that the Class label hit was to be the song "Over and Over" with a month and a half head start on the real hit, "Rock-in Robin."

—

Bobby Day "Rock-In Robin" July 1958

Style: Rhythm and blues
Where from: Texas
Where recorded: Los Angeles, CA
Suggested pairings: Charlie Jackson "Shake That Thing" 1925; Joe Liggins "Pink Champagne" 1950

Writer of "When the Swallows Come Back To Capistrano," Class label owner Leon Rene knew ornithology-based titles were hardly for the birds as proven by Bobby Day's "Rock-In Robin." Leon's son, Googie Rene, said, "Bobby Day came with a bunch of singers, five singers. My dad wrote a song, there was a rockin' robin in a tree top. I killed the bird you know; I popped him with a BB gun."

Originally written for Class country thrush Jeannie Mack, Bobby Day's "Rock-In Robin" with an unusual piccolo break by Plas Johnson, finally hit, and hit big. "I did stuff for Leon Rene," said Johnson. "I backed Bobby Day on 'Rock-In Robin.' I played piccolo, it was a solo, the whistle, the intro and stuff. I did work with Thurston Harris at the same time, even with different companies, if a record is a hit. 'Little Bitty Pretty One' sold pretty good; Bobby Day was hot at the time. Record companies would want that rhythm section or that soloist on the record." No doubt, because "Over and Over" had run its hit course on KFWB and Mighty 690.

Remakes: The Rivieras 1964; Ray Smith 1964; Freddie Cannon 1971; Michael Jackson 1972

—

Thurston Harris "Over and Over" Aladdin 1958

Style: Rhythm and blues
Where from: Indiana
Where recorded: Los Angeles, CA
Original version: Bobby Day

For the second time in a row, Thurston Harris covered Bobby Day, this time on the clever rocker about going to a dance, "Over and Over." Leon Rene's son, Googie

Rene, said, "It just happened that Aladdin figured they'd steal it, they did. Thurston Harris did it,"

Harris recalled, "I sneaked into the session and heard 'Over and Over'" with drummer Earl Palmer's machine gun like introduction. So Aladdin hired Palmer to do the same thing for Harris' cover. It worked, to an extent. In this instance, Harris chose the wrong side to **cover:** Day hit big with "Rock-in Robin" and Harris got local sales on "Over and Over," which charted on mightily on KGFJ and on the Mighty 690 in tandem with the Day original in early July. "Bobby told me as long as I'm alive he's not going to write another song," said a bemused Harris.

"We didn't particularly care for 'Rock-In Robin.' We felt we could steal 'Over and Over' a little better," said Al Frazier of the backing Sharps. "We saw Bobby Day after 'Over and Over' was released. He came up to Thurston and myself and said, 'Hey, why didn't you cover the A-side?'"

—

Evelyn Freeman & the Exciting Voices "Didn't It Rain" Bel Canto/United Artists 1958

Style: Gospel
Where from: Cleveland, OH
Where recorded: Los Angeles, CA

Founded in 1958 and located at 2919 S. LaCienega Blvd. in Culver City, Bel Canto turned out to be less interested in vinyl recordings than in newly marketed stereo, releasing their product line on just-introduced two-track reel-to-reel tapes, thought to be the wave of the stereo future.

After a single stiff on Dot, Evelyn Freeman applied her gospel training in an early R&B crossover. "Didn't It Rain" backed with "Swing Low Sweet Chariot," a thrilling vocal credited to Evelyn Freeman & the Exciting Voices, the first known 45 on Bel Canto.

According to Ellison White, Freeman & the Exciting Voices had as many as 14 singers, including White; Freeman's husband, Tommy Roberts; Gwen Johnson, sister of Ray and Plas Johnson; Johnny Woodson of The Kuff Linx; Margaret Bradford and bass man George Bledsoe on violin—who also backed Peggy Lee on "All Right, OK, You Win" in 1958.

In 1959, the Bel Canto two-track product line was converted to the more popular four-track format. TRW (Thompson Ramo Wooldridge, Inc.) bought out Bel Canto and also made deals with Liberty, Dot, Disneyland and Mercury to release their catalog on cartridge tapes. TRW also marketed the system needed to play the tapes. Out of this early phase came eight-track and cassette technology of the mid- to late 1960s. In early 1960, Bel Canto announced a move to Columbus, Ohio.

Though "Didn't It Rain" saw no chart action upon release, years later the tremendous vocals and throbbing bass line made it an underground hit, especially for those with in-car record players used to provide the soundtrack for cruising the local boulevards.

—

Eddie Cochran "Summertime Blues" Liberty 1958

Style: Rock 'n' roll
Where from: Bell Gardens, CA
Where recorded: Hollywood, CA

Eddie Cochran's most major guitar and vocal effort, "Summertime Blues"—with Guybo Smith, electric bass; Ray Johnson, piano; Earl Palmer, drums; the song's writer, Sharon Sheeley and Capehart on hand claps; and Warn Crosby of The Four Dots as Cochran's bass-voiced duet partner—broke in the Bay area in late July and nationally in early August.

"We did the record date as any record date, we go in we rehearsed the song to try and get some kind of instrumental hooks going to enhance the arrangement, we rehearsed it for a half hour to 45 minutes," Ray

Johnson recalled, "We laid it down, with Eddie singing lead and playing guitar. He very easy to work with, a very talented guitarist, singer."

"Summertime Blues" was released at the same time Ritchie Valens' similar "Come On Let's Go" came out, making the subject of influences moot.

There are two versions of the 45 rpm single. First released with an unaltered bass voice with the label notation, "vocal with orchestra," it was updated with echo added to the bass voice, identified by the notation, "voc. with orch." Further, there is a cold ending on the first version; on the second version, the ending fades out.

Remakes: The Princetons 1964; The Outsiders 1966; The Swingin' Apolloes 1967; Blue Cheer 1968; Tyrannosaurus Rex 1970; The Who 1970; Jim Mundy 1977

—

Ritchie Valens "Come On, Let's Go" Del-fi 1958

Style: Rock 'n' roll
Where from: Pacoima, CA
Where recorded: Hollywood, CA

Known as the "Little Richard" of the San Fernando Valley, Ritchie Valens attended schools in both the San Fernando Valley and Norwalk school districts and for a period was assigned to a remedial program, which undervalued his natural songwriting abilities.

It was said Valens rarely sang the same song the same way twice, making up a new style as he went along. About this song, Del-fi owner Bob Keene recalled, "He learned a few songs that had been out like 'Framed' and some of these things by Bo Diddley, which was his idol, but other than that, his own music, he'd sing a little different each time, really."

Valens was befriended as a youth by an equally young Roman Carter, later famous as leader of the blues band, The Carter Brothers. "Ritchie and I were solid friends since I was 11," recalled Carter. "I was on Norris Ave. and he was on Herrick St., and our houses were back-to-back and attached to each other. In 1957, I played against Ritchie in the Battle of the Bands at the recreation center at San Fernando at Recreation Park. He performed as Little Richard Valenzuela. "He used to sing Little Richard songs," said Carter. "Even when he was a kid, Ritchie would come out to play. He had a guitar in a sack. Little Julian Herrera was in our boys' club called The Saints. Julian Herrera and Ritchie Valens were related.

"We had an engagement in Pasadena [one] night," Carter continued. "I sang 'Long Tall Sally,' 'Further Up the Road.'" Ritchie was doing other people's stuff, he had just done his first recording, 'Let's stroll.' Ritchie had his band The Gents he was singing with; Danny Rosales was the key guy on piano and vocals."

Ritchie played lead guitar for The Silhouettes with Conrad Johnson, drums; Peter Medlin, alto sax; Joe Ponce, tenor sax and Gil Rocha, the leader of the Silhouettes, on tenor sax.

Keene recalled when he heard about the "Little Richard of San Fernando" from Doug Maccia, who delivered the Del-fi business cards. He went to a Pacoima theater to catch a show. From that first meeting, Valens was invited to audition and record, though when he showed up with The Silhouettes, Keene told him to lose the band, he wanted only Valens as a vocalist.

Macchia also recalled that the police harassed the band at Keene's Hollywood Hills home. on suspicion of being Mexican. According to Keene, Valens' car was stopped by the L.A.P.D., an officer from which supposedly uttered the memorable, "We don't like too many Mexicans in this area."

With a session band of Earl Palmer on drums, Carol Kaye on guitar, Rene Hall on electric bass, Red Callender on stand-up bass, Ernie Freeman on piano, Valens also on guitar, he sang "Come On, Let's Go" backed with his rhythmic remake of the Robins' "Framed" on-Del-fi.

Clearly, without Valens, Del-fi would not have lasted into 1959. Hall recalled, "When the session started, I would write in the current rock and roll trends. He would inject the Latin and wed the two together in a strange way as if they had been planned together. "He would tell me, 'Rene, you do the American, I'll do the Spanish. We'll be happily married.' I said, 'Good trick if you can do it' and he did."

In early August, "Come On, Let's Go" was a Mexican border and L.A. hit and even charted on R&B station KGFJ, as well as KFWB, where he was known as "Ricky Valance." As Keene noted, "A few weeks after the single charted on Billboard, I discovered a kid who worked at the distributorship was selling Ritchie's record out the back door. I told my distributor about it and he fired the guy. This was to have serious repercussions later on when I found out he was the brother of a radio biggie at KFWB. The kid blamed me for getting him fired and in revenge went to the Valenzuela family telling them I was cheating Ritchie. This would have been impossible since I had no control over the money. I was being financed by Allied Records, who were manufacturing and shipping all Del-fi releases at this time, and Allied received all receipts from any sales of Ritchie's records, or any other Del-fi records in release. Nevertheless, this caused a rift in my relationship with the Valenzuela family."

—

Don and Dewey "Ko Ko Joe" Specialty July 1958

Style: Rhythm and blues
Where from: Pasadena, CA
Where recorded: Hollywood, CA

Composed by Sonny Bono, Don and Dewey's "Ko Ko Joe" featured wild Dewey Terry piano backed with the doo wop-styled "The Letter," the latter much like Little Richard's "Send Me Some Lovin'," as if done by Johnny Ace with group backing. Playing it safe by being wild, that is. "In 1957, nobody knew how to write rock and roll music. The first person I saw doing rock and roll and hired by Art Rupe was Sonny Bono," said Dewey Terry. "I showed him how to write songs. He had no rhyme or reason to know how to write songs. God gave him a good ear and good business and he knew how to treat people… we're talking 1957. He was working for me as an A&R person and go-fer. I'd say, 'Sonny, go get some pop.' Sonny was driving a Ford with a retractable top that didn't retract. We'd go down Sunset to the studio with no top, rain or shine. He worked for Specialty Records; Sonny was assigned to Don and Dewey on a few of these things. He wrote that song 'Ko Ko Joe' also."

Remake: The Righteous Brothers 1963

—

Little Richard "True Fine Mama" Specialty 1958

Style: Rhythm and blues
Where from: Macon, GA
Where recorded: Los Angeles, CA
Original version: Little Julian Herrera 1958
Suggested pairings: The Dominoes "Have Mercy Baby" 1952; Joe Fritz "Honey Honey" 1953; The Cadets "Do You Wanna Rock" 1955

Little Richard used the Upsetters—Clifford Burks, Wilbert Smith and Grady Gaines, tenor sax; Nathaniel Douglas, guitar; Olsie Robinson, bass and Charles Connor, drums—on the relentless piano-backed vocal, "Ooh My Soul" backed with the equally outrageous rocker, "True Fine Mama" with backing by Guitar Slim's band—Lloyd Lambert, baritone sax; Joseph Tillman, sax; Oscar Moore, drums; William Pyles, Renald Richard and Clarence Ford, guitar and vocals by the Chimes—from a 1955 session on Specialty. Little Julian Herrera had already gotten the jump on Little Richard's then-unissued "True Fine Mama."

—

Little Richard "Ooh! My Soul" Specialty 1958

Style: Rhythm and blues
Where from: Macon, GA
Where recorded: Los Angeles, CA
Suggested pairings: Ritchie Valens "Ooh My Head" 1958; Led Zeppelin "Boogie With Stu" 1972

The manically paced flip side to Little Richard's "True Fine Mama," "Ooh My Soul" was turned into "Ooh My Head" by Ritchie Valens, and Led Zeppelin turned "Ooh My Head" into "Boogie With Stu" in 1975.

—

The Big Bopper "Chantilly Lace" D/Mercury July 1958

Style: Rock 'n' roll
From and recorded in: Texas
Original title: "That's What I Like"
Suggested pairing: The Wanderer "The Man In The Phone Booth" 1957

On his first recording, Jiles Perry Richardson cut his name down to Jape Richardson and the Japetts on the local hit, "Beggar To A King." He met Pappy Daily, who changed his name to The Big Bopper for a title originally called "That's What I Like," a B-side for "The Purple People Eater Meets The Witch Doctor," an answer to two #1 novelties, "The Purple People Eater" by Sheb Wooley and "The Witch Doctor" by David Seville, both of which end with the key lyric, "Tequila."

When released on Daily's D label, the spoken one-part phone conversation, "Chantilly Lace," was credited to The Big Bopper, who identified himself as such at the beginning of the record. Richardson was a prominent DJ at KTRM in Beaumont, Texas and was also a prolific songwriter of novelty hits like Johnny Preston's "Running Bear" and George Jones' "White Lightnin'."

Richardson died on tour on February 3, 1959 in the plane crash that also killed Buddy Holly and Ritchie Valens. This day was immortalized in Don McLean's song "American Pie" as "The day the music died."

Answers: Donna Dameron "Bopper 486609" 1959; Jayne Mansfield "That Makes It" 1964; Jive Bunny and the Mastermixers "That's What I Like" 1989
Remakes: Shorty Long 1967; R. Stevie Moore 1980

—

Bob & Earl "Gee Whiz" Class August 16, 1958

Style: Rhythm and blues
From and recorded in: Los Angeles, CA

"Leon Rene wrote the song 'Gee Whiz,'" said Bob & Earl's Earl Nelson. "Bobby and I decided it was a great group sound. The group was David Ford, Bobby Day lead, and Curtis Williams and Nelson background. Curtis left the group in 1959. I split from Bobby Day after 'Buzz Buzz Buzz,' then 'Gee Whiz,' that was the extent of it."

Bob & Earl's best and best-known ballad was this classic "Gee Whiz," dubbed with girl's voices and reissued by Bobby Day in 1960.

Remake: The Innocents 1960; Bobby Day 1960

—

The Miracles "Money" End August 1958

Style: Rhythm and blues vocal group
Where from: Detroit, MI
Where recorded: New York

Veteran Detroit vocalist Marv Johnson said, "The Matadors, The Chimes, were the two names chosen by The Miracles prior to them being The Miracles. As The Matadors and The Chimes, they appeared opposite us a lot in the theaters around town on amateur shows in the Hastings Street area, one of the better known ghetto areas in the City of Detroit. That was the breeding ground for some of the greatest artists ever to hit a stage, including Jackie Wilson."

Claudette Robinson said, "I didn't meet Smokey until he was 14. We came from different parts of town. He's from the north end. I was from the east side of Detroit. His neighborhood was more upscale. I lived in a single family home, we all lived in houses. Blue collar." Claudette and Smokey were married on November 7, 1959. "The idea of not going back to End, we never received any royalties. We had a two-record deal. The check was three dollars for all of us."

—

Duane Eddy "Ramrod" Jamie August 1958

Style: Rock 'n' roll
From and recorded in: Phoenix, AZ
Suggested pairing: Bob Taylor "Thunder" 1959

At 1 min 25 seconds, "Ramrod" was first out by Duane Eddy and his Rock-A-Billies on Ford, owned by Naomi Ford & Lee Hazlewood. Also at this Melrose Avenue, Los Angeles address at that time was Leiber & Stoller's Spark Records (with sales manager Lester Sill) and Quintet Music, and George Motola's Eagle Records and House Of Fortune Music. Hazlewood would have been only newly relocated from Phoenix AZ. Then came the alternate pressing with added instrumentation, a hit on Jamie out of Philly.

—

Donnie Owens "Need You" Guyden 1958

Style: Rock 'n' roll ballad
From and recorded in: Phoenix, AZ
Suggested pairings: Jesse Belvin "Goodnight My Love" 1956; Santo & Johnny "Sleep Walk" 1959; Rosie & the Originals "Angel Baby" 1960

Donnie Owens was a vocalist on this simple, swamp-beat ballad, "Need You," on which Duane Eddy played backing guitar. Owens was also rhythm guitar on many of Eddy's hits. This was an early Arizona release on the older sister label, Guyden, to Eddy's Jamie based in Philadelphia, which had been revived for this purpose.

—

The Zanies "The Blob" Era/Dore 1958

Style: Novelty
From and recorded in: Hollywood, CA

Though "The Blob" by The Five Blobs on Columbia was a national hit, "The Blob" (from the flick of the same name) backed with "Do You Dig Me Mister Pigmy" by the fantasy group called The Zanies with Don Wyatt and possible member Lou Bedell was a hit in L.A., where the Five Blobs did nothing. From the "The Blob" session came The Zanies' "The Mad Scientist" with "Dinner with Drac"-type vocals, a long sax break and all sorts of timely catch phrases like "fearless leader" and "they said it couldn't be done" backed with "She's A Winner" in 1958.

—

The Teddy Bears "To Know Him Is To Love Him" Dore 1958

Style: Pop doo wop
From and recorded in: Hollywood, CA

The Teddy Bears' "To Know Him Is To Love Him" was the first record release involving the talents of legendary producer Phil Spector and lead singer Annette Kleinbard, later known as Carol Connors—also her first recording—and Marshall Lieb. "I was living on Alfred St.," said owner of Dore, Lew Bedell. "I was sunning myself in the backyard, Donnie Kartoon leaned over from upstairs, said, 'Mr. Bedell there's a singing group at our school.'

"They came in to audition the next week. I told them, "We'll go down Friday after school at Gold Star, cut a couple of dubs, just to be a reference disc. They didn't finish one of the songs, wanted to come back Monday to finish." The trio recorded "'Don't You Worry My Little Pet," lifting the sound of Buddy Holly's "Rave On" with Spector on guitar and all three doing a "choo-wadda-wadda" chant. About "To Know Him Is

To Love Him", according to Kleinbard, Spector was so enamored with her delivery ("my voice kept cutting through," she later revealed), he merged two hits, "Teardrops" by Lee Andrews & the Hearts and Jack Scott's "My True Love" with "Red Red Robin," took the title "To Know Him Is To Love Him" from his father's tombstone and snagged The Teddy Bears name from a #1 hit ("Teddy Bear") by Elvis Presley and came up with a #1 hit. "Phil went out to see his father at the graveyard Sunday," said Bedell. "He told me, 'The hell with the other song, let's do this right now.'" At Spector's request, Kleinbard advanced him $10 for the session. With Sandy Nelson on drums. Kleinbard recalled doing the song "on the actual first take with the tape running. After we checked the balance on 'To Know Him Is To Love Him,' I walked out of the studio in 20 minutes—all of us. And that was the only tune that we recorded by itself like that."

"We took them to the courthouse, got them signed up and everything," said Bedell. "We had the hit, Phil came in, he insisted on doing a particular song, later did it on Imperial. He was very haughty, but without airplay he was modest."

Then came DJ support. "Charlie Boone in Fargo put it on. It got Minnesota airplay, they said 'send me 50,' next day, 200, looks good—next day, 18,000 in an area from Omaha to Minneapolis and Fargo. I called Dick Clark, told him, 'This makes it a million seller; it's a one and 1/2 percent area.' I called Philly, told the distributor to take Dick Clark a DJ copy."

—

Ritchie Valens "La Bamba" Del-fi 1958

Style: Rock 'n' roll
Where from: Pacoima, CA
Where recorded: Hollywood, CA
Earlier versions: Metropolitan Qt. "El Jarabe Veracruzano (Wedding In Vera Cruz)" 1904; Juan S. Garrido "The Veracruz Hop (La Bamba)" 1949
Suggested pairings: The Isley Brothers "Twist and Shout" 1962; The Routers "Let's Go" 1962; Jay & the Americans "Come A Little Bit Closer" 1964; The Vibrations "My Girl Sloopy" 1964; Dino, Desi & Billy "I'm A Fool" 1965; Merilee Rush "Angel of the Morning" 1965; The Kingsmen "Long Green" 1965; Wayne Fontana & Mindbenders "Game Of Love" 1965; The Rolling Stones "Get Off My Cloud" 1965; Bob Dylan "Like a Rolling Stone" 1965; Neil Diamond "Cherry Cherry" 1966; Bobby Fuller "I Fought the Law" 1966; The Barbarians "Moulty" 1966; The Monkees "I'm A Believer" 1966; The Troggs "Wild Thing" 1966; Neil Diamond "You Got to Me" 1967; The Music Explosion "A Little Bit Of Soul" 1967; James Brown "I Get the Feeling" 1968

The flip side of "Donna," Ritchie Valens' "La Bamba" was derived of a traditional huapango song of nonsense verses, the meaning of the lyrics often known only to the composer, and to be sung at weddings, was composed by Mariachi Vargas de Tecalitlán, MX. The lyrics to Ritchie Valens' "La Bamba" were changed to match his vocals

Remakes: Trini Lopez 1963; Eddie Cano 1967; Dusty Springfield 1968; The Sandpipers 1968; Neil Diamond 1970; Los Lobos, who took it to #1 in 1987

—

Ritchie Valens "Donna" Del-fi 1958

Style: Rock 'n' roll
Where from: Pacoima, CA
Where recorded: Hollywood, CA

Ritchie Valens' national breakthrough was theisromantic ballad about his girlfriend, Donna Ludwig. The flip side of "La Bamba," Valens' "'Donna' came out when Bob Keane of Del-fi had run out of money," said session player Rene Hall. "His label was on the verge of bankruptcy, he did this in the basement of his home. He was in hopes if he put this out, it could redeem him financially. From his distributors, he got the money, then we went to Gold Star Studios."

Keane recalled, "Just prior to his first U.S. tour, Ritchie called me on the phone to tell me that he had written a song for Donna Ludwig, a girl he liked at San Fernando High. He had even played an early version of it for her over the phone, though the song she heard surely bore little resemblance to the finished version released the next month."

Keane claimed Valens "had only the title and the first line figured out: 'I've got a girl, Donna is her name,' with no structure or lyrics to fill out the rest of the song. I told him to come on in to my studio and we'd work it out." With Hal Blaine on drums, Keene recalled he helped Valens finish the song and taped several versions of Valens singing the song on a portable 601-2 Ampex, with Ritchie accompanying himself on his guitar. By feeding one track to the other on the Ampex and developing a delay in the signal, Keane created echo and a reverb to Ritchie's voice. "I had never heard of this being done before, but I discovered it by looking for new sounds, even though my equipment was limited. I called this effect 'Delphonic Sound.'"

With early play on both border radio Mighty 690 and KFWB, "Donna" backed with "La Bamba" took off immediately and was on the charts when Valens died in a plane crash in Clear Lake, IA with Buddy Holly and The Big Bopper on February 3, 1959.

Answer: "Lost Without You" by Donna—Donna Ludwig, Ritchie's girlfriend, released on Huggy Boy's Pop label—1959

—

Eugene Church & the Fellows "Pretty Girls Everywhere" Class 1958

Style: Rhythm and blues
Where from: St. Louis, MO
Where recorded: Hollywood, CA
Suggested pairing: Jesse Belvin "Deacon Dan Tucker" 1958

"Pretty Girls Everywhere" by Eugene Church & the Fellows was released in late summer, but impacted local radio in the midwinter months. According to Church, "Tommy Williams, Buster and myself, we were rooming on Cochran Ave. We were just leaving the house, Buster was driving, and I was sitting on the passenger side, it was one of the first hot days of summertime, and everywhere we looked young ladies were stepping out in shorts, bikinis, little or nothing on and bro would tell me, 'Hey bro man, check this lady.' One lady walked by the car, I sang, 'everywhere I go I see a pretty girl,' she went on and she blushed, you should have seen her. 'Man that's a good idea for a tune,' that's how it was conceived.

"I brought the guitar home, playing the riff on it," Church continued. "After we had done the tune, we took the tune up to Bobby Day, told him I needed a record company. Bobby Day was right around the corner, Bobby said, 'Nobody should do this tune but you.' I took it to him; I was hoping he would say 'nobody but you.' He took us to Leon Rene's and that's where we recorded 'Pretty Girls Everywhere.'"

Lead singer Church and first tenor Tommy Williams used The Turks—Gaynel Hodge, tenor and Alex Hodge, baritone, and possibly Jesse Belvin, bass—on the session. "I always try to carry the sound," said Church. "I kept the Fellows with me most of the time. Richard Berry had a group named the Dreamers on 'Pretty Girls'" singing the "ahhhh" part.

"None of it was improvised," said Church. "I had the idea exactly what I was going to do before I got there; I always go over my songs, even the things that sound like they might be adlibbed, I throw them in, they're pre-planned, I know where they're going to hit. You might hit a lick, if you get what you call the spirit in a session, if that hits, you might add that. Actually that was well rehearsed. We took three or four takes. We was all live, include[d] all mistakes, the musicians, the singers."

"Pretty Girls Everywhere" broke first and big in the Bay Area in November, then nationally and in L.A. specifically in three months and Tijuana four months later. "It took a little while to break. It broke in the South, then in New York. I think it broke back East before it broke out here. When it broke, it stayed on the charts for eight months," said Church.

Remakes: Jimmie Cross 1961; Arthur Alexander 1963; The Walker Brothers 1964; The Chambers Brothers 1966

—

The Shadows "Under the Stars Of Love" Del-fi September 1958

Style: Latino doo wop
Where from: Wilmington, CA
Where recorded: Hollywood, CA

Brothers Jimmy Carlos and Pete Antoniano grew up in the harbor area town of Wilmington. "I went to Banning High School, then moved to Long Beach in '52," said Jimmy Carlos. "We were doing a lot of gigs for car clubs, we needed a name and picked a name that went with the era. We sang under the name The Shadows. Just sounded good.

"Pete entered a talent show at Wilmington Jr. High," Carlos continued. "He won it. We learned two songs and went to a talent show at a rented hall in Belmont Shore in Long Beach, won first place. The Debonaires invited us to a teen center at California Avenue and we competed against another group. We started performing for the Pharaohs Car Club, which I belonged to. Another car club offered us money, from there to another car club; we did a lot of things for the school, prom and stuff.

"We were listening to rhythm and blues groups, lot of the duets at the time. Some girls knew Hal Zeigler and the Red Cat (Red Gilson) who called us. They told us to come to El Monte Legion Stadium on Friday night. Ritchie Valens and Mondo & the Chili Peppers were headlining. We had a real quick rehearsal and sang two numbers. Red Cat told us to do a tape, 'Drop it off at my office, I'll see what I can do.'

"Ritchie said, 'You guys want to make records? Give me your telephone number. I'll talk to my manager,' Sunday we're home, Bob Keene called and told us, 'Come to my place on Silverlake and we'll audition.' I was 17; Pete was about 15. On the first session were some studio musicians. Rene Hall, guitar, he was on all our sessions. We did all our recording sessions in a one-week period of time," recording this doo wop ballad, "Under the Stars Of Love," backed with the uptempo "Jungle Fever" as The Shadows on Del-fi. "It came out in just a couple of days after the session" in September 1958.

"We were compared to The Five Satins by a guy at KFWB," Ritchie added. "We could not get airplay. Because we were called The Shadows, they thought we were black." So they changed their name to The Carlos Brothers.

—

The Flamingos "Lovers Never Say Goodbye" End October 1958

Style: Doo wop
Where from: Chicago, IL
Where recorded: New York, NY
Original title: "Please Wait for Me"

In 1956, The Flamingoes left Chess/Checker and signed with the mainstream Decca label, which proved to be a poor fit. "The Decca label was putting our records out, but Nate Nelson was still under contract to Chess in Chicago," recalled the Flamingoes' Terry Johnson. "We were expecting Decca to buy his contract out, we won our release. While we were waiting for Nate's contract run out, [we] ran into Richard Barrett at End Records.

When he got to End, George wanted us to fall into The Platters' style. George Goldner had a gambling habit, he would use our royalty money, the Chantels', Little Anthony & the Imperials' royalty money, so George sold the label to Morris Levy. Morris was backing him, George lost the company, so he had to join Morris Levy."

When The Flamingoes recorded this song first released as "Please Wait for Me," Johnson recalled, "George was rushing, because we sang 'Please Wait For Me'—George told us to call it 'Please Wait for Me.' We told him, 'No,' it was 'Lovers Never Say Goodbye.' George was mad because it was extra expense." A few copies with the "Please Wait For Me" title were released before the title change.

"I wrote the song, shared it with Paul Wilson, my best buddy at the time. It was about this young lady I fell in love with. We'd see each other every day, we were 19 or 20. She had to go to Europe, to go to a college her parents wanted her to go to, she was crying: 'I don't want to go, I don't want to say goodbye.' I said, 'Lovers never say goodbye. Ooh that stuck in my head. I said just say so long, because 'lovers never say goodbye, I went to the hotel, took my guitar, just used those words, came up with the chord structure."

—

Jackie Wilson "Lonely Teardrops" Brunswick October 1958

Style: Rhythm and blues/soul
Where from: Detroit, MI
Where recorded: New York
Suggested pairing: The Isley Brothers "Shout" 1959

After Jackie Wilson replaced Clyde McPhatter in The Dominoes, he went on his own as an important inventor of soul. Wilson's first two hits, the uptempo "Reet Petite" and the ballad "To Be Loved" as well as this rocking "Lonely Teardrops," which with its "say you will" refrain influenced "Shout" by The Isley Brothers, were written by Berry Gordy Jr., who parlayed his "Lonely Teardrops" profits to start his Motown empire in 1959.

Lamont Dozier of Holland-Dozier-Holland recalled, "Berry Gordy Jr. and Tyrone Carlo, at the time, we called Billy Davis, was part writer and assisted Gwen Gordy and helped write 'Lonely Teardrops.' All in all, we all came from very meager beginnings in Detroit and it was like a family affair. Everybody sung because there wasn't that much to do in Detroit." Mixed in that family affair was singer Marv Johnson, who was used to record demos at the time.

"'Lonely Teardrops' was one of the tunes Berry Gordy decided to send to Jackie. By us being around and able to sing and put it together, we were used on the demo," said Johnson, who had connections with one of the first black DJ's in Detroit, Senator Bristow Bryant. "He had a studio located on Alexandria Street. He allowed us to use his recording equipment to record a lot of our publishing tunes we were taking in. I would sing on a lot of things, we had all kinds of songs coming in from everywhere. We would send demos to New York."

Johnson continued, "In fact, the Jackie Wilson song, 'Lonely Teardrops' was picked up in Detroit by Jackie's Manager, Nat Tarnapol from New York. Eddie Holland, Robert Bateman and myself and a few others would just pitch in a make the demo. Eddie Holland had somewhat of a Jackie Wilson sound in his voice, he used to do a lot of Jackie Wilson material on talent day, we recorded the demo for 'Lonely Teardrops.' It was a group sound, somewhat slower than the arrangement eventually released. We did the initial idea with the melody intact as it was, the only [thing] we did was the 'shoodoowops' which gave the New York people ideas for arrangements."

It's been said that Dick Jacobs, the song's arranger, assigned the bass part to a tuba, so the low end could be heard over AM radio.

—

Cookie and His Cupcakes "Mathilda " Khourys/Judd October 1958

Style: Swamp rock
From and recorded in: Lake Charles, LA

Cookie and His Cupcakes, the first so-called swamp rock band to chart nationally, was an extension of The Boogie Ramblers with an additional tenor sax player/vocalist, Cookie, Huey "Cookie" Thierry—with Shelton Dunaway, sax and vocals; Sidney "Hot Rod" Reynaud, tenor sax; Marshall LeDee, guitar; Ernest Jacobs, piano; Joe "Blue" Landry, bass and Ivory Jackson, drums—debuted with "Mathilda." Said Thierry, "The title was not 'Mathilda.' I sang 'but still I cried and cried for you,' but they thought I sang 'Mathilda,' what they put on the label. I didn't know anybody named Mathilda, a white woman who lived on a hill, and I wasn't singing about her."

—

Elvis Presley "One Night" RCA October 1958

Style: Rock 'n' roll
Where from: Tupleo, MS
Where recorded: Los Angeles, CA
Original version: Smiley Lewis 1956

This grinding ballad of New Orleans-based Smiley Lewis original, Elvis Presley's "One Night" turned Lewis' ballad of regret into a demand for pleasure by changing one lyric: Lewis' "one night of sin is what I'm now paying for" became Elvis' "one night with you is what I'm now praying for." It was a big hit. Then Elvis went into the army.

Remakes: Fats Domino 1960; Roy Head 1976

—

Bill Parsons "All-American Boy" Fraternity October 1958

Style: Rock 'n' roll
Where from: Coalton, OH
Where recorded: King Records, Cincinnati, OH

This was a vocal by country crooner Bobby Bare, who had fallen in with Bill Parsons, an old friend from Coalton, Ohio, who was trying to get on a record. Parsons, who had just come back from army service in Germany, and Orville Lunsford had penned "All-American Boy," a thinly disguised talking blues about Elvis' fame and his military induction. Parsons asked Bare to perform the drawling first-person narrative on "All-American Boy" while Parsons himself delivered the vocal on the flip side, "Rubber Dolly," derived from an older folk song.

The Fraternity label purchased the masters, assigning full credit on both songs to Parsons. Bare was himself inducted, thus was unaware of this gaffe, which continued on for the life of the record to this very date.

—

James Brown and the Famous Flames "Try Me" Federal 1958

Style: Rhythm and blues
Where from: Macon, GA
Where recorded: Beltone Studios, New York, NY
Suggested pairing: Jerry Butler and the Impressions "For Your Precious Love" 1958

A smoothly pleading blues tune—with George Dorsey, alto sax; Clifford Scott, tenor sax; Ernie Hayes, piano; Kenny Burrell, guitar; Carl Pruitt, bass and "Panama" Francis, drums—James Brown and the Famous Flames—Johnny Terry, Bill Hollings, J.W. Archer and Louis Madison—hit big with "Try Me."

After nine records in a row failed to chart, with the exception of Johnny Terry, The Famous Flames essentially broke up, with new members added from Little Richard's backing band. There was talk about Brown being dropped from his label because of his hit drought since he last struck gold with "Please Please Please" in early 1956.

Brown later said he patterned "Try Me" after "For Your Precious Love" by Jerry Butler and the Impressions. After "Try Me" hit, Brown was able to assemble a new Famous Flames with several of the original members.

"Try Me" was such a success that Brown started the Try Me label, which among others, featured early work of Brown's girl singer, Tammy Montgomery, later Tammi Terrell, on "I Cried" in 1963.

Remake: James Brown, an instrumental version, 1965

—

LaVern Baker "I Cried a Tear" Atlantic 1958

Style: Rhythm and blues
Where from: Detroit, MI
Where recorded: New York
Suggested pairing: Chuck Willis "What Am I Living For" 1958

With a stroll beat by LaVern Baker, "I Cried a Tear" was a surprise hit for this chanteuse, really a duet with the saxophone of King Curtis.

—

The Crests "16 Candles" Coed 1958

Style: Doo wop
From and recorded in: New York
Original title: "21 Candles"

In 1955, The Crests were a black group with Patricia Van Dross, Harold Torres, Talmadge (Tommy) Gough and J.T. Carter, formed at Manhattan's P.S. 160 Junior High School. With the addition of lead singer Johnny Maestro, the Crests became an integrated group.

While singing on the Brooklyn Bridge subway station, the wife of orchestra leader Al Browne, who had backed up The Heartbeats, gave them her card.

With the Browne Orchestra, The Crests recorded the ballad "Sweetest One," which hit the charts in Boston in August 1957. Singer/songwriter/arranger Billy Dawn Smith brought them to music publisher George Paxton, who had just founded Coed Records. Patricia Van Dross, sister of soul singer Luther Vandross, was a 15-year old girl and not allowed to travel, so she had to drop out.

The Crests recorded the fine uptempo "Pretty Little Angel," which charted in Buffalo in March 1958. Their next was the ballad "Beside You," which had harmony, but little else going for it. When Alan Freed and Dick Clark flipped it over, they jumped on an evocative birthday song, "16 Candles," at first called "21 Candles," until marketing geniuses figured it was smart to go after the teenage audience. Charting in late November on New York's WMGM, "16 Candles" hit #2, as it did on L.A.'s KFWB in January and as it did on the national charts in February 1959.

Years later, Maestro founded the musical group The Brooklyn Bridge, perhaps in honor of the subway station where they were discovered.

—

Jim Bobo/Hank Mizell "Jungle Rock" EKO November 1958/King August 1959

Style: Rockabilly
Where from: Daytona Beach, FL
Where recorded: Chicago, IL

A rockabilly classic, "Jungle Rock" was first credited by mistake to Hank Mizzell's guitar player, Jim Bobo, while on the Chicago-based EKO label. This was corrected when reissued on King with the proper Hank Mizzell credit.

About "a jungle drummer doing a knocked-out beat," this recording is one of the most sought-after singles by the small legion of pure rockabilly collectors and stands alone as one of the final releases in this genre, while rock 'n' roll was quickly being swallowed by much more pop fare.

—

Lloyd Price "Stagger Lee" ABC/Paramount November 1958

Style: Rhythm and blues
Where from: New Orleans. LA
Where recorded: New York
Suggested pairings: Ma Rainey "Stack O'Lee Blues" 1926; Furry Lewis "Billy Lyons & Stack O'Lee" 1927; Mississippi John Hurt "Stack O'Lee Blues" 1929; Cab Calloway "Stack O'Lee Blues" 1932; Archibald "Stack-A-Lee " 1950; Tennessee Ernie Ford "Stack-O-Lee" 1951

Taken from the folk classic "Stack O'Lee Blues," Lloyd Price's "Stagger Lee" was a rollicking tale of shooting dice and murder by shooting, a best-selling version with "raunchy" lyrics, that had the ending changed by Dick Clark to play on national TV. Even though a violence-free version was created, it was not available on 45 at the time. "Stagger Lee" became the first censored song to reach #1.

According to Price, "Stagger Lee" was a bit he did in the army from his memories of the original song, a New Orleans standard, which he recorded as the record company needed a B-side for the expected hit, "You Need Love."

Parody: Spencer & Spencer "Stagger Lawrence" 1959
Remakes: P.J. Proby as "Stagger Lee" 1965; Ike & Tina Turner as "Stagger Lee & Billy" 1965; Wilson Pickett as "Stag-O-Lee" 1967; Pacific Gas & Electric as "Stag-O-Lee" 1970; Tommy Roe as "Stagger Lee" 1971; Dr. John as "Stack-A-Lee" 1972; The Grateful Dead as "Stagger Lee" 1978

Note: In 1973, a so-called "Bandstand version" of Lloyd Price's "Stagger Lee" was reissued on the ABC/Goldies label, then reissued in 1981 on MCA, with milder lyrics, sans the shooting and other references to violence, reduced to an argument and hurt feelings.

—

Eddie Cochran "C'mon Everybody" Liberty November 24, 1958

Style: Rock 'n' roll
Where from: Bell Gardens, CA
Where recorded: Hollywood, CA
Original title: "Let's Get Together"
Suggested pairing: Dave Dudley "Six Days On the Road" 1963; The Ramones "Suzy Is A Headbanger" 1977

On the heels of "Summertime Blues," Eddie Cochran—with Guybo Smith on electric bass, Earl Palmer on drums, Ray Johnson on piano and Cochran on vocal and guitar and maybe Capehart on tambourine—went with "Let's Get Together." Feeling the song wasn't dynamic enough. Eddie and his manager Jerry Capehart re-titled it with a new backing track using stops at the end of each verse to emphasize the song's new title, making "C'mon Everybody" Eddie Cochran's second most major local and national hit.

—

The Skyliners "Since I Don't Have You" Calico December 1958/Original Sound 1963

Style: Doo wop
Where from: Pittsburgh, PA
Where recorded: New York City, NY

Pittsburgh record distributor Joe Rock, at age 22, despondent over a recent breakup with his girlfriend Mercedes, who had decided to attend stewardess school in Oklahoma, was out driving around one night. At every stoplight, he wrote additional lyrics to his song of depression. With a melody he had created, Rock shopped a demo around to several record companies and was told the title was too negative.

Signing members of two groups, The Crescents led by Jimmy Beaumont and Janet Vogel of the El Rios, Rock put together the Calico label financed by a group of investors to record and release "Since I Don't

Have You." Rock booked time at Capitol Records' New York studio in December 1958, with a full string arrangement played by jazz stalwarts like Doc Severinson on trumpet, later the band leader on the Tonight Show, with Al Caiola, guitar; Trummie Young, trombone; George Auld, tenor sax, supplementing eight violinists from the New York Philharmonic Orchestra. It has been noted that instead of supplementing the vocal harmony, the strings actually became part of the harmony, dramatically finished with Janet Vogel's high soprano ad-libbed "You-ooo-ooo-ooo-ooo-ooo-ooo-ooooo!" thirteen yous in all, creating one of the first doo wop songs to use violins and clarinets in the background.

Needing a name for the group, Rock advocated for the title of one of his favorite songs, "Skyliner," a hit for saxophonist Charlie Barnet in 1945, and made The Skyliners name official. The Skyliners' "Since I Don't Have You" hit #1 on hometown KQV in January 1959, in March it went to #1 on WMGM in New York City, #2 on KFWB in L.A. and top 20 nationally.

—

The Jades "So Blue" Time December 1958

Style: Doo wop
Where from: Long Island, NY
Where recorded: New York

Originally called the Shades, The Jades were a Freeport High School vocal group with Lou Reed, rhythm guitar and background; Alan Walters, bass; Phil Harris, vocals "and held onto the guitar mostly for looks." Harris recalled, "The Jades wasn't a band, it was just one guitar and two other guys singing. I was in the background. I wrote the stuff, I didn't sing it. We would play shopping malls and some really bad violent places. I was always, like, tremendously underage, which was pretty cool.

"Lou and I met while we were in high school in our senior year," Harris continued. "We were in many of the same classes together and quite a few times we went over to his house to hang out. I don't think that we met prior to our senior year, but we were probably in some of the same classes together without realizing it. We were both interested in music and most of the "in" bands and groups of the time.

Harris added, "In our senior year, there was a variety show that the school puts on. Lou, another friend named Al Walters, and myself decided to get together to do a "Little Richard" act for the show. I sang lead. Lou and Al Walters sang background and Lou also played guitar. The skit was very successful based on the applause. After that show, the three of us decided to get together and try and come up with some songs that we could all participate in.

"One evening," Harris said, "at Lou's house, we started fooling around with some lyrics and during that evening, both "So Blue" and "Leave Her for Me" were written. In those days, it didn't take much imagination to come up with something that required great lyric development skills. You just thought of an experience that you might have gone through, and write it down."

Harris said, "When we got to the recording session, Bob Shad had gathered some musicians just for the recordings. King Curtis was part of that band. There was a piano player and drummer. Curtis can be heard on the intro to "So Blue" and throughout the song, and also on "Leave Her for Me."

Lou Reed said, "Our lead singer had to stand on a box so he could reach the microphone, 'cause they had a very big black guy singing the harmony parts with the rest of us. I'll always remember he was huge, and he had a giant mound of snot hanging out of his nose and we were too afraid to tell him."

Harris said, "We were still in school. We'd open supermarkets, shopping centers, things like that. The outfits we wore were classics of the '50s. Shades, peg pants, string ties, and jackets with glitter on them. It was what was called style; later on people would call it punk but at that time what we meant by punk was a pusher, y'know.

Harris noted, "Lou says that he got royalties of $.78. If that's so, he owes me $.26."

—

The Queen "Honky Tonky" Mercury December 1958
Style: Rhythm and blues
Where from: Tuscaloosa, AL
Where recorded: Chicago, IL

The Queen was a pseudonym for jazz and blues vocalist Dinah Washington, who was noted for her ballad style. The pseudonym was needed to keep jazz fans in the dark over this R&B release. The Queen's uptempo R&B rocker "Honky Tonky" was also recorded by The Drifters on an album only.

—

The Bell Notes "I've Had It" Time 1958
Style: Rock 'n' roll
Where from: Long Island, NY
Where recorded: New York

In 1957, saxophonist Carl Bonura and pianist Pete Kane of East Meadow High in Long Island and recently-graduated Ray Ceroni of Levittown were joined by bassist Lenny Giambalvo and drummer John Casey from West Hempstead to form The Bell Notes. Their debut, "I've Had It," kicked off with maracas, then the notes of Ceroni's guitar as he bent his way down the neck, creating an off-key yet intended effect. He wasn't the first to try this, for years axe men had obsessed over the sound of the record—over ways to incorporate such rebellious maneuvers into their own music with lyrics that convey a sense of being trapped and loving it.

Back on Long Island, DJ Alan Fredericks of the "Night Train" show on WGBB radio contacted Bob Shad, who signed them to his brand new Time label. In mid-December, "I've Had It" charted #6 on New York's WMGM, #5 on L.A.'s KFWB, and #4 on pop charts in late January '59.

—

Annette with the Afterbeats "Tall Paul" Disneyland December 1958
Style: Pop
Where from: Utica, NY
Where recorded: Hollywood, CA

Annette's march of a half dozen stiffs from '57 through '58 was cleanly broken at age 17 as Annette with the Afterbeats' scored on "Tall Paul," reputedly about her height-challenged pal, teen idol Paul Anka, backed with "Ma He's Making Eyes At Me" on Disneyland.

Annette was the first Mousketeer with a hit record, charting pop in the first week of 1959. It charted early in Buffalo, near her Utica hometown, though not convincingly in any market.

—

The Royaltones "Poor Boy" Jubilee 1958
Style: Rock 'n' roll instrumental
From and recorded in: Detroit, MI

Tenor sax player George Katsakis supplied the "laughing sax" for this Royaltones' instrumental rocking hit, "Poor Boy." The band, which also backed rocker Jack Scott on "My True Love" and the flip, "Leroy," also hit with the more rocking "Flamingo Express" in 1961, at a time they were also backing Del Shannon on some of his hits.

—

Hank Ballard & the Midnighters "The Twist" King December 1958

Style: Rhythm and blues vocal group
Where from: Detroit , MI
Where recorded: King Records studio, Cincinnati, OH
Suggested pairings: Clyde McPhatter & the Drifters "What'cha Gonna Do" 1955; The Midnighters "Is Your Love For Real" 1955

Ballard based "The Twist" on the on-stage dance The Midnighters did with one leg lifted. He said, "What inspired me, we were in Miami for a rehearsal, getting ready for a gig and The Midnighters were going through a routine, twisting their bodies. The title just came to me, that title sounds commercial, 'The Twist.' Once you get a title going for you, everything falls in place.

Ballard continued, "The 1955 hit, "What'cha Gonna Do" by Clyde McPhatter & the Drifters "inspired me to write 'The Twist.' I wrote it around his melody. Everybody was stealing from everybody, borrowing, yeah, borrowing. You hear a melody and you write around it. Don't break the law, bend it."

King Records made it the B-side of "Teardrops On Your Letter," a #16 R&B hit in the spring of 1959. "I couldn't convince the company 'The Twist' was the side," said Ballard. "They said 'Teardrops On Your Letter.' We had a little confrontation."

When Ballard first heard Chubby Checker's version, he thought it was his. Ballard made a deal with Dick Clark over "The Twist" that his next two 45s, "Finger Poppin' Time" and "Let's Go, Let's Go, Let's Go" got plugged on his show and thus became hits.

When Chubby's cover of the "The Twist" went #1 in 1960 and 1961, Ballard's King label made a deal with Times Square Records in New York City, which was ordering new pressings of oldies to satisfy the rage for older classic R&B and doo wop sides, causing Ballard's original to be reissued. Thus, Hank Ballard & the Midnighters' "The Twist" came out with two different versions, as the custom press for Times Square Records was a different take. "You can hear that baritone sax growling, that wasn't on the original cut. They added a couple of horns, plus a baritone sax," said Ballard. Then there was the false ending. "That was Ralph Bass' idea. It worked." It rated highly because, well, it was the Twist.

Remake: Chubby Checker 1961

The version by Ballard charted on KFXM, Riverside in December 1961 and #28 pop, but was badly beaten by Checker, thanks to Dick Clark's influential American Bandstand.

—

Frankie Avalon "Venus" Chancellor January 1959

Style: Pop
Where from: Philadelphia, PA
Where recorded: New York

Written for crooner Al Martino, who turned it down, Frankie Avalon, without holding his nose, managed his first #1 hit, this altered cha cha "Venus" on which the Philly vocal group, The Four Dates, sang back-up, as they had also done for Fabian.

—

Marv Johnson "Come To Me" Tamla/United Artists January 21, 1959

Style: Rhythm and blues
From and recorded in: Detroit, MI
Suggested pairing: Jimmy Jones "Handyman" 1959

On January 12, 1959, when Berry Gordy Jr. started Tamla Records with an $800 loan from his family and royalties earned writing for Jackie Wilson, Gordy originally wanted to name the label Tammy Records, after the hit song popularized by Debbie Reynolds from the 1957 film Tammy and the Bachelor. When he found the name was already in use, Berry decided on Tamla instead.

Tamla's first release, in the Detroit area, was Marv Johnson's "Come to Me" in 1959. "I was working in the 12th Street area of Detroit in a record shop," said Johnson. "'Come To Me' is a song written by myself and later in the production, I received quite a bit of help from Berry Gordy Jr. and his wife Raynoma, the mother of Motown. They would come in, shopping for music. The store had a piano, I was playing on a piano, working on some material because I was very much involved in music and wanted to advance myself if possible. He heard me rehearsing a young girls' group I had in the neighborhood. He asked me if I would come around to his apartment on Gladstone Street and play some music for him. I said I'd be happy to because I knew that was Berry Gordy Jr. and he was already doing good in his own right.

Johnson continued, "That same evening, I came around and played four or five songs for him, one of which was 'Come To Me.' He selected 'Come To Me' right away as something that would sound very commercial and something that fit the mode of the music. I came around several evenings after that to rehearse the tune, to go over it and put it together for recording."

Vocal backing was by the Rayber voices, "At this time, we had molded them down to a specific group, Robert Bateman, Briant Holland, Gwendolyn Murray and Raynoma, Berry's wife," Johnson explained. The distinctive flute sound was by Beans Bowes, "one of the noted Detroit musicians locally. He was with Bill Doggett's band and used to play a lot at the Flame Show Bar here in Detroit. Beans played baritone sax and flute and he did arrange 'Come to Me' too. It was selected as the first tune to be recorded by Berry for his company, which was Tamla at the time." Gordy then leased the master to United Artists as well as Johnson's contract.

Johnson then made the claim that Jimmy Jones' major hit, "Handyman" on Cub "was an effort on the part of East Coast people to copy us."

Remakes: Frances Burnett 1959; Mary Wells 1961; Thelma Houston 1978

—

The Falcons "You're So Fine" Flick/Unart January 1959

Style: Rhythm and blues vocal group
From and recorded in: Detroit, MI

Falcons' member Eddie Floyd recalled, "We did that session at a radio station with Senator Bristow Bryant, he was a gospel DJ. He had a little two tracks, we went in after hours and recorded that in a studio. Lance Finnie was guitar player. Lance always liked to hear Hank Ballard & the Midnighters with that little sound he had, it kind of worked together with Joe Stubbs and his voice."

Floyd added, "We didn't have a bass at that session, the bass player didn't show up. They had to take a guitar and tune it down and that was that really funny sound heard, a guitar trying to play bass. You might have thought it was lead, but it was another guitar trying to play bass."

—

Frankie Ford "Sea Cruise" Ace February 1959

Style: Rock 'n' roll
Where from: Gretna, LA
Where recorded: New Orleans, LA

At 18, Frankie Guzzo began playing in the clubs and met Joe Caronna, a local record hustler who became his manager and introduced him to Johnny Vincent at Ace's headquarters in Jackson, Mississippi. Vincent dubbed him Frankie Ford and booked him into Cosimo Matassa's New Orleans studio where he cut his first record, "Cheatin' Woman," with Huey Smith, piano; Alvin "Red" Tyler, sax and Frank Fields, bass.

The next single was "Roberta," with Ford's vocals dubbed over Huey "Piano" Smith and the Clowns' original backing track. For a flip-side, Huey brought in "Sea Cruise," which he wanted to record for himself. Vincent had Ford's vocals similarly dubbed over the original Clowns' track, with clanging bell and big foghorn sound effects added to the hot sax, piano and drums.

Local stations played around with it, but when WLAC in Nashville hit it heavy the record took off, landing Frankie on Dick Clark's American Bandstand.

Remakes: Mickie Most 1963; Herman's Hermits 1965; Ace Cannon 1966; Freddy Cannon 1968; Johnny Rivers 1971; Sha Na Na 1972; John Fogerty 1975; Robert Gordon with Link Wray 1978; Billy "Crash" Craddock 1980

—

The Fiestas "So Fine" Old Town February 1959

Style: Rhythm and blues vocal group
Where from: Newark, NJ
Where recorded: New York City, NY
Original version: The Sheiks 1955

"So Fine" was originally by The Sheiks with lead singer Jesse Belvin, writer's credit and produced by Johnny Otis on Federal from 1955. "So Fine" was rendered in unusual sing-a-long style as the first release by the Newark-based Fiestas—lead singer Tommy Bullock, tenor Eddie Morris, baritone Sam Ingalls and bass Preston Lane—who were often confused with The Falcons who recorded "You're So Fine" in 1959. When "So Fine" hit, Otis filed suit as J. Gribble, The Fiestas' manager got writer credit. "I wrote 'So Fine' and we recorded it not once but twice, with Mel Williams, Jesse Belvin and Harold Lewis, and it didn't do much," said Otis. "Years later, suddenly comes out a record on the Old Town label by The Fiestas and it's our record but they credited a songwriter named J. Gribble. So I called them and said, 'Man you got my song.' He said, 'Meet me in court,' and we did and that's the end of that. We won, we had a copyright dated a year before they claimed they wrote it."

Jesse Belvin, who was touring the area on "Guess Who," was called by Old Town's defense to testify he wrote the song, arguably correct, creating a chasm between Belvin and Otis from then on. Otis won as he had the paper copyright.

The Fiestas' version of "So Fine" was issued twice, first with a distinct piano intro; the second time with the group unison vocals at the start.

Remakes: The Hollywood Argyles 1960; The Santells 1964; The Premiers 1964; The Green Men 1964; The Hideaways 1965; The Corvets 1965; Paul Revere & the Raiders 1966; Dale & Grace 1967; Newbeats 1967; The Edgewoods 1967; Ike and Tina Turner 1968; The Stone Poneys 1968; The Elvin Bishop Group 1970; The Oak Ridge Boys 1982

—

Jesse Belvin "Guess Who" RCA February 1959

Style: Rhythm and blues
Where from: Texas
Where recorded: Hollywood, CA

In early 1959, Jesse Belvin's most major hit, "Guess Who," was out on RCA. "I would say 99 percent of Jesse's sound after he came with RCA was his own creation," said Belvin's RCA producer Shorty Rogers. "There was no attempt to change his sound. 'Guess Who' was one of the well known songs of Jesse's career. For the whole concept, Jesse needed someone to put it on paper for the vocal group parts. I didn't dream that up. Jesse did. 'I'd like to do this do you think it'll work?'"

The "Guess Who" session singers "were all friends of Jesse," Belvin continued. "He would bring them into the session, Gaynel Hodge and Gaynel's brother Alex Hodge, Obie Jesse, I think Gene Church would've been there too and Buster Williams. It was a great session. I rehearsed it with Jesse quite a bit. He had great input on the session. The things I put on paper were a collaboration between Jesse and me. I welcomed his thoughts they were good and valid. It went smooth because we had this preparation; they were ready to go, just a real happy deal."

On April 30, 1959, KGFJ's Big Jim Randolph wrote in the California Eagle, "In today's market, very few of the soft ballads sneak through, but recently a young man by the name of Johnny Mathis has had the appeal that is attractive to teenagers and adults. Well, he has just recently broken through with another one of the big hits in the country, 'Someone.' It should also be called the greatest steal in 1959. Columbia has come up with a tune that closely resembles the original. Once again, Mr. Mathis is up and running to the races. His interpretation of the song is superb. It's just unfortunate that he and Jesse Belvin must sing two songs that so closely resemble each other. We would like to wish them both luck, and, again, Johnny Mathis is out in front. For Jesse Belvin let us add that his version of "Guess Who" is like money in the bank."

—

Dale Hawkins "Class Cutter" Checker February 1959

Style: Rock 'n' roll
Where from: Louisiana
Where recorded: Chicago, IL

"That's me on the record," said Dells' bass singer, Chuck Barksdale of this rocking, juvenile delinquent hit, "Class Cutter" by Dale Hawkins. "I think it got $50 to come in. It's just me" singing lines like "when he heard the bell ring, he'd run the other way" with a nice sax break and other voices doing "yeah yeah yeah." At the end, Barksdale adds, "he thought he was cool, but he was only a fool."

—

Bobby Rydell "Please Don't Be Mad" Cameo February 1959

Style: Doo wop
From and recorded in: Philadelphia, PA

Bobby Rydell was an unknown commodity, having recorded two sides the very childish nonsense lyrics, "Fatty Fatty" and the marginally better "Happy Happy" with some Frankie Avalon yelps, just previous to this strong doo wop vocal, "Please Don't Be Mad," his very first on Cameo, his label of greatest success. On "Please Don't Be Mad," Rydell recalled the back-up vocal group was the Applejacks.

—

Bo Diddley "I'm Sorry" Checker February 1959

Style: Rhythm and blues
Where from: Mississippi
Where recorded: Chicago, IL
Suggested pairing: The Moonglows "Sincerely" 1955

"The Carnations were from Cleveland," said Harvey Fuqua of The Moonglows. "We were all one big family there, diversification, whatever you want to call it, everybody was there, buddies. Let's try this. That was the Moonglows in the background, we were singing background on that. We just sort of wanted to have the essence of 'Sincerely' in the background."

However, there was no consensus of the backing group on Bo Diddley's giant doo wop ballad fave, "I'm Sorry." "We used me, Johnny Keyes," said Johnny Keyes of the Magnificents. "L.C. Cooke and a guy out of the pool room."

—

Don and Dewey "Big Boy Pete" Specialty February 1959
Style: Rhythm and blues
Where from: Pasadena, CA
Where recorded: Hollywood, CA

Dewey Terry said, "We wrote 'Big Boy Pete' while traveling. We went to Seattle with guitarist Jimmy Nolen. They were shooting dice next door in the hotel." In Don and Dewey's version, "Pete gets cut right up in the midsection. Ernie Freeman did the arrangements on that tune and that's why it turned out more orchestrated than it was originally meant to... with a big eighteen piece band. Trial and error. That was an error. Effie Smith and John Criner had The Olympics. Both The Olympics and Don and Dewey were rehearsing at the house. They got our 'Big Boy Pete,' redid our tune and came out with it. We didn't do bad on the record, but we could've done better if it had been in the rock field."

Remake: The Olympics 1959

—

Don and Dewey "Farmer John" Specialty February 1959
Style: Rhythm and blues
Where from: Pasadena, CA
Where recorded: Hollywood, CA
Suggested pairing: Etta James "Tell Mama"

Don and Dewey's "Farmer John" was inspired by a well-known City of Vernon packing house. "I went to the meat packing place down in L.A.," Dewey Terry recalled. "The song just evolved from there." Don and Dewey's Specialty label career ended when the duet followed Sonny Bono to his brand new Rush label.

Remakes: Carl & the Commanders 1961; The Premiers 1964; The Tidal Waves 1966; Los Lobos 1987

—

Dion and the Belmonts "A Teenager In Love" Laurie 1959
Style: Doo wop
From and recorded in: New York
Suggested pairings: Del Vikings "Come Go With Me" 1956; The Crests "Wish She Were Mine" 1957; Ricky Nelson "Poor Little Fool" 1958

Dion and the Belmonts' "A Teenager in Love" was the first major hit penned by Doc Pomus and his partner, Mort Shuman, at the behest of the Laurie label. It was the perfect match of teenage and angst, just what pubescent record buyers required at the time. In fact, "A Teenager in Love" was written for the new Laurie act, The Mystics, but it was too good to waste on an unproven group, so when it was offered to Dion and the Belmonts, Pomus and Shuman wrote "Hushabye," The Mystics' consolation prize. Both records became major hits.

Remakes: Dion 1963; The Beach Boys 1978

—

Fabian "Turn Me Loose" Chancellor March 1959
Style: Rock 'n' roll
From and recorded in: Philadelphia, PA

Written by Doc Pomus and his partner, Mort Shuman, "Turn Me Loose" was teen idol Fabian Forte's calling card at the request of his management, creating Fabian's first hit. This was one of the earliest hits for Pomus and Shuman, who had great success with Dion and the Belmonts ("A Teenager In Love"), The Drifters ("Save the Last Dance For Me") and Elvis Presley ("Viva Las Vegas"), among many others.

Label owner Bob Marcucci heavily promoted "Turn Me Loose" with a series of advertisements saying "Fabian Is Coming," then "Who is Fabian?" then finally "Fabian is Here." It worked and "Turn Me Loose" went top ten. During the payola scandal, Fabian testified before Congress that his recordings had been doctored electronically to "significantly improve his voice."

—

Wilbert Harrison "Kansas City" Fury March 1959

Style: Rhythm and blues
Where from: Florida
Where recorded: New York City, NY
Original version: Little Willie Littlefield "KC Loving" 1952
Suggested pairing: Wilbert Harrison "This Woman Of Mine" 1952

From 1955 to 1959, blues vocalist Wilbert Harrison recorded for the Savoy label out of Newark, NJ. "I left Savoy, we wasn't getting along too well. I had options for five years, but Savoy's owner Herman Lubinsky didn't want 'Kansas City.' I said, 'I'm going to do it anyway.' I knew the record would be a pretty good record. I didn't know it was going to be as big as it was. He didn't want 'Kansas City,' too risqué. During that time it's hard to get a record like that across. He didn't want it, that was my most requested song at clubs I worked at in New Jersey."

Harrison continued, "I took the record to Bobby Robinson, he wasn't too interested in it either, he was interested in my two brothers. We had a little time left at the studio. 'Kansas City' took me a half hour to do the songs. Did 'Kansas City' once, the same way Little Willie Littlefield did it. They didn't like that, we had to change it, I changed it, they liked it the way I did it then.

"I took the record to the DJ, Pat the Cat, WNJR in Newark," Harrison added, "there was only one side on it... got a dub of it, took it to the disc jockey. I just slid the thing under the door, the place had closed, the disc jockey I wanted to see wasn't there. Pat the Cat started playing it, I didn't even know that the thing was being played. One morning, I was in my room, my landlady told me: 'They're playing your record.' I couldn't believe it. Lubinsky slapped a lawsuit dead on everybody. Had an injunction on it."

To Harrison, it was a hit because of "my beat, my voice. The way I did certain things. A certain word, I'd say 'aw mercy,' people thought it was 'mustang, mush, mercy,' mainly my beat. I actually was saying, like when you see a pretty girl, guys would say 'aw mercy,' people thought I was saying 'mustache, mustang,' whatever. I did it in a slang way. 'Aw mercy.'" Harrison also attributes the success to "the time and the beat. The beat in the key of D flat. A lot of people don't usually play in it. I did the record the way I did it in these clubs, people accepted it. There were seven covers on it. Hank Ballard couldn't get my groove. At the time, I knew, I'm not being selfish, I knew my version had it of all the versions I heard."

Wally Roker recalled, "'Kansas City' was the first record I promoted as a businessman after I left The Heartbeats. A lot of people over the years have done that record. It was just a song everybody loved and Wilbert Harrison captured the total commercial aspect of it and everybody was a little angry. 'We did this too, why couldn't we sell it?' Wilbert Harrison's was just flying out of the stores. It had a lot to do with that guitar player, Jimmy Spruill, he was that session guitar department for Bobby Robinson. He played on every session Bobby had, almost. He had a set of four or five guys who used to do the rhythm. Jimmy was outstanding. It had at least eight covers. Everybody thought it was such a natural record. They thought Bobby couldn't afford to press it. They figured they'd get a little action out of it since it would not be available in most places. Nate Duroff who owned Monarch Pressing extended $100,000 worth of credit, so he pressed up every record he needed. He did over two million copies on that record in the first run. Nate was sweating about his money."

While "Kansas City" was selling, people at the label "emptied the money out of the company as soon as it came in. I was doing $100,000 a month in billing with the combination of Wilbert Harrison, Tarheel Slim & Little Ann and different acts on the label," said Wally Roker. "Fats Lewis owned the Barbeque Pit in New York and was Bobby's backer at the time and actually gave him the money to cut some of these records. The people at Fury were stealing from each other, every time you'd turn around, one was writing a check, another was writing a check, soon as the money got into the account, they'd wipe it out. There was nothing to get."

Covers: Hank Ballard & the Midnighters; Rockin' Ronnie & the Rebels; Rocky Olson; a reissue of "KC Loving" by Little Willie Littlefield.

The cover by Little Richard was a different song. See Little Richard "Hey Hey Hey Hey."

—

Ritchie Valens "That's My Little Suzie" Del-fi March 1959

Style: Rock 'n' roll
Where from: Pacoima, CA
Where recorded: Hollywood, CA

Ritchie Valens' postmortem smash hit, this fine rocker "That's My Little Suzie," hit on border Mighty 690 on March 12 and pop on April 6, 1959. As of early 1959, Del-fi had few remaining Valens' sessions, so to add marketing punch, Keene created the "Valens Memorial Series."

On March 5, 1959, the Valley News Wax Tracks column opined about these tactics of Valens' retailing. "Several individual record stores have been using the death of the singers to boost sales figures. Some persons would buy the records purely because of the tragedy anyway, but these shops are throwing up big sales display, which play up the fact the singers were killed recently, hoping to pull in more 'sentimental sales.' Valens' album has been the top seller in this area for a couple of weeks. This is partially due, probably, to the fact he was a local boy. It's doubtful, though, that sales figures would have been as high if the accident had never happened. And you can bet many of the stores wouldn't have been pushing it so hard, either." Well, duh.

—

Tommy Dee "Three Stars" Crest 1959

Style: Country spoken word
Where from: Bakersfield, CA
Where recorded: Los Angeles, CA

After the February 3, 1959 deaths of Buddy Holly, Ritchie Valens and The Big Bopper, Riverside's KFXM DJ Tommy Dee cashed in quickly with a tribute to the "three stars" in a duet with Carol Kay & the Teen-Aires' entitled "Three Stars."

Donnie Brooks attempted to present the song to Era's Herb Newman. "He would never accept a song, but if he got the publishing, he'd take it. I told him about a song called 'Three Stars.' Dorsey Burnette did it, Johnny Burnette did it, Eddie Cochran did it. Then Tommy Dee had a big hit with it," said Brooks.

"He talked the lyrics," his duet partner Carole Kay said of Dee. "They needed a singer for the middle part and I just sang, two other singers were The Teen-Aires, older guys. I was floored about that. Tommy Dee presented the song, I was in the studio, I had to learn the song, it was very quick, I'm just guessing how I got involved. I believe it was the guitar strumming while he recited, then I sang my part. Probably not too many takes. I used to be very quick on learning something. I had been taken out of school to go sing; the kids knew I was a singer. It made me pretty popular at school, 45s were very popular at the time. Back then, I got half a cent a record. I must have made something, I recall some sort of problem because of half a cent."

"Three Stars" hit first on Mighty 690 and KFXM in mid-March, #11 pop on March 30.

—

Phil Harvey "Bumbershoot" Imperial April 4, 1959

Style: Jazz
Where from: Los Angeles, CA
Where recorded: Hollywood, CA

During a Teddy Bears session, production genius Phil Spector took on the identity of Phil Harvey (his middle name) with Spector, piano; Larry Taylor, bass and Elliot Ingber, guitar for this one-shot piano jazz instrumental "Bumbershoot," a slang term with female sexual implications backed with the similarly male double entendre phallic reference, "Willy Boy," thus creating a double double etendre.

In their April Fool's Day review, the Valley News missed the joke: "In the new release for Imperial by Phil Harvey, 'Bumbershoot' and 'Willy Boy' are both uptempo sides featuring guitar. In 'Willy Boy,' a wailing sax moves along with the guitars."

—

The Miracles "Bad Girl" Motown/Chess 1959

Style: Rhythm and blues/ soul vocal group
Where from: Detroit, MI
Where recorded: Chicago, IL

"We had a two record deal with End and a two record deal with Chess," said Claudette Robinson of The Miracles. "'Bad Girl' was a favorite in performing. Some are not big sellers, but audience appeal is good in performance. Smokey's voice was [a] naturally high voice, he sang with first soprano, not a falsetto. Sometimes he gets ideas from real life, sometimes he gets inspiration he sees on TV, a title, a line or he makes it up. He would be crying and pleading, real dramatic. Not a lot for the group to do, we'd mainly make motions, he'd be crooning away, girls would be screaming, yelling. I'd look at them, like why are they yelling? I was the artist, the wife.

Robinson continued, "Smokey did most of the negotiating. Berry talked to Smokey a lot about The Miracles. Basically that's how we got to Motown. It was on Chess for national distributorship only. Smokey was selling records out of his trunk around Michigan. He and Berry did those things in those days. As they were doing that in upper Michigan, it was cold, slippery and icy, their car slid under a truck. They went under there, they slid off the road, none of us knew about that until after the fact.

At that time, everyone had a job of some type," Robinson added. "Smokey worked with Berry, assisted him, taking records around, a go-fer, worked with him like others with him at the time. There was Raynoma, Berry's second wife, Robert Bateman, Eddie Holland was there. Probably by 1960, he was doing more."

—

The Mystics "Hushabye" Laurie April 1959

Style: Doo wop
From and recorded in: New York
Suggested pairing: Dion and the Belmonts "A Teenager In Love" 1959

Newly signed by Laurie records, which was hot with Dion and the Belmonts at the time, the song "A Teenager in Love" was promised to The Mystics, but instead was given to Dion and the Belmonts, a major hit. The consolation prize to The Mystics was this hastily composed "Hushabye" by the same writers they took from the lullaby, "All the Pretty Horses." Backing was by jazz session musicians, Al Caiola and Bucky Pizzarelli on guitars and Panama Francis on drums.

—

The Flamingos "I Only Have Eyes For You" End April 1959

Style: Doo wop
From and recorded in: Chicago, IL

One-time Flamingos lead singer Solly McElroy recalled that just prior to leaving the group, "we had been rehearsing 'I Only Have Eyes for You' and when Nate Nelson sang the song, if you heard me sing the song and heard him sing it, you'd swear it was one in the same. We had a thing about classical, we would take a number the average group wouldn't touch and put it into group harmony."

When McElroy left the group in 1954, the song was shelved. But it was resuscitated when Terry Johnson, who replaced Nate Nelson as lead singer in 1958, was on the road with the group. "I went to my hotel room, was laying in my bed, had my guitar. I would play a lot laying down. Fell asleep, I had a dream, don't remember what it was about. I heard this ethereal sound, 'de-bop-she-bop,' heard the way the chord structure should be, heard 'I only have eyes,' which was my part. Heard the whole arrangement in my head. At four o'clock in the morning, had the guitar at my chest, God gave me the chords. Woke up the guys up. 'Are you crazy?' We went to the studio without George Goldner's permission, and recorded it." Turned out, one of the inspirations for The Flamingos' "I Only Have Eyes For You" was the "Volga Boatman's Song (yo ho heave ho)."

—

Phil Phillips & the Twilights "Sea of Love" Khourys/Mercury April 1959

Style: Rhythm and blues
From and recorded in: Lake Charles, LA
Cover: Katie Webster 1959

At age 30, Phil Phillips, working as a bellhop at the Chateau Charles Motel in Lake Charles, was deeply taken with Verdie Mae, to whom he composed a song one night on her front porch. Creating the melody on his guitar, he improvised the lyrics: 'Come with me, my love... to the sea, the sea of love... I want to tell you how much I love you.' His attempts to woo her didn't work out at first, but he kept trying.

A couple of years later he found another use for the song. "I had my guitar, so I went and wrote this song, 'Sea of Love.' You see, she really didn't believe in me. But I felt if I could sing about it—a sea of love where it's quiet and peaceful—I could really show her how much I loved her and cared for her." A gas meter reader heard Baptiste practicing the song and told him to see a record producer named George Khoury, who had him record the song and convinced him to take the stage name Phil Phillips.

"Sea of Love" was released on Khoury's independent record label, Khoury grabbing half writer credit. "Sea Of Love" did so well in Louisiana that Mercury Records picked up the song to distribute nationally, where it became a big hit. Phillips claims he earned just $6,800 from the song, and he didn't even get the girl, which is OK by him. Said Phillips, "I married the right one though. It's a good thing I didn't marry that Verdie."

The famous harmony vocals on this song were performed by a group of friends Phillips brought to the studio. He had to teach them how to sing it. With members of Cookie & the Cupcakes involved in the session, Katie Webster backed Phillips on piano. Webster then claimed it was her song originally. It was the only major hit for Phillips, almost impossible to follow.

Remakes: Bill Deal and the Rhondels 1961; Cookie and His Cupcakes 1979; Del Shannon 1981; The Honeydrippers 1985

—

Dolly Parton "Puppy Love" Goldband 1959

Style: Swamp rock
Where from: Tennessee
Where recorded: Lake Charles, LA
Suggested pairing: Sugar Boy & the Cane Cutters "Jockomo" 1954

This was a debut recording by 13-year-old Dolly Parton with her uncle, Bill Owens, on guitar. According to her bio, she took a ten-hour bus trip with her grandmother, Rena Owens, from her home to Lake Charles to record the song she wrote at age 11. She wrote, "I don't think I'll ever forget the way the inside of that bus smelled. It was a combination of diesel fuel, Naugahyde and people who were going places."

—

Lloyd Price "Personality" ABC/Paramount April 1959

Style: Rhythm and blues
Where from: New Orleans, LA
Where recorded: New York City, NY
Suggested pairing: The Soul Stirrers "Wade In the Water"

With a melody adapted by the gospel "Wade In the Water," Lloyd Price had success with his "Personality," patterned after the "follow the bouncing ball" approach popularized by Mitch Miller's Sing Along with Mitch TV show.

—

The Drifters "There Goes My Baby" Atlantic April 1959

Style: Rhythm and blues vocal group
From and recorded in: New York City, NY
Suggested pairing: The Primettes "Tears Of Sorrow" 1960

In May 1958, Drifters manager George Treadwell fired the entire group. Lead singer of The Drifters, Bobby Hendricks, described how the replacement Drifters came into being. "That whole week, Tommy Evans and Frank Schiffman who was owner of the Apollo Theater and Tommy Smalls were having arguments about money and things like that. Tommy got out of hand and the report got back that these Drifters would have to go, he didn't want them in the Apollo Theater anymore. The Drifters had a contract for up to ten years and that was being threatened, the appearance at the Apollo was being threatened.

"On the show was Ben E. King and the Five Crows with their manager, Lover Patterson. George Treadwell asked how would they like to become The Drifters? Who wouldn't? They jumped on it. Three months later, 'There Goes My Baby' was released. I didn't care because I had recorded 'Itchy Twitchy Feeling' and it was a hit."

According to producer Mike Stoller, "That was a group called The Crowns that had just been turned into The Drifters magically. The Drifters was actually a hired group, owned by the manager. They hired the singers and paid them a salary. They got no royalties. They all disappeared, a new group called The Crowns signed with the managers and became the Drifters. The lead singer at that time was Ben E. King. It was the first time we worked with him, and they had this song, we worked a little bit on this song as well, co-writers on it, we had this idea that while we were rehearsing it, the changes led me into this kind of melody. Sounded like some orchestral pieces, I've said before it sounded like some Caucasian melody, we decided to use actual strings and we did. It was four fiddles and a cello. In the studio there was a tympani and the drummer was a drummer and not a percussionist."

Stoller recalled that there was no resistance to the breakthrough sound of "There Goes My Baby" by The Drifters after the label heard it. "We started getting involved with Brazilian rhythms, we were the first to introduce a little beat that the signature to rock 'n' roll, but was actually the Brazilian beat called the baion. They said, 'You can't hit a home run every time at bat, don't worry about it.' But we felt there was something in that record, even though they felt it was like listening to two radio stations at the same time. It's true, it wasn't a great mix that they heard. Tom Dowd, who was the engineer then before he became a producer remixed it, I think it was probably done in three takes.

"We had written the song with Ben E. King," continued Stoller. "I would say our contribution was important, but we were not going to take credit. Then we found out that his manager and road manager got credit as authors of this, one of whom was an accountant and I knew that they had not written a lick. And if they're getting credit why should we pass up credit of the young fellow, he's very nice, so we asked for credit and received it."

Before "There Goes My Baby," vocal group sessions were "strictly five or six guys in the background. Piano, sax, guitar and bass, violins were out of the question," said Bobby Hendricks. "'There Goes My Baby' was an experimental record with kettle drums and violins.

Hendricks continued, "Actually, there was a lot of arguing going on at Atlantic about whether that song would sell under the name The Drifters. They decided these songs have been recorded, we might as well release them. A lot of songs came out like that after. The melody lingered on. I loved what they were doing. We tried to keep what we were doing in the same vein. None of them were under contract, that's why I called them the supermarket group," said Hendricks. "That's what happened to Ben E. King. I was told he received $500 for singing lead on 'There Goes My Baby.' The big guys got the money, so Ben E. King quit. All the songs that came out after were on the shelf. He recorded up a bunch, then he split.

"I went back with the original Drifters," Hendricks added. "We started to reassemble, Bill Pinkney, Gerhart Thrasher, Andrew Thrasher and myself. We went on the road and I stayed with them for 15 years as Bill Pinkney's Original Drifters. So there was two Drifters, Ben E. King, they were doing the recording and we were doing the performing. That was the cause of a lot of controversy. In fact, today, it still is."

Remakes: Doc Bagby 1965; Jay & the Americans 1971; Donna Summer 1984

—

Bobby Darin "Dream Lover" Atco April 1959

Style: Rock 'n' roll
From and recorded in: New York City, NY
Suggested pairing: Steve Lawrence "Footsteps" 1960

With backing by the oft-used backup group, The Cues, who had backed LaVern Baker as The Gliders, Joe Turner as the Blue Kings and other Atlantic/Atco acts, the sound of Bobby Darin's "Dream Lover" was made unique by chimes played by Neil Sedaka.

Built on a Latin dance rhythm. Darin said of writing it, "I had just discovered the C-Am-F-G7 progression on the piano. I stretched them out and I like the space I felt in there, and the words just flowed."

Remakes: Frankie Sardo 1960; The Paris Sisters 1964; Sam Hawkins 1969; Anne Murray 1976; The Plasmatics 1979; Rick Nelson 1979; Tanya Tucker and Glen Campbell 1980

—

Chuck Berry "Back in the U.S.A." Chess 1959

Style: Rock 'n' roll
Where from: St. Louis, MO
Where recorded: Chicago, IL
Suggested pairing: The Beatles "Back In the USSR" 1968

It's a combination of Bobby Lester, The Dells, Etta James, we were all on this record," said Dells' bass singer Chuck Barksdale. "At one time, there was a record row from 14th and Michigan to 22nd Street, they had a number of record companies in Chicago. I was like a traveling salesman. I would go from one record company to another. 'Are you having a session today?' 'Oh yeah, you with The Dells. Are you guys available?'" Nobody knew it was The Dells singing background on I don't know how many records."

Remake: Linda Ronstadt 1978
Answers: "Back in the USSR" by John Fred and His Playboy Band 1969; Chubby Checker 1969

—

Big Jay McNeely "There Is Something On Your Mind" Swingin' May 2, 1959

Style: Rhythm and blues
Where from: Los Angeles, CA
Where recorded: Seattle, WA
Cover: The Hollywood Flames 1959
After years of label-hopping between various R&B imprints, tenor saxophone virtuoso Big Jay McNeely was without a label when he met blues vocalist Little Sonny Warner. Warner joined McNeely in Seattle, then Big Jay brought out a blues song written by Rocky Turner Wilson III of The Sharps. It was a "Fats Domino kind of song, triplets," which didn't call for one of McNeely's typically explosive tenor sax breaks, but he took an interest in the song and the singer, recording an acetate in January 1958. "I don't even honk once on that record," McNeely lamented. On the session was Bob McNeely on baritone sax; Wendell Johnson on guitar; Dillard McNeely on bass; Leonard Hardiman on drums and Warner on vocals.
After shopping the song around to various labels throughout 1958, McNeely visited DJ Hunter Hancock and his partner Roger Davenport, who were thinking of starting a label. This was their first release, and by March 1959, McNeely was soon hearing it on the radio. Unlike Art LaBoe, who took his acts like Sandy Nelson and Preston Epps to the studio, Hancock stocked his label with unreleased masters submitted by the musicians.

McNeely's "There Is Something On Your Mind" was released on Swingin' 614, as 6/14/1947 was the date Hancock began playing R&B on the radio, which directly led to his success.

About The Hollywood Flames cover of "There Is Something On Your Mind," KGFJ's Big Jim Randolph wrote in the April 23, 1959 California Eagle, "There's one side this week that's getting the real action in Los Angeles. This is a blues ballad entitled 'There Is Something On Your Mind.' There are two great versions. Perhaps you have your favorite, but for me, they are identical. The original is done by Big Jay McNeely with Little Sonny. The cover features The Hollywood Flames. Anyway, it's selling lots and lots of records, which is unusual today." This comment amounted to a slap in the face of KPOP DJ Hunter Hancock, on whose Swingin' label the Big Jay McNeely original was released. After this pressure play, in a few months, Hancock switched over to KGFJ.

Remake: Bobby Marchan 1960; Little Ray 1961

—

The Shirelles "Dedicated To the One I Love" Scepter May 1959

Style: Rhythm and blues vocal group
Where from: New Jersey
Where recorded: New York
Original version: The Five Royales 1957

Scepter label producer Wally Roker was in the Carolinas looking for regional material for The Shirelles, who had just started recording for the Tiara/Scepter labels. Roker purchased The Five Royales' original version of "Dedicated To the One I Love" and The Shirelles recorded it. Their remake of "Dedicated To the One I Love" stiffed in 1958 and that, they thought, was that.

With the emergence of the Shirelles' #1 hit, "(Will You Love Me) Tomorrow," Roker noticed that The Shirelles' "Dedicated To the One I Love" went to #1 in San Francisco before "(Will You Love Me) Tomorrow" went to #1 in San Francisco. "We had a #1 record on the East Coast, '(Will You Love Me) Tomorrow,' and a #1 record on the West Coast, 'Dedicated To the One I Love,'" said Roker. It charted in the Bay Area on January 2, 1961, just after The Shirelles' "Tonight's the Night" dropped from the charts. "It was based on promotion. '(Will You Love Me) Tomorrow' had people hearing 'Dedicated To the One I Love' and saying, 'Hey, we really never played this record. Let's play this record too.' We had the #1 record and the #5 record in the country at the same time," explained Roker.

Remakes: The Five Royales (with a dubbed in girl-group) 1961; Johnny Preston 1965; The Mamas and Papas 1967; The O'Kaysions 1968; Barbara Mason 1968; The Temprees 1972; Sweet Charles 1974

—

The Wailers "Tall Cool One" Golden West May 1959
Style: Rock 'n' roll
Where from: Tacoma, WA
Where recorded: Lakewood, WA

The Wailers were originally The Nitecaps, formed in 1958 by five high school friends: John Greek, rhythm guitar, trumpet; Richard Dangel, lead guitar; Kent Morrill, keyboards, vocals; Mark Marush, tenor sax and Mike Burk, drums. Seattle space age musician and songwriter Attilio Mineo connected them with Clark Galehouse, owner of Golden Crest Records of Huntington Station, Long Island, New York which released the band's moody, largely undanceable debut instrumental,

"Tall Cool One," hit big nationally, impressing the trades that a band on a New York label could make it big in Seattle, where it hit #2 on local KOL radio in mid-April 1959.

Adding lead vocalist "Rockin' Robin" Roberts from the Bluenotes, The Wailers then hit with the first rock remake of "Louie Louie," which inspired The Kingsmen of Portland, Oregon and Paul Revere & the Raiders to record the same song.

Remakes: Paul Revere and The Raiders 1961

—

Freddie Cannon "Tallahassee Lassie" Swan May 1959
Style: Rock 'n' roll
Where from: Boston, MA
Where recorded: Philadelphia, PA

After recording with the Boston-based Spindrifts on a Dion and the Belmonts—sounding "Cha Cha Doo" on Hot, reissued on ABC in 1958, Freddie Cannon became a single act, recording this booming novelty "Tallahassee Lassie" on Swan, a #6 hit in May 1959.

While being played by DJ Art LaBoe on L.A. radio, LaBoe asked East L.A. listeners to not complain as they misheard the lyrics as "my Tallahassee down in West L.A."

Cannon went on to record city-based titles "Okefenokee" and "Way Down Yonder In New Orleans" in 1959, and "Chattanooga Shoe Shine Boy" backed with "Boston (My Home Town)" in 1960.

Some copies of Cannon "Tallahassee Lassie" were issued under the name Freddy Cannon.

—

Bo Diddley "Crackin' Up" Checker May 1959
Style: Blues
Where from: Mississippi
Where recorded: Chicago, IL
Suggested pairing: Mickey & Sylvia "Love Is Strange" 1956

"I think ' Crackin' Up' was after 'Love Is Strange,'" said Bo Diddley. "I've got about six songs that carry that same type of melody. You know, different lyrics, that same wavelength." True enough.

—

Fabian "Tiger" Chancellor May 1959
Style: Rock 'n' roll
From and recorded in: Philadelphia, PA
Cover: Nick Todd—Pat Boone's brother 1959
Suggested pairing: Elvis Presley "Teddy Bear" 1957

Fabian's second major hit, the term "Tiger," with lines like "Growl—wow!" was in line with other animalistic titles like "Teddy Bear," "Running Bear" and "The Chipmunk Song," all #1 hits at the time.

—

Johnny Preston "Running Bear" Mercury June 1959

Style: Novelty rock 'n' roll
Where from: Port Arthur, TX
Where recorded: Gold Star studio in Houston, TX

With The Big Bopper, George Jones and producer Bill Hall making Indian sounds and whoops in the background, this hit about star-crossed lovers, Indian-style, "Running Bear," was recorded by Johnny Preston, who started an R&B band The Shades, which performed nights and weekends at local watering holes. Beaumont resident Jape "J.P." Richardson, The Big Bopper, caught their act and offered them a chance at "Running Bear," an eventual #1 hit.

—

Homer Escamilla "Battle Of Chavez Ravine" Sherri June 6, 1959

Style: Novelty
From and recorded in: Los Angeles, CA
Suggested pairing: Johnny Horton "Battle Of New Orleans" 1959

When the Brooklyn Dodgers moved to Los Angeles in 1957, it wasn't only their Flatbush fans who felt violated. In 1959, Mexican residents of an L.A. neighborhood called Chavez Ravine had their homes plowed under by prevailing political forces to claim land for Dodger Stadium. The plight of these displaced residents was generally overlooked or justified in the interests of clearing substandard housing.

That same year, one-time member of the Spike Jones ensemble, vocalist Homer Escamilla, issued this politically pointed country-styled novelty 45, inspired by Johnny Horton's recently popular #1 country hit, "The Battle Of New Orleans." In Escamilla's case, it was "Battle Of Chavez Ravine" on the Sherri label and was previewed on out-of-L.A. radio. Of course, that 45 got no play on L.A. radio, which found little advantage in upsetting local business and political forces.

—

Larry Hall "Sandy" Ever Green June 1959/ Hot July 1959/Strand August 28, 1959

Style: Rock 'n' roll
Where from: Garden Grove CA
Where recorded: El Monte, CA

Bob Summers had his original studio on Peck in El Monte: "We did local people who wanted to record bands." Summers recalled songwriter Hal Moffett had written a song called "Sandy" and brought Larry Hall to Summers to record. According to the label, "Sandy" was written by local country composer Terry Fell.

Summers used a cardboard box and got a hold of couple of brushes that drummers use and a stick. "I played an acoustic guitar over one track, recorded over that with a drum feel, brush and stick, bass guitar and electric guitar, made a track." Summers then had Hall sing to the track. "He was nervous; when I got done with splicing all these different tapes, it looked like a checkerboard." The result was this relaxed quasi-rocker, "Sandy," which hit big in August and September.

The Ever Green original had a notice on the label that all future copies would be on Hot. "A few months later, the songwriter came to the studio, told me it was a hit. I got about $450 for the session. Some of that fee went to the studio, some went to Summers' partner. Never thought of a producer royalty. Never heard from him again," said Summers.

From a fast start on KRLA, "Sandy" went from a summer hit to an end of the year charter.

—

Jivin' Gene and the Jokers "Breaking Up Is Hard To Do" Jin/Mercury June 1959

Style: Swamp rock
Where from: Louisiana
Where recorded: Ville Platte, LA

After one earlier release, "Up Up and Away," on Jin, Jivin' Gene and the Jokers recorded this moody swamp rock ballad, "Breaking Up Is Hard To Do" on Floyd Soileau's Jin label of Ville Platte, LA and was picked up for national distribution by the major Chicago-based Mercury label.

—

Ray Charles and His Orchestra "What'd I Say" Atlantic June 1959

Style: Rhythm and blues
Where from: Florida
Where recorded: New York City, NY
Suggested pairings: Ray Charles "Mess Around" 1953; Ray Charles "Sweet Sixteen Bars" 1960; The Shirelles "Boys"1960; The Hi Fi Dels "Some Other Guy"; The Link Eddy Combo "Big Mr. C" 1961

This was the ultimate call and response effort between Ray Charles and the Raeletts, his female vocal unit. Several variations of Ray Charles' original "What'd I Say" were released while it was charting. The yellow label 45 is a different take from the hit.

Cover: The Olympics 1959
Remakes: Ronnie Dio and the Red Caps 1960; Jerry Lee Lewis 1961; The Halos 1961; Bobby Darin 1962; Trini Lopez 1963; Elvis Presley 1964; Solomon Burke 1968

—

Bobby Rydell "Kissin' Time" Cameo June 1959

Style: Rock 'n' roll
From and recorded in: Philadelphia, PA
Suggested pairing: Chuck Berry "Sweet Little Sixteen" 1958

After two early bombs on the Cameo label, including the very fine doo wop "Please Don't Be Mad" earlier in 1959, Bobby Rydell finally hit in the summer. With background clapping supplied by Chubby Checker, the lyrics of Bobby Rydell's "Kissin' Time" were similar to Chuck Berry's "Sweet Little Sixteen," except Berry's were about dancing and Rydell's were about kissing in various cityscapes.

Remake: Kiss 1974

—

The Strangers "Caterpillar Crawl" Titan July 17, 1959

Style: Rock 'n' roll instrumental
Where from: San Diego, CA
Where recorded: Hollywood, CA
Original title: "Cockroach Crawl"
Suggested pairing: The Rumblers "Boss" 1962

The Strangers was started by guitarist Joel Scott Hill, who said, "I attended Steven Watts Kearny High school. I got together with another kid in school, Harold 'Strange' Kirby, who said he could play guitar." The Strangers were "Kirby on bass, John Callard on drums, Ron Lynch on sax and me on guitar." This slow, almost meandering "Caterpillar Crawl" on George Brown's brand new Titan, became a border instrumental hit, a cruising hit, then an L.A. hit.

Brown released it locally only, waiting for deals with the big boys. Kapp and Dot came calling, and when Brown hesitated, Kapp covered "Caterpillar Crawl," crediting it to Dave Dixon & the Roommates, which charted in Norfolk and Chicago. However, The Strangers' original held market share for decades as a cruising title. Hill went on to hit with "Little Lover" in 1960. "Caterpillar Crawl" featured a riff that influenced the intro of "Boss" by The Rumblers.

Later members of the Strangers were organ thumper Lee Eugene Michaels and drummer Johnny Barbata, who then joined The Sentinals. Michaels later had a successful recording career as Lee Michaels.

Cover: Dave Dixon & the Roommates

—

Arbogast & Ross "Chaos Pt. 1 & 2" Liberty 1959

Style: Novelty
From and recorded in: Hollywood, CA

The merciless spoof of top 40 radio, "Chaos Pt. 1 & 2" by Arbogast & Ross combined voiceover artist Bob Arbogast with comedic folk singer Stan Ross in this doomed venture, a two-part, six-minute-long spoof of KFWB-style fictional top 40 station KOS and KOS-AM. It featured DJ Speedy Clip, teen idols droning "Oh, Blanche," perky jingles, commercial breaks for "Pimple-On" and a news break to end all news breaks, which included the murder of a station engineer, live. The single reportedly sold 10,000 copies in three days before the radio industry realized how severely it was being savaged by this satire and hurriedly ordered it off their air.

"Top-40 people were so insecure, but we did not know that," said promotion man Don Blocker. "We cut a record with Bob Arbogast, a humorist around town, and gave 10,000 copies free to everybody at the [disc jockey] convention. Top-40 radio people resented it to the point that we got letters from stations written on toilet paper, saying, 'You guys are thieves, you stab us in the back, what are you doing, you can wipe that record with this.' That sort of thing. We took a big setback with that. We never released it commercially."

On June 11, the Valley News read, "From time to time, this column has commented on the ridiculous manner in which some of the local 'Top 40' radio shows are conducted with their 'color radio' blurbs, 'electronic news' capsules and frantic style of announcing. Now we'll no longer need to write anything but one word to sum up our feelings. That word is 'Chaos' and it's the title of a new 45rpm record released by Liberty. The record is a hilarious satire of the wild DJ shows. Written and recorded by Bob Arbogast and Stan Ross, 'Chaos' parodies these programs' commercials, mobile unit reports, announcing, weather and news reports and top tunes surveys. Also satirized are the singing groups which invariably are used to introduce everything on these shows. The group sings of 'KOS—Channel 4896341 ½.' Slogan of Station KOS is 'something for everyone 8 to 13.' And that seems to be the thinking of a lot of the for-real stations, too. It's a great record. The only trouble is that it probably won't change anything. An announcer on one of the for-real shows played 'Chaos' a few days ago, [and] stated 'wasn't that quite a satire,' then immediately spun one of those loud, irritating, recorded station messages. You just can't win."

In 1960, Stan Ross recorded rockabilly for World Pacific; Arbogast went to top 40 radio.

—

Bobby Vee & the Shadows "Suzy Baby" Soma/Liberty July 1959

Style: Rock 'n' roll
Where from: Fargo, ND
Where recorded: Minneapolis, MN

Bobby Vee & the Shadows' "Suzy Baby" was a pop rock performance based somewhat on the hiccuppy style of Buddy Holly, who died in the infamous plane crash in February 1959. The next day, Vee's band filled in for the rockers, who had been booked for a concert in his area. Vee went on to record with Liberty in a much more teen idol style to great success.

Bob Dylan, who played piano behind Bobby Vee in his early years, said Vee "had a metallic, edgy tone to his voice and it was as musical as a silver bell." Vee remembered that the musician he knew as Elston Gunnn [Dylan] "played pretty good in the key of C."

—

Bobby Vee & the Shadows "Flying High" Soma/Liberty 1959
Style: Rock 'n' roll instrumental
Where from: Fargo, ND
Where recorded: Minneapolis, MN

Bobby Vee & the Shadows on "Flying High" was a tough cruising-style instrumental with nary a hint of Vee's lightweight vocal skills.

—

Ray Sharpe "Linda Lu" Jamie 1959
Style: Rockabilly
Where from: Fort Worth, TX
Where recorded: Phoenix, AZ
Suggested pairings: Lillian Offitt "Miss You So" 1955; Jan & Dean "Batman" 1966

Black rockabilly singer and guitarist Ray Sharpe hooked up with Lester Sill and Lee Hazlewood, who produced Sharpe on his first, the rocker "Oh, My Baby's Gone" on Hamilton in 1958 with Duane Eddy and Al Casey playing guitar, perfectly matching his stuttering vocal on "Linda Lu," which has no less than two B-sides: "Monkey's Uncle" and "Red Sails In The Sunset," which was the first A-side.

When Dick Clark played "Linda Lu," Sill and Hazlewood changed the "Red Sails" side to Sharpe's own composition, "Monkey's Uncle," a Chuck Berry-inspired piece, to make more money on both sides of a hit.

Remakes: The Traits 1962; The Standells 1965; The Coachmen 1965

—

Santo & Johnny "Sleep Walk" Canadian American July 1959
Style: Rock 'n' roll
Where from: Brooklyn, NY
Where recorded: New York City, NY
Suggested pairing: Donnie Owens "Need You" 1958

This was a major instrumental hit by the guitar playing duet, the brothers Santo & Johnny Farina, creating a sleep-inducing electric guitar effect. They recorded this instrumental as a demo and it was picked up by the newly established Canadian American label, which had offices in both Manitoba Canada and New York City, thus Canadian American.

Vocal version: Betsy Brye of "Sleep Walk" on Canadian American August 1959

—

Jan & Dean "Baby Talk" Dore 1959
Style: Rock 'n' roll
From and recorded in: Los Angeles, CA
Original version: The Laurels "Baby Talk" 1959
First artist credit: Jan & Arnie

Artist credits on early pressings of Jan & Arnie's "Baby Talk" on Dore were quickly switched to Jan & Dean, to reflect the presence of Dean Torrence who replaced the army-bound Arnie Ginsberg as singing partner to Jan Berry. "Jan and Arnie were hot," said Torrence. "The record company hates to start over marketing-wise." The so-called mistaken use of Jan & Arnie's name "was the typical mentality of the record company exec., 'Gosh we have an established name we can't use.' It was like that almost with everybody, I think I agreed to it, thought it was the deal-breaker, maybe the record wouldn't come out. They were anticipating Arnie was considering it, wouldn't figure out why it was okay, he wouldn't care. He was considering it enough that we went ahead."

"We did the vocals in a garage with Jan on piano, then took that track into a studio and tried to put musicians on it," said Lou Adler. "Our favorite was doo wop," said Dean Torrence. "We wanted to be a vocal group, but no one was interested. Then, along came multi-tracking in the early 1960s, so we could become a vocal group and not split up a pie royalty-wise. We became a rock group with the two of us.

Adler continued, "It was Herb Alpert who discovered 'Baby Talk.' But we discovered it at the same time," as labels continued to send promo records to Jan Berry's fake radio station. With KJAN promos, "we had more access to indie labels, but we missed it." Finding new records to emulate "was the whole intent, going through them with a fine tooth comb to see if there was anything there we'd like to record. We were mining them."

Lee Silver, who first issued "Baby Talk" by The Laurels on his Spring label in 1959 recalled, "'Baby Talk' was written by Melvin Schwartz and The Laurels, which Mel also sang in. I received a call from Herb Alpert's brother, Dave Alpert, a friend of a friend. He said, 'My younger brother is recording Jan & Arnie.' He said, 'Is it possible for Herb to meet with you because he's looking for novelty material like "Short Shorts."' I said, 'Sure, he can meet with me. He came over to my place. I liked him. I said, 'There's a song I can't promote, if you like it, go ahead, see what you want to do with it.' He took it and played it for his partner Lou Adler, and at that point, he called me up. 'Lee we love the song, can we do it?' I said, 'Sure.' It became a very important record for Jan & Dean." Torrence said, "We knew how well we did with Herb. Herb and Lou became our managers and producers."

—

Skip & Flip "It Was I" Brent 1959

Style: Rock 'n' roll
Where from: Tucson, Az
Where recorded: Arizona

Gary "Flip" Paxton, real name Larry Wayne Stevens, and Clyde "Skip" Battin did not think up their own nicknames. As a teen, Paxton moved to Washington State, where he was picking peaches and working night clubs on the side. "I heard a song I had written on the radio and said, 'somebody stole my song.' I went to the radio station; they showed me 'It Was I'" by Skip & Flip, which had gone pop on June 22, 1959. "I called the label in New York. He said, 'That's you dummy, we've been looking for you for six months.' They told me a DJ from Allentown found it in stack of acetates at their office and told them to release it. They put it out, thinking, if it's not a hit, I'll never hear it and if it's a hit, I'll find them." He found them.

"Bob Shad, who owned Brent and Time Records, heard the demo and decided to release it, but needed a name. "They called us Skip & Flip because Bobby Shad's wife had two poodles at home named Skip & Flip. They asked me, 'Can you be here by Friday for Dick Clark's show and to Philly for the Bandstand Show?' They'd already contacted Clyde and he had a fake Skip & Flip in Tucson. They told me, 'Just go down to the airport and get on a plane.' I had never been in a building before more than two stories high. They sent this limo, took us to 7th & Broadway. I goobered, I had nothing, they bought me clothes; did the Dick Clark Show and Bandstand with Fabian and Bobby Rydell."

—

Chan Romero "The Hippy Hippy Shake" Del-fi July 1959

Style: Rock 'n' roll
Where from: Billings, MT
Where recorded: Hollywood, CA

Del-fi owner Bob Keane denied he was trying to replace the recently deceased Ritchie Valens with Hispanic rocker Chan Romero. When he arrived in L.A. from

Montana, through Keane, Romero was taken in by the Valens family and lived with them as a son for several years. "I started back in Butte, Montana. Elvis Presley inspired me. Got a guitar learned how to play. I was raised on country and my brother sang Chicano songs. I started a band called The Bell Tones, three friends of mine, the Williams brothers, Frank and Bobby, piano player and drummer; Little Joe played sax; now has a mariachi band.

"We were getting well known in the area," Romero continued. "One of the local disc jockeys, Weird Beard, kind of like Wolfman Jack on KBMY, the top rock station, came and heard us asked if we'd like to be managed; we were pretty excited.

Romero said, "When I started my first band Ritchie became my idol. I was amazed by his vocals. I didn't know he was Mexican at all. My manager thought I sounded like Ritchie. We were Hispanics, a lot of similarities between us." After Ritchie Valens was killed, "I sent a tape to Bob Keane with some of my songs including 'Hippy Hippy Shake' on it. Within a week he had us come out sign a contract. There was mixed emotion with him, discouragement and looking to the future."

Session guitarist Rene Hall said, "I played the bass guitar with the rhythm section and overdubbed with the Gretsch. Bob Keene was hoping he'd get a Ritchie Valens out of Chan, I don't think it worked out." Lifting a line from "a Nancy Kwon movie, she'd say 'for goodness sake,'" Chan Romero did "Hippy Hippy Shake," which was only a KFXM pick.

Remakes: The Swinging Blue Jeans 1964; The Georgia Satellites 1989

—

Tarheel Slim & Little Ann "It's Too Late" Fire/Checker (the Lovers) July 1959

Style: Blues
Where from: North Carolina
Where recorded: New York City, NY

Tarheel Slim, real name, Allen Bunn, and his duet partner and wife, Little Ann Sandford, had recorded as The Lovers on the dreamy hit "Darling It's Wonderful." After one release on Fury as Tarheel Slim, Tarheel Slim & Little Ann's first release on Bobby Robinson's brand new Fury subsidiary, Fire, was this intense blues duet, "It's Too Late," complete with a sobbing break in the vocal.

This was a major hit in New Orleans, enough that it was picked up the Checker label, which reverted to their Lovers identity upon release.

—

The Olympics "(Baby) Hully Gully" Arvee July 1959

Style: Rhythm and blues vocal group
From and recorded in: Los Angeles< CA
Suggested pairings: Herbie Alpert "Hully Gully" 1959; Fred Richards "Hullee Gullee" 1959; The Turks "Hully Gully" 1959; Johnny Otis "Three Girls Named Molly (Doin' The Hully Gully)" 1959; Rudy Ray Moore "Hully Gully Papa" 1959

The Olympics debuted on Arvee, named after its owner, Richard Vaughn's first and last initials (RV=Ar Vee), with "Private Eye," an answer to the Olympics' "Western Movies," which first hit the Mighty 690 charts for an unprecedented near six-month march to L.A. success.

After "Private Eye" sold out, Arvee began pushing the shoulder motion dance B-side, "Hully Gully," hardly a new dance. "It was just a throw-in, it wasn't even scheduled," recalled the Olympics' Walter Ward, who noted the songwriting was completed in the studio in 20 minutes by Fred Smith with suggestions by the group. "Charles Fizer and me said, 'Hey we know a tune.' The guys said, 'That's great, let's do it.'" From start to finish, it was on an eight-month charting track.

Note: Herbie Alpert's "Hully Gully" was a cheesy jazz instrumental that went nowhere. None of the earlier releases with that title had the "Hully Gully" beat.

Remakes: The Hollywood Argyles 1960
Answers: Jewel and Eddie "Doin' The Hully Gully" 1960; The Flares "Doin' The Hully Gully" 1962; Preston Epps "Hully Gully Bongo" 1960; Winston Wheaton "Hully Gully Every Day" 1960; The Seniors "Hully Gully Fever and The Flu Bug Too" 1960; Jasper Woods—really Richard Berry "Hully Gully Papa" 1961; The Dovells "Hully Gully Baby" 1962

—

Fabian "Got the Feeling" Chancellor August 1959

Style: Rock 'n' roll
From and recorded in: Philadelphia, PA

After release of the new Fabian hit, the first pressing of "Got the Feeling" was pulled as the slurred opening lyrics, which sounded like "when we were f*cking in the park," were completely excised, and replaced with the second line, "when were cheek to cheek," making the first press rare and a must for Philly rock 'n' roll and Fabe fans.

—

Sandy Nelson "Teen Beat" Original Sound August 10, 1959

Style: Rock 'n' roll instrumental
Where from: Santa Monica, CA
Where recorded: Hollywood, CA
Cover: Don Ralke

Sander Nelson was born in Santa Monica, CA and attended University High School, where he played drums with The Sleepwalkers with Bruce Johnston and others. As Sandy Nelson, he recorded with Kip Tyler & the Flips for Art Laboe's Starla label in 1957 and backed The Teddy Bears on the #1 "To Know Him Is To Love Him" in '58.

"Sandy was a drummer in one of the bands at El Monte," Laboe recalled. "He just played drums with some bands we had there, when the band would take an intermission, he'd stay on the stage, play his drums, the kids would dance to the riffs. I told him I've made a hit with 'Bongo Rock,' and I wanted the label to have original sounds, that's what I wanted 'Teen Beat' to be."

Laboe continued, "Sandy was painting our studio and came in all covered with paint with a tape in his hand, asking me to 'just listen.' It had a very fast upbeat, about four times faster than the record. It had Bruce Johnston on piano and Mike Deasy on guitar, I listened to it, thought it was pippy pappy sound. I signed the songwriter's agreement, told him I'd catch him later. I didn't want to play it as a march, told him to do it real slow, got him to the tempo I wanted, so we could do it. We had a guy named Guybo Smith, who tuned his bass to the drum beat, that's why it's so big, that was the bass married to the drum. We put lots of overdubs on it, then with Barney Kessell on guitar, we went in and overdubbed another session. You'll hear the duopoly there, Kessell on top of Nelson." Richie Podolor was also on guitar.

"I played on it and by virtue of how we put it together," said Bruce Johnston to 45Cat.com. "I qualify along with Richard Podolor as the writer with Sandy Nelson, but it didn't turn out that way 'cause we were too green to ask for a writing share." The result was "Teen Beat" on Original Sound.

Laboe recalled. "Sandy was underage, he said he had six months to go" before he could sign a contract. "I said, 'Let's wait six months' before he signed, it was a gentlemen's agreement." But before that happened, Nelson got an offer from Imperial, meaning there were no additional Sandy Nelson releases on Original Sound. "They didn't catch on how to make the sound,"

LaBoe said of his new label, Imperial. "We did lots of Barney Kessell overdubs on 'Teen Beat.' We went in and overdubbed another session, married Guybo Smith's bass to the drums." Imperial finally caught on to the teen beat with Sandy Nelson's second major hit, "Let There Be Drums," in September 1961

—

Barrett Strong "Money (That's What I Want)" Tamla/Anna August 1959

Style: Rhythm and blues
Where from: Mississippi
Where recorded: Detroit, MI
Earlier version: John Lee Hooker 1959

Barrett Strong's "Money (That's What I Want)" came from the collaborative efforts of receptionist Janie Bradford, whose Motown job moved from Berry Gordy Jr.'s apartment to a West Grand Boulevard building later famous as "Hitsville U.S.A." The first Barrett Strong record was "Let's Rock" on Tamla in April 1959, as described by song writer Janie Bradford. "It wasn't a hit, God knows. I had no idea. It was more R&B, but it didn't have the elements that 'Money' had. It was still in that flavor. Somebody must have changed my notes."

John Lee Hooker claimed to have written and first recorded "Money," which was the first major pop charting hit for Motown. With such strong early sales, it had to be farmed out to a label with national distribution.

Bradford heard her boss working on a new song with lyrics, "The best things in life are free, but you can give them to the birds and bees..." and the line that became the song's hook: "I want money... that's what I want!" Bradford came up with "Your love gives me such a thrill, but your love don't pay my bills..."

With these lyrics at hand, Barrett Strong and crew retired to Gordy Jr.'s newly opened studio. Strong hit the piano with an opening riff, drummer Benny Benjamin added a "tom-tom" beat. They gave the material "a gospel feel" as described by Claudette Robinson. "It had the gospel feel. People at the time wrote with the gospel feel."

By August 1960, "Money (That's What I Want)" was a big hit on Tamla, such a big hit, the newly founded label couldn't handle the sales. Gordy's sister Anna could as her Anna label had a distribution deal with Chess, which took the lion's share of the sales. Gordy finally broke that barrier with the national hit "Shop Around" by The Miracles, which was on Tamla from start to finish.

Remakes: Jerry Lee Lewis 1961; Joey Dee and the Starliters 1962; The Beatles 1964; The Rolling Stones 1964; The Kingsmen 1964; John Lee Hooker 1966; Larry Bright 1966; Little Richard 1967

—

The Rock-A-Teens "Woo-Hoo" Doran/Roulette August 1959

Style: Rock 'n' roll
Where from: Richmond, VA
Where recorded: Salem, VA
Suggested pairings: Arthur "Guitar Boogie" Smith "Guitar Boogie" 1947; The Virtues "Guitar Boogie Shuffle" 1959

Led by Vic Mizelle, vocals and guitar, The Rock-A-Teens—Bobby "Boo" Walke, guitar; Bill Cook, guitar; Eddie Robinson, sax; Paul Dixon, bass and Bill Smith, drums—were first known as high school band Boo Walke & the Rockets in 1956.

The band was rehearsing "Rock-A-Teen Boogie" at radio WEZL when DJ Jess Duboy began singing "woo hoo, woo woo hoo." They kept the vocal. Hoping to get a label deal, they shopped a demo to several labels and auditioned for George Donald McGraw, who owned a record shop in Salem, Virginia. McGraw was impressed by "Rock-A-Teen Boogie" with one of rock's first mid-tune drum solos. Retitled "Woo-Hoo," it came out on McGraw's Doran in August, the first pressings of which credited The Rock-A-Teens as the writers of "Woo Hoo." Then McGraw told the band that best-selling guitarist Arthur "Guitar Boogie" Smith was going to sue the group for plagiarism. McGraw offered to "buy the song off you guys and that way they can't sue you." Once McGraw struck a deal with Morris Levy at Roulette Records to reissue the record, composer credits went to G.D. McGraw.

—

Bobby Darin "Mack the Knife" Atco August 1959

Style: Pop
From and recorded in: New York City, NY
Original title "Moritat": Dick Hyman Trio; Richard Hayman and Jan August; Lawrence Welk; Louis Armstrong; Les Paul; Billy Vaughn (all 1956)

The original German version of this song is called "Theme from The Threepenny Opera," or "Moritat," which is the German word for "Murder Ballad."

All but the Armstrong version was an instrumental; Armstrong was the first to chart with a vocal rendition. Kurt Weill and Bertolt Brecht wrote this song in 1928 for the German play The Threepenny Opera. "Mack" is Macheath, the title character, portrayed as a criminal, with lyrics about a murderer.

Following the September 4, 1959 stabbing deaths of two teenagers by a 17 year old and other similar incidents of violence in New York City, WCBS radio in the Big Apple banned Bobby Darin's "Mack the Knife." Despite these setbacks, the enormous success of this pop evergreen forever changed Darin's style from that of a rocker to that of a mainline pop star and, eventually, into a folkie and social protest songwriter.

—

Bo Diddley "Say Man" Checker August 1959

Style: Blues
Where from: Mississippi
Where recorded: Chicago, IL

Considered one of the first rap records, Bo Diddley came with this guitar backed spoken word "Say Man" in which he traded "the dozens" with his maraca player Jerome Green.

Diddley resists the rap comparison: "It wasn't called rap, it was called signifyin." Not all the lyrics were clear to his fans, about which he said. "They can't understand, they say, 'my pretty baby said she was a bird,' they get the lyrics all screwed up, it's not that at all, but it sounds very much like that. It's 'my pretty baby said she wasn't for it.' I said 'for it.'"

Answer: Bo Diddley "Say Man, Back Again"

—

Ronnie Hawkins and the Hawks "Mary Lou" Roulette August 1959

Style: Rock 'n' roll
Where from: Arkansas; Hawks from Canada
Where recorded: New York City, NY
Original version: Young Jessie 1955

The Hawks were Jimmy Ray Paulman, lead guitar; Will 'Pop' Jones, piano; New York session player Sam Taylor, tenor sax and Levon Helm, drums, the latter of whom journeyed from this basic rocking heavy echo-chambered remake of Young Jessie's original "Mary Lou" into creating The Band, which backed Bob Dylan with great success.

—

Miss Toni Fisher "The Big Hurt" Signet September 1959

Style: Pop
From and recorded in: Los Angeles, CA

Signet's owner, husband of Fisher and songwriter Wayne Shanklin, who also wrote "Primrose Lane," which was still on the charts, invented what is known as "flanging," similar to "phasing" in which the sound appears lost to static, but still listenable, the very technique that took this piece of pop out of the ordinary.

Fisher recorded "The Big Hurt" at L.A.'s Gold Star studios with Heinie Beau's orchestra, but Shanklin felt there was something missing; he wanted the song to stand out and worked with the studio's engineers to come up with what he called a "gimmick sound." The end result used a tape-delay phasing effect (some have called it "flanging") sounding not unlike the distant, slightly distorted echo of a short wave radio tuning in a faraway signal. The recording was fantastically freakish by '50s standards.

Earliest examples of this hit show the artist as Toni Fisher; Miss Toni Fisher came later. DJ Wink Martindale supplied the "Miss" tag to Toni Fisher, as her voice was so strong it could be heard out of the background.

—

Neil Sedaka "Oh! Carol" RCA September 1959

Style: Rock 'n' roll
From and recorded in: New York City, NY
Suggested pairings: Paul Anka "Diana" 1957; Elton John "Crocodile Rock" 1972

Neil Sedaka named "Oh! Carol" for the songwriter Carole King with whom he went to Abraham Lincoln High in Brooklyn, New York, along with Neil Diamond. Aldon music producer and longtime friend Don Kirshner advised Sedaka, "Write a song with the girl's name in the title. Talk in the middle like The Diamonds did in 'Little Darlin.''"

Sedaka, whose publishing job was analyzing popular songs, said, "I looked at the #1 record in every country in the world and analyzed it. Howie Greenfield and I wrote 'Oh! Carol.' I took the beat, I took the drum licks, I took the guitar licks, I took the harmony changes, and I went to school on them. Howie wrote the lyrics in twenty minutes but was embarrassed. He thought it was terrible. But it was exactly what I wanted."

Answer: Carole King "Oh! Neil" 1960

—

The Isley Brothers "Shout" RCA 1959

Style: Rhythm and blues vocal group
Where from: Ohio
Where recorded: New York City, NY
Suggested pairings: Jackie Wilson "Lonely Teardrops" 1958; LaVern Baker "Saved" 1959; The Isley Brothers "Twist and Shout" 1961

The Isley Brothers patterned their "Shout" after the Jackie Wilson phrase, "say you will" he sang in his hit "Lonely Teardrops." The Isley Brothers turned "Shout" into call and response to the extent that church groups attempted to ban their performance, claiming secular lyrics shouldn't be sung in gospel form, not dissimilar to the reaction to LaVern Baker's "Saved."

Remakes: Joey Dee & the Starlighters 1962; The Shangri-Las 1964; Lulu & the Luvers 1964

—

Tommy Facenda "High School U.S.A." Legrand/Atlantic September 1959

Style: Rock 'n' roll novelty
From and recorded in: Norfolk, VA

One time back up vocalist for Gene Vincent's Blue Caps, Tommy Facenda recorded a rocking novelty vocal about local high schools in the Norfolk area,

"High School U.S.A." just in time for the new term in September 1959, on the Legrand label. The flip side was a doo wop, "Give Me Another Chance." Facenda's original was picked up by Atlantic, with a new B-side, "Plea Of Love." Atlantic had Facenda recorded 28 regionalized versions for many metro and rural areas, listing as many local high schools as the lyrics could accommodate. It charted first and nationally at #28 on October 19, 1959. The versions were released in this order:

The first "High School U.S.A." on Atlantic was a pick hit on WAVY, Norfolk, Virginia on October 30, 1959… then came… New York City; North and South Carolina; Washington-Baltimore area and Philadelphia versions, the latter charting on WIBG, Philadelphia on October 12, 1959. Detroit version charted nowhere. Pittsburgh, PA version charted on KQV, Pittsburgh on October 3, 1959. Minneapolis/St. Paul and the Dakotas hit on Minneapolis' KDWB on October 24, 1959. Florida version charted in November 5, 1959 on WPDQ, Jacksonville Florida. Newark, New Jersey version charted nowhere. Boston and Massachusetts area version charted on Boston's WHIL on October 12, 1959. Cleveland version charted on October 12, 1959 on WCUE in Akron and on October 19, 1959 on KYW, Cleveland, Ohio. Buffalo version charted on October 19, 1959 on WKBW, Buffalo at #2. Hartford version hit #1 on WPOP on October 19, 1959. Nashville version charted on November 1, 1959 on WKDA in Nashville. Indianapolis and Chicago versions charted nowhere. New Orleans version charted on November 29, 1959 on WAIL, Baton Rouge. St. Louis and Kansas City area version hit on November 29, 1959 on KWK, St. Louis. Alabama, Georgia and Cincinnati versions charted nowhere. Memphis version hit #4 on October 23, 1959 on WHBQ. Los Angeles and So Cal version hit on L.A.'s KRLA on October 16, 1959. Bay Area version hit on October 24, 1959 on KEWB, then KOBY and KYA on November 2. Texas version charted on December 24, 1959 on KNUZ, Houston. Seattle and Portland version hit on October 9, 1959 on KAYO in Seattle and on KISN, Vancouver, Washington on November 30. Denver version hit #1 on October 28, 1959 on KIMN, Denver. An Oklahoma version charted nowhere.

Then school was out (see Gary U.S. Bonds on Legrand).

—

The Revels "Midnight Stroll" Norgolde September 1959

Style: Novelty doo wop
From and recorded in: Philadelphia, PA
Original title: "Dead Man's Stroll"

In 1954, West Philadelphia High School students John Kelly, lead vocalist, John Grant, John Jones, Henry Colclugh and Bill Jackson formed the Re-Vels Quartette. The group had several releases on small local labels until, in 1958, the Re-Vels recorded the fine "False Alarm" for Chess, which was a regional seller. Back to the small local label, in this case, Norgolde Records, for which they recorded their droll novelty doo wop with midnight tolls and wailing ghosts, "Dead Man's Stroll," for Halloween 1959.

Scheduled to appear on Dick Clark's American Bandstand, Clark had them change the title to the more commercial "Midnight Stroll." It worked, it hit.

—

Freddy Fender "Wasted Days & Wasted Nights" Duncan/Imperial September 1959 Talent Scout 1963

Style: Swamp rock
From and recorded in: Texas

Freddy Fender recalled, "Wayne Duncan was, he isn't is anymore, was the first man who said, 'Freddy, you need to record.' I'd been recording in Spanish for Falcon Records. He's the first one to cut me in English. He had a jukebox route, that's as far as he knew about show business. That makes me know less than he did. He had the guts to take me all the way in his label. He had the guts to go all the way to New Orleans to talk to the distributors, things he never knew before."

The result was this Freddy Fender hit "Wasted Days and Wasted Nights" on Duncan, then leased to Lew Chudd's Imperial. Fender said, "I remember I went in front of Chudd. I had long sideburns, everybody had, like Elvis Presley. It wasn't a matter of trying to imitate Elvis Presley, everybody had long sideburns in the fifties. The first thing he told Wayne Duncan was, 'You got to tell your boy here to cut his sideburns off because he looks too much like a Mexican and I don't know if we can push him or not on the record thing.' He wanted me to look like a white boy which is an impossibility. Back then, it was a barrier to be a Mexican American artist."

—

Jimmy Jones "Handyman" Cub September 1959

Style: Rock 'n' roll
Where from: Birmingham, AL
Where recorded: Regent Sound Studios, New York City, NY
Suggested pairings: The Jones Boys "The Whistlin' Man" 1957; Marv Johnson "Come To Me" 1959; Sparks of Rhythm "Handyman" Apollo 1960; Jimmy Jones "Mr. Fix It" 1963

At age 12, Jimmy Jones moved to New York and attended George Washington High School. He brought his high tenor voice to vocal groups like the Berliners, a U.S. Army group formed in Germany with bass singer Andrew Barksdale, whom he had known in Birmingham. The Berliners became The Sparks of Rhythm and recorded "Stars in The Sky" for Apollo in 1955. After Jones left the group, in February 1956 they recorded "Handy Man" with Barksdale taking the lead. It wasn't issued at the time.

Jones then joined the Savoys on Savoy and The Pretenders on Rama and on Whirlin' Disc. Then the Pretenders became the Jones Boys, on which Jones recorded "Whistlin' Man" on Arrow, which was a lot like Jones' later "Handy Man." Jimmy Jones got together with songwriter Otis Blackwell again to record a demo of "Handy Man," with Otis doing the whistling as the flute player hadn't shown up. The demo was sold to a Cub subsidiary, which shot up to #2 on the national charts.

When "Handy Man" hit, Apollo released "Handy Man" by Andrew Barksdale and the Sparks of Rhythm for the first time, a song that sounded very little like Jones' hit. There was a lawsuit contemplated by Arrow against Cub. Marv Johnson, who had hit with "Come To Me" in January 1959, said, "Jimmy Jones and I became friends and he practically admitted to me that they were trying to get that 'come-a come-a' sound."

Remakes: Del Shannon 1964; James Taylor 1977

—

Marv Johnson "You Got What It Takes" United Artists September 1959

Style: Rhythm and blues
Where from: Detroit, MI
Where recorded: Cincinnati, OH
Original version: Bobby Parker "You Got What It Takes" 1957

Marv Johnson said, "'You Got What It Takes' is a composition written by Berry Gordy Jr., his sister, Gwendolyn, and Billy Roquel Davis, a writing partner of Berry's in early Jackie Wilson hits. Recorded originally by Bobby Parker for Vee Jay in 1958, Johnson stated, "I was given the song and belted it out the way I felt it. We recorded it here in a local studio called United Sound and it just seemed to have all the ingredients, all the magic was there. It turned out to be one of the biggest things I had the pleasure of doing. At the time, I was with United Artists, they had a tremendous promotional setup there."

With backing by The Rayber Voices, this rocking performance was a major pop and R&B hit starting out in Houston at #4 and Philadelphia at #3 in late October 1959. It was also recorded by Barrett Strong for Gordy's Tamla label a year later.

Remakes: Barrett Strong 1960; The Dave Clark Five 1967
Note: The 1965 hit, "You Got What It Takes," by Joe Tex, was an entirely different song.

—

The Miracles "Depend On Me" Tamla September 1959

Style: Rhythm and blues vocal group/soul
From and recorded in: Detroit, MI
Original title: "You Can Depend on Me"

No doubt the most re-recorded composition in their catalog, The Miracles' "The Feeling Is So Fine" backed with "You Can Depend On Me" was replaced with a new A-side, "Way Over There," with strings and Marvin Gaye on drums backed with a new version of the retitled "Depend On Me" in February 1960. Finally, the minor hit version of the Miracles' "Way Over There" and the earlier version of "Depend On Me" came on April 4, 1960. "I liked the instrumentation," said Claudine Robinson. "I remember there were two versions." Actually, there were three versions, with "Way Over There" reissued on Tamla in summer 1962, but to little success.

—

Bobby Rydell "We Got Love" Cameo September 1959

Style: Rock 'n' roll
From and recorded in: Philadelphia

With an avuncular beat similar to Lloyd Price's "Personality" from 1958, Bobby Rydell scored his second hit with "We Got Love."

—

The Drifters "Dance With Me" Atlantic September 18, 1959

Style: Rhythm and blues vocal group
From and recorded in: New York City, NY
Suggested pairing: The Distants "Answer Me" 1962

The Drifters were an unabashed influence on the Detroit-based Distants, later known as The Temptations.

—

Bob Grabeau "Charge" Magnolia October 2, 1959

Style: Novelty
Where from: Pittsburg, CA
Where recorded: Hollywood, CA
Suggested pairing: The Playmates "Beep Beep" 1959

Pop vocalist Bob Grabeau fronted big bandleader Horace Heidt on this novelty song to capitalize on the L.A. Dodgers winning the World Series. The song was about defeating the Pirates, the Braves, the Cubs, the Giants and the White Sox via the team's fan's chant, "Charge" (different from the Renegades' "Charge"), with organ backing and backed with "Angel Town" with label credit to Horace Heidt on the Magnolia label, which should have made the charts, except in the San Fernando Valley.

On October 24, 1959, KFWB printed the following disclaimer on its chart: "According to sales, the recording of 'Charge' by Bob Grabeau on Magnolia label should be included among the Fab 40. Because this is a topical novelty with highly fluctuating sales potential, it does not show among the established best selling records, since topical content excludes any realistic continuing sales quality." And blah, blah, blah, the survey read. To KFWB's eternal discredit, "Charge" became the long-lasting chant heard at sports events everywhere… with a half century's worth of popularity, certainly the polar opposite of KFWB's claims.

KFWB's attitude about playing baseball 45s changed radically when the Dodgers were into their next pennant drive. "D-O-D-G-E-R-S Song," a comic take on baseball by Danny Kaye on Reprise, reached #6 on September 29, 1962.

After these solid attempts, Grabeau continued on in obscurity, while Height's next was a novelty record by Dodger's play-by-play man, Vin Scully.

—

James Brown and the Famous Flames "Good Good Lovin'" Federal October 1959

Style: Rhythm and blues
Where from: Macon, GA
Where recorded: Cincinnati, OH

As fellow King/Federal recording act, Hank Ballard & the Midnighters hit with "The Twist" in late 1958, James Brown and the Famous Flames attempted a very early twist beat vocal on the appealing "Good Good Lovin'" on Federal, which hit in two markets: Buffalo, New York in late October and all three top 40 stations in the Bay Area in early November 1959.

Remake: Chubby Checker 1961

—

Charlie Ryan "Hot Rod Lincoln" 4-Star 1959

Style: Rock 'n' roll
Where from: Spokane, WA
Where recorded: Hollywood, CA
Original version: Charley Ryan and the Livingston Brothers 1955
Suggested pairing: Arkie Shibley "Hot Rod Race" 1951

Charley Ryan and the Livingston Brothers answered the 1951 country hit "Hot Rod Race" by Arkie Shibley and his Mountain Dew Boys as "Hot Rod Lincoln," first released on Souvenir out of Spokane, Washington in 1955. Re-recorded by Charlie Ryan for 4-Star, "Hot Rod Lincoln" told the second half of the "Hot Rod Race" story, as referenced by the opening: "Have you heard this story of the Hot Rod Race, when Fords and Lincolns was settin' the pace? That story is true, I'm here to say; I was drivin' that Model A."

While the song tells of a race between a Lincoln and a Cadillac on the Grapevine grade in California, to Ryan, the actual location was on the Lewiston grade in Idaho. The most iconic line from the song is "Son, you're gonna drive me to drinkin' if you don't stop drivin' that Hot Rod Lincoln!" Ryan's version of "Hot Rod Lincoln" charted in mainly in East Coast markets, starting in Syracuse in late December 1959. "Hot Rod Lincoln" was quickly covered by long-time country singer Johnny Bond on Republic, charting well in California markets only in late July 1960.

Cover: Johnny Bond 1960
Remakes: Commander Cody & His Lost Planet Airmen 1972; Asleep at the Wheel 1988

—

Ron Holden & the Thunderbirds "Love You So" Nite Owl November 1, 1959/Donna February 13, 1960

Style: Rock 'n' roll
From and recorded in: Seattle, WA

The start of the recording career of Ron Holden & the Thunderbirds was when Holden was arrested. "My band and myself were at a little high school sock hop. During the intermission, the boys in the band including myself went out. We jumped in our band car. We had probably a half pint of I.W. Harper and one of them funny little cigarettes. It was about ten of us, stuck in this little car. The police came over, checked us out, found out I was the only one over 18. I did my little odd job for the government. While I was in there, I met the forensic expert, the guy who took fingerprints. Every two hours or so, he'd take my fingerprints. I couldn't figure out what this guy was doin,' he was tryin' to get in my head. He heard me doo wopping in the can and he said, 'What was that song you were doing?' I told him I had just written a letter to my girlfriend explaining to her that I wasn't a bad guy. He said, 'I'm going to quit the sheriff's department. When you get out, come and visit me and we'll see if we can do something.'"

Fingerprint guy turned out to be Larry Nelson who was about to quit law enforcement and start the Seattle-based Nite Owl label. Nelson's partner was Chuck Markulis, who attended San Pedro High School and Everett Junior College in Washington and sang as The Shades on "Dear Lori" on Aladdin in 1959.

The Holden recording session took place on a Sunday morning "in Nelson's 10 x 12 feet living room. I had no idea what a studio was about. Chuck Markulis owned the stereo Roberts tape recorder; we had two channels to get 20 microphones in and all these guys. There was a dog in the room, it was real bizarre. We did it live. Every time we'd try to record, the dog would bark. Twenty hours later, we all hated each other."

Ron Holden's "Love You So" had a 38-second intro, perfect for a DJ a yak up before the vocals, on Nelson's new Nite Owl, which charted top 5 in black Seattle radio. Markulis and Nelson shopped the song to L.A. labels and the Challenge label pressed up 5,000 45s, but then backed out. To avoid litigation, Challenge sent 5,000 unlabeled discs to Seattle. Nelson and Markulis glued Nite Owl labels on them one-by-one. They then made a deal with Bob Keane, who released "Love You So" backed with "My Babe" on Donna, where it charted much higher than it did in Seattle, not to mention it was a big hit nationally.

Markulis moved back to So. Cal and opened the Hardtimes chain of pool halls.

—

Jimmy Reed "Baby What You Want Me To Do" Vee Jay November 1959

Style: Blues
Where from: Dunleith, MI
Where recorded: Chicago, IL

About Jimmy Reed's most recognized droning hit, "Baby What You Want Me To Do," sax session player Red Holloway said, "He never had a horn, just guitar players. I played on a few, on the record when his wife is singing some of the lyrics, when you hear a second voice, she's whispering the lyrics in his ears. I played on some of that material. A horn doesn't sound good on a record with him. He was a funny man, very nice to work with.

Holloway added, "Jimmy Reed used to drink all the time. We were trying to stop him from drinking. In Georgia or Florida, he would always find out where you could buy bootleg liquor. We'd tell him, 'We just heard that liquor you're drinking is poison. Twenty people have died.' Jimmy would be straight for two weeks. When he was sober, you couldn't stand him. 'Somebody buy him a drink.'"

—

Flip Sloan "Little Girl in the Cabin" Aladdin 1959

Style: Rock 'n' roll
Where from: Los Angeles, CA
Where recorded: Hollywood, CA
Suggested pairing: Elvis Presley "Too Much" 1957

While living with his parents in the Fairfax District of L.A., 14-year-old Flip Sloan got his big break in the mail. "My nanny, Freddi, received two flyers in the mail, they're looking for talent. One was from Specialty. Aladdin was the closest." Sloan went to audition and signed for one record under a name possibly conceived to confuse him with hit makers Skip & Flip. Flip Sloan, real name Phillip Schlein, debuted as a vocalist on a performance reminiscent of "Too Much" by Elvis Presley, "Little Girl in the Cabin," backed with "All I Want Is Loving" with backing by Clifton White, Herman Mitchell and Mike Deasy, guitar; Adolphus Alsbrook, bass; Larry Knechtel, piano and Bumps Blackwell, drums with The Blossoms on backing vocals. Sloan later became very well known as songwriter P.F. Sloan.

—

The Capris "There's a Moon Out Tonight" Planet/Lost Nite/Old Town/Trommers 1959

Style: Doo wop
Where from: Queens , NY
Where recorded: New York City, NY
Suggested pairing: The Danleers "One Summer Night" 1958

From Ozone Park, Queens, The Capris were Nick Santo lead baritone singer; Mike Mincelli, first tenor; Vinnie Narcardo, baritone; Frank Reina, second tenor and John Cassessa, bass. Named after the large Lincoln Capri, several producers heard them rehearsing and arranged for "There's a Moon Out Tonight" to be recorded at Bell Tone Studios. Finished in an hour, it only took three takes and they took the first one.

The ending of "There's a Moon Out Tonight" is known as a voice overlay with each Capri chanting the title in turn and slowing it down a little each time, creating one of the most memorable endings in doo wop recording history. "I don't think it was intentional," Mincelli recalled. "It was one of the mistakes. There were a lot of mistakes on that record."

Out on Planet Records, the disk bombed. By 1959, the Capris were no more. At the outset of the 1960/1961 oldies revival, Lost Nite bought the master for $200 and reissued it on red vinyl. With strong New York City play three years after it was first recorded and released and two years after the group broke up, it hit big.

Blues, Rhythm and Blues, Rock 'n' Roll, Garage, Soul, Surf, and Rock

1960s

Richard Berry & the Pharaohs "Have Love Will Travel" Flip January 11, 1960

Style: Rhythm and blues vocal group
Where from: New Orleans, LA
Where recorded: Los Angeles, CA

A title based on the CBS-TV series "Have Gun, Will Travel," this rhythmic bass vocal rocker "Have Love Will Travel" was a local L.A. hit for Richard Berry, who recalled, "Flip wanted everything to be close to R&B. When I took them 'No Room,'" the flipside, "I said, 'This is my soul.' Max Firetag, Flip's owner, said, "I don't give a damn about your soul." Berry said, "I can't write no more 'Louie Louie's.'" In response, Feirtag said, "I want another hit." And a hit he got.

Remakes: Paul Revere & the Raiders 1964; The Imperialites 1964; The Off-Beats; 1964; The Hollywood Hurricanes 1964; The Gallahads 1964; Lee Maye 1967, Tav Falco's Panther Burns 1990, Thee Headcoats 1992, The Sonics 1999; The Black Keys 2004

—

The Fendermen "Mule Skinner Blues" Cuca/Soma January 1960

Style: Garage rock 'n' roll
Where from: Madison and Niagara, WI
Recorded in Milwaukee, WI
Original version: Jimmie Rodgers "Blue Yodel #8" 1928
Suggested pairing: Joe D. Gibson "Good Morning Captain" 1958; The Bell Notes "I've Had It" 1959

"Mule Skinner Blues" was lifted from Jimmie Rodgers' legendary birth of country music, "Blue Yodel #8," in 1928. Over the years, various country and folk stars recorded versions, including the hit title "Good Mornin' Captain" by Joe D. Gibson on Tetra in 1958, the version which inspired the guitar duo The Fendermen—Jim Sundquist, lead guitarist from Niagara, Wisconsin, and Phil Humphrey, lead vocalist, of Madison, Wisconsin. Phil, the lead singer, who ad-libbed "ha-ha" and "yuk-yuk" silliness in a satirical yodeling technique, played rhythm player.

Jim, the lead guitarist of The Fendermen, named after their brand of guitar, created perhaps the first garage rock record. The ending was entirely lifted from the "cha cha cha" finish of The Bell Notes' "I've Had It" from early 1959. Released first on the regional Cuca label, which started out as the Swastika label before a pressing plant employee warned the owner of inherent problems with a swastika design, "Mule Skinner Blues" was reissued to the marginally more major Minneapolis label, Soma, for its national run, on which the Twin City's KDWB debuted it to #1 in May. It was also covered with aggressive skill by country veteran Rusty Draper on Mercury to little effect, the gag being a limited one.

Cover: Rusty Draper

—

Larry Bright "Mojo Workout" Tide January 1960

Style: Blues rock 'n' roll
Where from: Norfolk, VA
Where recorded: Hollywood, CA
Suggested pairings: Ann Cole "Got My Mojo Working" 1956; Muddy Waters "Got My Mojo Working" 1956

Julian Ferebree grew up in Corpus Christi, TX and Louisville, KY. Discharged from the Navy, in 1953 he relocated to L.A. where he played clubs and became Larry Bright. "Joe Saraceno saw me playing blues with

Elliott Ingber and Larry Taylor at the Sea Witch Club in Culver City. Saraceno invited me to his office. I was doing 'Mojo Workout.' Saraceno said, 'Rewrite it.'"

"Mojo Workout" was recorded "at Western Studios," continued Bright. "Marty Robbins was recording 'El Paso' at the same time. I recorded 'Mojo Workout' with Earl Palmer, drums; Red Callender, bass; Bill Pittman, guitar, Plas Johnson, sax and Ernie Freeman, piano. I told Billy to make an e chord. I patterned the breaks after 'Western Movies.'" The B-side, "I'll Change My Ways," used ex-Teddy Bears member Marshall Lieb, whose voice was overdubbed in the doo wop-style background.

Bright had no idea the session was sold as "Mojo Workout" to Tide Records for release until R&B radio station KGFJ began playing it. Promoter John Bloor then took the record to his brother, KFWB PD, Chuck Blore. "Ted Quillan and Gene Weed used to have meetings over what records to play on KFWB," said Bright. "I was sitting at a food stand with Phil Spector when I heard it on KFWB. Spector said, 'You've got a good one there.'" He was right. "Mojo Workout" hit KFWB at #15 on March 28 and pop at #90 on May 16, 1960.

"Larry Bright was a very talented white artist who sounded black," Rene Hall said. "He behaved as a black man and he did a very good imitation of many black artists currently popular at that time. It would've been the owner of her label, Ruth Strachborneo, and her stepsister who backed most of her artists and she still does."

Muddy Waters' publisher Arc Music later sued Tide over "Mojo Workout," and settled for half. When lawsuits and/or bricks began flying, the title was changed to "Mojo Workout (Dance)" by The Mojo Dancers on Tide. In 1973, Tide sued Arc Music for damages and apparently also won.

—

Stan Freberg "Old Payola Roll Blues" Capitol January 11, 1960

Style: Novelty
From and recorded in: Hollywood, CA

Stan Freberg's ultimate satire, this two-part "Old Payola Roll Blues," on Capitol was a virulent anti-rock 'n' roll playlet with Jesse White and Freberg creating record producer Barney Schlock and teen idol Clyde Ankle at a rock 'n' roll session, and begins when the producer steps out of the studio and grabs the first kid he sees, asking him if he can sing. "No." Clyde Ankle then warbles "high school oo-oo," which Schlock shops to jazz DJ Stanley. Rejected, Schlock slides out under the door and after a few parting cracks, Stanley resumes playing cool jazz.

With the L.A. Times actively railing against rock 'n' roll and the radio stations that spun it, it appeared the form was kaput, thus Freberg was nailing the coffin shut for all time. According to an Associated Press report on January 15, 1960, "Freberg dreamed up the record late last year on the beach at Laguna. 'I was trying to write another record on the quiz show scandals,' he recalled. 'Then the payola thing broke and I went to work on that, I had been attacking rock and roll since 1954, did four records on it until I finally concluded there was no use fighting it. When the payola scandal came up, I realized rock and roll was dying. I'd be delighted if I could drive a spear into the body.' This is not the first time Freberg has had problem getting his satires played. His 'Green Christmas,' a tirade against commercializing Christ's birthday, ran into opposition from Madison Ave. Yet it has sold 250,000 copies in the last two holiday seasons. 'Oh, well,' he sighed about his current imbroglio, 'anther day, another banning.'"

—

Bo Diddley "Road Runner" Checker January 1960

Style: Blues
Where from: Mississippi
Where recorded: Chicago, IL

Using the "beep-beep" taunt by the Roadrunner cartoon character, backing Bo Diddley on "Road Runner" were Jerome Green, maracas; Clifton James, Otis Spann, piano; Lady Bo, aka Peggy Jones, guitar; all on vocals with Chuck Barksdale of the Dells. There is no mention that the cartoon company pursued legal action. Bo Diddley called it "good highway music."

Remakes: Johnny Winter 1963; The Accents 1964; The Gants 1965

—

The Drifters "This Magic Moment" Atlantic January 28, 1960

Style: Rhythm and blues vocal group
From and recorded in: New York City, NY
Suggested pairing: The Dootones "Strange Love Affair" 1962; The Small Faces "Itchycoo Park" 1968

This song represents early use of lush strings in an R&B hit.

Remakes: Bobby Comstock 1965; Jay & the Americans 1968; Billy Joe Royal 1973; Richie Furay 1978

—

Freddy Fender "Holy One" Duncan January1960/Imperial April 1960

Style: Swamp rock
Where recorded: Brownsville, TX
Suggested pairing: The Moonglows "Sincerely" 1955

"I recorded 'Holy One' in Brownsville, Texas, in a radio station. I paid $50.00," said Freddy Fender. "It was me on the guitar; Louis Moody, the bass player from San Benito didn't have the money to buy a bass, so he played bass on a guitar. Little Herman was the drummer and then they also did the oohs and aahs as background singers. The backing of 'Holy One' reminded me of The Moonglows backing on 'Sincerely.' Most of the songs that we done like that, we called it the old G turn-around. Especially in '54 and '55, everything had the same harmony parts, everything was the same. 'Eddie My Love,' The Penguins' 'Earth Angel,' 'Holy One.'"

Fender continued, "I took it to a guy who had some money, hoping he would donate some money to get the record going. When he played the tape, he erased it. I had to go back to record it again. The original was better than the later one I did. He got my song, 'Holy One,' to #1 at KTSA, San Antonio; #2 on WNOE in New Orleans and WTIX in New Orleans and #4 on WAIL in Baton Rouge."

Fender's "'Holy One' on Duncan sold 280,000 copies in 1959, then it went on Imperial with Lew Chudd." Needing a new identity as he was doing time at Angola Prison at the time, Fender became Scotty Wayne for a redo of the song with a new title, "Only One," in 1963.

—

Marv Johnson "I Love the Way You Love" United Artists February 1960

Style: Rhythm and blues
Where from: Detroit, MI
Where recorded: New York City, NY

"'I Love the Way You Love' had the R&B and the sanctified religious type sound with the tambourine and the great driving church-like rhythm," said Marv Johnson. "The lead voice repeating more or less the basic parts of the song. We had the chemistry going, we followed suit. It came right behind 'I'm Comin' Home' and 'You Got What It Takes.' You can't put your finger on or explain exactly what causing this time of chemistry to sort of meld together, but we did have that sort of thing. Berry [Gordy's] productions were similar in a lot of ways. When we went in we knew what to do, we'd do the same thing. If you got the right chemistry, it always works like that. 'I Love the Way You Love' was that type of song that was good for me. The things we were doing were tailor made. We were a real close family-like group, everyone was together, there were no petty jealousies at that time, no concern about what was going on administratively, about anybody being cheated. We were just a group of young people satisfied to do what we want to please our audience."

—

Jesse Hill "Ooh Poo Pa Doo" Minit February 1960

Style: Rhythm and blues
From and recorded in: New Orleans, LA
Suggested pairing: The Isley Brothers "Nobody But Me" 1961

Earl King recalled how Jesse Hill's "Ooh Poo Pa Doo" started. "There was a bass player with Huey Piano Smith and the Clowns named Raymond Lewis, who had hit with 'I'm Gonna Put the Hurt On You' on Instant Records. Raymond was a guy who liked to talk a lot of trash in the car and Jesse Hill was playing drums with Huey. Every day, Raymond was talking trash about 'Ooh Poo Pah Doo,' using lines like 'I'm gonna ring a few bells in your head' or 'create a disturbance in your mind.' Raymond would say this to chicks he would meet and Jesse wrote them down and took the song to Toussaint to audition. He said, 'Look, I got this song, it don't make no sense, but I want you to come to my rehearsal.' Jesse sang the song, Alan [Toussaint] looked at him like he was crazy, but when he went back and heard the group and the rhythm he was playing, they put it together." "Ooh Poo Pah Doo" became a Mardi Gras fave, selling 800,000 copies.

Remakes: Ronnie Dio & the Prophets 1962; Sandy Nelson 1963; The Sisters 1964; Freddie Fender and by the Candy Johnson Show 1964; Paul Revere & the Raiders 1965; The Standells 1965; Trini Lopez 1966; The Canadian Rogues 1967; Nino Tempo & April Stevens 1968; Skip Easterling 1970; Ike & Tina Turner 1971

—

Ray Bryant "The Madison Time" Columbia March 1960

Style: Jazz
Where from: Philadelphia, PA
Where recorded: New York City, NY
Covers: Al Brown's Tunetoppers 1960; Les Brown and His Band Of Renown 1960

In 1948, jazz pianist Ray Bryant traveled with Tiny Grimes & his Rockin' Highlanders, a kilt-wearing R&B group, recording a few sides with them for the Gotham label in the summer of 1949. Bryant then started his own trio with brother Tommy and played at a number of Philly clubs. The Madison dance craze either began around 1957 in Columbus, Ohio or a few of years later in Baltimore, Maryland. Promoter, club owner and entrepreneur William "Bubbles" Holloway claimed credit for the line dance built around a left foot movement.

In 1959, organist Bill Doggett came up with an instrumental, "The Madison," on King Records, but it was a different approach. Bryant's "The Madison Time" turned the vocals over to DJ Eddie Morrison to explain the dance steps with specific moves, the label putting out an accompanying picture sleeve mapping the steps. Morrison instructed dancers to make moves like "The Rifleman... Cleveland Box... big strong basketball with the Wilt Chamberlain Hook… big strong Jackie Gleason (and away we go!)... how about a little stiff leg there?... double cross and freeze,'"while Brown's singing-and-speaking version called for dancers to make a "Boss turn, Birdland twice, reverse that bird, step back over... hit it, like a rug," which lasted until "The Twist" became the next big dance.

Remake: Richard "Groove" Holmes 1969

—

Jackie Wilson "Night" Brunswick March 1960

Style: Rhythm and blues
Where from: Detroit, MI
Where recorded: New York City, NY
Suggested pairing: Camille Saint-Saens' Samson et Delila "Mon coeur s'ouvre a ta voix" (My heart opens itself to your voice aka Softly Awakes My Heart)" 1877

Marv Johnson opined, "Jackie was just a tremendous artist, leader in rhythm and blues and popular music. He had a flexible voice that could really belt out any type of song you gave him. On the fast things, Jackie was a real driver with that 'hey hey' type of thing." Turned out, R&B fans preferred the flipside, the bluesey "Doggin' Around."

—

The Phantom "Love Me" Dot March 1960

Style: Rockabilly
Where from: Alabama
Where recorded: Gulf Coast Studio, Mobile, AL

This totally wild 93 seconds recorded in 1958 at the very tail end of rockabilly with lots of guitar and limited lyrical content, "Love Me" was The Phantom's only release. The Phantom was not Pat Boone's brother Nick as rumored, but a discovery of Pat's named Jerry Lott—with Frank Holmes, guitar; Pete McCord, bass; Bill Yates, piano and H.H. Brooks, drums. Lott told Derek Glenister of the session, "It was wild. The drummer lost one of his sticks, the piano player screamed and knocked his stool over, the guitar player's glasses were hanging sideways over his eyes." The Phantom didn't sell, despite the masked man picture sleeve.

—

Jerry Glenn "Holy One" Checker April 1960

Style: Swamp rock
Where recorded: Chicago, IL
Original version: Freddy Fender 1959

This song began charting in mid-April 1960 in San Bernardino, then in Boston. It is a cover of an original by Freddy Fender, who recalled, "Actually, he covered me on it, out of Chicago, I think. Chess Records. They tried to take it away from me, very common in the business. That's what he tried to do, but it didn't work. I guess it's a white boy. He was not that successful with it, but he sure gave it a good try."

Jerry Glenn was actually Jerry Kennedy, who was to record a remake of Johnny Otis' "Willie & the Hand Jive" in 1963.

Fender said, "I remember we were somewhere on the road and Wayne Duncan came in with the record, 'Look Freddy,' he put it on. That's when I knew we better put it on a label real quick or they were going to get it. Soon as that happened, he went to Lew Chudd on Imperial. We put it on Imperial." Which sold better, "Wasted Days & Wasted Nights" or "Holy One"? "Up to now, they have sold about the same. Three million each," Fender replied.

—

The Shirelles "Tonight's the Night" Scepter April 1960

Style: Rhythm and blues vocal group
Where from: New Jersey
Where recorded: New York
Covers: The Teenagers 1960; The Chiffons—not the "He's So Fine" Chiffons 1960

The Shirelles' "Tonight's the Night" was their first non-reissued major hit and was important enough to generate an answer, "(Will You Love Me) Tomorrow," an even bigger hit for those very same Shirelles.

Answer: The Shirelles "Tomorrow" 1961
Remake: Candy and the Kisses 1966

—

James Brown & the Famous Flames "Think" Federal April 1960

Style: Rhythm and blues
Where from: Macon, GA
Where recorded: Cincinnati, OH
Original version: The Five Royales "Think" 1958
Suggested pairing: The Four Seasons' "Dawn" 1964

In 1960, James Brown revived the Five Royales' rocking "Think" with stinging guitar work on the sister King label from 1958.

Remake: Wayne Cochran 1965

—

Hank Ballard & the Midnighters "Finger Poppin' Time" King April 1960

Style: Rhythm and blues vocal group
Where from: Detroit, MI
Where recorded: Cincinnati, OH
Suggested pairing: The Beach Boys "Do It Again" 1968

Said Hank Ballard, "I was in New York City at a bar and some lady walked in and asked the guy what time it was and he said 'ah baby, it's finger poppin' time.' Man I went straight to the hotel and wrote that song in 15 minutes. I did the Dick Clark show three times. He wouldn't let me bring The Midnighters on, kept them in the wings, 'My budget can't stand that, Hank. I can't let The Midnighters on." In exchange for not complaining about Chubby Checker's cover of "The Twist," that dance's originator Hank Ballard benefitted from heavy American Bandstand play of "Finger Poppin' Time" and his next two releases, all three of which were major hits.

Cover: The Stanley Brothers

—

The Olympics "Big Boy Pete" Arvee April 17, 1960

Style: Rhythm and blues vocal group
From and recorded in: Los Angeles, CA
Original version: Don and Dewey 1959

In 1960, Melvin King replaced Walter Hammond in The Olympics. Little Eddie of The Olympics recalled, "It [this song] was just a throw-in—it wasn't even scheduled. Charles and me said, 'Hey we know a tune.' That's what happened." The song, "Big Boy Pete," was already on the market by Don and Dewey on Specialty; however, that version had stiffed in 1959. "It was a throw-in after we was doing our session we needed another tune—did anyone know any tune? Charles and myself had another tune, 'Yeah we know a tune we've been rehearsing for a while.' The guys said, 'That's great let's do it.' We did it. After I seen it didn't do nothing with those guys, I said this could be a hit."

Dewey Terry of Don and Dewey recalled that both Don and Dewey and The Olympics rehearsed at their managers', John and Effie Criner, house, and that's how The Olympics knew of "Big Boy Pete."

The flipside, "The Slop," was promoted by KRLA upon release in early April, but Wallichs Music City broke the exciting "Big Boy Pete," who is shot at the fade.

Remakes: Rochel & the Candles 1964; The Tidal Waves 1966

—

The Safaris "Image Of a Girl" Eldo April 23, 1960

Style: Doo wop vocal group
Where from: San Fernando Valley, CA
Where recorded: Hollywood, CA
Cover: Otis Williams & the Charms

The Safaris were lead vocalist Jimmy Stephens, Richard Clasky from The Enchanters on Orbit, Sheldon Breier and Marvin Rosenberg. This white group began as Bilijean & the Angels' with "A Lover's Poem 'From Him'" with Darlene Love for Herb Alpert and Lou Adler's Tawney. The track from this session was supplied to The Untouchables, who were told to write a song over it, coming up with "Poor Boy Needs a Preacher." After a successful career on Capitol Records, R&B bandleader Johnny Otis and his partner Frank Gallo went across Vine St. to start the mainly R&B Eldo, which did best with the pop doo wop, easy-going metronome beat ballad "Image Of a Girl" by the Safaris on Eldo.

Otis spoke bemusedly of distancing himself from The Safaris' pop sound at El Monte Legion Stadium, though he didn't mention returning the checks their hit generated. "Image Of a Girl" was covered by Otis Williams & the Charms on King, over which Eldo sued, while King was suing over Cameo/Parkway's cover of "The Twist" by Hank Ballard & the Midnighters. Later, Otis was contracted by King to supply some L.A. sounds to that Cincinnati-based label, just as he'd already done for the King subsidiary, Federal, in 1954 and 1955. After "Image of A Girl" hit, The Angels' "A Lover's Poem 'From Him'" was issued to cash in that group's success.

—

Phil Sloan "If You Believe In Me" Mart 1960

Style: Rock 'n' roll
Where from: Los Angeles, CA
Where recorded: Beverly Hills, CA

Phil Sloan's rocking vocal with Buddy Holly-style guitar licks and inflections, "If You Believe In Me" was backed with the Ritchie Valens-style rocker "She's My Girl" with the Hylton Shane Orchestra; Bill Pittman, guitar; Steve Douglas, sax and Sandy Nelson, drums and was issued on Marty Melcher/Doris Day's Mart, a subsidiary of Arwin. Sloan recalled, "Jan & Arnie were on Arwin, so were The Pets and were on the radio. I noticed the address; it was an office building, Canon Drive. They had to be in my bus radius, I could take a bus there. I had my guitar in a pillow case, asked them if they were looking for songs or recordings. The secretary sent me to the head of A&R, who brought me to see Marty Melcher, who said 'sign him and record him' to Hylton Shane, a young guy, 23, collegiate with a sincere looking face. It got some radio station play. KFWB played it once in a battle of the records." This was when Sloan was 14; later he succeeded as songwriter P.F. Sloan.

—

The Hollywood Argyles "Alley Oop" Lute May 1960

Style: Novelty rock 'n' roll
Where from: Gary Paxton, Tucson, AZ; Dallas Frazier and Billy Mize, Bakersfield, CA
Where recorded: Hollywood, CA
Covers: Dante & the Evergreens 1960; The Dynasores 1960

This Dallas Frazier composition, "Alley Oop," was the earliest collaboration of Gary Paxton and Kim Fowley. When Paxton first came to town, "Dallas Frazier recognized me and said, 'I write songs.' He had a country song, wanted The Olympics or The Coasters to record it; he liked that kind of stuff."

Kim Fowley, who had just graduated from high school, ran into Paxton and "told me, 'you can come stay at my place,'" recalled Paxton. "It was a flophouse on Cahuenga. I had to close the door, pull the bed down, took the backseat out of my car, locked the hallway door every night at midnight. Next morning, he'd get up, unlock the door, I'd put my backseat in the hallway. I got arrested twice for loitering."

Paxton, being under contract to the Brent label as Skip & Flip, named the band The Hollywood Argyles, after the street corner where they recorded. "Other than myself, there were no actual Hollywood Argyles," said Paxton, who drawled The Coasters-style vocal with several Bakersfield session players—Dallas Frazier, Billy Mize, and Scotty Turner as well as Diana Mutz, who according to Fowley was Paxton's girlfriend from church, and Dave Martinez from Tucson singing background vocals—and an uncredited mostly black band—Gaynel Hodge on piano, Harper Cosby of Gerald Wilson's Jazz Orchestra and the Johnny Otis Show on standup bass, Bobby Rey on, saxophone, Lloyd Price's drummer Ronnie Selico who was on 'Big Boy Pete ' by The Olympics, and Sandy Nelson," who had already hit with "Teen Beat" did percussion with striking the drums with wine bottles emptied by the band before and during the session, and a bass line added by Pat Vegas. Paxton said, "We paid $25 apiece for the session."

Where to place the song? Al Kavelin told Paxton, "You and me and Kim could start a new label called Lute, Lute's gonna make a lot of loot, but there was no loot after 'Alley Oop.' Al Kavelin disguised himself, claimed to be a Jehovah Witness preacher," said Paxton. Out as "Alley Oop" by The Hollywood Argyles on Lute, a label run by Al Kavelin, "a crook. Al Kavelin was working at Daywin Records with Marty Melcher, told me that Lute was part of Daywin, but never paid me a penny. He cheated me out of 'Alley Oop.'"

Bakersfield top 40 station KAFY offered to make it a pick hit or as a future bomb in late April 1960. It then charted a sister station to KAFY, KFXM in Riverside, at Wallichs Music City at Sunset and Vine in early May. By month's end, it was #1 in all the land.

According to Paxton, the Lute label was created to release "Alley Oop" by The Hollywood Argyles. Paxton noted Lute's numbering system was intentionally confusing. After the success of "Alley Oop" on Lute (5905) in early 1961, Lute issued simultaneous 6000/5800 series beginning with Gary Paxton & the Hollywood Argyles' "You're Ruinin' My Gladness" backed with "The Way I See" on Lute (5801). According to Paxton, the changes were "by design to keep lawyers from coming in" through re-sequencing and back-numbering what appeared to be the label's release schedule. "Kavelin and Bernstein bankrupted Lute to get out of paying, then bought farmland in Bakersfield." The bloom came off the rose as King Features Syndicate, owners of the rights to the Alley Oop character sued, collecting much of the songwriter's and label's payday. "Soon as we cut the record," recalled Paxton. "King Features contacted us, we ended up paying up 1/4 of 1 cent per record. When 'Alley Oop' suddenly took off, people wanted to book us for concerts, but there was no such group." To avoid possible litigation by the Brent label to which Paxton was signed as half of Skip & Flip, when "Alley Oop" hit, publicity furnished by the Lute label purposely changed details of the session. Local musicians like sax player Rey, drummer Gary Webb, guitarist Deary Weaver, Ted Winters, bass and vocalist Ted Marsh, and pianist Marshall Leib from The Teddy Bears were hired to take "Alley Oop" on the road as the touring Hollywood Argyles, identified in all publicity as singers on the hit.

Answers: The Pre-Historics "Alley Oop—Cha-Cha-Cha" 1960

Satires: The Hong Kong White Sox "Cholly Oop," a racist satire recorded at the "Alley Oop" session with Paxton, Mize and Frazier, which charted in Bakersfield in August 13, 1960; Gary Paxton "Alley Oop Was A Two-Dab Man" 1962

—

Roy Orbison "Only the Lonely" Monument May 1960

Where recorded: Nashville, TN
Suggested pairings: The Fleetwoods "Come Softly to Me" 1959; The Crystals "Uptown" 1961; The Beatles "Please Please Me" 1963; Mark Dinning "Come Back To Me My Love" 1960

With strings and the Anita Kerr singers, Orbison hit big with this evocative "Only the Lonely," which he had attempted to first sell to Elvis Presley and The Everly Brothers, who suggested Orbison record it himself. As there might have been confusion with Frank Sinatra blues ballad, "Only the Lonely," Orbison's effort was subtitled "Know the Way I Feel." This was recorded with backing by the A team Nashville session players, with Bob Moore bass player and arranger.

—

Pete Roberts "Twinkie Lee" Rendezvous May 23, 1960

Style: Rock 'n' roll
Where from: Virginia
Where recorded: Hollywood, CA
Suggested pairing: Johnny Faire "Bertha Lou" 1957

On the heels of Larry Bright's major hit "Mojo Workout," Bright promptly skipped labels. According to Bright, when he couldn't get cooperation from his first label, Tide, he got drunk and recorded for Highland as Pete Roberts. "Ray Terry was a promoter for Rendezvous," said Bright. "Me and drummer Dan Belski and Marshall Lieb did this song, named after Chuck Blore's daughter's cat Twinkie Lee. On commercial copies, Pete Roberts was credited on "Twinkie Lee" on Rendezvous, but on promo copies, it was Larry Bright on this rocking Bay Area hit.

Bright recalled, "John Marascalco sued over "Twinkie Lee," said it was too close to 'Bertha Lou.'" a local hit by Johnny Faire from '57. In a provocation to their established reissue label partner, the Rendezvous label, which had issued the side as by Pete Roberts in 1963, Talmadge credited Larry Bright on "Twinkie-Lee" on Highland. At about this time, Tide label owner Ruth Strachborneo reported to the police that Bright had driven by and pitched a rock through her plate glass window.

—

Donnie Brooks "Mission Bell" Era 1960

Style: Rock 'n' roll
Where from: Texas
Where recorded: Hollywood, CA

The hit "Mission Bell" was incomplete when singer Donnie Brooks received it. Brooks worked for song-poem Fable Records. He recalled, "We had this one writer, William Michaels, who was in the stock business and very wealthy. He would write songs every day and come in with ten or twelve songs. He'd say, 'I want to record them now.' They were horrible… 'let me kiss the chocolate drops from your sweet, sweet lips.' We'd say, 'That's sickening.' So my writing and producing partner Jesse Hodges would take them home and rewrite the whole song. He was a very good writer. William Michaels wrote a song… 'put another nickel in the wishing well, the wishing well,' sort of like Sheriff John's 'put another candle on my birthday cake…' Jesse Hodges rewrote it as 'my love is higher than a mission bell.' Michaels would say, 'What are you doing to my songs?' We'd say, 'We're just putting them in order.'"

Brooks continued, "When we got it ('Mission Bell'), it had no bridge. We took it around to several labels because it was a folk song. They said, 'There's no bridge, so we're going to pass on it.' John Marascalco and Scotty Turnbull wrote the bridge, 'give me your heart of gold.' Era liked it, 'You go in and cut it.' I said, 'I'm a pop singer. It's a folk song.' They said, 'You do everything else,' so I went in, got the background tracks put down by Hal Blaine, drums; Glen Campbell, Jerry Cole and maybe James Burton, guitar; Ray Pohlman, bass and Danny Gould on strings. I said, 'I'll come in tomorrow and do my vocals.' I came in the next day. They said, 'Everything is fine, you don't have to come in.' I said, 'What do you mean?' 'Your vocal turned out fine.' I said, 'I don't remember doing the vocal.' I was leading the vocal, singing 'my love is higher than a mission bell.' I'm conducting the girls (the Carousels with Vivian Roberts), so they took that. I was angry. I never got to do my vocals. They just took what I did with the girls. It was a live thing. They were happy with it."

Out as "Mission Bell" by Donnie Brooks on Era, it hit #1 at Wallichs Music City on May 9, a full month prior to hitting L.A. radio or the national charts, where it hit in June. "Mission Bell" hit "real slow which was good for the artist, not for the company," said Brooks. "It kept my name going as a single. It sold 400,000 to 700,000 copies nationwide. A year later, it did well in Canada at #5 and Australia at #4, but not in England. It gave me a calling card, kept me in the oldies thing. I got established as Donnie Brooks and had a five-year deal with Era and I kept coming out with records."

—

The Gamblers "LSD-25" World Pacific 1960

Style: Instrumental rock 'n' roll
Where from: Los Angeles, CA area and Canada
Where recorded: Hollywood, CA

The Gamblers were lead guitarist Derry Weaver, who came to L.A. with Paul Revere & the Raiders before being deported to Canada; Larry Taylor, bass; Elliot Ingber, rhythm guitar and Rod Schaffer on drums, all of whom had backed The Enchanters on Orbit and Bruce Johnston on piano for their first release and first hit, "Moon Dawg," backed with "LSD-25" on World Pacific, the B-side title inspired by a *Life* magazine article on LSD.

The A-side, "Moon Dawg" charted on KFXM in late May 1960 and on KFWB and KRLA in mid-June in the top 15. According to Taylor, "Derry Weaver was from Canada. We got connected with him. He didn't sing, wrote instrumentals. He thought up a unique way of guitar playing around L.A. He was one of first guitar players to tune his strings down, gave it a different sound when he recorded."

Written by Derry, "Moon Dawg" was an instant classic—a blasting guitar rocker with a stunning drum intro and some nice dog howls courtesy of Nick Venet who, according to the label, "arranged and directed" the recording. "Nicky didn't arrange anything except the deal with World Pacific in exchange for the publishing," said Taylor. "We'll let him have that one. He also did the dog howl. Great job. We were all standing around the mike singing 'ah-ah-ah-ah-ah-ah' and Nick howled. Great overdub! One take."

Venet added, "Yes, LSD-25 was about a drug that made mice chase cats. It was being experimented with at some universities. It was made from rye bread. I never got into any drugs." Venet then convinced naïve label execs that the title, "LSD-25," was about a Naval ship, like JFK's PT-109. The Gamblers became The Hollywood Gamblers and moved on to other labels.

—

The Rockin' Rebels "Wild Weekend" Marlee/Swan June 1960

Style: Instrumental rock 'n' roll
From and recorded in: Buffalo, NY

The four member Rebels were brothers Jim Kipler, guitar; Mickey Kipler, sax; Paul Balon, bass and Tommy Gorman, drums out of Baker-Victory High School in Lackawanna, near Buffalo, NY. DJ Tom Shannon at Buffalo, New York's Top 40 WKBW recorded them on an instrumental variation on his radio theme, titled "Wild Weekend" for which Shannon and fellow DJ Phil Todaro's came up with a new label, Mar Lee, the names of their girlfriends.

"Wild Weekend" hit #7 on WKBW in March 1960. As there was possible conflict with Duane Eddy's Rebels, the band became The Rockin' Rebels. After an appearance on American Bandstand, The Rockin' Rebels' "Wild Weekend" was picked up by Swan Records of Philadelphia, charting #3 on WKBW in

November 1962, hitting nationally at #8 on December 29, 1962. Shannon and Todaro made money; the band, not so much.

—

The Bosstones aka Boss-Tones "Mope-itty Mope" Boss/V-Tone June 1960

Style: Doo wop
From and recorded in: Philadelphia, PA

The Boss-Tones were a Philadelphia vocal group responsible for the bass heavy novelty doo wop "Mope-itty Mope," first out on the Boss label in June 1959, reissued on V-Tone in January 1960, but with negligible sales, even in its hometown. Then came 1961, when the 100,000 watt Mighty 690, XEAK, out of Tijuana, Mexico, a signal that had blanketed the western half of the United States with rock 'n' roll since 1957, changed format. Probably because of new top 40 L.A. competition from KFWB, which went top 40 in 1958, and KRLA, which had just gone top 40 in 1961, XEAK decided to go all news. To get some sort of attention, for about two weeks, when they announced the latest Chuck Berry, Everly Brothers, Jan & Dean or Ricky Nelson, the record played was "Mope-itty Mope" by the Boss-Tones. Every artist and record was announced, but for two straight weeks, "Mope-itty Mope" was the only sound heard other than the news.

Remake: The Dovells "Mope-Itty Mope Stomp" 1962

—

Bobby Marchan "There's Something On Your Mind" Fire June 1960

Style: Rhythm and blues
Where from: New Orleans, LA
Where recorded: New York, NY
Original version: Big Jay McNeely "There Is Something On Your Mind" 1959

Bobby Marchan, a stage name for a vocalist and female impersonator born in Youngstown, Ohio, got his start with Huey Piano Smith and the Clowns, a legendary New Orleans act. In 1960, he recorded a more or less cover of Big Jay McNeely's moody original hit, "There Is Something On Your Mind," changing the title slightly to "There's Something On Your Mind," but changing the content wildly, adding an almost comedic spoken bridge about shooting his woman's boyfriend, then shooting her, then vocalizing her last words, "hmmm hmmm."

—

Wanda Jackson "Let's Have A Party" Capitol June 1960

Style: Rockabilly
Where from: Tulsa, OK
Where recorded: Hollywood, CA
Suggested pairing: Little Richard "Rip It Up" 1956

Wanda Jackson recalled, "This song, 'Let's Have a Party,' was from a movie. I worked with Elvis off and on for a couple of years, '55 and '56, when he signed with Victor and came out to Hollywood." Recorded in about 1957, Wanda Jackson said of her rocking remake of a rather droll Elvis Presley original, "Let's Have a Party," with the first title "Party." "That one signifies rockabilly. The last verse in that song, I didn't even know the right words, I couldn't understand Elvis Presley, what he said. I kind of had to make up some words. People would ask me, 'What are you saying on that last line... got the parson in the pot?' Or was it 'everybody run, got the possum in the pot.' Really it was, 'everybody run, taste the possum papa shot.' I had a terrible cold when I recorded that, so I didn't do it any harm. I used the song as an opening song. I had my own band, did club work, seemed like a natural song. I had my band there, piano is Big Al Downing, guitarist Vernon Sandusky, Skeets McDonald on bass and Buck Owens on acoustic guitar."

—

Paul Chaplain and His Emeralds "Shortnin' Bread" Harper June 1960

Style: Garage rock 'n' roll
Where from: Massachusetts
Recorded in: New York
Suggested pairing: Etta James "Shortnin' Bread Rock" 1956

At the apex of folk and traditional material being arranged into rock 'n' roll vocals and instrumentals, Paul Chaplain's fine vocal of "Shortnin' Bread" was released in June 1960. When picked up for national distribution, "Shortnin' Bread" charted in August in all major markets, then hit #1 on WJJD and WLS in Chicago.

Cover: The Bell Notes 1960
Remakes: The Blisters 1963

—

Chubby Checker "The Twist" Parkway June 1960

Style: Rock 'n' roll
Where from: South Carolina
Where recorded: hiladelphia, PA
Original version: Hank Ballard & the Midnighters 1959

Chubby Checker was given his recording name by Dick Clark's wife Barbara, as a spoof on Fats Domino's name. Growing up in Philadelphia, Chubby was signed to Cameo-Parkway by Kal Mann, who penned Checker's debut, "The Class," showcasing his impersonations of Fats Domino and The Coasters, hitting the local WIBG charts in April, peaking at #38 in June 1959. Next came "Private Eyes," a clone of The Coasters' "Searchin'" from 1957.

Chubby Checker then redid a moderate hit by Hank Ballard & the Midnighters with vocal backing by The Dreamlovers. Checker's version of "The Twist" was a note-for-note copy, so faithful to the original that Hank Ballard thought he was listening to himself when he first heard it on the radio. Ballard's "The Twist" hit #2 on KYA and KEWB between June and August 1960. In summer 1961, Checker's "The Twist" backed with "Toot," loosely based on Royal Tones' "Short Shorts" from 1957, hit #1 on WMGM in New York City and KRLA in L.A., as well as hitting #1 nationally and #2 R&B. Mann decided to develop a dance to go along with the song, which Checker demonstrated on the Saturday August 6, 1960 Dick Clark Show.

Promoted not only to the teenage audience but also to the adult discotheque audience in New York, "'The Twist' dance rage exploded into the adult world," wrote Billboard. In January 1962, Parkway reissued "The Twist" with a new flip, "Twistin' USA," going to #1 all over again.

Remakes: Ernie Freeman 1961; Sam Cooke 1961; The Fat Boys with Chubby Checker "The Twist (Yo, Twist!)" 1988

—

The Paradons "Diamonds & Pearls" Milestone June 18, 1960

Style: Rhythm and blues vocal group
Where from: Bakersfield, CA
Where recorded: Hollywood, CA
Covers: The Escos; The Turbans

The Bakersfield-based Paradons emerged as a play on words from their gospel roots as The Dons of Heaven, according to member Charles "Chuck" Weldon. "We would sing gospel on Sundays, then at school we became The Paradons." Original members were lead tenor West Tyler, Billy Myers, Billy Powers and Edwin Scott, who joined the group with a song in hand.

"Edwin told me he wrote 'Diamonds & Pearls,' went to show the song to his mother and the local minister was having coffee with her," said Kim Fowley who later produced Scott. "Those were his two witnesses. The Paradons came over, he taught it to them. When I came in, they fired Scott. He took it very hard. Everyone treated Scott bad, we were teenagers. He wasn't one of us." With Weldon taking Scott's place, the group began "singing around the parks," said Weldon, "putting different songs together," one of them being "Diamonds & Pearls," which Scott had written. After Scott left the group, the song underwent some changes, but it remained basically the same as when Scott taught it to the group.

They went to L.A. with Ricky Lee & the Barons, who told them, "We're going to L.A. to record. If we get done early you can record some songs." With members Ricky Lee, lead guitar and vocalist; David Pearson, tenor sax; Jim Burris, baritone sax and Randy Curley, bass, Ricky Lee and the Barons backed The Paradons on "Diamonds & Pearls." Weldon said of "Diamonds & Pearls," a national hit on Milestone, operated by Werly Fairburn & Madelon Baker, "We must have done four or five songs in the first session. Milestone got it on vinyl and the record came out. After the song hit, producer Kim Fowley put Scott in touch with an attorney, "Walter Hearst organized another lawyer to become a lawyer for Edwin Scott, pursued all the actors in the lawsuit. He had a one record deal, lot of compromises, number of names as writer. In the settlement, it was him and others who were alleged to have co-wrote it. Turned out The Paradons were only a one hit wonder, after all that work," said Weldon.

—

Ike & Tina Turner "A Fool In Love" Sue July 1960

Style: Rhythm and blues
Where from: Clarksdale, MS and East St. Louis, IL
Where recorded: St. Louis, MO

"I was doing a song for Art Lassiter, he's a singer in St. Louis. I wrote 'A Fool in Love' for Art," said Ike Turner. "Tina and I were buddies, I would take her with me everywhere I go. Tina and I wasn't like man and wife, we was like sisters and brothers. We had little arguments and stuff, we was always together 24 hours a day. When you don't agree. We never agreed with nothing, Lassiter borrowed $90 to get some car tires. I'd been working on the song at the house with him and he didn't show up in the studio. I think they only had one or two tracks then. Tina knew the words just sitting around the piano with me when I was doing it with him. The guy at the studio, he had two tracks, 'Why don't you let me put her voice on it as a guide and I'll put it on one track and I'll put the band on the other track.' So that's what we did.

Ike Tuner added, "I think that bass came from, that pattern, that running line like that came from quartets that sang 'howm bow, howm bow,' like singing spirituals. I'm sure that was where it had to come from, because there was nothing like that around, man. When I put the scream in 'A Fool in Love,' on the part of Tina hollering in the record, in those days, they didn't have limiters and all that stuff. This guy, he'd never cut a record before with a band. We went in there and rented the Techsonic Recording Studio, all he knew was commercials, jingles, stuff like that. When Tina got to her part, he said, 'Damn it, don't holler in my mike.' She got scared. Kind of faded it down."

"I carried it to the Club Imperial in St. Louis," Ike Turner continued, "and all the kids there said, 'Put it out like it is.' I gave it to a disc jockey in St. Louis, Dave Dixon, he sent it to Juggy Murray. Juggy came down, he wanted the record and in one month, it was gone."

Vocalist Bobby Hendricks recalled Ike Turner first contacted Bobby Robinson at Fury/Fire Records. Hendricks said, "The tape was floating around New York. Juggy decided, 'I'll get this group Ike and Tina Turner,' but he did not sign them to a contract. Or whether he signed them or not, it was broken and they got away from him. [the] Sue [label] didn't want to jump on them because they didn't know how good that sound would work. Juggy asked me, I listened to some of the tapes, said, 'Why not, they sound good enough.' I was told that most of that was recorded in St. Louis, they came to New York with these sounds on tape."

—

Sam Cooke "Chain Gang" RCA July 26, 1960

Style: Soul
Where from: Chicago, IL
Where recorded: Hollywood, CA
Suggested pairings: The Untouchables "Raisin' Sugar Cane" 1961; Roy Orbison "Workin' For the Man" 1962

Sam Cooke's career was refashioned into more of a soul sound with this highly influential "Chain Gang" with the Sims Twins who recalled "Some of the Soul Stirrers" in the background. "J.W. Alexander was back there with a little stick or something. He started hitting and Sam said, 'Keep it up.'"

Sam Cooke's "Chain Gang" first hit Inland Empire radio charts in early August 1960, L.A. charts in September. It is supposedly based on Cooke encountering a real chain gang while on the road in the South. As producer Luigi Creatore told Rolling Stone, "We made one record with him and nothing happened. Then we said, 'Listen, Sammy, you write some things and bring them in the next time we do a session.' So he did. He came by and played several things. Not everything he wrote was good. We just said, 'That's nice, what else have you got?' He said, 'Well, I'm working on a thing and it goes like, 'Uh, ah, uh, ah, I hear the sound of the men working on the chain gang.' We postponed the session, he finished that, and of course 'Chain Gang' was a smash for him."

Answer: Theola Kilgore "That's the Sound of My Man" 1961

—

The Revels "Church Key" CTI/Impact July 1960

Style: Instrumental rock 'n' roll
Where from: Santa Maria, CA
Where recorded: Hollywood, CA and Los Angeles, CA

Originally Gil Serna and the Rockets, sax player Norman Knowles took over the Santa Maria instrumental combo named The Revels, with Sam Eddy on piano; Dean Sorenson, lead guitar; Paul Sorenson, rhythm guitar; Knowles, sax and Jim McRae, drums.

Said the label owner Tony Hilder, "The Revels came up to me; had no material. I met them at Gold Star, we created 'Church Key.'" The term "church key" referred to a metal beer can opener with a sharp point to break the top, thus the Duane Eddy-styled instrumental, which began with the whoosh sound associated with opening a beer can, the giggle of Barbara Adkins and probably Hilder's voice intoning the title "Church Key" on CTI, a label partnership between Hilder and DJ Charles Trammell. Hilder then released it on his own Impact, which hit big in the Inland Empire.

"The Revels guitarist Dan Darnold had a riff. I took the riff and built 'Church Key.'" said Hilder. "Darnald was using the goodie bar, that's the song. I put it together, took it to Gold Star, then I finished it up at Ted Brinson's garage, had session sax player Plas Johnson do the horn."

—

Paul Revere & the Raiders "Beatnik Sticks" Gardena July 29, 1960

Style: Rock 'n' roll instrumental
Where from: Boise, ID
Where recorded: Hollywood, CA

Just another instrumental band, Paul Revere & the Raiders came to L.A. courtesy Gary Paxton. "I first met Mark Lindsay in late '58, early '59, when Skip & Flip played in Boise. When 'Alley Oop' hit, we went on tour," said Paxton. "Paul Revere's Dick and his wife owned an A&W and Paul Revere was to be our backup band. Paul asked us to take him to Hollywood. Moon was guitar; Mark Lindsay, sax and vocals; Paul on piano and a bass player. I took them with me and they lived in my apartment on Hayworth off the west side of the Strip near the Whisky for over a month.

Paxton added, "… Paul met John Gus who owned a pressing plant in Gardena at a gig. I talked to him about pressing the record, putting it on his label." The rocking topical title was the "Chopsticks" piano boogie, "Beatnik Sticks" backed with "Orbit (The Spy)," with an ear-splitting high-pitched tone lead-in.

—

Jerry Butler "He Will Break Your Heart" Vee Jay August 1960

Style: Soul
From and recorded in: Chicago, IL
Suggested pairings: the Everly Brothers "When Will I Be Loved" 1960; Steam "Na Na Hey Hey Kiss Him Goodbye" 1969; Dawn "He Don't Love You" 1975

After leaving the Impressions, soul practitioner Jerry Butler hit big with this avuncular vocal, "He Will Break Your Heart.... But wait." It was retitled and re-charted on and off for 15 years.

—

Johnny Kidd and the Pirates "Shakin' All Over" Apt August 1960

Style: Rock
From and recorded in: England

This was an early UK rockabilly release, "Shakin' All Over," by Johnny Kidd & the Pirates, Johnny Kidd, vocals; Alan Caddy, guitar; Brian Gregg, bass; Clem Cattini, drums and Joe Moretti, lead guitar. It was written as a B-side to a scheduled song; considered a throwaway.

Kidd said, "When I was going round with a bunch of lads and we happened to see a girl who was a real sizzler we used to say that she gave us 'quivers down the membranes.' It was a standard saying with us referring to any attractive girl." In remake, it was also the debut single by aptly named The Guess Who, based on members searching for a name, coming up with Guess Who, meant by the Canadian label to throw off record buyers at the onset of the British Invasion.

Remake: The Guess Who 1964

—

Maurice Williams & the Zodiacs "Stay" Herald August 1960

Style: Rhythm and blues/doo wop/beach
Where from: The Carolinas
Suggested pairing: Billie & Lillie "La Dee Dah" 1958

Maurice Williams & the Zodiacs were an extension of The Gladiolas, who originated the song "Little Darlin'" in 1957. As the Excello label owned The Gladiolas' name, the group had to change to The Zodiacs, based on a Ford import, which only was around for a year. To get a deal with the Herald label, Williams had to drop the lyric "if we have another smoke" to "another dance." At only one minute, 37 seconds, "Stay" was by far the shortest top five hit. It ends with a reference to the title "La Dee Dah," a hit by Billie & Lillie in 1958.

Remakes: The Hollies 1963; The Four Seasons 1964

—

James Brown & the Famous Flames "This Old Heart" Federal August 1960

Style: Rhythm and blues
Where from: Macon, GA
Where recorded: Cincinnati, OH
Suggested pairing: Ray Charles "Sticks & Stones" 1960

James Brown hit with this percussive "This Old Heart," reminiscent of Ray Charles' "Sticks & Stones," also from 1960.

—

Johnny Love "Chills and Fever" Startime/Dot August 1960
Style: Proto soul
Where from: Los Angeles, CA

When this proto-soul vocalist hit on L.A.'s KRLA in September 1960 with "Chills and Fever" backed with the fine swamp ballad, "No Use Pledging My Love" on the Startime label, he was Johnny Love. "Chills and Fever" charted for a good four months.

The original Startime release credited Johnny Love, but when it was picked up for national distribution by Dot Records, artist credit was changed to Ronnie Love. Some claim Love was really Detroit hit songwriter Ron Dunbar. However, hints on the Startime label indicate a relationship to the owner of the about-to-vanish Aladdin label out of L.A., a hit factory since the 1940s. Almost part two of Little Willie John's "Fever," "Chills & Fever' was a national hit in January 1961.

Remake: Tom Jones 1966

—

The Drifters "Save the Last Dance For Me" Atlantic August 1960
Style: Rhythm and blues vocal group
From and recorded in: New York City, NY
Suggested pairings: The Turbans "When You Dance" 1955; Arthur Alexander "You Better Move On" 1960; Ben E. King "Spanish Harlem" 1960; Ben E. King "First Taste Of Love" 1960; The Shirelles "Tomorrow" 1960; The Jarmels "A Little Bit Of Soap" 1961; Elvis Presley "Just Tell Her Jim Said Hello" 1962; Sam Cooke "Another Saturday Night" 1963

As songwriter Doc Pomus was crippled with polio, he reflected on not being able to dance with his bride at their wedding. Written by Pomus and Mort Shuman for Jimmy Clanton, The Drifters' Latin tempo highly orchestrated vocal "Save the Last Dance For Me" was their only #1 hit. At first, it was the B-side to "Nobody But Me," but hit when flipped. Label credit was given to Ben E. King, the only time on a Drifters' release, telegraphing the label's plan to promote King's records.

Answer: Damita Jo "I'll Save the Last Dance for You" 1960
Remake: The DeFranco Family 1974

—

Hank Ballard & the Midnighters "Let's Go, Let's Go, Let's Go" King September 1960
Style: Rhythm and blues vocal group
Where from: Detroit
Recorded in Cincinnati, OH
Suggested pairings: The Midnighters "That House On the Hill" 1955; The Vibrations "The Watusi" 1961

"Well, Fats Domino found a thrill on 'Blueberry Hill,'" said Hank Ballard. "There's something happening on those hills." In 1961, the Vibrations hit with "The Watusi" with an identical guitar intro on the Checker label. "We took them to court. If they had one more bar, we would have won the case. I want another bar."

Answer: Hank Ballard & the Midnighters "(I'm Goin' Back To) The House On The Hill" 1963

—

Gary U.S. Bonds "New Orleans" Legrand September 1960
Style: Rhythm and blues
From and recorded in: Norfolk, VA
Suggested pairing: Johnny Horton "Battle of 'New Orleans" 1959

When "New Orleans" was written by Royster, a country writer, "that was the first song they brought to me to record," said Bonds. "It was a Hank-type country thing. I said, 'I don't think I could do that' or The Bravados would kill me. I could never go back to a black neighborhood again, so we changed it around." It went from a country music answer to Johnny Horton's 'Battle of 'New Orleans' to rhythm and blues. Upon release of 'New Orleans,' the label indicated 'buy—b-u-y U.S. Bonds,' they thought it was a public service announcement." The strategy was that radio stations could promote the record and get credit for mandatory public service announcements required of radio stations by the FCC via the U.S. Bonds name.

—

James Booker "Gonzo" Peacock September 1960

Style: Rhythm and blues instrumental
From and recorded in: New Orleans, LA
Suggested pairing: The Primitives "The Ostrich" 1965

James Carroll Booker made his recording debut as Little Booker on "Doin' the Hambone" in 1954 on Imperial, a label that used him as session pianist with Fats Domino, Smiley Lewis and others. In 1960, Booker's instrumental "Gonzo" hit #43 and #3 R&B, starting with the Bay Area in early September, where it hit #2 on KYA and #1 on KEWB.

Booker then recorded "Smacksie," then ironically went to the slammer for drug usage, smack being a euphemism used by druggies, as was "Cool Turkey," the B-side of "Gonzo." In and out of trouble, he formed a relationship with DA Harry Connick Sr., who was also Booker's lawyer. Connick helped Booker avoid a prison sentence in exchange for piano lessons for Connick's son Harry Connick Jr.

—

Mary Wells "Bye Bye Baby" Motown September 1960

Style: Rhythm and blues
From and recorded in: Detroit, MI

A teenaged nightclub singer, Mary Wells wrote this driving vocal, "Bye Bye Baby" for R&B star, singer Jackie Wilson. When Berry Gordy Jr., who also wrote for Wilson, heard the song, he signed Wells to his fledgling Motown label. Songwriter and talent scout Johnnie Mae Matthews claimed "Mary Wells was 14 years old when she came to me. She came with about four lines of 'Bye, Bye Baby' and asked me if I would finish it up for her, and I finished it up for her. I wrote that record. I never got any credit for that!"

Betty Lavett recalled, "Johnnie Mae was in her 30s. She was a very coarse, hard, lying and deceitful woman."

—

Aretha Franklin "Today I Sing the Blues" Columbia September 12, 1960

Style: Rhythm and blues
Where from: Detroit, MI
Where recorded: New York

Groomed by the Columbia label as a pop/jazz vocalist, Aretha Franklin's debut in the secular realm and her first hit, albeit minor, was this moody "Today I Sing the Blues."

—

The Coasters "Shoppin' For Clothes" Atco 1960

Style: Rhythm and blues vocal group
Where from: Los Angeles, CA
Where recorded: New York
Suggested pairing: Kent Harris "Clothesline" 1956

This Coasters minor hit, "Shoppin' For Clothes," was a wry comedic visit to a clothing store to buy a suit. In both of their shopping songs ("Clothesline" and "Shoppin' For Clothes") when the protagonist's credit "didn't go through," he was left sans suit.

Kent Harris recalled working and writing for the credited songwriters Leiber-Stoller during his days at American Music. Leiber-Stoller later claimed that Billy Guy came to that session with the lyrics he had just heard on the radio, though he had forgotten the details of the record.

—

Joe Jones "You Talk Too Much" Ric/Roulette October 1960

Style: Rhythm and blues
From and recorded in: New Orleans, LA
Cover: Frankie Ford 1960

"Ric Records was already in existence" before Joe Jones recorded "You Talk Too Much," said producer Harold Battiste. "We had Ric before Joe Banashak's label, Minit. I was thinking about what I thought we could do." Ric's owner, "Joe Ruffino was associated with Joe Assunto, who had a one stop there. I don't know why Ruffino started a record label. When we promoted the record, Joe Jones and I went out on the road, wound up in New York, broke. Lloyd Price was involved with Roulette Records. When we got to New York, we had 29 cents in our pocket and a subway token. We got out to Coney Island. We got a penny from a guard at the subway station. Lloyd rescued us. He was playing at Coney Island. At the time, the original Ric label pressing of the record was way up the charts. When Lloyd realized this, he said, 'I'm going to put you in touch with some guys.' We met Morris Levy at Roulette Records. I don't know what the contractual arrangements we had with Joe Ruffino. Joe Jones and I were frightened at the situation because we had the impression we were dealing with people who were way beyond our expectations of what business people are and they said they would call. They sent for Joe Ruffino and Joe came to New York. When the smoke cleared, the record had gone to Roulette. The transition to Roulette was just what the powers were doing."

Answers: Martha Nelson "I Don't Talk Too Much" 1960; Joe Jones "One Big Mouth" 1960

—

Cleveland Crochet and His Hillbilly Ramblers "Sugar Bee" Goldband October 1960

Style: Cajun/rock 'n' roll
From and recorded in: Lake Charles, LA
Suggested pairing: The Boogie Ramblers "Cindy Lou" 1956

Goldband label owner Eddie Shuler had been searching for a Cajun band that could play rock 'n' roll, and had just about given up, as he told Mike Leadbitter in "From the Bayou," when violin player Cleveland Crochet and his band walked into his office "They had something they wanted me to hear and we went out to the studio. They told me they had spent three years developing the sound. I knew at last I found what I was looking for. We set a date and the result was 'Sugar Bee,'" the perfect melding of Cajun performance to a rock 'n' roll beat. "All we had done was to take a French song and give it a driving steel-guitar and rock and roll back beat, but the wailing sounds coming over the speakers told me the record was in," and a hit, for that matter.

Members of the band were Jay Stutes, vocal and steel guitar; Shorty LeBlanc, vocal and accordion; Bradley Stutes, string bass; Clifton Newman, drums; Mickey Broussard, drums; Rufus Thibodeaux, electric bass and violin; S.J. Barrio, rhythm guitar and Crochet, violin.

—

Dion "Lonely Teenager" Laurie October 1960

Style: Rock 'n' roll
From and recorded in: New York

This was Dion's debut in the single artist realm after leaving The Belmonts and his first hit as a single, albeit minor. This very rocking "Lonely Teenager" scraped the charts, but not much more.

—

The Miracles "Shop Around" Tamla October 1960

Style: Rhythm and blues vocal group/soul
From and recorded in: Detroit, MI
Suggested pairing: The Miracles "My Mama Done Told Me" 1958

When "Shop Around" by The Miracles was released, Tamla owner Berry Gordy Jr. listened to it on a car radio. Not liking what he heard, he recruited the group back into the studio to re-record a new version, which was subsequently released. The first version, which was also released, had more guitar than the second. "It took so long to release, that's why Motown did release 'Shop Around,'" said Claudette Robinson of The Miracles. "By me being in the group I'd sing the lead his part—people thought I was Smokey they never saw us before at the time of "Shop Around,'" There were a few main reasons I didn't lead. I felt Smokey had the best voice. Smokey felt I had the best voice. I was extremely shy. I thought being [a] girl in background was unique."

The first, later withdrawn, version has become a hot collector's item; the hit version, less so.

—

Richie Marsh "What Chance Have I" Rosco October 1960

Style: Rock 'n' roll
Where from: Salt Lake City, UT
Where recorded: Hollywood, CA

Before he became Sky Saxon with the Seeds, Ritchie Marsh arrived in L.A. in 1960 with Elvis tendencies. As Richie Marsh, he recorded on the rocking Van Winkle, DeLory, Darian-composed teen ode, "What Chance Have I" with a Buddy Holly backbeat for Bob Ross' Rosco in October 1960. Marsh said, "To get to record, I had to lay echo chamber tile for Bob Ross' studio. I never made anything on those records."

As Richie Marsh & the Hoodwinks on "Baby, Baby, Baby" backed with "Half Angel" in duet with teen movie star Darla Hood with the Bob Roberts Orchestra on Acama, "We were backed by The Blossoms. I had Darla singing on it; that was her husband Jose Granson's label," Marsh recalled. "For releasing 'Half Angel,' Bob Ross moved me out to his house and had me dig him a swimming pool." Darla Hood was best known as a child actress in the Our Gang comedies.

—

Gene Pitney "(I Wanna) Love My Life Away" Musicor November 1960

Style: Rock 'n' roll
From and recorded in: Connecticut

Gene Pitney had already recorded two duets as Jamie and Jane and as Billy Bryan in 1959 before he hit pay dirt. It was a time of experimental sounds like "Witch Doctor" by David Seville in 1958; "Susie Darling" by Robin Luke and "The Big Hurt" by Miss Toni Fisher in 1959, gaining so much traction that Gene Pitney built his own tape recorder to record his first hit, "(I Wanna) Love My Life Away," playing several instruments and multi-tracking the vocals.

—

Buster Brown "Fannie Mae" Fire November 1960

Style: Blues
Where from: Georgia
Where recorded: New York City, NY
Suggested pairings: The Beach Boys "Help Me Rhonda" 1965; The Rolling Stones "West Coast Under Assistant Promo Man" 1965

Moving from Georgia to New Jersey, Buster Brown found a few small clubs willing to let him perform for tips at night while making the rounds of independent New York record companies by day. Signed by Bobby Robinson's Fire, the producer booked session players Jimmy Lewis, bass; Riff Ruffin and Jimmy Spruill, guitar, who'd played on "Kansas City." They put together a rocking blues with Buster's patented 'wooos' and a strong Brown harmonica break.

"A 65-year-old man with a limp," was how Fire label promo guy Wally Roker described Brown. "I hated the record. I took the record to Big Bill, a blues disc jockey on WBMX on the west side of Chicago. It was like an off-brand station. He loved it, went crazy on it, started playing it. Went back to New York the next day, United Distributors ordered 30,000 copies, 'They're screaming for it.'"

Remakes: The Righteous Brothers 1965; Mighty Sam 1966

—

The Shirelles "(Will You Love Me) Tomorrow" Scepter November 1960

Style: Rock 'n' roll
Where from: New Jersey
Where recorded: New York City, NY
Suggested pairings: The Drifters "Save the Last Dance For Me" 1959

This song about a day following an implied intimate encounter as previewed in 'Tonight's the Night" by The Shirelles, "(Will You Love Me) Tomorrow" was the first #1 hit by a black female group despite being banned by radio stations for mildly sexual content, and sold over a million copies.

Said Little Eva, "I sang the Shirelles' song, '(Will You Love Me) Tomorrow.' They didn't want me to babysit if I couldn't sing." Wally Roker, who promoted "Tomorrow," recalled, "Carol King wrote that song and we loved it, wanted to do it. She did the arrangements also. King Curtis was the leader on the session. Carol King did the strings, Luther Dixon did the rhythm."

Before Scepter owner Florence Greenberg pulled out this hit, Roker recalled, "she was about $25,000 into her father and was having a complete coronary breakdown on the phone with me every 15 to 20 minutes, trying to figure out what we're going to do, whether we're going to survive, are we going to make it, what am I going to say to my parents about paying back this $25,000 I owe my father. When '(Will You Love Me) Tomorrow' busted wide open, it ended all that."

Answer: The Satintones "Tomorrow & Always" 1961
Remakes: Charlie McCoy 1964; The Escorts 1964; Bunny Sigler 1966; The Bachs Lunch 1967; The Four Seasons 1968; Linda Ronstadt 1970; Cher 1971; The Uniques 1972: Little Eva 1972; Melanie 1973; Donnie Elbert 1976; Dana Valery 1976; The Mike Curb Congregation 1978; Millie Jackson 1989

—

Rosie & the Originals "Angel Baby" Highland 1960

Style: Rock 'n' roll
Where from: San Diego, CA
Where recorded: San Marcos, CA
Covers: Charles Brown 1961; Sandra Teen 1961

Rosie Hamlin grew up in Alaska and arrived in San Diego as an elementary school student, later attended Mission Bay High School and performed in clubs as early as age 13. As vocalist with the teen garage band Rosie & the Originals, Hamlin scored her first chart hit with this unlikely ballad, "Angel Baby," backed with the blues "Give Me Love" sung by an uncredited Bluford Wade on Highland.

Hamlin said, "A lot of the songs were 'baby this or baby that.' My boyfriend, Robert Foster, used to call me his 'little baby,' make little endearments like that. He was 16, I was 14. I used to write poetry, but it was real secret; I wrote the song as a poem for him, we were very shy, we were allowed to sit on the front porch and that's about it. We sat there and talked until somebody yelled for us to 'break it up, come in now.' Long after we'd broken up, I had an old used piano and that's when I learned the old 4 chord progression and I put it to that. It was a shy way of expressing your inner feelings."

Members of The Originals, said Hamlin: "Noah Tafolla was lead guitar, my boyfriend, he did sing. David Ponce, rhythm guitar, Tony Gomez, sax, he could sing a teeny bit; Carl Van Guda, our drummer. I lived in National City, some of the guys lived in Logan Heights, one guy lived in Pt. Loma. There were no recording studios out there, but we found an old building that had been an aircraft hangar in Santee, way out there. The quality of the record speaks for the era itself. Everything was 4 track, it's typical of that era."

Band members took acetates of the song to various record shops and other venues. At a local shop, Rosie met a salesman who took an acetate that had a scratch on it as it had been played at parties. It was that defective copy that Highland Records pressed up for release. "Alan Freed on KDAY got it started," said Hamlin. "He was given half the publishing for a period of time, it broke on the East Coast for the same period of time." In mid-November, "Angel Baby" charted on Wallichs Music City and went to #1 on border radio Mighty 690 and KCBQ, close to where the song was created.

Remake: Angelica 1991

—

Rochel & the Candles "Once Upon a Time" Swingin November 1960

Style: Doo wop
Where from: Texas/Louisiana
Where recorded: Hollywood, CA

Rochel Henderson moved to L.A. in 1956 and sang with The Chosen Gospel Singers, who at that time included baritone Lou Rawls, before forming Rochel & the Candles with lead tenor Johnny Wyatt and baritone Rochel Henderson. The Candles was chosen because Rochel wanted something bright and The Hollywood Flames had just lit up the charts for Ebb.

Songwriter Jimmy Johnson, who had cut "Lone Ranger Gonna Git Married" for Class, also penned "Once Upon a Time," a plaintive ballad of lost love, which he taught to Wyatt. Johnson recalled the song so enraptured Wyatt that he came to Johnson's house for several months to practice singing it. While Wyatt learned the melody, Rochel was hustling up a vocal group, Melvin Sasso and T.C. Henderson—no relation to Rochel—bass. Henderson contacted DJ Hunter Hancock and, according to Johnson, they signed a contract, recording "Once Upon A Time."

Remake: Johnny Wyatt 1966

—

The Fugitives "Freeway" Arvee November 1960

Style: Rock 'n' roll
Where from: Phoenix, AZ
Where recorded: Hollywood, CA

Alan Smith, piano, formed The Fugitives at Tempe, AZ Union High School with Henry Spencer, tenor sax; Dale Reynolds, guitar and Kay Lines, drums. "Dale was out of high school, I might have been a sophomore, Kay was year ahead of me, lead drummer in the high school band. The Fugitives came before that name," said Smith. "We went to Audio Recorders of Arizona and recorded a demo, 'Freeway,' 'Blue Moon,' 'My Pad to Yours'… the 4th one was 'Fugitive.' Russell Sims of Sims Records might have been hanging out at the studio. Russell Sims showed up at my house on 17th St. in Tempe with Leroy Van Dyke and said he wanted to re-record the song. We loaded our piano onto a truck, and I was playing the piano on the way to the studio. I had a history of all kind[s] of stunts. Used to jump off of buildings. Sims wanted that piano to re-record the record. We headed toward Canyon Recorders and played the song. I knew something was wrong when the engineer came over and asked, 'Could you not play the cymbals, they're not recording well.' I didn't like it, maybe that ended the relationship.

Smith continued, "Sims' brother was a country DJ in Phoenix at the time. On a whim, Dale and I broke into Sims' house to recover our contracts. Since he had the stampers made from the master tape of the same record he put it out on Sims with different mastering. He went to Memphis." After breaking into and breaking off with Sims, "we went back and recorded 'Fugitive.' We hired a bass player. Then we owned the master.

"In 1960 and 61, I asked my mom if I could drive the family Hudson Hornet over to L.A., where I started hitting the labels. I had a lot of 45s, so I knew what labels to visit. I went to Del-fi, don't remember how I stumbled into Arvee, but I remembered that label. I met John Powell, who later told me he was trying to get in my underwear."

Once released, "Freeway" by the Fugitives, an appropriate name considering the break-in at Sims' house, hit in late October 1960. Smith added, "Russell Sims made stampers unbeknownst to myself and then ran out of Phoenix, saw dollar signs and released the same session on his Sims."

—

Bo Diddley "Gunslinger" Checker November 1960

Style: Blues
Where from: Chicago, IL
Where recorded: Washington, DC

About "Gunslinger," "It's a song I came up with after the movie 'The Magnificent Seven' was released," said Bo Diddley. His wife, Kay, helped him record "Gunslinger" for his own Bo-Kay label (meaning a "bouquet of people"—his family) in the basement of his DC home on a two track Presto Recorder, all live, no dubbing—with backing by The Jewels. "I had to splice out all the bad notes," Kay noted.

Lady Bo, Peggy Jones, was leader of The Jewels, not to be confused with the "Opportunity" Jewels. She was replaced with another female guitarist, The Duchess, who was really Norma Jean Richardson. "Bo passed her off as his sister." Kay and Bo moved to Chicago in 1964 where they were married on May 6, 1965. "We decided to make it legal," said Kay, Bo Diddley's second or third wife, depending on whether annulments count.

—

Hank Ballard and the Midnighters "The Hoochi Coochi Coo" King November 1960

Style: Rhythm and blues vocal group
Where from: Detroit, MI
Where recorded: Cincinnati, OH

Hank Ballard and the Midnighters' "The Hoochi Coochi Coo" was recorded as a dance. "That's the one with a lot of fire in it," said Ballard. "I like to open with that tune for some reason, it smokes." The term coochi is problematic in some street slang, a reference to a vagina.

—

The Sevilles "Charlena" J-C/Galaxy November 1960

Style: Rhythm and blues vocal group
Where from: Los Angeles, CA
Where recorded: Hollywood, CA

According to one-time Paramounts members James Lanier, The Sevilles, who recorded "Charlena," were fellow ex-Paramounts, Ernest Hamilton and Robert Baker and Baker's friend, James Spencer, and Manny Chavez of the Jaguars on guitar. The group might have also involved tenor Johnny White, ex-Shields' member Charles Wright, ex-Turks' member Tommy "Buster" Williams and Johnny Morisette, who had sung with The Medallions and The Sliders and other vocal groups.

"Nobody would record 'Charlena,'" recalled Chavez, whose girlfriend was the namesake Charlena, who lived in Bellflower and was as described in the lyrics of the song. "We sang that song for everybody for more than a year," said Chavez. "Cliff Goldsmith had it all set up. I walked into the studio to do it on the day I shipped out" to the army. "It was supposed to be a Jaguars record, but because of the timeframe, we weren't able to pull it off."

Remake: The Trippers 1967; Los Lobos 1987

—

Buzz Clifford "Baby Sittin' Boogie" Columbia November 21, 1960

Style: Rock & roll
Where from: Berwyn, IL
Where recorded: New York City, NY
Original title: "Baby Sitter Boogie"

In 1957, Buzz Clifford recorded the male shop style, "14 Karet Fool," followed by the hotter rockabilly, "Pididdle (The Car With One Light)," both for Bow. He then recorded the teen ballad "Hello, Mr. Moonlight" with The Ray Conniff Singers for Columbia. Then came the fine Winfield Scott and Lincoln Chase compositions, "Driftwood" with the rocking novelty, "Baby Sitter Boogie" with occasional "goo-goos" sprinkled throughout this Columbia label release, the title of which was quickly changed to "Baby Sittin' Boogie," which hit #8 on WABC in August 1960; #4 on KRLA in February '61.

—

Bob Arlin "East L.A." Olympia November 25, 1960

Style: Rock 'n' roll
Where from: Santa Monica, CA
Where recorded: Hollywood, CA
Cover: Solid Jackson

About this tough rocker, "East L.A." by Bob Arlin on Olympia, writer, guitarist and biker enthusiast, John Orvis said, "Bob Arlin was about 21 or 22, when his dad Max Arlin, a dentist came to me, fronted the money for him to record the song. Bob Arlin liked Chuck Berry and blues. He used to live in my neighborhood in Santa Monica." Orvis recorded him on "East L.A." with references to "high riser bars, they go so fast, they don't know where they are.' KFWB liked it, but they wouldn't play it with those lyrics, "fifty dollar bills, gonna snuff you out." though Orvis insisted it was true, that in East L.A., "at the time, that's all it took to have someone snuffed, fifty bucks." Apparently, the reference was little problem for "East L.A." getting play elsewhere, like the Inland Empire… a long way from L.A.

Orvis approached the Candix label first, that label booked the session to be recorded by Orvis, who reconsidered, giving the material to Arlin. At the last minute, comedic actor and co-creator of "Chaos" by Arbogast & Ross, Stan Ross, was brought in as Solid Jackson to cover "East L.A.," backed with "Speedy Gonzales" on Candix. Session tenor sax man "Steve Douglas wanted to play horn with us," said Orvis. "He played horn on the Solid Jackson instead."

In the mid-1960s, Orvis recorded "East L.A." as J.O. & the Soulfools on Arc, but the new arrangement had scant connection to the Arlin original. "It was blues, blues, blues, the way Canned Heat did the blues about a year or so later."

Orvis continued, "Jerry owned Arc, a freak, right on Tweedy Blvd., he was just weird. I played at the Penthouse on Long Beach Blvd in 1962. I lived on east 61st in Maywood, right behind Bethlehem Steel, just like Huntington Park used to be. The Soulfools were Shakey Walls, drums, Jamie Shane, bass. Orvis also played in Lynwood at the Harum Club on Long Beach Blvd. His act featured "Norman Brown, the dancing drummer. He was into swing music. He'd jump off the stage, jump up and dance on the drums. I had to jump off the stage, play guitar behind my back. Swing was still popular." The audience consisted of motorcycle clubs and "'chucos" (pachucos), Mexicans who were later known as lowriders. "They didn't have that much rivalry. They came to hear the music. Everybody used to ride together, there was a certain respect" between clubs.

Later lead singer of the successful L.A. garage band The Leaves, Arlin next recorded the topical instrumentals "707" backed with "708" on Olympia in 1961 and "Mushroom Machine" for Tiki in 1965.

Remake: J.O. & Soulfools 1965

—

The Drifters "I Count the Tears" Atlantic November 30, 1960

Style: Rhythm and blues vocal group
From and recorded in: New York City, NY
Suggested pairing: The Grassroots "Let's Live For Today" 1967

In the midst of strings backing a series of R&B releases came the Ben E. King lead voice on this Drifters' "I Count the Tears," which set the stage for the departure of King from The Drifters and major success as a single artist.

—

Ben E. King "Spanish Harlem" Atco December 1960

Style: Rhythm and blues
From and recorded in: New York City, NY
Suggested pairing: The Drifters "Save the Last Dance For Me" 1959

Just split from The Drifters, Ben E. King, who grew up mere blocks from Spanish Harlem, was eager to make an auspicious solo debut on October 27, 1960, and insisted on cutting this rare collaboration between himself, Phil Spector, Jerry Leiber and Mike Stoller, who would now exclusively produce both Ben and the Drifters,. From that session came "Spanish Harlem" backed with "First Taste Of Love," "Young Boy Blues" and, with only 20 minutes to spare, "Stand By Me." "Spanish Harlem," with its baion rhythm, made the Top 10.

Remake: King Curtis—instrumental track of Ben E. King version—1965

—

Solomon Burke "Cry To Me" Atlantic December 1960

Style: Rhythm and blues
Where from: Philadelphia, PA
Where recorded: New York City, NY

This was the first hit for major soul talent Solomon Burke.

—

The Church Street Five "A Night With Daddy G" Legrand December 1960

Style: Rhythm and blues
From and recorded in: Norfolk, VA
Suggested pairing: Gary U.S. Bonds "Quarter To Three" 1961

Daddy G was local preacher Daddy Grace, but saxophone player Gene Barge took that Daddy G identity for his rollicking party-oriented effort, "A Night With Daddy G," credited to The Church Street Five—Earl Swanson, sax and Emmitt Shields, drums—Church Street being a famed party byway in Norfolk, VA.

The bed of "A Night With Daddy G" was the instrumental bed for Gary U.S. Bonds' #1 hit, "Quarter To Three" in 1961. According to Bonds, "Gene Barge was one of the jazz players, sax player, as well as Nap Shields, Melvin Glover. They were strictly into jazz bop. Rock 'n' roll was really, really new. They were much older guys. We got them together, the only musicians we knew, gave them five or ten bucks apiece, 'Let's go record.'"

Bonds added, "Daddy G used to be about the Daddy Grace Church. Long fingernails, the long Cadillac, he'd sit back, 'Bring me money and I will save you from something.' Sweet Daddy Grace's church was on Church Street, I guess that's where it came from. From being called Gene Barge, I guess that's where Daddy G came from."

—

Etta James "At Last" Argo December 1960

Style: Rhythm and blues
Where from: Los Angeles, CA
Where recorded: Chicago, IL
Original version: Glenn Miller and his Orchestra with vocals by Ray Eberle 1941
Earlier version: Richard Berry and the Dreamers "At Last" 1954

The songwriting team of Mack Gordon and Harry Warren wrote this song "At Last" for the musical Sun Valley Serenade in 1941. It was re-recorded by Richard Berry and the Dreamers in 1954. In 1961, Berry's early singing partner on "Roll With Me Henry," Etta James, recorded "At Last" for the jazz-oriented Chess subsidiary, Argo. "Chess initially picked her songs," said James' one-time manager and spouse, Billy Foster. "They mandated which songs she did. But she had a strong presence, so if she didn't like a song, she wouldn't sing it right, she would tell them, so they wouldn't invest time and money if they didn't think she'd sing it to the best of her ability."

With violin orchestrations, this one she must have liked, a lot.

—

Kathy Young & the Innocents "A Thousand Stars" Indigo 1960

Style: Doo wop
Where from: Long Beach, CA
Where recorded: Hollywood, CA
Original version: The Rivileers 1956

Kathy Young was 15 years old when she and her mother attended the Wink Martindale Show, a daily dance program on Los Angeles TV that featured The Innocents performing their current hit, "Honest I Do." Kathy approached the group to congratulate them and mentioned she was a vocalist. Jim Lee, the Innocents' manager, as well as the owner of their record label, took one look at the photogenic teenager and invited her to come to his studio the following week for an audition.

When Kathy and her mom showed up with at Lee's Indigo Records office, she sang one of her favorite songs, "A Thousand Stars," an original by The Rivileers, a black doo wop vocal group from Queens, NY. Jim Lee knew Kathy needed a background group to fill out her sound… and he had the perfect candidate: The Innocents.

As Kathy Young & the Innocents, they debuted with the redo of "A Thousand Stars" on Martindale's KRLA show, rendering "A Thousand Stars" an almost instant hit as of late September 1960 when it went #1 on all local charts and #3 nationally. It also became a favorite in the local press. The December 6, 1960 Press Telegram reported, "While 'A Thousand Stars' has become a most popular recording in the Southland, the other side of Kathy Young's 45 called 'Eddie, My Darling' has found favor in other parts of the country. It could be possible for this side, another slow-beat ballad which Miss Young composed herself, to send it back up the survey." On January 21, 1961, the Press Telegram headline was "L.B. girl, 15 (xxxx Downey Ave.), makes her mark as teen star with hit disc."

—

Johnny Burnette "You're Sixteen" Liberty 1960

Style: Rock 'n' roll
Where from: Memphis, TN
Where recorded: Hollywood, CA

Johnny Burnette's pop teen rocker, a Richard and Robert Scherman composition, "You're Sixteen" was backed by Bobby Gibbons, Vincent Terri and Alfred Viola, guitars; Ernie Freeman, piano; Red Callender, bass; Jerry Allison, drums; two violas and eight violins.

Remake: Ringo Starr 1974.

—

Four Young Men "You Been Torturing Me"
Crest December 16, 1960
Style: Novelty
Where from: Louisiana/Iowa/Salt Lake City, UT
Where recorded: Hollywood, CA
Cover: The Hollywood Argyles 1961

The Four Young Men were Gib Guilbeau, Darrell Cotton, Ernie Williams and Wayne Moore, lead guitar. A laconically rendered novelty "You Been Torturing Me" was about a guy tortured by his cheating girlfriend and how he would torture her. The December 6, 1960 Press Telegram reported, "The Four Young Men combine the 'Alley Oop and 'Time Machine' techniques in an attempt at a hit in a new disc, 'You Been Torturing Me.' We believe that this record, a rather hard one to explain, will be on the leading surveys before long because of the fun listening it provides."

—

Shelby Flint "Angel On My Shoulder"
Valiant December 17, 1960
Style: Pop
Where from: North Hollywood, CA
Where recorded: Hollywood, CA
Original version: Jerry Wallace 1960

In 1958, Shelby Flint, a 19 year old Birmingham High School in Van Nuys graduate, was attending Pierce College in Woodland Hills when she signed a contract with Cadence. Flint's debut recording was "Oh, I Miss Him So" on Cadence which most consumers missed acquiring.

The Valley News reported on February 12, 1959, "In spite of her recent success in show business, Shelby plans to give up her recording career in favor of leading folk singing in the adult community musical seminars in the South. Last summer while working at the Highlander Folk School in Monteagle, Tenn., Shelby realized the great need for organized projects in the small southern cities, and she intends to devote much of her time to the development of such projects. 'I would like to be an integral part in relieving the tensions that exist between the colored and white persons,' [she said]."

Returning from relieving Southern tensions, Flint hooked up with former Cadence label mate Barry DeVorzon, who recorded as John Buck & the Blazers on the instrumental "Forbidden City" in 1959, and started Valiant with Flint's soft vocal on a cover of Jerry Wallace's flip side ballad, "Angel On My Shoulder," which was a major hit in 1960 and in 1965. "Shelby Flint was my first arrangement," recalled Perry Botkin "There was no drummer on 'Angel on Shoulder' because Shelby's voice was so light. We used three violins with Sid Sharpe. He was a working fool and a terrific classical violinist. There were no rock & roll string players." Jerry Wallace's "Angel on My Shoulder" was on Challenge, a hit on KFWB, XEAK, KRLA, KFXM and pop in November.

—

Aretha Franklin "Won't Be Long"
Columbia December 23, 1960
Style: Proto soul
From and recorded in: Detroit, MI
Suggested pairing: Phillip Upchurch "You Can't Sit Down" 1961

Aretha Franklin's "Won't Be Long" was her first up-tempo jazz vocal, her most successful during her half-century tenure on Columbia. While Etta James was on an upswing, her Detroit counterpart, Aretha Franklin, was stuck in a rut as Columbia didn't know how to record her.

—

Slim Harpo "Rainin' In My Heart" Excello January 1961

Style: Blues
Where from: Baton Rouge, LA
Where recorded: Crowley, LA

With this stop-time blues, "Rainin' In My Heart," Slim Harpo created a new genre, swamp blues with a spoken bridge in the middle and his one-man harmonica/guitar talents solidly displayed.

Remake: The Pretty Things 1965

—

The Marathons "Peanut Butter" Arvee 1961

Style: Rhythm and blues
From and recorded in: Los Angeles, CA
Suggested pairing: The Olympics "Hully Gully" 1959

"H.B. Barnum and I wrote 'Peanut Butter,'" said the song's co-producer Marty Cooper. "It was my idea. H.B. and I worked on it and hired The Vibrations. We did as a parody, made a deal with them and Arvee owner Richard Vaughn."

For this recording, The Vibrations were re-named The Marathons, patterned after The Olympics, whose "Hully Gully" became the template for their "Peanut Butter," an almost instant sensation. "It's not The Olympics. We were tied up in the East Coast and the company needed a single out," said Olympics lead singer Walter Ward. "The producers got another group to do it and got our same sound."

When the song hit, Leonard Chess of Chess records contacted Cooper about recording his Vibrations group. "Marty, we got a mess here. Why don't you just come along with me," Chess said, hoping to get Arvee to license the song to Chess. Instead, "Peanut Butter" was re-recorded as by "The Vibrations, known to others as The Marathons" as was printed on the label of the new version released on Argo and Chess. Said Carl Fisher of the Vibrations about this confusion, "'Peanut Butter' was a joke. H.B. Barnum wanted the group to do a demo of that song, next thing we knew was he put it out. Chess Records found out, so we decided to record it again as The Vibrations, it was an inside deal between Chess and whoever was in control of The Marathons." To this day, some "experts" assert "Peanut Butter" was by The Olympics.

To capitalize on their hit, Arvee rush-released a Marathons LP recorded by a Marathons group then recently out of Fremont High School, who later recorded as The Younghearts for Bobby Sanders

—

The Vibrations "The Watusi" Checker 1961

Style: Rhythm and blues
From and recorded in: Los Angeles, CA
Suggested pairing: Hank Ballard & the Midnighters "Let's Go, Let's Go, Let's Go" King September 1960

Matt "Guitar" Murphy started playing guitar in high school, near Lamont, MS. He hung out with Jim Richard, Fred Richard and Richard Boyd out of Chicago. Murphy said, "That's me playing guitar on that; Richard Boyd's playing bass. That introduction came from Hank Ballard, that's exactly where we got it, 'Thrill on the Hill.' I find that on a lot of tunes, that's all there is to that."

—

The Drifters "Up on the Roof" Atlantic 1961

Style: Rhythm and blues
From and recorded in: New York City, NY

The vocals on The Drifters' "Up on the Roof" were backed by Dionne & Dee Dee Warwick, after Dionne met Burt Bacharach during The Drifters "Mexican Divorce" session. It is a super elegant urban proto-soul performance with strings.

—

Bobby Bland "I Pity the Fool" Duke January 1961

Style: Blues
Where from: Memphis, TN
Where recorded: Houston, TX

Guitar backing for Bobby Bland on "I Pity the Fool" was by Wayne Bennett, who recalled, "I think the guitar was always present for Bobby down through the years. When I went to Duke/Peacock, writer, arranger Joe Scott did all of Bobby's top-notch songs, 14 hits back to back. We credited The Texas Empire Band, started in 1959, the band lasted until 1965."

—

The Goodtimers "Pony Time" Arnold January 1961

Style: Rhythm and blues
From and recorded in: New York City, NY

The Goodtimers' "Pony Time" vocal was by songwriter Don Covay on his original of a dance released just prior to Chubby Checker's charting version. It got lost in the stable.

—

Chubby Checker "Pony Time" Parkway January 1961

Style: Rock 'n' roll
Where from: South Carolina
Where recorded: Philadelphia, PA
Original version: Don Covay "Pony Time" 1959

"Pony Time" was a remake of a Don Covay original, much like The Midnighters' "Sexy Ways" from 1954. "Pony Time" was easier to dance to than "The Twist." But after this twistless period, Checker found his future within the twist, as "The Twist" went to #1 a second time, as did his "Let's Twist Again" as well as his major "Slow Twistin'" with an uncredited Dee Sharpe.

—

Ernie K-Doe "Mother-In-Law" Minit 1961

Style: Rhythm and blues
From and recorded in: New Orleans, LA
Suggested pairing: Neil Sedaka "Sweet Little You" 1961

Recording first as a member of The Blue Diamonds in 1954, R&B vocalist Ernie Kador adopted the name Ernie K-Doe for this drolly performed Allen Toussaint composition and #1 hit, "Mother-in-Law," with vocal backing by Benny Spellman, with whom he dueted on Spellman's "Lipstick Traces" in 1962. "Spellman was doing the bass thing on K-Doe's 'Mother In Law,'" said noted performer and New Orleans R&B historian Earl King. "Also on K-Doe's 'A Certain Girl' and he also did the bass thing on my 'Trick Bag' and 'Don't Lose It.' That's Benny."

—

The Marcels "Blue Moon" Colpix February 1961

Style: Doo wop group
From and recorded in: Pittsburgh, PA
Original version: Connee Boswell 1935
Doo wop original: The Emanons 1956

Formed at Oliver High School in north Pittsburgh, PA, The Marcels were Cornelius Harp, lead singer and guitar; Fred Johnson, bass; Ron Mundy, first tenor; Gene Bricker, second tenor and Fred Knauss, baritone. Named after a popular hairstyle of the day, The Marcels were signed by Colpix, which gave them vintage material, "Heart & Soul," which they didn't know. Asked what they did know, they gave "Blue Moon" a try, which went straight to #1 with their rocking doo wop remake of the Tin Pan Alley standard, already put to doo wop by The Emanons on Josie in 1956, but not with the same punch. There was also an opening element similar to "Zoom Zoom Zoom" by the Collegians from 1958.

"Blue Moon" by the Marcels charted and went to #1 on WABC, New York in February 1961 and KFWB and KRLA in L.A. in April, the same month "Heart & Soul" by both The Cleftones and Jan & Dean hit the charts, just not as hard. The Cleftones' version reached #3 on WABC in New York, while West Coasters' Jan & Dean hit #1 on KFWB and #3 on KRLA in L.A. about a month later. It was that kind of year.

It was said this wild version of "Blue Moon" was a threat to the sanity of songwriter Richard Rodgers.

—

B. Bumble & the Stingers "Bumble Boogie" Rendezvous February 1961

Style: Instrumental rock 'n' roll
Where from: L.A. area, CA
Where recorded: Hollywood, CA
Original version: Jack Fina 1946

Fresh from backing the Ernie Fields hit "In the Mood" on Rendezvous, The Ernie Freeman Combo, sans Fields who was recording under his own name for Rendezvous, next adapted the classical "Flight Of the Bumble Bee" by Rimsky-Korsakov, which pianist Jack Fina adapted as "Bumble Boogie" on Mercury in '46.

Producer Kim Fowley recorded Freeman on two tracks, one with a grand piano for the rhythm part, the other with a modified upright piano with tacks attached to the hammers to create a tinny "honky tonk" sound. Based on several non-existent session bands like The Renegades and The Hollywood Gamblers, who had recorded for American International, Fowley gave them the make-believe identity, B. Bumble & the Stingers, who turned "Bumble Boogie" into a top 40 a piano-based instrumental hit. This approximate combination recorded under names like The Mar-Ketts for Union and Liberty and The Routers for Warner Brothers and inspired other fantasy groups like the Piltdown Men on Capitol and The Link Eddy Combo on Reprise. The success of "Bumble Boogie" spawned several early '60s rock instrumentals derived from classical themes: "Like Long Hair" by Paul Revere and the Raiders; "Nut Rocker" by Jack B. Nimble and covered by B. Bumble & the Stingers and "Asia Minor" by Kokomo on Felsted.

—

Gary U.S. Bonds "Not Me" Legrand February 1961

Style: Rhythm and blues
From and recorded in: Norfolk, VA

Bonds said, "We sold 800,000 copies of 'Not Me.' It was banned. They said it was dirty lyrics, again, a church going guy. Don't know why they pinned it on me." In fact, the censorship was handled in a unique way. The lyric, "well, she called me yesterday about a quarter to one/She said come on over daddy, let's have some fun/I said now what about your husband, he come back from the gym?/She said come on over daddy, don't worry 'bout him" was changed to "Well, she called me yesterday about a quarter to one/She said come on over daddy, let's do the Madison/I said now what about your boyfriend they call Battlin' Jim?/She said come on over daddy, don't worry 'bout him." However, the voice doing the new lyrics was obviously and clumsily dubbed in, making for a confused performance. Not so the successful redo by The Orlons, which stuck to the original lyrics, which were not a problem two years later.

Remake: The Orlons 1963

—

The Frogmen "Underwater" Candix

Style: Instrumental rock 'n' roll
Where from: Culver City, CA/Westchester, CA
Where recorded: Hollywood, CA

The Frogmen had two guitarists, James Young (b. 1943), who lived in Culver City and went to Chaminade High School in Cheviot Hills, and Dennis Farley, who went to St. Bernard's High School in Westchester. Young's cousin Mike Anderson of Sherman Oaks played drums; Larry Wnuk played accordion, "and" said Young, "we tried to get him play the piano" with Ray Sullivan, alto sax; Larry Bartone, sax and Frank DeLuna, guiro and engineer on the "Underwater" session.

"We originally were called The Corsairs," said Young. A promoter, Jack Andrews, "heard us, wanted to promote the record. We had recorded this instrumental. He took it to the studio, added reverb, added the frog sound and tried to get credit for writing the song because he added reverb and sound effects." Without notice, The Corsairs were changed to The Frogmen on their only instrumental, "Underwater," backed with a session instrumental by violinist Sidney Sharp with The Ernie Freeman Combo, "The Mad Rush" on Candix, a label incorporated in August 1960 and owned by twins Robert and Richard Dix and William Canaday Silva with Joe Saraceno. "The Dix brothers were part of it, but I'm not sure," said Bruce Morgan. "My dad wasn't as serious about his labels as Candix was about theirs," said Morgan, referring to distribution.

"We had the name painted on a drum, we all called the stations and asked them to play the hit," said Young. "The label wanted us to go on American Bandstand, but our parents wouldn't let us go back, as school was still in session. That's when the label stepped in and hired The Royal Impalas out of Bakersfield, "called them The Frogmen, put them in wetsuits, used our names when they were interviewed by Dick Clark. They were going to use them to go on tour because we were too young," said Young.

—

Rosie & the Originals "Lonely Blue Nights" Brunswick February 18, 1961

Style: Rock 'n' roll
Where from: San Diego, CA
Where recorded: New York
Original version: Rosie & the Originals 1961

Upon the success of "Angel Baby," Rosie & the Originals redid "Lonely Blue Nights" backed with "We'll Have a Chance" for Brunswick with whom they signed in early 1961 to do a quickie LP with songs they had yet to write. In New York for a recording session, the band found out at the last minute they had to write about 10 songs overnight. As Rosie, she recorded "My Darling Forever" backed with "The Time Is Near" on Brunswick, her final 45 for the label.

—

The Velveteens "Dog Patch Creeper" Emmy

Style: Latino doo wop
Where from: Pomona, CA
Where recorded: Cucamonga, CA
Suggested pairing: Johnny Otis "Midnite Creeper" 1957

Mexican-American musician Johnny Valenzuela put together a band he dubbed The Velveteens. "My dad was musician, I started playing trumpet in junior high, then I switched to saxophone. When I was around 13 or 14, I went to El Monte Legion Stadium, saw Ritchie Valens; I was Hispanic, he was too. I saw him in a concert in the summer of 1958 playing guitar, I was just stunned by him. He did 'Hi Tone,' 'Donna' and 'Come On Let's Go.'

Valenzuela continued, "At the time, I was forming a group… age 13… already had a little knowledge, heard the doo wop sounds, picked up their melodies and chord progressions. He's [Valens] the one who made me switch to guitar. At the time, Danny Espinoza, sax; Danny Valenzuela played drums; I was playing piano at the time, chord progressions were so simple; Rod Rodriguez on guitar; Pauly Rodridguez on bass. At home, I used to sit down and really practice, lyrics and instrumentals. The area we lived at on 7th in Pomona we used to call Dog Patch." Thus The Velveteens' first release was the instrumental "Dog Patch Creeper" backed with "Johnny's Jump" on Emmy, owned by Paul Buff in his Pal Recording Studios in the Inland Empire city of Cucamonga, where Frank Zappa soon arrived to invent a new kind of rock 'n' roll.

"My dad helped us, somehow got connections through somebody, he heard about the recording studio," said Valenzuela. "My dad pressed out 2,000 45s and Paul Buff got in the deal some way or another." Buff said, "I remember them. They were a Chicano band that had a lot of saxophones, played funky music. That came about from them. I opened the studio myself to help them out. They did three sessions, brought this girl in once. I charged them $12.50 an hour or $15 for stereo. We didn't have a record mill, we were trying to do things that we thought might happen. Probably pressed not more than 500. Could've been a thousand records.

Buff continued, "Either a group came in like The Velveteens, or more typically I'd record myself and Aerni on surf, Zappa and Buff on Zappa music." In later interviews with rock historian David Reyes, Frank Zappa was very high on the band.

—

Ray Charles "One Mint Julep" Impulse! February 1961

Style: Jazz instrumental
Where from: Florida
Where recorded: Hollywood, CA
Original version: The Clovers 1952
Suggested pairing: Little Stevie Wonder "Fingertips" 1962

In late 1960, Long Beach resident Jim Lamarand was working the jazz department of Wallich's Music City in Lakewood. He recalled that evening many employees were out for dinner break when a black limo pulled up in the parking lot. The black driver got out, came into the store, looked around and returned to the limo, bringing back Ray Charles. Charles then walked into the space of Al Kalie Music and sat down at an organ. He then proceeded to test the instrument, playing an impromptu concert. As Hody's Drive-In was just across Lakewood Blvd, Lamarand did his best to summon employees back to hear the concert. After about an hour or so, Charles got back into the limo and left. Shortly thereafter, Charles recorded a pounding organ instrumental version of the Clovers' 1952 drinking/ pregnancy vocal "One Mint Julep" with Charles adding a shout, "just a little bit of soul" instead of the "just a little bit of soda" the producer wanted.

—

Del Shannon "Runaway" Big Top February 1961

Style: Rock 'n' roll
Where from: Detroit, MI
Where recorded: Bell Studios 237 West 54th Street New York City, NY
Suggested pairing: Scandal "Goodbye To You" 1982

Del Shannon and keyboard player Max Crook, who played a keyboard called a Musitron, came up with this while playing a club in Battle Creek, Michigan. On the song. Crook hit an A minor and a G. Shannon said, "Max, play that again, it's a great change." The drummer, Dick Parker, followed them and after 15 minutes, the manager of the club shouted, "Knock it off, play something else."

Backing Del Shannon's high falsetto "Runaway" vocals were session players Al Caiola, lead guitar and Milt Hinton, bass; Joe Marshall, drums, Max Crook, Musitron and Bill Ramal, saxophone. It was produced by Embee Productions, Irving Micahnik and Harry Balk, who steered Shannon's 1960s career. Engineered by Bill McMeekin and arranged by Bill Ramalctually—a split session with Crook recording the very next Big Top 45, "The Snake" backed with "The Wanderer" credited to Maximillan.

Remakes: Lawrence Welk and His Orchestra 1962; The Malibu's 1966; The Mad Lads 1967; The Small Faces 1972; Bonnie Raitt 1977; Narvel Felts 1978

—

Link-Eddy Combo "The Big Mr. C" Reprise 1961

Style: Jazz instrumental
Where from: L.A. area, CA
Where recorded: Hollywood, CA
Suggested pairing: Ray Charles "What'd I Say" 1959

In 1960, Frank Sinatra had left Capitol to begin his own Reprise, with L.A. session players Ed Cobb and Lincoln Mayorga coming along for the ride. The two had recorded at all Four Preps sessions on Capitol and later linked up as The Piltdown Men for Capitol. The contraction of the names of Link (Lincoln) and Eddy came together as the Link-Eddy Combo, which also suggested the names of popular rock 'n' roll guitarists Link Wray and Duane Eddy on an instrumental tribute to Ray Charles' giant hit "What'd I Say," entitled "The Big Mr. C" as the second release on Reprise. It hit early in the Bay Area on KYA and KEWB. Charles sued over the infringement "The Big Mr. C" and the case was settled in a way that wasn't exactly satisfactory to the big Mr. Charles, who was found to have rights to the lyrics, but not the melody, which Charles had never bothered to copyright; that in turn was awarded to Cobb/Mayorga.

—

The Pips "Every Beat Of My Heart" Huntom/Vee Jay March 1961

Style: Rhythm and blues vocal group
From and recorded in: Atlanta, GA
Original version: The Royals 1952
Covers: Henry Booth & the Midnighters—reissue of original by the Royals 1961; Gladys Knight and the Pips 1962

"Gladys Knight and the Pips recorded it and it became a big hit," said Johnny Otis of "Every Beat Of My Heart" he wrote for The Royals in 1952. The Pips' recording of "Every Beat of My Heart" on the Atlanta-based Huntom label was leased to Vee Jay, which released it as The Pips, scoring a #1 hit.

In this case, the group competed against itself, with a second version of "Every Beat of My Heart" credited to Gladys Knight & the Pips on Fury.

One-time Heartbeats member, a group named after The Royals' "Every Beat of My Heart," Wally Roker was working for Bobby Robinson's Harlem-based Fury label. "The song itself was very good, she was very good. We bought it from Henry who was a promoter in Atlanta. The guys we bought it from had the rights. He had the rights, he was a very wealthy person, backed the whole situation. The other master was found out not to belong to who sold it to the other company, Vee Jay, which had another copy of that master. It only made Gladys a little hotter, a little stronger. She had two companies working on it. It directed more attention to Gladys."

Remakes: Little Willie John 1962; James Brown & the Famous Flames 1963

—

Jimmy Reed "Big Boss Man" Vee Jay March 1961

Style: Blues
Where from: Dunleith, MI
Where recorded: Chicago, IL

At the time of "Big Boss Man," when sober, Jimmy Reed never had much to say. Said Red Holloway, "He was too quiet. First thing, you'd say, 'something is wrong with Jimmy.' When drinking, he'd always have something to tell you. 'Red, I sure like the way you play saxophone.' He had that real drawl. When he was sober, you could hardly get him to say hello. When you'd riding down the highway, he'd never make a sound."

Remakes: Charlie Rich 1963; The Pretty Things 1964; Willie Cobbs 1964; The Standells 1965; Erma Franklin 1967; Elvis Presley 1967; B. B. King 1985

—

Dee Clark "Raindrops" Vee Jay March 1961

Style: Rhythm and blues
Where from: Blytheville, AR
Where recorded: Chicago, IL

Dee Clark was reportedly inspired to write this song after a late night drive through a heavy rainstorm. Accordingly, the opening and closing of the song both feature heavy rain and thunder sound effects, with the closing augmented by Clark's powerful, swooping falsetto in which he shouts "it keeps on fallin'" followed by final clap of thunder. Backing Clark were Al Duncan, drums; Quinn Wilson, bass; Earl Skarritt and Phil Upchurch, guitar.

Spanish version: Bobby Pares "Gotas De Lluvia (Raindrops)" 1961

—

Shep and the Limelites "Daddy's Home" Hull March 1961

Style: Doo wop
From and recorded in: New York
Suggested pairing: The Heartbeats "A Thousand Miles Away" 1956

An extension of The Heartbeats, Shep and the Limelites was James "Shep" Sheppard, Clarence Bassett and Charles Baskerville, who recorded "Daddy's Home" as an answer to The Heartbeats' "A Thousand Miles Away." Problem was, according to Heartbeats member, Wally Roker, Sheppard plagiarized himself by lifting too much of "A Thousand Miles Away" into this answer. As a result, Rama Records, which had purchased "A Thousand Miles Away" from Bea Kaslin's Hull, sued Kaslin and won the copyright, driving the smaller Hull straight out of business.

"Daddy's Home" was a Big Apple hit from the beginning, reaching #2 on WABC and #3 on WMGM in March 1961.

Remakes: The Duke of Earl 1962; Chuck Jackson and Maxime Brown 1967; Jermaine Jackson 1972

—

Little Caesar & the Romans "Those Oldies But Goodies" Del-fi March 1961

Style: Doo wop
Where from: Los Angeles, CA
Where recorded: Hollywood, CA

Carl Burnett sang lead and David Johnson of the Upfronts did the recitation with other ex-Upfronts, Leroy Sanders, Johnny Simmons and Early Harris, all of whom were also with The Cubans on the only major hit Little Caesar & the Romans ever had. "I had a buddy named Jimmy Dodd, he and me was running buddies, he was from Bakersfield," said Burnett. "One night me and him was kicking it, we went to the movies, 'Hey let's go by my buddy Paul's house, he's having a party.' Went over to Paul Politi's house to party, he stayed on Temple, had a house on a hill. His old running buddy, Nick Curingas, was there. Paul was the type of guy who loved to fool around, had this song him and Nick wrote. He was trying everybody out, they just didn't come on like the way they wanted the song to be sung. Jimmy knew I doo wopped and said, 'Let my buddy try it.' I didn't want to sing. They drug me over there, I got over there, do this first verse, if I don't like it, you can back and forget about it. First I listened to him, he told me how it'd go, I started singing it. He said, 'That's it! That's the way I wanted it to go.' Everybody started clapping. I did the rest of the part, when we got done, everybody said yeah and went home.

"Paul went to the studio the next day," Burnett said. "Week later, they invited me and Jimmy and some of the girls to do that song. He had The Upfronts at first, he didn't use them, he called this other background group called The Romans, which I chose. At first they were going to sing the background of the group."

With demo disc in hand, it still wasn't easy for songwriter Politi to get "Those Oldies But Goodies" on a local label. Because he picked up the Oldies But Goodies phrase from Art LaBoe's successful series of Original Sound LPs begun in 1958, he took it to first to Original Sound, but LaBoe turned it down. "I liked the song, but I didn't like the way it was done," said LaBoe. "I told Paul Polito to make a better rendition, I'd put it out. "He took it over to Bob Keane," who released "Those Oldies But Goodies (Remind Me Of You)" on Del-fi, the first major hit about recent oldies. "I found myself announcing the song in the top ten," LaBoe admitted.

Answer: Sonny Knight "Those Oldies But Goodies Are Dedicated To You" 1962

—

Roy Orbison "Running Scared" Monument March 1961

Style: Rock 'n' roll
Where from: Texas
Where recorded: Nashville, TN
Suggested pairings: Bobby Vee "Run to Him" 1961; The Shangri-Las "He Cried" 1964

Another operatic Roy Orbison ballad, Orbison was able to express fear of lost love in this vocal, "Running Scared."

—

The Jive Five "My True Story" April 1961

Style: Doo wop
Where from: Brooklyn, NY
Where recorded: New York
Suggested pairings: Spaniels "You're Gonna Cry" 1957; The Paragons "Twilight" 1958

In 1959 Eugene Pitt put together his own group, The Jive Five, with neighborhood friends, Jerome Hanna, tenor; Richard Harris; Thurmon "Billy" Prophet and Norman Johnson, bass. In early '61, all the five jivers auditioned for Les Cahan and Joe Rene at the Beltone Studio on Broadway in New York. Cahan, who'd been running the studio for several years, decided to branch out with Beltone Records and made a spectacular splash shortly afterwards with Bobby Lewis' "Tossin' and Turnin,'" the biggest hit of the entire year.

One of the songs the Jive Five sang that day was an original ballad by Pitt and Oscar Waltzer, "My True Story," based on Eugene's own experience of losing a girlfriend to one of his (former?) pals. While young, the guys were named by neighborhood girls from Brooklyn's Bedford-Stuyvesant, who told them, "You are just a jive five." The name stuck.

When introduced to the owners of the new startup, Beltone Records, the group was asked what songs they had. Lead singer and songwriter Eugene Pitt said, "We sang other songs we had, but they didn't like it. 'Anything else?' We told them, 'My True Story,' but we didn't like the song. We sang it and they said, 'That's the one.'" One thing about "My True Story" was that the title was not found anywhere in the lyrics, which according to Pitt, was true, though "names have been changed."

Doo wop was at the peak of its early 1960s "revival," a time of renewed interest in many '50s recordings. "My True Story," with backing by Rene's band, had an addicting 'Cry, cry-y-y...' vocal hook (often resulting in record store customers who didn't know the actual title offering their own wailing "Cry-cry-cry" in attempts to identify the song). It captured the essence of older doo wop but got off to a slow start at the beginning of summer '61; by September, though, it had gained momentum, moving into the top ten on the pop charts while hitting number one R&B. Pitt rejects the term doo wop. "When I started out, it was rhythm and blues."

—

Gary U.S. Bonds "Quarter To Three" Legrand April 1961

Style: Rhythm and blues
From and recorded in: Norfolk, VA
Suggested pairings: The Church Street Five "A Night With Daddy G" 1960; Dion "Runaround Sue" 1961; Chubby Checker "Dancin' Party" 1962

As to the premise for "Quarter to Three," Gary U.S. Bonds said, "The Church Street Five's 'A Night With Daddy G' was released and it wasn't selling that much. Guys played it, but that don't count. One day we were hanging around the studio, 'Why don't we put some lyrics to the thing?' I said 'okay.' We went in and wrote probably the greatest lyric you ever heard if you can understand it. Took about ten minutes, lyrics, that's all. I just started writing about me and Daddy G and the Church Street Five and how much fun we were having.

Bonds continued, "They said it was dirty, one of the reasons it sold so much. The beginning part is what they thought was dirty. It doesn't say anything. Just me and Daddy talking, 'how you doin'?' They thought we was talking about naked women and stuff. We knew what was going on. The liquid refreshment part was certainly true. It took about eight or ten takes before we could get the little drunks together. That was 1961 when it hit the charts. Legrand was very happy. They got a chance to get a four track machine."

After the success of 'Quarter To Three,' Bonds changed his recording name to Gary (U.S.) Bonds as some deejays had assumed U.S. Bonds was a vocal group.

Remakes: Sir Douglas 1966; The Strangeloves 1967; The Executives 1973; Clarence Clemons 1989

—

LaVern Baker "Saved" Atlantic April 1961

Style: Rhythm and blues
Where from: Detroit, MI
Where recorded: New York
Suggested pairing: Bessie Smith "Careless Love Blues" 1925

This song includes Phil Spector on guitar, behind the big bass drum, while LaVern Baker shouted about being saved. According to co-composer Mike Stoller, "Saved" got him in trouble with the gospel crowd for making light of their material and actually got banned on some radio.

—

Ben E. King "Stand By Me" Atco April 1961

Style: Rhythm and blues
From and recorded in: New York
Suggested pairings: Soul Stirrers "Stand By Me, Father" 1959; Don Covay "See About Me" 1961; The Marvelettes "Don't Mess With Bill" 1965; The Police "Every Breath You Take" 1983

Though based on the gospel "Stand By Me, Father," most recently recorded by the Soul Stirrers in 1959, vocalist Ben E. King and Glick, a penname for Jerry Leiber and Mike Stoller, were credited for this composition, "Stand By Me," on which Phil Spector played guitar. "Stand By Me" hit on WABC at #3 in mid-April 1961 and KRLA #9 and KFWB #5 in May 1961.

Remakes: Don Shirley 1962; Cassius Clay 1964; Chuck Jackson 1964; Earl Grant 1965; Little Eva 1965; The Tangents 1966; Spyder Turner 1966; Johnny Jones 1968; David & Jimmy Ruffin 1970; John Lennon 1975; Syl Johnson 1978; Mickey Gilley 1980; Maurice White 1985

—

The Blue Jays "Lover's Island" Milestone April 21, 1961

Style: Doo wop
Where from: Venice, CA and Santa Monica, CA
Where recorded: Hollywood, CA

Leon Peels came to California at age 12 and graduated from Venice High in 1955. The Blue Jays formed when Peels met Alex Manigo, a Santa Monica High graduate. "We used to sing on the corners and over at the Oakwood Playground in Venice. They used to give dances, we sang there," said Peels. "That's how we got started in about 1958, just the guys in the neighborhood." Peels sang lead with Manigo, baritone; Verner Richardson, second tenor and Leonard Davidson, bass.

Peels continued, "Alex and I put it together. I was 24 at the time. I guess we liked to practice, we wanted to have it together when we went into the studio. We had that distinctive R&B sound. 'Lover's Island' was written by Alex Manigo and myself, we were on the Venice pier, sitting down there, back in those days they had the Rosemary Theater and the Dome Theater. Alex said, 'Let's write a song,' I came up with 'on lover's island,' he came up with another, we got the lines together, before long we had the song out," said Peels.

"Lover's Island" on Milestone had great local sales. The Blue Jays appeared at an unprecedented Hollywood Bowl rock 'n' roll concert in 1961. "At the first note of 'Lover's Island,' the kids went to scream," said Peels. Peels made very little money during this period. Owners of Milestone, "the Bakers had some problems with The Paradons, I believe they had to use the money from 'Lover's Island' to fight in court." Other Blue Jays discs sold, but none reached the top ten. After just a handful of releases and the crib death of his infant son, Peels gave up recording.

—

Gene & Wendell "The Roach" Ray Star May 1, 1961

Style: Rhythm and blues
From and recorded in: Los Angeles, CA

Gene & Wendell teamed with The Sweethearts on this dance, "The Roach," on Ray Star, a label owned by Ray Rindoni and Art LaBoe's ex, Starla Kay, after he named his Starla label after her. "Rindoni was a garment manufacturer," said Ray Star arranger Nick Venet. "He wanted to go into the business because of her. I named the label Ray Star, it took off. They were in the same offices as KDAY on that little street between Sunset and Hollywood. They didn't know anything about the business."

"The Roach" charted eight months late, and did best in Seattle. Venet said, "They performed at the 5/4 Ballroom. Alonzo Willis took me back there. There were sex change guys who'd get out and perform, every one was great; would make James Brown look like he was standing still.

"'The Roach' was the black Twist," explained Venet. "I wrote down the steps, put them on the jacket. The song was Alonzo's idea in a sense, he had stolen the melody from another song. Alonzo's idea was how a roach took his girlfriend away, mine was they got a new dance. We went into the studio with three instruments: Sonny Knight on piano; Jesse Sailes, drums and Rene Hall on guitar, and did the arrangements and Bones Howe did the engineering at Radio Recorders.

Venet continued, "I took Gene & Wendell on the road because it was big there, hopped into a Cadillac, drove to New Orleans. The guys slept with rags around their necks, kids ripping the convertible top with knives, place was packed on the south side. They went on the stage, these guys were seasoned, they had performed a lot in L.A. without a record, had the police come and take them off the stage. One of them had his fly down, the girls were going nuts. Girls were packed in the room, some as young as 12. They surrounded the guys and tore off their clothes. I'm not sure what happened because girls were all over them."

Answer: Gene & Wendell "Roach Stomp" 1961

—

Ann-Margaret "I Just Don't Understand" RCA June 1961

Style: Pop
Where from: Valsjöbyn, Sweden
Where recorded: Nashville, NY
Suggested pairing: Marty Robbins "Don't Worry" 1960

Actress Ann-Margaret's hit "I Just Don't Understand" was an early example, perhaps the second, of the fuzz guitar on record, after Marty Robbins' "Don't Worry" from 1960. The guitar was courtesy Billy Strange of The Wrecking Crew with Charlie McCoy on harmonica.

—

The Mar-Keys "Last Night" Satellite/Stax June 1961

Style: Rhythm and blues instrumental
From and recorded in: Memphis, TN

Originally dubbed The Royal Spades, "The Mar-Keys came from the fact Stax was in a movie theater and the marquee [was] out in front," said Mar-Keys' member Stax label session guitarist Steve Cropper. Cropper continued, "We were arguing about the French spelling of it, 'queue' or however it goes. [I said,] 'Let's do it simple where everybody can get it.' It means nothing. The Mar-Keys. I know when were wrote the song, the title came later. The song came out of a riff that Jerry Lee 'Smoochie' Smith was playing on the piano. Charles Axton came up with the 'da da,' I came up with the drum fills, you can almost sing the drum roll." Cropper also noted he helped Smoochie Smith play the organ, by holding down a key while playing a solo. Cropper just reached over and helped out. He said, "Somewhere in the session, we were kidding with Floyd Newman about somebody had a hangover because they were out late last night: 'ooh last night,' that's where it came from, we had him sing it during the record."

Mar-Keys bass player Duck Dunn recalled, in the early days, "There was a record shop out front that paid the bills. Miss Axton put in a recording studio, we'd go in, a one track machine." About "Last Night," Dunn said, "They erased some of it and some of it had to be spliced, so I think it's in two parts. I didn't think it was good enough to be released. We had the rhythm section on it. Jerry Wexler said, 'If you put horns on it, it'll work.' I think that was the time we were recording Don Covay. I think he was the first artist to come in." Shortly after this 45 hit, a pre-existing Satellite label contacted them, thus Satellite became Stax, a positive change.

—

The Dreamlovers "When We Get Married" Heritage 1961

Style: Doo wop
From and recorded in: Philadelphia, PA

Named after the Bobby Darin hit, The Dreamlovers recorded "For the First Time" for the Len label in 1960, and "Home Is Where the Heart Is" and "May I Kiss the Bride" on V-Tone, prior to hitting the national charts with this romantic ballad, "When We Get Married," charting first at #14 on Philly's own WIBG in early July 1961.

Remakes: The Intruders 1970; Joe Bataan 1970; Larry Graham 1980; The Persians 1973

—

Roy Orbison "Candy Man" Monument July 1961

Style: Rock 'n' roll
Where from: Texas
Where recorded: Nashville, TN
Suggested pairing: Jimmy Reed "Big Boss Man" 1961

Roy Orbison and his band, The Candymen, created a unique sound with two guitars, two harmonicas, a bass guitar, a set of drums, and backing vocals on this upbeat paean to pleasure.

—

Van McCoy "Mr. DJ" Rock N July 1961

Style: Proto soul
Where from: Washington, DC
Where recorded: Philadelphia, PA

In 1961, Van McCoy owned Rock N Records as a way of putting out his first single, "Hey Mr. DJ," an appealing spoken-sung performance that failed to chart. He shut down Rock N when Scepter Records hired him as a staff writer. Later, he had sales with Chris Bartley and with The Ad Libs on Vando Records, co-owned with Philly D.J Jocko Henderson, and Maxx label with Gladys Knight & the Pips. In 1976, McCoy went to #1 with disco era "The Hustle."

—

Lee Dorsey "Ya Ya" Fury July 1961

Style: Rhythm and blues
Where from: Portland, OR
Where recorded: New Orleans, LA

There was no special meaning in these lyrics, "sittin' on my la la, waiting for my ya ya." It was self-explanatory. Though Earl King did give some background: "'Ya Ya' was written off some phrase someone had heard called gumbo ya ya. It's connected somehow to some kind of voo doo stuff. Phrases mean different things to different people in different locales. You may take a phrase indigenous in certain locales and people may not be aware of it away from there."

—

The Supremes "I Want a Guy" Tamla 1961

Style: Proto soul vocal group
From and recorded in: Detroit, MI

"'I Want a Guy' was my idea," said Freddie Gorman. "'Forever' was Lamont Dozier's idea. I had come in the evening as usual, into the studio portion of where we did our recording. Brian Holland was there, he had this group of girls, four of them, another girl, Barbara Martin. They had been in a meeting with Berry Gordy and he had said he didn't want any girls groups. He didn't want any more. I had the song, 'I Want a Guy.' Brian and I started playing it, started teaching it to them. Diana Ross was singing lead. Berry walked into the studio and said, 'You girls still here? Didn't I tell you I wasn't into a girls group.' Brian or myself said, 'Berry, wait a minute, hear them sing this song.' He did, he loved it, went on to joining us to finishing the song, it was their first release. I had two verses and a bridge, he probably wrote the last verse, straightened it around. It got them their contract. They were very determined. It sure did a lot for me."

Gladys Horton of The Marvelettes said, "When we went to Motown, The Supremes were already there," "They had 'I Want a Guy' that The Marvelettes recorded. The Supremes recorded it first. We were so innocent in those days, I don't think the Supremes minded. They were one of the more established groups there, The Miracles and The Supremes. Marv Johnson, Andre Williams, Mary Wells was there. Barrett Strong was a good friend of Berry's, they wrote tunes together."

—

The Supremes "Buttered Popcorn" Tamla July 1961

Style: Proto soul vocal group
From and recorded in: Detroit, MI

Some take the Supremes' "Buttered Popcorn" as an ode to masturbation. What is known is that the B-side, "Who's Loving You" is the most recorded of the label's songs, by The Miracles, by The Jackson Five and by The Supremes, never to chart.

—

The Temptations "Oh, Mother of Mine" Miracle 1961

Style: Proto soul vocal group
Where from: Alabama
Where recorded: Detroit, MI

The Distants came over to Motown in need of a new moniker. They were given the name The Temptations, but the material they were given, "Oh, Mother of Mine," was ordinary and didn't tempt many record buyers to this release on Miracle, likely named after The Miracles, the only hit vocal group the label had at the time.

A second Temptations release, "Check Yourself," was also on Miracle, but also wasn't, a miracle, that is. "Dream Come True" by The Temptations, a stronger song, represented the debut of the Gordy label in early 1962, but also didn't burn up the charts. The label decided to try a new name and new label, The Pirates, on the fine rocking version of the Nolan Strong and the Diablos' classic, "Mind Over Matter" on Mel-o-dy. Whichever name hit, The Temptations or The Pirates, would be their name. The Pirates were deep sixed; The Temptations it was.

—

Dick & Dee Dee "The Mountain's High" Lama/Liberty July 1961

Style: Rock 'n' roll
Where from: Santa Monica, CA
Where recorded: Hollywood, CA
Suggested pairings: The Cookies "In Paradise" 1956; Marv Johnson "Move Two Mountains" 1960; The Miracles "Way Over There" 1960; Big Country "In A Big Country" 1983

One of the most successful recording acts of the early 1960s was Dick & Dee Dee. Dick St. John had recorded at least two records on the Rona label prior to joining with Dee Dee (real name: Mary Sperling), whom he met while at Paul Revere Junior High, then reconnected as employees of an ice cream store in Santa Monica. "She was named Dee Dee because it's better than Dick and Mary," said St. John. "This is when you had two tracks. We would sing it, then ping pong it, then mix it as we went along. All records of this era did that."

One of many hits about mountains, this medium tempo with lots of drumming by Allen Breneman, "The Mountain's High," about frustrated love backed with the ballad "I Want Someone" by Dick & Dee Dee was issued on Lama, a label owned by the Wilder Brothers, who made a deal for release in the U.S. and worldwide on Liberty in all markets, except for San Francisco and Seattle, where it was promoted on Lama. In L.A., it was released on Liberty. In the Bay Area, Tom Donahue and Bob Mitchel heard it and played the B-side. "It was #1 on the West Coast long before it was #1 on the East Coast," said St. John. It hit #2 nationally about a month later.

Dick & Dee Dee commenced on a tour of Texas with Ray Peterson, Gary U.S. Bonds, The Hollywood Argyles and Kathy Young. As he was black, "Gary would have to stay in one place, we in another," said St. John.

—

The Duals "Stick Shift" Star Revue/Sue July 1961

Style: Rock 'n' roll
Where from: Los Angeles, CA
Where recorded: Hollywood, CA

Likely inspired by the vocal cruising/speeding car sound effects created by Vernon Green in The Medallions' "Buick 59" and "Speedin.'" The Duals were dual black guitar slingers Henry Bellinger and Johnny Lageman, who recorded this sound effects-laden (rumbling engine, power shift, squealing wheels and police sirens) perfect-for-cruising hot rod instrumental "Stick Shift" backed with "Cruising" on one-time Meadowlarks' vocalist Ron Barrett's Star Revue label, then on Sue for national distribution.

—

Jimmy Reed "Bright Lights Big City" Vee Jay August 1961

Style: Blues
Where from: Dunleith, MI
Where recorded: Chicago, IL

During a Jimmy Reed performance, "he'd be real nervous, sweat a lot," said sax man Red Holloway. "He'd go in one turn to the next. His personality was never brought out like it should be." When drunk, "he would really get loose, really a fantastic player. Strictly his own style." His wife, Mama Reed, "was giving him the lyrics" to "Bright Lights, Big City," his final major hit. "He had a little taste, he couldn't remember the lyrics, she'd whisper the lyrics in his ear. He wrote a lot of material," as did his wife.

—

The Dovells "Bristol Stomp" Parkway August 1961

Style: Rock 'n' roll vocal group
From and recorded in: Philadelphia, PA
Suggested pairing: The Students "Everyday Of the Week" 1958

The Dovells had exactly one record, the uptempo "No, No, No," selling poorly when they performed at a record hop in Bristol, PA and noticed the teens were doing a stomp dance to an oldie, "Everyday Of the Week" by The Students out of Indianapolis. The rest was easy: Lead singer Len Barry and The Dovells wrote new lyrics to The Students' melody, including a reference to the record hop, and the rest was chart action. Having no flip side, they reused the "No, No, No," the fine doo wop ballad B-side, "Letters Of Love" as the "Bristol Stomp" B-side, until they could come up with a new B-side, "Out In The Cold Again" for "Bristol Stomp."

—

The Impressions "Gypsy Woman" ABC August 1961

Style: Soul
From and recorded in: Chicago, CA

"I think I wrote 'Gypsy Woman' when I was about 15," said Impressions' lead vocalist Curtis Mayfield. "A lot of things, the first 'I love you,' the first feelings within self, the first recognizing of what is beautiful and appealing, the first good western movie where there was this gypsy lady dancing around the campfire light, her eyes were like that of burning embers, all of those different things, that's what brought about 'Gypsy Woman.'"

Remakes: The Fabulous Peps 1968; Jay and the Americans 1969; Brian Hyland 1970; Bobby Womack 1986

—

Chubby Checker "The Fly" Parkway September 1961

Style: Rock 'n' roll
Where from: South Carolina
Where recorded: Philadelphia, PA

"We were at a record hop," said John Madara, "we saw the kids doing the dance The Fly to Ron Holden's 'Love You So.' We immediately went back and wrote the song and got it out in three days. We had recorded it with Carl & the Commanders. We brought it in to Cameo to sell as a master. Kal Mann, who had written a lot of songs for Chubby Checker, said, 'This has got to be the next Chubby Checker record.'"

David White said, "That was the only time Cameo/Parkway used an outside track. Cameo gave us an ultimatum, 'Either let us use your track or we'll write our own Fly and blow you out of the water.' Well, okay. They had the power then. We just took Carl's voice off, put Chubby's on. We produced the music for Chubby, Johnny's electric razor was the fly." The same track was then reused for John Zacherle's "The Bat."

—

Ray Charles "Hit the Road Jack" ABC September 1961

Style: Rhythm and blues
Where from: Florida
Where recorded: Hollywood, CA

Ray Charles asked one-time R&B hit maker and songwriter Percy Mayfield if he had any songs for Charles to record. Mayfield offered up "Hit the Road Jack." The snarling female duet voice was Margie Hendricks of The Raelettes, whose affair with Charles produced a son in 1959.

"Ray Charles was a tremendous entity in rhythm and blues, planning on going pop," said arranger and guitar player Rene Hall. "He thought going to ABC was an entree into the pop market. ABC distributors were not rhythm and blues oriented people. They didn't have the contact with black deejays and radio stations Atlantic had; they sweetened the pot with the black deejays. ABC didn't have that connection at that time, that was the reason it didn't get off the ground as fast as more of the pop things. Ray is a genius, he was then, is now. You never get past four or five measures that he doesn't inject changes to... for the better. He has to hear what you have written to enhance his ideas into it. 'Right there, I think we should change...'" Reversing the lyrics of "Hit the Road Jack," Charles fired Margie ("hit the road") from The Raelettes in 1964.

—

Dion "Runaround Sue" Laurie September 1961

Style: Rock 'n' roll
Where from: The Bronx, NY
Where recorded: New York
Suggested pairings: The Elegants "Please Believe Me" 1959; U.S. Bonds "Quarter To Three" 1961; Chubby Checker " Dancin' Party" 1962

"After 'Quarter To Three,' everybody started picking up on what we were doing, especially those guys in Philadelphia," said Gary U.S. Bonds. "I was a little ticked. I was rich then, who cares? I named a few friends of mine, Bobby and Chubby, they hated me. 'Runaround Sue' was 'Quarter To Three,' and Chubby did 'Dancin' Party'" in 1962. "I could demand monies, but we weren't getting any, so nobody could do anything." With the record "Copy Cat," "I kind of got even with everybody. A couple of them came to me and said, 'We're going to kill you.' Good thing I had The Bravados with me. We had jackets, orange, black and gold. Like a shield, nice Itali type shield, Mexican name. Hatchet and stiletto. They went to jail, most of the other guys, Moose and other guys went into the service."

—

The Showmen "It Will Stand" Minit September 1961

Style: Retro soul vocal group
Where from: Norfolk, VA
Where recorded: Washington, DC

One of the great examples of rock 'n' roll/rhythm and blues/soul paying tribute to the music itself. When they were signed, "the group was already formed," said Showmen lead singer General Johnson. "We were like a neighborhood group, doo woppers in the neighborhood. We were called The Humdingers. A little guy in Norfolk named Noah Biggs. Norfolk has a lot of very talented people, they had no outlets to do their thing. Although he was unorthodox, Noah did try. In his place, a lot of people passed through.

All of us were friends: U.S. Bonds, James McLease aka Jimmy Soul, he came through there. Swampdog. There's a lot of people who later became successful who would hang out at that place called Nimrods. It was a record store in the front of the place, in the back he had tape recorders, guitar amps, microphones, stuff we liked to see. It was open to anybody who had talent. On the weekends, sometimes he'd give shows. He got us a recording deal with Minit Records. They didn't like the name The Humdingers.

"I wrote 'Country Fool,' Johnson continued. "Noah gave me the title, it was the A-side of the record. Noah Biggs sent a tape of 'Country Fool' to Jae Banasak in New Orleans. He sent it to Alan Toussaint in Washington, DC. We met him there, cut a demo, whatever came out on Minit is from that session. We were all excited. Nothing happened with 'Country Fool.' We thought it was all over. A disc jockey in San Francisco turned over 'Country Fool' and played 'It Will Stand,' which was the beginning of my serious professional career. That was one of the first really good songs I'd written. I write real earthy, things that teach the emotion to people. I was trying to write an anthem. The title was 'Rock and Roll Will Stand.' They changed it to 'It Will Stand.' They did it to a couple of other songs on Minit. At such a young age, I was happy to have a record out. I didn't care what they named it. I fought for 'Rock and Roll Will Stand.' I found out why Minit Records changed the song. 'It Will Stand' is a lot more clever title than 'Rock and Roll Will Stand.' In the early things I was doing, I was writing from the heart and not as scientific when it came to titles. When 'It Will Stand' was first released, Imperial and Minit were having their problems and it wasn't promoted properly. It was #1 in a lot of different places, but not at one time. It would be a hit in San Francisco, then a hit in L.A. much later. It was a hit in Pittsburgh or Detroit until 1964."

—

The Marvelettes "Please Mr. Postman" Tamla September 1961

Style: Proto soul vocal group
From and recorded in: Detroit, MI
Suggested pairing: Dee Dee Sharpe "Mashed Potato Time" 1962

"Our first names were The Cantsingyets. 'Let's say we can't sing yet.' One day, but not yet," said Gladys Horton, lead singer of The Marvelettes. "When he heard that name, Berry Gordy Jr. said they can't use that name. Berry said, 'We thought of a name for you girls.' It came from The Marvelous Marvelettes. We liked it, we were happy he was pleased with us. It sounded pretty good.

Horton continued, "We had no original tunes. Brian Holland and Robert Batemen auditioned us, they said you girls sounded good but you've got to get something original. We got a bad girls group, The Supremes. This isn't good enough. You've got to get something original. When went back to Inkster, Georgia Dobbins was with the group, we had two Georgias then, we didn't have Wanda. Georgia went back, 'You heard what they said, we got to get something original.' She knew William Garrett, she called a rehearsal, William came over with all these tunes. We asked him to sing, it was altogether different, it was a blues thing. She asked him, 'Can I reconstruct the song?' 'Take anything you want to do with it.' This was his title 'Please Mr. Postman' only. Georgia reconstructed it, said, 'Gladys I'm not going to be able to be with the group, I want you to lead the song.' She taught me the song, we went back to Motown, then the co-writers listened to the song, said, 'Girls we think you got something.' They rehearsed us and rehearsed us. It did come out to be good song.

"A lot of the groups used to come in to do foot stomps and handclaps on songs," Horton explained. Our very first tune, one of The Supremes, Florence, came to me, The Supremes were there, it was on a Saturday and The Supremes happened to come by the studio. Florence came to me, said, 'Gladys, I hear something you can be doing in those some of those spots you're leaving open. Why don't you put a little "oh yeah."'" I did it. If she knew, she could put her name on the song. I caught on with a little something of my own. She helped me out, it was a #1 tune, she gave me a little something to add in there."

Remakes: The Beatles 1964; The Pat Boone Family 1974; The Carpenters 1974

—

Dick Dale and the Del-Tones "Let's Go Trippin" Deltone September 1961

Style: Instrumental rock 'n' roll
Where from: Massachusetts
Where recorded: Hollywood, CA
Original title: "Let's Go Trippen"

In the start of a major career move, Dick Dale & the Del-Tones went from vocalist to instrumentalist with this mega-influential single, "Let's Go Trippin,'" on Deltone. Dale was always dissatisfied with his big guitar sound reduced to a vinyl 45. "I used to run the Deltone Record Store across the street from the Rendezvous. When I heard 'Let's Go Trippin',' I threw it across the record store. It didn't sound like me on stage. In those days, they used limiters in recording sessions. That's why I stopped recording," said Dale. "Any engineer who heard the big sound that came out of my guitar bleeding through the board would use limiters, which made it sound tinny"—a sore spot not unfamiliar to Johnny "Guitar" Watson back in the mid-50s.

The Long Beach Press-Telegram wrote on November 5, 1961, "The hottest thing out seems to be Dick Dale's Deltone recording of 'Let's Go Trippin.' It has been a long time since a rock and roll instrumental has caused such a commotion."

—

The Miracles "Everybody Gotta Pay Some Dues" Tamla September 19, 1961

Style: Soul vocal group
From and recorded in: Detroit, MI
Original title: "Everybody's Gotta Pay Some Dues"

"It was another title," said Claudette Robinson of The Miracles. "In those days, the longer the title, the better the sales. Smokey and Berry probably changed the title." In fact, "Everybody's Gotta Pay Some Dues" became "Everybody Gotta Pay Some Dues" and, for a short period, "You Gotta Pay Some Dues."

—

Eddie Holland "Jamie" Motown October 1961

Style: Soul
From and recorded in: Detroit, MI

Even though he had already recorded for Mercury, United Artists and Tamla, Eddie Holland wasn't a born stage performer, owing to stage fright. Therefore he had much more of a future as a songwriter under the HDH moniker, hitting with only one song, the lighthearted rocker "Jamie," which was issued twice, in accordance of Motown owner Berry Gordy's preference for getting the song right over getting the song out quick.

—

The Tokens "The Lion Sleeps Tonight" RCA October 1961

Style: Pop doo wop vocal group
From and recorded in: New York City, NY
Original title: "Wimoweh"
Suggested pairings: Solomon Linda & the Evening Birds "Mbube" 1939; Gordon Jenkins and the Weavers "Wimoweh" 1951; Yma Sumac "Wimoweh" 1952; Kitty White "Wimoweh (the Lion Sleeps)" 1960

A hunting song originally sung in Zulu, the original title was "Mbube," which means "lion." Written by South African singer Solomon Linda, who recorded it in 1939 with his group, The Evening Birds, this African chant refers to King Chaka—The Lion—who lies in sleep and will awake one day.

In the 1950s Linda sold the rights to this song to Gallo Records of South Africa for 10 shillings (about $1.70), as apartheid laws did not allow blacks to negotiate. In 1951, Gordon Jenkins recorded a big band arrangement of "Wimoweh" with Pete Seeger's Weavers. The Tokens—Hank Medress, Jay Siegel, and Phil and Mitch Margo, who had several hits but no label deal—sang "Wimoweh" for producers Hugo and Luigi. Impressed, Hugo and Luigi and George Weiss rewrote the song and changed the title to "The Lion Sleeps Tonight," which session singer Kitty White had already mostly changed to "The Lion Sleeps" one year previously. Opera singer Anita Darien was brought in for the soprano during the sax solo of the pop doo wop version by The Tokens, who were apparently embarrassed with the new title and lyrics and fought the release of the recording. They felt better when it made #1 on the pop charts and major markets in October 1961. In 1971, The Tokens sang backup on the Robert John version, also a #1 hit.

Remake: Robert John 1971

—

Buddy Guy "Stone Crazy" Chess 1961

Style: Blues
Where from: Mississippi
Where recorded: Chicago, IL

"Chess was the big leagues," said Buddy Guy. "My first session was with Willie Dixon, came got me from Cobra Records with me on some stuff he had, 'I Got My Eyes On You' and 'Slop Around'" on Chess, both released in 1960. "Muddy Waters had heard about me then. Leonard Chess would get ready to record Muddy, Muddy would say 'I gotta have that kid play with me.' Leonard would say, 'We want somebody old who really knows the old blues." Muddy would say, 'I'm telling you who to get.' That's how I got next to Leonard cause he thought I didn't know that, but I know that stuff, but just to improve myself with Buddy Guy['s] standpoint, when you up there. Now I feel Muddy, I feel Walter, because these are the fathers of the blues. 'Stone Crazy' was done at the studio, recording at 1:30 or 2:30 in the morning at Chess. The last verse of that song is I'm going back down somewhere where the weather suits my clothes. It was supposed to be freezing, not subfreezing. The next day it was 13 below zero, tuned the radio on, first thing I heard was "going back down somewhere where the weather suits my clothes."

—

Charles McCullough & the Silks "My Girl" Dootone September 1961

Style: Rhythm and blues group
Where from: Houston, TX
Where recorded: Los Angeles, CA

Charles McCullough, who came to L.A. in 1949 and graduated from Centennial High School in 1956, recalled, "I just played in a school band, whenever we recorded, I was playing 'My Girl.' At that time, I'd sit down at the piano, I was thinking about different things. My mother played piano real good, so I picked it up real good. I set my own trend, I was just fooling around, I was young. I looked at 'Zorro,' sat at a piano and wrote that. Never heard about the show, but I thought maybe one day I could get it played on TV when they showed it. When me and the group got together, we just came up with The Silks name."

Members of this group were "Jesse Ford, soprano and first tenor, who could go down to a bass; Ike Hillery, bass and Sammy Young, baritone. Charles McCullough and the Silks auditioned for Dooto. McCullough recalls, "We went down there on Central and Hooper, where they split off, took a chance on a Saturday. He had a lot of groups come in and he liked the song and he wanted to sign us." Their debut was the moody, emotive ballad, "My Girl." Sax player Elliott Shavers recalled, "Charles McCullough worked with me on guitar, The Silks, Happy Roy Easter, he was the leader, Elroy Haley, piano player, and the drummer, Ron Green. I was in and out of the group most of the time."

After three releases, McCullough gave up recording. "I've got mixed emotions about Dootsie Williams," owner of Dootone Records, McCullough recalled. "We wasn't getting nowhere with him and I quit showing up."

—

Prince La La "She Put the Hurt On Me" A.F.O. September 1961
Style: Rhythm and blues
From and recorded in: New Orleans, LA
Original title: "You Put The Hurt On Me"

This earliest release on the brand new A.F.O. label, initials of All For One, was set up by mainly black New Orleans musicians, a city which previously had almost no homegrown record labels, and had some great early success with both Barbara George and Prince La La, real name Lawrence Nelson. Backing him on "You Put the Hurt on Me" were Nat Perrilliant and Red Tyler, tenor sax; Harold Battiste, piano; Melvin Lastie, trumpet; Roy Montrell, guitar; Chuck Badie, bass and John Boudreaux, drums.

According to Battiste, "The Prince La La record was an accident because it was supposed to be Barbara George." After a few weeks in release, the title was changed to "She Put The Hurt On Me."

Answer: Little Herman "I'm Gonna Put The Hurt On You" 1964

—

Jimmy Dean "Big Bad John" Columbia September 22, 1961
Style: Country
Where from: Plainview, TX
Where recorded: Nashville, TN
Original title: "Big John"

This song is perhaps the most altered release that ever went to #1. At first, the title on the promotional label was "Big John," but was changed because The Shirelles had a "Big John" on the market, in honor of President John Kennedy. Secondly, the corrected "Big Bad John" was lightly censored to change the ending line from "lies one hell of a man" to "lies a big, big man." Perhaps as few as 10,000 copies or as many as 40,000 copies with the hell ending were pressed. According to Dean's roommate, the song was intended to be a joke. Floyd Cramer was to play piano, but wound up hitting a chunk of steel with a hammer instead. It was Floyd's idea to make the switch.

Answer: Dottie West "My Big John" 1961
Satires: Frank Gallup "Ballad Of Irving" 1961; Phil McLean "Small Sad Sam" 1961

—

Barbara George "I Know (You Don't Love Me No More)" A.F.O. October 1961
Style: Rhythm and blues
From and recorded in: New Orleans, LA
Suggested pairings: Elder Chas. Beck "Just A Closer Walk With Thee" 1949; Jimmy Norman "I Don't Love you No More" 1962; The Shirelles "Everybody Loves A Lover" 1962

A.F.O. producer and session pianist Harold Battiste said, "The Prince La La record was an accident because it was supposed to be Barbara George. She came to audition, Prince La La was accompanying her. She couldn't get the song together, so he showed her how to sing "She Put The Hurt On Me." We decided let's record him. Was going to be four sides, so he did those two, and we did the other two on Barbara, 'I Know' and another song."

—

James Ray "If You Gotta Make a Fool Of Somebody" Caprice October 1961

Style: Rhythm and blues
Where from: Washington, DC
Where recorded: New York City, NY

James Ray Raymond recorded first in 1959 as Little Jimmy Ray on a blatant steal of Little Willie John's "Fever" from 1956 entitled "You Need to Fall in Love." Songwriter Rudy Clark rediscovered Ray, who'd been sleeping on an apartment building roof, and had him to audition for Gerry Granahan, owner of the brand new Caprice Records. The only R&B hit with dominant tuba backing, James Ray's "If You Gotta Make a Fool of Somebody," had veteran bandleader/piano banger Hutch Davie supplying the instrumental background as he had done with "The Green Door" by Jim Lowe from 1956.

—

The Sims Twins "Soothe Me" SAR October 13, 1961

Style: Rhythm and blues
From and recorded in: Los Angeles, CA
Suggested pairing: The Soul Stirrers "Lead Me, Jesus" 1961

Previously recording gospel as The Sims Brothers with "God Can Set The World On Fire" on Dootone in 1954, The Sims Twins, Ken and Bob Sims, were discovered by Sam Cooke at the California Club. "Sam liked our sound," said Bob. "He said, 'I'll record you all.'" Ken said, "He heard us sing, so he asked us to background him on 'Cupid' the next night, so that was it. While we were recording him, we did 'Cupid,' he decided to show us 'Soothe Me' and we did it right there on the spot."

A gentle mid-tempo ballad, the flipside to "Soothe Me" was a remake of a Johnny Morisette hit, "I'll Never Come Running Back To You" which, in turn, was an answer to Sam Cooke's much earlier hit, "I'll Come Running Back To You" Ken Sims said, "I think Sam wrote 'I'll Never Come Running Back To You' for Johnnie Morisette' and he gave it to us. Sam gave us $80, he said, 'You take this, get out of here.'"

On December 10, 1964, at a show in Birmingham, Alabama with Johnnie Taylor, Johnnie Morisette and Bobby Womack, Ken recalled, "'Soothe Me' was so hot, the man did not want us to come on first, he wanted us to come out last. We turned the club out. Bobby Womack and none of them got a chance to sing that night." The same night, Sam Cooke was killed at a Los Angeles motel. "In the paper the next morning was 'Shoot Me Baby.'" said Bobby Womack.

—

The Ikettes "I'm Blue (The Gong-Gong Song)" Atco November 1961

Style: Rhythm and blues group
Where from: St. Louis, MO
Where recorded: Los Angeles, CA
Suggested pairing: Ike & Tina Turner "So Blue Over You" 1968

Ike Turner's all-female backing vocal group, The Ikettes, backed Tina Turner under her new name on her debut, "A Fool In Love," in 1960, albeit anonymously. "I think I patented the Ikettes name in 1955," said Ike Turner. "They couldn't really sing, they were good doing background." Members were Robbie Montgomery, Delores Johnson, "the one [who] did 'gong gong gong,' she was from Dallas," and Eloise Hester. On The Ikettes "I'm Blue," Tina Turner sang backup. "We was under contract to Juggy Murray" at Sue Records, said Ike Turner, referring to Ike & Tina Turner releases only. Since they couldn't use the name Ike & Tina Turner, "Jerry Wexler put the song out as the Ikettes on Atco. When I put in 'gong gong,' he didn't want to do it."

—

Gene Chandler "Duke Of Earl" Vee Jay November 1961

Style: Rhythm and blues
From and recorded in: Chicago, IL

"They were The Dukays when I met them," said Gene Chandler. "I was singing with a group at school. The group in the neighborhood were The Dukays, 'You should be singing for us, it's where you live.' It was one of the convincing things. I came to them coming out of the service. Now here's our second recording session, I wanted to be a single artist, I made a decision to become The Duke. At [record label] Nat, Carl Davis was producing me. We had two records to choose from. A group of people who would distribute it across the country, this company would choose what they thought would be a hit record, we recorded "Nite Owl" and "Duke Of Earl." The guys chose the 'Nite Owl,' turned down 'Duke Of Earl.' Calvin Carter, brother of Vivian Carter, wanted to hear what 'Nite Owl' sounded like, Carl and Bunky needed money to get it out. 'What else have you recorded,' he then said he wanted to buy it, the lead singer of Duke is the lead singer of all songs, he's with The Dukays. Would he come with us, he's also the lead. It was a hell of a choice, either ['Duke of Earl' or] 'Nite Owl,' which was going up the charts, it was a heck of chance. We already had a hit with 'The Girl's A Devil.'" Chandler chose "Duke Of Earl." Once it hit, "I remember going to California, when I got off the plane, they had a red carpet, Rolls Royce, Hawaiian girls dancing in San Francisco. We went to do a movie in L.A. 'Don't Knock the Twist.' All these people with top hats and capes on. I'm making money on all of those."

Answers: The Pearlettes "Duchess Of Earl" 1962; The Duke of Earl "Walk On With the Duke" 1962; Rod Mckuen "Oliver Twist Meets The Duke Of Oil" 1962; Dorothy Berry "Girl Who Stopped The Duke Of Earl" 1962; Dipsy & the Doodles "Duke Of Nothin'" 1963

—

Chubby Checker "The Twist" Parkway November 1961

Style: Rock 'n' roll
From and recorded in: Philadelphia, PA

In late 1961, the Parkway label reissued Chubby Checker's "The Twist" with a new B-side, "Twistin' U.S.A." replacing "Toot" and proving the label marketing geniuses, as the song reached #1 for the second time in two years, a feat never duplicated before or since.

—

The Marketts "Surfer's Stomp" Union/Liberty 1961

Style: Rock 'n' roll
Where from: Los Angeles, CA
Where recorded: Hollywood, CA

The classic surf instrumental genre was given a swell ride by the black Ernie Freeman Combo as the Mar-Kets on this medium tempo shuffle, "Surfer's Stomp" backed with "Start" on Joe Saraceno-owned Union, sold in Southern California only. Nationally, "Surfer's Stomp" backed with "Start" was reissued on Liberty, complete with a diagram as to how to do the dance.

Songwriter and session rhythm guitar player Mike Z. Gordon posted on YouTube writer's credits on "Surfer's Stomp," which showed Gordon as the writer and producer. But when it hit, his name disappeared, and was replaced by Saraceno's name. "He finally got caught and they won a $500,000 judgment against him and took all of his songs," Gordon posted.

—

The Beach Boys "Surfin'" Candix/X 1961

Style: Rock 'n' roll
Where from: Hawthorne, CA
Where recorded: Hollywood, CA

When "Surfin'" was recorded by music publisher Hite Morgan in mid-September, the band was known as

The Pendletons, and included brothers Brian, Carl, and Dennis Wilson from Hawthorne, cousin Mike Love and neighborhood friend Al Jardine, who lived in Torrance.

About the name change to The Beach Boys, Bruce Morgan, son of song publishers Hite and Dorita Morgan, who first recorded the band, recalled, "The whole concept behind The Beach Boys was my parents' idea." For years, their father Murry Wilson visited the Morgans to pitch his songs. "My mom was tired of listening to Murry's songs. He was in our living room all the time with 'moon June spoon' songs. My mom said, 'Let's shift the focus to the boys.' Dennis was a surfer. She asked Dennis to make a list of surfing terms to learn something about surfing, so she sat down with Dennis, coaxing him to writing surf themes to music. At that time Brian wasn't interested, so mom asked him, 'What kind of music do you like?' His favorite was 'Duke Of Earl,' and that was the genesis of The Beach Boys. Murry didn't want any association with The Beach Boys because he thought their music was terrible. So he said, 'Don't tell anybody about that group.' He was a real asshole, the way he talked about his own kids. I used to hide when he visited. There was a lot of controversy at the time, lot of argument because they wanted to be called The Pendletons. That argument went on until my dad said, 'You're gonna be The Beach Boys.' The groups back then had uniforms and they bought these Pendleton jackets, so that was their Beach Boys' uniform. They had one session.

Hite Morgan, who was a friend of mine, came out with this thing in the front room, where they had the mastering studio," said Tony Hilder. The first record as The Beach Boys was "Surfin'" backed with "Luau" on Candix, also pressed on X, which nibbled at the charts for three months. Apparently, the X label issue of "Surfin'" was pressed up by Murry Wilson to sell at Venice beach. The first known mention of The Beach Boys in the press was in the February 1, 1962 Press-Telegram Teen Tempo column: "'Surfin" by The Beach Boys and 'Surfer Stomp' by The Mar-kets are both in the local top ten. The latter is even making headway where surfing is a distant dream."

In February 8, 1962, Jaguars member Val Poliuto of the City of Commerce filled in for tenor Mike Love when they recorded "Karote" [*sic*], "Surfin Safari," "Surfin," "Little Surfer Girl," "Luau" and "Judy" for Morgan's Deck Records at Keene Studios, 8715 W. Third St Los Angeles, which were never released as singles. "Hite had this a capella tape with them doing 'Surfin.'" said Tony Hilder. "Dorinda did 'Little Surfer Girl.' Capitol fucked over Hite; I went to court on that. Capitol was trying to say it was a different version." The Beach Boys never again recorded for Candix—or for X or for Deck for that matter—but they were soon very, very big on Capitol.

—

The Primettes "Tears Of Sorrow" Lu Pine December 1961

Style: Soul vocal group
From and recorded in: Detroit, MI
Suggested pairing: The Drifters 1959

Already renamed The Supremes, The Primettes with lead singer Diana Ross copped the melody of The Drifters' recent hit, "There Goes My Baby" into the recording of "Tears Of Sorrow," just as The Distants had done with The Drifters' recent "Dance With Me" in creating "Answer Me."

According to songwriter Lamont Dozier, "The Primettes, originally there were four, the other girl, Barbara, how soon we forget. The group used to be sort of the low act on the totem pole at Motown," having been eclipsed early by The Marvelettes and Martha and the Vandellas. This sole Primettes recording was issued to counter the debut of The Supremes on Tamla.

—

The Falcons and Band (Ohio Untouchables) "I Found a Love" Lu Pine January 1962

Style: Soul vocal group
From and recorded in: Detroit, MI

Falcons' member Wilson Pickett said of "I Found aLove," which possessed a gospel flavor, "I wrote that. We had Joe Stubbs in there, lead singer of 'You're So Fine.' He was brother of Levi Stubbs of The Four Tops."

Remake: Wilson Pickett 1967

—

Bruce Channel "Hey! Baby" LeCam/Smash December 1961

Style: Rock 'n' roll
Where from: Texas
Where recorded: Fort Worth, TX
Suggested pairings: The Beatles "Love Me Do" 1963; The Beatles "Please Please Me" 1963

Around 1959, Bruce Channel wrote "Hey! Baby" with a friend, Margaret Cobb, and had been performing the song in the clubs for two years before he finally taped a demo and sent it to a retired Air Force Major Bill Smith, an independent record producer and owner of the LeCam label in Fort Worth. Major Bill invited Channel to his studio to rerecord the song. Not liking the guitar intro on the demo of "Hey! Baby," Major Bill Smith asked Delbert McClinton to play harmonica on the track, while Ronnie Dawson played drums. It took 15 minutes to record three takes.

Major Bill liked the ballad side better and took a tape of both songs to a DJ conference in Nashville to get it off and running. Decca's Paul Cohen offered to buy the "Hey Baby" side. Major Bill thought he could improve the song and put it on his own LeCam label, which sold well, then was leased to Smash. First played on KRUX in Phoenix, it charted on December 31 and reached #1 in a few weeks. Nationally, "Hey! Baby" hit nationally in late January; hit #1 on March 10, 1962. A year later came a similar harmonica passage in The Beatles "Love Me Do" and later, "Please Please Me."

Remakes: The Toronados 1966; José Feliciano 1969

—

Big Sambo and the House Wreckers "The Rains Came" Eric December 1961

Style: Swamp rock
Where from: Texas
Where recorded: New Orleans, LA

Huey P. Meaux produced Big Sambo's first and biggest hit record, "The Rains Came," in 1961. "We recorded 'The Rains Came' at Cosimo Matassa's studio in New Orleans," recalled Meaux. "He had an unusual voice, the vocal we had on the record was really haunting. As soon as we recorded it, I knew we were gonna have a hit."

Big Sambo recorded other songs, like "Barking Up The Wrong Tree," as James Young and the Housewreckers, but Meaux never got a chance to work with him again. Meaux said, "His heart was the same color as his saxophone—gold." Always known as Big Sambo, which must have become an embarrassing moniker, he changed to Big Sam in later issues under the distribution arm of the London label, but not before creating a swamp rock classic, redone by several high profile Texas/Louisiana acts.

Remakes: Sir Douglas Quintet 1965; Soul Brothers, Inc. 1968; Mighty Joe Young 1970; Joe Hughes 1975; Freddy Fender 1977; Warren Storm 1988

—

Etta James "Something's Got a Hold On Me" Argo January 1962

Style: Soul
Where from: Los Angeles, CA
Where recorded: Chicago, IL
Suggested pairings: Sam Cooke "Bring It On Home To Me" 1962; The Miracles "You've Really Got a Hold On Me" 1962

This song was done in the quasi-gospel similar to other hits of the day by Sam Cooke and by The Miracles, both of which came later. "That was her big record," said her one-time husband, Billy Foster. "She used to sing it with The Kinfolks, she used to close her shows with the song."

—

Arthur Alexander "You Better Move On" Dot January 1962

Style: Rhythm and blues vocal
Where from: Sheffield, AL
Where recorded: Muscle Shoals, AL

As June Alexander, Arthur Alexander recorded a soundalike to Brook Benton's "Kiddio" entitled "Sally Sue Brown" for Judd in 1960. In fact, June was intended to be printed as Junior. Alexander recorded the slow, almost menacing blues, "You Better Move On," in a rented abandoned studio/warehouse with an all white backing band, Dan Penn and the Pallbearers, later famous for the Muscle Shoals Sound. Selling about 800,000 copies, it funded the better known Muscle Shoals studio, which was to record hits by Tommy Roe, The Tams, Joe Tex, Wilson Pickett, Aretha Franklin and Jimmy Hughes.

In late January 1962, "You Better Move On" was an early pick hit on Inland Empire KFXM in far-away California. In 1965, after Penn and Co. left for Nashville, the famous "Swampers" became the Muscle Shoals rhythm section, playing on many soul classics and starting their own studio in the area in 1969.

—

King Curtis & the Noble Knights "Soul Twist" Enjoy February 1962

Style: Rhythm and blues instrumental
Where from: Ft. Worth, TX
Where recorded: New York

Tenor saxophone session genius King Curtis, who had backed any number of sessions by The Drifters, LaVern Baker and The Coasters, among others, recorded this instrumental smash hit, combining two elements in the title, the currently popular twist with the just-arriving soul music, into "Soul Twist" with Ernie Hayes, organ; Billy Butler, guitar; Jimmy Lewis and Ray Lucas, drums.

—

Chubby Checker "Slow Twistin'" Parkway February 1962

Style: Rock 'n' roll
Where from: South Carolina
Where recorded: Philadelphia, PA

This best-selling duet with Chubby Checker on this appealing "Slow Twistin'" was with an uncredited Dee Dee Sharpe and two of the female Orlons, Rosetta Hightower and Shirley Brickley, who had just recorded "Mr. 21," but were on their way to hitsville with "Wah Watusi" in May 1962 as was Sharpe with "Mashed Potato Time" in February 1962.

—

Nathaniel Mayer and the Fabulous Twilights "Village Of Love" Fortune/United Artists February 1962

Style: Rhythm and blues vocal group
From and recorded in: Detroit, MI

Patterned after James Brown, Nathaniel Mayer offered a raw, highly energetic vocal style and wild stage show. At

Fortune Records, he was label-mate with Nolan Strong and Andre Williams. Mayer would stay with the label for six years, recording a handful of records. At age 18 in 1962, Nathaniel Mayer and the Fabulous Twilights scored a Top 40 hit record with this aggressive bass-led vocal rocker "Village of Love" on Fortune Records, who then leased the record to United Artists Records. Along with "You're So Fine" by The Falcons, "Village Of Love" stands as the most impressive answer to the smoother teen oriented Motown sound, which owed its very existence to records like these. This was R&B; everything later was soul.

—

Mary Wells "The One Who Really Loves You" Motown February 8, 1962

Style: Soul
From and recorded in: Detroit, MI

This spectacular cha cha beat performance by Mary Wells set her style as a rocking vamp after her rough start with "Bye Bye Baby" in 1960.

Answer: Charmaine "Young Girl" 1963

—

The Crystals "Uptown" Philles February 14, 1962

Style: Proto soul vocal group
From and recorded in: New York

In 1961, Phil Spector recorded a Brooklyn girl group called The Crystals with lead singer Dee Dee Kinnebrew on two hits, "There's No Other (Like My Baby)" on his new Philles label and "Uptown," with an excess of strings, both of which charted in 1961 and 1962. Then the Crystals recorded one entirely non-commercial hit, "He Hit Me (And It Felt Like a Kiss)" in July. Spector dropped the first Crystals from Brooklyn, recorded The Blossoms from L.A. in their place, and renamed the L.A. group The Crystals for their releases on his label, while for the most part they remained The Blossoms on all other labels with which Spector was not associated. During this period, they did a few releases as The Wildcats and The Girlfriends, but those were one-offs. It's never simple when it comes to this group.

—

Dee Dee Sharpe "Mashed Potato Time" Cameo 1962

Style: Proto soul
From and recorded in: Philadelphia, PA
Suggested pairings: Nat Kendricks "Mashed Potatoes" 1959; The Marvelettes "Please Mr. Postman" 1961; Little Eva "The Locomotion"1962; Bobby "Boris" Pickett "Monster Mash" 1962

Dee Dee Sharpe debuted as an uncredited duet partner with Chubby Checker on "Slow Twistin'" in late January 1962. In very early February 1962, Dee Dee Sharpe was credited on a number one hit with group backing by two of the female Orlons, Rosetta Hightower and Shirley Brickley, who had just put out their second single, "(Happy Birthday) Mr. Twenty-One." Sharpe's "Mashed Potato Time" was a popular dance move at the time, sounding very little like "(Do the) Mashed Potatoes" by Nat Kendrick & the Swans, an alter ego to James Brown, from very late 1959.

In L.A., first appearing in March, this song went to #1 on KFWB and KRLA and #1 on WABC in New York. It only reached #3 in hometown WIBG in Philly. Then came the lawsuit. "'Mashed Potato Time' was obviously very close to 'Please Mr. Postman' by The Marvelettes," said Freddie Gorman. "In order to infringe on the rights of another song, you have to use the melody for so many bars. They went farther than they should have. It was proven it was the same melody. Once that's proven, the song belongs to the originators of the first one."

—

Bertha Tillman "Oh My Angel" Brent March 12, 1962

Style: Proto soul
Where from: San Diego, CA
Where recorded: Hollywood, CA

June Jackson of J.J. Jackson & the Jackals met Bertha Tillman at a recording session in 1961. Tillman was a salesgirl at a local department store and frequented the same district in San Diego where the group was based. "Bertha was sweetheart to Wilfred Eldridge, a street singer. He was the top singer at 30th & Imperial" in the heart of the black district of San Diego. "She had class and dignity." Hank Blackman was so enamored of Bertha that he convinced Jackson to have her audition. "Can you sing?" he asked her. At the time, Jackson was writing a song called "Nightmare," which he refashioned into "Oh My Angel" for her. "I wrote it in fifteen minutes."

Prior to the RCA recording session in Hollywood, Eldrige secreted Tillman to Tijuana. "He was kind of jealous of me," said Jackson. However Tillman managed to return to her mother's home. After a false start or so, Jackson and Tillman's mother persuaded her to accompany the group to Hollywood. At the same time, Jackson also met Eddie Williams at the Plaza Hotel in downtown San Diego. Jackson had seen Williams on the Johnny Otis TV Show and introduced himself. Williams who had previously sung with The Aladdins and with The Penguins knew of The Jackaels' release and also agreed to attend the session at the RCA/Victor studios in Hollywood.

During a marathon session, which lasted from 7 p.m. to 2:30 a.m., four acts recorded vocal group arrangements. H.B. Barnum did some arrangements. Hank Levine worked with Eddie Williams. With backing by J.J. Jackson & the Jackels, Bertha Tillman recorded this classic love anthem on "Oh My Angel" on Bob Shad's Brent label. Jackson was dubious when Shad reported that none of his efforts from this session sold especially well. "They'd sell your record in another part of the country where you didn't know it was a hit. That way they could tell you it didn't sell," claimed Jackson about the spotty sales track of this and other vocal group hits.

—

Felix & the Escorts "The Syracuse" Jag March 1962

Style: Rock 'n' roll
From and recorded in: Syracuse, NY

Founder of the Young Rascals, Felix Cavaliere first recorded as leader of Felix & the Escorts on the Syracuse-oriented dance, not surprisingly, "The Syracuse," which charted on Syracuse radio.

—

Otis Redding & the Pinetoppers "Shout Bamalama" Orbit March 1962/Confederate April 1962/Bethlehem February 1964/King 1968

Style: Rhythm and blues vocal
From and recorded in: Georgia
Suggested pairing: Little Richard "Bama Lama Bama Loo" 1959

Otis Redding was in full Little Richard mode on this shouter "Shout Bamalama," joining such R&B and soul luminaries as James Brown, Don Covay, Joe Tex, Dee Clark and even the Beatles as impersonators of the Georgia Peach, as well as Larry Williams and Don and Dewey, who were signed for their Little Richard-style wildness. Ironically, as a leading exponent of black soul music, Redding's debut single was on a label designed to glorify the confederacy and named after that tradition.

—

The Shirelles "Soldier Boy" Scepter 1962
Style: Proto soul
Where from: New Jersey
Where recorded: New York
Suggested pairings: Charles Brown "You Are My First Love" 1947; The Orlons "I'll Be True" 1961; The Beatles "P.S. I Love You" 1964

Does anyone know who played guitar on Soldier Boy? It sounds similar to Duane Eddy. I can't remember where I heard this, but someone told me that the back story to this song is that the boy had already died overseas (perhaps in Vietnam?—some U.S. troops were there in '62) and she's saying she considers him her one and only and will never marry. Has Florence Greenberg ever said anything about this, or is it just hearsay?

The song isn't about a boy going off to war, just going off to the army. There was a peacetime draft in 1962 and virtually all young men served in the military. There was no war for the "Soldier Boy."

—

Walter Brennan "Old Rivers" Liberty 1962
Style: Country spoken word
Where from: Lynn, MA
Where recorded: Hollywood, CA

Having had three moderate sellers on Dot from 1960 and 1961, TV's "Real McCoys" character actor Walter Brennan was panning for vinyl gold, which came in the form of the recitation "Old Rivers." Musical director and "Old Rivers" songwriter Cliff Crofford said, "He was a black man in my hometown in Texas. Rivers was his name, there was one other black in the town. I'd been on the Johnny Cash tour, ran into Cliffie Stone, sold him 'Old Rivers,' which I meant to get to Johnny Cash." Crofford was at Liberty in 1962 when "a guy stuck his head in arranger Snuff Garrett's office, 'We're doing Mr. Brennen tomorrow night.' As he turned to leave, the arranger Snuff said, 'Wait, what songs do you have?' 'Nothing.' He turned to me, 'Have you reached Cash?' 'No he's been on tour.' 'Oh hell yeah, let's do it.' Leon Russell did the demo, I asked him to do the demo. Four guitars, Glen Campbell, Tommy Allsup and couple of pop jazz guitars; Jerry Allison, drummer; Red Callender, bass; Earl Palmer, drums; Ernie Freeman was directing. 'John Glenn' was supposed to be the A-side, a Beverly Hills doctor wrote that," Crofford recalled. "I worked on that John Glenn song for two and a half hours, big session, only had two takes on 'Old Rivers.' Thirty minutes, two takes, it was good.

Crofford continued, "When we get to end, on that very last line, Snuff asked Walter, 'Can you give us something there?' When we got to the last part, when I looked at him, there were tears, when we said 'cut,' Brennan lifted his leg, laughed like hell… scared me to death."

Walter Brennan's "Old Rivers" backed with "The Epic Ride Of John H. Glenn" was thus released on Liberty, hitting in the Inland Empire in March 1962 and #5 pop on April 7, 1962.

—

Mongo Santamaria "Watermelon Man" Battle March 13, 1962
Style: Latin instrumental
Where from: Havana, Cuba
Where recorded: New York

Born Ramon Santamaria Rodriguez in Havana, Afro-Cuban conga man Mongo Santamaria was given the "Mongo" nickname by his father. Showing a preference for percussion, he joined the Perez Prado band when he moved from Cuba to Mexico City in 1948. Prado began recording for RCA Victor in New York City in 1950 with Santamaria's conga playing featured on many of his early recordings. Mongo's own band used 22-year-old Herbie Hancock as fill-in on piano. On Hancock's "Watermelon Man," Santamaria improvised his own rhythms to a packed dance floor, full of whoops and hollers from dancers in this impromptu jam. Hancock issued a competing version, but Santamaria had seized the momentum, and a jazz classic was born. Lyrics were added in the Hancock and Gloria Lynne version in 1965.

Remakes: Xavier Cugat 1963; Gloria Lynn 1965; Mel Taylor; Count Basie 1965; Monk Higgins 1968; Fred Wesley & the JBs 1972; Herbie Hancock 1974; Herbie Mann 1978

—

The Rivingtons "Papa Oom Mow Mow" Liberty March 16, 1962

Style: Novelty vocal group
Where from: Los Angeles, CA
Where recorded: Hollywood, CA

Founded out of The Sharps, The Rivingtons hit after bass singer Rocky Turner Wilson III was locked up with a fellow inmate who was singing a nonsense lyric, "oom mow mow." Wilson picked up on it, recalled Rivingtons' leader Al Frazier. "Rocky came up with that 'oom mow mow' and he was going down the line, 'a- mow mow ,' b- mow mow' and 'c- mow mow' until he got to 'oom-mow mow.' "We got to playing with it. It got to be a chant. Then we started making the trumpet sound, 'dit-dit-dit.' We kept going, it sounded great. We would rehearse in my garage; they were fooling around, everybody had a little taste and stuff, thought it was funny, ten hours later we came up with it. Then we started seriously thinking about lyrics and putting a lead over it. By accident, Carl said 'man that's the craziest thing I ever heard.' That's how the thing started. We just cracked up laughing. 'Can't even understand what it means, what's it mean man? Don't mean nothin.'"

Producer Kim Fowley picks up the story: "A few months later, at 7 a.m., Al Frazier called and sang 'Papa Oom Mow Mow' to me over the phone. He said, 'The whole group wants to be recorded today, you can produce us again.' I ran them over to Pan Or Productions, an arm of Beechwood Publishing where the VP, Jack Levy, and Adam Ross got all excited over 'Papa Oom Mow Mow.' I became a talent scout, got an override, got in the studio, it got recorded, somehow Mickey Goldston got the sheet music, at the height of Elijah Muhammad, got photo'd with the Rivingtons, took everyone's shares of production money."

Frazier said, "I knew Adam from The Starwood days when I was over there. They were going bananas over it. They went up and got me an advance of about $1,500. Wow, $1,500, at that time, the guys were going ape." As Capitol had first refusal at anything from Beechwood, Levy offered it to them, but was turned down. "They thought it was way out of line because it was a completely new and hard sound," said Frazier. "Little did we know it would turn into a dance called 'The Bird.' Adam Ross was riding on Jack Levy's coattails. They had the connections, hooked us up with Capitol, actually Beechwood, Capitol was scared to touch 'Papa Oom Mow Mow' thought it was a little bit far-fetched. They went over to Liberty and talked to Al Bennett and Bob Scaff. They were a really young company and had promotion staff with Tommy Laploma. They put the song down in one take at Radio Recorders."

For "Papa Oom Mow Mow," they were dubbed The Rivingtons, after a street in New York where Levy and Ross had spent part of their childhood. Frazier later found out that after the session, piano player, Gaynel Hodge immediately took the riff to another session where he was backing John Maus; John Stewart, guitar and Scott Engel, bass, who recorded the same nonsense lyrics, called it "The Moongoon Stomp" by The Moongooners.

"It took us six months to get 'Papa Oom Mow Mow' played—before KFWB would touch it," said Frazier. Before it hit, they made an appearance in San Bernardino where they found out about "The Moongoon Stomp" After forcing "Moongoon Stomp" off the market, The Rivingtons' "Papa Oom Mow Mow" took off, though with little thanks to L.A.'s most influential R&B station. "We went around L.A. doing shows for all the KGFJ disc jockeys, Hunter Hancock, Herman Griffin and Rudy Harvey. KGFJ would play it if we would make personal appearances at their disc jockey nights. All them disc jockeys had a disk jockey nights at some club. If we'd make a freebie appearance, they'd play our records."

—

The Temptations "Dream Come True" March 16, 1962

Style: Soul
Where from: Alabama
Where recorded: Detroit, MI

Replacing Paul Williams, The Temptations used falsetto Eddie Kendricks as lead singer with bass Melvin Franklin, who took a brief solo just before the outro of "Dream Come True," The Temptations' first recording on the new Gordy label. It included background vocals by Melvin Franklin, Paul Williams, Al Bryant, and Otis Williams with Musitron and Ondioline instrumentation by Berry Gordy Jr's wife, Raynoma Liles Gordy supplementing The Funk Brothers who, according to Freddie Gorman, were Bennie Benjamin, guitar; James Jamerson, Fender bass; Joe Hunter or Earl Van Dyke, keyboards; Uriel "Yule" Jones, drums and Eddie "Bongo" Brown, congas.

—

Rene & Ray "Queen Of My Heart" Donna March 1962

Style: Duet low rider doo wop
Where from: Pomona and Glendora, CA
Where recorded: Cucamonga, CA

Put together by Johnny Valenzuela of the Pomona-based group The Velveteens, "Ray Quinones was Ray," said Valenzuela. "Rene was a Puerto Rican named Paul (real name: Pablo Venezuela) from Glendora, who introduced himself as a singer. I didn't put him in the band because I wanted to keep it Hispanic," said Valenzuela, who later realized that Puerto Ricans were Hispanic, though he assumed they were black.

Eddie Davis was working with with Bob Keane when Rene & Ray showed up. "They were out of Pomona. They just came into the studio one day, they had a sound, couple of guys. They left a tape. Bob called them right away. Bob had a keen ear for hit records."

"I was the producer on Rene & Ray," said Paul Buff of the Pal Studio in Cucamonga. "It was put together with Rene & Ray and me in the studio, Zappa's vibes were there, I played those," said Buff. "A lot of that might be my sound, I had almost a sound of my own. I did half of that myself, maybe piano, drums and vibes. Rene & Ray came in; let me produce their stuff." Buff recalled, "I shopped it to Del-fi. I never got any royalties."

—

James Brown & the Famous Flames "Night Train" King March 1962

Style: Rhythm and blues
Where from: Macon, GA
Where recorded: Cincinnati, OH
Original version: Jimmy Forrest 1962

James Brown & the Famous Flames turned their version of jazz standard "Night Train" into a chugging instrumental with Brown shouting out various big city stops associated with his career, "Atlanta, Georgia, Miami, Florida," adding "don't forget New Orleans, the home of the blues."

—

Little Stevie Wonder "I Call It Pretty Music But the Old People Call It the Blues"

Style: Soul
From and recorded in: Detroit, MI

An exciting live number by Little Stevie Wonder, this rousing "I Call It Pretty Music But the Old People Call It the Blues" was this enduring performer's debut single, but hardly a hit.

—

Freddy Cannon "Palisades Park" Swan April 1962

Style: Rock 'n' roll
Where from: Boston, MA
Recorded in: Philadelphia, PA

After a string of hits on Swan Records, Freddy Cannon recorded this Chuck Barris composition, "Palisades Park," about the famed New Jersey amusement zone, complete with sound effects of roller coasters and screaming riders in the background.

Released on April 20, "Palisades Park" wasted little time zooming up Philly's WIBG charts to #1 on April 23, 1962. However, it took a little longer to chart nationally, so reputedly Barris, who was an ABC-TV network honcho at the time, made a deal with Dick Clark to move his American Bandstand to Hollywood as Clark desired in exchange for Bandstand plays of "Palisades Park," which Clark accommodated. As of February 1964, Bandstand was in Hollywood and "Palisades Park" was a proven hit.

—

Kenny & the Cadets "Barbi" Randy April 1962

Style: Pop group
Where from: Hawthorne, CA
Where recorded: Silver Lake, CA

This companion piece to "Surfin'" was created by Beach Boys members Brian Wilson, Carl Wilson and Al Jardine as a tribute to the Mattel doll. "Barbi" was a sugary pop sound ala Dion & the Belmonts/Elegants as Kenny & the Cadets on Randy. "I had a tune with The Beach Boys as Kenny & the Cadets, worked in the editing room at Stereo Masters, I would do my stuff and I would just hang there," recalled Tony Hilder.

The Alley Kats redid "Barbie" on Impact. "Hite Morgan was a friend of mine, came out with this thing in the front room, where they had the mastering studio," said Hilder. "Hite had this a capella with them doing 'Surfin.' Dorinda did 'Little Surfer Girl.' They fucked over Hite, I went to court on that. Capitol was trying to say this was a different version. He had the a capella, I brought in a lousy band, so bad I pulled them off, had them do the instruments over the Wilsons and that came out and the master that was done there, that I finished off in the front room on Melrose, put up the drums and cymbals. It was #1 in Sweden. Hite sold it somewhere. Murry pushed him, that might be Brian." The single was likely never released as years later, a stock of mint original singles was located by collector Dave Antrell, who sold black vinyl examples for about $15 and colored vinyl 45s for about $75. The colored vinyl 45s now sell for about $1,500 and the black vinyl for around $200 to $500. Note: I didn't like the songs, so I didn't buy it dirt cheap in any color.

—

The Orlons "The Wah-Watusi" Cameo May 1962

Style: Proto soul vocal group
From and recorded in: Philadelphia, PA

The Orlons' lead singer Rosetta Hightower, in high school with Shirley Brickley and Marlena Davis, discovered fellow student Stephen Caldwell, lead singer of a local group called The Romeos. Impressed, they invited him to join their group in 1960 and named themselves The Orlons as a tongue-in-cheek nod to the friendly rivalry they had with a popular group at their high school, The Cashmeres. Orlon was a brand name for the widely used synthetic fiber acrylic. In the lyrics, "The Wah-Watusi" critiques three other dances, "Mashed Potato Time" by Dee Dee Sharpe as well as "The Twist" and "The Fly" by Chubby Checker, all released on the same Cameo/Parkway family of labels. In-house advertising with a twist, so to speak.

—

John Lee Hooker "Boom Boom" Vee Jay 1962

Style: Blues
Where from: Clarksdale, MS
Where recorded: Chicago, IL
Suggested pairings: Big Joe Williams "Please Don't Go" 1935; Howlin' Wolf "Who's Been Talkin?" 1957; Count Five "Psychotic Reaction" 1966

While performing a series of dates at the Apex Bar in Detroit, a bartender named Luilla would use the phrase, "boom boom, you're late again" whenever Hooker showed up late. "Then one night she said, 'Boom boom, I'm gonna shoot you down.' She gave me a song but she didn't know it. After I got it copyrighted, I could do it in the bar. So then if anybody got the idea to do it I had them by the neck, because I had it copyrighted. About two months later I recorded it. That barmaid felt pretty good. She went around telling everybody 'I got John Lee to write that song.' I gave her some bread for it, too, so she was pretty happy." Other important lyrics were "pow pow pow pow."

This song was recorded in a session with Motown's session players, bassist James Jamerson, drummer Benny Benjamin, baritone saxophonist Andrew "Mike" Terry and tenor saxophonist Hank Cosby, later known as The Funk Brothers.

Remake: The Animals 1964

—

Dick Dale and The Del-Tones "Miserlou" Deltone April 1962

Style: Rock 'n' roll instrumental
Where from: Massachusetts
Where recorded: Hollywood, CA

Dick Dale said, "'Miserlou' means an Arabic dance… 'where is my sweetheart' in Arabic. I used to listen to that, my uncle played that and my other uncle played the oud, a stringed instrument. They would play 'Miserlou' slow for belly dancers. When I opened the Rendezvous Ballroom, the first 17 kids were the 17 kids I was surfin' with. They asked me, 'Can you play something on a single string?' I chose 'Miserlou' and it didn't sound full, so I added Gene Krupa style drums, with a bass player, it went BAM!"

—

Pattie La Belle and the Blue Bells "I Sold My Heart to the Junkman" Newton April 1962

Style: Girl group vocal
From and recorded in: Chicago, IL

This is the purported debut of Philadelphia-based Patti LaBelle and the Blue Belles, though the group was really The Starlets, who had hit with the Ikettes-style "Better Tell Him No" in 1961. As the song, an original by the L.A.-based Basin Street Boys from the 1940s, "I Sold My Heart To the Junkman," was hit, there was a need for a group to go along with it, but The Starlets weren't available. A female group auditioned and was hired as The Blue Belles, renamed Patti LaBelle and the Blue Belles on their next hit, "Down the Aisle." Reissues of "I Sold My Heart To the Junkman" were credited to the badly misspelled Pattie La Belle and The Blue Bells.

—

The Isley Brothers "Twist and Shout" Wand April 1962

Style: Rhythm and blues vocal group
Where from: New Jersey
Where recorded: New York
Original version: The Top Notes 1961

The song "Twist and Shout" was cut first by Phil Spector on the Philadelphia-based doo wop vocal group The Top Notes on Atlantic, but that version was too fast and a little on the bubble gum side to sell well. Then, according to Wally Roker, "Atlantic was out of that game" when The Isley Brothers recorded a much more raucous party sounding version of "Twist and

Shout." Roker recalled, "That was a brawling session. Started early in the morning, 5, 6 o'clock and ended up about 3, 4 o'clock in the morning, a total disaster. Everybody being very unhappy and upset, going crazy and wild, breaking up chairs and abusing each other's mind with words of you know what, everybody left the session very disturbed and upset. Might've done 30 or 40 takes, it was words, crashing chairs, going crazy, being upset at each other, somebody was showing them what to do, they were trying to say they didn't need to be shown what to do.

Roker continued, "The Isley Brothers are very different at times, one for all, all for one whether they're right or wrong. It ended up being done Luther Dixon's way. He produced all the hits for Scepter/Wand, except the Burt Bacharach stuff. Luther stayed in the studio, mixing, checking and working on it and came in the next day, said, 'What do you think of this?' I said, 'Hey, let's try it, sounds good.' Made an acetate, gave it to me, next day I went down, saw Jerry Blavat in Philadelphia, said, 'Send me about 10,000 of the thing you dropped off down here.' Bert Berns was a creative person, he knew what he wanted. The Isley Brothers also in a way were creative and thought they knew what they wanted. It was a combination of creative people fighting creative people and Luther was in the middle trying to create peace, trying to get a flow going, he ended up getting the best out of it, with The Isley Brothers fighting Bert, it ended up being a creative feeling record."

Remakes: The Beatles 1964; The Shangri-Las 1964

—

The Miracles "I'll Try Something New" Tamla April 9, 1962

Style: Soul vocal group
From and recorded in: Detroit, MI

About Smokey Robinson and his several hits with The Miracles, his wife Claudette said, "His greatest asset was his play on words. he's good that way. It's amazing when you hear those songs. 'I'll Try Something New' was something he wrote at a baseball game. His dad loved the Cleveland Indians, they were at a game."

Remake: Diana Ross and the Supremes 1969; The Temptations 1969

—

The Marvelettes "Playboy" Tamla April 9, 1962

Style: Soul vocal group
From and recorded in: Detroit, MI

"That was the one I wrote for The Marvelettes," said group's lead singer Gladys Horton. "It went number seven. 'Twistin' Postman' was out, basically, they were trying to keep it a dance, it was a dance tune for the twist. It didn't last as long as 'Postman,' we were on to something else. I was only trying to do what Georgia was trying to do with 'Postman,' take a lot of words and rhyme them. Berry [Gordy Jr.] used to say, 'You know what makes a good story, you have to keep those hits coming.' We had one hit, I got to think of something quick. 'Playboy' is kind of catchy, I just put the words that made 'Playboy' work. I thought of the title. 'The false joy,' that's the line Mickey Stevenson put in, 'watch'a de playboy, he bringing de false joy.'"

—

The Duke Of Earl "Walk On With the Duke" Vee Jay April 1962

Style: Soul
From and recorded in: Chicago, IL

"In the very beginning, I wanted 'London Town'" as the A-side, Gene Chandler recalled. "They wanted 'Walk On With the Duke.' That was going too far, it's not for me to walk on with the duke, I didn't think that would sell. They wanted to name me The Duke of Earl, I really resisted, said, 'I'm planning on doing a lot of music you haven't heard, I need a name to go along with these records and not The Duke of Earl.' A lot of people didn't know that Gene Chandler was The Duke

Of Earl. I convinced them not change me to The Duke of Earl. I had to fight out of the original outfit. They wanted me to look like [a] Revolutionary War figure, [put a] gray haired wig on me. Hand down in shirt, holding a triangle hat Napoleon style. I wanted to be a modern day duke."

—

Claudine Clark "Party Lights" Chancellor May 1962

Style: Rock 'n' roll
Where from: Macon, GA
Where recorded: Philadelphia, PA
Suggested pairing: The Sensations "Let Me In" 1962

Claudine Clark began recording at age 17, though she didn't hit pay dirt until she complained about "Party Lights" and not being invited. In 1958, Clark debuted "Teenage Blues" on the Herald label. She later appeared on the small Philadelphia label Alma with a children's record, "The Get Set Song," then as Joy Dawn, based on two popular brands of detergents for Swan. Her first single was a ballad, "Disappointed," but Clark insisted on access to a swingin' party. Claudine Clark's "Party Lights" was about her mom who wouldn't let her join in the fun.

"Party Lights" went to #4 on WIBG in Philly in May 1962 and hit #3 on KRLA, Los Angeles in August.

—

Sam Cooke "Having a Party" RCA May 1962

Style: Soul
Where from: Mississippi/Chicago, IL
Where recorded: Hollywood, CA

Radio initially ignored a soul classic "Bring It On Home To Me" in favor of this lighter twist-beat, "Having a Party," which referenced "Soul Twist" by King Curtis and "I Know" by Barbara George as the potential hit. "We was in the studio," said the Sims Twins' Ken Sims of the "Having a Party" session, "Sam told us to come back him up."

—

Sam Cooke "Bring It On Home To Me" RCA May 1962

Style: Soul
Where from: Mississippi/Chicago, IL
Where recorded: Hollywood, CA
Suggested pairings: Charles Brown & Amos Milburn "I Wanna Go Back Home" 1961; The Miracles "You've Really Got a Hold On Me" 1962

Sam Cooke switched from a frothy "Twistin' the Night Away"/"Having A Party" to a much deeper soul sound, this call and response "Bring It On Home To Me" in duet with old gospel buddy Lou Rawls with Ernie Freeman, piano; René Hall and Tommy Tedesco, guitar; William Green, saxophone; Ray Pohlman, bass and Frank Capp, drums with five violins, two cellos and one viola.

Cooke's producer Rene Hall said, "I wasn't familiar with the Charles Brown record. We were after the Soul Stirrers thing done with Kylo Turner and Sam Cooke in gospel, we were trying to create that flavor in a rhythm and blues recording. Lou was also a gospel singer with The Pilgrim Travelers, he and Sam would jam together, different type gospel things, they worked this out between them. "It's clean, as a matter of fact is so closely blending, you'd think it was an overdub, instead of two separate individuals, it was well rehearsed over what we did by walking into the studio and doing vocally. The chord structure is similar, the melody is a little different, you could say they stole the idea from this record if they were exposed to it."

It first hit in San Francisco, a month later in other markets. In a sense, with this Sam Cooke hit, soul music was born and the deep stuff was what record buyers began insisting on.

—

Barbara Lynn "You'll Lose a Good Thing" Jamie May 1962

Style: Rhythm and blues
Where from: Beaumont, TX
Where recorded: Cosimo Matassa's J&M studios, New Orleans, LA

Born Barbara Lynn Open, Barbara Lynn hit playing left handed guitar on this plaintive woman's blues "You'll Lose a Good Thing." Lynn recalled, "I started at Ebert High School in 1960. I broke up with this guy, we had a little problem," said Lynn. "I told him on the telephone, 'If you lose me, you'll lose a good thing.' A few days later, we had a little squabble. I went home and wrote the song, put in some words and rhymed it up. The time I was called on to do a song, it was the song I used. He knows I wrote that for him."

Cut in New Orleans, the "You'll Lose a Good Thing" session included Mac Rebbeneck, aka Dr. John, on piano under the auspices of producer Huey P. Meaux, whom Lynn met through singer Joe Barry, who introduced her to Meaux, who took half writer credit on her first best-selling composition. Referring to Meaux, Lynn said, "My manager put it on Jamie, then my manager took the lease to Atlantic."

—

Don Gardner and Dee Dee Ford "I Need Your Lovin'" Fire May 1962

Style: Rhythm and blues duet
Where from: Philadelphia, PA
Where recorded: New York City, NY

Drummer and singer Don Gardner had been recording since the 1940s, with a multiplicity of sides on about a dozen labels when he and Dee Dee Ford from Louisiana were "discovered" by Fire label head Bobby Robinson at Smalls Paradise in New York City. The extended version of their night club pleaser, "I Need Your Loving," with a feverish 'Wo-wo-wo-wo... wo...WO!' by Don at the halfway part was spotted by Robinson as the song to record. When it came out, Don Gardner found out the first three minutes of their song were placed at the introduction, beginning it with the "wo-wo-wo" midpoint and scoring a major hit.

—

The Genteels "Take It Off" Stag/Capitol May 19, 1962

Style: Rock 'n' roll instrumental
Where from: Inland Empire, CA
Where recorded: Cucamonga, CA

The Genteels recorded the barroom chant about strippers and girls in wet T-shirts, "Take it Off," on the Inland Empire Stag label. Band members—Lenny Angelo, lead guitar; Carl Hubert, drums and Jerry Martin, bass—recorded this mainly instrumental at Pal Studios. Martin had also played with Dino Dupre on "Ambrosia" in 1959.

—

The Beach Boys "Surfin' Safari" Capitol May 26, 1962

Style: Rock 'n' roll group
Where from: Hawthorne, CA
Where recorded: Hollywood, CA

The Beach Boys debuted on Capitol with this doo wop sounding "Surfin' Safari" which sold best in non-surfin' deep waters of doo wop saturated New York City. In a September 6, 1962 story about the local band The Casuals, which became The Dartells, the Oxnard Courier noted an upcoming battle with The Beach Boys, "whose record 'Surf and Safari' is the number one record in Southern California listings."

—

The Beach Boys "409" Capitol May 26, 1962

Style: Rock 'n' roll group
Where from: Hawthorne, CA
Where recorded: Hollywood, CA

This Beach Boys hot rod ode, "409," about a 409 cubic inch W-series V8 engine popular with hot rodders of the time, was mostly written by Gary Usher complete with hot rod sound effects played by Usher's Chevrolet 348, the predecessor to the 409. This release set the pattern for the next two Beach Boys hits: a surf song for the East and West Coasts and hot rod/car song for the Midwest and Southeast record-buyers.

—

Chris Montez "Let's Dance" Monogram May 28, 1962

Style: Rock 'n' roll
Where from: Hawthorne, CA
Where recorded: Hollywood, CA

Influenced by Ritchie Valens, whom he met once, vocalist Chris Montez, real name, Ezekiel Christopher Montanez, grew up in Hawthorne and graduated from Hawthorne High School. Montez played teenage dances with a trio called The Rhythm Dukes with Bill Boyd and Mike Garcia. "I don't know if I was Ritchie Valens' protégé, but I was one of his big fans when I was growing up. We have sort of the same range of voice, sort of the same style, his style was easy for me to sing, his ballads and interpretation was very close. I did all the selections you'd hear Ritchie Valens do. I got to see him one time at this auditorium in Inglewood. I was waiting for him to do this song, surprised to see him there, looked to my right, he was standing next to me. 'Aren't you Ritchie Valens?' He said yes and smiled. And then I never saw him again."

Montez's first recording break came as a result of "hustling, trying to get someone to listen to me. I went into a studio, it cost me $15, we did a two track one time only, 'She's My Rocking Baby' and something in the form of 'They Say.' Someone played it for someone in the studio when I left. I talked over these people for a few months, they said no, so I went to a publisher." Eventually Chris Montez's "They Say" in the school of Valens balladry backed with "I Lost My Baby" was released on Guaranteed, a two sided, two city Arizona charter. "I remember 'They Say' being popular, 'Now here's a song that's getting lots of requests.' I remember jumping for joy, it was great excitement for me."

Montez went on to duet with Kathy Young, whose first record also appeared in this very same time frame. Montez hit the charts hard with this infectious organ-drum-guitar-backed rocker, "Let's Dance," inspired by Valens' "Come On Let's Go," which "was something the label wanted to do."

—

Little Eva "The Loco-Motion" Dimension June 1962

Style: Soul
Where from: North Carolina
Where recorded: New York City, NY
Suggested pairings: The Marvelettes "Please Mr. Postman" 1961; Dee Dee Sharpe "Mashed Potato Time" 1962; Nathaniel Mayer & the Fabulous Twilights "Village Of Love" 1962

This song was written about a dance that didn't exist. "I made the record 'The Loco-Motion' because The Cookies got me the job babysitting for Carole King," said Little Eva. "'The Loco-Motion' was an accident. I was introduced to Carole King and Gerry Goffin through The Cookies and I had an audition. She was looking for a babysitter, but they also needed a fourth voice for The Cookies. They got this contract to write a song for Dee Dee Sharpe, who had 'Mashed Potatoes' out at the time. She needed a follow-up record. Carole and Gerry got the right to write her a song and they wrote 'The Loco-Motion.' I even put in a few words. I helped to make up the dance. 'Jump up, jump back.' I just threw in a word or two. It wasn't anything big. They wrote the song, I didn't co-write it. I just helped make up the dance.

"Then they asked me to do the dub which was a demonstration record to take to the producer of Dee Dee Sharpe," Little Eva continued. "Carole King and I did the dub, there was just piano. They took the dub in and Donnie Kirschner, who at the time was their producer, listened to it. He thought it was great, the dub with me singing. They put it on the air that very night on some station in New York. It took off overnight. Little Eva was born overnight."

Two extant versions exist, one including handclaps during the verses, the other with no handclaps.

Answers: The Locomotions " Little Eva" 1962; Oliver & Twisters "Locomotion Twist" 1962; Rachel & the Revolvers "The Revo-Lution" 1963; Little Eva "Old Smokey Locomotion" 1963; The Four Buddies "Slow Locomotion" 1963; The Tornadoes "Like Locomotion" 1963; The Riviaires "Mocolotion" 1964
Remakes: Grand Funk Railroad 1974; Carole King 1980

—

Tommy Roe "Sheila" ABC June 1962

Style: Rock 'n' roll
Where from: Atlanta, GA
Where recorded: Nashville, TN
Suggested pairing: Buddy Holly "Peggy Sue" 1957

Thomas David "Tommy" Roe first recorded the novelty rocker "Caveman" for the Mark IV label, picked up by Atlanta-based Judd Records, run by Jud Phillips, the brother of Sam Phillips of Sun Records. Tommy Roe then recorded the misspelled "Shelia" for Judd in 1960. It didn't chart. But when Roe accepted a deal with ABC-Paramount, "Sheila" was re-recorded by label producer Felton Jarvis with a different arrangement, featuring an insistent "Peggy Sue"-style bassline, which dominated the release. Jerry Reed was on guitar; Buddy Harman, drums; Wayne Moss, guitar and Bob Moore, bass. The backup singers were The Jordanaires, who sang behind Elvis Presley on many of his hits. "Sheila" was released as the B-side to the more subdued vocal, "Save Your Kisses." DJs flipped the record and started playing "Sheila" instead, the song took off, debuting on KFXM at #2 on June 16, 1962

Remake: Greg Kihn 1981

—

The Tornados "Bustin' Surfboards" Aerturn June 30, 1962

Style: Surf rock
Where from: Redlands, CA
Where recorded: Pal Studios, Cucamonga, CA

A Redlands High School band first known as The Vaqueroes with George White on sax; Norman Saunders, lead guitar; brother Gerald Saunders, bass and vocals; cousin Jesse Saunders, rhythm guitar and Leonard Delany, drums became The Tornados, named after weather conditions in Saunders' home state of Alabama, which was subject to tornados.

Using KFXM radio weather sound effects in their debut effort, this very surfy instrumental "Bustin' Surfboards" on Dave Aerni and George Tauton's brand new Aerturn label was recorded at Riverside Airport.

The British instrumental group The Tornados hit with "Telstar" on many of the same stations in November 1962 and went to #1 pop, a chart the local Tornados never cracked. Therefore, it was up to the Inland Empire band to become The Hollywood Tornados, because the British Empire band created by Joe Meek remained The Tornados.

—

The Four Seasons "Sherry" Vee Jay July 1962

Style: Pop doo wop vocal group
Where from: New Jersey
Where recorded: New York City, NY
Suggested pairings: Dion & the Belmonts "A Teenager In Love" 1959; The Tokens "The Lion Sleeps Tonight" 1961; Bruce Channel "Hey! Baby" 1961; The Contours "Shake Sherry" 1962; Del Shannon "Sue's Gotta Be Mine" 1963; Jan and Dean "Linda" 1964; Billy Joel "Uptown Girl" 1981

On May 29, 1954, Billboard had this to say about Frankie Valley and the Travelers' new release, "Somebody Else Took Her Home," on Mercury: "The label has come up with a new singer with an exciting style and a sound somewhat to the vein of the early Johnnie Ray." The record stiffed, but Valli and the group continued to record as Frankie Valley and the Romans, the Four Lovers, the Village Voices, and the Topics, among many other names as well as Valli recording as Frankie Tyler. Nothing hit big.

In 1960, The Four Lovers auditioned at the Four Seasons bowling alley in New Jersey. They were turned down, but kept the name of the alley. After stiffing with a remake of "Bermuda," Valli performed a new song over the telephone for producer Bob Crewe, who liked it, but not the title. They considered "Jackie Baby" after Jackie Kennedy, "Peri" after a record label Crewe had a stake in, and "Teri," but settled on "Sherry," the daughter of one of Crewe's best friends, New York DJ Jack Spector. The lyrics were about coming to a twist party, allowing the group to become first white artists to sign with Vee-Jay, and going straight to #1.

Answer: Tracey Dey "Jerry I'm Your Sherry"

—

Booker T & the MGs "Green Onions" Volt/Stax July 1962

Style: Soul instrumental
From and recorded in: Memphis, TN
Suggested pairings: Bill Davis & the Legends "Spunky Onions" Peacock 1960; Joey Dee & the Starlighters "Hot Pastrami & Mashed Potatoes" 1963; Sam Cooke "Shake" 1964; The Rolling Stones "Stoned" 1964

Booker T. Jones was said to have told Stax owner Jim Stewart about the title, "Why 'Green Onions'?" Jim asked. Booker T: "Because that is the nastiest thing I can think of and it's something you throw away." While on NPR, Booker T. said, "The bass player thought it was so funky, he wanted to call it, 'Funky Onions,' but they thought that was too low-class, so we used 'Green Onions' instead."

This tune is a 12-bar blues with a rippling Hammond organ line. The guitarist Steve Cropper used a Fender Telecaster on "Green Onions" as he did on all of The M.G.'s instrumentals. According to Cropper, the title is not a marijuana reference; rather, the track is named after the Green Badger's cat, Green Onions, whose way of walking inspired the riff. According to Booker T. Jones, who grew up in Memphis and used the Satellite Record Shop as his place to pick up records, he recalled the owners intended to make Satellite into a country label. Jones spotted a Hammond organ in the studio and played a nightclub blues riff entitled "Behave Yourself" for his first A-side on Volt. When a DJ on the local WLOK flipped it, the response to "Green Onions" was so positive, the label switched "Green Onions" to the A-side, reissuing the tune on Stax.

—

The Crystals "He Hit Me (And It Felt Like a Kiss)" Philles July 6, 1962

Style: Soul
Where from: Brooklyn, NY
Where recorded: New York

This song with its controversial subject matter glorifying domestic abuse on the part of label owner and producer Phil Spector made for an easy-to-censor release, and thus minimal sales.

—

Timi Yuro "What's a Matter Baby" Liberty July 9, 1962

Style: Soul
Where from: Chicago, IL
Where recorded: Hollywood, CA
Suggested pairing: The Crystals "He's a Rebel" 1962

With a piano vamp that would go to #1, Timi Yuro hit big with this bitter wall-of-sound rocker, "What's a Matter Baby." Though credited to Clyde Otis as producer, it was really produced by Phil Spector on his way out from the Liberty label.

—

The Marvelettes "Beechwood 4-5789" Tamla July 11, 1962

Style: Soul vocal group
From and recorded in: Detroit, MI

"There was a lot of controversy about that phone number," said Marvelettes' lead singer, Gladys Horton. "It was someone's number too, yes it was. That song was written by Marvin Gaye and Mickey Stevenson. We thought it was a cute idea, they were just thinking of the numbers that go together well. That sound, 45789, lyrically."

—

The Routers "Let's Go" Warner Brothers July 20, 1962

Style: Rock 'n' roll instrumental
Where from: Los Angeles, CA
Where recorded: Hollywood, CA
Suggested pairing: Ritchie Valens "La Bamba" 1958

A variation of the Mar-Ketts, Joe Saraceno also produced The Routers—Mike Gordon, guitar with session players Plas Johnson, tenor sax; Earl Palmer, drums; Ray Johnson, piano; Scott Engel, bass and Tommy Tedesco, guitar—on this football game chant hit.

The later Routers involved only Gordon from the original players. As Jimmie Maddin recalled, "I was working with another guy, Joe Saraceno, for Warner Brothers. He was making rock records; he had a bunch of instrumental hits. He was cutting instrumentals. I was the Nighthawks group. I worked as a Routers for him one night, that was [the] studio group."

—

Marvin Gaye "Stubborn Kind Of Fellow" Tamla July 23, 1962

Style: Soul
Where from: Washington, DC
Where recorded: Detroit, MI

Several releases into his Motown/Tamla career, Marvin Gaye's first hit was this hitchhike beat "Stubborn Kind Of Fellow" with vocal backing by Martha and the Vandellas. "Chester Simmons was taking care of Bo Diddley's business," said Tammi Diddley. "When Harvey Fuqua came into DC, Bo would use three people. He would go to the projects to pick up Marvin Gaye, who used to valet for Bo in the late 1950s, and Reese Palmer to take them to the Howard while Chester was getting dressed."

Wishing to emulate the smooth ballad style of Nat King Cole and Sam Cooke, Gaye didn't want to sing an upbeat song, especially with a scream attached to it, so he was told it was only a demo for Gino Parks, who had a recording track record with the label. Then the label released it by Gaye. Martha and the Vandellas continued to accompany Gaye on "I'm Crazy 'Bout My Baby," "Hitch Hike" and "Pride & Joy."

—

Bobby (Boris) Pickett & the Crypt Kickers "Monster Mash" Garpax August 1962/Parrot

Style: Novelty rock 'n' roll
Where from: Massachusetts
Where recorded: Hollywood, CA

Previous to this hit, vocalist Bobby Pickett was in several Paxton-produced groups like The Stompers and The Cordials. Pickett had a way of acting out monster roles ala Boris Karloff, a talent for which Gary Paxton created this song he released as Bobby Pickett & the Crypt Kickers' "Monster Mash," not an easy record for Garpax's Paxton to promote. Backing Pickett were "George Motola's wife, Ricky Page, me and Hal Davis were on 'Monster Mash," recalled Marc Gordon. "We did background for Gary Paxton." With sound effects and session players like "Billy Riley on harmonica and guitar; Gary Paxton, piano; Jesse Sailes, drums and Chuck Hamilton, bass," according to Gordon, though others have cited Leon Russell, organ; Mark Andes, bass and Mel Taylor, drums, Paxton took the record around to L.A. radio stations.

"I pressed it on Garpax, took it to KFWB and KRLA, they turned it down," said Paxton. "One program director said, 'That's even stupider than 'Alley Oop.' I drove to Fresno with 4,000 copies and picked out seven or eight record stores, and in each one, talked to the girl who stocked records and gave each store 10 copies apiece. Then we went to Oakland and San Jose and did the same thing. We told radio stations in the area it was in all the record stores, and when they called, they found out they all had the record, so they played it. "It was becoming a hit and George Sherlock, head of London Records in L.A., made an offer. I wanted $100,000; he offered $50,000. I told him I wanted 14 percent royalty and to keep it on Garpax. He wasn't sure he could do that. I told him that they had Felsted and Buck Ram's label, so why not put it on my Garpax. He agreed."

—

Scotty Wayne "Only One" Talent Scout 1962

Style: Swamp rock
Where recorded: Texas

After he was sprung from Angola Prison, Freddy Fender's label still had a problem, really two problems. He wasn't ready to have his name used on the release, because of negative fame, being an ex-con and all that. "I was not available when Wayne Duncan changed the name from Freddy Fender to Scotty Wayne. I was not working with him anymore, I was somewhere else. He had a son named Scotty, his name was Wayne, so he put the name Scotty Wayne on it." Duncan wanted to keep Fender material on the market, but because of well publicized problems, chose to give him that pseudonym. "I didn't really appreciate the new name. I'm not the kind of guy to get ruffled up about things. I let it sink in a little bit. After that, if it's worth getting ruffled up about, maybe I'll do something. Otherwise, I'll go on my way. I don't just blow up immediately."

The original title, "Holy One," was also controversial, thus became "Only One." Fender recalled, "There was a time we were having a lot of no no's from the DJs because the song 'Holy One,' the title they thought was too close to a religious thing, so they changed it to 'Only One.' It seemed like a[n] appropriate title to me. You can write a song like 'Holy One' in Spanish, and it doesn't sound as touchy as it does in English because of the language thing."

—

The Contours "Do You Love Me" Gordy August 11, 1962

Style: Soul vocal group
From and recorded in: Detroit, MI
Suggested pairing: The Isley Brothers 'Twist and Shout" 1961

"We were considered the most dynamic group out of Motown," said Joe Billingslea of The Contours. "Five dancing singers with splits, somersaults, back-over flips while we were performing. We patterned ourselves after Hank Ballard & the Midnighters, who was my idol. We used to go watch them at the Madison Theater in Detroit and were awed by their stage presence. A lot of our routines were adapted from their style and from Jackie Wilson's style, which formed the Contours style."

According to Billingslea, on this Contours' first hit and third release, "Do You Love Me," the false ending sold the rough and ready church-like vocals. "We were first called The Blenders after we left The Majestics. A guy named Wes Higgins was the manager of The Falcons. He wanted two of our songs, but he didn't want the group. While we were leaving the door, I noticed the name of the company on the door, Flick and Contour. We took a vote and the group decided to go with the name The Contours.

Billingslea continued, "If you listen to 'Do You Love Me' closely, it's similar to 'Twist and Shout" by the Isley Brothers, that's what Berry Gordy wrote the tune off of. I think also what sold the song was our lead singer's voice, that harsh church voice and also the part that was put in by Berry, where the bass would cut out and come back in with that 'boom boom boom' part. That was the tricky part of the song that caught on good for us.

Billingslea recalled, as The Temptations had yet to score their first hit, "'Do You Love Me' was intended for The Temptations and they couldn't sing the song the way Berry Gordy wanted the song sung, so he in turn asked us to try the song, he liked the way it was done, it was our first million seller."

—

The Crystals "He's a Rebel" Philles August 14, 1962

Style: Soul vocal group
Where from: Los Angeles, CA
Where recorded: Hollywood, CA
Original version: Vikki Carr 1962
Suggested pairing: Timi Yuro "What's a Matter Baby" 1962

Producer Phil Spector chose "He's a Rebel" for The Crystals, a song Latina vocalist Vikki Carr had already recorded for Liberty, giving her a head start. Spector got wind of the competition and hired The Blossoms who had just been dropped by Challenge—Darlene Wright, whom Spector renamed Darlene Love on lead vocals; Fanita James, Edna Wright, Gracia Nitzsche and Cher to cover Carr's "He's a Rebel" as The Crystals on Philles.

The B-side, "I Love You Eddie," was recorded by the original Brooklyn-based Crystals and was an answer song to "He's a Yankee" by The Sweethearts on Brunswick, and was also rendered as "I Love You Betty" by Terry Day on Columbia.

—

Danny & Gwen "Submarine Race" Liberty August 29, 1962

Style: Novelty
Where from: Rosemead, CA/Texas
Where recorded: Hollywood, CA

Named after producer Snuff Garrett's two-year-old daughter, Gwen was Mexican-American thrush Vikki Carr and Danny was Jerry Naylor of The Crickets. Danny & Gwen recorded this novelty duet centered around the lover's lane seduction line, "Submarine Race." It probably was a bit too racy for hit status. Carr's next song, "He's A Rebel," charted, but was soon swamped by The Crystals' version. It was clear that this was the summer of novelty sounding releases.

—

Les Cooper "Wiggle Wobble" Everlast August 1962

Style: Rhythm and blues instrumental
Where from: Norfolk, VA
Where recorded: New York City, NY

Les Cooper began his career singing with doo wop groups The Empires and The Whirlers, and was the manager of The Charts, who hit with "Deserie" in 1957. In 1962, Cooper released the instrumental single "Wiggle Wobble" as Les Cooper & the Soul Rockers, produced by Bobby Robinson and featuring the tenor saxophone of Joe Grier formerly of The Charts.

—

Herb Alpert & the Tijuana Brass "The Lonely Bull" A&M 1962

Style: Pop instrumental
Where from: L.A. area, CA
Where recorded: Hollywood, CA

Hardly the first instrumental or novelty release by Herb Alpert, Herb Alpert & the Tijuana Brass' "The Lonely Bull" set his style for decades to come, also causing his A&M to grow into a legendary label for decades to come. After a debacle with a singer named Mallory Sands, whom Alan Freed promised to play on his radio show just prior to getting fired in the previous month, Herb Alpert "was very down," said songwriter Lee Silver, who had just been a partner with Alpert in the Lash label. "Then I had to go to New York. When I came back, he and Jerry Moss played 'Lonely Bull' for me in his garage."

Originally entitled "Twinkle Star," Alpert heard a mariachi band at a Tijuana bullfight, from which he recorded crowd responses and the fanfare of the brass musicians by way of his trumpet and renamed the song "The Lonely Bull." Silver added, "Herb said, 'You know, Lee, the future is in albums.' I said, 'Go ahead and release it.'" He did, as "The Lonely Bull (El Solo Toro)" backed with "Acapulco 1922" by Herb Alpert & the Tijuana Brass, basically ground zero for the A&M label and the success of Herb Alpert. In the short run, dozens of ersatz Mexican sounding releases by domestic combos with bullfighting and matador titles flooded the 45 rpm market and stiffed uniformly.

—

Bettye LaVette "My Man, He's a Lovin' Man" Atlantic September 1962

Style: Soul
From and recorded in: Detroit, MI

"I was 16 years old in Detroit and getting involved in recording was a typical thing to do," said Bettye LaVette. "Everybody else was doing it. Everybody was making records, people were putting things to together. In '62, segregation was very big, so everybody knew everybody." As early as 1959 came some great Detroit records that hit the top ten, "You're so Fine" by The Falcons and "Money" by Barrett Strong, the first Motown label record to place well on the charts. But when LaVette entered the music game in '62, Motown was hardly the mighty Hitsville U.S.A. it became. The Supremes were freshly minted from The Primettes and The Temptations were one record away from their career as The Primes, then as The Distants. LaVette added, "I knew everybody who got [their] start at the time. We were all in the exact same place at the very same time. Everybody was older. Except Stevie Wonder, who was younger than me."

LaVette hit the national charts with her first release, backed by The Falcons. "My Man, He's A Lovin' Man" was done in a youthful voice she describes as sounding like Minnie Mouse. "I never sounded like a woman. Early on, I sounded like Minnie Mouse, then straight to sounding like James Brown."

—

The Drifters "Up on the Roof" Atlantic September 1962

Style: Rhythm and blues vocal group
From and recorded in: New York City, NY
Original version: Little Eva 1962

Supposedly inspired by scenes from "West Side Story," Carole King wrote "Up on the Roof" for Drifters' lead singer Rudy Lewis, with vocal backing by Dionne & Dee Dee Warwick. Dionne then met Burt Bacharach at The Drifters "Mexican Divorce" session.

Remakes: The Sidekicks 1966; The Cryan' Shames 1968; Laura Nyro 1970; Carole King 1970; Ralfi Pagan 1972; James Taylor 1979

—

The Vells "You'll Never Cherish a Love So True" Mel-o-dy October 1, 1962

Style: Soul
From and recorded in: Detroit, MI

The Vells were previously known as The Del-Phis when they recorded "It Takes Two" for Check Mate in 1961. With a "Hitch Hike" beat, "You'll Never Cherish a Love So True" by The Vells never charted nationally.
The lead singer was "a lady named Gloria Williams," said Freddie Gorman, who co-wrote The Vells' release. The group singing in the background became The Vandellas when Martha Reeves, who had also sung with the Del-Phis, re-joined the group. "Gloria was the first lead singer, but never pursued her career any further. That's when they changed their name from The Vells to Martha and the Vandellas and they re-recorded that song. That was an upright bass, just a little before James Jamerson came with the Fender. He was a fine musician and great bass player and what he did with the Fender Rhodes bass, he revolutionized it." The name Vandellas was chosen by Martha to combine where she lived, Van Dyke Blvd., with Detroit gospel singer Della Reese.

—

Little Stevie Wonder "La La La La La" Tamla October 3, 1962

Style: Soul
From and recorded in: Detroit, MI

This was an unusual approach by accomplished lyricist Stevie Wonder, in that his "La La La La La" consisted mainly of those very lyrics along with "one more time." With a backbeat similar to Mongo Santamaria's "Watermelon Man," the Temple City, CA band The Blendells turned these very lyrics into a decent hit in 1966.

Remake: The Blendells 1966

—

The Drew-Vels "Tell Him" Capitol October 7, 1963

Style: Soul vocal group
Where from: South Carolina
Where recorded: Chicago, IL

The short-lived vocal group, The Drew-Vels—Patti Drew, lead; Carlton Black, bass and baritone; Lorraine Drew and Erma Drew—had the first version of this emotive ballad, "Tell Him," which Patti Drew revived as a solo act with uncredited group backing almost four years later. This "Tell Him" was in no way connected to The Exciters more frantic "Tell Him," a hit at the same time.

Remake: Patti Drew 1967

—

The Diddley Oohs "Hooray for the Big Slow Train" Dore October 1962

Style: Novelty
From and recorded in: Hollywood, CA

"Herb Alpert needed $400, so he approached Lou Bedell with a song by The Diddley Oohs," said co-composer Don Drowty, also known as Dante. "It was terrible, but Bedell bought it anyway because Alpert needed the dough." The result was this tribute to the just-opened Seattle World's Fair (held April 21, 1962 to October 21, 1962). "Hooray for the Big Slow Train" backed with an apropos generic instrumental title, "Like Terrible," on Dore.

Before The Diddley Oohs disc was pressed, Alpert had already hit big as the leader of the Tijuana Brass. However, it is doubtful this 45 was put out other than on promotional copies.

—

The Pastel Six "Cinnamon Cinder" Zen
October 13, 1962

Style: Rock 'n' roll
Where from: Southern California
Where recorded: Hollywood, CA

The Pastel Six had one single on Downey Records when they were signed to record a 45 rpm commercial for a teen club chain in the Valley, Long Beach, and Orange County, this "Cinnamon Cinder (It's A Very Nice Dance)" on Russ Regan's Zen.

"When I started playing with The Pastel Six, we played in the Pomona Gardens. I heard about the Cinnamon Cinder on Ventura Blvd when I was working in Van Nuys at the Peppermint Stick," said sax player Dave Kadison. "The leader was Bob Toten, guitar; Tony Tilman, lead guitar and vocal; Ricky Rodriguez, bass and trumpet; Dave Kadison, tenor and piano; Eric Frickert, baritone sax; Lynn Hamm, drums and vocals Bill Myers, tenor sax."

—

The Atlantics "Remember the Night" Linda
October 13, 1962

Style: Retro doo wop
Where recorded: Hollywood, CA

Barry & Bobby, Barry Richards and Bobby Hart, recorded the oldies tribute lyrics, "Remember the Night" on Goliath, which was almost instantly covered by The Rivingtons as The Atlantics on Linda; the B-side also issued backed with "Tracy (All I Have Is Yours)" by Barry White & the Atlantics on Faro in 1963. "In the other session, there were different singers in there with The Rivingtons. They hadn't become The Rivingtons at that time," said Eddie Davis. "When they did 'Flame Of Love,' they were The Rivingtons. 'Papa Oom Mow Mow' was going at the same time. There were so many records that sounded like that. On all the records, it's the same musicians playing on all the records. It's all the same musicians on the back of all the things where you have the vocalists in front of the music. From East L.A., they were all self-contained groups, the vocals and the music all came out of the group. In these sessions, we had hired musicians. Bobby Gross playing drums, Gaynel Hodge on piano, Earl Palmer, Red Callender; they played all the sessions... you always get that group, 'Hully Gully' and 'Western Movies,' they did them all, for everybody."

Said Larry Tamblyn, "We met the Rivingtons. Randy Thomas had a copy of 'Flame Of Love.' He was a friend with Bobby Hart. He was just there, I used to look up and Eddie would bring these guys, a kid on the block that couldn't sing. We used the old Wurlitzer, electric keyboard we wanted, so we let Bobby Hart sing. Randy Thomas then joined The Hondells."

—

The Rumblers "Boss" Downey October 13, 1962/Dot 1963

Style: Rock 'n' roll
Where from: England/Norwalk CA
Where recorded: Downey, CA
Suggested pairings: Link Wray "Rumble' 1958; The Strangers "Caterpillar Crawl" 1959

Adrian Lloyd emigrated from England to Long Beach in about 1958. He recalled, "I attended Long Beach Poly High School, class of 1963," but didn't graduate. Then came The Rumblers from nearby Norwalk, named after Link Wray's hit, "Rumble" from '58. "When I got with The Rumblers, they'd not done anything," said Lloyd. In 1961, The Rumblers were Mike Kelishes and Johnny Kirkland, guitar; Wayne Matteson, bass and Eddie Braracco, drums, whom Lloyd replaced with Bob Jones added on sax in 1962.

Lloyd added, "I met them at Johnny Kirkland's house on Gridley Road in Norwalk. I was about a year older than Johnny, I was 18; they were 17." While working at the Record Room, "I got to know Sid Talmadge, head of Record Merchandising, who told me, 'If you guys cut anything, let me hear it.' We recorded at Garrison Studio in Long Beach. He didn't like 'That's It' the original flip of 'Stompin' Time.' He said, '"Stompin' Time" sounds pretty good, get me a better thing for the other side, I'll put it out.' Mike wrote 'Intersection'" on Syd Talmadge's Highland Records in 1962. "After that, we kept going back, but we never made anything on that. We were all green at that time. I'd heard of Wenzel's Music Town from Bill Myers of The Pastel Six," Lloyd recalled. "Wenzel's had done the recording of 'Cinnamon Cinder.' I took in a copy of 'Stomping Time" for him to hear. We played 'Rumblin,' recorded it, put it on the shelf." Mike Kalishes' father Nick became their manager.

Lloyd continued, "Bob Jones thought up 'Boss.' Bob was into the surfing scene. We wanted a title that was something real good in surfer terms, Bob said, 'How about "Boss"?'" For the "Boss" vocal flip side, "Nobody could sing. They said, 'The guy's got a great set of drums and he can play,'" referring to Lloyd. "I stuck a microphone between my legs and sang 'I Don't Need You No More'" as the B-side. The Rumblers' "Boss" with an intro lifted from "Caterpillar Crawl" by The Strangers from '59 ("there's a familiarity") backed with a bluesey Lloyd vocal on "I Don't Need You No More" was issued on Downey in the L.A. market; nationally on Dot in '63.

Answer: The Rumblers "Boss Strikes Back" 1963

—

The Exciters "Tell Him" United Artists October 18, 1962

Style: Soul vocal group
From and recorded in: New York City, NY
Original versions: Gil Hamilton "Tell Her" 1962; Ed Townsend "Tell Her" 1962
Suggested pairing: The Masterettes "Follow the Leader" 1961

Bert Berns, using the pseudonym Bert Russell, wrote this song as "Tell Her." Versions by Johnny Thunder and Ed Townsend were released in 1962, but they both stiffed.

When the production team of Jerry Leiber and Mike Stoller left Atlantic Records to work for United Artists, they produced a new version by The Exciters, a New York quartet featuring three female vocalists. Released later in 1962 as "Tell Him," it became a big hit, reaching its chart peak on January 19, 1963. The Exciters followed with "He's Got The Power" (#57), and a "Tell Him" clone called "Get Him" (#76). They also recorded the original version of "Do-Wah Diddy."

—

Jim Cava "Humpty-Dumpty Heart" Royalty October 20, 1962

Style: Rock 'n' roll
Where from: England/Norwalk CA
Where recorded: Downey, CA

Jim Cavalier, born in Youngstown Ohio in 1944, arrived in Southern California at "three or four," then moved to the San Joaquin Valley "for a while. My parents had a friend, a country DJ in Visalia, CA. I cut some demos, not much happened. In 1961, we moved to Long Beach." He attended Millikan High School, where "we did a Thadus dance with The Dartells. My dad, Jess, worked across the street from Wenzel's at Lakewood Pipe. In late summer 1961, I recorded two songs with The Pastel Six, piano, sax and guitar, the Wenzel's in-house band. The studio had been opened for some time. I recorded Bobby Vee's 'Walkin' with My Angel' and 'Class of 62,' which Bob Luman had out as 'Class of 59.' They were just demos. The Chantays were recording there. The Rumblers with Adrian Lloyd. I liked him. He was a nice guy. Wenzel had the right idea, he would break the song and sell it to Dot. He'd get the royalties. After I did the Wenzel's thing, it was way cool, I had a record player in the car, my mom, Anna got 50 demos from Wenzel's and sent them to every record company in the country. I was working in a Gardena body shop. One day, my mom called, 'Jim get home, you have an audition with Royalty Records in Hollywood.'

Cavalier continued, "I met Vito Gazzi. I was a pretty mild kid; he looked like a gangster." Cavalier later found out "the Genovese from an East Coast would send people out here, get investors to invest in the record, get a half million dollars and when it didn't hit, they wouldn't have to pay them back. He played this song like 'Purple People Eater' on his tape recorder, 'What do you think? Would you like to record that song?' 'No.' 'You don't understand what you're turning down.' 'I would not record this fuckin' record if it was the last one on earth.' Gazzi called again. My mom told me, 'He wants to see you. I won't be going with you.'

"Gazzi took me to the Hollywood Hills, here's this auburn haired woman in coveralls, Rickie Page. Gazzi introduced me to George Motola who I knew wrote 'Goodnight My Love.' I sat there for 15 minutes. Gazzi and Motola were talking. George said, 'Rickie go get that song you wrote for Bobby Vee.' Motola told me Vee's brother was his manager and 'I don't get along with his brother.' We signed a contract; we were on our way. That was in July. Recorded it at Gold Star in two sessions. We had Glen Campbell and Leon Russell on that; Rickie Page and the Crypt Kickers." The Rickie Page-Bobby Plaisted, aka Bobby Please composition "Humpty-Dumpty Heart" backed with "Take-A-Way" by Jim Cava was a Vito Gazzi production and a Fresno pick hit. "Vic Gazzi didn't plan on dealing with my mom when they started giving me the runaround. I got a phone call from Robert W. Morgan in Fresno, 'I've got some bad news; we can't get your record. I've gotten calls, but we can't get the record in the stores and it's going to die a natural death.' I went to Gazzi, he said, 'Take this check to Merit music, get a box,' First man I ever saw with long hair, Sonny Bono waited on me, he told me, 'They're not pressing it. This check will take care of 500 copies, but they're not pressing it. We're getting calls.'

"Me and my mom went to some labels. Liberty told us, 'We don't need another Bobby Vee.' We went to Art LaBoe's office; then we went to Dot. This woman told me, 'You get me the master, we'll put you on the charts.' I should have gone to Goldstar or to Merit to get the master. My mom went to Gazzi to get the master, then she got an attorney. Gazzi and Royalty disappeared. Vito Gazzi hasn't been heard from since a few months after 'Humpty-Dumpty Heart' was released and started to get good airplay."

—

Four Seasons "Big Girls Don't Cry" Vee Jay October 27, 1962

Style: Pop doo wop vocal group
Where from: New Jersey
Where recorded: New York

The idea for this Four Seasons' title, "Big Girls Don't Cry," was lifted from dialogue in a John Payne western, which gave The Four Seasons their second chart topping hit in a few months.

—

Mary Wells "Two Lovers" Motown October 29, 1962

Style: Soul
From and recorded in: Detroit, MI

The cha cha beat vocal by Mary Wells turned this song, "Two Lovers," into an unexpected story of a split personality.

—

Jan Bradley "Mama Didn't Lie" Formal/Chess November 1962

Style: Soul
Where from: Byhalia, MI
Where recorded: Chicago, IL
Suggested pairing: The Miracles "Shop Around"

Addie Bradley grew up in the Chicago suburbs. As Jan Bradley, she recorded songwriter Curtis Mayfield's "We Girls" for the Formal label, named after owner Angelo Giardini's tux business. Next, Mayfield wrote the putative answer to the hit, "Shop Around" by The Miracles on Tamla from 1960 and gave the breezy "Mama Didn't Lie" to Bradley to record on Formal in 1962, amounting to the female answer to the male attitude displayed by The Miracles' "Shop Around."

This was Mayfield's only recording on Chess, the very label that had turned down Mayfield and his Impressions in 1958. In later interviews, Mayfield made it clear he was not a fan of the Chess label because of the turndown, but he had nothing to do with the song being leased to that label.

Bradley's "I'm Over You" on Chess hit the pop and R&B charts in early 1965.

Remake: The Fascinations "Mama Didn't Lie" 1962

—

Otis Redding "These Arms Of Mine" Volt November 1962

Style: Soul
Where from: Georgia
Where recorded: Memphis, TN

"The day I first heard Otis Redding," said Steve Cropper, "unbeknownst to me, I thought he was the driver for Johnny Jenkins and the Pinetoppers. They had him up there. We were trying to get a repeat record on him. He had a song called 'Love Twist' he had a lot of success with. They thought bringing him to Stax Records increased his chances of getting another hit single. This guy, I didn't see him really. I saw him around in the lobby, he kept after Al Jackson all day long. He want us to hear him sing. Sometimes you do that, sometimes you can't. We were wrapping up the session pretty early. Al Jackson came down, said, 'You gotta listen to this guy, he's been after me all day long.' We said, 'Okay, let's go, where is he?' He sat down at the piano and started singing 'These Arms Of Mine' and the rest is history, seventeen singles in a row."

—

Dick Dale and His Del-Tones "Peppermint Man" Deltone November 1962

Style: Rock 'n' roll
Where from: Massachusetts
Where recorded: Hollywood , CA

Dick Dale recalled, "I had this striped shirt Billy Barber got me, and when the kids saw me wearing it, they went 'ooh peppermint man.'" Songwriter Alonzo Willis heard about this description and wrote "Peppermint Man," which featured Dale's aggressive vocals.

—

The Tornados "Telstar" London November 1962

Style: Space age instrumental
From and recorded in: England
Suggested pairings: Dave "Baby" Cortez "The Happy Organ" 1959; Jean Ledrut "La Marche d'Austerlitz" 1962 (lawsuit filed); Boston "More Than A Feeling" 1976

Prior to the U.S. arrival of the Beatles, producer Joe Meek's U.K. band The Tornados hit #1 in America. With an idea to create an instrumental theme for the just-launched Telstar communications satellite that would establish a new standard for communication in the coming years, Meek ran an ad in Melody Maker seeking musicians. Alan Caddy and Clem Cattini, former members of Johnny Kidd and the Pirates, were teamed with three others, forming The Tornados to create an instrumental with space sound effects. A Clavioline keyboard played by Geoff Goddard duplicated a sound similar to Dave "Baby" Cortez' #1 hit, "The Happy Organ." Goddard also supplied the "humming" vocal at the end of the song, Meek added an "ah ah" voiceover and a backwards tape of a flushing toilet, meant to evoke the effect of a space bound rocket.

Recorded in two days, when "Telstar" hit #1 in the U.S., a Redlands, CA-based Tornadoes surf group had to change to The Hollywood Tornadoes, even though they had been The Tornadoes since 1959. Owners of the theme of the film, "The Battle of Austerlitz," sued Meek over a similarity between the first seven notes of each tune. The suit was decided in Meek's favor. On February 3, 1967, during an argument, 37-year-old Meek shot and killed his landlady, then did the same to himself.

Remakes: Apollo 100 1974; The Spitballs 1979

Answers: Margie Singleton "Magic Star" 1962; The Tornadoes "Life On Venus (Telstar II)"; The Astronomers "Relay-Son Of Telstar" 1963

—

The Contours "Shake Sherry" Gordy November 15, 1962

Style: Soul vocal group
From and recorded in: Detroit, MI

The Contours' Joe Billingslea said, "'Shake Sherry' was written by Berry Gordy Jr. on the strength of 'Sherry' by The Four Seasons. It sounded nothing like The Four Seasons, it had The Contours sound and Berry Gordy was then one of the gifted songwriters I have known. Everything that came out of Motown in '60, '61 or '62 was picked by the kids. He would invite them in the studio and they were awed by the studio. They got to meet celebrities in the studio and they were served pop and potato chips, they'd listen to the songs, dance to the songs and they would ask them what songs they liked the best. Then he'd go back to his staff and producers and he'd go with the majority of songs and nine times out of ten, it was a hit."

—

Johnny Thunder "Loop De Loop" Diamond December 1962

Style: Soul
Where from: Leesburg, FL
Where recorded: Bell Studios, New York City, NY

Born August 15, 1932, vocalist Gil Hamilton recorded "Pretty Baby," pretty much a combination of Marv Johnson's "You Got What It Takes" and Jimmy Jones' "Handyman," on Fury in 1960. Hamilton also recorded the excellent "Twist and Shout" clone "Move & Groove" for Vee Jay in 1962. Both records stiffed. Hamilton recorded the entirely original "Tell Her" for Capitol in 1962. It didn't sell. He changed it to "Tell Him," and the song was soon a major hit for The Exciters. In 1963, songwriter and record producer Teddy Vann gave Hamilton a new name, persuading him to record a novelty version of the traditional children's nursery song "Loop de Loop," also known as "Looby Lou," under the name Johnny Thunder. That was the hit he needed.

—

Chantays "Pipeline" Downey/Dot December 1962

Style: Surf rock
Where from: Santa Ana, CA
Where recorded: Pal Recording Studio in Cucamonga, CA

The Chantays out of Santa Ana High School were guitarists Bob Spickard and Brian Carman, who wrote "Pipeline"; Bob Welch, drums; Warren Waters, bass and Rob Marshall, keyboard. A cranking "ghostly" guitar surf instrumental about a perfect surf wave, "Pipeline" was originally "Liberty's Whip" and later "44 Magnum." After seeing a surf flick about the notorious Hawaiian Pipeline, they named their tune "Pipeline." The demo was shopped around to various labels and was picked up by Downey Records at Wenzel's Music in Downey, which was just beginning to notice the instrumental surf craze.

—

The Miracles "You've Really Got a Hold On Me" Tamla December 1962

Style: Soul vocal group
From and recorded in: Detroit, MI
Suggested pairings: Sam Cooke "Bring It On Home To Me" 1961

"Smokey admired Sam Cooke a lot. Sam influenced him a lot," said Smokey Robinson's ex-wife Claudette Robinson. "I discovered Smokey had a bluesy side to him. I never thought about 'Bring It On Home To Me.' By now, every song on the Tamla label was by Yhe Miracles, Marvin Gaye, The Marvelettes, or Stevie Wonder. You couldn't put the release on one label, you could release a Tamla, then a Motown, then a Gordy."

—

Marvin Gaye "Hitch Hike" Tamla December 1962

Style: Soul
Where from: Washington, DC
Where recorded: Detroit, MI
Suggested pairings: Chubby Checker "Popeye The Hitchhiker" 1962; Redbone "Come & Get Your Love" 1974

Based on a popular dance of the day, with backing by Martha and the Vandellas, Marvin Gaye's "Hitch Hike" was somewhat of an answer to the Chubby Checker hit "Popeye The Hitchhiker," from summer 1962, and later echoed in the Redbone hit, "Come & Get Your Love" in 1974.

Remake: The Spiders—an early Alice Cooper identity 1965

—

Albert Collins "Defrost" Hall-Way December 24, 1962

Style: Blues
Where from: Leona, Tx
Where recorded: Beaumont, Tx

Albert Collins debuted with the blues guitar instrumental "Freeze" for Kangaroo in June 1958, establishing a trend for additional titles like "Frosty" and "Defrost." Collins said, "I was cutting instrumentals in those days. I wasn't doing singing too much. That was Booker T. & the M.G.'s' days, 'Green Onions,' instrumentals were selling. That's when I cut 'Frosty.' Pretty good seller. I got that from my dad's car. I had a bass player, we come from Corpus Christie, Texas one night. It started raining and my windshield fogged up. 'Why don't you turn your defroster on?' I looked at my dashboard, maybe I can do a tune called 'Defrost.' That's how that music got started. We're gonna keep you cold, man."

—

McKinley Mitchell "The Town I Live In" Midas/One-der-ful 1962

Style: Soul
From and recorded in: Chicago, IL

McKinley Mitchell's blues ballad "The Town I Live In" became anthemic, especially in L.A., because of a haunting remake by Thee Midniters. According to legendary blues songwriter Willie Dixon, "Chicago has kind of been like the blues capitol of the world, because so many people from all over the world came to Chicago to introduce their music. They could always find a place to let it loose around there and people appreciated it, even if it was on the streets." Dixon recalled McKinley Mitchell as one of many Chicago-based vocalists who never got their due. "McKinley Mitchell and all those guys. They wasn't getting no publicity back in those days. And they're getting it today, although they're dead."

—

Ron Roman "Love Of My Life" Aerni 1963

Style: Doo wop
Where from: Chino, CA
Where recorded: Cucamonga, CA

Ron Roman was Joe Macaluso, who attended high school in Chino and was backed by Johnny and Ronnie Williams on guitar on this Frank Zappa-composed doo wop, "Love Of My Life," the only release on Dave Aerni's Daani. Just 50 copies were pressed, an original 45 is very rare.

Remake: Ruben & the Jets 1968

—

The Dartells "Hot Pastrami" Arlen/Dot January 25, 1963

Style: Rock 'n' roll group
Where from: Oxnard, CA
Where recorded: Hollywood, CA
Suggested pairing: Nat Kendricks "Mashed Potatoes" 1960

As of early 1960, The Hysterics from Hueneme High School in Oxnard, described in the press as a "jazz combo," began performing at local events. The Hysterics became The Casuals, which were promoted in a September 6, 1962 article in the Oxnard Courier on how get a record into national sales and about a promised battle with the Beach Boys, "whose record 'Surf and Safari' is the number one record in Southern California listings. Their manager, Tom Ayers, said he contracted the Arlen Records company in Culver City to make a record with the band. The result is a firm commitment to record The Casuals and promote 5,000 copies of the record where Arlen Records has regional offices. The record will be made during this month."

The Casuals became The Dartells. On January 28, 1963, the Oxnard Courier wrote about a new version of a rock 'n' roll dance called the "mashed potato." It all started out as a joke, according to Dick Burns, guitar-playing member of the six-man combo and spokesman for the group: "Last September the band members, Hueneme High School students Randy Ray, 18, Doug Philips, 18 and Gary Peeler, 18, Santa Clara High School graduate Dick Burns, 19 and Dick Peil, 20, stationed with the Navy at Pt. Mugu, arranged a recording session with Arlen Records in Culver City and were forced to change their name because another dance band was called The Casuals. The teenagers chose The Dartells. The Dartells placed high hopes tor fame on a song they wrote and performed with an all-out effort titled 'Dartell Stomp'" backed with "Hot Pastrami." In spite of the record company's promotional efforts in major record outlets throughout the country, the 'Dartell Stomp' just did not sell.

Then, one day, a disk jockey in Northern California flipped the record over and played the other side which features a song The Dartells had not even planned to record." It was "Hot Pastrami," a song The Dartells improvised from the "mashed potato" dance beat to "warm up with before the recording session," Dick explained. Doug Phillips, the vocalist on 'Hot Pastrami," just "felt the beat and made up words as he went along," according to The Dartells' manager, Tom Ayres, co-owner with actor Glenn Sipes of the Audio Record Bar. The lyrics were mainly "girls" and "dance." Ayres said hc received offers from five major record companies that made bids to buy The Dartells' one-year recording contract.

—

The Crystals "(Let's Dance) the Screw Pt. 1 & 2" Philles January 30, 1963

Style: Novelty soul vocal group
Where from: Los Angeles, CA
Where recorded: Hollywood, CA

After the success of "He's A Rebel," Spector promptly sacked the original Brooklyn Crystals group, except for having them record "(Let's Dance) the Screw Pt. 1 & 2" on Philles as payment to erstwhile partner Lester Sill who was owed one more record in their partnership dissolution. The Blossoms became The Crystals, meaning few Blossoms records would be released until The Crystals' hit string ran out, which took about two years.

Sill was the only person intended to hear "(Let's Dance) the Screw," as he was selected as the only person to get a copy. The performance amounts to the group chanting "dance," "let's do it," "to the right, to the left" but never the title, a job left up to a male voice proclaiming the title in a truly offensive manner. Multiple copies exist as the pressing plant had a minimum order size. The remaining records were intended for destruction, which did not account for archive copies kept by the record company or the pressing plant, pressing plant employee souvenirs and/or records that were possibly shipped, eventually purchased as "warehouse" stock by collectors or jobbers.

—

The Surfaris "Wipe Out" DFS January 1963/Princess February 1963/Dot March 1963

Style: Surf rock instrumental
Where from: Glendora, CA
Where recorded: Pal Recording Studio in Cucamonga, CA
Suggested pairings: Preston Epps "Bongo Rock" 1959; The Expressos "Teenage Express" 1960

The Surfaris were Jim Fuller, lead guitar; Bob Berryhill, rhythm guitar; Pat Connolly, bass. "We met at a talent show, Fuller, Connolly and me," said Berryhill. "In September 1962, Connolly called me, would you like to be in a band? Got a dance at Pomona Catholic High and we'll meet the drummer." They found drummer Ron Wilson, a member of the Charter Oaks High School Marching Band. Wilson led the drums-heavy surf-lingo instrumental with a cracking sound—meant to sound like a breaking surfboard—a maniacal laugh and the only two words: "wipe out," slang for being knocked off a board by a wave, "Wipe Out" was backed with the deadpan vocal, "Surfer Joe" on their manager, Dale F. Smolin's DFS label.

"'Wipe Out' was originally called 'Switchblade,'" said Berryhill. "Fuller went to Tijuana the week before, pulled out a switchblade, clicked it over the mike. The engineer said it had no pizzazz. We needed something like 'Bustin' Surfboards.' We broke a cement plasterboard from an old Cucamonga house over the mike, Smolin let out a witch's laugh… didn't want any credit for it. In fact, in shows, he'd do the laugh on the mike offstage." The DFS original was pressed to give away at live shows by The Surfaris, when it was hit in big Fresno, John Marascalco picked up the DFS label original and released it in its original form on Princess in order to sell to a major label.

Donnie Brooks recalled, "John Marascalco offered me 'Wipe Out' for $500. Marascalco wanted to keep

'Surfer Joe,'" but Donnie didn't have the money, so he had to turn it down.

Told by Dot it was too long for them to release. Marascalco released a shorter version on Princess in February, re-issued by Dot in March, reissued again on Dot All Time Hits.

—

The Surfaris "Surfer Joe" DFS January 1963/Princess February 1963/Dot March 1963

Style: Surf rock group
Where from: Glendora, CA
Where recorded: Pal Recording Studio in Cucamonga, CA

Ron Wilson was the vocalist on his own composition, "Surfer Joe," about a beach bum who, with "a green surfboard and a woody to match" won the Huntington Beach surfing contest, went into the Marines and drew KP duty.

Ron Wilson told me he had a dream about Surfer Joe," said Berryhill, "We sat down at Dale Smolin's studio and finished the lyrics." One verse was dropped from the Dot reissue in hopes of increased airplay. But the flip B-side, the instrumental "Wipe Out," won the day.

—

The Chiffons "He's So Fine" Laurie February 1963

Style: Soul vocal group
From and recorded in: New York City, NY
Suggested pairings: Edwin Hawkins Singers "Oh Happy Day" 1969 (lawsuit won); The Intrigues "In A Moment" 1969; George Harrison "My Sweet Lord" 1970; Gary Wright "Really Wanna Know You" 1970; Frank Zappa "A Little Green Rosetta" 1979

The Chiffons debuted with this uptempo brightly rendered Brill Building classic, "He's So Fine," which enriched copyright lawyers, and to a lesser extent, the original songwriters, for decades. (For more on the lawsuit, please see George Harrison's "My Sweet Lord.")

—

The Rip Chords "Here I Stand" Columbia February 16, 1963

Style: Rock 'n' roll duet
Where from: Inglewood, CA
Where recorded: Hollywood, CA
Original version: Wade Flemons 1958

"Phil Stewart was a little ahead of his time," said harmony partner Ernie Bringas. The idea of the two teaming up "came from looking at some old records; I noted Jan & Arnie. I knew they were not singing at Arwin anymore; Jan & Dean had moved to Dore." Phil Stewart opined, "Maybe Arwin needed us to take their place. We went to that label, my 'middle name is Jan, we're Jan & Ernie.' We had a song we had written called 'Raindrops,' it was soft and melodious, they liked the song, Doris Day threatened to do it, they gave us an audition at Columbia with Terry Melcher." Melcher had great connections. Stewart signed a writer contract at $50 a week. "Terry said, 'I want to record you guys, as The Opposites, the preacher and the private eye."

As The Opposites, Stewart recalled, "they jerked the record off after three days, flip side was 'Karen.' When we recorded 'Here I Stand,' there was a TV show called 'Rip Cord' at the time."

Melcher recalled The Rip Chords' name. "We got it from putting the 'h' into it; made it kind of exciting; parachuting struck me as an exciting spine-tingling thing to do; rip has a feel to it.

According to Ken Barnes in Radio & Records, The Rip Chords' first real release was originally 'Wynema.' Terry said there's more Karens."

—

Martha and the Vandellas "Come and Get These Memories" Gordy February 22, 1963

Style: Soul vocal group
From and recorded in: Detroit, MI

The first hit for Martha and the Vandellas was "Come and Get These Memories." Co-writer with Brian and Eddie Holland, Lamont Dozier said, "I was looking for another sound, something different. I figured there were other plateaus for it to go. I thought it needed to grow and my background was somewhat from a classical background, my grandmother and aunt played this type of music. Classical music was around me all the time while I was a kid, so I listened to 'Clare De Lune' and Nat Cole and people like that. I figured it was time to give rock a little class because to me it was a little loose. That was the partly the reason for '"Come and Get These Memories.' I wrote these lyrics on a piece of Kroger sack, you know the shopping bag you get. I used to cut these papers up and write, so I wrote this lyric, 'come and get these memories' on a Kroger sack and that's how I took it to Motown. I like to think this was the real tone or the real roots of Holland-Dozier-Holland and somewhat the Motown sound as well, because of the technique of writing. I came up with this idea purely out of feeling sick and tired about a lot of things and I think a lot of people think that way, a lot of girls I know. I was the cause of making them feel that way. So I got some of these stories back from them time to time and this was one of this. A little bit from three or four different girls and I came up with "Come and Get These Memories."

Lead singer Martha Reeves told Mojo magazine taht the song was "part jazz, the way the harmony is structured. Lamont played the keyboards to teach us the song, Eddie Holland did the vocals for the lead, and Brian Holland added the harmonies for the background. So the three of them working with us, we came up with a beautiful song. Whenever I hear it I always marvel at the ways that everything blends, the voices, the music. There's this instant entrance where you have to count to catch [it] but it works every time."

—

The Beatles "Please Please Me" Vee Jay February 25, 1963

Style: British Invasion
Where from: Liverpool, England
Where recorded: London, England
Suggested pairing: Bing Crosby "Please" 1933

When the Beatles attempted to break into the American charts with a successful Capitol, their label's U.S. affiliate, which had first refusal, exercised that option. That allowed another label to step in, and Chicago-based Vee Jay, most recently a top indie label thanks to The Four Seasons, but with a rich tradition of R&B and blues, signed them up. Their "Please Please Me" was a sped up take on Roy Orbison's distinctively moody "Only the Lonely" from 1960 and Chris Kenner's lively "I Like it Like That" from 1961. The "come on, come on..." part is reminiscent of two traditional folk songs: "New's Evens Song" and "Come Fair One." The theme was rumored to be about oral sex. The Beatles denied this, since they had a very clean image to maintain at the time.

Lennon said of the song, "I was always intrigued by the double use of the word 'please.'" Speaking of doubles, their name was misspelled "Beattles" on the record label on the first American release.

—

The Beach Boys "Surfin' U.S.A." Capitol February 26, 1963

Style: Rock 'n' roll group
Where from: Hawthorne, CA
Where recorded: Hollywood, CA
Suggested pairing: Chuck Berry "Sweet Little Sixteen" 1958

The Beach Boys' "Surfin' U.S.A." revealed 15 or 16 surfing spots ("Redondo Beach, L.A.") in California, Australia and Hawaii backed with the drag race story in "Shut Down," co-written by Roger Christian. Christian wasn't impressed with "409" so he created a drag race between a Super-Stock 413 cubic inch-powered '62 Dodge Dart and a fuel injected '63 Corvette Stingray.

On February 1, the Long Beach PT wrote, "The Beach Boys bring back 'Sweet Little Sixteen" with their latest effort—only in a way that has never been done before. The tune is the same, but the lyrics have been altered to correspond with the new title of 'Surfin' U.S.A.' It has great potential and the old Chuck Berry hit was about to be revived anyway." Apparently, both songs were promoted separately, with the surf song promoted prior to the hot rod song. Chuck Berry then sued for songwriter credit and won, apparently easily.

—

The Penguins "Memories Of El Monte" Original Sound February 27, 1963

Style: Retro doo wop vocal group
Where from: Los Angeles, CA
Where recorded: Cucamonga, CA

At the apex of the start of the oldies but goodies revival of 1962 and 1963, The Penguins, really The Viceroys with a Cleve Duncan lead, warbled this Frank Zappa co-composition, "Memories Of El Monte," for Art LaBoe's Original Sound. Out of Jefferson and Cathedral High Schools, The Viceroys were James Conwell, Andrew "Jack" White, Charles Jones, Oliver Williams and Herbert White, who cut "Dreamy Eyes" for Original Sound in 1961. "It was a local hit, we started traveling with Art Laboe and Hal Zeigler," said Viceroys member James Conwell. "We became The Penguins, traveled the south as The Penguins, did 'Memories Of El Monte.' Frank Zappa was a young kid, hanging around the studio, trying to sell songs."

Ray Collins, the song's co-writer, revealed the title was taken from a best-selling "Memories of El Monte" LP on LaBoe's Starla label, which featured songs sung by El Monte Legion Stadium groups, the very subject of the song. "It came from the title of that album. Frank said he and a friend of his had thought of writing a song from that title, so I just sat down at the piano and said, 'Let's do it.' So we did it. We sat down, and I remember the first line coming out, 'I'm all alone, feeling so blue...' Then we wrote it, and actually, Art Laboe's responsible for adding in the different groups' names and The Penguins impersonating those different groups," said Collins, referring to Duncan's spoken part which mentioned mainly local R&B songs and groups. "It could have been just as good without it, I believe," said Collins. LaBoe responded, "I felt the thing got boring after it got going, I put this montage in there. I had this group that would do it, The Viceroys." Collins answered, "Art Laboe's always had this thing about people recording R&B ballads too slow, so I think that he overcompensated and made 'Memories of El Monte' too fast."

LaBoe remembered, "Zappa used to store his vibraphone in the building where he recorded. I made him play on 'Memories Of El Monte' for the rent. He was all right, always had that acid personality. I got him out of jail when he got in trouble," likely the Studio Z raid in Cucamonga. "It was pretty innocent stuff, but nobody would get him out. It cost about thirty dollars." Zappa recalled to Les Carter on KPPC that he and Collins were working at the Troubadour in Hollywood on talent night "as Loeb and Leopold, singing about pimples and other things The Mothers were doing, but haven't been back since then... disgusting."

—

Johnny Fortune "Soul Surfer" Park Avenue February 28, 1963

Style: Surf rock instrumental
Where from: Inland Empire, CA
Where recorded: El Monte, CA

Guitarist Johnny Fortune recorded mostly at Pal Studios in the Inland Empire; however this session was conducted at an El Monte studio owned by Bobby Summers, with backing by Jim O'Keefe, sax; Fortune's 10-year old brother, drums and Fortune overdubbing the bass line on "Soul Surfer" backed with "Midnight Surf" on a label owned by John Fisher, Park Avenue.

—

Zip and the Zippers "Where You Goin,' Little Boy" Pageant March 1963

Style: Soul vocal group
From and recorded in: Philadelphia, PA

For reasons unknown, The Orlons recorded as Zip and the Zippers on this minor hit, "Where You Goin,' Little Boy."

—

Barbara Lewis "Hello Stranger" Atlantic March 1963

Style: R&B vocal
Where from: Detroit, MI
Where recorded: Chicago, IL

The Chicago-based Dells supplied the chu-wops to this engaging bit of balladry, "Hello Stranger" by Detroit-based Barbara Lewis; by far, her most major hit.

—

Solomon Burke "If You Need Me" Atlantic 1963

Style: Soul
Where from: Philadelphia, PA
Original version: Wilson Pickett March 1963

Before he joined the Atlantic label, Wilson Pickett recalled that Atlantic "had Solomon Burke. He was the ballad singer. They didn't have a follow-up to his song 'Just Out Of Reach.' So I brought 'If You Need Me.' They bought the song from me. $500. They promised to put it out on me, but then they put it out on Solomon Burke. So my manager, Mr. Golden, didn't like that. We went to Harold Logan and Lloyd Price, who owned Double L Records. They put the song out on me, so me and Solomon had the song at the same time."

—

Ray Barreto Y Su Charanga Moderna "El Watusi" Tico March 1963

Style: Latin jazz funk
From and recorded in: New York City, NY

Conga player Ray Barretto came up with the exciting "El Watusi," not about a dance, but a vocal jazz composition in Cuban street Spanish with various chattering voices describing a scary-looking biggest and baddest man in Havana, Wito Cortwright, a guiro player. "El Watusi" was issued as the novelty B-side of the charanga "Ritmo Sabroso," at the height to the charanga rage in Spanish Harlem. Willie Torres was the other voice in the extended spoken vamp that led up to the instrumental part, making it one of the first rap records. The opening rap was made up as they went along, according to Torres. In that it was released for sales in Spanish Harlem, where residents still had 78 rpm players, this was possibly the final 78 rpm record issued in the U.S., excepting vanity pressings done decades later.

—

The Righteous Brothers "Little Latin Lupe Lu" Moonglow March 1963

Style: Blue-eyed soul duet
Where from: Santa Ana, CA and Anaheim, CA
Where recorded: Hollywood, CA

Albert van Hoogten, owner of Ronnex Records in Belgium, sent his brother Rene Jan van Hoogten to the United States in the mid-1950s to set up a label here and to become Ray Maxwell. Ray came out to L.A., settled in Anaheim and started Moonglow Records in Hollywood. "He was driving around and when he came out of a market, Ray heard a P.A. system blasting, some guy singing, followed the sound to a garage, in there were four guys called The Paramours, one of the members was Bill Medley. 'I like you guys, like the way you sound.' 'We're on Mercury.' 'I'll buy your contract,' very low keyed, never got excited, 'Gonna start a label, put you on a label.' No sooner does he pay for the contract with Mercury, 'Don't want to sing with those guys, I found another guy,' that was Bobby Hatfield," said Dick Monda of Moonglow.

Arranger Rene Hall said, "Nat Goodman, a former Mercury A&R man, had a contract with Bill Medley, and I helped him put this combination together in my office. They were rehearsing, putting together this combination, writing out the chords for the musicians to play. There were only two or three studios popular in Hollywood at the time. Bill was very talented; he had this R&B projection, which was unusual for a white singer. It was a cross between rhythm and blues and gospel. This was their original stylizing quality. The Righteous Brothers were trying to imitate The Isley Brothers. If you listen carefully, you notice the close relationship to their presentation and The Isley Brothers' lead singer."

After two Paramours singles, Hatfield and Bill Medley came up a new name they reportedly picked up singing for black Marines in an Orange County club. The debut disc as The Righteous Brothers was this uptempo "Little Latin Lupe Lu" on Moonglow, a major local smash… and a national hit in a month and a half. The vast majority of deejays thought they were black, and when they showed up to promote the record, some stations that programmed all-black music had to apologize to the brothers that they had to pull the record from rotation. Despite that, the act performed successfully at the California Club and was mentioned in the KGFJ Soul Magazine, inventing a brand new "blue eyed soul" category.

Remakes: The Kingsmen 1964; The Chancellors 1965; Mitch Ryder & the Detroit Wheels 1966

—

The Rumblers "Boss Strikes Back" Downey/Dot March 8, 1963

Style: Rock 'n' roll
Where from: England/Norwalk CA
Where recorded: Downey, CA

Adrian Lloyd's final release with The Rumblers was "Boss Strikes Back" backed with with Lloyd's vocal on "Sorry (For The Way I Treated You)" on Downey, then on Dot. "I wrote 'I Don't You Need No More' and 'Sorry' with Mike Kalishes," said Lloyd. "I left; they said they fired me; the truth was I was tired of not getting paid, I hustled most of the jobs, else we wouldn't have gotten anything. I threw a fit. Bill Wenzel locked me in a recording studio. They said, 'You're not leaving until you record.' I said, 'I'll throw this microphone through this window. I'll call the cops.' The other Rumblers stayed on; six months later, Bob Jones, the sax player, quit. I left, I didn't want to leave, those guys were living at home, they had more money than me, my grandmother paid my rent. 'Boss' was out and I was washing dishes at Woolworths. I couldn't afford a starter for my '41 blue Plymouth coupe, so I'd park it downhill so I could start it. I would date some of the girls at Wilson High and have the girls push me sometimes. Wenzel's didn't want me to work at Woolworths; they wanted me to tour. Paul Smith, the boss at Woolworths, told me not to quit, 'You're crazy.' We did the Sam Riddle Show and as leader of the band, Sam Riddle gave me a check. Wenzel took the check, said it was for publicity. I got a $57 check from Wenzel's. Wenzel came up with The Chantays and dropped us," but "Boss" persisted.

Answer: The Rumblers "Boss Soul" 1965

—

The Four Jewels "Loaded With Goodies" District/Start/Checker March 1963

Style: Rhythm and blues vocal group
Where from: Washington, DC
Where recorded: Chicago, IL

Sandra Bear, Grace Ruffin, Margie Clark and Carrie Mingo formed this act at Theodore Roosevelt High School as The Impalas. With help from Grace's cousin, Billy Stewart, a pianist for Bo Diddley, they recorded "For the Love of Mike" for Checker in 1961. That's when they found out about a different Impalas, who had sold a million copies of "Sorry (I Ran All the Way Home)" in 1959, so they changed to The Jewels. Then Bo Diddley took The Jewels to Chicago with him. By then, their lead singer, Gloria Jolivet, had married Bo's nephew Ricky Jolivet, who worked as Bo Diddley Jr. As The Four Jewels, they hit in Baltimore with this ballad, "Loaded With Goodies." Then they became The Jewels and had a national hit, "Opportunity."

—

The Drifters "On Broadway" Atlantic March 1963

Style: Soul vocal group
From and recorded in: New York City, NY

Lifted from the title of the Walter Winchell column, "On Broadway," a Jerry Leiber-Mike Stoller/Barry Mann-Cynthia Weil collaboration, was written for The Cookies, and was among the last Drifters songs featuring lead singer Rudy Lewis, who replaced Ben E. King who left the Drifters to be a solo act in 1961. Lewis died of a heart attack in 1964. Phil Spector was an apprentice to Leiber and Stoller at the time, and he played the guitar solo for "On Broadway." Spector learned many of his production techniques watching Leiber and Stoller produce The Drifters.

"Later on, he'd gone pretty much on his own with his own label. We bumped into him on the street and asked him to come by a sit on something we were doing with The Drifters. He played the guitar solo on 'On Broadway,'" said Stoller. "We didn't work a lot together. He just watched us to see what we did and later, Jerry got him his first recording production deal. We had been asked to produce Ray Peterson." Later, Spector had the Crystals record "On Broadway" for an LP.

Remake: George Benson 1978

—

James Brown & the Famous Flames "Prisoner Of Love" King March 1963

Style: Soul
Where from: Macon, GA
Where recorded: Bell Sound Studios, New York City, NY
Original version: Perry Como 1949

"Prisoner Of Love" was the only one of James Brown's releases under Rene Hall's supervision.
Hall said, "He had an orchestra. His orchestra happened to be busy. Sammy Lowe who had done all of James Brown's things asked me, 'Could you cover for me, he wants to record "Prisoner Of Love."' It was in E flat, originally, the orchestration. He found that key quite comfortable. When they got to the bridge, it modulates into the key of G minor, then G major. James told me, 'I don't like it when you change keys on me, why do you change keys on me?' I told him, 'That's the way the tune goes, James.' 'No. No, stay in the same key.' 'I can't stay in the same key, because that will not fit the melody.' 'I'll show you, just play the chords.' I did, he sung it. 'That's going to be quite laughable, because everybody knows it, James.' 'I don't care, if you write it that way, can't you write it that way.' I did and it was a hit, believe it or not."

—

Baby Ray & the Ferns "How's Your Bird" Donna March 30, 1963

Style: Novelty rock 'n' roll
Where from: Pomona, CA
Where recorded: Cucamonga, CA

In the first of three 45s Frank Zappa produced for Bob Keane's Donna label, Baby Ray & the Ferns was Ray Collins with Zappa on this tribute to Steve Allen, "How's Your Bird" backed with a hard-hitting doo wop vocal, "The World's Greatest Sinner," taken from a movie Zappa supposedly had in production on Donna. Other Zappa-involved Donna 45s were by The Heartbreakers and Bob Guy.

—

The Heartbreakers "Every Time I See You" Donna April 1963

Style: Retro doo wop
Where from: Texas/Inland Empire, CA
Where recorded: Cucamonga, CA

"The Heartbreakers were Benny and Joe Rodriguez from Texas," said Max Uballez of The Romancers. "Billy Cardenas [their producer] found them in a church carnival singing in Spanish. They never appeared with instruments." Thus on their several recordings, Uballez supplied The Romancers' band. "The Heartbreakers were part of The Romancers entourage that also included The Sisters and Robert and Ray."

Benny Rodriguez said, "We were too young, back in '59," the year they arrived in L.A. from El Paso. "I was 14, my brother was 12. My brother went to Belvedere Junior High, I went to Roosevelt High. We'd been singing since we were kids, played family parties, people starting noticing us. We both played guitars, trio style done duet. Billy gave us that name, The Heartbreakers," that it was the natural consequence of romance.

Billy Cardenas said, "The Heartbreakers didn't know a lot of songs in English, they wanted to do 'Cradle Rock,' which they remembered from Texas," an original by The Rhythm Heirs on El Paso-based Yucca in 1959. "The Heartbreakers messed it up," said the song's writer, Virgie Gallegos. "They couldn't understand my English, there's a real moral of my song, to help young girls have pride in their body and not have sex to prove their love to a boy."

Uballez said, "The Romancers backed the session. We recorded at Pal Studio. Zappa came in, he had a song he wanted the Heartbreakers to do and Bob Keane had sent us in to do the Zappa song," "Every Time I See You."

—

The Crystals "Da Doo Ron Ron (When He Walked Me Home)" Philles April 1963

Style: Soul vocal group
Where from: Brooklyn, NY or Los Angeles, CA
Where recorded: Gold Star Studios Hollywood, CA
Suggested pairings: The Shirelles "I Met Him On A Sunday" 1958; The Angels "My Boyfriend's Back" 1961

A major hit for The Crystals, "Da Doo Ron Ron (When He Walked Me Home)" drew from recent successful girl group themes. Songwriters Jeff Barry and Ellie Greenwich changed "met him on a Sunday" to "Monday" in this Phil Spector production. The refrain "da doo ron ron" came from nonsense syllables they stuck in as filler, but it was exactly what Phil Spector was looking for, since he didn't want a cerebral lyric getting in the way of his massive production and the tidy boy-meets-girl story line.

Sonny Bono, also a record producer, who hung out at the sessions, recalls Spector asked if the song was "dumb enough," accessible to the teens, the target audience. Spector knew he had a hit with this one, telling Bono on playback, "That's solid gold coming out of that speaker."

Darlene Love said she sang lead on "Da Doo Ron Ron," but her voice was wiped off the tape, Spector replacing her with Crystals lead singer Dolores "La La" Brooks when Darlene asked him for an artist's contract. "When I went to the studio to do 'Da Doo Ron Ron,' Phil taught me the song," said Brooks. "When I walked in the studio, all the musicians were there," packed into a 19 x 24 feet room. As they put down the track, "me and Cher went out to get something to eat. We come back, they're still putting down the track. All of the sudden, when the track is finished, Phil says, 'La La, go in the booth and put down the song now.' I went in there, put down the song. I had trouble with 'Yeah, yeah, yeah, yeah, yeah.' I had trouble because he liked my ending, because it was my ending in my head, and he said, 'I want that again.' I had to double it, and it was hard for me to double it, because I couldn't get together with the 'Yeah, yeah, yeah, yeah,' and then (in lower voice), 'Yeah, yeah, yeah, yeah.' It was confusing. He said, 'La La, try it again.'" And she did.

Remakes: The Ikettes 1966; Ian Matthews 1972; Bo Donaldson & the Heywoods 1974; Shaun Cassidy 1977

—

Bobby Hatfield "Hot Tamales" Moonglow April 26, 1963

Style: Rock 'n' roll
Where from: Anaheim, CA
Where recorded: Hollywood, CA

While their "Little Latin Lupe Lu" was hitting the charts, The Righteous Brothers' tenor Bobby Hatfield recorded "Hot Tamales" as a single with a novelty vocal group backed effort.

—

The Beatles "From Me To You" Vee Jay May 6, 1963

Style: Rock 'n' roll vocal group
Where from: Liverpool, England
Where recorded: England
Suggested pairing: Roy Orbison "Anything You Want (You Got It)" 1989

John Lennon and Paul McCartney wrote this on a bus while The Beatles were touring with Helen Shapiro, a 16-year-old who was more popular in America at the time than they were. They wrote the song as a message to The Beatles' fans, "from me to you." This was the first song to feature The Beatles' falsetto "whoooo." This was a big part of many of their early hits, including "I Want To Hold Your Hand." Paul McCartney learned the "whoooo" from listening to Little Richard.

—

The Essex "Easier Said Than Done" Roulette May 1963

Style: Soul vocal group
Where from: Camp LeJeune, NC
Where recorded: Bell Sound studio, New York City, NY
Suggested pairing: The Grassroots "Sooner Or Later" 1971

This male group with the female Essex lead Anita Humes were five Marines stationed at Camp LeJeune. assigned to the aircraft carrier Essex. The song writer recalled working in the communications department with several teletype machines, which when all were running together, created a beat, which inspired the beat of 'Easier Said Than Done." The flip, "Are You Going My Way," was the designated hit side.

"Easier Said Than Done" was so short that parts of the song had to be spliced together to produce a finished master recording. The song's progression was used in The Grassroots' "Sooner Or Later" in 1971.

—

Marvin Gaye "Pride & Joy" Tamla May 1963

Style: Soul
Where from: Washington, DC
Where recorded: Detroit, MI
Suggested pairings: The Cookies "In Paradise" 1956; The Midnighters "Let's Go Again" 1961

Marvin Gaye's "Pride & Joy" was the third straight and final single by Gaye to use Martha and the Vandellas for background vocals just weeks before "Heat Wave" made that girl group a hit-making act, no longer available for backing.

—

Brian Lord & the Midnighters "The Big Surfer" Vigah/Capitol May 15, 1963

Style: Novelty rock 'n' roll
Where from: Inland Empire, CA
Where recorded: Cucamonga, CA

Pal Studio owner Paul Buff, Frank Zappa and Dave Aerni played guitar behind KFXM DJ Brian Lord & the Midnighters with vocal support by Buff, Zappa and Ray Collins on this JFK spoof, "The Big Surfer," which contained lyrical references to the Peace Corps being sent to Alabama backed with "Not Another One!" about the need for still another B-side title on this JFK-inspired novelty.

Buff and Zappa bought all the copies at local stores to prove to Capitol it was a hit. It was played as a pick hit for seven weeks on radio station KMEN in San Bernardino, CA, likely because Brian Lord was a KMEN DJ. Impressed, Capitol released the 45, pressed 400 copies, then recalled it two weeks later when civil rights activist Medgar Evers was killed in Mississippi on June 12, 1963.

—

Ned & Nelda "Hey Nelda" Vigah 1963

Style: Novelty rock 'n' roll duet
Where from: Inland Empire, CA
Where recorded: Cucamonga, CA

"Hey Nelda" by Ned and Nelda (Frank Zappa and Ray Collins) was an over-the-top parody of Paul & Paula's "Hey, Paula" backed with the even sillier "Surf Along With Ned and Nelda" on Vigah.
After JFK's death in November 1963, there was no more Vigah.

In the '70s, both sides were reissued on a Moxie ep in 1975.

About this, record collector Richard Gibson recalled, "My brother, David Gibson had Moxie Records. He pressed 500 copies of the Zappa; Zappa called him up and said, 'I'm really flattered you printed up my record, but don't do that again.'" He didn't.

—

Jan & Dean "Surf City" Liberty May 17, 1963

Style: Rock 'n' roll duet
Where from: Bel Air, CA
Where recorded: Hollywood, CA

Jan & Dean hit #1 for the first time with this rock & roll creation that became reality, "Surf City" with duet harmonies by "Surf City" writer Brian Wilson of the Beach Boys, which caused many to think the Beach Boys and Jan & Dean's harmonies were what surf music was all about.

"It was a great thing for Brian," said Jan & Dean's Dean Torrence. "He wasn't going to complete the song because he was tired of it. We all got along. We were fans of theirs; they were fans of us. 'Would you like to help us with the tracks?' You can hear Brian's voice, we thought we had disguised it." This was also a hit with the term "oldie but a goodie" in the lyrics.

With a switch in labels (Dore vs. Liberty) came the hits, according to the duo's Dean Torrence. "All in all, when it was all geared up, Liberty was the right choice, they were learning as they were going along too, lot further ahead on the learning curve than Dore, had Liberty been distributed by a major, we would have been further along, didn't have the juice a major label had. Our friends The Beach Boys had a major label, they had advertising, merchandising and PR."

When "Surf City" was released, distributors contacted Capitol about the new Beach Boys 45, which caused Capitol to order Wilson not to do outside sessions, an order later rescinded. After Surf City" hit, session drummer Earl Palmer was re-called for all additional Jan & Dean hits.

—

Bill Medley "If You're Lying, You'll Be Crying" Moonglow May 24, 1963

Style: Rock 'n' roll
Where from: Santa Ana, CA
Where recorded: Hollywood, CA

About a month after Bobby Hatfield's debut 45, bass voiced Bill Medley of The Righteous Brothers was also broken out as a single on this fine blues rocker "If You're Lying, You'll Be Crying."
After the tepid results of this experiment, it was back to the Righteous Brothers for Hatfield and Medley.

—

The Baggys "El Surfer" Pipeline May 31, 1963

Style: Novelty
From and recorded in: Hollywood, CA
Suggested pairing: Ray Barretto "El Watusi" 1963

Still another studio group involving producer Joe Saraceno, who had created The Mar-Kets and The Routers with Russ Regan, The Baggys, surfer slang for shorts, sang this to the tune of "El Watusi" by Ray Barretto, with KFWB DJ Gene Weed challenging a heavily accented Mexican ("hey gremmie") on how to surf on the waves in "El Surfer," taken from The Chantays' hit.

—

Johnny Niles "Donna I Understand" Mercury 1963/Spindle Top 1963

Style: Rock 'n' roll
Where from: Brooklyn, NY
Where recorded: Hollywood, CA

Harry Nilsson recorded first as Johnny Niles on this soft teen ballad with a spoken break, "Donna I Understand" backed with the "Short Shorts"-derived rocking novelty with girl group "yea yea" backing and a stinging guitar break titled "Wig Job" with a possible outtake of this material with a sax replacing the guitar break.

The record was reissued by Harry Nilsson on Spindle Top. Nilsson then partnered with John Marascalco as Bo-Pete and the Foto-Fi Four.

—

The Perez Brothers "I'm Truly Truly Yours" Olfies/Wolfie May 31, 1963

Style: Latino doo wop duet
From and recorded in: Pacoima, CA
Original version: Robert & Johnny 1958

Ralph "Gordy" and Louis "Donsie" Perez were the Perez Brothers, who recorded this Chicano/low rider anthem, "I'm Truly Truly Yours" on Olfies, owned by Ofie Martinez, a woman who broadcast on KVFM from her record store in the Pacoima area of the San Fernando Valley, according to Billy Cardenas.

Vibes player Gil Rocha recalled that, after his band The Silhouettes lost vocalist Ritchie Valens, the Perez brothers approached him. "They were from Canoga Park," said Rocha. "They were local, started singing really young with a local group, named after a guy that played sax. We played all around town. Ofie saw them and put up the money to record them." The Perez Brothers were backed by The Gents with Danny Rosales on piano and Sal Barragan from The Silhouettes on sax and conga; Hector Barragan, keyboard; Ralph, guitar and timbales and Louie doubled on bass.

—

Bobby Jameson "Gotta Find My Roogalator" Penthouse 1963

Style: Rock 'n' roll
Where from: Glendale, CA
Where recorded: Hollywood , CA
Suggested pairing: Larry Bright "Mojo Workout" 1960

Frank Zappa arranged Bobby Jameson on a redo of the Lowell Fulson blues classic, "Reconsider Baby." Zappa then wrote and arranged Jameson on "Gotta Find My Roogalator," a term Jameson picked up from a Johnny Rivers record on Penthouse, owned by Mattel Toys heir Ken Handler. "I believed roogalator was similar to 'mojo,' like 'Got My Mojo Working.' I started fiddling around with the word and told Johnny I had written a pretty good song, but never got him to record it. I think John may have written his own version, but I've never heard it," wrote Jameson. "I talked to Frank about doing another record, and told him Handler was sorry for not giving him credit on 'Reconsider Baby.' Frank really didn't seem to care all that much about it, but I assured him he'd get credit if we did anything else. I asked Frank to listen to 'Gotta Find My Roogalator' and he liked the song. He said he knew exactly who he would use on the session."

The session included Wrecking Crew members Louis Morell, guitar; Robert West, guitar; Carol Kaye, bass; Larry Knechtel, piano; Gene Estes and/or John Gueri, drums. "Frank played guitar and arranged the song," Jameson wrote. "In reality, Frank and I produced the record, but of course were not given credit, but Frank was at least credited as the arranger." Then the release was pulled because of Handler's special proclivities. Penthouse owner Handler promised to promote the record, and invited Jameson to his house for a meeting. 'I'd like you to spend the night here Bobby.' 'I looked at him closely and said, 'Why, what'd you have in mind?' He said, 'I want you to stay here with me.'" Jameson rebuffed him, and the record was as dead as Jameson's faith in Handler.

—

The Crossfires "Fiberglass Jungle" Capco 1963

Style: Rock 'n' roll group
Where from: Westchester, CA
Where recorded: Hollywood, CA

Later known as The Turtles, The Crossfires had two lead vocalists, Westchester High School schoolmates Mark Volman and Howard Kaylan, who doubled as the band's twin sax players. The group also included Al Nichol, lead guitar, vocals and keyboard; Jim Tucker, rhythm guitar; Chuck Portz, bass; and from Inglewood High School, Don Murray, drums and harmonica.

In summer 1963, they cut this hot rod-entitled instrumental "Fiberglass Jungle" on Capco, a recording deal doubtless set up by their employer DJ Reb Foster who owned the local Revelaire Club, where they worked through their conversion from The Crossfires to The Turtles two years later in summer 1965.

—

Stevie Wonder "Fingertips" Tamla 1963

Style: Soul
Where from: Detroit, MI
Where recorded: Regal Theater, Chicago, IL

At age 12, Stevie Wonder was part of a Motown package tour called "The Motortown Revue," which on March 10, 1963 visited the Regal Theatre in Chicago, where Wonder's performance was recorded. At song's end, when Wonder was being pulled off the stage to give way to the waiting Marvelettes, Wonder fed off the crowd reaction and he picked up the song "Fingertips," again a riff from "Mary Had a Little Lamb" on the harmonica with additional backing by The Marvelettes' band, who were just taking the stage and finished enough of the song to create part two of "Fingertips," a title lyric that appears nowhere in the song, probably titled off the overall sound.

—

The Orlons "Not Me" Cameo June 1963

Style: Soul
From and recorded in: Philadelphia, PA
Original version: Gary U.S. Bonds 1962

The Orlons' "Not Me" contained the original, not the revised lyrics found in the second issue of The Bonds' original "Not Me."

—

Major Lance "The Monkey Time" Okeh June 1963

Style: Soul
From and recorded in: Chicago, IL

"With The Impressions, we didn't have a hit record," said Curtis Mayfield. "The fellows used to pout lots of time, 'Hey that could've been our song.' It wasn't meant for us. I couldn't see The Impressions, we were too into our thing to do the tune, we paid the consequences, he had a hit, we didn't." Even so, the uncredited group on "The Monkey Time" was The Impressions. "Major Lance had a good habit of going into the closet, pulling out the songs I threw in there, saying this'll never happen," added Mayfield.

—

Doris Troy "Just One Look" Atlantic June 1963

Style: Soul
From and recorded in: New York City, NY

Having twice recorded as Doris Payne, Doris Troy, born Doris Higginson in the Bronx, hit big with this rhythmic soul rocker, "Just One Look," as a songwriter demo. No recording session was scheduled, so the demo was quickly released, and it charted right away.

Remake: The Hollies 1964

—

The Ran-Dells "Martian Hop" Chairman June 1963

Style: Novelty doo wop group
Where from: Wildwood, NJ
Where recorded: Bell Studios, New York City, NY

Space age and novelty combined for "Martian Hop" by The Ran-Dells, brothers Robert and Steven Rappaport and cousin John Spirt. While Steven attended Brandeis University in Waltham, Mass, he had access to the school's recording equipment. Taking the sound effects of "Moon Maid" from the album Electronic Music by the Dutch outfit The Electrosoniks, which merged electronic music and jazz, Steven put nonsense doo wop style lyrics over it. With the help of songwriter Gerry Goffin, the three got a deal with Don Kirshner, who had just begun the Chairman label, with distribution by London Records. As "My Favorite Martian" was a popular CBS-TV show, the single almost took orbit.

—

Wilson Pickett "It's Too Late" Double L June 1963

Style: Soul
Where from: Detroit, MI
Where recorded: New York City, NY
Original version: Solomon Burke 1963

When Wilson Pickett's version of "It's Too Late" was shopped to the Atlantic label, they wanted the song, but not the singer, so "It's Too Late" was given to Solomon Burke, who recorded it first, then it was covered by Pickett. Both versions charted, with Burke competing against Pickett, who was later signed by Atlantic.

—

Inez & Charlie Foxx "Mockingbird" Symbol June 22, 1963

Style: Soul
Where from: Greensboro, NC
Where recorded: New York City, NY
Suggested pairing: Aretha Franklin "Mockingbird" 1967 (recorded prior to Inez & Charlie Foxx)

As with "Bo Diddley" by Bo Diddley, the story of a promised diamond ring in "Mockingbird" is based on a traditional American folk song/lullaby sometimes known as "Hush Little Baby." Though Inez Foxx had several recordings, including the understated blues vocal "A Feeling (That I Can't Explain)" on Brunswick in 1960, Inez and Charlie Foxx were untested as a brother and sister act when they approached Juggy Murray of Sue Records. In the finished "Mockingbird" session, Inez sang, Charlie answered and the compelling back-and-forth wordplay was a national hit.

Remakes: Aretha Franklin 1967; Barry Goldberg featuring Clydie King 1972; Carly Simon & James Taylor 1974

—

The Supremes "A Breathtaking Guy" Motown June 1963

Style: Soul vocal group
From and recorded in: Detroit, MI
Original title: "A Breath Taking, First Sight Soul Shaking, One Night Love Making, Next Day Heartbreaking Guy"

The emergence of The Supremes was anything but breathtaking. First issued with an unheard of 15-word title, this song was quickly shortened, creating an instant collector's item. The first title was taken from the lyrics of this cha cha beat.

This was The Supremes' most major hit to date after five previous Supremes 45s, three of them on Motown. A fave of low riders and cruisers, "A Breathtaking Guy" charted first in the Inland Empire and in L.A. in June 1963.

—

Garnet Mimms & the Enchanters "Cry Baby" United Artists July 19, 1963

Style: Soul vocal group
From and recorded in: Philadelphia, PA

In 1957, 24-year-old Garnet Mimms put together his own post-military doo wop quintet, The Gainors, with an Evening Star singer, Samuel Bell; and three other singers; soon-to-be soul star Howard Tate, Willie Combo and John Jefferson, on "You Must Be an Angel" for Red Top, a small local label. Signed by Cameo Records, The Gainors released "The Secret." Zola Pearnell, a Philly native who'd been performing for some time in Europe, and Charles Boyer joined Garnet Mimms for his next release. Bert Berns and Jerry Ragovoy helped create "Cry Baby," especially the spoken passage ("... even though you made a fool of me so many times before...") with gospel warblers Cissy Houston, Sylvia Shemwell and Dee Dee Warwick replacing The Enchanters, who probably hadn't even been named yet.

—

Billy Abbott & the Jewels "Groovy Baby" Parkway July 1963

Style: Soul vocal group
From and recorded in: Philadelphia, PA

Billy Abbott's subtle ballad "Groovy Baby" had backing by The Jewels, who were actually The Tymes using a pseudonym.

—

The Angels "My Boyfriend's Back" Smash July 1963

Style: Girl group rock 'n' roll
From and recorded in: New York City, NY

Songwriter Bob Feldman witnessed an altercation between a girl and a tough-looking boy who wore a leather jacket. The girl yelled at him for telling lies about her at school and actually said the two phrases that would become lyrics to the song, "My boyfriend's back and you're gonna be in trouble... you're gonna be sorry you were ever born." Feldman took the phrase to writing partners Jerry Goldstein and Richard Gottehrer, from which "My Boyfriend's Back" was created. Recorded as a demo intended for The Shirelles, The Angels' demo was released as a single on Smash and quickly hit #1.

An oldies version (a reissue after the hit has run its course) was also released, on which the lyrics, "My boyfriend's back, he's gonna save my reputation" is heard twice, once before and once after the break. On the hit version, the ending section comes in immediately after the "hey la"s that follow "If I were you I'd take a permanent vacation."

—

Martha and the Vandellas "(Love Is Like a) Heat Wave" Gordy July 1963

Style: Soul vocal group
From and recorded in: Detroit, MI
Original title: "Heat Wave"
Suggested pairing: Lovin' Spoonful "Do You Believe In Magic" 1966

"Heat Wave" was about desire, not the weather. The title of the 1963 single was "Heat Wave" with no reference to love, which was added on after the fact. Some hear gospel roots with call and response vocals in this song. Regardless, it amounted to a great summertime hit.

—

Mr. Clean "Mr. Clean" Original Sound July 1963

Style: Novelty rock 'n' roll
Where from: Ontario, CA or San Gabriel/Pomona, CA
Where recorded: Cucamonga, CA
Suggested pairing: Richard Berry & the Pharaohs "Have Love Will Travel" 1959

With vocal backing to the approximate tune of Richard Berry's "Have Love Will Travel" by the most-apropos Sweethearts with Berry's ex, Dorothy Berry, Mr. Clean sang at Pal about "Mr. Clean" backed with the doo wop blues "Jessie Lee" for Original Sound. "I don't know if he had a name, that's all I knew him by," said Paul Buff. "He was a black guy," bald headed like the Mr. Clean character of TV commercial fame. He was backed by "some people he'd brought in. Zappa was connected with them at the time. Likely Mr. Clean was from Ontario or San Gabriel, Pomona. I didn't have anything to do with him, Zappa did." Zappa told Dr. Demento Mr. Clean was Bob Davis, taking his act to small clubs in the area, who then joined the Marines in 1970.

—

The Beach Boys "Surfer Girl" Capitol July 16, 1963

Style: Rock 'n' roll
Where from: Hawthorne, CA
Where recorded: Hollywood, CA
Suggested pairing: Snow White & the Seven Dwarves "When You Wish Upon A Star" 1939

The Beach Boys' first ballad was this Brian Wilson composition about his girlfriend at the time, "Surfer Girl," with David Marks replacing Al Jardine and Mike Love on lead backed with the hot rod "Little Deuce Coupe" about a modified 1932 Model B Ford (with a lyric about "pink slip daddy" by KFWB DJ Roger Christian) known as a deuce coupe with Hal Blaine's drumming dubbed over Dennis Wilson's drumming.

—

The Righteous Brothers "My Babe" Moonglow July 20, 1963

Style: Rock 'n' roll
Where from: Orange County, CA

After an aborted attempt to break out the duet's Bobby Hatfield and Bill Medley as single artists, this second 45 by The Righteous Brothers was "My Babe" backed with "Fee-Fi-Fidily-I-Oh" on Moonglow, which took a little less than two months to hit. "Several labels wanted to distribute it nationally, this guy from Vee Jay wanted to distribute," said Dick Monda, "but Ray Maxwell couldn't understand everything, Then Maxwell found a distributor to take his records, he goes back, Vee Jay thinks he doesn't like the deal, upping the ante, up and up, selling records like crazy, he gets an enormous advance, does okay nationally, not great, they lost a little faith. They only did a one record deal with him, 'My Babe' comes out, selling records the same, in late 1963, Atlantic makes the real deal with him, handles all the records with him. That's when Moonglow entered into a distribution agreement with Atco Records."

—

Hollywood Persuaders "Tijuana Surf" Original Sound August 1963

Style: Surf instrumental
Where recorded: Pal Studio, Cucamonga, CA
Suggested pairing: The Marketts "Surfer Stomp" 1961; Herb Alpert & the Tijuana Brass "The Lonely Bull" 1962

The first of three-in-a-row Original Sound singles with Frank Zappa involvement was Hollywood Persuaders on "Tijuana Surf," a collaboration of Pal Studio's Paul Buff of Alta Loma and Frank Zappa who lived in the studio. Buff recalled of the title that may well have been influenced by Herb Alpert's uber popular Tijuana Brass, "'Tijuana Surf' was all me on piano, bass, drums and organ. I went to a music store and rented an alto sax, cost $15, took it back to my studio, spent the weekend learning how to play sax, took it back Monday. In the process, learned how to play it and recorded 'Tijuana Surf.' Maybe LaBoe named it. I had this tendency to sound Chicano. Maybe I heard a cha cha group or something. I ended up as partner with Art LaBoe in his studio."

Reissued on the Mexican Gamma label, "that record was #1 in Mexico for nine months." Zappa recalled. "'Tijuana Surf' sold 5,000 to 8,000 copies in Fresno and eating it in the rest of the U.S. Some wise dude decided to release it in Mexico, where it sold 150,000 copies and was #1 for 17 weeks," said Zappa to Les Carter on KPPC.

—

The Crystals "Then He Kissed Me" Philles August 1963

Style: Soul vocal group
Where from: Los Angeles, CA
Where recorded: New York City, NY
Suggested pairings: James Booker "Gonzo" 1959; Bobby Darin "18 Yellow Roses" 1963; The Darnells "Too Hurt To Cry, Too Much In Love To Say Goodbye" 1963; The Beach Boys "Sloop John B" 1966; Bruce Springsteen "Racing in the Street"

For this and other songs, Phil Spector used his "Wall Of Sound" technique, meaning long hours in the studio for the musicians. As recalled by his engineer Larry Levine, Spector didn't allow them to take breaks on the theory that if they tired, their playing wouldn't be "individualistic," but blend in to the wall.

Original member and new lead singer La La Brooks of the first Brooklyn-based Crystals sang lead on "Then He Kissed Me," as she was the only member who could sing "He's a Rebel" at live performances, recreating L.A.-based Crystals member Darlene Love's hit vocal. Spector asked 15-year-old La La had she ever been kissed. "Yeah," she replied. "My little boyfriend at 13 years kissed me on my mouth at the door. But not kiss kiss—you know what I'm saying?" Spector dimmed the lights in the studio and instructed, 'Think of somebody kissing you.'" Love recalled, "I was a kid, so I'm not going to think like that. So he would turn off the lights, I would have a little light on my music, on my words, and then he said, 'Now, concentrate.' 'Well, he walked up to me and he asked me if I wanted to dance.' Spector said, 'That's the way you do it!' So I guess he had to train my mind to think that I was talking about a boy. He knew how to get things out of you."

After this hit, Spector lost interest in The Crystals and turned his attention to The Ronettes, kiss or no kiss.

—

Roy Orbison "Mean Woman Blues" Monument August 1963

Style: Rock 'n' roll
Where from: Texas
Where recorded: Nashville, TN
Original version: Elvis Presley 1957
Earlier version: Jerry Lee Lewis 1957
Suggested pairing: Elvis Presley "Hard Headed Woman" 1958

Issued on LP and EP only, "Mean Woman Blues" began on the soundtrack for Elvis Presley's 1957 movie "Loving You." After a Jerry Lee Lewis version in 1957, "Mean Woman Blues" was issued as the flipside to Roy Orbison's hit "Blue Bayou," which hit #5 on the Billboard Hot 100 music charts.

—

The Ronettes "Be My Baby" Philles August 1963

Style: Soul vocal group
Where from: Spanish Harlem, NY
Where recorded: Gold Star, Hollywood, CA
Suggested pairings: Frankie Lymon & the Teenagers "Why Do Fools Fall In Love" 1956; The Beach Boys "Don't Worry Baby" 1964; The Four Seasons "Rag Doll" 1964

After a remarkably short career as Ronnie and the Relatives with "I Want A Boy" and " I'm Gonna Quit While I'm Ahead" in 1961 and 1962, the group became The Ronettes with "Silhouettes" in May 1962. But after their "Good Girls," The Ronettes quit while not ahead in early 1963. As pre-teens, Ronnie's mother demanded her release from Colpix and got it, mainly because there were no hits. That all quickly changed. Phil Spector flew Ronnie Bennett to Hollywood to record the just-composed "Be My Baby," inspired by the flame generated by Phil and Ronnie. Leaving the other two Ronettes behind, she laid down the lead track with backing voices of Cher, Sonny, Darlene Love and about 10 other singers, all of whom were multi-tracked.

Ronnie based her unique "uh oh" hiccup on the unique hiccup used by local singer Frankie Lymon & the Teenagers in the mega doo wop hit "Why Do Fools Fall In Love" from 1956. With this hit, Spector transferred his efforts from The Crystals to The Ronettes.

Remakes: Andy Kim 1970; Cissy Houston 1971

—

Paul Revere & the Raiders "Louie Louie" Sande/Columbia August 25, 1963/ November 2, 1963

Style: Rock 'n' roll
Where from: Boise, ID
Where recorded: Portland, OR

After about three years in L.A. and a few chart records, Paul Revere & the Raiders returned to hometown Idaho, where they helped spark the Northwest rock sound with their first garage-style remake of Richard Berry & the Pharaohs' R&B classic "Louie Louie" backed with "Night Train" on the one-release Sande, an early hit in Boise. "Louie Louie" was reissued on Columbia, which led to Paul Revere & the Raiders being signed by that label as their first 1960s rock act, predating The Byrds and all other late '60s rockers that took Columbia to the top of the charts.

—

The Rotations "The Cruncher" Original Sound August 31, 1963

Style: Rock 'n' roll instrumental
From and recorded in: Cucamonga, CA

Also with Frank Zappa involvement, Paul Buff played all The Rotations instrumentation on this organ instrumental "The Cruncher" with surf sound effects with a "Peter Gunn" progression and a Mike Dineri sax break backed with the surfer guitar-based "Heavies" with wave sound effects on Original Sound. According to Paul Buff, "'The Cruncher' is me, except the sax, the other side was me and Dave Aerni."

—

The Impressions "It's All Right" ABC September 1963

Style: Soul vocal group
From and recorded in: Chicago, IL

"It just came natural," said Curtis Mayfield of his debut hit with The Impressions after several false starts. About this easy-going moderate tempo, "It's All Right," songwriter and lead singer Mayfield said, "It made me realize my talents wasn't so much my trying to be talented, it was a gift I found early in life and I chose to follow it."

—

The Beatles "She Loves You" Swan September 16, 1963

Style: Rock 'n' roll group
From and recorded in: England
Suggested pairings: Elvis Presley "All Shook Up" 1956; The Isley Brothers "Twist and Shout" 1962; Bobby Rydell "Forget Him" 1963

In a sense an answer to Bobby Rydell's "Forget Him," The Beatles on "She Loves You" was about a different suggestion over a love affair. As Paul McCartney said, "I'd planned an answering song where a couple of us would sing 'She loves you' and the other ones would answer 'Yeah Yeah.' We decided that was a crummy idea but at least we then had the idea of a song called 'She Loves You.' Regarding the falsetto exaltation that occurs at the song's manic peak, McCartney once explained, "The 'wooooo' was taken from the Isley Brothers' 'Twist and Shout.' We stuck it in everything." Some hear an edit between the lines "I think it's only fair" into "pride can hurt you too."

—

Marlow Stewart and His 4 Guitars "Riptide" Variety Productions 1963

Style: Rock 'n' roll instrumental
Where from: Anaheim, CA
Where recorded: Hollywood, CA
Suggested pairing: Dick Dale "Miserlou" 1962

Marlow Stewart, also known as Marlow Hendrix, was born "just outside of Watts in 1939," then lived in an area of Anaheim in 1955, which became Stanton in 1956. He attended Pacifica High School in Anaheim near Garden Grove. He came from a show-biz background: "Mark Hendrix, my dad was from North Carolina and managed various theaters in Los Angeles and was the host of 'Rocket To Stardom.' I was playing guitar since I was eight. At age 14, I did 'Riptide.' The day before we did it, my dad told me about a deal he had [with] a low-profile FM radio station, KNAC, in Lakewood. 'I've got time at the station, can you write a song real quick?' I had one day, that's what you come up with when you get a day to write a song. I used four guitars, they called me Marlow Stewart" to avoid nepotism charges. "I had a Hawaiian steel guitar and an old singing cowboy guitar that glowed in the dark and played all four of the guitars. They couldn't all be tuned, so they were overdubbed at Garrison Recording studio, a little four-track place in Long Beach.

In mid-August, it was apparently released untitled and a contest was held at his dad's theater. At contest's end in October, the instrumental was titled "Riptide'" backed with the earliest known example of extreme sports, "Sky Surfin'" by Marlow Stewart & His 4 Guitars on Variety Productions.

Stewart added, "I ripped off Dick Dale on 'Riptide.' He was my hero. There's a lot of 'Miserlou,' it took me a long time to double pick." His father arranged for Marlow to do a photograph session at Compton Airport for the picture sleeve. There was more promotion. "At that time, Long Beach was a Navy town," Stewart recalled. "If you buy my record, you get a free ticket, buy a ticket, get a free record." Not too many intact sleeves exist as a coupon had to be cut out of the sleeve to get the free ticket. "The guys in the Navy took them all over the world."

Soon, Stewart was playing with the Long Beach-based Illusions on "Ooh Poo Pah Doo" and doing radio, having taken over his father's interview show for about a year. "They gave me a script and I played a record. You played music to cover up the sound of a scratchy record. When I had a radio show, I interviewed Dick Dale. He still calls me Mark."

—

Sky Saxon & the Soul Rockers "Go Ahead and Cry" Conquest September 1963

Style: Rock 'n' roll
Where from: Utah
Where recorded: Hollywood, CA
Suggested pairing: Freddy Cannon "Palisades Park"

Sounding like Bobby Vee or Lou Christie, Sky Saxon & the Soul Rockers were on this girl group and bass man doo wop backed rocking teen ode out of Freddy Cannon's "Palisades Park" entitled "Go Ahead and Cry" backed with and a similarly teen rockaballad, Ritchie Marsh's "They Say," co-composed by Pat Vegas with a big horn finish on Conquest in September 1963. "Conquest was my label," said Saxon. "Pat Vegas and I hung out together, they were really good guys, we were all hanging around Hollywood. When the name Sky was suggested, at the time it had more of a country and western feel. Saxon was a name we came up with after going through a series of words."

—

The Trashmen "Surfer Bird" Garrett 1963

Style: Garage rock
From and recorded in: Minneapolis, MN
Suggested pairings: The Rivingtons "Papa Oom Mow Mow" 1961; The Rivingtons "The Bird Is the Word" 1962

First known as Jim Thaxter & the Travelers on "Sally Jo" for Ariel, The Trashmen copped two songs from the Rivingtons, an R&B group out of L.A., combining their "The Bird Is the Word" and "Papa-Oom-Mow-Mow" in this wild garage rock vocal with all random noises like clucks and shrieks and whatnot, "Surfer Bird." The Trashmen were Tony Andreason, lead guitar and vocals; Dal Winslow, guitar and vocals; Steve Wahrer on drums and vocals and Bob Reed on bass guitar. When they got word of "Surfer Bird," The Rivingtons were not amused despite The Trashmen's claims they heard the songs played by Wisconsin-based The Sorenson Brothers. The Rivingtons won the inevitable lawsuit.

This song reportedly sold 30,000 copies in its first weekend.

After all this, the urban legend that the song had been written by Leonard Bernstein to show his disdain for rock 'n' roll by proving that any song could become a hit was just that, a legend.

Remakes: The Ramones 1977; The Cramps

—

The Kingsmen "Louie Louie" Jerden/Wand October 1963

Style: Garage rock
From and recorded in: Portland, OR
Original version: Richard Berry & the Pharaohs 1957
Suggested pairings: The Rockyfellers "Killer Joe" 1963; The Vibrations "Dancing Danny" 1963; The Premiers "Farmer John" 1964; The Kinks "You Really Got Me" 1964; The Vibrations "My Girl Sloopy" 1964; Bob Dylan "Like a Rolling Stone" 1965; The Rolling Stones "Get Off My Cloud" 1965; The Remains "Why Do I Cry" 1965; Dino, Desi & Billy "I'm A Fool" 1965; The Troggs "Wild Thing" 1966; Rare Breed "Beg Borrow and Steal" 1966; The Righteous Brothers "You've Lost That Lovin' Feeling" 1966; The Royal Guardsmen "Snoopy Vs. Red Baron" 1966; Frank Zappa "Plastic People" 1967; Lou Reed "Vicious" 1972; Hot Chocolate "Brother Louie" 1973; The Outlaws "Don't Tread On Me" 1975; Bruce Springsteen "Sherry Darling" 1980; Rick James "Super Freak" 1981; GG Allin "Don't Talk To Me" 1983
Other "Louie Louie" versions: Rockin' Robin Roberts 1963; Paul Revere & the Raiders 1963

After Rockin' Robin Roberts got some Seattle play with his garage remake of "Louie Louie," another Pacific Northwest band, The Kingsmen, gave the song a try with Jack Ely on lead vocals. The Kingsmen's version was so garbled, with mistakes such as Ely coming in early on one verse, that imaginary fake lyrics began to appear, "Every night and day, I play with my thing. I f--k you girl, oh, all the way. On my bed, I'll lay her there. I feel my bone, ah, in her hair."

The alleged dirty lyrics were submitted to the FBI by some concerned citizens, which the agency compared against the copyrighted published lyrics. The offensive lyrics the FBI lab workers were listening for were: "Lou-ai Lou-ai Oh, no, Grab her way down low. There is a fine little girl waiting for me, She is just a girl across the way, When I take her all alone, She's never the girl I lay at home. She had a rag on, I moved above It won't be long she'll slip it off I held her in my arm and then And I told her I'd rather lay her again. A fine little bitch, she waits for me; she gets her kicks on top of me. Each night I take her out all alone; she ain't the kind I lay at home Each night at ten, I lay her again; I f--k my girl all kinds of ways. And on that chair, I lay her there; I felt my boner in her hair. If she's got a rag on, I'll move above; It won't be long, she'll slip it off. I'll take her in my arms again; tell her I'd rather lay her again."

When the Indiana governor declared it pornographic, the FBI launched an extensive investigation in 1964 and asked the Indiana Broadcasters Association to ban it. The investigation spanned offices in several states, with technicians listening to the song at different speeds trying to discern any obscene lyrics. None were found. The FBI eventually declared it "unintelligible at any speed."

Paul Revere and The Raiders, also on the Northwest touring scene, recorded their version the day after The Kingsmen at the same studio for release on Sande, which was picked up, along with the band, by Columbia. Ely later tried to capitalize on the success of "Louie Louie" by releasing similar songs on his own, including "Louie Louie 66," "Love That Louie," and "Louie Go Home."

—

The Pyramids "Penetration" Best October 1963

Style: Rock instrumental
From and recorded in: Long Beach, CA

The Long Beach Polytechnic High School rock band called The Pyramids hit big with this surf-styled instrumental, "Penetration," their second release for a local label, Best. The Pyramids—Skip Mercier, lead guitar; Willy Glover, rhythm guitar; Steve Leonard, bass guitar; Tom Phillips, saxophone and Ron McMullen, drums—took their name from the pyramid symbol of an on-campus fraternity. "Skip was in a fraternity called Sphinx, since he was in that, we called ourselves the Pyramids," said Glover.

They were recorded by John Hodge. "John Hodge went to another school, used to live by the Los Alamitos racetrack, he had a lot of kids in his family, he was a very poor kid," said Glover. "He said, 'I'm gonna make you a star.' I said, 'Okay.' Two to three weeks later, we're in the recording studio, we're doing The Pyramids. I don't know where he got the money from. As far as I can remember, we were called Willie & the Pyramids. "We put the 'Pipeline' rhythm to 'Penetration.' That wasn't supposed to be the hit. DJs were told to play 'Here Comes Marsha.' They flipped it over, played the instrumental, boom!"

Though often grouped with surf hits, Glover recalled "the title came from a group member who was very sexual. He said, 'Let's think of all the titles that have to do with sex... 'Contact,' 'Pressure' 'Penetration.'

This song hit first in the Inland Empire, and months later in L.A.

—

Otis Redding "Pain In My Heart" Volt October 1963

Style: Soul
Where from: Macon, GA
Where recorded: Memphis, TN
Suggested pairing: Irma Thomas "Ruler Of My Heart"

One of Otis Redding's better and most soulful ballads, "Pain In My Heart" wasn't a major hit, but is an enduring classic.

—

Betty Everett "You're No Good" Vee Jay October 1963

Style: Soul
From and recorded in: Chicago, IL
Original version: Dee Dee Warwick 1963

Buddy Guy said of Betty Everett, "What a great singer. I'd talk to her and Otis Rush who gave me hope." Before Vee Jay, Everett recorded for the blues label Cobra. "At that time, Cobra didn't have a talent scout," said Guy. "The president, Eli Toscano, would go out and get everything he had, engineering it all himself. I didn't know if that made it better for blues players, but you get ready to record, you go straight to the horse's head. You didn't have to go through anybody else, we had Willie Dixon hanging around then. It was great fun in those days."

Remakes: The Swinging Blue Jeans 1964; The Three Souls 1965; The Moon-Dawgs 1966; Rosie and the Originals 1973; Linda Ronstadt 1974; Elvis Costello 1989

—

Hank Jacobs "So Far Away" Sue October 1963

Style: Soul instrumental
From and recorded in: Los Angeles, CA

After several years of collaboration, organ player Hank Jacobs and Kent Harris hooked up with Sue Records owner Juggy Murray. Harris said, "I produced him on 'So Far Away.' He was a kid who played organ in a church choir, he was 16 or something, eastside around Central Ave. 'East Side.' That was the title he wanted, the other side was 'Monkey Hips & Rice,' we thought that side was going to be a hit. Juggy came out here on a convention, I told him I had a master I had, he bought it on the spot."

—

Marvin Gaye "Can I Get a Witness" Tamla October 1963

Style: Soul
Where from: Washington, DC
Where recorded: Detroit, MI
Suggested pairings: The Three Sounds "Here We Come" 1962; Billy Storm "Baby, Don't Look Down" 1964; Leon Haywood "The Truth About Money" 1964

With uncredited backing by The Supremes, Lamont Dozier said of the inspiration for Marvin Gaye's "Can I Get a Witness" was "a phrase that was quite prominent in the church I attended and most black churches in Detroit, those revival meetings so to speak. The preachers would often yell out over the crowd, 'Can I get a witness?'"

—

Tommy James & the Shondells "Hanky Panky" Snap/Red Fox/Roulette 1963/1966

Style: Rock 'n' roll group
From and recorded in: Michigan
Original version: The Raindrops "Hanky Panky" 1963
Suggested pairing: Swingin Medallions "Double Shot Of My Baby's Love" 1965

Tommy James heard "Hanky Panky" performed by a local band in Michigan. Working at a record shop, he found that "Hanky Panky" had been recorded by The Raindrops with the flip side, "That Boy John," about President John F. Kennedy, and withdrawn from the market when JFK was assassinated. James had his band, The Shondells, the name of which was taken from singing star Troy Shondell, recorded "Hanky Panky" on the small local Snap label. Somehow, the record found its way to Pittsburgh, PA, where it was played on the air and sold as many as 80,000 copies on the bootleg Red Fox label before James was contacted. When he arrived in Pittsburgh, he was a big star without any Shondells, so he recruited a new band previously known as The Reconteurs. From there, James and the Shondells went to New York and signed with Roulette, which reissued "Hanky Panky" into a number one hit.

—

The Marketts "Out of Limits" Warner Brothers

Style: Rock instrumental
From and recorded in: Los Angeles, CA
Original title: "Outer Limits"

The Marketts were in fact the so-called Wrecking Crew, the assemblage of the most successful session musicians in the L.A./Hollywood area. The name Wrecking Crew was supposedly applied to drummer Hal Blaine, about whom a more established Capitol label musician accused of "wrecking popular music with rock and roll."

To support their latest hit, the Warner Brothers label sent out teenaged combos to play as the Marketts. In one instance, when a new Marketts single came out, the band was on the road and had yet to hear it, so they called the label, which played it to them over the phone so they could learn it well enough to include it in their next concert. While the record was out, the TV series *The Outer Limits* threatened legal action, so the title was changed to "Out Of Limits."

—

The Exciters "Do-Wah Diddy" United Artists November 1963

Style: Soul vocal group
From and recorded in: New York

Intending to repeat the success of their composition, "Da Doo Ron Ron," by The Crystals, Jeff Barry and Ellie Greenwich and came up with "Do-Wah Diddy," which they intended for themselves as the Raindrops, under which name they had already recorded the original "Hanky Panky." "Do-Wah Diddy," which was recorded by The Exciters, sold moderately. It was not properly promoted by the label, and soon forgotten.

Remake: Manfred Mann "Do Wah Diddy Diddy" 1964

—

The Supremes "When the Lovelight Starts Shining Through His Eyes" Motown November 1963

Style: Soul vocal group
From and recorded in: Detroit, MI
Suggested pairing: Bo Diddley "Bo Diddley" 1955

"When the Lovelight Starts Shining Through His Eyes" was written by Holland–Dozier–Holland and recorded by The Supremes. Coming off the Phil Spector-inspired "Run, Run, Run," which sold well, it meant The Supremes might benefit from more of the same. "The Supremes were sort of feeling their way as far as direction was concerned," said Lamont Dozier. "Brian Holland and I thought that since The Ronettes were hot at the time, that accounts for the 'Run, Run, Run' sounding so similar to the Phil Spector era, and 'When the Lovelight Starts Shining Through His Eyes' was another one that was influenced by the Phil Spector sound."

—

Bob & Earl "Harlem Shuffle" Marc 1963

Style: Soul duet
From and recorded in: Los Angeles, CA
Sly and the Family Stone "Dance To the Music" 1967

Los Angeles-based vocal group singers Bobby Relf and Earl Nelson were Bob & Earl on this breakout hit, "Harlem Shuffle." "We took the title 'Harlem Shuffle' from Round Robin's 'Slauson Shuffle,'" said Relf. "But we made it Harlem, so we'd get sales on both coasts." It worked; it was a bi-coastal and a national hit.

"In 1963, we went to San Francisco to do 'Harlem Shuffle' and they had a band backing us up," said Earl Nelson. "It was led by a disc jockey on the big San Francisco soul station. He hadn't done any major recording yet. His name was Sly Stone. They brought us out with our horn introduction and he asked us if we minded if he used that 'Harlem Shuffle' opening sometime. We didn't care so we told him it was okay and that's how he began his first big hit 'Dance To the Music.'"

Remakes: Bob Kuban & the In-Men 1966; The Traits 1966; Wayne Cochran 1970; The Rolling Stones 1986

—

Major Lance "Um Um Um Um Um" Okeh 1963

Style: Soul
From and recorded in: Los Angeles, CA

About this Major Lance hit, "Um Um Um Um Um," the writer, Curtis Mayfield, recalled, "Major Lance was good at that pulling out this tune I wrote while riding in a car. I have no idea why I even wrote this song. But the song made sense. Major saw qualities in it. It happened for Major. It allowed myself another avenue of expression I wouldn't have had otherwise."

—

The Tams "What Kind Of Fool (Do You Think I Am)" ABC-Paramount November 1963

Style: Soul vocal group
Where from: Atlanta, GA
Where recorded: Fame studio, Muscle Shoals, AL

The Tams first recorded "Untie Me" in summer 1962, but hit big with the eminently danceable vocal, "What Kind Of Fool (Do You Think I Am)," an instant beach music fave. With a flute sound beginning and underlying the performance, this broke a tradition of sorts, a white Atlanta female flutist backing a black Atlanta male vocal group. This was perhaps the first success out of the legendary Fame studios, later the source of much southern soul.

—

Kai Winding "Time Is On My Side" Verve November 1963

Style: Soul
Where from: Denmark
Where recorded: New York City, NY

Jazz player Kai Winding was backed on this soulful "Time Is On My Side" by The Gospelaires with members Cissy Houston, Dionne Warwick, and Dee Dee Warwick, who filled in for Garnett Mimms and the Enchanters, who were credited on the label. After this original with few lyrics other than the title, songwriter Jimmy Norman was recruited to add extra lyrics.

Remakes: Irma Thomas 1964; The Rolling Stones 1964

—

Shorty Long "Devil With the Blue Dress" Soul 1963

Style: Soul
Where from: Mississippi
Where recorded: Detroit, MI

Born Frederick Earl Long in Birmingham, AL on May 20, 1940, he sang at the Birmingham Baptist Church, and was tutored by Alvin "Shine" Robinson and "Father of the Blues," W. C. Handy on piano, organ, drums, guitar, trumpet, and harmonica. His nickname based on his stature, Shorty Long moved to Detroit in 1959. When Berry Gordy acquired the Tri-Phil/Harvey/Anna family of labels, Shorty landed at Motown's Soul subsidiary, recording "Devil With the Blue Dress On" as the debut of the new Motown-owned imprint, Soul. Backing was supplied by a below-the-radar vocal group called The Originals. "We got together in the latter part of 1964," said Freddie Gorman. "We went to Motown and signed a contract in 1965." The conservative, plodding "Devil With the Blue Dress" was later turned out as a rocker by Detroit-based Mitch Ryder & the Detroit Wheels.

Remake: Mitch Ryder & the Detroit Wheels 1966

—

Shirley Ellis "The Nitty Gritty" Congress 1963

Style: Soul
From and recorded in: New York City, NY
Original title: Shirley Elliston "The Real Nitty Gritty"

Shirley Elliston was credited on the soft ballad, "Love Can Make You Know" on the Shell label. Completely changing her style to a rocking novelty this song was first titled "The Real Nitty Gritty" by Shirley Elliston, and quickly changed to "The Nitty Gritty" by Shirley Ellis. It reached #3 on KRLA in November 1963, #3 on KFWB in December 1963, and #3 on WMCA, New York in January 1964.

Remake: Gladys Knight & the Pips 1969

—

The Dave Clark Five "Glad All Over" Epic December 27, 1963

Style: Rock 'n' roll
From and recorded in: England

Lead vocalist Mike Smith came across a '50s recording, "Glad All Over," by Carl Perkins and wrote a new song with the same title. The Dave Clark Five's "Glad All Over" vocals were by Smith in unison group vocals, a sax blaring underneath, and a beat described as an "air hammer" in a production dubbed the "Tottenham Sound." The band's leader, Dave Clark wasn't on vocals, but on drums, though there might have been a different drummer on the recorded song.

—

Scott English and the Accents "High on a Hill" Sultan/Spokane 1964

Style: Doo wop
Where from: Brooklyn, NY
Where recorded: New York City, NY

Scott English was a white high tenor lead fronting the black Accents on this classic ballad, "High on a Hill." It was released on Sultan as of November 1963, where it charted on KFXM in Riverside, CA. With a label change to Spokane, "High pn a Hill" hit big in January 1964, #4 on KRLA and #14 on KFWB in L.A. The flipside, "When," was first used as the flipside of The Dedications novelty, "Ugly Pills" from 1962.

—

The Jewels "Opportunity" Dimension 1964

Style: Soul vocal group
Where from: Washington, DC
Where recorded: New York

Having been around as The Four Jewels for several years, they shortened their name to The Jewels and, as a trio, recorded this mainly sing-a-long ala "So Fine" by the Fiestas, "Opportunity," for the almost brand new Dimension label.

—

Barbara Mason "Yes I'm Ready" Arctic 1964

Style: Soul
Where from: Philadelphia, PA
Suggested pairings: Major Lane "The Monkey Time" 1962; The Sequins "Hey Romeo" 1970

Amounting to an answer record, young Philly songwriter and vocalist Barbara Mason answered Major Lance's hit, "The Monkey Time" lyric with "Are you ready?" To which Barbara Mason answered with "Yes I'm Ready." Considered by many to be the first record to have the Philadelphia sound, Mason went on to record other similar soft ballads like "Sad Sad Girl," easily influenced by The Impressions "Sad Sad Girl and Boy" in 1966.

—

The Beatles "I Want To Hold Your Hand" Capitol January 1964

Style: Rock 'n' roll
From and recorded in: England

Reputedly, Bob Dylan thought the line "I can't hide" from the Beatles "I Want To Hold Your Hand" was "I get high," and a reference to marijuana. He was surprised to learn they had never tried pot, and it became part of Beatles lore when he introduced them to it.

This was one of John Lennon's favorite Beatles songs.

—

The Beatles "I Saw Her Standing There" Capitol 1964

Style: Rock 'n' roll
From and recorded in: England
Suggested pairings: Chuck Berry "Talkin' Bout You" 1958

The Beatles borrowed a significant riff from Chuck Berry, just before the bluesier Rolling Stones had a chance to return the favor, on this flipside hit, the woo-heavy "I Saw Her Standing There."

—

Sam Cooke "Good News" RCA 1964

Style: Soul
Where from: Chicago, IL
Where recorded: Hollywood, CA
Suggested pairings: Ray Charles "I've Got a Woman" 1954; Little Richard "Ain't That Good News" 1955

Sam Cooke delivered a rollicking vocal on "Good News" with backing by René Hall, John Pisano, Clif White and Howard Roberts, guitar; John Ewing, trombone; Jewell Grant, William Green and Edgar Redmond, saxophone; Joseph Gibbons, guitar and banjo; Eddie Tilman, bass; Sharkey Hall, drums and Emil Radocchia, marimba and tympani.

—

The Temptations "The Way You Do the Things You Do" Gordy January 23, 1964

Style: Soul vocal group
Where from: Alabama
Where recorded: Detroit, MI

In early 1964, Smokey Robinson and fellow Miracles member Bobby Rogers co-wrote and produced "The Way You Do the Things You Do" for The Temptations with Eddie Kendricks on lead, creating The Temptations' first major hit, which was referenced in James Brown's "Out Of Sight" in August 1964.

Remakes: Diana Ross & the Supremes with the Temptations 1969; Stoney & Meatloaf 1971; Dion 1976; Evie Sands 1976; Rita Coolidge 1978; UB40 1993

—

Terry Stafford "Suspicion" January 31, 1964

Style: Rock 'n' roll
Where from: Amarillo, TX
Where recorded: El Monte, CA
Original version: Elvis Presley 1963

"When I was growing up, I was a big Elvis fan, just came from Amarillo, Texas. I picked up his 'Pot Luck' album with 'Suspicion' and a George Jones record in Covina," said Terry Stafford. "I recorded 'Suspicion' in El Monte with Bob Summers, Mary Ford's brother. I had tried to sell the master of 'Suspicion' to Capitol and the record companies. A&M had that master," but didn't release it. The A&M office was Herb Alpert's garage. A&M gave me the master back and gave cab money. I lived in Whittier. I went four or five blocks, caught a bus, kept the money. I might have been a little anxious, maybe it was a foolish move getting the record back. When they gave me the master back, John Fisher put it out."

Redo: Terry Stafford "Sospeto"—Italian version 1964

—

Chuck Berry "Nadine (Is It You?)" Chess February 1964

Style: Rock 'n' roll
Where from: St. Louis, MO
Where recorded: Chicago, IL
Suggested pairings: Chuck Berry "Maybellene" 1955; Chuck Berry "Dear Dad" 1964; Rick & the Ravens "Geraldine" 1964

At the tail end of a period when authorities were cracking down on rock 'n' roll acts, from October 1961 until October 1963, Chuck Berry was in prison for violating the Mann Act, bringing a teenage girl across a state line for immoral purposes. During this time in stir, Berry penned "Nadine," "You Never Can Tell," "Promised Land" and "No Particular Place to Go."

Marshall Chess, son of Chess Records founder Leonard, said to the Independent newspaper, "I was his road manager in 1963 when he came out of prison and we were desperate because he was our biggest star. He came right from jail, looking raggedy. My dad gave me $100 and said, 'Take him down to State Street and get him some new clothes.' Then he came right back to our studio and recorded 'Nadine,'" the story of a man catching sight of a woman and spending the rest of the song trying to catch up with her.

—

The Vibrations "My Girl Sloopy" Atlantic February 1964

Style: Soul vocal group
Where from: Los Angeles, CA
Where recorded: New York
Suggested pairings: Ritchie Valens "La Bamba" 1958; The Kingsmen "Louie Louie" 1963; Jimmy Holiday "Baby I Love You" 1966; Neil Diamond "Cherry Cherry" 1966; The Righteous Brothers "You've Lost That Lovin' Feeling" 1966; Merilee Rush "Angel Of the Morning" 1968

Lead singer of the Vibrations, Carl Fisher, recalled about "My Girl Sloopy," the songwriters "Bert Berns and Wes Farrell used conga player Mongo Santamaria and timbale player on the session. It had a cajunto rhythm section behind them." Berns and Farrell added crow noises to the session. After "the guys came in and produced it and shopped it around," the song was picked up by Atlantic. Berns and Farrell, who began the Bang label about a year later, gave the song to the McCoys, retitled as "Hang On Sloopy" to match the lyrics. As of 1966, the song was forever known under that title, or as "Sloopy" or "Sloop Dance."

"My Girl Sloopy" remakes: Little Caesar & Consuls 1965; Killer Joe Orchestra 1965
"Hang On Sloopy" remakes: The McCoys 1966; Arsenio 1966; Ramsey Lewis 1966; Count Basie 1967; The X-Citers Unlimited 1967; The Lettermen 1970; Brooks Arthur Ensemble 1971; Foster Sylvers 1974
"Sloop Dance" remakes: The Vibrations 1964; The Atlantics 1965
"Sloopy" remakes: Ronnie & Pomona Casuals 1964; David Porter 1972
Answers: Johnny Thunder "Everybody Do The Sloopy" 1965; Billy Young " Do The Sloopy" 1965; The Debs "Sloopy's Gonna Hang On" 1965; The Secret Agents "I Saw Sloopy" 1966; Hank Ballard "Sloop and Slide" 1966; Bobby & the Expressions "Slooptime USA" 1966; Mister Hipp "Sloopy and The Red Moron" 1967

—

The Rolling Stones "Stoned" London February 1964

Style: Rock 'n' roll group
From and recorded in: England
Suggested pairing: Booker T & the MGs "Green Onions" 1962

This instrumental was not unlike Booker T & the MGs' "Green Onions" from 1962, but the title, "Stoned," with hard drug implications was potent enough to get The Rolling Stones' debut record banned in the U.S.

The Lennon-McCartney B-side vocal, "I Wanna Be Your Man" subsequently was used on the next Stones' 45, " Not Fade Away," so as not to discard a potential hit.

—

The Salas Brothers "Darling (Please Bring Your Love)" Faro February 1964

Style: Latino doo wop duet
From and recorded in: Los Angeles, CA
Original version: Phil & Harv 1961

The Salas Brothers were Rudy Salas and Steve Salas. "We started singing with our family on these big reunions; Mom taught us harmony," said Rudy. "We sang in Spanish, but we didn't speak Spanish. The Percussions needed singers. Steve was 9, I was 11. We did fiestas, but we were very young; we were working in clubs until 3 or 4 a.m. Eddie Davis was looking for talent, talked us into the studio, we could appreciate that market." The Salas Brothers debuted on the redo of "Darling (Please Bring Your Love)," originally by Phil & Harv on Rampart, a sister label to Faro. The Salas Brothers were the nucleus of Tierra in the 1970s.

—

Tommy Tucker "Hi-Heel Sneakers" Checker February 1964

Style: Blues
Where from: Ohio
Where recorded: New York
Suggested pairing: Jimmy Reed "Big Boss Man" 1962

Producer Herb Abramson operated A-1 Sound Studios in New York, where many popular R&B artists recorded. He leased Tucker's "Hi Heel Sneakers" with guitar by Dean Young to Checker Records, which released it as a single in 1964. Encyclopedia of the Blues states, "This now-familiar rhythmic chord progression of accenting the beat a la 'Hi-Heel Sneakers' was in turn incorporated into many cover versions of 'Big Boss Man,' and ironically influenced how the Jimmy Reed standard is typically played today."

Referenced in James Brown's "Out Of Sight" in August 1964
Answer: Sugar Pie Desanto "Slip-In Mules" 1964
Remakes: The Three Souls 1964; The Surfaris 1965; Ramsey Lewis 1966, Jimmy Hughes 1967; Jose Feliciano 1968; Elvis Presley 1969

—

The Swinging Blue Jeans "Hippy Hippy Shake" Imperial February 1964

Style: Rock 'n' roll group
From and recorded in: England
Original version: Chan Romero 1959
Suggested pairing: The B-52s "Dance This Mess Around" 1979

This manic version of the rocker "Hippy Hippy Shake" was made by the one-time skiffle band, The Swinging Blue Jeans, a band that specialized in remaking classic U.S. rock sounds.

Remake: The Georgia Satellites 1989

—

Bo-Pete "Baa Baa Blacksheep" Crusader 1964

Style: Novelty rock 'n' roll
From and recorded in: Hollywood, CA

After a Mercury label one-shot as Johnny Niles on "Wig Job," Harry Nilsson became Bo-Pete on this wall of sound ala Bob B. Soxx & the Blue Jeans' nursery rhyme 45, "Baa Baa Blacksheep."

According to songwriter John Marascalco, "Harry Nilsson was in Tommy Sands' band with Hal Blaine. He was writing with Scotty Turner as an ASCAP writer and looked me up, said, 'I'd like to do some writing with you.' We started writing a couple of things. Harry met me, we started to write, checked in at Vineland apartment." Next came The Foto-Fi Four, more Bo-Pete and Nilsson.

A reissue of "Baa Baa Blacksheep" by Harry Nilsson was on Marascalco's Lola in '64.

—

Rosa Lee Brooks "My Diary" Revis February 1964

Style: Rhythm and blues
From and recorded in: Los Angeles, CA

Member of The Ribbons, Rosa Lee Brooks, recalled meeting Jimi Hendrix: "I was at the California Club at an Ike & Tina Turner show, turned around, a man was staring at me, until I got embarrassed because we were that turned on. I got up to go to the lady's room, he said some naughty stuff. When I got back, he asked me to join him at our table. He introduced himself as a guitar player for the Little Richard Band. We were enjoying our show and vibing off of each other. At the end of the evening, I drove my '59 Chevy Impala north to Sunset and we were joking about Little Richard being the queen of rocking rhythm.

"Jimi Hendrix was staying at the Wilcox Hotel. Got to know him intimately. I was 20, Jimi was 21. We were staying at the Franklin Motel at Yucca and Franklin. Next morning, he [Hendrix] picked up his guitar, started strumming 'love notes.' Sang 'My Diary.'

"The session was held about a couple of weeks later in mid-January 1964. I knew of Billy Revis at the California Club. We let Billy Revis and his wife hear the song. He wrote out his address. We came over to his house on 40th & Cimarron. He had a converted garage into a studio. He asked me and Jimi, did we know other singers and musicians we could get. I knew Arthur Lee for two or three months, knew he was trying to start to band. I called Arthur Lee, [who] lived at 29th & Arlington. Could he do background vocals? I introduced him to Jimi, who wasn't really pleased, Arthur was a pretty man. Didn't know he was a threat. Jimi got real quiet. Arthur sat in the back seat, went to Billy Revis' place, got guys who played horns and girl singers. The high falsetto was by Arthur Lee. I sang 'My Diary' in two takes, [the] horns are sloppy. After we finished 'My Diary,' Jimi spontaneously began playing this rhythm. I'd been shown the dance, make a U and a T like 'the Madison.' That move that Jimi does when bends his knee, that's 'The Utee.' Arthur worked with The Blossoms on 'The Utee'"

—

Caesar & Cleo "The Letter" Vault February 22, 1964/October 1965

Style: Rock 'n' roll duet
From and recorded in: Los Angeles, CA
Original version: Don and Dewey 1959

Thanks to Sam Cooke's Soul Station, Cher debuted with Sonny Bono as Caesar & Cleo. In early 1964, "Sam Cooke rented a place where writers could come in and write songs," said Bobby Womack. "He had this band out of Louisiana, bring in a New Orleans sound, we'd all meet there, we were all going. I think it was on Vermont. Dr. John, other people would come on in. All the writers on Sam's label came in there. Johnny Morisette, Johnnie Taylor didn't write, Mel Carter, Billy Preston was everywhere."

Harold Battiste returned to L.A. in 1963. "I connected back with Sam. Sam had started his own label. I wanted to start a place in the black community that would make it convenient for talent than having them travel to Hollywood. So we developed a concept called the Soul Station, a little storefront at 37th and Vermont that would allow people to come in. The Valentinos, whatever people he had, would come in. Mary Love started out there. The plan was to have Soul Station #1 and Soul Station #2. The biggest thing that came out of the Soul Station was Sonny & Cher, known then as Caesar & Cleo. "They came down and asked if I would do something on them," said Battiste. "I put together a thing called 'The Letter,' a song Sonny had written; something he was going to redo for Cher. This cat named Jack Lewerke had a label called Vault and released it." Bono had written "The Letter" for Don and Dewey who had recorded it. Caesar & Cleo's "The Letter" backed with the instrumental, "Spring Fever" by Vincente, a Bono pseudonym. The Caesar & Cleo billing was changed to Sonny & Cher on the reissue of "The Letter" backed with "Spring Fever" on Vault, which hit pretty big in October 1965.

—

The Beatles "Do You Want To Know a Secret" Vee Jay 1964

Style: Rock 'n' roll group
From and recorded in: England
Original version: Billy J. Kramer & the Dakotas 1963.
Suggested pairings: Snow White & the Seven Dwarfs "Wishing Well"; The Stereos "I Really Love You" 1961

This was the first major Beatles hit on the Vee Jay label, when Capitol successfully claimed all post-1964 titles by The Beatles, including "Do You Want To Know a Secret." As Vee Jay was unable to fill massive orders, that caused the demise of both Vee Jay and its Tollie subsidiary, as distributorships, aware of the loss of Beatles product, failed to pay for accounts receivable.

—

Jan & Dean "Dead Man's Curve" Liberty March 1, 1964

Style: Rock 'n' roll
Where from: Bel Air, CA
Where recorded: Hollywood, CA

When Jan & Dean's satire of death rock hits, "Dead Man's Curve," collided with the charts, there was no way they could have predicted how this bit of humor could take on a reality of its own when Jan Berry crashed his 'Vette two years later, effectively ending the career of this hit making duet.

Dean Torrence called this a "doo wop record. We wanted to do a tongue in cheek drama about teenage risk taking. Nobody died."

—

Manfred Mann "5-4-3-2-1" Prestige March 2, 1964

Style: Rock 'n' roll group
From and recorded in: England

The lyrics "5-4-3-2-1" were from the opening of the Ready Steady Go! ITV show, for which Manfred Mann wrote the theme song and released as a single.

—

The Beatles "Twist and Shout" Tollie March 2, 1964

Style: Rock 'n' roll
From and recorded in: England
Original version: The Top Notes 1960
First hit version: The Isley Brothers 1962

The Beatles redid the much more energetic version of "Twist and Shout" by the Isley Brothers, making it a hit for the second time out of three attempts on the material by different groups.

—

The Standells "The Shake" Liberty March 3, 1964

Style: Garage rock 'n' roll
Where from: Bel Air, CA
Where recorded: Hollywood, CA
Suggested pairings: The Ronettes "Be My Baby"1963; Bobby Freeman "C'mon and Swim" 1964

With their first label deal, the newly renamed Standells, vocalists Larry Tamblyn and Tony Valentino; Gary Leeds, drums and Gary Lane, bass turned garage, though, at the time, the sound was more like a live au-go go sound. "I was still underage at the time, undercover cops came in, demanded to see our ID," said Tamblyn. "The guy tells me I'll be back tomorrow to check your ID. We drove to Tijuana, got a fake ID, fake draft card, just got back. I filled it out, typed it up myself with a phony address in Cincinnati, Ohio, guy just glanced at it. We were doing 'Louie Louie,' 'Money,' 'Kansas City,' we did Four Seasons and Chuck Berry stuff. I started off as a guitarist, switched to keyboards." When they signed with Liberty, "our manager, Bert Jacobs was involved in organized crime. He was a bookie before he was a manager, he was Liberty's bookie."

According to Jerry Heller in his Ruthless For Life, "Bert Jacobs' major claim to fame was that he was proud of point shaving and fixing some basketball games in the '60s. We were actually the first group to sport long hair. A teen magazine came over to do an article. They took pictures of us."

In 1964 The Standells signed with Liberty and recorded the undistinguished variation on "The Swim" called "The Shake," with help from a girl group, active organ backing, a "Be My Baby" break and a false ending.

—

The Rolling Stones "Not Fade Away" London March 6, 1964

Style: Rock 'n' roll group
From and recorded in: England
Original version: The Crickets 1957
Earlier version: Bobby Fuller 1962
Cover: Dick & DeeDee 1964
Suggested pairing: Bo Diddley "Bo Diddley" 1955

Rolling Stones' drummer Charlie Watts said about the band's hit remake of "Not Fade Away," a Crickets original, "We did it with a Bo Diddley beat, which at the time was very avant-garde for a white band to be playing Bo Diddley's stuff. It was a very popular rhythm for us in clubs, looking at it from the drumming point of view. So we did it in this slightly different way than Buddy Holly did it."

Remakes: Black Oak 1972; The Everly Brothers 1973; Bo Diddley 1976; Tanya Tucker 1978; Gary Busey 1978

—

Mary Wells "My Guy" Motown March 13, 1964

Style: Soul
From and recorded in: Detroit, MI

"Everything that came out of Motown in 1960, '61, '62 was picked up by the kids," said Joe Billingslea of The Contours. "Berry Gordy Jr. would invite them in the studio and they were awed by the studio. They got to meet celebrities in the studio and they were served pop and potato chips. They'd listen to the songs and dance to the songs and they would ask them what songs they liked the best, and he'd go back with his staff and producers and he'd go with the majority of songs and nine times out of ten it was a hit."

After having recorded as Little Iva for the Miracle label in 1961, Berry Gordy Jr.'s ex-wife, Raynoma, was assigned to the Motown office in New York in 1963. Strapped for cash, but needing to meet demand for Mary Wells' #1 hit, "My Guy," she authorized pressing of 5,000 copies of this song to sell to record stores. She was turned in to the FBI for bootlegging the record by the home office. To avoid prosecution, she signed away her rights to any claim against Motown. Then with her new husband, Eddie Singleton, she formed the Shrine label in Washington, DC, a warehouse that was destroyed in the DC riots of 1968.

—

The Dave Clark Five "Bits and Pieces" Epic March 20, 1964

Style: Rock 'n' roll group
From and recorded in: England
Suggested pairings: Kenny Dino "Your Ma Said You Cried In Your Sleep Last Night" 1961; Chubby Checker "Hooka Tooka" 1963; The Thundermen "Thunderbeat" 1964; Herman's Hermits "Can't You Hear My Heartbeat" 1965

Dave Clark recalled to Uncut, "Bits and Pieces" derived from live shows, "with just the drums going, with everybody in the band stomping. All the audience would start to stomp, and you can imagine what it was like." Venue owners wouldn't let them play "Bits and Pieces" at concerts as they feared fans would jump up and down in time to the beat and cause damage similar to the July 17, 1981 Kansas City balcony collapse, which killed 114. That collapse was caused by participants swaying in time to the music, making venue owners' fears well founded.

—

The Hollies "Just One Look" Imperial March 1964

Style: Rock 'n' roll group
From and recorded in: England
Original version: Doris Troy 1962

This Brit band named after Buddy Holly, The Hollies, was led by Graham Nash. The first release, "Stay," stiffed, but after switching labels they had success with "Just One Look."

—

Bonnie Jo Mason "Ringo I Love You" Annette 1964

Style: Novelty rock 'n' roll
From and recorded in: Hollywood, CA

Responding to the British Invasion and #1 hits by the Beatles, Phil Spector brought Sonny Bono and Cher Sarkiasian into the studio as Bonnie Jo Mason to record a tribute to The Beatles, "Ringo I Love You" backed with the instrumental, "Beatle Blues," on a label named after Spector's wife at the time, Annette, which was rush-released and sold best in Buffalo.

—

Gene Cornish & the Unbeetables "I Wanna Be a Beetle" Dawn March 1964

Style: Novelty rock 'n' roll
From and recorded in: Upstate New York, NY

Future member of the Young Rascals, Gene Cornish, attempted to catch on to the oncoming British rock goldrush with the intentionally misspelled, I Wanna Be a Beetle," a minor hit locally.

—

The Foto-Fi Four "Stand Up and Holler" Foto-Fi 1964

Style: Novelty rock 'n' roll
From and recorded in: Hollywood, CA

To cash in on The Beatles invasion with a picture cover that sure looked like a Beatles release, The Foto-Fi Four were created for the two-part single, the Bo Diddley-beat "Stand Up and Holler" on Foto-Fi, a music track designed to be synchronized to the accompanying 8mm film of The Beatles' arrival in America with packaging that instructed "play this side with film" with the synching notes. This song was put together by Harry Nilsson and John Marascalco, who recalled, "We approached the documentary people, who said, 'We want you to write us a song.' Harry and I wrote the song. I produced that and Harry did the singing."

"Stand Up and Holler" was then covered by the soul group The Originals and re-titled "All For the Beatles (Stand Up and Holler)."

—

The Kinks "Long Tall Sally" Cameo April 1, 1964

Style: Rock 'n' roll group
From and recorded in: England
Original version: Little Richard 1956

The Kinks' debut was this remake of Little Richard's giant hit "Long Tall Sally," from 1956, not the only Little Richard British Invasion remake in April of that year.

—

The Swinging Blue Jeans "Good Golly Miss Molly" Imperial April 1964

Style: Rock 'n' roll group
From and recorded in: England
Original version: The Valiants 1957
Earlier version: Little Richard "Good Golly Miss Molly" 1957

This was one in a series of '50s rock 'n' roll compositions by The Swinging Blue Jeans.

—

The Dave Clark Five "Do You Love Me" Epic April 1964

Style: Rock 'n' roll group
From and recorded in: England
Original version: The Contours 1962

The Dave Clark Five had success with this thumping version of the soul hit.

—

Brenda Holloway "Every Little Bit Hurts" Tamla 1964

Style: Soul
Where from: Los Angeles, CA
Where recorded: Hollywood, CA
Suggested pairing: Ketty Lester "Love Letters" 1963

Brenda Holloway had already recorded about a half dozen 45s for Brevit, Catch and Donna when she became Motown's big West Coast find on this Ed Cobb-composed soul ballad, "Every Little Bit Hurts" on Tamla.

Marc Gordon, who ran the L.A. Motown operation with Hal Davis, recalled, "Hal discovered Brenda and Brenda came over to Motown as a result. I started Motown out here in '62; Brenda Holloway was the catalyst that got me with Motown. That impressed Berry to the extent that he was willing to open the L.A. office. Berry hired us to enhance their album marketing, to give his artists a chance to be produced by major artists here. He had us produce Marvin Gaye and The Supremes with big orchestras that they didn't have in Detroit. He wanted to make it a West Coast big sound."

According to Holloway, the song was presented to her by Ed Cobb, who had written the very similar 1963 hit "Love Letters" for Ketty Lester. "Ed Cobb wrote the song for Ketty Lester," said Holloway. "I didn't really want to do that song. Barbara Wilson, Frank Wilson's first wife, did the demo. She had a great sound. I just thought the song was for her. I was crying when I was actually recording the song."

—

The Beatles "Love Me Do" Tollie April 27, 1964

Style: Rock 'n' roll group
From and recorded in: England
Suggested pairing: Bruce Channel "Hey Baby" 1962

This was Ringo's first appearance, playing tambourine, with session drummer Andy White adding a skiffle beat. Before they recorded this, Lennon always sang the lead vocal, but when his harmonica part was added, McCartney had to sing lead because Lennon was on a harmonica in a solo gleaned from Bruce Channel's #1 "Hey Baby" from 1961. Session drummer Andy White filled in, shoving Ringo to the tambourine, though Ringo's drumming made the single.

—

The Premiers "Farmer John" Faro/Warner Brothers May 2, 1964

Style: Latino rock 'n' roll group
Where from: San Gabriel, CA
Where recorded: Hollywood, CA
Original version: Don and Dewey 1959
Suggested pairing: The Kingsmen "Louie Louie" 1963

With Lawrence Perez on guitar and his brother, John Perez, drums; Frank Zuniga, bass and George Delgado, rhythm, they were The Premiers, a name John chose "starting out and premiering at places we're going to play at." The Premiers recorded what amounted to the first major national East Side Sound hit. According to Faro's Eddie Davis, "It was different, something new at that time. Live recording was just a thing that was coming into its being. We had just done The Mixtures at Rainbow Gardens, with legendary people in the recording industry. We heard Don and Dewey's old recording of 'Farmer John' and said, 'There's a recording we out to do," and the next time I saw Billy Cardenas, he had The Premiers play it for me. I thought it was great."

Cardenas added, "The influence was because 'Louie Louie' was a big hit at that time, so I told the guys, 'Hey man, let's put the same beat, rhythm,' because it was a turnabout that Don and Dewey used to do, they used to do uptempo. And I broke it down to a 'Louie Louie' beat; it fit right in there. The guys kept arguing, 'It's not going to work.'"

Davis added, "When I heard it I said, 'We've got to go record it,' so we went to record it, but The Premiers weren't the best singers in the world and the record had such a groove.... I was going to shelve it. Bruce Morgan. the engineer said, 'You can't shelve it, something like that is too great.' 'What are we going to do, we can't change the singers?' The Premiers had a girls' car club, The Chevelles, they used to follow them everywhere, they would start all this screaming and hollering, always, at The Premiers, it was really exciting group to be with in person... Margie... and [I] just got the idea, 'Let's make this a live recording, maybe we can get enough noise in there so the groove will carry through.' At the recording studio we had all the kids come down and we had a little party, a little schnapps, everybody was having a good time. We put the record on and played it, in those days we had 3-track recording, put the record on and while they were in there having a party we just recorded the crowd on top of it."

Cardenas added, "At that time we purchased a club in Fullerton called the Rhythm Room, so we decided to call it 'Live at the Rhythm Room,' just to plug the Rhythm Room. "Davis added, "It made the place very popular, until Fullerton ran us out of town.

Cardenas continued, "The Premiers worked for a record store out of San Gabriel and at that time there was a very popular thing called the Teenage Fair and the Teenage Fair had booths and groups that were playing and The Premiers worked at this record store and they were selling the record on site. I walked over to KFWB and I talked to Don Anti and we immediately put it as 'Duffy's Blues' when we recorded it" backed with a noisy redo of Don and Dewey's "Farmer John" on Faro, and rolled out with 40,000 or 50,000 records in a week or so, and then Warner Brothers called."

Lawrence said, "We had a few sax players, we went through a lot of sax players. Basically, we ended up as a four member group. Joe Whiteman was the one who created 'Duffy's Blues.'" According to Davis, all Premiers flip sides like "Duffy's Blues" were "usually blues and we named them all after Billy Cardenas' daughters."

Remake: Los Lobos in 1981
Answer: The Salas Brothers with The Jaguars "The Return Of Farmer John" 1964

—

Johnny Rivers "Memphis" Imperial 1964

Style: Rock 'n' roll
Where from: Louisiana
Where recorded: Hollywood, CA
Original version: Chuck Berry 1959

After a one-record career, "Two By Two," under his real name, Johnny Ramistella, Johnny Rivers was given a new name by DJ Alan Freed with record releases on various labels, sounding like Elvis on Gone, a folk style on Guyden and Era, a rocking sound on Cub, Chancellor and Capitol, from 1958 through 1963 when he relocated to L.A. Despite having about a dozen flops, as his on-line bio contends, "Johnny's first single, a cover of Chuck Berry's 'Memphis,' came from the 'Johnny Rivers At the Whisky a Go Go' album. His version, more driving and bluesy than Berry's original, was so popular that Johnny had to play it three times a night at the Whisky. The so-called "live" or "go go sound" translated into live sounding hits by other artists, including Trini Lopez, The Blendells, The Premiers and the various versions of "Land Of A Thousand Dances" by several Hispanic bands.

—

The Animals "Baby, Let Me Take You Home" MGM 1964

Style: Rock 'n' roll group
From and recorded in: England
Original version: Hoagy Lands "Baby Let Me Hold Your Hand" 1963

Their U.S. debut, The Animals' "Baby, Let Me Take You Home" with a strong guitar intro was a redo of Hoagy Lands' "Baby Let Me Hold Your Hand" on Atlantic from 1963. "Baby, Let Me Take You Home" charted best in Sacramento and in L.A. on KRLA.

—

The Impressions "Keep On Pushing" ABC May 1964

Style: Soul vocal group
From and recorded in: Chicago, IL

"You might say that 'Keep On Pushing' was actually a gospel song, the only differences was instead of saying 'God gave me my strength,' that 'I've got my strength to "Keep On Pushing."' Isn't one related to the other?" asked Curtis Mayfield, who said the gospel community never resisted such messages in a soul context.

—

Die Beatles "Sie Liebt Dich (She Loves You)" Swan May 21, 1964

Style: Rock 'n' roll group
From and recorded in: England

"Sie Liebt Dich (She Loves You)" by Die Beatles is nothing more than the Beatles' "She Loves You" sung in German.

—

The Valentinos "It's All Over Now" SAR May 1964

Style: Rock 'n' roll group
Where from: Cleveland, OH
Where recorded: Hollywood, CA

The Valentinos' most influential "It's All Over Now" on Sam Cooke's SAR label took months to chart. Bobby Womack said, "It was me and Cecil, guitar; Harry, bass; Earl Palmer on drums." Contrary to the style of the day, there were no horns or strings. "With horns, you'd sound like everybody else. Strings would get in the way of your voices because they are so close. Johnny Morisette was sitting there with a newspaper, hitting it, howling real loud. I asked Sam to keep him down, Sam said let him go. Every time he felt the spirit, he'd holler as loud as he could. I thought he was trying to mess the session up. He laughed a lot and Sam said, 'Leave Johnnie in there.'"

Cover: The Rolling Stones 1964

—

Chuck Berry "No Particular Place To Go" Chess May 1964

Style: Rock 'n' roll
Where from: St. Louis, MO
Where recorded: Chicago, IL
Suggested pairings: Chuck Berry "School Day" 1957; The Beach Boys "I Get Around" 1964

"No Particular Place To Go" was written at a time when Chuck Berry had literally no place to go. He was in prison. This story is about cruising in his automobile and his frustration with undoing his "safety belt" so he can make love to his female companion. That is the end of a rather contrived story about cruising, safety and sexual frustration.

—

The Rolling Stones "Tell Me (You're Coming Back)" London June 12, 1964

Style: Rock 'n' roll group
From and recorded in: England

For this first Jagger-Richard composition, the pair was reportedly locked in a room by their manager and told to come up with something. As Keith Richards recalled, "'Tell Me' which was pulled out as a single in America, was a dub. Half those records were dubs on that first album, that Mick and I and Charlie and I'd put a bass on or maybe Bill was there and he'd put a bass on. Let's put it down while we remember it and the next thing we know is, 'Oh look, track 8 is that dub we did a couple months ago.' That's how little control we had."

Mick Jagger said, "Keith was playing 12-string and singing harmonies into the same microphone as the 12-string. We recorded it in this tiny studio in the West End of London called Regent Sound, which was a demo studio. I think the whole of that album was recorded in there. But it's very different from doing those R&B covers or Marvin Gaye covers and all that. There's a definite feel about it. It's a very pop song, as opposed to all the blues covers and the Motown covers, which everyone did at the time."

—

Jan & Dean "The Little Old Lady From Pasadena" Liberty June 13, 1964

Style: Rock 'n' roll
Where from: Bel Air, CA
Where recorded: Hollywood, CA

Inspired by a popular TV commercial for a local Dodge dealership, Jan & Dean recorded this most topical "The Little Old Lady From Pasadena" backed with KFWB's Gene Weed's composition "My Mighty GTO," a total of two car makes on one 45. "The Dodge dealers should have embraced it," Dean Torrance recalled. "We would've given it to them for free."

P.F. Sloan recalled, "Lou Adler of Screen Gems asked Steve Barri and me to become Jan & Dean's background singers. Steve was working at a record store, had a child, needed to make money. I wound up singing all of Dean's parts on all of the records, I sang on 'Little Old Lady.' I didn't want to be known as the person singing Dean's parts."

—

The Drifters "Under the Boardwalk" Atlantic June 1964

Style: Soul vocal group
From and recorded in: New York City, NY

The Drifters' "Under the Boardwalk" was first sung as "we'll be makin' some love," and changed by blue noses to "we'll be having some fun," evoking the carefree sounds of the shore. Johnny Moore was a last-minute lead singer replacement, on account of their regular lead Rudy Lewis dying of a heroin overdose in his hotel room the night before the session.

—

The Supremes "Where Did Our Love Go" Motown June 17, 1964

Style: Soul vocal group
From and recorded in: Detroit, MI
Suggested pairing: The Supremes "Baby Love" 1964

"We were offered a song, it was The Supremes first number one," said Gladys Horton. "The Marvelettes were offered either 'Too Many Fish In The Sea' or 'Where Did Our Love Go' by Holland Dozier Holland. 'Girls, we've got two songs, pick the one you want.' They played just the music track. They played both songs. 'Too Many Fish In The Sea' [had] the bongos and all the music; in 'Where Did Our Love Go,' Diane carried the melody, so it was basically just the rhythm. We don't want that one, we want the one with all the bongos. When we heard it by The Supremes, that's a fantastic song. When The Supremes got going, they surpassed everyone. They held on. It must've been for us to walk up there, they had been there for two or three years, we walk in there. Diane asked us, 'Where do you girls come from?' That's just the way she felt. 'Wait a minute, I've been down here.' They had more time to rehearse, so their voices were more polished than ours. It's not always how good you sound that it's going to be a smash or not. She just came out and said, 'Who do you think you are, coming in there, getting a hit record before us?' We laughed it off. After talking to Diane, she explained, 'You girls a[re] great, but we've been trying.' I told her, 'Don't even worry about it, because you are going to make it someday.' She had to talk about it. 'This is a surprise to us too, so don't get mad.' It was a surprise to Berry, it was the right song for him at the right time. The foot-stomping beat was the result of two boards being banged together."

—

The Animals "House of the Rising Sun" MGM July 1964

Style: Rock 'n' roll group
From and recorded in: England
Original version: Clarence "Tom" Ashley and Gwen Foster "Rising Sun Blues" 1933
Suggested pairing: The Callahan Brothers "Rounder's Luck" 1935

The Animals' second release and very first #1, with the menacing combination of vocals by Eric Burdon and organ by Alan Price, gave "House of the Rising Sun" about a New Orleans brothel the right amount of blues rock. Taken from folk and blues standards, when the Animals' 45 of "House of the Rising Sun" was about to be released, Price told the group that demand meant a rush release and there wasn't time to put all the writers' names on the already crowded label, so writer credit was given to Price only, with Burdon claiming he "nicked" the credit and was able to retire on his earnings.

About 90 seconds of this original U.K. single were excised, not censored, to suit the needs of U.S. radio.

The Animals' "House of the Rising Sun" was first heard on KMEN in San Bernardino, where it charted #1 in mid-July.

Remakes: Frijid Pink 1969; Claude King 1969; Dolly Parton 1981

—

The Four Tops "Baby I Need Your Loving" Motown July 10, 1964

Style: Soul vocal group
From and recorded in: Detroit, MI
Suggested pairings: The Foundations "Baby Now That I Found You" 1967; Joe Jeffrey "My Pledge Of Love" 1969

About a year after the failed single "What Goes Up, Must Come Down," which The Four Tops recorded with Holland-Dozier, they scored with this sincerely rendered rockaballad, "Baby I Need Your Loving," which hit the Detroit top five in July; L.A. and New York City in August.

"The Four Tops and I are very tight," said songwriter Lamont Dozier. "We've been very close since 'Baby I Need Your Loving,' one of the first recordings we did in 1964. I just love the harmony."

Answer: The Righteous Brothers "You've Lost That Lovin' Feelin'" 1964

—

The Blendells "La La La La La" Rampart/Reprise July 11, 1964

Style: Latino rock 'n' roll group
Where from: Temple City, CA
Where recorded: Hollywood, CA
Original version: Stevie Wonder 1962
Suggested pairing: The Kingsmen "Louie Louie" 1963

When Stevie Wonder came to the Paramount Ballroom in East Los Angeles and performed "La La La La La," Eddie Davis, owner of Rampart Records, said to producer Billy Cardenas, "'Somebody ought to record that.' The next time I saw Billy," Davis continued, "he had it together with The Blendells. All it was was a drum-beating situation and we put it in a groove. Brought it down to the East Side Sound."

The Blendells—Mike Rincon, bass out of Cathedral High School; Ronnie Chipres, drums; Rudy Valona, lead guitar; Don Cardenas, sax; Tommy Esparza, rhythm guitar and lead singer Sal Murillo—recorded this highly rhythmic cover of Stevie Wonder's "La La La La La" backed with a powerful instrumental tribute by guitarist Andy Tesso to local DJ Huggy Boy, "Huggie's Bunnies," on Rampart and reissued on Reprise. Between takes, "Andy Tesso, did the riff" to "Huggie's Bunnies," according to Tony Valdez. "Billy, Max Uballes and Eddie did the backgrounds on 'Huggie's Bunnies.'"

Though the label claims "La La La La La" was recorded live at the Rhythm Room in Fullerton, it was actually done at Stereo Masters' Recording Studio with the band's mainly female fan club, organized by Margie Cabrera, to come in and scream. The part about the Rhythm Room was just a plug for Davis' teen club, which Davis and Cardenas claim was chased from Fullerton by anti-Latino civic leaders and cops.

The Blendells then backed Cannibal & the Headhunters on "Land of 1000 Dances" in early 1965.

Note: An aggressive version of "Huggie's Bunnies" by Frankie Olvera was issued in 1964.

—

The Beatles "A Hard Day's Night" Capitol July 13, 1964

Style: Rock 'n' roll group
From and recorded in: England

The Beatles' "A Hard Day's Night" uses long, repeating notes uncommon in pop music. The melody resembles the Irish folk song "Donall Og," with the same pentatonic, as well as small glissandos like glissandos found in the English ballad "Three Babes."

—

The Rolling Stones "It's All Over Now" July 24, 1964

Style: Rock 'n' roll group
Where from: England
Where recorded: Chicago, IL
Original version: The Valentinos 1964

Two months after the original version of this song by The Valentinos developed in the soul marketplace, The Rolling Stones came up with their cover version, over objections of Valentinos' leader, Bobby Womack. The Stones' version featured the very unique sound of a baritone guitar. As Keith Richards recalled, "We cut that in Chess Studios the first time in Chicago. The year before we were playing bars in England, you know. And then we're walking into Chess Studios which was where all of these records that had been made that were so important to us. Now and again in life you get this feeling that you've died and gone to heaven. Luckily, neither was true. American studios at that time were so much more together than in England. I mean, they had some good stuff in England but they didn't have knowledge of how to record it. We were lucky. There were a couple of guys like Glyn Johns in England who had a rough idea of recording. But the way you'd get a sound in an American studio in those days was the difference between day and night, compared to working in England or Europe. I mean these cats, in America, they'd done it already. So to work in Chess was our first taste of American record."

Remakes: The C & C Boys 1964; The Uniques 1968; Rod Stewart 1970; Waylon Jennings 1971; Molly Hatchet 1976

—

James Brown and His Orchestra "Out of Sight" Smash July 1964

Style: Soul
Where from: Georgia
Where recorded: New York
Referenced: Tommy Tucker Hi Heel Sneakers" 1964; Sugar Pie Desanto "Slip-In Mules" 1964; The Temptations "The Way You Do the Things You Do" 1962

"Out of Sight" was one of a few titles James Brown recorded with the Smash label before his first label, King/Federal reclaimed his contact. Saxophonist Maceo Parker was featured on this twelve-bar blues number, written by Brown under the pseudonym "Ted Wright." The stuttering, staccato dance rhythms and blasting horn section riffs of its instrumental arrangement were an important step in funk development. In his 1986 autobiography Brown wrote that "Out of Sight" was another beginning, musically and professionally. "My music—and most music—changed with 'Papa's Got a Brand New Bag,' but it really started on 'Out of Sight.' You can hear the band and me start to move in a whole other direction rhythmically. The horns, the guitars, the vocals, everything was starting to be used to establish all kinds of rhythms at once. I was trying to get every aspect of the production to contribute to the rhythmic patterns."

King Records filed a lawsuit and in October 1964, a judge ruled Smash Records could issue only instrumental recordings by Brown, and all masters of Brown vocals were property of King Records.

—

The Shangri-Las "Remember (Walking in the Sand)" Red Bird July 1964

Style: Girl group rock 'n' roll
Where From and recorded in: New York
Suggested pairings: Skid Row "I Remember You" 1989; The Beatles "Free As A Bird" 1995

This was a dramatic reading of a lost love scenario mixed with seagull-like sound effects taken from a sound effects record, according to the producer.

—

Solomon Burke "Everybody Needs Somebody to Love" Atlantic July 1964

Style: Soul
Where from: Philadelphia, PA
Where recorded: New York

Burke started preaching at the age of seven and often recorded his vocals from behind a pulpit. He attacks this song in the style of a fire-and-brimstone Southern preacher, calling out for a witness and testifying to the power of love.

Remakes: The Rolling Stones 1965; The Five Cards Stud 1966; Knights Of Day 1966; The Bad 1966; Thee Midniters 1967; Wilson Pickett 1967; The Blues Brothers 1990

—

Chuck Berry "You Never Can Tell" Chess July 1964

Style: Rock 'n' roll
Where from: St. Louis, MO
Where recorded: Chicago, IL
Suggested pairing: Mitchell Torok "Caribbean" 1959

With very little guitar, driven by piano and saxophone, and a dab of Cajun influence, Chuck Berry's "You Never Can Tell" is about a teenaged couple, Pierre and the mademoiselle, marrying and making it stick, with a nice record collection, a Coolerator "crammed with TV dinners and ginger ale" and some Roebuck furniture. It was written from the perspective of young people, as Berry often did, who supply advice to the older generation: "'C'est la vie,' say the old folks."

—

Martha and the Vandellas "Dancin' in the Streets" Gordy July 31, 1964

Style: Soul vocal group
From and recorded in: Detroit, MI
Suggested pairings: The Larks "The Jerk" 1964; The Rolling Stones "Street Fighting Man" 1968

The Vandellas were one-time singing Motown secretary Martha Reeves, Annette Sterling and Rosalind Ashford. At her secretarial job, Reeves taught background singers, leading to her own trio and her first hit, "Come and Get These Memories," in 1962. When co-writers Mickey Stevenson and Marvin Gaye rode through Detroit, they saw the city opening up fire hydrants for children to play in the water, looking like they were dancing in the water in the streets. At the session, the third writer, Ivy Joe Hunter, felt the drum track was weak, and needed more bump and grind. He brought in a crowbar, sat on a concrete floor, said, "roll tape" and slammed the tool against the concrete floor on the downbeat to create one of the most defined and distinctive drumbeats in the Motown catalog. The lyrics incorporated many urban areas like Philadelphia and New York City, to increases sales there.

Lamont Dozier recalled, "Whoever had the best tune on a groove would get the release, that was the competitiveness of the Motown scene and kept all of us on our toes." Written for Kim Weston, Mary Wells was also offered this song, but she turned it down. Lamont Dozier recalled, "One year, we'd didn't have a release on Martha and the Vandellas. Ivy Jo Hunter wrote ' Dancing in the Streets' and we did a song called 'Jimmy Mack' that at the time everybody thought 'Dancing in the Streets' was better than 'Jimmy Mack,' which went into the can and stayed for about four or five years."

Dozier noted Gordy "was good and still is at picking songs, him being a songwriter himself, extraordinaire, he knew songs, he felt them and he knew how to direct the release of songs. That was a tremendous help to all the producers and songwriters and he made us all look good."

Written at the height of the civil rights movement, Afro Americans heard in "Dancing In The Streets" as "Demonstrate In The Streets" in the cities mentioned in the song.

Don Julian used the dance aspect for his top ten hit, "The Jerk" by the Larks in late 1964, and it inspired The Rolling Stones on "Street Fighting Man" in 1968.

Remakes: The Grateful Dead 1977; Teri DeSario With K.C. 1980

—

The Yardbirds "I Wish You Would" Epic August 7, 1964
Style: Rock 'n' roll group
From and recorded in: England
Original version: Billy Boy 1955
Original title: "I Wish You Could" (first pressing and picture sleeve printing error)

On this first release by The Yardbirds, the title was wrong and overdone echo drowned out lead singer Keith Relf's voice. The Yardbirds were famed for experimenting with distortion and other effects in their quest for an updated blues sound. Guitarist Jimmy Page, who later joined The Yardbirds, would later use them with Led Zeppelin.

—

Manfred Mann "Do Wah Diddy Diddy" Ascot August 1964
Style: Rock 'n' roll group
From and recorded in: England
Original: The Exciters "Do-Wah Diddy" 1963

The band Manfred Mann took The Exciters' moderate hit "Do-Wah Diddy," added an extra Diddy and took "Do Wah Diddy Diddy" to a #1 spot.

—

The Beatles "Slow Down" Capitol August 24, 1964
Style: Rock 'n' roll group
From and recorded in: England
Original version: Larry Williams 1957

This was a fast remake of a Larry Williams non-hit, rendered in the style of Little Richard. For The Beatles, it was their final chart hit of vintage material. From this point on, it was all Lennon-McCartney compositions, for the most part at least.

—

The Kinks "You Really Got Me" Reprise August 26, 1964
Style: Rock 'n' roll group
From and recorded in: England
Jimmy Giuffre "The Train and the River" 1957; The Champs "Tequila" 1958

Ray Davies, who wrote "You Really Got Me" with the help of his brother, Kinks guitarist Dave Davies, played it for Dave on piano, and Dave tried it on guitar. When recording "You Really Got Me," Dave got the dirty guitar sound by slashing the speaker cone on his amp with a razor blade. The vibration of the fabric produced the "fuzz" effect, which became common as various electronic devices were later invented to distort sound. Lacking such devices, Davies kicked or mistreated his amp to get the desired sound. Producer Shel Talmy brought in session musician Bobby Graham to play drums and Jimmy Page on rhythm guitar.

The first line was originally "You, you really got me going." Ray Davies changed it to "Girl, you really got me going" to appeal to the teenage girls in their audience. Dave Davies, who got the idea for the guitar riff from "Tequila" by The Champs, was trying to write something similar to "Louie Louie," which was a big hit for The Kingsmen.

Remake: Van Halen 1978

—

The Rolling Stones "Time Is On My Side" London September 25, 1964
Style: Rock 'n' roll group
Where from: England
Where recorded: Chicago, IL
Original version: Kai Winding 1963
Earlier version: Irma Thomas 1963

Keith Richards said of this song, "In America we were basically known for heavy, slowish kind of ballads. 'Time Is On My Side,' 'Tell Me,' 'Heart of Stone,' that was what we were known for. Strangely enough that was our thing. Every single was a slow song. Who would believe it? You'd think they'd be clamoring for out-and-out rock and roll, but no, it was the soul ballads that happened for us in America." Apparently, two versions of "Time Is On My Side" were released. The first used organ backing; the second guitar backing.

—

Herman's Hermits "I'm Into Something Good" MGM September 1964

Style: Rock 'n' roll group
From and recorded in: England
Original version: Earl Jean—member of the Cookies 1964

The youthful exuberance on this track is very real, as the band was very excited to be cutting a single. "On the record you can hear the enthusiasm of this band who believe that they were going to be heard on the radio," lead singer Peter Noone said in his Songfacts interview. "When the record was on the radio, we thought we'd made it." The hand claps on this song were done into the same microphone where Peter Noone was recording his vocal. They aren't always in time to the beat, but that's part of the appeal of the recording, as it's unrefined, but jubilant.

Remake: Donny Osmond 1971

—

The Shangri-Las "Leader of the Pack" Bang September 1964

Style: Girl group rock 'n' roll
From and recorded in: New York

This song combines death, motorcycles and gangs. Who can beat that combo?

George "Shadow" Morton found the inspiration for this song at a diner in Hicksville, New York. "Bikers, hotrodders, gum-smacking ladies," he said, "not careful at all about their language." Producer Morton, credited on the composition with Jeff Barry and Ellie Greenwich, brought a bike into the studio for the motorcycle sounds. The sound of the motorcycle is the engineer's Harley Davidson driven through the lobby of the hotel and up to the floor of the recording studio. No one was arrested, but a ticket was issued. However, in an interview four decades later, Shangri-Las lead singer Mary Weiss said the motorcycle sound was taken from an effects record. This song was censored by the BBC, likely because of its death theme, although some think it might encourage violence between mods and rockers.

Satire: The Detergents' "Leader of the Laundromat"

—

The Supremes "Baby Love" Motown September 1964

Style: Soul vocal group
From and recorded in: Detroit, MI
Suggested pairings: The Supremes "Where Did Our Love Go" 1964; The Lovin' Spoonful "Daydream: 1966; Thelma Houston "Baby Mine" 1966

Written off The Supremes' just-previous #1 hit "Where Did Our Love Go," co-writer, Lamont Dozier said, "I would collaborate with Eddie on lyrics and with Brian on melodies. Then Brian and I would go into the studio and produce the actual record although Eddie should have been put down as one of the producers because he helped teach the artists the tune when the lyric was finished." With Diana Ross on lead vocals, Berry Gordy thought it incomplete, so he had her dub in the starting semi-lyric, "oooooh."

In testimony about a Lorenzo Pack lawsuit against Motown in 1966 over his song "I'm Afraid," he alleged Holland-Dozier-Holland plagiarized for "Baby Love." Brian Holland testified, "When we write a song, we try to express real feelings about a real situation. In writing the song for The Supremes it was obvious that we were writing for pretty young girls, of whom one is the so-called lead singer. Therefore, in writing 'Baby Love,' we pictured a simple story about a girl whose boyfriend has left her and who loves him very dearly and who would like the boy to come back. The music fits this simple story." As with other Motown releases, "Shop Around" by The Miracles and "Jamie" by Eddie Holland, at least two versions of "Baby Love" were issued. The more quieter version with a different instrumental break was replaced by a more aggressive sound, supplemented by Mike Valvano's foot stomping, to keep energy and chart position up.

—

The Sunrays "Car Party" Tower September 1964

Style: Rock 'n' roll
Where from: Hawthorne, CA and South Bay, CA
Where recorded: Hollywood, CA

After Murry Wilson was fired by the Beach Boys, he took over management of The Sunrays, who recorded his song "Car Party" backed with "Outta Gas" as the debut 45 on the brand new Tower. The Sunrays were Rick Henn, guitarists Eddy Medora and Byron Case, keyboard player Marty DiGiovanni, and bassist Vince Hozier. Medora recalled, "I think we reached our peak as a garage band and musicians. We knew hundreds and hundreds of songs. When Murray mentioned that he wanted us to sing harmonies, we said, 'This is an opportunity for us to learn.' It was tough because when you're a band you say, I wanna do what 'I' wanna do, but a lot of bands don't make it because of that. There's gotta be one chef in the kitchen cooking. You get too many chefs and you get a lot of arguments and that's what happened with Murray and his sons. Murray wrote 'Car Party' and we all wrote the flip side, "Outta Gas," together. He wanted The Beach Boys to do his car song. And we went 'oh my god, a car song.' We all loved cars and we just thought the car song thing had had it. But at the same time, when you think about car songs, other than the Rip Chords, Jan & Dean, and The Beach Boys—at that time, those were the only groups that were doing those type of songs. Herb Albert used to come in quite a bit… Phil Spector. And Larry Marks, who was the number one engineer—we cut all the lights out, tried to get that wall-of-sound… which we did. We had a very, very huge sound. We would lay down our tracks ourselves, then they would bring in the 'wrecking crew' to tweak it up."

—

The Larks "The Jerk" Money October 1964

Style: Soul vocal group
From and recorded in: Los Angeles, CA
Suggested pairings: Martha and the Vandellas "Dancin' in the Streets" 1964; Major Lance "Girls" 1964; Clyde & the Blue Jays "The Big Jerk" 1964; The Miracles 'Come On and Do the Jerk" 1964

Don Julian's career busted wide open when he split his singing Larks from his Meadowlarks band. Julian readily admitted he wrote "The Jerk" as a bit of an answer to Martha and the Vandellas' major Motown hit "Dancing in the Streets." Julian sang lead vocals with backing by Charles Morrison and Ted Walters as The Larks on this mega-hit.

"I had taken 'The Jerk' to Warner Brothers Records," said Julian. "Bob Krasnow was the guy making the deal with me, I was waiting on the final word from him, I called his office three days in a row, couldn't get in touch with him, took one copy by Vee Jay, took another copy to Dolphins of Hollywood. A guy walked in and wanted to buy the record right there on the spot." Dolphin's put it on the air that night." "The Jerk" hit #1 on KRLA on October 10 and #7 pop on November 14, 1964. Three days later Warner Brothers Records put out their version of "The Jerk'" as "The Big Jerk" by Clyde & the Blue Jays on Loma. "I think they were trying to beat me.

"During the time the record was a hit, we had a show at the 5/4 Ballroom with The Supremes, The Miracles and myself with The Meadowlarks band. We did a show in Oakland, did a show with The Miracles and The Supremes. The response was so great, The Miracles recorded 'Come On and Do the Jerk,' which created a little concern with the Motown machinery; we were bound to be crushed under the Motown monster. Smokey's tune was a good tune, it was real fast; mine had a dancing in the street beat, kept mine alive, we were able to overcome Bobby Sanders, able to overcome the Miracles."

—

The Supremes "Come See About Me" Motown October 27, 1964

Style: Soul vocal group
From and recorded in: Detroit, MI
Suggested pairings: Mid South Singers "Lord Come See About Me" 1953; Don Covay & the Goodtimers "See About Me" 1961; Nella Dodds "Come See About Me" 1964

The Supremes recorded this song, "Come See About Me," for inclusion in their upcoming album. That's when Nella Dodds recorded the first version on a single, which began to move up the charts. To staunch the loss of a fine song, Motown rush released The Supremes' version out on a 45 and it became the group's newest #1 hit, cutting Nella Dodds off at the turntable.

Remakes: Mitch Ryder & the Detroit Wheels 1967; Jr. Walker & the All Stars 1968

—

The Righteous Brothers "You've Lost That Lovin' Feelin'" Philles 1964

Style: Blue-eyed soul duet
Where from: Orange County, CA
Where recorded: Hollywood, CA
Suggested pairing: The Four Tops "Baby I Need Your Loving" 1964

The supposed most-played song in the history of radio, The Righteous Brothers' "You've Lost That Lovin' Feelin'" was released on Phil Spector's Philles label. Recorded on three or four tracks, "You've Lost That Lovin' Feelin'" underwent about a dozen overdubs which meant it lost that many generations from the original source recording. Some thought it an answer to "Baby I Need Your Lovin'" by The Four Tops. "Ray Maxwell told me he thought Barry Mann and Cynthia should do it," said Dick Monda of Moonglow. "To me it sounded as if the needle were dragging." Monda recalled Ray Maxwell of the Moonglow label "made a deal with Spector. The brothers were leased to Philles. He just allowed Phil Spector to put them on Philles, he paid Bobby and Bill. Every other Righteous Brothers record was issued either on Philles or on Moonglow."

In a move for maximum top 40 radio play, Spector changed the song's actual playing time shown on the label from 3:50 to a more DJ-friendly 3:05. It began on KRLA on November 22, 1964, where it went to #1.

—

Don Covay "Mercy Mercy" Rosemart October 1964

Style: Soul
Where from: Orangeburg, SC
Where recorded: A-1 Sound 56th Street, New York City, NY

This was recorded in a studio owned by Herb Abramson, one of the founders of Atlantic, and the WWRL DJ "the Magnificent Montague," on a three-track Presto tape deck. The record came out on Rosemart, which was named after Montague's wife, Rose and his son Martin, with a then unknown guitar player James, Jimi Hendrix, on lead guitar.

—

The American Four "Luci Baines" Selma October 1964

Style: Rock 'n' roll
From and recorded in: Los Angeles, CA
Suggested pairings: The Isley Brothers "Twist and Shout" 1961; The Vibrations "My Girl Sloopy" 1964

A vehicle for Arthur Lee, The American Four recorded this satirical vocal "Luci Baines," an assumed reference to President Johnson's daughter, backed with a mainly organ instrumental "Soul Food." Arthur Lee went on to form the highly respected psychedelic band Love.

—

Marvin Gaye "How Sweet It Is" Tamla November 4, 1964

Style: Soul
Where from: Washington, DC
Where recorded: Detroit, MI

With a phrase popularized by Jackie Gleason, "How Sweet It Is," for this song Marvin Gaye used The Andantes—Marlene Barrow, Jackie Hicks and Louvain Demps—on background vocals and The Funk Brothers on piano and percussion with guitar by The Miracles' Marv Tarplin.

Remake: Marvin Gaye "Wie Schön Das Ist"—German language version 1964

—

The Animals "Boom Boom" MGM November 1964

Style: Rock 'n' roll
From and recorded in: England

A recent rocking blues classic by John Lee Hooker, the Animals' take on this vocal, "Boom Boom," had middlin' success on the WMCA and KFXM charts in November, 1964.

—

Alvin Cash and the Crawlers "Twine Time" XL/Mar-V-Lus November 1964

Style: Soul instrumental
Where from: St. Louis, MO
Where recorded: Chicago, IL
Suggested pairing: Jr. Walker & the All Stars "Shotgun" 1965

Alvin Cash and his eight brothers and sisters attended Sumner High in St. Louis where Annie Mae Bullock also attended before recording as Tina Turner. "I used to sit behind Tina and kick my knee in her butt all the time," Cash told the Chicago Sun-Times. "She'd turn around and say, 'Alvin Cash, would you cut that out!'" Alvin formed The Crawlers with three of his younger siblings in East St. Louis, and in 1963, went to Chicago to see if his act could cut a record. Andre Williams caught the act and asked Cash about yelling some lines on a new dance disc called "The Twine," based on dance moves local kids were making. Cash came in with The Nightlighters, a band he was touring with at the time. This back-up unit subsequently changed its name to The Crawlers, and later, to The Registers. "Twine Time" was a pleasantly crude instrumental with an unstoppably funky groove; sales of the disk came close to a million. Jr. Walker and the All Stars gave it a big-time mention ('it's twiiiine time!') on their group's springtime smash "Shotgun."

—

Chuck Berry "Promised Land" Chess November 1964

Style: Rock 'n' roll
Where from: St. Louis, MO
Where recorded: Chicago, IL
Suggested pairings: Roy Acuff "Wabash Cannonball" 1938; King Cole Trio "Route 66" 1946; Moon Mullican "Greyhound" 1952; Elvis Presley "Mystery Train" 1955; Chuck Berry "Memphis" 1959

Written by Chuck Berry in prison in the early 1960s, "Promised Land" is a tale of a poor boy who heads to California from his home in Norfolk, Virginia. The journey takes him by bus, train and airplane through much of the United States; "got through Mississippi clean." When he finally arrives, he calls back home to tell them he made it.

Remake: Elvis Presley 1974

—

The Ad Libs "The Boy From New York City" December 1964

Style: Soul vocal group
Where from: Bayonne, NJ
Where recorded: New York City, NY

As The Creators—Hughie Harris and Danny Austin, James Wright, John Alan and bass singer Chris Coles—recorded a doo wop ballad, "I'll Never Never Do it Again," on T-Kay, and "Yeah, He's Got It" on Philips in 1962. Two members left; Norman Donegan and Dave Watt joined as did Mary Ann Thomas, who took lead as they became The Ad Libs on this snappy "The Boy from New York City" ("Ooh-wah-ooo-wah, cool, cool kitty..."). They took a demo to Broadway in Manhattan where Jerry Leiber and Mike Stoller heard a hit and signed them to Red Bird Records, placing it on their new Blue Cat subsidiary. The rest was the history of a hit, #7 on New York's WMCA in December, #4 on L.A's KRLA in January and #11 on L.A.'s KFWB.

—

The Beau Brummels "Laugh Laugh" Autum December 1964

Style: Rock 'n' roll
From and recorded in: San Francisco, CA

The Beau Brummels, who took their name from the dandy of literature, cashed in on the idea of claiming a British-sounding name, and alphabetically their records would be placed next to The Beatles in record store browser bins, jacking up their sales. This marketing tactic was denied by Valentino and those who worked with the band. Led by Sal Valentino, vocals, the group included Ron Elliott, guitar; Ron Meagher, bass guitar; Declan Mulligan, rhythm guitar and John Petersen, drums. Valentino first recorded as Sal Valentino & the Valentines on "I Wanna Twist" on Falco in 1962. Discovered and signed by San Francisco disc jockeys Tom Donahue and Bobby Mitchell, produced by Sylvester Stewart, later known as Sly Stone, The Beau Brummels' folkish, yet rocking "Laugh Laugh" was the very first hit of the coming Haight-Ashbury Sound. This song hit #1 on Sacramento and San Jose charts; #3 in their Bay Area hometown; #1 in L.A.; and barely cracked the New York top 20.

—

The Kinks "All of the Day & All of the Night" Reprise December 9, 1964

Style: Rock 'n' roll
From and recorded in: England
Suggested pairings: Paul Revere & the Raiders "Just Like Me" 1966; The Who "I Can't Explain" 1964; The Doors "Hello, I Love You, Won't You Tell Me Your Name" 1968

Jim Morrison of The Doors approached keyboard player Ray Manzarek about an idea for a song: "Jim said, 'I got this new song, "Hello I Love You."' He wrote it for a girl, we're sitting at the beach, this absolutely foxy black American, white, black, she was everything, she had mixed blood. He said, 'Here's how it goes.' I'm thinking, 'Hold it, that's "All Of the Day" by the Kinks. Jim knew music, but he didn't know it that well, that's in the back of his brain, he applied those words to that melody, he didn't know where it came from. It was just something floating around in his head, I thought, let him sing. It's not quite 'All of the Day...' where we're going to get sued. I talked to Ray Davies about it once in '73. I said, 'Listen man, thanks a lot for "Hello I Love You..." He said, 'Whadaya mean mate?" "I said, 'Well, "Hello I Love You..." is like "All of the Day, All of the Night." You're not going to sue us are you?' He said, 'Get out of here. Fine. So what. Copyright that? Enjoy. God bless, glad you guys made it.'"

—

The Who "I Can't Explain" Decca December 1964

Style: Rock
From and recorded in: England
Suggested pairings: The Kingsmen "Louie Louie" 1963; The Kinks "You Really Got Me" 1964; The Kinks "All Day and All of the Night" 1964; The Nazz "Open My Eyes" 1969; The Clash "Guns On the Roof" 1979

After one release as the High Numbers, the UK-only single "Zoot Suit," The Who debuted with a "Louie Louie" riff on the intro of "I Can't Explain," Pete Townshend's alleged answer to the Kinks' garagey "You Really Got Me" about an 18-year-old who can't admit love to his girlfriend as he's too high on dexies, aka speed. The Who's Pete Townshend acknowledged the performance "can't be beat for straightforward Kink copying. There is little to say about how I wrote this. It came out of the top of my head when I was 18 and a half." To achieve that Kinks sound, the Who hired Kinks' producer Shel Talmy, who produced and secured session players, including Jimmy Page, later of Led Zeppelin, on rhythm guitar. "It's pretty well known that Pete deliberately wrote 'I Can't Explain' with a 'Kinks' leaning to get my attention—and he did!" said Talmy.

—

The Rolling Stones "Heart Of Stone" London December 19, 1964

Style: Rock 'n' roll
From and recorded in: England
Suggested pairing: The Rolling Stones "Under My Thumb"

With a distinct blues feel, "Heart Of Stone" was the second composition written by The Rolling Stones' members, credited to Mick Jagger and Keith Richards. Richards, Bill Wyman and Brian Jones also sang backup vocals with Jimmy Page, guitar, and L.A. producer and Phil Spector associate Jack Nitzsche, piano and tambourine.

—

The Temptations "My Girl" Gordy December 21, 1964

Style: Soul vocal group
Where from: Alabama
Where recorded: Detroit, MI

While traveling as part of the Motortown Revue, Smokey Robinson and fellow Miracles member Ronnie White wrote "My Girl," recorded in the fall of 1964 with David Ruffin singing his first lead vocal for the group. "Smokey declared it was written to capture Ruffin's vocal chops," said Claudette Robinson. "'My Girl' really was for The Temptations. He really wanted to use David Ruffin's voice, he thought David was one of those untapped resources. Because people knew Eddie Kendricks' voice, he wanted people more to be more familiar with David Ruffin's voice."

This song had nothing to do with Mary Wells' #1 hit, "My Guy." Right, sure.

—

Sam the Sham and the Pharaohs "Wooly Bully" XL December 1964/MGM February 1965

Style: Rock 'n' roll
Where from: San Antonio, TX
Where recorded: Phillips Recording Service Memphis, TN

Sam was Domingo Samudio, and Sam the Sham and the Pharaohs were an all Mexican-American band formed in 1961, at one time including Trini Lopez, that impersonated an Egyptian rock outfit. The countdown is "uno dos tres quarto" which suggested their Spanish background, and the one lyric, "don't be L7," interprets to don't be square, using fingers to create a square. Some obscure lyrics like "Wooly Bully" were assumed sexual and banned by some radio stations.

Remakes: Canned Heat 1971; Disco Tex & The Sex-O-Lettes 1977
Answer: The Soul Brothers "Wooly Bully Again" 1966

—

Sam Cooke "A Change Is Gonna Come" RCA December 1964

Style: Soul
Where from: Chicago, IL
Where recorded: Hollywood, CA

Along with The Impressions' "People Get Ready," the success of Sam Cooke's "A Change Is Gonna Come" took the civil rights issue from the political arena to more commercial venues, pushing it to anthem status. Starting off in gospel, "Sam Cooke made the transition," said his producer Rene Hall. "He came from a religious background, they had this afterthought that doing pop music was sinful."

Remakes: Brother Jack McDuff 1966; The Meditation Singers 1966; Brenton Wood 1969; Paris [Mr. Tears] 1970; The 5th Dimension 1970; Bobby Womack 1977; Billy Preston 1981: Solomon Burke 1981; Jennifer Holliday 1983

—

Moody Blues "Go Now" Deram December 1964

Style: Rock 'n' roll
From and recorded in: England
Original version: Bessie Banks

Moody Blues guitarist and "Go Now" vocalist Denny Laine recalled to Gibson.com how the band came to cover this song: "It came in one of these suitcases full of records from America. A friend of B. Mitchel Reed, who was a DJ, would send this stuff across. So I picked that one out especially because Mike Pinder was a piano player. We'd always get the gig where the piano would be out of tune and we'd get the slow handclap because they were waiting to tune the piano. We did 'Go Now' because it was a song with a piano in it."

—

Thee Midniters "Land of a Thousand Dances" Chattahoochee December 26, 1964

Style: Latino rock 'n' roll
Where from: Los Angeles, CA
Where recorded: Hollywood, CA
Original version: Chris Kenner 1962

When Thee Midniters recorded "Land of a Thousand Dances," Lil' Ray was gone and Lil' Willie G Garcia was the full-time lead singer. "It was just one of the songs in their repertoire and it was being recorded," said Billy Cardenas, who was associated with Eddie Davis of Rampart Records which had released The Cannibal and The Headhunters version: "That was the battle of the bands at East L.A. College and everything was taped. So when Eddie Davis came out with Cannibal's 'Land of a Thousand Dances,' they covered it."

One-time Midniters vocalist Lil' Ray Jiminez stated, "I was supposed to do the big show at East L.A. College. I got stuck at a show the night before in fog in Bakersfield and couldn't make it. At that time, Eddie Torres went to Chattahoochee, started to roll a little, we were mad," said Cardenas. "Ruth Conti of Chattahoochee decided to put it out, which worked out good because KRLA had a contest, which is the best one, and Cannibal won by quite a bit." "Huggy Boy played it seven times a night," said Torres. "He kept saying '"Thee Midniters"' on "Land of a Thousand Dances.'" Rock radio split on which version to support. According to Eddie Davis, "You find out who your friends are.... I'm talking about radio people who are supposed to be your friends. Chattahoochie really worked hard trying to develop that record, they did a lot of advertising in Billboard and the trades. With Cannibal, I bought a '65 airport limousine and threw them in the car, we went on the road." Cardenas said, "It was a competition thing and it really helped." Davis said, "Thee Midniters was a band; Cannibal was four individuals. They were a vocal group, and were visual, very visual." At the same time, according to Cardenas, "Hank Ballard & the Midnighters were recording and they were working up a hit, 'Land of a Thousand Dances,'" which was never issued. Thee Midniters' "Land Of A Thousand Dances" was reissued backed with "Ball O' Twine," which members of Thee Midniters denied was recorded by them.

—

Cannibal & the Headhunters "Land of 1000 Dances" Rampart/Date January 14, 1965

Style: Latino rock 'n' roll
Where from: Los Angeles, CA
Where recorded: Hollywood, CA
Original version: Chris Kenner 1962

The zenith of the East L.A. sound occurred in early '65, when two little known Hispanic groups, Cannibal & the Headhunters and Thee Midniters debuted with a giant local and, eventually, national hit. In the case of Thee Midniters, there had been one previous recording as Lil' Ray & the Midniters; however the band had to change the spelling, adding the "Thee" to avoid conflict with the earlier Hank Ballard & the Midnighters, which also underwent a forced name change from The Royals to The Midnighters after a conflict with The Five Royales in 1954. This song was a redo of "Land of a Thousand Dances" (Thee Midniters) or "Land of 1000 Dances" (Cannibal and the Headhunters) of a New Orleans-based Chris Kenner original which was a minor hit in 1962. In the case of Cannibal & the Headhunters vs. Thee Midniters, what set the former apart was the "na na na na na na" chant at the opening because Cannibal & the Headhunters lead singer Frankie G forgot the lyrics.

According to Robert "Rabbit" Jaramillo of the group, "Frankie was Little Cannibal because his brother was Big Cannibal. He got in a fight and bit someone." Rabbit recalled he had a shrunken head on the dash of his '52 Chevy. "Eddie Davis saw that, The Head Hunters were born. "I knew Cannibal was a gangster, same gang I was in, Primera Flats," said producer Johnny Jay. "He was from the Pee Wees, I was from the Midget Dukes of Primera Flats; he lived on Cincinnati Street in Boyle Heights. Cannibal learned how to play piano, I took him in as one of my key singers." Rabbit said, "'Land Of 1000 Dances' took us out of the projects. Other members were Richard "Scar" Lopez, Yo Yo Jaramillo and Little Frankie G Garcia. "I recorded it with Cannibal & the Headhunters and Thee Midniters recorded it on their own; all these things were taking place at the same time," said Billy Cardenas.

Cardenas continued, "I started to cover the record, but I hesitated, I didn't want to do that, although it was a funky version of it. It was The Blendells who were to back up The Headhunters on that hit record. "The nonsense lyric, that's Frankie," said Cardenas. "He very simply forgot the words at a performance, he started "na na na na," it's a thing that caught on instantly. Everybody started doing it, Thee Midniters picked it up and it was part of their repertoire before a recording was ever made."

Eddie Davis of Rampart Records recalled, "Cannibal's backup group was The Rhythm Playboys and Billy Cardenas managed The Rhythm Playboys, and the night of the recording session, he wouldn't let the group come. So we're sitting there in the studio getting ready to record and there's no band to record except for the bass player, Billy Watson, and he said, 'Billy Cardenas told us not to come, but I came anyway.' This was Wednesday night and The Blendells always rehearsed on a Wednesday night, so I called them up at their home and said, 'I'm in trouble down here, why don't you play this thing for Cannibal?' and they came. There's two basses, Billy Watson and Mike from The Blendells, and they wound up backing Cannibal... it became successful. If the Playboys had come, maybe the record would never have happened."

According to talent scout and Flash Records clerk Rudy Benevidez, "I was a consultant to a lot of sessions. They brought 'Land Of 1000 Dances' to me. He couldn't get no airplay, came to me when I was at Flash Records. I said, 'The intro is too long, clip it.' He went back into the studio and he edited it. It was a hit overnight, but stayed on some charts for over four months."

—

Them "Gloria" Parrot January 1965
Style: Rock 'n' roll
Where from: Belfast, Ireland
Where recorded: England
Suggested pairings: Mike Evans "Gruesome" 1967; Suzi Quatro "Lipstick" 1981; AC/DC "Jailbreak" 1984

This group named themselves Them after the 1954 sci-fi horror film, with the lead voice of Van Morrison. The title lyric spelled out, "G-l-o-r-i-a." The song is about a girl who comes by a lot, possibly for sex, which caused some banning of the song. It was released as the B-side of the Them single "Baby Please Don't Go," a cover of a blues standard.

Remakes: The Blues Magoos 1967; The Shadows of Knight 1967; Patti Smith 1975; The Doors 1983

—

The Animals "Don't Let Me Be Misunderstood" MGM January 1965
Style: Rock 'n' roll
From and recorded in: England
Original version: Nina Simone 1964

As lead vocalist Eric Burdon told Rolling Stone, "It was never considered pop material, but it somehow got passed on to us and we fell in love with it immediately." The Animals turned "Don't Let Me Be Misunderstood" into an earnest plea that caused it to chart on WMCA in February and hit #9 on KFWB in March 1965.

Remake: Santa Esmeralda 1982

—

The Primitives "The Ostrich" Pickwick City January 1965
Style: Rock 'n' roll
From and recorded in: New York
Suggested pairing: James Booker "Gonzo" 1960

After The Jades, Lou Reed was subjected to shock treatment, went to college, graduated with honors from Syracuse University's College of Arts and Sciences and ended up in Greenwich Village. "The Ostrich," a parody of popular dance songs of the time, which included lines such as "put your head on the floor and have somebody step on it" to the bass line taken from James Booker's New Orleans instrumental hit "Gonzo," played by The Primitives—Welsh musician John Cale, viola, keyboards and bass, who had recently moved to New York to study music and was playing viola in La Monte Young's Theatre of Eternal Music, along with Tony Conrad. Cale and Conrad were on "The Ostrich," Reed tuned each string of his guitar to the same note, which they began to call his "ostrich guitar" tuning. This technique created a drone effect like their experimentation in Young's avant-garde ensemble. Cale contributed to Reed's early repertoire, i.e. "Heroin," and a partnership began to evolve. Reed and Cale lived together on the Lower East Side, and invited Reed's college acquaintance, guitarist Sterling Morrison, and Cale's neighbor drummer, Angus MacLise, to help form their new group, The Velvet Underground.

—

Jr. Walker & the All Stars "Shotgun" Soul January 14, 1965
Style: Soul instrumental
Where from: Blytheville, AR
Where recorded: Detroit, MI

Born in 1931, tenor sax player Junior Walker, real name Autry DeWalt Mixon Jr., first signed with Harvey Fuqua's Harvey label in 1961, recording several instrumentals. Fuqua said Walker thought up his own stage name. In 1964, when Harvey was absorbed by

Motown, Walker was assigned to the subsidiary Soul label and was encouraged to try a few vocals, like the searing sax heavy signature vocal "Shotgun." Fuqua recalled, "I might have had something to do with it. I give most of the credit to Johnny Bristol, who really wanted him to start singing. He wanted him to sing more as opposed to playing." The session featured The Funk Brothers' James Jamerson on bass and Benny Benjamin on drums, and there was a dance that went along with it.

—

The Impressions "People Get Ready" ABC February 1965

Style: Soul vocal group
From and recorded in: Chicago, IL

Curtis Mayfield combined a reference to train travel and the civil rights struggle into this anthemic "People Get Ready," every bit the equal to Sam Cooke's "A Change Is Gonna Come," though not a claim made by songwriter Mayfield himself. "I believe any song that's good enough to sing in church, broken down in its proper lyric form, is good enough to perform in a tavern, being that there are human beings in both. If you're going to straighten out people, where is it you should perform it?" The flipside, I've Been Trying," was influential in the success of Billy Stewart.

Remakes: The Chambers Brothers 1972; The Persuasions 1972; Sonny Terry & Brownie McGhee 1973; Bob Marley & the Wailers 1977; Jeff Beck & Rod Stewart 1985

—

Billy Stewart "I Do Love You" Chess February 1965

Style: Soul
From and recorded in: Chicago, IL
Suggested pairing: The Impressions "I've Been Trying"

After limited success with releases like "Strange Feeling" and "Reap What You Sow" in 1962, Billy Stewart hit stuttering ballad style pay dirt with the evocative "I Do Love You," a take-off on the Impressions' "I've Been Trying" and the first of several hits for him.

—

The Marvelettes "Too Many Fish in the Sea" Tamla 1965

Style: Soul vocal group
From and recorded in: Detroit, MI

"It was still a great song, everyone loved it on stage," said Gladys Horton from The Marvelettes, whose "Too Many Fish In The Sea" was a minor hit. The crowd would say, "We want the one with the bongos."

—

Martha and the Vandellas "Nowhere To Run" Gordy February 5, 1965

Style: Soul vocal group
From and recorded in: Detroit, MI

When Mary Wells missed a session date, Motown secretary Martha Reeves stepped in for her, and with The Vandellas, took on "Nowhere to Run," a panicked vocal about obsessive love with massive percussion, supplemented by snow chains in the midst of Detroit's deep winter environment. Co-writer Lamont Dozier described "a lot of urgency there, a lot of desperate need, again from old girlfriends and their troubles thrown upon me, which I was partly responsible for. I took advantage of that and wrote songs from it along with Eddie and Brian. She definitely had the voice to get that urgency across, that need was very convincing."

—

The Beatles "Eight Days a Week" Capitol February 15, 1965

Style: Rock 'n' roll
From and recorded in: England

As opposed to an ending fade, this one fades in at the beginning.

—

The Whispers "Never Again" Dore February 21, 1965

Style: Soul vocal group
From and recorded in: Los Angeles, CA

The Whispers were Walter and Wallace "Scotty" Scott out of Jordan High School, both of whom had sung with The Utopians on Imperial in 1962. "They never sounded like each other," said James Faulkner "The twins wasn't getting along, there was a conflict." Walter tried to organize another group while Wallace sang on the ballad "Never Again" backed with the instrumental "Slow Jerk."

—

Gene Chandler "Nothing Can Stop Me" Constellation March 1965

Style: Soul
From and recorded in: Chicago, IL

"Gene Chandler came on the scene through Carl Davis," said the writer of "Nothing Can Stop Me," Curtis Mayfield. "He was on Constellation. I believe this label was owned by Abner after he moved on from Vee Jay. Gene was one of his main artists, Little Curtis was always around, I'd been doing things for Abner, Vee Jay, Jerry Butler, The Impressions, even Dee Clark. I met Gene, I'd show him a few of my songs. He had his power at the company, he'd get it over."

Chandler added, "Curtis Mayfield wrote it, it wasn't for me. Curtis Mayfield was showing me some songs, 'Man's Temptation' and 'The Monkey Time.' Years later, after 'The Monkey Time,' he's playing these songs he wrote for Major Lance. One was 'Nothing Can Stop Me.'"

Though the lyric "nothing can stop me" was used in Chandler's first hit, "Duke Of Earl," Mayfield said, "The thoughts in mind pertained to the lyric matter of the song, just about my own person[al] ego and pride of what I was about with this young lady and 'nothing can stop me.'"

—

The Miracles "Ooo Baby Baby" Tamla March 5, 1965

Style: Soul vocal group
From and recorded in: Detroit, MI

"We had started singing that melody on stage, we would just say that phrase," said Claudette Robinson of "Ooo Baby Baby" by The Miracles. "It ended up developing into a song. Smokey would kind of do this, almost ad-libbing between songs. Often lead singers would have phrases or terms used to say something to the audience, more female than male—'ooh baby baby' was one of the phrases."

—

The Rolling Stones "The Last Time" London March 13, 1965

Style: Rock 'n' roll
From and recorded in: England
Suggested pairings: The Staple Singers "This May Be The Last Time" 1955; James Brown "Maybe the Last Time" 1964; The Verve "Bitter Sweet Symphony" 1997

Their earliest use of original material, in fact, this Rolling Stones' hit, "The Last Time," was an adaptation of the gospel "This May Be The Last Time" by The Staple

Singers from 1955. Producer Phil Spector assisted with this effort. A similar guitar rift found in "This Could Be the Last Time" by The Staple Singers was recycled in the Beatles' "Day Tripper" in late 1965. When Pops Staples found out about The Stones' hit, supposedly the statute of limitations had expired.

—

The Guess Who "Shakin' All Over" Quality (Canada)/Scepter March 1965

Style: Rock
From and recorded in: Canada
Original version: Johnny Kidd & the Pirates 1959

A debut single by aptly named The Guess Who, based on members searching for a name, coming up with Guess Who, was used by the Canadian label to throw off record buyers at the onset of the British Invasion. This first release as The Guess Who, "Shakin' All Over," was led by Chad Allen on this remake of the British-based Johnny Kidd & the Pirates.

Remakes: The Swinging Blue Jeans 1964; Mae West 1966; Billy Idol 1987

—

Bob Dylan "Subterranean Homesick Blues" Columbia March 1965

Style: Folk rock
Where from: Minnesota
Where recorded: New York
Suggested pairing: Chuck Berry "Too Much Monkey Business" 1956

Apart from being derived from Chuck Berry's 'Too Much Monkey Business," Bob Dylan's "Subterranean Homesick Blues" was also influenced by "some of the scat songs of the forties," Dylan said. John Lennon once said of the track that it was so captivating it made him wonder how he could ever compete.

—

Sir Douglas Quintet "She's About a Mover" Tribe March 1965

Style: Rock 'n' roll
Where from: San Antonio, TX
Where recorded: Houston, TX
Suggested pairings: Ray Charles "What'd I Say" 1959; Marvin Gaye "Can I Get a Witness" 1963

The Sir Douglas Quintet was another ersatz Brit sounding band calling the lead singer Sir. Sir Douglas was Doug Sahm, who formed this San Antonio band in 1964. Sahm had recorded as Little Doug in 1955, then as Doug Sahm and the Sprits. With Augie Meyers on Vox Continental organ, they came up with this debut hit, "She's About a Mover," by Sir Douglas Quintet.

Remakes: Trini Lopez 1965; Otis Clay 1968; Billy "Crash" Craddock 1976; Ringo Starr 1994

—

The Beatles "Ticket To Ride" Capitol April 19, 1965

Style: Rock 'n' roll
From and recorded in: England

John Lennon claimed that this composition of his was the first heavy-metal song. For his part, McCartney played lead guitar. "We almost invented the idea of a new bit of a song on the fade-out," he said of "Ticket." "It was quite radical at the time."

—

The Four Tops "I Can't Help Myself" Motown April 23, 1965

Style: Soul vocal group
From and recorded in: Detroit, MI
Suggested pairings: The Supremes "Where Did Our Love Go"; Funkadelic "Fish & Chips" 1970

"It was one of the lyrics Eddie Holland and myself collaborated on and when I came up with 'I Can't Help Myself.' The first thing that came out of my mouth as

I sat at the piano, 'Sugar Pie Honey Bunch,' bam, that was it," said song's co-writer Lamont Dozier. "Eddie took it from there, that's the first thing we muttered out and it stuck as we finished it off." The Motown rhythm section, The Funk Brothers were Bennie Benjamin, drums; James Jamerson, bass; Earl Van Dyke, piano; Robert White, guitar; Joe Messina, guitar; Eddie Willis, guitar; Clarence Isabel or James Gittens on vibes. "It was incredible how they knew each producer, they knew what HDH [Holland-Dozier-Holland] wanted, so if HDH came on the scene, they'd give us a little tease, okay, which one will it be today?"

—

The Byrds "Mr. Tambourine Man" Columbia April 1965

Style: Folk rock
From and recorded in: Los Angeles, CA
Original version: Bob Dylan
Suggested pairing: Paul Revere & the Raiders "Kicks" 1966

In a sense, album rock started with the folk rock Beefeaters that had just failed at Elektra and debuted as The Byrds with their harmonic take on Bob Dylan's "Mr. Tambourine Man" on Columbia. The Byrds were Jim McGuinn, lead guitar; Gene Clark, tambourine; David Crosby, rhythm guitar; Chris Hillman, bass guitar and Michael Clarke, drums. Despite their proficiency, producer Terry Melcher decided to bring in The Wrecking Crew, Hal Blaine, drums; Larry Knechtel and Glen Campbell or Jerry Cole, guitar and Leon Russell, piano, who had backed many of Phil Spector's hits along with McGuinn's guitar.

From KHJ in 1965 to KPPC in 1969, many folk rock groups inspired by The Byrds like the Mamas & Papas and Crosby Stills & Nash took to the charts in a big way and dominated the sound. Through the Eagles into the 1980s with their gentle album-oriented releases, the day of the 45's dominance as a market trend leader was slowly ebbing away. Session producer Terry Melcher recalled, "By the time we got to 'Kicks' by Paul Revere & the Raiders, I threw the bass guitar sound into the intro of 'Kicks,' which had a strong similarity to the intro of "Mr. Tambourine Man." By this time, Melcher also decided The Byrds were worthy of playing instruments on their sessions.

—

Them "Here Comes the Night" Parrot April 1965

Style: Rock 'n' roll
Where from: Ireland
Where recorded: England

Van Morrison vocalized with Them on "Here Comes The Night," amounting to a two tempo performance with Jimmy Page, guitar.

—

Roy Head & the Traits "Treat Her Right" Backbeat April 1965

Style: Blue eyed soul
Where from: Three Rivers, TX
Where recorded: Houston, TX
Suggested pairings: Ray Charles "What'd I Say" 1959; Booker T & MGs "Green Onions" 1962; The Dartells "Hot Pastrami" 1962; Joey Dee and the Starliters "Hot Pastrami With Mashed Potatoes" 1963

This was a rocking example of "blue eyed soul," a soulful black sound by a white artist. With Roy Head on vocals, The Traits were Johnny Clark, lead guitar; Frank Miller, rhythm guitar; Gene Kurtz, bass; Dan Buie, keyboards; Danny Gomez and Tommy May, tenor sax; Johnny Gibson, trumpet and Jerry Gibson, drums.

—

The Rolling Stones "(I Can't Get No) Satisfaction" London 1965

Style: Rock
From and recorded in: England
Suggested pairings: Chuck Berry "Thirty Days" 1955; The Soul Sisters "I Can't Stand It" 1964; Martha and the Vandellas "Nowhere To Run" 1965

Not about sex, but about teenaged rebellion, "Satisfaction" was the Stones' first use of the fuzz box. Mick Jagger said, "It sounded like a folk song when we first started working on it and Keith didn't like it much. He didn't want it to be a single, he didn't think it would do very well. I think Keith thought it was a bit basic. I don't think he really listened to it properly. He was too close to it and just felt it was a silly kind of riff." The fuzz guitar sound stayed, the horn section didn't.

In 1966, The Stones performed "(I Can't Get No) Satisfaction" on The Ed Sullivan Show. The line "Trying to make some girl" was bleeped out by censors.

Remakes: Otis Redding 1967; Jimmy McGriff 1968; Devo 1978; The Residents 1978

—

The Strangeloves "I Want Candy" Bang May 1965

Style: Rock 'n' roll
From and recorded in: New York
Suggested pairings: Bo Diddley "Bo Diddley" 1955; Mickey & Sylvia "Love Is Strange" 1956

After recording as The Pygmies in 1963, songwriters Richard Gottehrer, Bob Feldman and Jerry Goldstein created The Strangeloves in 1964, named after the Mickey & Sylvia hit, "Love Is Strange." As The Strangeloves, they hit with this Bo Diddley beat "I Want Candy," with tom tom backing, both songs with Bo Diddley roots. Feldman did a narration with a fake English accent, the idea being the band was part of the British Invasion, claiming to come from Aboriginal Australia.

—

Thee Midniters "Whittier Blvd." Chattahoochee May 15, 1965

Style: Latino rock 'n' roll
Where from: Los Angeles, CA
Where recorded: Hollywood, CA
Suggested pairings: The Rolling Stones "2120 South Michigan Avenue" 1964; The Ambertones "Cruise" 1964; Godfrey "Down Whittier Blvd." 1966

"Whittier Blvd." by Thee Midniters became an ultimate cruising anthem with Little Willie G's historic shout, "Let's take a trip down Whittier Blvd." According to Little Willie G, with a honk, a cry and the manic "arriba" laugh apparently supplied by "Ronnie Figueroa, the organ player, who was always cutting up. He had taken acting classes, when we conceived the idea of 'Whittier Blvd,' all the horns, the cruising, the talking, he came in to supervise what somebody would probably do if they were out partying on a Friday night." Thee Midniters' manager Eddie Torres said, "We were going to do 'Evil Love' for Sonny Phillips. It was too melodic. I said, 'Let's do "Whittier Blvd.," keep it going." The kids used to tell me, 'Why don't you do "Whittier Blvd."?' 'It's just an instrumental.' I told Ronnie Figueroa, 'Why don't you do that laugh, do that instrumental?'"

According to Willie G, the band often warmed up with "2120 South Michigan Avenue," so when they were told the needed a B-side for "Evil Love," Little Willie G broke into his spoken intro and the band fell in with the instrumental.

Billy Cardenas recalled, "Eddie Torres put it together, Eddie asked me to help him. I took him out to KRLA, talked to Dick Moreland. I got the record on the air right away, took a trip down the 605 Freeway, here comes the record 'Whittier Blvd.'" As a consequence, it became a cruising anthem, much to the consternation of the LAPD and the L.A. County Sheriff, both of whom each patrolled sections of Whittier Blvd.

KTYM DJ and Huggy Boy associate, Godfrey, recorded a commentary over the track, entitled "Down Whittier Blvd." on Whittier in 1966.

—

Manfred Mann "My Little Red Book" Ascot May 26, 1965

Style: Rock
From and recorded in: England
Original version: Manfred Mann 1965
Suggested pairing: Pink Floyd "Interstellar Overdrive" 1967

Written off the newsworthiness of Mao's Little Red Book, Hal David and Burt Bacharach framed the title around a dumped guy finding a new girlfriend in his phone book for the movie *What's New, Pussycat?* in 1966. The film version of the song was performed by Manfred Mann. Bacharach said, "Manfred Mann had the right changes but it was a bad record. I made the record with them. It's just a very nervous sounding record. They were uncomfortable with that song. Manfred had a tough time playing it. It took forever to make that record."

Remake: Love 1966

—

The Contours "First I Look at the Purse" Gordy June 23, 1965

Style: Soul vocal group
From and recorded in: Detroit, MI

"First I Look at the Purse" was written for The Contours by Smokey Robinson and Ronnie Rogers of The Miracles," said The Contours' Joe Billingslea. "The irony of the song, Smokey wanted to do the song, him and Berry Gordy sat down and decided the song wouldn't fit The Miracles' image. We were such a rowdy group at the time, our routines were so rambunctious, they decide to give up the song and we're glad to this day they gave us the song. The first time we performed at the Apollo Theater, we were singing 'First I Look at the Purse.' All of a sudden the women started throwing purses on the stage to us. It was a shock at first, then we made it part of our act where we would come out on the stage and the purse would be laying off the side of the stage and one guy would open the purse, look through the purse, he'd find 25 cents or food stamps or something to make the crowd laugh."

—

The Miracles "The Tracks Of My Tears" Tamla June 23, 1965

Style: Soul vocal group
From and recorded in: Detroit, MI

"I think [this song] started with the rhythm and Marvin Tarplin, one of many songs he and Smokey collaborated on like 'I'll Be Doggone' by Marvin Gaye," said Smokey Robinson's wife and Miracles member, Claudette Robinson.

Remake: Aretha Franklin 1969

—

Wilson Pickett "In the Midnight Hour" Atlantic June 1965

Style: Soul
Where from: Detroit, MI
Where recorded: Memphis, TN
Suggested pairings: Wilson Pickett "I'm Gonna Cry" 1964

"Come all the way back from the gospel times," said Pickett. "We used to sing 'I'm going to call Jesus in the midnight hour,' so it followed on and on. When I stopped singing gospel, I went over into the rhythm and blues, these words still lingered with me. I decided if I can sing about Jesus in the midnight hour, I can sing about a girl in the midnight hour." In fact, Wilson Pickett sang those key title lines at the fade out of his previous 45, "I'm Gonna Cry," something Stax session guitar player Steve Cropper recognized when he prepared for a session with Pickett, whom he had never met. Cropper found a copy of "I'm Gonna Cry," suggesting to Pickett they expand those lyrics for the next session. Apparently Pickett agreed that this conversation happened.

Remakes: Little Mac and the Boss Sounds 1965; Billy Preston 1966; The Electrons, The Wanted, The Swamp Rats 1967; The Mirettes 1967; Cross Country 1973; The Insiders 1974; Roxy Music 1980

—

Bob Dylan "Like a Rolling Stone" Columbia June 28, 1965

Style: Folk rock
Where from: Minnesota
Where recorded: New York
Suggested pairing: Hank Williams "Lost Highway" 1951

Chicago-based Paul Butterfield Blues Band guitarist Mike Bloomfield joined up with Al Kooper out of The Royal Teens, who had hit in 1958 with "Short Shorts," on Hammond organ to back Bob Dylan on "Like a Rolling Stone." Invited to the session as an observer, Kooper wanted to sit in on guitar, his primary instrument. When he heard Bloomfield, the session guitarist, warming up, clearly Bloomfield was a much better guitarist, so Kooper went into the control room and inveighed upon the producer, Tom Wilson, to play organ, so keyboardist Paul Griffin moved from the Hammond organ to piano. Kooper's organ came in an eighth note behind the other members of the band, which Kooper followed to make sure he was playing the proper chords. It worked. Dylan said at session's end, "Turn the organ up!"

The record was first issued as a six minute A-side, but recalled and released in two parts of 3:02 each to accommodate itself onto a 45. Even so, because of listener demand, radio was forced to play the entire six minute performance. At 6:13, it was a breakthrough when this got radio play and became a hit, since many stations refused to play songs much longer than 3 minutes. It was also rare for a song with so many lyrics to do well commercially. The title is not a reference to The Rolling Stones. It is taken from the phrase "A rolling stone gathers no moss." Dylan got the idea from Hank Williams' "Lost Highway" line, "I'm a rolling stone, I'm alone and lost."

—

James Brown "Papa's Got a Brand New Bag" King June 1965

Style: Funk soul
Where recorded: North Carolina

According to Earl King, who already had "Trick Bag" on the market, "I met James Brown one day. He was headed to a studio in New Orleans. He said, 'Earl, I want you to write me a song in the vein of "Trick Bag."' I kept procrastinating and then James came out with 'Papa's Got a Brand New Bag.'

Considered one of the sparks of funk, "Papa's Got a Brand New Bag" was Brown's first recording to feature Jimmy Nolen on stinging guitar. The taped recording of "Papa's Got a Brand New Bag" was edited and sped up for its single release, increasing the tempo and raising the pitch by a half step.

—

The Turtles "It Ain't Me Babe" White Whale July 1965

Style: Folk rock
Where from: Hawthorne, CA
Where recorded: Hollywood, CA

The Crossfires were the house band at the Revelaire Club operated by DJ Rob Foster, "who had us audition for Ted Feigin and Lee Lassiff, two of his record distributor friends," said Crossfires/Turtles drummer Don Murray. According to Don Drowty, "Feigin was working for Herb Alpert and Lou Adler on the East Coast. They had a studio at LaBrea," and were planning to form their own record label "and use their clout with distribution syndicates to get their records in the stores and on the radio," added Murray. "We passed the audition, recorded Bob Dylan's 'It Ain't Me Babe' on a shoestring budget, and cracked the national fop five, all without the assistance of a major label. The Turtles signed their record contracts in July 1965."

The Turtles' "It Ain't Me Babe" was on the just-created White Whale. "White Whale didn't want to sign us to a binding contract until they were sure the record was going to be a hit." During the changeover from The Crossfires to The Tyrtles—based on the alternate spelling of the Byrds, who had debuted a month earlier with another Dylan composition—then to The Turtles, the Revelaire Club marquee was similarly changed, but fans soon found out they did exactly the same show as the week previous.

—

Barry McGuire "Eve of Destruction" Dunhill August 4, 1965

Style: Protest rock
Where from: Oklahoma City, OK
Where recorded: Los Angeles, CA

Composed by P.F. Sloan for The Turtles, with backing by Grass Roots, a growling Barry McGuire hit true gold on "Eve Of Destruction" on Dunhill. Reaction to the theme of the song was swift and not kind, especially to teenaged Sloan, who still lived with his parents in the Fairfax District of Los Angeles. "Picture the nightmare, the most dangerous man in America, for 30 years. John Birch was the face of it, all these things were hidden. We were under threat. Label was under threat. It's huge. I'm a threat to American society. I received a letter from one of those guys, apologizing to make a quick buck, they realized they were part of the hate group, and they apologized," said Sloan. "I think the who[le] thing was a divine play. The song gave the vote to 18 year olds, a senator quoted my line, I was the messenger of it. First and only. How do I deal with the nuclear threat, the world, the only woman who loves me is a black woman who cleans my parents' house. The song was banned all over the country and all over the world. Heartfelt. If you're a young label, and your record is being banned by every radio station and every country in the world. It was like a volcano, they were trying to put a cover on top of it. Radio Caroline played it five times an hour. Number one. Metaphorical record."

Answer: The Spokesmen "The Dawn of Correction" 1965

—

The Spokesmen "The Dawn of Correction" Decca 1965

Style: Anti-protest
From and recorded in: Philadelphia, PA

"WIBG radio newsman Ray Gilmore thought there needed to be an answer to 'Eve Of Destruction,'" said songwriter John Madara. "We needed a positive answer to a negative song. We worked all night on that. We didn't have anyone to sing, so we put ourselves to be the vocalists." It broke on L.A.'s KHJ and KRLA, hitting the top 30 in August 1965, doing the same on WIBG in September.

—

Otis Redding "Respect" Volt August 15, 1965

Style: Soul
Where from: Macon, GA
Where recorded: Memphis, TN

In a duet with William Bell, "hey hey," Otis Redding's original version of "Respect" omitted the extended refrain that helped propel the Aretha Franklin remake, which was about the whole issue of respect, while Redding simply wanted respect from his family when he returned home from work. The original version of "Respect" was produced by Steve Cropper, who also played guitar with William Bell and Earl Sims on backup vocals. On this session, Duck Dunn was on bass. "Otis Redding, in all his sessions, just made a better player out of all the musicians. On 'Respect,' that's his horn line. His sense of timing, his sense of rhythm. We would be playing, we would just watch him, his energy. He had fun. A lot of that stuff, we'd be in the studio, ten to six. It got to be a job. Every time Otis came in, it was fun, completely fun."

Remake: The Rationals 1966; Aretha Franklin 1967; The Vagrants 1967; Jimmy Smith 1967; Dick Hyman 1968; Zinga Washington 1982

—

The Dave Clark Five "Catch Us If You Can" Epic August 15, 1965

Style: Rock 'n' roll
From and recorded in: England
Suggested pairing: The Monkees "(Theme From) the Monkees" 1966

This catchy uptempo riff, was used in the movie *Having A Wild Weekend.* The riff, the finger snaps, a key lyric, "here we come again," was adapted by the Monkees.

—

The Animals "We've Gotta Get Out Of This Place" MGM August 1965

Style: Rock 'n' roll
From and recorded in: England

An anthem popular among those drafted for service in Viet Nam, the most topical "We've Gotta Get Out of This Place" by The Animals had success in July, 1965, hitting #5 on KMEN, San Bernardino, #15 on WMCA, New York and a peak of #9 on KHJ, KFWB and KRLA in August.

—

The Miracles "My Girl Has Gone" Tamla September 22, 1965

Style: Soul vocal group
From and recorded in: Detroit, MI

One of his better ballads, released far ahead of Smokey's separation from Claudette Robinson, The Miracles' "My Girl Has Gone" was thus not autobiographic in theme or performance.

—

Fontella Bass "Rescue Me" Checker September 1965

Style: Soul
Where from: St Louis, MO
Where recorded: Chicago, IL

Fontella Bass was the daughter of Martha Bass, a member of The Clara Ward Singers who toured with Aretha Franklin's father, the Rev. C.L. Franklin. She first recorded for local St. Louis labels: "Bad Boy" for Little Milton's Bobbin label; and two for Ike Turner labels, "I Love the Man" for Sonja and "Poor Little Fool" in duet with Tina Turner for Prann. About "Rescue Me," a rocking gospel-inspired plea, Bass told the New York Times her call-and-response vocals for were from a memory lapse. "When we were recording that, I forgot some of the words. Back then, you didn't stop while the tape was running. I remembered from the church what to do if you forget the words. I sang, 'Ummm, ummm, ummm' and it worked out just fine." Backing on "Rescue Me" included drummer Maurice White, who a decade later would form Earth, Wind & Fire; Louis Satterfield, bass; Leonard Caston, piano; Sonny Thompson, organ; Pete Cosey and Gerald Sims, guitars and Minnie Riperton on background vocals. One of the producers of the song, Billy Davis, came up with a novel idea for the ending. Instead of having the engineer fade the song, he walked the studio floor, tapped each musician on the shoulder when he wanted him to stop playing, so the instruments stopped individually.

Answers: Fontella Bass "Recovery" 1965; Aretha Franklin "Since You've Been Gone" 1968

—

Len Barry "1-2-3" Decca September 1965

Style: Blue-eyed soul
From and recorded in: Philadelphia, PA
Suggested pairing: The Supremes "Ask Any Girl" 1965

The lead singer of The Dovells on "Bristol Stomp" in 1961, Leonard Borisoff, took the stage name Len Barry for a remake of Lavern Baker's "Jim Dandy," followed by "Hearts Are Trump," penned by Barry with producer Jimmy Wisner. Then came "Let's Do it Again," a retread of "You Can't Sit Down" with totally different lyrics for Mercury. A switch of Decca on timely variation on the Shirley Ellis hit, "Name Game," entitled "Lip Sync (To The Tongue Twisters)" made #20 in Philly in May 1965. But the big hit was this rhythmic single, "1-2-3," for which songwriters Madara-White wrote the bridge a half hour before the session. It had that smooth blue eyed soul sound that brought it to #3 on Philly radio in August 1965, then #2 on WMCA in New York and #1 on Boss Radio in L.A. in September. It topped out #2 nationally in September. Then came problems.

"Motown thought it sounded similar to a Supremes B-side, 'Ask Any Girl,'" said David White, co-writer of "1-2-3." "We settled with them. Now Holland-Dozier-Holland are part owners of "1-2-3" along with Madara-White. Never met them." Added Madara, "They didn't want anyone to duplicate their sound. The basis of the lawsuit was we tried to duplicate their sound," adding that the opening horn part came from TV's *The Defenders*, the E.G. Marshall series. "The arranger came up with that figure, Jimmy Wisner," said White.

—

The Seeds "Can't Seem To Make You Mine" GNP Crescendo September 27, 1965

Style: Garage rock 'n' roll
Where from: Salt Lake City, UT/Detroit, MI
Where recorded: Los Angeles, CA

Led by singer Sky Saxon, real name Ritchie Marsh, L.A.'s greatest second-time-around garage band, The Seeds' first two 45s flopped at first, then both hit as reissues. "I started a band called The Vikings with imitation fur vests in 1965, couldn't afford the helmets, didn't make it without the helmets," said Saxon. "People thought we looked really seedy, I wasn't into dressing up like The Beatles. The Seeds were from Farmington, Michigan. It was a package deal, to get Darryl Hooper, keyboards, I had to take Rick Andridge, drums; later we worked it out and we became great. With Jan Savage, guitar, we had a sound."

Jimmie Maddin recalled, "I was walking down Hollywood Blvd. I had a group, they're Sky Saxon, The Celts. He was a Mormon from Salt Lake City. The Byrds had hit with 'Tambourine Man.' I was a DJ at Mighty 690. I controlled the Beatles Fan Club right in front of KFWB. I owned the Sundown, then the Summit. I was running Beatles films. I brought the group in, had them perform between the movies. Sky and I thought of the name The Seeds because they looked so seedy. I went into Western Recorders to cut their album. He took that name, he wanted to be like the American Beatles. I did it with my own money, he wrote that song on the front seat of my car."

Saxon added, "After The Seeds got going, we couldn't get a record deal. We already tried. Jimmie Maddin took me to Atlantic and to GNP, both were offering $4,000. GNP's Gene Norman said he would be like my father." L.A. producer Denny Bruce told Bomp magazine, "There was another guy hanging around at that time, from Salt Lake City, Sky Saxon! Sonny Bono was thinking of recording Sky. At that time he was sounding like Dee Clark, 'Just Keep It Up.' He was Richard Marsh then, that's right. The next time I saw him he asked me if I'd play on The Seeds' sessions and produce. I told him I didn't want to do that, and he ended up telling me he'd pay me just to come down and be at the sessions."

The Seeds debuted with this garage rocker "Can't Seem To Make You Mine" backed with the proto-rockabilly, "Daisy Mae" on Norman's GNP Crescendo. Saxon added, "I really wrote it for Little Richard." To that extent this Seeds release could be considered the first L.A. garage 45 of importance. "A hit on KBLA radio helped break through the Spector sound," said Saxon. "Can't Seem To Make You Mine" charted for the Seeds in 1967 after their "Pushin' To Hard" first made the charts on its second time around.

—

The Barbarians "Are You a Boy Or Are You a Girl" Laurie September 1965

Style: Garage rock
Where from: Provincetown, MA
Where recorded: New York

The Barbarians, with one handed drummer Victor "Moulty" Molton, who used a prosthetic hook in place of his missing left hand to hold his drumstick, with Ronnie Enos, lead guitar; Bruce Benson and Jerry Causi debuted with this biting satire of long-haired exponents of the British Invasion, "Are You a Boy or Are You a Girl?" with references to The Stones, Liverpool, hair styles and skintight pants.

—

The Grass Roots "Mr. Jones ('Ballad of a Thin Man')" Dunhill September 1965

Style: Folk rock
Where from: San Francisco, CA
Where recorded: Los Angeles, CA

The Grass Roots rearranged and retitled Bob Dylan's "Ballad of a Thin Man" into "Mr. Jones (A Ballad of a Thin Man)" on Dunhill. At the onset, The Grass Roots were little more than P.F. Sloan and Steve Barri, who had most recently recorded as The Fantastic Baggys on "Tell Em I'm Surfin" in summer 1964. "I was the Grass Roots," said Sloan, who also worked for New York based music publishers. "I put that together. Bob Dylan wanted to meet me. He was afraid they were going to kick him off the label, I gave him some advice, he told me to pick any song off the album, I'll give it to you. I picked 'Ballad of a Thin Man,' recorded it with a studio band, the label nixed the idea of me singing it, I went to San Francisco, found a group and produced it. Wild Bill Fulton only recorded three songs. Dunhill doesn't pay anybody, the group left, they told Wild Bill they'd pay him if he'd sing 'Where Were You,' didn't pay him, we put an ad in the newspaper, Rob Gill and a few other guys, they were sort of working together at the time.

"Jan & Dean may have put L.A. on the map," added Sloan. "There wasn't any act that came out of L.A. that got any respect. The Doors, Byrds, Grass Roots, every group that came out of L.A. was considered third rate."

—

James Brown "I Got You" October 1965

Where recorded: Criteria Studios Miami, FL
Suggested pairing: Yvonne Fair and James Brown Band "I Found You" 1962

Yvonne Fair was one of Brown's backup singers on the road, who recorded "I Found You," produced by James Brown in 1962. This is the song that became Brown's signature tune and gave him his famous catch phrase, "I Feel Good." Brown had been promoting "I Got You" on the road, and on The T.A.M.I. Show, Shindig, and the movie, Ski Party, so he recorded a new version of the song in May 1965 at Criteria Studios in Miami. Released by King Records, it shot to the top of the R&B charts and #3 on the pop charts. The original 1964 version of this song had no guitar. In the Brown 1965 redo, there was a distinct guitar presence; his screams were more pronounced as well as more of Maceo Parker's sax. Other players were Maceo's brother, Melvin Parker, drums; Nat Jones, organ and Bernard Odum, bass.

—

The Bobby Fuller Four "I Fought the Law" Mustang October 1965

Style: Rock 'n' roll
Where from: El Paso, TX
Where recorded: Hollywood, CA
Original version: The Crickets 1961
Earlier versions: Paul Stefen & the Royal Lancers 1963; Sammy Masters 1964

After The Bobby Fuller Four had recorded The Crickets' "I Fought the Law" on the New Mexico-based Exeter label in 1964, Bobby Fuller came to L.A. to audition for Bob Keane. "He was a pretty good engineer," Keane recalled. "He had a little studio in the back of his house in El Paso. When I heard them, there was something there, he had a great sound, but it wasn't all put together." After releasing Fuller's eerie "Those Memories Of You" backed with "Our Favorite Martian" on Donna, Keane recalled, "I didn't hear the hit potential and told him he should work on his music and when he got some more stuff, to give me a call. It was almost a year later when he came back and said, 'Here's some new things.'" After charting locally only with "Let Her Dance," Fuller gave "I Fought the Law" another try with Coke bottles used for the gunshot sound effects.

"Bobby didn't agree with what we were doing," said Keane. "He didn't like the Coke bottle thing and he didn't like to have the galloping guitar that was the sound that would happen and it turned out it did very well. It was rockabilly oriented and it went to #1 in Detroit before anywhere else." As with Ritchie Valens, Bob Keane lost another star on the verge of greatness to unexpected death. On July 18, 1966, Fuller was murdered in Hollywood. Keane claimed another label wanted Fuller in their stable and later accused the LAPD of botching the investigation of his death, which involved inhalation of gasoline, labeling it a suicide, though his body appeared battered; his right finger was broken, as if it had been bent back, all of which did not point to suicide.

Remakes: The Hoodoo Rhythm Devils 1973; Sam Neely 1975; Hank Williams, Jr. 1978; The Clash 1979; The Nitty Gritty Dirt Band 1992

—

The Leaves "Hey Joe, Where You Gonna Go?" Mira November 1965

Style: Garage rock
From and recorded in: Los Angeles, CA
Original version: Tim Rose 1966

The Leaves issued the first version of this garage classic "Hey Joe, Where You Gonna Go" about guns and premeditated murder, and its was authorship claimed by a West Coast balladeer, Billy Roberts, who copyrighted it in 1962. When The Leaves redid the song as "Hey Joe" in the more turbulent garage-heavy month of April 1966, it went from tepid to red hot. In the case of the competing versions, the original "Hey Joe, Where You Gonna Go?" was a Wallichs pick hit as the newer remade "Hey Joe" first hit the charts. Niela Miller, a girlfriend of [Roberts'] in the late fifties, insists that her song "Baby Please Don't Go to Town" was plagiarized by Roberts, who altered the lyrics to "Hey Joe, where you goin' with that gun in your hand?" Miller said, "My music publisher at the time advised me against suing Billy." According to Martin Cohen, the lawyer who administers the rights to the song, it was first cut by the singer Dino Valente who, confusingly, also assumed co-writing credits for a while and was paid composer's royalties. Folkie Tim Rose claimed "Hey Joe" as his; in 1966 he added a verse and slowed it down. "I was essentially writing a new song."

"Hey Joe" remakes: The Leaves 1966; Jimi Hendrix 1967; Cher 1967; The Stillroven 1967; Love 1967; The Marmalade 1968; The Music Machine 1968; Wilson Pickett 1969; Patti Smith 1974

—

Bob Kuban and the In-Men "The Cheater" Musicland U.S.A. November 1965

Style: Blue-eyed soul
From and recorded in: St. Louis, MO

After the Bob Kuban Band stiffed with the fine dance "Jerkin' Time," a cross between Bob & Earl's "Harlem Shuffle" and The Larks' "The Jerk," came a fabulous rocking blue-eyed soul vocal, "The Cheater," with vocals by Walter Scott and leader Bob Kuban on drums, which hit #1 on St. Louis radio KXOK. The body of Scott was later stuffed into a cistern after his murder by his ex and her boyfriend.

—

The Who "My Generation" Decca November 20, 1965

Style: Rock
From and recorded in: England

The Who's "My Generation" was banned from the BBC because Roger Daltry's vocals resembled stuttering, which might have offended actual stutterers. Some at the BBC also opined the line "Why don't you all f-f-f-fade away" suggested another f-word. Regardless, "My Generation" became an anthem for many in the Who's generation.

—

Stevie Wonder "Uptight (Everything's Alright)" Tamla November 22, 1965

Style: Soul
From and recorded in: Detroit, MI
Suggested pairing: Bill Cosby "Little Ole Man (Uptight, Everything's Alright)" 1967

Not the first use of this title for Motown, in 1962, Herman Griffin had the same title, but it was an organ instrumental patterned after Barrett Strong's "Money," probably by Earl Van Dyke, as Griffin was a vocalist only. "Uptight (Everything's Alright)" was a title based on a slang expression and generally considered a negative, i.e. "she's just uptight," meaning hard to communicate with.

As Wonder's voice began to change, Sylvia Moy and Henry Cosby took one of Wonder's instrumental riffs to devise a new song, depicting a poor young man's appreciation for a rich girl's seeing beyond his poverty to his true worth. During the session, because Wonder's inability to read the lyrics, Moy sang the lyrics of "Uptight" into Wonder's earphones, making sure she was singing a line ahead of his vocals, so he could catch up with the lyrics.

With uncredited backing by the yet-to-be named Watts 103rd St. Rhythm Band, Bill Cosby's comedic redo of "Uptight" as "Little Ole Man (Uptight, Everything's Alright)" was a hit in 1967.

—

Slim Harpo "Baby Scratch My Back" Excello December 1965

Style: Blues
Where from: Baton Rouge, LA
Where recorded: Crowley, LA

"Baby Scratch My Back" by blues one-man-band Slim Harpo is mostly instrumental with laconic monologues and harmonica fills by Harpo. The backing has been described as "a loping beat with tremolo laden guitar, wood block maracas, and snapping snare drum sound."

—

The Standells "Dirty Water" Tower December 1965

Style: Garage rock
From and recorded in: Los Angeles, CA
Suggested pairing: The Rolling Stones "The Last Time" 1965

After Standells releases on Liberty and Vee Jay, "we signed with Ed Cobb, he signed us to Tower," said Standells' vocalist Larry Tamblyn. "Through our manager, we started off pretty well, Ed was pretty easy to work with, he showed us 'Dirty Water' in a pretty raw form, we put [it] together and put the guitar lick on it. Dick Dodd did the chant at the beginning, 'wanna tell you about our town.'" Some claim the song was influenced by "The Last Time" by The Rolling Stones from 1965, which in turn was based on a gospel song of the same title. With "Dirty Water" lyrics having to do with the River Charles in Boston, many assumed The Standells were from Boston, not just singing about "our town" to this day.

Tamblyn added, "Our manager Bert Jacobs had a dispute with Ed Cobb and Ray Harris who had a partnership" called Greengrass Productions under Attarack, whose president was Seymour Heller. "It caused a big legal dispute. They contacted Dick Dodd, told him, 'We can make you a star without them.' Dick was young, wanted to be up front, didn't want to be behind the drums. Our contract said, if one member remains, he gets the name. By the time litigation was cleared up, we ended up with the name." To date, "Dirty Water" is still played at Boston sporting events.

—

The Miracles "Going to a Go-Go" Tamla December 6, 1965

Style: Soul vocal group
From and recorded in: Detroit, MI

The Miracles uptempo vocal on "Going to a Go-Go" was a reference to the Washington, DC area "Go-Go" style, an offshoot of funk and R&B, emphasizing percussion, accounting for the bongos and jam style. Heard in go-go clubs, the music was supplemented by go-go dancers in cages, protecting them from fans.

Remake: The Rolling Stones 1982

—

The Beach Boys "Barbara Ann" Capitol 1965

Style: Rock 'n' roll/doo wop
Where from: Hawthorne, CA
Where recorded: Hollywood, CA
Original version: The Regents 1961

Dean Torrence from Jan & Dean sang lead on this doo wop remake of The Regents' giant 1961 doo wop. Capitol Records released this without naming the band as The Beach Boys were trying to establish credibility as a serious musical act, and didn't want to be known for putting out such a simple song.

—

Frank Wilson "Do I Love You" Soul December 23, 1965

Style: Soul
From and recorded in: Los Angeles, CA

"Do I Love You" by Frank Wilson is by far the rarest of all soul records. Wilson, who sang with the family group The Wil-Sones on Highland and The Remarkables on Audio Arts, joined Motown in late 1965 when it moved west. When he recorded this sole soul single, Motown owner Berry Gordy Jr. told Wilson to make a decision: either you're a vocalist or a songwriter. When Wilson chose writer, Gordy stopped the release, but two copies remained in the label's files, one of which was filched in a transaction that involved drugs and a drug-addled employee of the firm who took Quaaludes from a medical professional for the label's file copy of this 45. The doctor collected '50s vocal group harmony records and turned it around in a big trade. That copy sold for over $20,000. Another of the two surviving copies circulate in collector's circles and most recently sold for £25,742 (over $30,000 in U.S. dollars).

—

The Elgins "Darling Baby" VIP December 31, 1965

Style: Soul vocal group
From and recorded in: Detroit, MI

Robert Fleming, Johnny Dawson, Cleo "Duke" Miller and Norman McLean recorded as The Downbeats on "Your Baby's Back" for the Tamla label in 1962. Motown suggested that they add female lead vocalist Saundra Mallett, who had recorded unsuccessfully for the label, backed by The Vandellas, after winning a talent contest. As The Elgins, their first single release was this heavily romantic ballad, "Darling Baby." Several very early copies credited The Downbeats. As the boss, Berry Gordy Jr. wanted to use the name Elgins, one of the names used by The Temptations. It was pressed, issued as the Elgins and became a monster hit.

—

The Isley Brothers "This Old Heart Of Mine (Is Weak For You)" Tamla January 28, 1966

Style: Soul vocal group
Where from: New Jersey
Where recorded: Detroit, MI
Suggested pairings: The Four Tops "Shake Me, Wake Me (When It's Over)" 1966; The Impressions "Can't Satisfy" 1966

This was destined to be the B-side of the next single by The Supremes said song's co-writer Lamont Dozier. "They only wanted #1 one records. After that, everybody we wanted to record, everything we wanted to record, everyone else wanted it. We did overpower. We couldn't get the songs. We did 'Reach Out,' they gave it to The Four Tops. We wanted our own label, so that it wouldn't happen again." About one week after the release, the very similar "Shake Me, Wake Me (When It's Over)" by The Four Tops was released. On The Isley Brothers' "This Old Heart Of Mine (Is Weak For You)," the lead singer was Ronald Isley with O'Kelly Isley, Jr. and Rudolph Isley with uncredited background vocals by The Andantes—Jackie Hicks, Marlene Barrow and Louvain Demps. The Impressions' "Can't Satisfy" came out six months later, in July 1966, and was met with legal action, which Motown won.

—

Paul Revere & the Raiders "Kicks" Columbia February 28, 1966

Style: Rock
Where from: Idaho/Portland, OR
Where recorded: Hollywood, CA
Suggested pairing: The Byrds "Mr. Tambourine Man" 1965

After The Byrds hit with "Mr. Tambourine Man," producer Terry Melcher came up with this anti-drug themed release by Paul Revere & the Raiders, "Kicks," which had been intended for The Animals. "I thought Mark Lindsay had a kind of Jagger voice. By the time was got to 'Kicks' by Paul Revere & the Raiders, I threw the bass guitar sound of 'Mr. Tambourine Man' into the intro of 'Kicks'"

—

Great Society "Someone to Love" Northbeach February 1966

Style: Rock
From and recorded in: San Francisco, CA
Suggested pairing: Jefferson Airplane "Somebody to Love" 1967

The song, originally entitled "Someone to Love," was written by guitarist Darby Slick and recorded by his group, Great Society. When lead singer Grace Slick left that group to replace vocalist Signe Anderson of Jefferson Airplane, she recorded the title with a slight change, "Somebody to Love" with a more aggressive style. Written by Great Society guitarist Darby after his girlfriend left him, Slick first performed the song by that band. The song made little impact outside of the club circuit in the Bay Area, and it is not known to have been sold away from the Bay.

—

The Syndicate of Sound "Little Girl" Hush February 1966/Amy April 1966

Style: Garage rock
From and recorded in: San Jose, CA

Syndicate of Sound took first place at a San Francisco Bay area battle of the bands in 1965; the prize, a one-shot recording deal with Bob Keane's Del Fi Records, which had produced "Prepare For Love" on Scarlet. Then came their droll "Little Girl" on Hush, which advised "other girls did it too… it's all over for you." Don Baskin, the band's vocalist, told classicbands.com, "We couldn't get 'Little Girl' played anywhere. We decided to release it on our producer's label, Hush, which was a rhythm and blues label out of Richmond, California. Our producer's parents had owned that label. He decided, 'Let's put it out locally and see how it does,' and we sold 5,000 copies in the first week. An incredible number for that day and time in and around the Northern California area. A big station in San Francisco really broke our first record—KYA. That's what really made us take off. We had our first big, big break-out in Oklahoma City and it started from there."

—

The Temptations "Get Ready" Gordy February 7, 1966

Style: Soul vocal group
Where from: Alabama
Where recorded: Detroit, MI
Suggested pairing: The Rolling Stones "Bitch" 1971

A Smokey Robinson composition, The Temptations' "Get Ready" had special meaning to So. Cal. street gangs, as when it was played on the radio, the dedication was a warning about a gang showdown… as in "get ready, 'cause here I come."

Remake: Rare Earth 1969

—

Robert Parker "Barefootin'" Nola March 1966

Style: Soul
From and recorded in: New Orleans, LA

"That was plagiarized, period. I wrote the song for the guy who did it," said Earl King of Robert Parker's hit, "Barefootin'."They changed the words around in it and went somewhere else with Wardell when they had Nola Records. I just chalk that up as another experience."

—

Love "My Little Red Book" Elektra March 1966

Style: Rock
From and recorded in: Los Angeles, CA

Writer of "My Little Red Book," Burt Bacharach said to Record Collector magazine, "Love had a hit with it. Wrong changes and all, and I never loved that. There were a couple of chords that were wrong and it would have been better with the right chords. It's called people reading music, people reading a lead sheet, then you know what the right chord is. But I liked their energy on the song and I liked that it was a hit."

—

Sam & Dave "Hold On! I'm a Comin'" Stax March 14, 1966

Style: Soul duet
Where from: Miami, FL
Where recorded: Memphis, TN

Once, when songwriter and producer David Porter of Sam & Dave was in the bathroom, his songwriting partner Isaac Hayes yelled at him to hurry up so they could get back to work, as they had made little progress that day. A song title was born when Porter responded, "Hold on man, I'm coming." Porter told

Hayes that "Hold On, I'm Coming" would be a great title. Supposed sexual lyrics caused it to be banned by some radio stations.

—

Bob Dylan "Rainy Day Women #12 & 35" Columbia March 24, 1966

Style: Rock
Where from: Minnesota
Where recorded: New York
Suggested pairings: Gene Autry "The Rheumatism Blues" 1929; Ray Charles "Let's Go Get Stoned" 1966; Napoleon XIV "They're Coming To Take Me Away" 1966

From the lyric, "Everybody must get stoned," the assumption is the song is about smoking pot. "I have never and never will write a 'drug song,'" said Dylan. It was more likely about relationships or Biblical meanings (i.e., "let he who is without sin cast the first stone"). Dylan answered a question about people interpreting this song to be about getting high in a 2012 Rolling Stone article: "These are people that aren't familiar with the Book of Acts." But the drug charge stuck, and some stations refused to play it. Dylan burst out laughing in this session, which is clearly heard. According to Down the Highway: The Life of Bob Dylan by Howard Sounes, "The musicians were having a lot of fun in the studio, passing around joints and swapping instruments as they kept the mood light and jovial with a marching bass line beat." Guitarist/bassist Charlie McCoy, who played the trumpet, recalled to Uncut magazine, "Tonight he wants to do a song with a Salvation Army sound, 'We need a trumpet and trombone.'" In 1966, Napoleon XIV's "They're Coming to Take Me Away" revived that very marching bass line from the intro. The discordant bleary trombone and harmonica riff is borrowed from an early and obscure blues recording, Gene Autry's "The Rheumatism Blues," from 1929.

—

Wilson Pickett "634-5789 (Soulsville, U.S.A.)" Atlantic March 1966

Style: Soul
Where from: Detroit, MI
Where recorded: Memphis, TN

Written by Eddie Floyd and Steve Cropper, Wilson Pickett's "634-5789 (Soulsville, U.S.A.)" was first issued on his 1966 Atlantic Records album The Exciting Wilson Pickett. The single reached #1 on the "Black Singles" chart and #13 on the "Pop Singles" chart.

Answer: Joe Tex "S.Y.S.L.J.F.M. (The Letter Song)" 1966

—

The Young Rascals "Good Lovin'" Atlantic March 1966

Style: Blue-eyed soul
Where from: Upstate New York, NY
Where recorded: New York City, NY
Original version: The Olympics 1965

The L.A.-based Olympics hit with "Good Lovin'" on the Loma label in Philly and New York, then in L.A. just before the Watts Riots. "The Rascals heard it, wanted to record it," said Olympics' lead singer Walter Ward. "Bob Krasnow was our producer. We had money trouble, Bob said, 'Nobody's running Loma.' At that time, they were just changing over. Bob said, 'I've got to go somewhere else.' Loma was not promoting the record. Loma was new under Warner Brothers, they didn't even know they had the record. Bob Krasnow gave it to The Young Rascals, but we both had success on it," Ward recalled. Helping to improve The Rascals' version was the false ending the original version by The Olympics didn't have.

Cover: Brenton Wood 1966

—

The Young Rascals "Mustang Sally" Atlantic 1966

Style: Blue-eyed soul
Where from: Upstate New York, NY
Where recorded: New York City, NY
Original version: Sir Mack Rice 1965

"Mustang Sally" was written about the drummer for Della Reese. She wanted to buy him a Lincoln for his birthday and he wanted a Mustang. Aretha Franklin's contribution was the name change from "Mustang Mama" to "Mustang Sally." First recorded by the song's writer, Sir Mack Rice, it was then covered by The Rascals. "That was written by Sir Mack Rice, who was one of The Falcons," said Wilson Pickett, "from Detroit, Michigan. I was the lead singer of The Falcons for years before I went on my own. Mack Rice cut a demo, he was trying to get it out himself." In fact, Rice recorded the song for the Blue Rock label in 1966. Felix Cavaliere of The Young Rascals said The Rascals recorded "Mustang Sally" before Wilson Pickett. Atlantic Records cut the song from them and gave it to Wilson Pickett. Pickett picked up the tempo, playing the song a little faster than The Rascals' rendition.

—

Percy Sledge "When a Man Loves a Woman" Atlantic March 1966

Style: Soul
Where from: Alabama
Where recorded: Sheffield, AL
Suggested pairings: Procol Harum "A Whiter Shade Of Pale" 1967

Percy Sledge was a hospital orderly and part-time singer with The Esquires Combo who entertained at university frat rows. One of his songs was the plaintive ballad, "Please Don't Leave Me," which was retitled "When a Man Loves a Woman," the first #1 Southern soul hit.

Answer: Little Esther "When a Woman Loves a Man" 1967

—

The Capitols "Cool Jerk" Karen March 1966

Style: Soul vocal group
From and recorded in: Detroit, MI
Suggested pairings: The Del Vikings "Cool Shake" 1958; The Contours "Can You Do It" 1964; The Strangeloves "Night Time" 1966; Pharrell Williams "Happy" 2013

Vocalist Sharon McMahon did the clapping on this song with Telma Hopkins, Deon Jackson and Karen label owner Ollie McLaughlin; Ray Monnette, guitar; Johnny Griffith, piano; Bob Babbitt, bass; Mike Terry, sax and George McGregor, drums.

Remake: The GoGo's 1984

—

The Beach Bums "The Ballad of the Yellow Beret" Are You Kidding Me April 1966

Style: Protest rock
From and recorded in: Michigan

An early vehicle for rocker Bob Seger, The Beach Bums recorded this satirical "The Ballad of The Yellow Beret" in 1966, mocking draft evaders and Barry Sadler's #1 hit, "Ballad of the Green Berets." Even though it was a spoof, Sadler and his record label, SRCA, threatened a lawsuit and the recording was withdrawn from the market.

—

Joe Tex "S.Y.S.L.J.F.M. (The Letter Song)" Dial April 1966

Style: Soul
Where from: Baytown, TX
Where recorded: New York
Suggested pairing: Wilson Pickett "634-5789 (Soulsville, U.S.A.)" 1966

The message of Joe Tex's "S.Y.S.L.J.F.M." was "Save Your Sweet Love Just For Me," amounting to an answer to Wilson Pickett's very recent hit, "634-5789."

—

Wilson Pickett "Ninety-Nine and a Half (Won't Do)" Atlantic May 9, 1966

Style: Soul
Where from: Detroit, MI
Where recorded: Memphis, TN
Original version: The Original Gospel Harmonettes "99 1/2" 1956

Schooled in gospel, Wilson Pickett went soulful in the early 1960s, borrowing some gospel themes like "Ninety-Nine and a Half (Won't Do)," and turning the lyrics into a secular message.

Remakes: The Standells 1967; The Trammps 1976

—

The Players "He'll Be Back" Minit May 1966

Style: Soul vocal group
From and recorded in: Chicago, IL

The Players did not perform on this going-to-war ballad, as recalled by Dells' bass singer, Chuck Barksdale. "Michael McGill, Vern Allison, Jack Carter and myself did the complete background. Sad to say, the real Players could not sing. We did ' He'll Be Back.' We were the premier background group in Chicago. We got paid fairly well."

—

The Contours "Just a Little Misunderstanding" Gordy May 1966

Style: Soul vocal group
From and recorded in: Detroit, MI

Said Joe Billingslea of The Contours, "'Just a Little Misunderstanding' was written by Stevie Wonder. Joe Stubbs liked the song, so we decided to let Joe have it since he was so interested and enthused about doing the song. He did a decent job on the song. A minor hit, it made a little noise for us." Said Joe Stubbs, "That didn't. The group had gone different ways, the guys went into different groups, then I went into 100 Proof, other than background on a couple of things."

—

Captain Beefheart & His Magic Band "Diddy Wah Diddy" A&M May 23, 1966

Style: Rock 'n' roll
Where from: Glendale, CA
Where recorded: Hollywood, CA
Original version: Arthur "Blind" Blake "Diddie Wa Diddie" 1929

Captain Beefheart, real name Don van Vliet, grew up in the Antelope Valley of California and played with The Omens and The Blackouts, the latter band formed by Frank Zappa, who arranged for him to record at the Pal Recording Studio in Cucamonga as The Soots, seeking support from a major label. It didn't work, labels weren't ready for a white rocker who sang like Howlin' Wolf. The debut single was to be "Electricity" from the "Safe as Milk" album, which A&M's Jerry Moss rejected as being "negative," unsuitable for his 13-year-old daughter to hear on the radio. To be sure Beefheart's lascivious growl and spooky Theremin are not for the faint-hearted, yet the song has a prophetic lyric that meanders to compare man's ability at harnessing his innate powers with his never ending quest to exploit the earth's resources, and his (perhaps untapped) potential to create meaningful brotherhood. Moss plumped for the traditional Blind Blake blues, "Diddy Wah Diddy," which he felt was safe enough for his daughter's young ears, unaware of the sexual lyrics.

The Magic Band was primarily a R&B band, led by ex-Omens' member Alexis Snouffer and Jerry Handley, bass; with Doug Moon, guitar and Vic Mortenson, drums.

—

Ray Charles "Let's Go Get Stoned" ABC 1966

Style: Soul
Where from: Florida
Where recorded: Hollywood, CA
Original version: Chuck Bernard & the Satellite Band 1965
Earlier version: The Coasters 1965

With substantial vocal backing by The Raeletts, Ray Charles recorded this funky "Let's Go Get Stoned" with Billy Preston on organ. Banned by pop radio, but not by L.A. soul radio, the very commercial "Let's Go Get Stoned" dropped off all local radio charts after two weeks. "I auditioned with Ray. I was a little hot," said Vermetta Royster, who came over from the gospel Clara Ward Singers with whom she had sung between 1957 and 1965 and sang with Raeletts members Merry Clayton, Lillie Ford, Gwen Berry and Clydie King. About the material, "It had such a feeling. Gospel has a feeling, it's a rhythm, not about a bottle of gin." From this role, Royster joined The Ikettes, and with Ford and Berry, formed The Sisters Love.

Remakes: James Brown 1966; Big Mama Thornton 1967; Lowell Fulson 1968

—

The Troggs "Wild Thing" Atco/Fontana May/June 1966

Style: Rock
Where from: England
Where recorded: London, England
Original version: The Wild Ones 1965
Suggested pairings: Ritchie Valens "La Bamba" 1958; Kingsmen "Louie Louie" 1963; Tommy James "Crimson & Clover" 1968

Songwriter Billy Vera told about fellow songwriter Chip Taylor asking him to help out with an all night writing session for Christopher & The Wild Ones, who were holding a recording session the next day. As Vera had a concert commitment, he couldn't help, so Taylor wrote by himself. Apparently, Taylor came up with the most simplistic title he could think of, made it rhyme in an equally simplistic manner and came up with "Wild Thing," which rhymed with "sing" and "everything," and for the break, declared "I love you." Presto, it was done and recorded by The Wild Ones, and stiffed.

The Troggs replaced the whistling in The Wild Ones' version with an ocarina. The way The Troggs' version stops and starts again was supposedly inspired by Elvis Presley's "Heartbreak Hotel."

The Troggs' hit was released simultaneously on two labels in the USA, Atco and Fontana, the former taking a chance on the song; the latter, having the first rights to issue the song, which they did in a secondary sort of way. The tiny difference between the Atco and Fontana versions: The Atco release has a click at 2:09 right after [Reg] Presley says "you move me" and before the next note; the Fontana label version doesn't have that sound.

Remakes: Fancy 1974; The Skids 1980; Sam Kinison 1985; X 1989; by Hank Williams, Jr. 1995
Satirical **remake:** Senator Bobby 1967

—

Grateful Dead "Don't Ease Me In" Scorpio July 1966

Style: Haight Ashbury rock
From and recorded in: San Francisco, CA

In 1965, The Warlocks were Jerry Garcia and Bob Weir, guitar; Ron McKernan, keyboard and harmonica. After playing as The Warlocks, the Jerry Garcia-led Haight Ashbury band with Phil Lesh, bass and Bill Krentzmann, drums became The Grateful Dead on the very much Chuck Berry-style single "Don't Ease Me In" on Scorpio. Apparently that Grateful Dead name stuck.

Not many copies of this were pressed and this was re-released as a bootleg 45 in the early 1970s.

—

Napoleon XIV "They're Coming To Take Me Away, Ha-haaa" Warner Brothers 1966

Style: Novelty
Where **From and recorded in:** New York City, NY
Suggested pairing: Bob Dylan "Rainy Day Women #12 & 35" 1966

A comedic deadpan reading over a thumping beat similar to Bob Dylan's slightly earlier "Rainy Day Women #12 & 35," Jerry Samuels as Napoleon XIV recited a tale of being committed to the funny farm in "They're Coming To Take Me Away, Ha-haaa" on Warner Brothers. Long before there was a Dr. Demento, his alter-ego, Barry Hansen, heard Samuels hum the piece, "da da dat dat da dat da da da da da..." and Samuels said, "Yeah, that's 'The Campbell's Are Coming,' and I thought, 'they're coming to take me away, ha ha.' There it was, and by understanding what I could do with a Variable Frequency Oscillator, I wrote this thing." After the novelty wore off, the song began being banned by many radio stations, yet had sold well enough to already become a classic. The flip, the A-side done backwards, was entitled "Aaah-Ah, Yawa Em Ekat Ot GnimoC Er'yheT."

This song wasn't covered, which is done under compulsory licensing, as it wasn't considered music. "Since this has no melody, they were able to copyright it as a lecture intended for oral delivery instead of as a song. This meant other record companies couldn't copy it without permission," Samuels told Songfacts.

—

Eddie Floyd "Knock On Wood" Stax July 13, 1966

Style: Soul
Where from: Washington, DC
Where recorded: Memphis, TN

"I met a guy named Al Bell in Washington, DC years later," said Eddie Floyd. "He went down to Memphis to work as a promotion man for Stax. We wrote some songs for Carla Thomas who was in college then at Howard University. We practiced some songs at a radio station, we'd always had good luck at radio stations. We went to Memphis, I wrote some songs, Carla was my in to Stax. We did the 'Knock On Wood' thing. I thought it should be for Otis Redding. I didn't think they'd put it out on me, it was like a demo for me. Everybody says it sounds like a record, so they gave it to Al Bell. He released it in Washington, DC, also Memphis. Deejays would pick it up, town to town, state to state, took about eight months, then it happened. Took almost a year."

—

The Impressions "Can't Satisfy" ABC July 18, 1966

Style: Soul
From and recorded in: Chicago, IL
Suggested pairing: The Isley Brothers "This Old Heart Of Mine" 1966

When Curtis Mayfield wrote "Can't Satisfy" for The Impressions, he was unconsciously influenced by The Isley Brothers on "This Old Heart Of Mine." As a result, legal action was taken and "Can't Satisfy" ended up with Motown writer credits.

—

The Beach Boys "Wouldn't It Be Nice" Capitol July 29, 1966

Style: Rock 'n' roll
Where from: Hawthorne, CA
Where recorded: Hollywood, CA

"I gathered 23 musicians in one studio, an extraordinary number for a pop record, everyone played simultaneously," said Wilson in his autobiography of the A-side title. "The different sounds bleeding into one another, producing a rich, heavenly blanket of music." Among the 23 were Larry Knechtel, organ; Carole Kaye and Ray Pohlman, bass; Hal Blaine, drums; Jay Migliori and Leonard Hartman, sax; Lyle Ritz, string bass; Carl Fortina, accordian; Frank Marocco, clarinet; Bill Green, woodwinds with Leonard Malarsky and Sidney Sharp, violins, who in 1961 fiddled on the Johnny "Guitar" Watson "Posin'" session for King.

The presumed Beach Boys' hit was the A-side, "Wouldn't It Be Nice" backed with "God Only Knows," a B-side many consider definitive.

—

The Beach Boys "God Only Knows" Capitol July 29, 1966

Style: Rock 'n' roll
Where from: Hawthorne, CA
Where recorded: Hollywood, CA
Suggested pairing: Lovin' Spoonful "You Didn't Have To Be So Nice" 1965

When the Beach Boys recorded "God Only Knows," by legend, the song's writer Brian Wilson, who'd been inspired by the Lovin' Spoonful on "You Didn't Have To Be So Nice" from 1965, was nervous about the use of the word "God" in the title of a pop song, despite an earlier use of that same title by Philly doo wop group the Capris in 1954.

—

Count Five "Psychotic Reaction" Double Shot August 1966

Style: Psych rock
Where from: San Jose, CA
Where recorded: Los Angeles, CA
Suggested pairing: John Lee Hooker "Boom Boom" 1962

A very early example of garage becoming psych, "Psychotic Reaction" by Count Five was vocalized by Sean Byrne, who rejected that label saying the band was clean cut and didn't do drugs. It was "about a love that's gone bad." Byrne had just moved to San Jose from Dublin, met up with some local musicians, and "worked out in the garage, until we got good enough for the clubs." They then became Count Five, riffing on band names like the Dave Clark Five, when Byrne "just happened to say Count Five and it stuck."

While playing an opening spot for the Dave Clark Five at West Valley College in San Jose, Kenn's dad approached KLIV DJ Brian Lord who liked the act and got them an audition for Irwin Zucker's Double Shot Records. "Lord got us the shot at it. Six record companies turned us down; Capitol twice. 'There's something missing,' they said." Zucker signed the group; Psychotic Reaction" was their first release.

—

Question Mark & the Mysterians "96 Tears" Pa-Go-Go/Cameo 1966

Style: Garage/psych rock
Where from: Michigan
Where recorded: Living room in Bay City, Michigan
Original title: "69 Tears"

This Hispanic band started with "?," for the band's frontman, who wanted anonymity. Some say he invented the name Rudy Martinez to collect royalties. The Mysterians were Larry Borjas, guitar; Borjas' cousin Robert Balderrama, bass and Robert Martinez, guitars, bongos and drums from the Saginaw Valley area of Michigan. Robert Martinez and Lary Borjas were drafted just before recording, so Bobby recruited Eddie Serratto, drums and Frank Lugo, bass with Bobby Balderrama switching from bass to guitar. At one point, "?" referred to the individual band members only by three-letter names (at one point, the band was known as XYZ).

One of the most recognizable organ riffs in rock, ? Mark & Mysterians' "96 Tears" helped define the sound of that era. Often thought to be a Farfisa, keyboard player, 14-year-old Frank Rodriguez, used a Vox Continental. Texas-based Pa-Go-Go Records, owned by the group's manager, Lillian Gonzales, pressed 500 copies so they could distribute them to southern Michigan DJs, then licensed "96 Tears" to Cameo because their logo was ?'s favorite color, orange.

—

The Four Tops "Reach Out I'll Be There" Motown August 18, 1966

Style: Soul vocal group
From and recorded in: Detroit, MI

The Four Tops employed an unusually aggressive arrangement on their breakthrough vocal, "Reach Out I'll Be There." Said co-writer Lamont Dozier, "'Reach Out I'll Be There' was quite exciting at the time because it was a new direction for us, something we were trying out and it was a breakthrough. It transcended anything we had done before." An almost-instant pick hit in tiny Escondido, CA, "Reach Out I'll Be There" was top five in L.A., and hit #1 in New York City.

—

The Chambers Brothers "Time Has Come Today" Columbia September 1966

Style: Psych rock
Where from: Mississippi by way of Boston, MA
Where recorded: Los Angeles, CA

Formed in 1954 by four brothers, George, Willie, Lester and Joe Chambers, they came to L.A. in the 1960s and backed various doo wop singers. They also recorded with folk singer Hoyt Axton. "Time Has Come Today" was written by Joe and Willie Chambers from a dream they both shared about the younger generation fighting for civil rights, social justice and an end to the Vietnam War. The lyrics are considered ambiguous, but the repetition of the word "time!" indicates a call to action.

The original version of this Chambers Brothers' funky rocker, "Time Has Come Today," had no psych sound effects, which were used in the updated hit version in late 1968.

—

The Music Machine "Talk, Talk" Original Sound September 10, 1966

Style: Garage rock
Where from: San Pedro, CA
Where recorded: Hollywood, CA

Built on folk roots, as frontman Sean Bonniwell of San Pedro played with The Wayfarers; Keith Olsen, bass had backed folkie Gale Garnett; and Ron Egar, drums had played with The GoldeBriars, after whom the band modeled their black attire. These three founded The Ragamuffins in 1965, then recruited organist Doug Rhodes and lead guitar Mark Landon to form The Music Machine. Bonniwell said, "I ended up calling us The Music Machine was in order to stop the managers, or whoever was in control of where we were playing, from coming up in between songs, saying 'play The Turtles' or something like that. We would be onstage for an hour and ten minutes, wall-to-wall music, just non-stop, just like a Music Machine."

Producer Brian Ross caught them playing at the Hollywood Legion Lanes. Bonniwell explained, "We were sitting in that bowling alley lounge, and decided to record those two songs I was rehearsing with the band before we went in. We used to rehearse eight to ten hours a day like The Wayfarers did. This standard, this pursuit of excellence, was something that was very much a part of my persona. I rehearsed The Music Machine mercilessly. So when we got in the studio, we were really fine-tuned. I mean, there's just no question about it. Brian gave us all the wrong advice. 'Be sure and change your strings.' Well, you don't do that before a recording session, because strings take time to stretch, and instruments are going out of tune all the time."

Ross took them to the RCA recording studio C where Bonniwell had once recorded with The Wayfarers. "'Talk Talk' took two takes. And it took one take for 'Come On In,'" which was the original A-side for the record. "The whole session cost $150. Only took three hours. Then I took a copy of the tape over to Dot Records, which was then on the brink of extinction. This guy wouldn't let me out of the office. He yelled at me, he said, 'That record is so bad it's good!' He said, 'I have no idea what that is, but I know it's a hit.' He almost threatened to lock the door to his office until I signed a contract. Of course, I couldn't, because I'd just signed a producer's contract with Brian Ross. Brian had gone to his friend Art LaBoe at Original Sound and made a deal. He made an 8 percent deal, of which Brian took half. So I sat there with him after everybody was gone at three o'clock in the morning in this bowling alley. I told him, how do you expect me to keep my group together, splitting four cents five ways? He just didn't care. He was zeroed in his profit. That's all he cared about. And I have to tell you that that was true for the duration of The Music Machine. Nobody gave a damn about how I wrote my songs, how we recorded them, the longevity of the band, nothing, from our management to the record company. They could care less." KRLA played the 45 of the garage classic "Talk, Talk" backed with "Come On In" when The Music Machine appeared at the Cinnamon Cinder, which drew long lines.

—

The Beach Boys "Good Vibrations" Capitol September 28, 1966

Style: Psych rock
Where from: Hawthorne, CA
Where recorded: Hollywood, CA
Suggested pairings: Miklos Rozsa "Spellbound" 1945; Paul Revere & the Raiders "Good Thing" 1966; The Beach Boys "Here Today" 1966

The Beach Boys' first stab at psych included replacing sometimes scary Hitchcock-like "Spellbound" Theremin-based vibes with "Good Vibrations" purportedly also designed to both overcome the hits of Phil Spector and/or answer the production skills of The Beatles. Songfacts.com said Brian Wilson called this song "the summation of my musical vision. A harmonic convergence of imagination and talent, production values and craft, songwriting and spirituality." Wilson reportedly wrote it while on LSD, which explains why the song is the musical embodiment of a spectacular acid trip.

Credited co-writer and Beach Boys lead singer Mike Love told songfacts.com, it was "basically a flowery poem." Love admitted that the psychedelic vibe was an influence on his words. Said Love, "It was this flowery power type of thing." Released about three months after it was scheduled, "Good Vibrations" reflected Brian Wilson's unstoppable perfectionism—when it came to record releases, at least. The name Brian Wilson represented the shocking and skyrocketing costs in time and money of recording sessions, two months to record using around 90 hours of studio time in six studios and 70 hours of tape in 17 sessions, costing about $50,000 to make.

Except for Brian, no Beach Boys played on "Good Vibrations." Instead, a dozen members of The Wrecking Crew, including Glen Campbell and/or Al Casey, guitar; Ray Pohlman, electric bass; Lyle Ritz, double bass; Jim Horn, piccolo; Hal Blaine, drums; Larry Knechtel, organ; Al de Lory, piano; Jesse Ehrlich, cello; Tommy Morgan, harmonica and Paul Tanner, Electro-Theremin.

Remakes: Floyd Cramer 1967; The Troggs 1975; Todd Rundgren 1976

—

Gene Chandler "I Fooled You This Time" Checker October 1966

Style: Soul
From and recorded in: Chicago, IL

"It's not controversial" how Gene Chandler recorded for two labels, Chess and Brunswick, at the same time. "I was on the Constellation label with Ewart Abner, who was going out of biz and sold all his rights to Leonard Chess. I was in the middle of negotiations with Brunswick. My contract was up with Abner, I owed them an album, Chess wanted that album from me, so I asked them if one [album] would hold them off. One was for Brunswick. I didn't have to do that one, Chess just wanted that album, I talked them into it. I actually had no problem with Nat Tarnapol of Brunswick. The problem came from people who had less strength than I had, [I] didn't take nothing from anybody, if you go to people, get favors, you are beholden."

—

The Seeds "Pushin' Too Hard" GNP Crescendo October 1966

Style: Protest rock
Where from: Salt Lake City, UT/Detroit, MI
Where recorded: Los Angeles, CA
Original title: "You're Pushing Too Hard"

Sometimes, unexpected events can help groups and songs succeed where they never had a prayer before. The Seeds Featuring Sky Saxon stiffed with the original "You're Pushing Too Hard" on GNP Crescendo in November 1965. "It was the answer to Pandora's Box, it happened because it was also for a girl that was pushing me," said Sky Saxon, who under Ritchie Marsh wrote a theme song, "Pushin' Too Hard" in 1963 or 64. "I sold the masters to GNP Crescendo Records," said Jimmy Maddin. "I owned the masters. I was close to a deal with Capitol Records." The Seeds' original version was retitled "Pushin' Too Hard," taking to the charts in its second incarnation and more or less coincided with, but actually preceded, most of the weekend Sunset Strip riots, which at times involved as many as 2,000 youths and began on Saturday. "The minute I got the hit 'Pushin' Too Hard,' they screwed me," said Maddin. "They said it wasn't selling, then made a deal to cash in for ten grand. The disc jockey Lord Tim on KFWB stepped in, signed The Seeds, took them away from me. They never had another hit." Saxon recalled he turned down the role in the movie Riot On the Sunset Strip. "The premise was you lock up people over 30. I wanted to be true to the people." The Standells appeared in the Seeds' role.

—

Blues Magoos "(We Ain't Got) Nothin' Yet" Mercury October 1966

Style: Psych rock
From and recorded in: New York
Suggested pairing: Rick Nelson "Summertime" 1962

First known as the Bloos Magoos, not after Mr. Magoo, but after moogoo gai pan, this group was New York City's first psych band of any consequence. The Blues Magoos—lead singer/guitarist Peppy Castro (real name, Emil Thielheim); Ronnie Gilbert, bass; Dennis LaPore, guitar; Ralph Scala, organ and John Finnegan, drums—recorded "People With No Faces" for Verve/Folkways and "Who Do You Love" for Ganim. Signed by Mercury Records, "Bloos" was dropped, and became the Blues Magoos when they recorded John D. Loudermilk's "Tobacco Road," already a Nashville Teens hit. They then borrowed the intro into Rick Nelson's "Summertime" from 1962 to build into the vocal of "(We Ain't Got) Nothin' Yet," charting big in Cleveland and the rest of Ohio in October.

—

The Electric Prunes "I Had Too Much to Dream (Last Night)" Reprise November 1966

Style: Psych rock
Where from: Woodland Hills, CA
Where recorded: Hollywood, CA

First known as The Sanctions, a surf combo, then as Jim and the Lords, this fake Brit band—lead singer and rhythm guitarist James Lowe, bassist and keyboard player Mark Tulin and lead guitarist Ken Williams—formed the core of the group with Michael "Quint" Weakley as drummer. They debuted with a cover of The Gypsy Trips' "Ain't it Hard." They used a Bigsby Wiggle Stick (motorcycle racer/guitar maker Paul Bigsby had invented a device that when connected to an electric guitar creates a vibrato sound), thus they combined psych effects with a surf guitar on the intro to the trippy "I Had Too Much to Dream (Last Night)," by far their biggest hit.

—

Dyke & the Blazers "Funky Broadway" Artco October 1966/Original Sound November 1966

Style: Funk
Where from: Buffalo, NY
Where recorded: Phoenix, AZ
Suggested pairings: James Brown "There Was a Time"

Dyke Arlester Christian, vocalist; Alvester "Pig" Jacobs, guitar; J.V. Hunt and Clarence Towns, saxophone; Alvin Battle, bass and Willie Earl, drums were stranded in Phoenix where they merged with The Three Blazers' Bernard Williams tenor saxophonist; Rich Cason, organ and Rodney Brown, drums. As Dyke & the Blazers, they recorded this two-part vocal, "Funky Broadway" about Broadway in Buffalo and Broadway in Phoenix on their manager Art Barrett's Artco label.

According to Original Sound's Art LaBoe, "Tony Evans, a Phoenix DJ, came to my sales manager with a finished product. It was making a little noise in Phoenix. I didn't think too much of it, thought it was too slow. This black kid named Charles in my shipping department heard it and said, 'What is that?' When he began to dance to it, I knew we had something." They did. A hit in December, Dyke and the Blazers' "Funky Broadway Pt. 1 & 2" on Original Sound was the first national hit to use "funky" in the title, and was banned on local pop radio.

Remakes: Jimmy Smith 1967

—

Albert King "Crosscut Saw" Stax November 14, 1966

Style: Blues
Where from: Mississippi
Where recorded: Memphis, TN
Original version: Binghampton Blues Boys—instrumental
Suggested pairing: Led Zeppelin "Lemon Song" 1969

This was the first major Stax label hit by Albert King, who recalled about the deep blues "Crosscut Saw" from 1966, "Gave me a little money every now and then to keep my damn mouth shut. Didn't give me no royalties for eight years." So he left.

Remake: John Hammond 1968

—

Chain Reaction "The Sun" Date November 1966

Style: Rock
Where from: Yonkers, NY
Where recorded: New York

This was an Early Yonkers band with lead singer Steven Tallarico performing in a folksy style with harmonica well before Tallarico became Steve Tyler, and Aerosmith was born.

—

Jimmy Castor "Hey Leroy, Your Mama's Callin' You" Smash November 1966

Style: Latin soul
From and recorded in: New York

"Leroy was made up," said Jimmy Castor of this surprise hit. "I needed something on that rainy Saturday morning. I don't have time to go to the bridge," not meaning Brooklyn, or any bridge like that, but a bridge on the song. "The cowbell was played by Johnny Pacheco," Castor added.

—

Wilson Pickett, "Mustang Sally" Atlantic November 1966

Style: Soul
Where from: Detroit, MI
Where recorded: Fame Studios Muscle Shoals, Alabama

"I think The Rascals were way later." No, Pickett, they recorded it first. On his own, after Pickett finished his final "Mustang Sally" take, the tape flew off the reel and broke into pieces. But engineer Tom Dowd calmly cleared the room and told everyone to come back in half an hour. Dowd pieced the tape back together, saving one of the funkiest soul anthems of the era.

Bonny "Mack" Rice wrote the song as a joke while teasing Reese. He called the early version "Mustang Mama" but the title was changed when Aretha Franklin suggested that he change the title to "Mustang Sally." Rice, who composed the song, was the first to record the song in 1965, though Pickett claimed that the Blue Rock label version was only a demo, thus he had it first. As Pickett was alleged to have carried a pistol to settle arguments, a contrary opinion was unlikely.

—

The Fifth Dimension "I'll Be Loving You Forever" Soul City December 3, 1966

Style: Soul vocal group
Where from: St. Louis, MO and Philadelphia, PA
Where recorded: Hollywood, CA

The Fifth Dimension were LaMont McLemore and Marilyn McCoo from The Versatiles, and Billy Davis Jr., Ron Townsen and Florence LaRue. Having departed Bob Keane's Bronco label, the group was at a crossroads, said Harry Elston. "I was a photographer for Motown, Marc Gordon was president of Motown on the West Coast and said, 'Come over and audition.' He gave us some old Smokey songs, took some reject songs, had us do them so Berry Gordy Jr. could hear it. The group chipped in money for me to go to Detroit for Berry to hear the songs. He wouldn't see me, kept putting me off, I told Berry, 'I have to see you, I can't go back without seeing you.' I got up at seven in the morning, I was waiting on the steps for Berry to come to work. He heard the songs, said, 'You guys can really sing, but I don't hear no hits.' Then, Johnny Rivers said, 'If you come with me, you won't got lost in the Motown shuffle.'" And they weren't.

The Fifth Dimension debuted on "I'll Be Loving You Forever" on Rivers' Soul City. "We were the foundation of the West Coast sound," said the group's manager and Motown executive Gordon. "Eddie Beale, who had worked with The Platters and Lou Rawls, did the rehearsals and arrangements. Rene DeKnight cultivated the sound of The Fifth Dimension, he groomed the sound, he was perfect in my universe when I needed him."

—

The Casinos "Then You Can Tell Me Goodbye" Fraternity December 1966

Style: Blue-eyed soul group
From and recorded in: Cincinnati, OH
Original version: Don Cherry 1962
Earlier versions: Johnny Nash 1964; John D. Loudermilk 1965

Led by vocalist Gene Hughes with many members who came and went over the years along with a couple of group names before settling on The Casinos. Hughes had dubbed his group The Capris, switching to The Casinos after becoming aware of two other Capris groups, especially the one with the hit "There's a Moon Out Tonight" in 1961. Harry Carlson's Cincinnati-based Fraternity Records signed The Casinos in '65, debuting with "She's Out of Sight" with Fraternity artist Lonnie Mack on guitar. The Casinos had this one major hit, a sentimental, almost emotional rendering of John D. Loudermilk's composition, "Then You Can Tell Me Goodbye," from 1962.

Remake: Eddy Arnold 1968

—

Spencer Davis Group "Gimme Some Lovin'" United Artists December 1966

Style: Brit blue-eyed soul group
From and recorded in: England
Original version: The Jordan Brothers 1966
Suggested pairings: Homer Banks "Ain't That A Whole Lot Of Love" 1965; Tommy James "Getting' Together" 1967; The Knack "My Sharona" 1979

Written "on the fly" by the group's lead singer, 17-year-old Steve Winwood, who also played the Hammond B-3 organ on this super intense "Gimme Some Lovin,'" it was completed in the first or second take. In Rolling Stone magazine, bassist Muff Winwood said, "Steve had been singing, 'Gimme some lovin',' just yelling anything. It took about an hour to write, then down the pub for lunch."

The line thought to be, "you'd better take some clothes off, 'cos the place is on fire" did not fare as well with some radio censors, though it could well have been "you'd better take some time off."

A first version of "Gimme Some Lovin'" by the Frackville, PA-based Jordan Brothers was released a couple of weeks before the Davis Group. The Jordan Brothers had been summoned to New York by the Philips label, which played them the Davis demo, which they had received through mysterious channels. The Jordan Brothers learned the song and recorded it, with some good response, until being quashed by the Spencer Davis Group cover, which had a somewhat more "soulful" sound.

—

Brenda and the Tabulations "Dry Your Eyes" Dionn December 19, 1966

Style: Soul vocal group
From and recorded in: Philadelphia, PA
Suggested pairing: Johnny Ace "Never Let Me Go" 1954

Brenda Payton was lead singer of The Tabulations, which featured her husband and a male guitarist. The name Brenda and the Tabulations was chosen with the hope of tabulating all the money the group would earn with their first hit, "Dry Your Eyes," with Brenda performing a powerful spoken bridge on a composition formed around a key line in Johnny Ace's "Never Let Me Go" on Duke from 1954 and also inspired by another Philly classic, "Dry Your Eyes" by The Inspirations, the title of which was changed for Wanda Burt as "Your True Love Is Standing By" from 1961 on Music City.

—

Cannonball Adderley "Mercy, Mercy, Mercy" Capitol December 1966

Style: Jazz funk
Where from: Tampa, FL
Where recorded: Capitol Records studio ("The Club") Hollywood, CA
Suggested pairing: Fred Hughes "You Can't Take It Away" 1965

Alto saxophone player Cannonball Adderley's funky riff on this Joe Zawinul composition, "Mercy, Mercy, Mercy," was an irresistible, mellow groove recorded before a live, invitation-only audience at Capitol Records tower in Hollywood. The group included Nat Adderley and Zawinul, keyboards; Victor Gaskin, bass and Roy McCordy, drums. The riff was very similar to the R&B hit "You Can't Take It Away" by Compton vocalist Fred Hughes from 1965. The single was trimmed from five to three minutes and reached the R&B top ten and pop top 20, hitting first in Baltimore in December 1966, then it went to #2 on KFWB and KGFJ.

Remakes: The Buckinghams 1967; Marlena Shaw 1967; Count Basie and His Orchestra 1967; Larry Williams & Johnny "Guitar" Watson 1967; Willie Mitchell 1968

—

Buffalo Springfield "For What It's Worth" Atco December 1966

Style: Protest rock
Where from: Los Angeles, CA
Where recorded: Hollywood, CA

The third single by the Buffalo Springfield, this Stephen Stills composition, "For What It's Worth," was a topical subject that became a major hit and put the band at rock's forefront for a short period. Guitarist Stills, most recently of the New York-based Au Go Go Singers, arrived in L.A., and invited fellow Au Go Go Richie Furay to play rhythm guitar for a new group he was thinking of forming. Stills and Furay were stuck in a traffic jam on April 6, 1966 when they spotted a black hearse with Canadian license plates driven by guitarist Neil Young, who Stills knew in Canada, with a fellow Canadian passenger, bassist Bruce Palmer, formerly with Jack London & the Sparrows. "The most remarkable karmic event ever," said Palmer. Country drummers Dewey Martin filled out the lineup of The Herd, a name they changed from a name on a parked steamroller. Buffalo Springfield became the house band at L.A:s Whisky a Go-Go.

The band's recording contract with Atco was a $12,000 advance, unheard of at the time.

Their first 45 was the Young composition "Nowadays Clancy Can't Even Sing," generally a stiff, a middling hit on KHJ and KFWB in August 1966, but charting well in Palmdale, where the action wasn't. "It was too sophisticated for AM radio," said an insider. "When 'Clancy' bombed, we all panicked," said Furay. "We really began to have communication problems and grew further and further apart." Then came the similarly folkish vocal, "Burned," in November, which did even more poorly.

Then the band began to rock with "For What It's Worth" about young folks protesting the closing of the Sunset Strip club Pandora's Box on November 12, 1966. The song's writer, Stills, heard about the protests from his band mates and set out to write up the incident, as recalled by P.F. Sloan. "I was with Stephen Stills," who wrote it "more like a news report. Step back. It scared the shit out of Stephen. We were in the night club listening to Love when the riots broke out."

Featuring Neil Young's sinister-sounding lead guitar, "For What It's Worth" took the band to local charts, #3 on KFXM and #2 on KHJ in late December, #4 on KFWB in early February and the national top ten at #7 in January. After "For What It's Worth" became a hit single, it replaced "Baby Don't Scold Me" on re-issues of the album. Shortly after this success, the band broke up at a Long Beach Arena concert, tensions still the name of the game.

Remakes: The Staple Singers 1967; King Curtis and The Kingpins 1967; Cher 1969; Crosby, Stills and Nash 1983

—

Aaron Neville "Tell It Like It Is" Parlo December 1966

Style: Soul
From and recorded in: New Orleans, LA

"I heard 'Tell It Like It Is' and I said, 'Bro, this is the shit right here,'" said Art Neville. Aaron was working as a longshoreman when he cut this sublime ballad. He originally felt something so sweet wouldn't catch on in an era of gritty R&B. "A lot of people come up to me and say, 'That song got me and my wife together,'" he recalled, "and others say, 'It broke me and my wife up.'"

—

Cream "I Feel Free" January 1967

Style: Rock
From and recorded in: England

This was the debut release by the Eric Clapton-led Cream, a serious rock band that quickly changed rock 'n' roll, sneaking up to the thunder brought about by Led Zepplin one year hence.

—

Tommy James "I Think We're Alone Now" Roulette January 1967

Style: Rock
Where from: Michigan
Where recorded: New York City, NY
Suggested pairing: The Everly Brothers "Wake Up Little Suzie" 1957

Tommy James' "I Think We're Alone Now" would endure almost automatic censorship from the title alone, just like the selectively censored "Wake Up Little Suzie" by the Everly Brothers from 1957.

Remakes: The Rubinoos 1977; Tiffany 1987
Satire: "Weird Al" Yankovic "I Think I'm a Clone Now" 1988

—

The Doors "Break On Through" Elektra January 28, 1967

Style: Rock 'n' roll
From and recorded in: Hollywood, CA

The Doors—Jim Morrison on vocals, Ray Manzarek from Rick & the Ravens on keyboards, John Densmore and Robbie Kreiger—debuted with "Break On Through" backed with "End Of the Night" on Elektra. "It was April or so, there was really not that much going on," said Manzarek. "We had released the record in January, 'Break On Through' had reached 106 on the Hot 100, those 10 records [101-110] were called bubbling under, we never bubbled up to the Hot 100, we needed something man, 'Let's get this record off the ground.' Three months later, we had the #1 song in America."

—

Arthur Conley "Sweet Soul Music" Atco February 1, 1967

Style: Soul
Where from: Atlanta, GA/Baltimore, MD
Where recorded: Muscle Shoals, AL
Suggested pairings: Al Caiola "Theme From the Magnificent Seven" 1960; Sam Cooke "Yeah Man" 1965

Credited to Arthur Conley and Otis Redding as writers, "Sweet Soul Music" was a soulfully rocking tribute to several soul hits of the day, "Going to a Go-Go" by The Miracles "Love's a Hurtin' Thing" by Lou Rawls, "Hold On I'm Coming" by Sam & Dave, "Mustang Sally" by Wilson Pickett and "Fa-Fa-Fa-Fa-Fa (Sad Song)" by Otis Redding. The late Sam Cooke's business partner J.W. Alexander sued for plagiarizing the melody. A settlement was reached in which Cooke's name was added to the writer credits, and Otis Redding agreed to record some songs in the future for Kags Music, a Cooke and Alexander company.

—

Aretha Franklin "I Never Loved a Man (The Way I Love You)" Atlantic February 1967
Style: Soul vocal
Where from: Detroit, MI
Where recorded: Muscle Shoals, AL

Aretha Franklin's career on Atlantic began with Jerry Wexler. Wexler said, "In 1966, I was in Muscle Shoals recording Wilson Pickett, when I got a call from gospel DJ Louise Williams, who said, 'Call this number, she's waiting to hear from you.' Next week, we signed a five year contract" with Aretha Franklin. He "took her to Muscle Shoals, Chips Moman helped me a lot, came up with the guitar break." The session involved Aretha Franklin, piano and vocals, with her sisters, Carolyn Franklin and Erma Franklin, and The Sweet Inspirations doing background vocals; King Curtis and Charles Chalmers, tenor saxophone; Willie Bridges, baritone and tenor saxophone; Gene Chrisman, drums; Tommy Cogbill, bass; Jimmy Johnson, guitar; Melvin Lastie, trumpet, cornet; Chips Moman, guitar and Dewey Oldham, keyboards.

After a dispute with a white trumpet player over a supposed racial slur with Aretha's husband, Ted White, she left Muscle Shoals, having recorded only one side. Franklin and many of the same Muscle Shoals musicians were flown in to back her on the B-side, "Do Right Woman—Do Right Man," in New York several weeks later. This song hit first in St. Louis on February 16, 1967, and was a national #1 a very short time later.

—

Wilson Pickett "I Found a Love" Atlantic March 1967
Style: Soul vocal
Where from: Detroit, MI
Where recorded: Muscle Shoals, AL
Original version: The Falcons 1962

Between early 1967 and 1969, Wilson Pickett and Aretha Franklin alternated single soul 45s on the Atlantic label, making them both Detroit products, recording mainly in the South, as the Queen and King of soul music. In the case of Wilson Pickett, his recording of "I Found a Love" was a redo of his days as lead singer of The Falcons, based out of Detroit.

—

Jay and the Techniques "Apples, Peaches and Pumpkin Pie" Smash March 1967
Style: Pop soul vocal group
From and recorded in: Philadelphia, PA

"What I saw was, this is not the kind of song I want to sing, about fruit," said Jay Proctor of Jay and the Techniques. "I was a Temptations lover, I was into James Brown and the whole stone soul type of thing. "'Apples, Peaches and Pumpkin Pie' and things didn't sound very soulful to me. I really wasn't all that enthused about doing the song; however I never recorded for anyone before. I left a lot in Jerry Ross' hands. This guy know what he's talking about. I'm not going to squash this opportunity to record, so we did the song. It's not soul, it's not pop, they didn't have a name for it. It didn't have a message. It was about love, but it wasn't about love." With Ashford & Simpson and Melba a Moore supplying background vocals, the intended A-side, "Stronger Than Dirt," was written by a New Jersey DJ who played it all the time. "Someone came in the studio and inadvertently played 'Apples, Peaches and Pumpkin Pie' and liked it."

—

Brenton Wood "Oogum Boogum Song" Double Shot 1967
Style: Soul vocal
Where from: San Pedro, CA
Where recorded: Hollywood, CA

When producer/songwriter Hal Winn set up his own label, "originally we had called it Sure Shot Records, 'shot heard around the world,'" but a pre-existing Sure Shot owned by Don Robey out of Houston put a stop to that plan; thus, Double Shot. "The initial release was going to be 'Psychotic Reaction' by The Count Five," said Winn.

Brenton Wood confessed that though he was comfortable in a recording studio, he had never performed on stage and had difficulty learning those ropes. Backing Wood was Kent Sprague, later of Kent & the Candidates, who played keyboard behind him. "They had a group that backed him on early sides," said Winn. "I was searching for a good hit song to enter the music market, only thing I could think of was write everything that's around you, then go in and jumble the words, that's what I did with 'Oogum Boogum.'" said Wood. "The title was an accident, frustration, sitting down at a piano singing 'oogum boogum.' Someone happened to hear me, said, 'What's that?' It dawned on me. It caught his ear. Maybe it would catch somebody else's ear. It happens like that. I substituted 'Oogum Boogum' for the title 'Abra Cadabra.'"

On early pressings, label credit showed "Brenton Woods," but was soon corrected to Brenton Wood when "Oogum Boogum" began to sell.

Winn said, "We took it immediately to Herman Griffith in Dolphin's of Hollywood. He played the record; people came in to buy the record, bought 25 copies of it. Overnight success. I'd been writing songs for 12 year[s] prior to that."

—

Jefferson Airplane "Somebody To Love" RCA March 1967
Style: Haight Ashbury
From and recorded in: San Francisco, CA

The song, originally titled "Someone to Love," was written by guitarist Darby Slick (Grace Slick's sister-in-law) and recorded by his group, The Great Society. When lead singer Grace Slick left to replace vocalist Signe Anderson of Jefferson Airplane, she recorded the title with a slight change, "Somebody to Love, with second person lyrics and a more aggressive style. Previous records from the Haight-Ashbury scene (Great Society, Grateful Dead) were distributed and sold locally; Jefferson Airplane's "Somebody To Love" was the first on a major label with charting action, thus Haight-Ashbury went worldwide instantly.

—

The Rascals "Groovin'" Atlantic April 6, 1967
Style: Blue-eyed soul group
Where from: Upstate New York, NY
Where recorded: New York City, NY

Felix Cavaliere sang lead on The Rascals' "Groovin'" with conga backing, a Cuban-influenced bass guitar line from session musician Chuck Rainey and a haunting harmonica by session man Michael Weinstein. Atlantic's head Jerry Wexler did not want to release "Groovin,'" but DJ Murray the K intervened. "They didn't originally like the record because it had no drum on it," said Cavaliere. "We had just cut it, and Murray came in the studio to say hello. After he heard the song, he said, 'Man, this is a smash.' So, when he later heard that Atlantic didn't want to put it out, he went to see Jerry Wexler and said, 'Are you crazy? This is a friggin' No. 1 record.' He was right, going to #1 for four straight weeks."

The lyric "you and me endlessly" was misheard as "you and me and Leslie." In June, the Rascals' "Groovin" was issued in Spanish and in Italian.

Remakes: Booker T. and The M.G.'s 1967; Wilson Pickett 1978: El Chicano 1982; War 1984

—

Aretha Franklin "Respect" Atlantic April 1967

Style: Soul
Where from: Detroit, MI
Where recorded: Stax Studios, Memphis, TN
Original version: Otis Redding 1965
Earlier version: The Rationals 1966

Franklin's remake of Otis Redding's original, "Respect," turned his request for respect when he comes home to a feminist declaration by way of sisters' Carolyn and Emma Franklin chanting the added "sock it to me" refrain at the end of every phrase, as well as a strong sax bridge supplied by King Curtis to the approximate melody of Sam & Dave's hit "When Something Is Wrong With My Baby." It has since become an anthem of rights—female, racial and whatever rights might concern the listener.

Remakes: The Roy Meriwether Trio 1967; The Vagrants 1967; Rotary Connection 1969

—

Strawberry Alarm Clock "Incense and Peppermints" All American/UNI April 1967

Style: Psych rock
Where from: Burbank, CA
Where recorded: Hollywood, CA

Thee Sixpence—with Ed King, lead guitar; Michael Luciano, vocals; Lee Freeman, rhythm guitar, harmonica, vocals; Gary Lovetro, Steve Rabe, guitar, vocals and Randy Seol, drums, vibes, percussion, vocals—recorded several 45s. Then the band changed their name to Strawberry Alarm Clock, recording the first #1 L.A.-based psych 45, "Incense and Peppermints," possibly inspired by the psych title, "Strawberry Fields Forever" by The Beatles in February 1967. They were managed by local rockabilly singer Fat Daddy Holmes. "Incense & Peppermints" hit big nationally when picked up by Uni, a new psych and rock-oriented subsidiary of the more established MCA label.

—

The Doors "Light My Fire" Elektra May 3, 1967

Style: Rock
Where from: South Bay, CA and Venice, CA
Where recorded: Hollywood, CA

The Doors kicked in with this keyboard-heavy Morrison vocal "Light My Fire." As described by Ray Manzarek, "Robbie brought it in. Actually, it was a folk rock song.... Robbie had a [hums], kind of like that... it's nice, the chords are nice, Densmore says, 'Let's give it a kind of Latin thing.' John took off on that Latin part, I started playing Latin behind him with that left-handed piano bass I play, we're doing Latin, 'Let's go into hard rock.' John jumps into a four and Robbie had only one verse, Jim had to contribute the verse, 'our love becomes a funeral pyre,' throw in a little death, blood and fire, right on the money.

Manzarek, continued, "[Dave] Diamond is the guy who said, 'You got to cut this song down. I'm getting all kinds of requests for 'Light My Fire,' but I can't play it because it's 6 minutes 45 seconds long... we just don't do it. We can't do it, we play 3 minute songs.' It worked. In that context, it works. If I'm going to hear this song by the AM radio, the cut was clear, you couldn't tell where the cut was made, there was no extra beat added, Paul and Bruce were right on the money, 'Sounds OK, if we have to..." As usual, L.A. market leader Boss Radio KHJ was conservative in featuring "Light My Fire," not charting for almost two months.

KRLA's early advocacy of this record also applied to the flipside, "The Crystal Ship." Traditional AM rock & roll station KFWB was about to change format to all-news in March 1968; KRLA didn't play extended tracks and KHJ was conservative in charting the newest sound, so the opportunity for a new rock station was wide open in November 1967, thus underground FM KPPC in Pasadena eventually changed the whole scene, from singles to LP tracks.

The old KHJ-FM became "oldies" KRTH five years later.

Remakes: Chet Atkins 1968; José Feliciano 1968; Rhetta Hughes 1968; Gerald Wilson 1968; Julie Driscoll 1969; Brian Auger & the Trinity 1969; The Watts 103rd Street Rhythm Band 1969; Peter Duchin 1969; Woody Herman 1969

—

Van Morrison "Brown Eyed Girl" Bang May 1967

Style: Irish blue-eyed soul group
Where from: Ireland
Where recorded: New York, NY

This was the debut release by blue-eyed Irish soul singer Van Morrison after he departed Them and signed with the Bang label, whose owner, Bert Berns, backed Morrison on "Brown Eyed Girl" after The Sweet Inspirations left the session. Joining Berns in the background was songwriter Jeff Barry. As a key lyric was thought to be about premarital sex ("Makin' love in the green grass"), radio stations refused to air "Brown Eyed Girl," so the label changed to acceptable lyrics ("Laughin' and a-runnin,' hey hey"), and made it Van's first hit.

—

Albert King "Born Under a Bad Sign" Stax May 14, 1967

Style: Blues
Where from: St. Louis, MO
Where recorded: Memphis, TN

About his most major hit, "Born Under A Bad Sign," Albert King said, "All of those songs came from when I went to Stax. Didn't get nothing out of them. Got $250,000 front money, then I bussed."

—

Smokey Robinson & the Miracles "More Love" Tamla May 26, 1967

Style: Soul vocal group
From and recorded in: Detroit, MI

"The song he wrote for me was 'More Love,'" said Claudette Robinson of Smokey Robinson, her husband at the time. "Over the years, people would say, 'What did you do to him? Was that song about you? Are you ever going to write a song about us?' Maybe so, forever. This is for us. Sort of like an anthem for The Miracles."

—

Ohio Express "Beg, Borrow and Steal" Cameo June 1967

Style: Rock
From and recorded in: Ohio
Original release: Rare Breed 1966
Earlier release: The Demotrons 1967
Suggested pairing: Richard Berry "Louie Louie" 1957

A non-existent band, the Ohio Express, was credited with this hit of the "Louie Louie"-beat "Beg, Borrow and Steal." First out by The Rare Breed on Attack from 1966, which had recorded the song as The Conquests, they were unaware it had been released. When they started hearing the song on New York City radio, credited to The Rare Breed, then leased to Cameo, for which producers Jeff Katz and Jerry Kasenetz renamed the group The Ohio Express, it was already a hit.

The producers sent out others to tour on the hit, making The Ohio Express whomever Katz and Kasenetz hired. This way creating the so-called bubble gum sound, which included The Music Explosion, the 1910 Fruitgum Company and The Archies, the latter from another producer.

—

Procol Harum "A Whiter Shade Of Pale" Deram June 1967

Style: Rock
From and recorded in: England
Suggested pairings: Percy Sledge "When a Man Loves a Woman" 1966

Procol Harum's lyricist Keith Reid got the idea for this title at a party, which gave him a starting point. Reid told Songfacts.com, "At our first session, we cut four tracks, and 'Whiter Shade of Pale' was the one that recorded best. In those days it wasn't just a question of how good is your song, it was how good of a recording can you make. Because it was essentially live recording, and if you didn't have a great sound engineer or the studio wasn't so good, you might not get a very good-sounding record. And for some reason everything at our first studio session came out sounding really good."

The song includes lyrical references to the "Vestal Virgins," the six virgin holy priestesses of Vesta, goddess of the hearth and home. The Vestal duty brought great honor and afforded greater privileges to women who served in that role. The lyric "As the miller told his tale" sounds like a reference to "The Miller's Tale," from Chaucer's English novel, The Canterbury Tales. This tale is well known to English students as a vulgar or bawdy story, told by the miller. Given this, the line, "And so it was that later as the miller told his tale, that her face, at first just ghostly, turned a whiter shade of pale" is an attempt by a young man, who has just caused a girl to turn pale by telling some vulgar story, to explain away her signs of disgust as due to other things such as the dancing, the drinking."

—

The Gentrys "Keep On Dancin'" Youngstown June 1967/MGM August 1967

Style: Rock
From and recorded in: Memphis, TN
Original version: The Avantis 1963

The Gentrys' "Keep On Dancin'" was first on Youngstown, a local label owned by Chips Moman and Don C, who wanted to have a Memphis scene similar to Motown. "The Avantis were a three-man group, Memphis' answer to The Isley Brothers, in the 1960s, we all enjoyed R&B," said Gentrys' leader Larry Raspberry. The Avantis leader was "Willie Young, slightly older, removed by age by us." When the Gentrys covered "Keep On Dancin," they added a false ending The Avantis original didn't have. "I played guitar, sang lead in the group."

The Gentrys were Larry Wall, drums; Pat Neal, bass; Jimmy Johnson, trumpet and organ; Hammond organ, Farisa organ and sax; Bobby Fisher. Jimmy Hart and Bruce Bowles were the backup singers. "George Klein, who had the 5 to 6 shift on WHBQ, sponsored the band. When Chips came back to Memphis, George Klein told him about us. We were eating at a place close to his radio station, George Klein walked in with Chips and introduced him to us. George Klein had a TV talent party show that aired locally, where you had to lip synch. Chips supplied resources, gave us performance tapes, that's how we got recording experience. We would lip synch on George's show, 'let's do a real record, we'll record it on local label, so it gets picked up by a major.' Chips Moman understood the record business, we understood the garage band world. We were seniors at Treadwell High School when we recorded. Chips knew we were a popular teenage garage band, we were Beatles clones, we duplicated that look and sound, tons of kids with money for music, who couldn't drink."

After The Gentrys' "Keep On Dancin'" hit nationally, Gentrys member Jimmy Hart recorded a cover version of "Keep On Dancin'," which he credited to The Gentrys on the local sound-a-like Hit label. "I got called by those Hit label people, decided not to do it. I knew if you were in the band, you had the right to use the band's name. It's markedly different by the way Jimmy approached my voice at the time."

Remake: The Gentrys on Hit 1967

—

The Hombres "Let It Out" Verve July 1967

Style: Rock
From and recorded in: Memphis, TN
Original title: "Let It All Hang Out"
Suggested pairing: Red Ingle & the Natural Seven "Cigareets, Whuskey and Wild, Wild Women" 1948

With an opening quote from "Cigareets, Whuskey and Wild, Wild Women" by Red Ingle & the Natural Seven, this song gave way to an organ-backed droll vocal with the title exclamation, "let it all hang out." Of The Hombres, Gentrys' leader Larry Raspberry said, "The Hombres were the band who had hits with 'It's A Gas' and 'Let It All Hang Out.' The also performed as Ronny & the Daytonas. I booked The Hombres, The Gentrys and The Daytonas. Gary McKuen went to the same high school I did. He was a fantastic guitarist, great musician. Jerry Masters was a member of The Hombres with vocals by one time, longtime member of Jerry Lee Lewis' band, "B.B. Cunningham, who was Mr. Hombre, when I booked them."

—

The Box Tops "The Letter" Mala July 1967

Style: Blue-eyed soul group
From and recorded in: Memphis, TN

There was no group called The Box Tops when "The Letter" was first released. The song is about a letter from a former love interest that causes the protagonist to fly out to see her immediately, based on the very first lyrics written, "Give me a ticket for an aeroplane," a lyric embellished with jet plane sound effects. At 16, blue eyed soul lead singer Alex Chilton was the youngest of the group. After the session, a group member suggested, "Let's have a contest and everybody can send in 50 cents and a box top." Producer Dan Penn thus dubbed them The Box Tops. On "The Letter," Chilton, age 16, moaned like a gruff soul man. He credited the performance to his producer, Memphis legend, Penn. "He coached me pretty heavily on singing anything we ever did," Chilton said. "In a lot of cases, it sounds more like him singing than it sounds like me."

Remakes: The Arbors 1969; Joe Cocker 1970

—

The Youngbloods "Get Together" RCA July 1967

Style: Folk rock
Where from: New York City, NY and Boston, MA
Where recorded: San Francisco, CA
Original title: The Folkswingers "Amor A Todos" 1963
Earlier versions: The Kingston Trio 1964; We Five "Let's Get Together" 1965

An anthem of the new counter-culture, songwriter Dino Valenti aka Chet Powers recorded "Get Together" in January 1964. Recorded live at the Hungry I in San Francisco by the Kingston Trio that same year, We Five changed the title to "Let's Get Together" and had some sales. Recorded by Jesse Colin Young's band, The Youngbloods, it hit the charts, then went away. Then in 1969, the National Conference of Christians and Jews decided to send it to radio and TV stations to support Brotherhood Week. As broadcasters were required to run public service announcements for the public good, this was a natural, and because of this exposure, The Youngblood's' "Get Together" shot to #5 on the pop charts on August 31, 1969.

After the September 11, 2001 terrorist attacks, the media conglomerate Clear Channel Communications put The Youngbloods' "Get Together" on a list of "lyrically questionable" songs that was sent to its 1,200 radio stations. So it was back to the starting point for the song and the band. Obscure, publicized then censored, depending on the temperature at the moment.

Remake: Judy Clay 1969
Remakes as "Everybody Get Together": The Sunshine Company 1968; The Staple Singers 1968; The Stonemans 1970; The Dave Clark Five 1970; Skeeter Davis & George Hamilton IV 1970; The Wonder Stuff 1990; Big Mountain 1996

—

The Beatles "All You Need Is Love" Capitol July 1967

Style: Rock
From and recorded in: England

With an opening from the French national anthem, "La Marseillaise," The Beatles supposedly recorded "All You Need Is Love" on Our World, a six-hour TV satellite broadcast seen by 400 million viewers, for which the song was written. They used a prerecorded backing track and John Lennon's vocal was redone a few hours later. Eric Clapton mimed guitar during the special. "It was for love and bloody peace," Ringo Starr said. The backing choir included Mick Jagger, Keith Moon and Donovan. At song's finish, Paul McCartney sang the chorus to "She Loves You",,, "yeah yeah yeah."

—

Brenton Wood "Gimme Little Sign" Double Shot 1967

Style: Soul vocal
Where from: San Pedro, CA
Where recorded: Hollywood, CA
Suggested pairings: Wilbert Wade "You Can't Fool Me" 1965

Brenton Wood recalled, "I wrote that song ["Gimme Little Sign"] when I was 16 years old. We kicked that song around five or six years." A Compton track star, Wilbert Wade recorded two Wood compositions, "You Can't Fool Me" backed with "Come Here, Girl," for Liberty in 1965. "Nothing happened with it. He didn't have the punch."

On Wood's second major hit, "Gimme Little Sign," Maurice "Mighty Mo" Rogers played Farfisa organ and recalled, "I was on all his hits but 'Oogum Boogum.' [Did] the solo on 'Gimme Little Sign' and piano too. Solos on 'Baby You Got It' and all his stuff. I was in a soul band that became the band for Double Shot," Kent & the Candidates. Double Shot owner Hal Winn added, when we "put out 'Gimme Little Sign,' I said, 'you gotta add brass and add strings."

—

Canned Heat "Rollin' and Tumblin'" Liberty July 29, 1967

Style: Boogie blues
Where from: Torrance, CA; Boston, MA and So Cal, CA
Where recorded: Hollywood, CA
Original version: Hambone Willie Newbern "Roll and Tumble Blues" 1929
Earlier versions: Baby Face Leroy 1950; Muddy Waters 1951; Elmore James and His Broomdusters 1966

Named after a Tommy Johnson song and formed in the mid-1960s by Johnny Otis, white blues band Canned Heat was created around blues record collector vocalist Bob "The Bear" Hite and guitarist Henry Vestine. Bass player Larry Taylor said, "They were first called The Canned Heat Jug Band when Bob put it together in 1965 and played the Topanga Corral and later the Ashgrove. Henry Vestine was a big record collector, Bob Hite was a big record collector and [they] were friends and liked pre-war blues. Henry collected blues and used to canvas the south to find these records. They loved the music so much they formed Canned Heat. That was their dream. John Fahey brought Al Wilson from Boston and introduced him to Canned Heat." The first iteration of Canned Heat on Liberty was "Al, Bob, Henry, Frank Cook, drums; Stuart Brotman, bass, who later played with Kaleidescope, and was replaced by Mark Andes, who went to Spirit." Taylor said, "I met Henry at the Seawitch, my trio The Cajuns, I used to watch Henry play. I came in then when the band signed with Liberty."

Canned Heat's redo of the Muddy Waters' early 1950 rockin' blues hit "Rollin' and Tumblin'" got hot in Phoenix, then top ten in Salinas, then it was over.

Remake: Johnny Winter 1969

—

Jackie Wilson "(Your Love Keeps Lifting Me) Higher and Higher" Brunswick July 29, 1967

Style: Soul vocal
Where from: Detroit, MI
Where recorded: Chicago, IL/New York
Original version: The Dells 1967

"The backing track for "(Your Love Keeps Lifting Me) Higher and Higher" was recorded on July 6, 1967 at Columbia's studios in Chicago, and produced by Carl Davis. The session, arranged by Sonny Sanders, featured bassist James Jamerson, drummer Richard 'Pistol' Allen, guitarist Robert White and keyboardist Johnny Griffith, all members of the Motown Records house band, The Funk Brothers, who often moonlighted on sessions for Davis to augment the meager wages paid by Motown.

Apparently, The Dells used this track for their version. According to Carl Davis, "The Funk Brothers used to come over on the weekends from Detroit. They'd load up in the van and come over to Chicago, and I would pay 'em double scale, and I'd pay 'em in cash."

Similarly, two of Motown's house session singers, the Andantes—Jackie Hicks and Marlene Barrow along with Pat Lewis—performed on the session for "Higher and Higher." Davis brought the track to New York City for Wilson to add his vocal; Davis recalled Wilson originally sang the song "like a soul ballad. I said that's totally wrong. You have to jump and go with the percussion. If he didn't want to sing it that way, I would put my voice on the record and sell millions." After hearing Davis' strong advice, Wilson cut the lead vocal for "Higher and Higher" in a single take.

—

Fantastic Johnny C "Boogaloo Down Broadway" Phil-L.A. of Soul August 1967

Style: Soul
Where from: Greenwood, SC
Where recorded: Philadelphia, PA

With inspiration from Dyke and the Blazers' "Funky Broadway" from 1965, Johnny Corley, also known as The Fantastic Johnny C, hit big with this percussive vocal, stop and go dance hit "Boogaloo Down Broadway" on Phil-L.A. of Soul Records, run by famed San Francisco soul producer Jesse James, who attended the same Macedonia Baptist Church as did Corley. Featuring Leon Mitchell and the band later known as MFSB with drummer Earl Young, both sides leaned on the same instrumental track.

—

Sam & Dave "Soul Man" Stax August 21, 1967

Style: Soul
Where from: Miami, FL
Where recorded: Memphis, TN

For the follow-up to "Hold On, I'm Comin'," writer-producers Hayes and Porter decided to tinker with the Sam & Dave style when Porter asked singer Sam Moore to give him "the Bobby Bland squall." With Steve Cropper on guitar and the blast of the Memphis Horns, "we had no idea how good we were," Hayes said of the working crew.

—

Marvin Gaye & Tammi Terrell "Your Precious Love" Tamla August 1967

Style: Soul duet
Where from: Philadelphia, PA
Where recorded: Detroit, MI

Female soul vocalist Tammi Terrell recorded four sides under her real name, Tammy Montgomery, from 1961 through 1964, prior to catching on with Motown as Tammi Terrell with "I Can't Believe You Love Me" in November 1965, "We were in Wildwood, NJ with The Supremes, breaking in the act, just before going in the Copa," said Mabel John. who worked with Berry Gordy. "We went to a club to see Steve Gibson and the Red Caps, Tammi was singing with Steve. A young girl, she was wonderful looking and sang great. I asked her if she'd like to make some records. She said, 'Of course.' She came down, we talked and talked. After they closed there, about two weeks later, I had her come to Detroit. She wanted to sing with Marvin Gaye, most girls did, that was how we came about it." But first, there was the matter of her name, Tammi Montgomery. The Montgomery thing just sounded strange. Tammi Montgomery, come on. Tammi Terrell sounded interesting and luscious, like she was. People sat around the room, they threw out some names..."

—

Aretha Franklin "A Natural Woman" Atlantic September 1967

Style: Soul vocal
Where from: Detroit
Where recorded: Muscle Shoals, AL

Songwriter Gerry Goffin was leaving the Oyster House and Jerry Wexler of Atlantic, passing in a car, yelled out, "Why don't you write a song called 'Natural Woman'?" Goffin and partner/wife Carol King felt the title was distinct and important, they gave Wexler a piece of it, about which Jerry said, "Isn't it amazing what those kids gave me? The checks keep coming in and I'm really happy about it," referring to knowing how much he added to the song, not really as a third writer but the title and the inspiration of what was to be a great song. Speaking of pieces coming together, this song's vocal backup included Aretha's sisters, Erma and Carolyn. Erma's biggest hit at the time was the original "Piece Of My Heart."

—

Erma Franklin "Piece Of My Heart" Shout October 1967

Style: Soul vocal
Where from: Detroit, MI
Where recorded: New York City, NY

The older sister of soul empress Aretha Franklin, the closest thing Erma Franklin had to a hit was this powerful rendition of this blues song associated with Janis Joplin, "Piece of My Heart."

Remake: Janis Joplin 1968

—

Wilson Pickett "Stag-O-Lee" October 16, 1967

Style: Soul
Where from: Detroit, MI
Where recorded: Muscle Shoals, AL
Original hit: Lloyd Price "Stagger Lee" 1959

Bobby Womack's fine guitar backing played a large part in the success of Wilson Pickett's "Stag-O-Lee."

—

Bobby Womack "Broadway Walk" Minit October 25, 1967

Style: Soul
Where from: Cleveland, OH
Where recorded: Muscle Shoals, AL

Womack said, "'Broadway Walk' was a Wilson Pickett type song, he would have done that," had Womack not recorded it first. "Darryl Carter was an engineer, the only black guy in the studio," Womack added. "I asked them if I could join the group, I just loved the creative part, started playing with them, played on The Box Tops, stayed at a motel, cut four sessions, the money wasn't a problem." On that session, it was Tommy Cogbill, "the hottest bass"; Reggie Young; Bobby Wood and Bobby Simmons, who came out of Nashville. They was so hot and bad, Aretha Franklin, The Stones came in, Elvis Presley came in."

—

Etta James "Tell Mama" Cadet October 1967

Style: Soul
Where from: Los Angeles, CA
Where recorded: Muscle Shoals, AL
Original version: Clarence Carter "Tell Daddy" 1967

To remove her from local temptations in Chicago and L.A., the Chess label had Etta James record this throbbing rocker, "Tell Mama," in Muscle Shoals, Alabama with area musicians Barry Beckett, organ; Junior Lowe, guitar; David Hood, bass; Roger Hawkins, drums and Spooner Oldham, keyboards. "Rick Hall was the producer on 'Tell Mama,'" said Etta James' ex-spouse and manager at the time, Billy Foster. "He was the one who did Aretha Franklin, "I Never Loved A Man.' They still had segregated bathrooms down there, so Rick would try to get us in to avoid exposure to that kind of element right there at the studio, Aretha's old man got all upset and left down there, they put him on a plane back to Detroit. Etta recorded 'Tell Mama' after Aretha. We went down there twice. Rick Hall made us comfortable at the studio, we stayed at an apartment in the studio he had arranged for artists, he was hospitable, we liked Rick, he was a nice guy. I think the sound Rick Hall produced—Chess felt there were only certain artists who could handle Rick Hall's type of producing, Etta was one of them, bluesy cross-over artists. The Dells and Billy Stewart had big hits, there was a girl working at the desk, Minnie Riperton who would soon become a major hit maker before dying at an early age. We knew 'Tell Mama' was a good kicking record and they picked that."

—

Etta James "I'd Rather Go Blind" Cadet October 1967

Style: Soul
Where from: Los Angeles, CA
Where recorded: Muscle Shoals, AL

"At a period of my life, I got in a lot of trouble, and ended up at Soledad Prison," said Billy Foster. "I went to the music room, that's where I met Fugi, Ellington Jordan, we used to go to the music room, he was playing 'I'd Rather Go Blind.' I liked the way that goes, we sat down, he had a majority of the lyrics already made, I put in a few lyrics and I forgot about it.

"When I was released, I opened up an office on LaCienega and first met Etta, and booked her on a show. First time I saw her I was selling gowns and I had a Missy Lee gown and I went backstage at the 5/4 Ballroom and I had this gown, told Miss Dakota Canada I gotta gown for Etta James, so come in the dressing room and she was in her girdle, she was hefty, and I told her I got a gown for Etta James. She commenced to putting the gown on, she was hefty, I said, 'Oh oh be careful, don't break it,' but she got it on over the parts. She said, 'Okay I'll buy it,' so I sold it for $45. That was my initial connection to Etta."

Foster continued, "I guess it was a year later I met again her under circumstances of coming to my office, but people were telling me she's late to her gigs, but her talent was so magnificent. When I would go to the California Club to see her where she was performing she would give me chills, something about her demeanor and Etta doesn't have to sing, but just walk up on the stage and her presence would amplify. We ended up being together. When I got with Etta, I got a letter from Fugi. I told him I'm dealing with Etta, he said can you get 'I'd Rather Go Blind' with her. They let him mail me the cassette tape of the song, I submitted it to Leonard Chess and he liked it. Phil Walden had just recorded Aretha Franklin in Muscle Shoals, and they played the song for Phil and he liked the song. In that whole 'Tell Mama' era, it rode the hit as the B-side. When we was traveling down there, Otis Redding was getting ready to record 'I'd Rather Go Blind' and Rick Hall was going to produce it. I talked with him on the telephone in Chicago, and a week later [Otis] ended up in the accident" that caused his death.

Foster explained, "There was eight of us in the car, we were in Opaluses Louisiana. Jimmy Green went down there with his entourage. We were all in a stupor. The promoter had run off. We tried to catch the promoter going to New Orleans, it was 4 in the morning and there was a sign said New Orleans that way, and Jimmy tried to make that curve, Jimmy was driving, Etta was in the middle and I was on the passenger side. I remember the car flipping over and my life passing in front of my face. We hit a bayou of sand, if we hit any other kind of obstacle, we would have been killed."

—

The Golliwogs "Porterville" Scorpio/Fantasy October 1967/January 1968

Style: Rock
From and recorded in: the East Bay, CA

Active since 1964, the Golliwogs had recorded a half dozen songs before coming up with "Porterville," a reference to a Northern California city, a title that's not once mentioned in the lyrics, the hook of which was 'I don't care." Golliwogs' leader and chief songwriter, John Fogerty, said it marked a shift in songwriting style. "Everything changed after that," he said. "I gave up trying to write sappy love songs about stuff I didn't know anything about, and I started inventing stories." The last Golliwogs single on the Fantasy label subsidiary, it was re-released in January 1968 as the first single credited to Creedence Clearwater Revival.

—

Smokey Robinson and The Miracles "I Second That Emotion" Tamla October 1967

Style: Soul vocal group
From and recorded in: Detroit, MI

"I second that motion" is a common phrase heard at meetings in America where policy is being determined. It's what Motown producer Al Cleveland meant to say when he was on a shopping trip with Smokey Robinson.

One morning in 1967, Robinson and Cleveland were shopping at Hudson's, a Detroit department store. Robinson found a set of pearls for his wife, Claudette. "They're beautiful." he said to the salesperson. "I sure hope she likes them." Cleveland then added, "I second that emotion." Both songwriters laughed at Cleveland's malapropism; he had meant to say, "I second that motion." The two were immediately inspired to write a song using the incorrect phrase.

In songwriting circles, this one is often studied for its use of secondary rhymes and melodic intricacy. Smokey Robinson sprinkled in words like "notion" and "devotion" to compliment the title, all while rhyming verses with phrases like "kisses sweet" and "no repeat." The guitar line also perfectly accents the vocal.

—

John Fred & His Playboy Band "Judy In Disguise" Paula October 1967

Style: Psych rock
Where from: Louisiana
Where recorded: Robin Hood Studios Tyler, TX
Suggested pairing: The Beatles "Lucy In The Sky With Diamonds"

This was the first hit title based on mishearing another title. Recording since 1959, John Fred's first major hit, "Judy In Disguise," was a parody of "Lucy In The Sky With Diamonds" by The Beatles, which many understood as "Lucy in disguise with diamonds." "We were playing in Florida and the girls at the time had these big old sunglasses," said Fred. "One of the guys was hustling this chick. She took off these glasses and she could stop a clock. I said, 'She's kind of in disguise.'"

Lyrics included the Playtex commercial inspired "Cross your heart with a living bra," "Come to me tonight" and "Unzipper the strings of my kite." Radio didn't catch on to the sexual innuendo matched with porno sound effects coming before the first and last choruses.

Using brass, a sitar, piano, bass, guitar, drums, breathing sounds and dissonant string sounds, other members of The Playboy Band did not like the slowed-down, yet abrupt ending, "I guess I'll just take your glasses."

—

Archie Bell & the Drells "Tighten Up" Ovide November 1967/Atlantic February 1968

Style: Soul vocal group
From and recorded in: Houston, TX

According to Bell, the group and the band were two different things. "We never let people know, the band behind us was The TSU Tornados, which used to use it as a break song. I was rooming with Billy Butler, one of The Drells, he started doing the dance, so I gave him half of the writer's fees. Cut by The TSU Tornados, we would use 'tighten up' like a slang word. I heard a San Antonio DJ say, 'Nothing good ever came out of Texas since JFK was assassinated.' We answered, 'We're as good as we want.'" The TSU Tornados, which cut several records on Atlantic, were Jerry Jenkins and Pete, bass; Robert Sanders, organ; Darryl Busby, sax; Clarence "Creeper" Harper, trumpet; Leroy Lewis, sax; Nelson Mills, trumpet and Dwight Barnes, drums. Bell explained that lead vocalist and guitarist, Cal Thomas, who had previously played in an R&B band called the Arabian Knights, came up with the guitar part. Cal's brother, Will Thomas, was also guitar and vocals. "Eight guys with three horns," said Bell.

The owner of Houston-based Ovide was "Skipper Lee Frazier, who changed it to O.V. Frazier. He had developed the East West label. Skipper Lee made the deal, I was in the military, in Germany," when the song went to #1, therefore Bell couldn't tour or make appearances to advance his career. "They gave us a pretty good deal, screw you later down the line. Jeff Hubbard out of Indy called me, told me we had to sign these papers, never heard nothing about it, got $50 or $60."

—

Aretha Franklin "Chain of Fools" Atlantic November 1967

Style: Soul
Where from: Detroit, MI
Where recorded: New York
Suggested pairing: Rev. Elijah Fair & the Sensational Gladys Davis Trio "Pains Of Life"

Composed by Don Covay, Aretha Franklin's "Chain Of Fools" featured gospel-inspired opening guitar licks by Joe South, while Ellie Greenwich filled in the harmony with The Sweet Inspirations and Aretha's sisters, Carolyn Franklin and Erma Franklin. In February 1968, Don Covay's band, The Good Timers, were then credited on an instrumental version, using the guitar-based instrumental bed with dubbed in shouts and cheers on the same Atlantic label, well after Aretha's version had cooled off.

Remakes: The Good Timers 1968; Jimmy Brown 1968; Tommy Ferguson 1968; Jimmy Smith 1968; The Commitments 1991

—

Sly and the Family Stone "Dance to the Music" Epic November 1967

Style: Soul
Where from: Vallejo, CA
Where recorded: Hollywood, CA
Suggested pairings: Huey Smith & Clowns "Don't You Just Know It" 1958; Bob & Earl "Harlem Shuffle" 1963; The Four Tops "It's the Same Old Song" Motown July 9, 1965; Delaney & Bonnie "Only You Know and I Know" 1971

"In 1963 we went to San Francisco to do 'Harlem Shuffle' and they had a band backing us up it," said Bob & Earl's Earl Nelson. "It was led by a disc jockey on the big San Francisco soul station. He hadn't done any major recording yet. His name was Sly Stone. They brought us out with our horn introduction and he asked us if we minded if he used that 'Harlem Shuffle' opening sometime. We didn't care so we told him it was okay and that's how he began his first big hit, 'Dance To the Music.'"

Sly's sax player Jerry Martini said, "We moved to New York to make it. We weren't that popular in San Francisco. A previous album that stiffed and a single, 'Underdog,' that went along with it, it was a little premature, the rhythms, everything we're trying to do was a little early. After our first record, I remember walking down the halls with Sly. He was really upset. He said, 'I'm going to put something together that's total formula, that's what they want, that's what they're going to get.'" In fact, the lyrics are very simplistic, introducing each band member's instrument. "The 'boom boom' part, that originally only came in the middle of it. At the last minute, the record company spliced that and put it on the beginning of the song and it had a lot to do with the catchiness of it. Then we got 'Dance To the Music' to hit on the East Coast."

—

The Soul Survivors "Expressway To Your Heart" Crimson 1967

Style: Blue-eyed soul group
From and recorded in: Philadelphia, PA
Suggested pairings: Lovin' Spoonful "Summer In The City" 1966; Madeline Bell "I'm Gonna Make You Love Me" 1967

The Soul Survivors first played together in New York under the name The Dedications, founded by members Kenny Jeremiah and Richie and Charlie Ingui, who released several singles under this name in 1962 and 1964. In a move to Philadelphia, they became The Soul Survivors, signed to the Crimson label, who got them with Gamble & Huff.

"Expressway to Your Heart" hit first on Philly soul radio, then L.A.'s KGFJ, until their album came out, showing their race as white. Suddenly soul radio dropped their hit. Jay Proctor of Jay & the Techniques recalled, "There's a line in the song, identical line, 'love and affection, coming in your direction' borrowed from 'I'm Gonna Make You Love Me.' Happens all the time," said Proctor.

The use of urban expressway sound effects, pioneered by The Lovin' Spoonful, were heard in "Summer In The City."

—

Jimi Hendrix "Hey Joe" Reprise 1967

Style: Psych rock
Where from: Seattle, WA
Where recorded: De Lane Lea Studios, London, England
Original version: Tim Rose 1966
Earlier versions: The Enemys; Thee Sixpence; The Surfaris; Sammy Lee & the Summits; The Leaves (all 1966)

When ex-Animals bass player Chas Chandler saw Tim Rose perform his version of "Hey Joe," which he claimed had deep folk roots, at the Cafe Wha? in New

York City, he began looking for an artist to record a rock version. That artist was Jimi Hendrix, who himself played at the Cafe Wha? in 1966 and had performed a "Hey Joe" arrangement inspired by Rose's rendition. Chandler used this record to debut Hendrix, who recorded the song in England in September 1966, and to turn the guitarist into a star. Radio station owners, Clear Channel Communications, barred "Hey Joe" after 9/11 because of its violent subject matter.

Remakes: Cher 1967; The Stillroven 1967; Love 1967; The Music Machine 1968; The Marmalade 1968; Wilson Pickett 1969; Patti Smith 1974

—

Small Faces "Itchycoo Park" Immediate 1967

Style: Rock
From and recorded in: England
Suggested pairings: The Everly Brothers "I Wonder If I Care As Much" 1957; Miss Toni Fisher "The Big Hurt" 1959; The Drifters "This Magic Moment" 1960

Later known as Faces, Rod Stewart's backing band, Steve Marriott and Ronnie Lane formed the Small Faces and wrote their first smash, "Itchycoo Park," about skipping school to hang out at Itchycoo Park, the nickname of Little Ilford Park in London, either full of stinging nettles or stinging wasps, depending on the version told. With lyrics like "What did you do there? I got high," the band denied that it was about drugs. "We just got high from not going to school." Even so, it was at some time BBC banned, though it was constantly played on the BBC Top of the Pops Show. It was one of the first pop singles to use flanging or phase-shifting production, which you can hear when the vocals and drums become distorted in the song, heard in the bridge section after each chorus.

—

The Bar Kays "Soul Finger" Volt 1967

Style: Soul instrumental group
From and recorded in: Memphis, TN
Suggested pairings: Little Richard "Lucille" 1957; Otis Redding "Mary Had Little Lamb" 1963; J.J. Jackson "But It's Alright" 1966; Ray Parker Jr. "Ghostbusters" 1984; Huey Lewis & the News "I Want A New Drug" 1984

Named as a variation of a Bacardi Rum ad, The Bar-Kays' "Soul Finger" is the first single released by this R&B group, a studio session group first known as The River Arrows, who had most success backing Otis Redding. "Soul Finger" begins with the melody to the popular children's song a "Mary Had Little Lamb" redone by Otis Redding, followed by a line from J.J. Jackson's hit "But It's Alright," goes to a high trumpet trill similar to Little Richard's "Lucille" from 1957, then into a chorus of neighborhood kids who hung around the recording studio and were instructed to shout the title lyric.

—

Bill Cosby "Little Ole Man (Uptight Everything's Alright)" Warner Brothers 1967

Style: Novelty soul
Where from: Philadelphia, PA
Where recorded: Hollywood, CA
Original version: Stevie Wonder

Bill Cosby hit with this humorous take on Stevie Wonder's "Uptight" as "Little Ole Man (Uptight Everything's Alright)" on Warner Brothers. About the session, Charles Wright recalled, "He [Cosby] needed 'Uptight' redone. They were so happy with the band I was playing with, a studio band James Carmichael and Arthur Wright assembled from time to time. "We made a bunch of hits, Bettye Swann, Leon Haywood, Jackie Lee, 'Neki Hokey' by P.J. Proby, a whole bunch of people. We had no name for that band, we had a formula. That particular day, Fred Smith and Cosby were particularly happy with the situation, they stayed all day, at the end of the day, they announced they wanted us to do his single, we did the single. It was a novelty thing, but with the single, they wanted the band to back him up wherever he'd go, so he started out with my band when he came to see me, live. We were the Wright Sounds, actually, he came to see us perform. He was so happy with our performance band, he wanted us to back him at his live shows," naming them The Watts 103rd Street Rhythm Band.

—

Cream "Sunshine Of Your Love" Atco December 1967

Style: Rock
From and recorded in: England
Suggested pairings: Creedence Clearwater Revival "Proud Mary" 1967; Creedence Clearwater Revival "Bad Moon Rising" 1969

Cream was Eric Clapton, guitar; Ginger Baker, drums and Jack Bruce, bass. Clapton and Bruce wrote the music to "Sunshine Of Your Love," with a guitar break with elements of "Blue Moon." Thought by some to be about LSD, the lyrics, either "till my seas are dried up" or "till my seeds are dried up," were written by beat poet Pete Brown, also lyric writer for "I Feel Free" and "White Room." Clapton's grungy blues guitar solo and Bruce's song-carrying bass line came together at the last minute in the studio.

—

Otis Redding "(Sittin' On) The Dock of the Bay" Volt January 8, 1968

Style: Soul
Where from: Augusta, GA
Where recorded: Memphis, TN

Otis Redding recorded "(Sittin' On) The Dock Of The Bay" with Booker T. & the M.G.'s, the Stax house band. Just before the session, Stax Records had recently purchased a 4-track recorder, which made it easy to add the extra beach-y sound effects, waves, seagulls, which were dubbed in after the recording. Redding died in a plane crash on December 10, 1967, three days after he recorded this song and a month before its January 8, 1968 release. Describing what he saw when he was in San Francisco for a concert, "Dock Of The Bay" was by far his biggest hit. During the session, Otis and the song's co-writer, guitarist Steve Cropper, didn't have a last verse, so Redding whistled it. The plan was to return to Memphis and fill in the verse after performing in Madison, Wisconsin, but Redding died before he had the chance. Later, Cropper said mixing that track to record was the most difficult thing he had to do.

—

The Beatles "Lady Madonna" Apple March 18, 1968

Style: Rock
From and recorded in: England
Suggested pairing: Humphrey Lyttleton "Bad Penny Blues" 1955

This song was famously inspired by a picture of an African woman suckling her kid, over the caption "Mountain Madonna." It was lifted from Humphrey Lyttleton's "Bad Penny Blues," a 1955 Brit jazz classic with similar piano riffs and bass line. British jazz musicians were brought in on short notice to play the saxophone parts. John Lennon, Paul McCartney and George Harrison faked a brass solo by singing through their cupped hands. Paul overdubbed bass; John and George added a very distinctive guitar riff by playing their guitars through the same amp. This was the last Beatles Capitol Records release. The next ones were on Apple Records, the label The Beatles created.

Remake: Fats Domino 1968

—

Tommy James and The Shondells "Mony Mony" Roulette March 1968

Style: Rock
Where from: Michigan
Where recorded: New York

Tommy James spotted the name MONY on a New York skyscraper, an abbreviation for Mutual Of New York, an insurance company. It turned into a sizeable hit.

—

Steppenwolf "Born To Be Wild" May 1968

Style: Rock
Where from: Canada
Where recorded: Hollywood, CA
Cover: Kim Fowley 1968

The first single by Steppenwolf, "Sookie Sookie," flopped. Then came this hit. The line "Heavy Metal Thunder" meant "Born To Be Wild" by Steppenwolf was the first popular song to use the phrase "Heavy Metal," which became a term for hard rock. William Burroughs coined the phrase in his 1961 novel The Soft Machine, calling a character the :Heavy Metal Kid." Burroughs told The Paris Review, "I felt that heavy metal was sort of the ultimate expression of addiction, that there's something actually metallic in addiction, that the final stage reached is not so much vegetable as mineral." Intended as a folk ballad about life on the open road, "Born To Be Wild" was written by Mars Bonfire, who saw a "Born to Ride" poster with a picture of a motorcycle erupting out of the earth like a volcano with fire all around it. It went from folk song as the tempo of the backing of the organ increased to create a rock classic, used in the 1969 movie Easy Rider, a counterculture classic starring Dennis Hopper and Peter Fonda as bikers who ride from Los Angeles to New Orleans.

Remakes: Wilson Pickett 1969; Blue Oyster Cult 1973

—

Shorty Long "Here Comes the Judge" Soul May 7, 1968

Style: Soul
Where from: Mississippi
Where recorded: Detroit, MI

Backed by The Originals, Shorty Long scored with "Here Comes the Judge," based on a Pigmeat Markham skit. Long emceed many Motortown Revue shows and Smokey Robinson was the only Motown artist able to produce his own recordings.

—

The O'Kaysions "Girl Watcher" North State/ABC May 1968

Style: Blue-eyed soul group
Where from: Wilson, NC
Where recorded: Pitt Sound Studio, Greenville, NC

Now known as beach music artists, The O'Kaysions first formed as The Kays in 1959. This fanciful dance step tune, "Girl Watcher," was first released on John I. Whitfield's North State label, then was released nationally by ABC Records. As the studio was a budget outfit, the original tape was missing, so the ABC release was recorded from a North State single, creating a master tape one generation away from the original.

Answer: Ginger Thompson "Boy Watcher" 1968

—

The Rolling Stones "Jumpin' Jack Flash" London June 1, 1968

Style: Rock
From and recorded in: England

Keith Richards told Rolling Stone in 2010, "The lyrics came from a gray dawn at Redlands. Mick and I had been up all night, it was raining outside, and there was the sound of these boots near the window, belonging to my gardener, Jack Dyer. It woke Mick up. He said, 'What's that?' I said, 'Oh, that's Jack. That's jumping Jack.' I started to work around the phrase on the guitar, which was in open tuning, singing the phrase 'Jumping Jack.' Mick said, 'Flash,' and suddenly we had this phrase with a great rhythm and ring to it."

Mick Jagger said, "It's about having a hard time and getting out. Just a metaphor for getting out of all the acid things."

Remakes: Johnny Winter 1971; Aretha Franklin 1986

—

Wilson Pickett "I'm a Midnight Mover" Atlantic June 17, 1968

Style: Soul
Where from: Detroit, MI
Where recorded: Memphis, TN

Writer of "I'm a Midnight Mover," Bobby Womack recalled the song was produced by Chips Moman. "Pickett was there, sitting there waiting, Pickett ain't got no material, nothing going on, I had all of these songs, the songs United Artists gave me the deal for. Pickett ate them up, Those are the ones, he [Womack] gave all his songs to Pickett. Whether I grow as a producer, writer or artist, it will come together." However, giving all his songs to Pickett was a major problem for United Artists.
Why was it a major problem? Womack was signed to record his own material. By giving most of them to Pickett, he was out of material.

—

The Doors "Hello, I Love You, Won't You Tell Me Your Name" Elektra June 1968

Style: Rock
From and recorded in: Los Angeles, CA
Suggested pairings: The Kinks "All Of the Day All Of the Night" 1964; Paul Revere & the Raiders "Just Like Me" 1966

The Doors hit big with an over the top vocal with this title on early pressings, "Hello, I Love You, Won't You Tell Me Your Name." Ray Manzarek said, "Jim said, 'I got this new song, "Hello I Love You."' He wrote it for a girl, we're sitting at the beach, this absolutely foxy black American, white, black, she was everything, she had mixed blood. She was walking, 17 years old, tiny little bikini, strutting, looked absolutely gorgeous, Jim said, 'Hello baby, I love you...' He didn't go up to her to follow through, but five days later he said, 'I got the song, remember that chick we saw? The Dusky Jewel?' That's the line, 'do you have to make her see you fool, do you hope to pluck this dusky jewel?' Sort of coffee colored dusky jewel. He said, 'Here's how it goes.' I'm thinking, 'hold it.' I didn't say anything. 'Hold it, that's "All Of the Day" by the Kinks. Jim knew music, but he didn't know it that well, that's in the back of his brain, he applied those words to that melody, he didn't know where it came from. It was just something floating around in his head, I thought, let him sing. It's not quite 'All of the Day' where we're going to get sued." Oh, yeah? Kinks' producer, Shel Talmy said, "Morrison and whomever settled out of court with payment for plagiarism."

—

The Dells "Stay In My Corner" Cadet 1968

Style: Soul vocal group
From and recorded in: Chicago, IL
Original version: The Dells "Stay In My Corner" Vee Jay 1964

"The Dells recorded 'Stay In My Corner' for Vee Jay in 1964," said Dells' bass man Chuck Barksdale. "We had been doing it around the country, it was such tremendous response from the audience for it. We were in the studio finishing an album, we needed an extra tune. The rest is history. We recorded the song live with an orchestra. The holding of the note Marvin did was not on purpose, it was just one of those things that happens spontaneously in the studio. He just happened to have the lungs and the talent to do it. It was the first long playing R&B record. It was 6 minutes, 10 seconds."

—

The Rascals "People Got To Be Free" Atlantic July 1968

Style: Blue-eyed soul group
Where from: Upstate New York, NY
Where recorded: New York City, NY
Suggested pairing: Dawn "Candida" 1971

On April 4, 1968, Martin Luther King, Jr. was gunned down in Memphis, and Robert F. Kennedy was assassinated on June 5 in Los Angeles. Riots and civil disruptions broke out. In response, Eddie Brigati and Felix Cavaliere of The Rascals wrote "People Got To Be Free," ala King and Kennedy, calling for unity and understanding. Cavaliere claimed that he had to fight for this song, since Jerry Wexler at Atlantic Records was worried a message song would hurt The Rascals' career. Cavaliere prevailed and the song became the group's biggest hit, reaching #1 in America in August 1968. This was the third #1 hit for the group. As The Young Rascals they had scored with "Good Lovin'" and "Groovin',' but this was their first #1 under their original name, as between 1966 and 1967 they were credited as The Young Rascals, as Atlantic Records chose "to avoid confusion" with the Harmonica Rascals.

—

Bobby Womack "Fly Me to the Moon" Minit July 1968

Style: Soul
Where from: Cleveland, OH
Where recorded: Memphis, TN
Suggested pairing: Joe Harnell "Fly Me to the Moon Boss Nova" 1962

The bossa nova classic, "Fly Me to the Moon Boss Nova," was first recorded as a jazz instrumental by Joe Harnell, followed quickly as a vocal by Edie Gorme in November 1962. About "Fly Me to the Moon," Bobby Womack said, "United Artists gave me a deal for $75,000. Where do you want me to record? I looked in my bag, ain't got no more songs. United Artists called. I had no songs at all, band was sleeping on me, took 'Fly Me to the Moon,' just speed it up, each [of the] guys kept waking up, picking up their instruments. Willie Mitchell played trumpet. Gave the song to United Artists. "Is that the original 'Fly Me to the Moon? That's not why we signed you, where are the other songs?" Despite the reluctance, United Artists placed it on Minit and it sold well.

—

Canned Heat "On the Road Again" Liberty August 3, 1968

Style: Boogie blues
Where from: Torrance, CA; Boston, MA and So Cal, CA
Where recorded: Hollywood, CA
Suggested pairings: Tommy Johnson's "Big Road Blues" 1929; Floyd Jones' "Dark Road" 1952

"Blind" Al Wilson's vocals on their first smash based on Tommy Johnson's "Big Road Blues" from 1929 and Floyd Jones' "Dark Road" from 1952, this drolly rocking "On the Road Again" with a raga intro backed with Hite's gravelly vocal on "Boogie Music" proved their blues collector credentials.

—

The Band "The Weight" Capitol August 8, 1968

Style: Rock
Where from: Canada
Where recorded: Upstate New York, NY

Known popularly as The Band, this hit version of the Bob Dylan composition, The Weight," was not released as The Band, but with artist credit to Jaime Robbie Robertson, Rick Danko, Richard Manuel, Garth Hudson, Levon Helm; Music From Big Pink. They were a Canadian band, earlier known as The Hawks behind rocker Ronnie Hawkins from 1958 to 1963, Paul London & the Capers in 1962, Levon & the Hawks and The Canadian Squires in 1964, then hooked up with Bob Dylan in 1965.

Remakes: Jackie DeShannon 1968; Spooky Tooth 1968; Rotary Connection 1969 Diana Ross & the Supremes 1969; The Temptations 1969; Aretha Franklin 1969

—

Crazy World of Arthur Brown "Fire" Atlantic August 1968

Style: Rock
From and recorded in: England

This Crazy World of Arthur Brown's volcanic rocker, "Fire," was the result of a bad trip, as Brown told the Chicago Tribune's Dave Hoekstra. The song's co-writer Vincent Crane was dosed with LSD at a party. "For a long number of years, he never came back. He talked in numbers for a day and a half. He had to return to England for mental attention." Drachian Theaker "used to kick his drums offstage during an act; he would run by hotels, pressing his vital parts against the windows! After that, we became unmanageable," and backed by an organ, of course.

—

Gene Chandler "There Was a Time" Brunswick August 1968

Style: Soul
From and recorded in: Chicago, IL
Suggested pairing: James Brown "There Was a Time"

About the original of "There Was a Time" by James Brown, Gene Chandler stated in his remake, "I patterned it after him."

—

Cream "White Room" Atco August 1968

Style: Psych rock
From and recorded in: England
Suggested pairing: Nancy Wilson "In A Long White Room" 1968

Powered by Eric Clapton's wah-wah work, the unnerving psychedelic imagery came from Pete Brown, co-writer of "White Room" emerging from a period of drug and alcohol excess. "It was in my white-painted room that I had the horrible drug experience that made me want to stop everything." Then along came Nancy Wilson, singing and similar yet guitar-less opening lyric "In A Long White Room" from Zorba the Greek, a film that was much more dated.

—

Bill Deal & Rhondells "May I" Beach/Heritage August 1968

Style: Beach style rhythm and blues
Where from: Portsmouth, VA
Recorded in Warren Miller's Studio Virginia Beach, VA
Original version: Maurice Williams & the Zodiacs 1965

The song "May I" was redone by Bill Deal & the Rhondells on Deal's Beach label, with about 3000 copies pressed. Only a few went to local DJs; the balance was sold directly to record shops and audiences. Heritage

Records acquired the master in August of 1968 and reissued it with a different B-side.

—

Big Brother & the Holding Company "Piece Of My Heart" Columbia August 1968

Style: Blues rock
Where from: Texas
Where recorded: San Francisco, CA
Original version: Erma Franklin 1967

After a half dozen releases credited to the Haight Asbury rock band Big Brother & the Holding Company on the Mainstream label starting in 1966, this was Janis Joplin's explosive blues-drenched vocals on the remake of Erma Franklin's soul hit, "Piece Of My Heart," on Columbia, with no Janis Joplin label credit, a situation that was about to change in a major way when she departed the band. In fact, in a L.A. Free Press review of an early Big Brother & the Holding Company concert, Joplin was referred to as "the chick singer."

—

The Beatles "Hey Jude" Apple August 26, 1968

Style: Rock
From and recorded in: England
Suggested pairings: Jerry Butler "He Will Break Your Heart" 1960; The Drifters "Save the Last Dance For Me" 1960.

The Beatles' "Hey Jude" was about John's feelings for his son Julian during a rough divorce period. Recorded with a 36-piece orchestra, members of which clapped and sang on the fadeout—earning them double their normal rate for their efforts. At 7 minutes and 11 seconds, the Beatles' "Hey Jude" was by far the longest of their single releases, four minutes of which was the "na na na na" fade. Paul 'hit a clunker on the piano and said a naughty word' during the recording of 'Hey Jude.' It was John's idea to keep the expletive in the song but bury it in the background: 'Nobody else will hear it but we'll know it's there.' No known censorship resulted.

—

The Beatles "Revolution" Apple August 26, 1968

Style: Rock
From and recorded in: England

Considered the first overtly political Beatles song, "Revolution" amounted to a response to the Vietnam War by John Lennon, who said, "I wanted to talk, I wanted to say my piece about revolution. I wanted to tell you, or whoever listens, to communicate, to say 'What do you say? This is what I say.'" The title "Revolution" is mentioned just once, in the first line of the song. Wanting his vocals to have an unusual sound, Lennon recorded most of them lying on his back in the studio. The famous scream at the beginning is a double-tracked recording of Lennon. Lennon wanted it to sound loud to the point of speaker distortion. Producer George Martin tried to dissuade Lennon, saying that radio stations would reject the record if it sounded distorted. Martin was wrong. The political left viewed this song as betraying their cause, so when the album version came out in three months later, the phrase "count me out" became "count me out, in" to appease critics or to indicate how times had changed after the 1968 Chicago riots. Speaking of which, unlike The Rolling Stones' "Street Fighting Man," Chicago radio was allowed to spin the Beatles' "Revolution," which shot to #1 on all Windy City rock outlets as well as nationally.

—

The Rolling Stones "Street Fighting Man" London August 30, 1968

Style: Rock
From and recorded in: England
Suggested pairing: Martha and the Vandellas "Dancin' In the Streets" 1964

Chicago mayor Richard Daley ordered local radio stations not to play this Rolling Stones' single "Street Fighting Man" during the National Democratic Convention, in anticipation of the rioting that did occur during the convention. The ban gave the song huge publicity, air play and sales, most likely elsewhere. "Street Fighting Man" did not hit the charts on the two top 40 stations in Chicago, WLS or WCFL, or any Illinois radio, as of August or September 1968. A week or so earlier, The Rolling Stones' "Jumpin' Jack Flash" was a big hit on both stations as was The Beatles' "Revolution." Despite charting in the top 20 in New York and L.A., the lack of Chicago radio play hurt national sales and "Street Fighting Man" reached a tepid #48.

—

Wilson Pickett "I Found a True Love" Atlantic September 1968

Style: Soul
Where from: Detroit, MI
Where recorded: Muscle Shoals, AL
Original version: Bobby Womack 1965

Songwriter Bobby Womack, who had already recorded the rocker "I Found a True Love" for Checker in 1965 said, "It was easy to write for Wilson Pickett, he came from a gospel background, he wasn't afraid to try something."

—

Canned Heat "Going up the Country" October 1968

Style: Boogie blues
Where from: Torrance, CA; Boston, MA and So Cal, CA
Where recorded: Hollywood, CA
Suggested pairings: Texas Alexander "Farm Hand Blues" 1927; Henry Thomas "Bull Doze Blues"; Cannon's Jug Stompers "Springdale Blues" 1928

Members of Canned Heat, especially Bob Hite and Henry Vestine, were given access to the Aladdin, Imperial and Liberty vaults once Liberty was acquired by United Artists, and the word liberty applied when it came to these so-called united artists like Canned Heat helping themselves to vaulted rare records and one of a kind acetates. However, they used that access to advantage, in that the band was the impetus behind the Legendary Masters Series that reissued blues and doo wop collectors' items in LP form for the first time, in the heyday of interest in vintage recordings of all genres. Possibly the best-known blues record with a flute break, this steady rocking "Going up the Country" with a flute part lifted from "Bull Doze Blues" recorded by Henry Thomas, was deemed by some the unofficial Woodstock anthem. After two major hits, Canned Heat was booked at Woodstock and paid $15,000; however their act was already set and they didn't need the exposure. "Going up the Country" was issued in two ways, with the flute part extended or the flute part cut short.

Remake: Jim Ed Brown 1970

—

Marvin Gaye "I Heard It Through the Grapevine" Tamla October 30, 1968

Style: Soul
Where from: Washington, DC
Where recorded: Detroit, MI
Original version: Gladys Knight & the Pips 1967

After Gladys Knight & the Pips hit with "I Heard It Through the Grapevine" in 1967, it was recorded by The Miracles for the 1968 LP Special Occasion. The insistent Marvin Gaye vocal was lifted from his 1968 album In the Groove, gaining it attention of radio DJs. Motown founder Berry Gordy reluctantly decided to release it as a single in October 1968, and it went to #1.

Remakes: Red Prysock 1968; Ray Johnson 1968; Sam Taylor Jr. 1969; Creedence Clearwater Revival 1975; Earl Klugh 1977; The Slits 1979; The California Raisins 1987

—

Sly and the Family Stone "Everyday People" Epic November 1, 1968

Style: Psych soul
Where from: Vallejo, CA
Where recorded: San Francisco, CA

Taking some inspiration from Mother Goose, adding a twist to the traditional nursery rhyme "rub-a-dub-dub," Sly Stone wrote this song about how everyone is essentially the same, regardless of race or background, even Billy Preston who was on organ. The familiar three men in a tub, the butcher, the baker, the candlestick-maker, became the butcher, the banker, the drummer. In the spirit of the song's message of solidarity of all people, Sly added, "Makes no difference what group I'm in."

Remakes: The Different Strokes 1968: Joan Jett & the Blackhearts 1983; Aretha Franklin 1991

—

Creedence Clearwater Revival "Susie Q" Fantasy November 1968

Style: Rock
From and recorded in: the East Bay, CA
Original version: Dale Hawkins 1957

After several years struggling as the Golliwogs, who had a small local East Bay hit with "Porterville," Creedence Clearwater Revival finally hit pay dirt with a remake of Dale to wide stereo separation, feedback and vocal distortion, making vocalist John Fogerty sound like he was singing through a megaphone. Before it was pressed, the band brought a cassette tape of the song to a San Francisco DJ, who played it in appreciation for the group's earlier support of a DJ strike.

—

Tommy James and The Shondells "Crimson and Clover" Roulette December 1968

Style: Rock
Where from: Michigan
Where recorded: New York
Suggested pairing: The Troggs "Wild Thing" 1966

This was the song that made Tommy James a psych album act after about five years as a pop radio 45s act. James recalled a visit to WLS Chicago with a tape demo of "Crimson and Clover," which he played for DJ Larry Lujack, who stealthily recorded the song and put it on the air as an exclusive. That deprived James of completing the finished record. The demo of "Crimson and Clover" with a "Wild Thing" guitar break was released at about 2 1/2 minutes, so to get underground radio play, an extended version was spliced together from the master tape, which had some really bad edits. Fans of the song have imputed all sorts of hidden sexuality into the title: "crimson is the color of love" in the woman. Clover is the grass in which to make love, or a blossom that tastes like honey." All about early sexual experiences.

Remake: Joan Jett and the Blackhearts 1982

—

The Chambers Brothers "Time Has Come Today" Columbia December 1968

Style: Psych rock
Where from: Mississippi by way of Boston, MA
Where recorded: Los Angeles, CA
Suggested pairing: Santana "Black Magic Woman" 1970

This was the second try on this composition, earlier released without psych effects in 1966. The Chambers Brothers' remake of "Time Has Come Today" with extra psych instrumentation along with the shout of "cuckoo," a cowbell used to imitate a ticking clock, was cut from 11:06 on the LP to 3:05 (and also to 4:45), for the 45. "And my soul has been psychedelicized."

—

MC5 "Kick Out the Jams" Elektra December 1968

Style: Rock
From and recorded in: Detroit, MI

The opening line from this proto-punk gem (along with the offending word printed on the album's inside cover) caused a ruckus when the MC5 released their debut album in 1969: "It's time to... kick out the jams, motherf–er!" The original edition of the LP was removed from store shelves and replaced with two versions: one with a censored cover and audio and another with the censored cover but uncensored audio (to be sold from only behind the counter). But Detroit-based Hudson's department stores refused to carry any version of 'Kick Out the Jams,' which morphed into a ban on all records from MC5's label, Elektra Records. To retaliate, the band took out full-page ads in Ann Arbor and Detroit newspapers with the words "F–Hudson's!" Elektra then dropped the group.

"Kick Out the Jams" began as one of 500 free singles given away to attendees of the "Elektra free concert" for MC 5 at the Fillmore East, December 26, 1968. According to Rob Tyner, "As the band members made their way toward the cars Elektra had sent to ferry them back to their hotel, the crowd's verbal abuse crossed the line into physical ugliness. They angrily showered the vehicles with rocks, debris, and the 45s that had been given away at the show."

—

Crazy Elephant "Gimme Gimme Good Lovin'" Bell January 1969

Style: Rock 'n' roll
From and recorded in: New York

At the peak of the second British Invasion, Crazy Elephant on this bubble gum vocal, "Gimme Gimme Good Lovin'" was rolled out as a group of Welsh miners. In fact, they were a group of New York studio singers led by former Cadillacs vocalist Robert Spencer, produced by Jerry Kasenetz and Jeff Katz of Super K Productions, who hit with similar studio groups: The Music Explosion, The 1910 Fruitgum Company and The Ohio Express.

—

Creedence Clearwater Revival "Proud Mary" Fantasy January 1969

Style: Rock
From and recorded in: East Bay, CA
Suggested pairings: Jimmy Wilson "Big Wheel Rolling" 1958; Cream "Sunshine Of Your Love" 1967

"Proud Mary" by Creedence Clearwater Revival helped set their style as backwoods bayou-style rockers. John Fogerty intended Mary to be a maid working for the rich. "She gets off the bus every morning and goes to work and holds their lives together," he explained. "Then she has to go home." After watching the television show Maverick, about a riverboat gambler, member Stu Cook decided it should be about a riverboat. Another TV series, Rawhide, had a 'rollin,' rollin' on the river" theme. Some radio assumed some of the lyrics to be about marijuana.

Remakes: The Checkmates Ltd. featuring Sonny Charles and Solomon Burke 1969; Ike & Tina Turner 1971

—

Spirit "I Got a Line On You" Ode January 18, 1969

Style: Rock 'n' roll
From and recorded in: Hollywood, CA

Guitarist/vocalist Randy California, jazz drummer Ed Cassidy and keyboard player John Locke formed The Red Roosters, which performed Chuck Berry-style folk rock at Randy's uncle Ed Pearl's Ashgrove. Cassidy and California went to New York, where they met and jammed with Jimi Hendrix at the Café Wha?. Meanwhile, bass player Mark Andes left Canned Heat in 1966 and hooked up with percussionist/vocalist Jay Ferguson to form Western Union, which performed Jay's songs at the Sea Witch on the Sunset Strip. After Western Union broke up, Ferguson wanted to go solo. "John Locke was a fan of Gibran, they played a few gigs under that name." With Ferguson handling vocals, Spirit moved to Topanga Canyon, where they began a commune and were signed to Lou Adler's Ode, for which they recorded "Mechanical World" on Ode. Their first hit, with a lyric line added by Dr. Demento, who was part of this scene, was "I Got a Line on You."

According to a December 8, 2012 L.A. Times obituary of Cassidy, "Jimi Hendrix incorporated Spirit guitar solos into performances and fans took notice of similarities between Led Zeppelin's 'Stairway to Heaven' and Spirit's 'Taurus,' which was released first. When Led Zeppelin played their first gig in the U.S. in 1968, they opened for Spirit." Big legal action resulted; Spirit lost.

—

The Isley Brothers "It's Your Thing" T-Neck February 1969

Style: Soul vocal group
Where from: Ohio
Where recorded: New York
Suggested pairing: Watts 103rd St. Rhythm Band "Do Your Thing" 1968

The Isleys fled Motown to revive their T-Neck label, unleashing the free-will funk of "It's Your Thing," and earning a lawsuit from Motown's Berry Gordy Jr, who claimed he owned the song.

—

El Chicano "Viva Tirado" Gordo/Kapp March 23, 1970

Style: Latin jazz
From and recorded in: Los Angeles, CA
Original version: Gerald Wilson

In late 1969, Eddie Davis took in a performance by the Latin-jazz outfit called the VIPs—Bobby Espinosa, keyboards; Freddie Sanchez, guitar; Mickey Lespron, guitar; Andre Baeza, percussion and John De Luna, drums—who performed at the Kabuki Lounge on Crenshaw in Los Angeles.
Interested, he took the tape to Flash Record Shop counterman Rudy Benavidez, who would often refer talent and evaluate new releases. "Eddie gave me the cassette, I took it home, played it overnight."

When the time came to release the new VIPs record, Benavidez had a suggestion. "People don't know who gave El Chicano their name," said Benavidez. "I did." As the record was about to be pressed as "El Chicano" by the VIPs, a man at the pressing plant recognized the tune as a Gerald Wilson composition, "Viva Tirado." Instead of being the song, El Chicano became the band. The VIPs hated the name, until sales reports began to come in on "Viva Tirado Pt. 1 & 2" on Eddie Davis' relatively new Gordo label. Then they loved it.

—

Sly and the Family Stone "I Want To Take You Higher" Epic March 24, 1969

Style: Psych soul
Where from: Vallejo, CA
Where recorded: Hollywood, CA
Suggested pairings: Billy Preston "Advice" 1966; Sly and the Family Stone "Higher" 1968; The Ohio Players "Fire" 1974

Sly and the Family Stone's "I Want to Take You Higher" opens with a bluesy guitar riff played by Freddie Stone. Said band member, sax player Jerry Martini, "'I Want to Take You Higher' was not a drug song, it was not about that, it was about taking you higher musically. He just got caught up with what was going on at the times, a product of our times and culture. He was fine until he moved to New York City, where people and bands he hung out with offered him free candy. By that point, everybody was catering to him and he wouldn't listen to anybody. He'd become Sly Stone, as opposed to my good friend, Sylvester Stewart. There was a personality transformation."

Remake: Ike & Tina Turner 1970

—

The Beatles With Billy Preston "Get Back" Apple April 1969

Style: Rock
Where from: Liverpool, England
Where recorded: London, England
Suggested pairings: Chuck Berry "Roll Over Beethoven" 1956; Jackie Lomax "Sour Milk Sea" 1968

The Beatles' "Get Back" represented a return to their rock 'n' roll roots, including the false ending.

—

Jr. Walker & the All Stars "What Does It Take (To Win Your Love)" Soul April 1969

Style: Soul
Where from: Indiana
Where recorded: Detroit, MI

"I wrote half the lyrics," said Harvey Fuqua of "What Does It Take (To Win Your Love)" by Jr. Walker. "Should be three writers on there, Johnny Bristol, Vernon Bullock and myself. It took him almost forever to do that. He comes in, said 'I'm stuck on two lines.' I said to Johnny Bristol, 'Johnny, sing duet with him, it might sound better.'" A Motown quality control meeting rejected this song for single release, but radio station DJs made the track popular, resulting in Motown releasing it as a single, whereupon it reached No. 4 on the Hot 100 and No. 1 on the R&B chart.

—

Creedence Clearwater Revival "Bad Moon Rising" Fantasy April 1969

Style: Rock
From and recorded in: the Bay Area, CA

"This song is definitely not about astrology," Fogerty once joked about "Bad Moon Rising," saying that is was "scary, spooky stuff." With violence at home and a war abroad, the analogy to a bad moon on the rise—not a bathroom on the right—was thought by many to be apt.

—

Zager and Evans "In the Year 2525 (Exordium & Terminus)" Truth 1968/RCA May 1969

Style: Jesus rock
Where from: Lincoln, NB
Where recorded: Odessa, TX

A supposed born-again story of the future in 1010-year intervals from 2525 to 6565, in this song, disturbing predictions are given for each selected year. The overriding theme, of a world doomed by its passive acquiescence to and overdependence on its own overdone technologies, struck a resonant chord in millions of people around the world in the late 1960s. Horn overdubs on both versions were mixed louder on the Truth release than on the RCA where the horns were buried way deep in the mix. They pressed about 11,000 of these, 1000 in the original pressing then 10,000 additional on Truth, perhaps for regional release, either during the time or before RCA took over the distribution.

—

Edwin Hawkins Singers "Oh Happy Day" Pavillion May 1969

Style: Gospel
From and recorded in: Berkeley, CA
Suggested pairing: George Harrison "My Sweet Lord" 1970

Designed as a fundraiser to help members of the Ephesian Church of God In Christ in Berkeley choir compete in an annual choir competition, the original recording of "Oh Happy Day"—with Dorothy Morrison, led and backed by Elaine Kelly, Margarette Branch, Tramaine Davis, Reuben Franklin, Donald Cashmere, Betty Watson and Ruth Lyons—was released locally by the Northern California State Youth Choir in LP form only, "Let Us Go In The House Of The Lord" on LaMont Branch's custom label, Century 70 Records. After a California DJ spun the track to extremely high response, the master was sold to Buddah Records, then released as the Edwin Hawkins Singers on Pavillion.

Remake: Glen Campbell 1970

—

Tommy James & the Shondells "Crystal Blue Persuasion" Roulette May 1969

Style: Rock
Where from: Michigan
Where recorded: New York City, NY
Covers: Joe Bataan 1969; The Kelly Bros 1969

According to Tommy James, co-writer of "Crystal Blue Persuasion" this is a semi-religious poetic song with a "conga drum, a bongo, a tambourine, a flamenco guitar, and a very light-sounding bass" as well as a Hammond keyboard. Based on imagery out of the Book of Revelation, about the lake of crystal, the idea became 'crystal blue persuasion.'" Although those words aren't used together, "it was what the image meant to me." The lyrics, "It's a new vibration," are about James becoming Christian, but many listeners had their own drug-induced interpretation, causing some radio playlist banning, but not much.

Remakes: The Invincibles 1970; The Naturals 1974; Gonzales 1977

—

The Beatles "The Ballad Of John and Yoko" Apple June 4, 1969

Style: Rock 'n' roll
Where from: Liverpool, England
Where recorded: London, England
Suggested pairings: Johnny Burnette Rock N' Roll Trio "Lonesome Tears In My Eyes" 1956; ABBA "Ring Ring" 1973; Dwight Yoakam's "Fast as You Can" 1993

This rockingly manic auto-biographical tour of John and Yoko's relationship gave radio two chances to censor: "trying to get a little peace" and/or "piece" and the more dicey "Christ you know it ain't easy" lyrics.

—

Wilbert Harrison "Let's Work Together" Sue July 1969

Style: Soul
Where from: Florida
Where recorded: New York City NY
Original title: "Let's Stick Together" 1962

"I had another record out, 'Let's Stick Together,' during the movement," said Wilbert Harrison. "I just figured I'd take the record and redo it with different words. Canned Heat did it. It was all right. I never did meet them, never did perform with them."

Remakes: Canned Heat 1970; Bryan Ferry 1976; Dwight Yoakam 1991; George Thorogood & the Destroyers with Elvin Bishop & Johnny Johnson 1995

—

Sly and the Family Stone "Hot Fun in the Summertime" Epic July 21, 1969

Style: Psych soul
Where from: Vallejo, CA
Where recorded: San Francisco, CA

Sly and the Family Stone's "Hot Fun in the Summertime" is a dedication to the fun and games to be had during the summer. This song is known for its rare use of strings in a Sly and the Family Stone song: violins played in the upper register. "He just kept whipping them out," said sax player Jerry Martini. "He had so many songs in his head and on paper he never got a chance to record."

—

Steam "Na Na Hey Hey Kiss Him Goodbye" Fontana August 1969/Mercury 1975

Style: Rock
Where from: Connecticut
Where recorded: Mercury Sound Studios New York
Suggested pairing: Jerry Butler "He Will Break Your Heart" Vee Jay August 1960

"Na Na Hey Hey Kiss Him Goodbye" was written as a throwaway B-side, but became a high profile musical goodbye. It was written by Gary DeCarlo, Dale Frashuer and Paul Leka, who had been in the Chateaus vocal group in the early '60s. Another group member, Dale Frashuer, suggested they use their 1961 song "Kiss Him Goodbye." That song didn't have a chorus, so Leka wrote one, inserting "na na"s instead of actual words. After this all-night session, they emerged with the completed song.

Bob Reno, the A&R man at Mercury, needed material for the subsidiary Fontana Records, so the song was released on that label and credited to the group Steam. The group chant asks a girl to kiss off the guy she's with and get with him, since he will appreciate her. Likewise, singer-songwriter Paul Leka was feeling frustrated in the late '60s when what he felt were his best songwriting compositions kept constantly getting overlooked by radio DJs, who'd play the flip side of his singles instead. Gathering together a bunch of studio musicians for a one-off single, he decided to make a B-side so unlistenable stations wouldn't possibly play it, and worked on the result for a long time, layering what he considered ridiculous effects like "a piano sped up to sound like a bunch of mosquitoes." He was effectively disgusted by the result, but it became by far his biggest hit, rocketing straight to #1 while the A-side, "It's the Magic in You Girl," still remains largely forgotten.

Becoming a popular chant among baseball fans when an opposing pitcher was in trouble, "Na Na Hey Hey Kiss Him Goodbye" was reissued as a White Sox theme in the Chicago area only in 1975.

—

The Originals "Baby, I'm For Real" Soul August 1969

Style: Retro soul vocal group
From and recorded in: Detroit, MI

"When we formed The Originals, it was Ty Hunter, Walter Gaines, C.P. Spencer and myself," said group member Freddie Gorman. "Ty was under contract to Chess and they would not give him a release. Hank Dixon, who had sung with Walter and C.P., was just coming out of the service, so he was in the group that did 'Baby, I'm For Real.' We were rehearsing one evening, kicking names around, Walter Gaines' wife said, 'You're all originals, you should call yourself The Originals,"

Though they had several early issues, including a rocking take on "Good Night Irene" and a tip of the lyrical hat to The Temptations in the lyrics of "We've Got A Way Out Love," and the mellow ballad "Green Grow The Lilacs," which owed a debt to the progression and key lyrics in "My Girl," The Originals didn't catch on until this doo wop throwback Marvin Gaye-composed "Baby, I'm For Real" in late 1969. "That's the Marvin Gaye production," said Gorman. "He didn't get the credit on that first record. He didn't have a producer's contract. Marvin Gaye was a member of The Moonglows, so that's how far he reached for that. When we recorded that song, it must have sat there a year before it was released. The company had an office called quality control. Everything they released went through there first. I think it got bogged down there. When we finished and heard the song, I know secretaries with the company that heard it, and shook their heads and said, 'Oh my goodness.' We began to believe it wasn't what we thought. After we finished it, we played it over and over at Marvin's house and never got tired of it. They didn't release it, they put the album out and the single, 'Green Grow The Lilacs.' They thought that was going to be the hit. The disc jockeys took 'Baby, I'm For Real' off it, so they changed the name of the album to 'Baby, I'm For Real.'"

—

Diana Ross & the Supremes "Someday We'll Be Together" Motown October 1969

Style: Soul vocal group
From and recorded in: Detroit, MI
Original version: Johnny & Jackey 1961

The Supremes, Mary Wilson and Cindy Birdsong, did not back Diana Ross on this song, "Someday We'll Be Together," a remake of an early Detroit minor hit by Johnny & Jackey that Berry Gordy Jr. planned to have Jr. Walker & the All Stars record. Harvey Fuqua of The Moonglows and owner of Tri-Phi on which the original Johnny & Jackey version appeared, and who produced this session, said, "I think this girl named Linda took Florence's place at the time. Maybe Tammi Terrell might have done something with it." West Coast vocalists Patrice Holloway, Maxime Waters and Julia Waters backed Ross, assisted by the song's writers, Johnny Bristol and Jackey Beavers. In fact, Bristol's voice is heard, coaching Ross to get it right. "Sing it pretty" and "You better."

Remakes: Bobby Darin 1971; Jackey Beavers 1971

—

The Beatles "Come Together" Apple October 6, 1969

Style: Rock
Where from: Liverpool, England
Where recorded: London, England
Suggested pairing: Chuck Berry "You Can't Catch Me" 1957

In need of a campaign slogan in the race for governor of California against Ronald Reagan, Timothy Leary asked John Lennon to write a campaign song. A rotary phone sound effect was employed before each verse, and after the chorus Lennon copped the key line "here come old flattop" from Chuck Berry's automotive themed "You Can't Catch Me" from 1957. The sales of The Beatles "Come Together" prompted Berry's publisher, Morris Levy, to sue. In an out-of-court settlement, John Lennon agreed to record an album of oldies titles for Levy. But when the LP, "John Lennon Sings the Great Rock and Roll Hits," was issued without his permission in 1975, more legal filings ensued and Lennon took ownership of the recordings, releasing them on his own Apple label as the "Rock and Roll" LP and several singles.

—

The Jackson 5 "I Want You Back" Motown October 7, 1969

Style: Soul vocal group
Where from: Gary, IN
Where recorded: Los Angeles, CA
Original title: "I Want to Be Free"

As of 1970, the three acts that kept Motown afloat were Marvin Gaye, Diana Ross and the Jackson 5, who were partly discovered by Diana Ross. The Jackson 5's switch from Steeltown to Motown was a true new label triumph. Originally penned for Gladys Knight, "I Want You Back," released October 7, 1969 seemed advanced for Michael Jackson's pre-teen voice. Originally entitled "I Want To Be Free," Motown's Berry Gordy Jr. changed it to "I Want You Back," making it more of a love song. The B-side was the blues ballad "Who's Loving You," a composition used as the B-side of The Miracles' "Shop Around" on Tamla and The Supremes' "Buttered Popcorn" on Tamla.

"I Want You Back" hit #1 pop and #1 soul in mid-November 1969.

—

Shocking Blue "Venus" Colossus November 1969

Style: Rock
Group From and recorded in: Holland
Suggested pairings: The Big Three "The Banjo Song" 1963; The Who "Pinball Wizard" 1969

With Mama Cass Elliot with Tim Rose and Jim Hendricks, The Big Three was one of the root groups of The Mamas and the Papas. Rose reworked Stephen Foster's "Oh Susanna" into "The Banjo Song," which was reworked into "Venus" by the Dutch band The Shocking Blue, a band founded in 1967 by Robbie van Leeuwen and lead singer Mariska Veres from the beat scene Motions.

Remake: Bananarama 1986

—

Norman Greenbaum "Spirit in the Sky" Reprise December 1969

Style: Jesus rock
Where from: Malden, MA
Where recorded: San Francisco, CA

Norman Greenbaum began his musical career while he was a student at Boston University, playing area coffeehouses before relocating to the West Coast during the mid-'60s and forming the psychedelic jug band Dr. West's Medicine Show & Jugband that hit with "The Eggplant That Ate Chicago," but broke up in 1968. Greenbaum described himself as a Jewish musician who dug gospel music, writing "Spirit in the Sky" with lyrics about the afterlife and several references to Jesus. Greenbaum used a Fender Telecaster with a fuzz box built into the body to generate the song's characteristic bass line.

—

Chairmen of the Board "Give Me Just a Little More Time" Invictus December 1969

Style: Soul vocal group
Where from: Norfolk, VA
Where recorded: Detroit, MI

Lead singer of The Showmen, General Johnson, who had hit with "It Will Stand," formed Chairmen of the Board with Danny Woods, Eddie Custis, and Harrison Kennedy, who was lead vocalist of the Chairmen of the Board on "Chairman of the Board." Each member took lead vocals, Johnson's hiccuppy vocals sold "Give Me Just a Little More "(You've Got Me) Dangling on a String," "Everything's Tuesday," "Pay to the Piper" and "Finders Keepers." Operated out of the Cadillac Towers in Detroit with studios at the old Grand Rivers movie theater, Invictus owner Lamont Dozier spoke of the problems he had with Motown. "It's amazing they had a label just like Berry Gordy had," said Johnson. "When we came in to ask for the same things they felt they were deprived of, they chose not to give them up. Because were doing a lot of work over there, from '70 to '76, I think I had five gold records, we just didn't feel that we went too far without us getting what we felt we were supposed to get. I chose to leave the company. We're talking about a penny per record, production fees, maybe your own split publishing. All the publishers were fighting not to do that."

—

Screamin' Jay Hawkins "Moanin'" Philips 1969

Style: Novelty soul
Where from: Cleveland, OH
Where recorded: New York City, NY
Original title: "Constipation Blues"

Somewhere in the era of "underground radio" and counterculture attitudes came this brave attempt at an unlikely hit with shock value by a proven talent. To the extent that Hawkins fans were hardly clamoring for toilet habit vocals meant no sales. The record company changed the title to "Moanin'"; still no sales.

Soul, Rock, Funk, and Punk

1970s

The Originals "The Bells" Soul January 9, 1970

Style: Retro soul vocal group
From and recorded in: Detroit, MI

As with "Baby I'm For Real," The Originals' "The Bells," with a unique spoken ending, was written by and produced by Marvin Gaye. In 1972, C.P. Spencer left the group. Ty Hunter was in a group called The Glass House that wasn't doing anything, so we got Invictus Records to give his contract back and he joined The Originals, again," said Freddy Gorman.

—

Charles Wright & the Watts 103rd St. Rhythm Band "Loveland" Warner Brothers March 1970

Style: Funk soul group
From and recorded in: Los Angeles, CA
Original version: Al Hibbler "Love Land" 1958
Earlier version: Don Trotter 1969
Suggested pairing: James Gadson "Got To Find My Baby" 1972

When the Watts 103rd St. Rhythm Band recorded the fine "Loveland," band leader Charles Wright was under the impression it was an original by Don Trotter of The Untouchables, who had recorded it under his own name on Josie in October 1969. "That song was originally done by Al Hibbler, I didn't know it when he brought it to me as an old doo wop song. Great idea, but it's too far behind the times for today's market, so 'I'll rewrite it and share it with you,' and he agreed. I spent a year rewriting that song and two and a half years re-recording it, over and over again, to get the right feel I wanted it to have until one day, I convinced the band to do it. That song caused me more problems and money. I recorded that song over and over again, every time we went in the studio, trying to get this right feeling; finally we did. I let the drummer James Gadson who had a wonderful voice sing the song and the only reason I did that is because when I was working on this, the drum beats, the 16th notes on the hi hat, this is the first record that ever had that. I created this drum beat to go along with this upbeat version of doo wop and he and I had to have him come over to the house all the time to try to do this and I was wearing his patience out, so I said, 'I'm going to let you sing the song' by him coming over working on it."

The Watts 103rd St. Rhythm Band with Charles Wright recorded "Loveland," which hit biggest on border radio XPRS and Boss Radio KHJ. Wright recalled, "When the record became a hit and I was traveling up and down the road, some guy kept following me around asking, 'Aren't you going to give my brother some of that song?' I said no, 'I don't know your brother. Me and some guy way out in California wrote this song, I don't know what you're talking about.' He began to get on my nerves, he surfaced just about everywhere I'd go, asking, 'Aren't you going to give my brother some of that song?' So finally they sued me. At this time, I'm sure Don Trotter had spent his share of the royalties. My attorney was trying to make money off of it too, [the guy] finally showed me a lead sheet couple of years later. When I saw the lead sheet, I threw up my hands. The guy's brother had actually written the song and it was recorded by Al Hibbler as a B-side in 1958. Mr. Trotter thought nobody would suspect since it's a B-side, that they'd never notice anything. These guys appreciated what I'd done to it, so they left me half of the song. I'm only the half owner of the song, these other two guys own the other half.

Wright added, "After it was a hit, James Gadson came to me and said one night in the studio, 'I'm ready to go off on my own now because of this song.' Went off on his own and recorded same exact song all over again, kind of killed his singing career. It was the exact duplicate of 'Loveland.' He called it 'Got To Find My Baby.'"

—

Eric Burdon & War "Spill the Wine" MGM May 13, 1970

Style: Funk soul group
Where from: England/Compton, CA, Long Beach, CA, and San Pedro, CA
Where recorded: Hollywood, CA

One time lead singer of The Animals, Eric Burdon debuted as Eric Burdon & War on this rhythmic "Spill the Wine" on MGM. Jerry Goldstein, who had produced and sung on a variety of East Coast doo wop and pop hits like "My Boyfriend's Back" by The Angels, put Burdon and War together. "Eric Burdon had left The Animals," said War keyboard player Lonnie Jordan. "We were playing as The Nightshift behind Deacon Jones. Jerry walked in the club looking for a band for Eric Burdon. We were playing 'Hang Em High,' he knew the original Ikettes singing background with Deacon Jones. Eric and Lee Oskar came up on stage, we thought Lee was Eric. Jerry asked us if we'd like to come into the studio." They did.

War got their name during a visit to Tokyo. "We were walking down the street on a back alley, Steve Gold was the manager. The band was walking in front of him, we were young, all had Afros. Steve said, 'I'm glad I know you guys, I'd walk the other way, you look like you just came off a battlefield.' He said 'War.' We said, 'That's too radical.'" They later changed their minds. The first War session took place at Wally Heidler's studio "on Cahuenga right next to Shelley Mann's jazz club," said Jordan. "I already laid down the tracks, while trying to create lyrics, we spent a lot of money, you could hear Hampton Hawes and Milt Jackson next door through the wall, while I was trying to do the track. I'm also watching Eric improvise and come up with lyrics. Carmen, a Puerto Rican girl, very nice looking" was with Burdon. "I never saw her face. That was the problem that night. Eric was in the singing booth against the wall, she had beautiful hair, I never saw her body, just saw her head. I was behind the board in the control room, smoking weed, watching the back of Carmen, watching Eric sing, I was hypnotized, dazed and confused, started pouring this wine in a Styrofoam cup, all of a sudden I saw it spill in the board, starting smoking, everyone jumped up, Eric thought it was a joke, started singing 'spill the wine, spill the wine spill the wine.'" A hit.

"I ended up paying $25,000 later on. Eric couldn't continue on with us because of political problems he had with MGM; we weren't with MGM, Eric was." Burdon's final MGM 45 was a blues duet with Jimmy Witherspoon.

—

Edwin Starr "War" Gordy June 1970

Style: Soul
From and recorded in: Detroit, CA

This anti-Vietnam War protest, "War," was first recorded by The Temptations with more of a traditional soul rendition on their Psychedelic Shack LP. Once it reached the anti-war audience came a demand it be released as a single. The label and the group hesitated. Not wanting to characterize The Temptations with a political issue, "War" was handed off to Edwin Starr, who executed a more strident version, just what the song's public had demanded. "We backed Edwin Starr's 'War,'" said Freddie Gorman of The Originals.

Remake: Bruce Springsteen and The E Street Band 1986

—

Mungo Jerry "In the Summertime" Janus June 1970

Style: Skiffle blues
From and recorded in: England

"In the Summertime" is the debut single by British rock band Mungo Jerry, the alter-ego of lead singer Ray Dorset, who played acoustic and electric guitar and a shaker instrument called cabasa; with Paul King, banjo and jug; Mike Cole, string bass and Colin Earl, piano. Dorset stomped his foot to the rhythm. The "motorcycle" at song's end was a Triumph sports car driving past the studio while the engineer was holding the microphone. "So he got the stereo effects from left to right or right to left, whatever." The song was a great, unique summertime hit.

—

King Floyd "Groove Me" Chimneyville September 1970

Style: Soul
Where from: New Orleans, LA
Where recorded: Malaco Records Studio Jackson, MI

King Floyd III was born in New Orleans in 1945. In the mid-60s, Floyd was recording for Original Sound and Pulsar in the L.A. area. While working at a box company he composed what became "Groove Me" for a flirtatious female co-worker, who left the job before he could give it to her. "I decided to give up the business in 1969," said Floyd. "I went to New Orleans, met CP Love, I had 12 or 13 songs in my head. CP told my manager, Elijah Walker, to record me. Chimneyville was the name of the Jackson label owned by Malaco, which made a deal with Atlantic through DJ George Vinnet of WYLD, New Orleans."

Backing King Floyd on this session were Wardell Quezergue, organ; Jerry Puckett, guitar; Vernie Robbins, bass and James Stroud, drums. "They were playing the A-side, 'What Our Love Needs' When Vinnet played 'Groove Me.' I told him, 'George you're playing the wrong side.' It was too dry, funky. It had been done in one take. The other side had strings. It was about to bite the dust. Malaco, too," said Floyd, but when Atlantic took over the record, "they made a million dollars off 'Groove Me.'"

—

Van Morrison "Domino" Warner Brothers October 1970

Style: Rock
Where from: Belfast, Northern Ireland
Where recorded: Hollywood, CA

No longer with Bang, Van Morrison combined Irish Celtic with gospel to create his own style in this tribute to Fats Domino called "Domino."

—

The Osmonds "One Bad Apple" MGM November 1970

Style: Pop rock
Where from: Utah
Where recorded: Muscle Shoals, AL

When Mike Curb took over operations of MGM, he made big news by dropping what he called "drug oriented acts." Having come over from Sidewalk Records, for whom Curb had attempted to sign The Osmonds, where he brought some songs to the negotiations with their manager, Andy Williams' brother, Joe Williams, who rejected Sidewalk, saying, "I can get this junk anywhere." Once Curb had them signed, they recorded this uptempo Jackson 5 clone, "One Bad Apple," which went straight up the charts. The dropping of "druggie" acts reached the President, so when Nixon was re-elected, Curb wrote, congratulating him. Mike had a meeting with Nixon, and Mike was always liberal, but suddenly became a staunch Republican. With his political chops set up by Nixon, from 1979 to 1983, Curb was Republican Lt. Governor of California under Democratic Governor Jerry Brown.

—

George Harrison "My Sweet Lord" Apple November 25, 1970

Style: Rock
Where from: Liverpool, England
Where recorded: London, England
Original version: Billy Preston 1970
Suggested pairings: Bach "Toccata and Fugue in D-minor"; The Chiffons "He's So Fine" 1963; Edwin Hawkins Singers "Oh Happy Day" 1969; The Intrigues "In A Moment" 1969; George Harrison "This Song" 1976

Shortly after The Beatles disbanded, lead guitarist and songwriter George Harrison wrote "My Sweet Lord" in praise of the Hindu god Krishna, at the same time intending the lyrics to serve as a call to abandon religious sectarianism through his deliberate blending of the Hebrew word hallelujah with chants of "Hare Krishna" and Vedic prayer. This song had the Wall of Sound treatment of Phil Spector, who also sang backup, featuring Harrison's slide guitar technique.

In 1971, Bright Tunes, which owned the 1963 hit "He's So Fine" by The Chiffons, sued Harrison. In 1973, Bright Tunes won a settlement, which Harrison dealt with in an uptempo, piano-driven boogie, "This Song," which reflected his frustration of the infringement case with satirical lyrics. "This Song" featured Billy Preston on piano and organ, and Monty Python's Eric Idle, whose satire was to call out in falsetto, "Could be 'Sugar Pie, Honey Bunch'—No, sounds more like 'Rescue Me'!" Harrison's erstwhile partner, Alan Klein, bought the Bright Tunes catalog and tried to collect, but was rebuffed by the court.

Remakes: Billy Preston 1970; The Ronnie Kole Trio 1971; Nina Simone 1973; Ray Anthony 1974; The Chiffons 1975

—

Ike & Tina Turner "Proud Mary" United Artists January 1971

Style: Soul
Where from: Mississippi and St. Louis, MO
Where recorded: Los Angeles, CA
Original version: Creedence Clearwater Revival 1968

Ike Turner recalled of his remake of "Proud Mary" with Tina on vocals, "It came from when I was messing around with Spector. If you notice, 'rolling, rolling,' that one and one beat, that's the way Spector records. We cut that record down at United, I didn't even like that record, man, I was just doing something to get a side. The other side must be the 'Tweeter,' that's the side I was going with. On 'Proud Mary,' we went to the fast part, didn't want to do that. Everything I do is always right, we always laugh about it.... I have an inferiority complex... whenever you sing in the microphone, 'girl you got choices.' When we cut the album, we were lacking a few tunes, so we said, 'Well, let's just put in a few things that we're doing on stage.' That's how 'Proud Mary' came about. I had loved it when it first came out. We auditioned a girl and she had sung 'Proud Mary.' This is like eight months later, and Ike said, 'You know, I forgot all about that tune.' And I said let's do it, but let's change it. So in the car Ike plays the guitar, we just sort of jam. And we just sort of broke into the black version of it. It was never planned to say, 'Well, let's go to the record shop, and I'd like to record this tune by Aretha Franklin.'... It's just that we get it for stage, because we give the people a little bit of us and a little bit of what they hear on the radio every day."

Remake: The Ohio Players 1971

—

Marvin Gaye "What's Goin' On" Tamla January 1971

Style: Soul
Where from: Washington, DC
Where recorded: Detroit, MI

Marvin Gaye had worked hard to play pro football, and as a result, was good friends with Detroit Lions players Mel Farr and Lem Barney, who sang backup on "What's Going On," the title taken from a black slang greeting as well as other black street slang, "right on, right on" and "wh'as happenin'" in the sax-heavy opening. Entirely a social consciousness theme, Motown owner Berry Gordy Jr. rejected the song for release, until he found out about the impressive sales when the 45 was snuck out. As Gaye recalled, "They didn't like it, didn't understand it, and didn't trust it. Management said the songs were too long, too formless, and would get lost on a public looking for easy three-minute stories. For months they wouldn't release it. My attitude had to be firm: 'Put it out or I'll never record for you again!'"

—

Van Morrison "Blue Money" Warner Brothers January 1971

Style: Rock
Where from: Belfast, Northern Ireland
Where recorded: Hollywood, CA

In his fascination with Fats Domino in his previous hit, "Domino," perhaps it's little wonder that Morrison came up with this "Blue Money" title, perilously close to Fats' "Blue Monday."

—

The Rolling Stones "Brown Sugar" Rolling Stones April 1971

Style: Rock
Where from: England
Where recorded: Muscle Shoals, AL
Suggested pairing: Foreigner "Hot Blooded" 1978

About slavery disguised as a woman, Mick Jagger wrote this as "Black Pussy." Deciding it was a little too direct, he changed it to "Brown Sugar." In Keith Richards' 2010 autobiography, Life, her floats a theory as to what the lyrics "Scarred old slaver know he doin' alright" are all about. Some poor guy at their publishing company probably came up with that transcription for the lyrics, but Jagger was most likely singing, "Skydog Slaver," as "Skydog" was a nickname for Muscle Shoals regular Duane Allman, since he was high all the time.

On this song, Bobby Keys was on saxophone. This was the first song released on Rolling Stones Records, The Stones' subsidiary of Atlantic Records.

—

John Lee Hooker & Canned Heat "Whiskey and Wimmen" United Artists May 1971

Style: Rock 'n' roll
Where from: Detroit, MI, So Cal, CA
Where recorded: Hollywood, CA
Original version: Wilbert Harrison "Woman and Whiskey" 1956

John Lee Hooker & Canned Heat recorded "Whiskey and Wimmen." Band bass player Larry Taylor said, "Skip Taylor found John Lee Hooker, put us together in 1971." In the November 1970-February 1971 issue of R&B Magazine, Bob Hite stated that the Hooker sessions were "something the late Al Wilson and I always wanted to do. Alan for the joy of playing with John and myself to record John the way he hasn't been recorded properly in 15 years, Hooker is recorded by himself and with Alan Wilson playing both harp and guitar, and even piano. The band is added for a few tracks. It's a pretty loose funky sound and I don't think the hard Hooker fan will object."

—

The Staple Singers "Respect Yourself" Stax October 1971

Style: Soul
Where from: Chicago, IL
Where recorded: Muscle Shoals, AL

Frustrated with the state of the world, songwriter Luther Ingram said, "black folk need to learn to respect themselves." Fellow writer Mack Rice liked the comment so much that he built a funk groove around it, then gave the song to The Staple Singers. "We hooked up with Stax, about 1970, '71. Al Bell got The Staple Singers," said Pops Staples. "He came to Chicago, he was a disc jockey in Arkansas when he first met us. He was top man in Memphis, Memphis was his spot. Money talks and he talked big money. We never did get out of the religious thing, but the biggest record we had was trying to tell the children, 'Respect Yourself.' When I was a kid, I had to respect older people, whether they was my parents or not. Trouble today, we don't have no respect for ourselves or nobody else."

—

Don McLean "American Pie" United Artists November 1971

Style: Retro rock
Where from: New Rochelle, NY
Where recorded: New York

The song that kick-started the nostalgia trend of the early 1970s when it hit #1, "American Pie" was the only hit Don McLean ever had. He's never revealed real meaning to the many references in the song he called "The Day the Music Died." Clearly it is about the February 3, 1959 plane crash that killed Buddy Holly, The Big Bopper and Ritchie Valens, all of whom were on top of their careers as rockers. On the UK show Songbook, McLean explained, "For some reason I wanted to write a big song about America and about politics, but I wanted to do it in a different way. As I was fiddling around, I started singing this thing about the Buddy Holly crash, the thing that came out, "Long, long time ago, I can still remember how that music used to make me smile.' I thought, Whoa, what's that? And then the day the music died, it just came out. And I said, 'Oh, that is such a great idea.' And so that's all I had. And then I thought, 'I can't have another slow song on this record. I've got to speed this up.' I came up with this chorus, crazy chorus. And then one time about a month later I just woke up and wrote the other five verses. Because I realized what it was, I knew what I had. And basically, all I had to do was speed up the slow verse with the chorus and then slow down the last verse so it was like the first verse, and then tell the story, which was a dream. It is from all these fantasies, all these memories that I made personal. Buddy Holly's death to me was a personal tragedy. As a child, a 15-year-old, I had no idea that nobody else felt that way much. I mean, I went to school and mentioned it and they said, 'So what?' So I carried this yearning and longing, if you will, this weird sadness that would overtake me when I would look at [the] album, The Buddy Holly Story, because that was my last Buddy record before he passed away."

At 8 minutes 32 seconds, this is the longest song to hit #1 on the Hot 100. The single was split in two parts because the 45 did not have enough room for the whole song on one side. The A-side ran 4:11 and the B-side was 4:31—you had to flip the record in the middle to hear all of it. Disc jockeys usually played the album version at full length, though there was an alternate DJ version which dropped the "Helter skelter" verse, went to the "generation lost in space" verse through most of the chorus, then added an alternate ending where it sounded as if the chorus was about to repeat, but it faded quickly.

—

Al Green "Let's Stay Together" Hi November 1971

Style: Soul
Where from: Arkansas
Where recorded: Memphis, TN
Suggested pairing: Marvin Gaye "What's Goin' On" 1971

Wine drinking experts create a noisy background. When the track at was cut at Royal, Mitchell brought in a group of neighborhood winos who used to linger outside the studio to serve as Green's audience and to supplement the insistent rhythm section—Howard Grimes and Al Jackson, Jr. drums; Leroy Hodges, bass; Charles Hodges, organ and piano and Teenie Hodges, guitar as well as Wayne Jackson, trumpet; Andrew Love and Ed Logan, tenor saxophone; James Mitchell, bass and baritone saxophone and Jack Hale, Sr., trombone with Charles Chalmers, Donna Rhodes and Sandra Rhodes on backup vocals. "Willie wanted Al to have people here," recalled the song's organist Charles Hodges to Mojo magazine. "Sometimes, when you sing about something, if you look at people, you can relate with the song a little more compassionately. You'd be surprised what you can project from that. You feed on what you're looking at."

Green hated the "thin" sound of his falsetto on it. Producer Willie Mitchell recalled, "The only fight I ever had with him was about 'Let's Stay Together,' because he thought 'Let's Stay Together' was not a hit."

Remake: Isaac Hayes 1971; Tina Turner 1984

—

Isaac Hayes "Shaft" Enterprise November 1971

Style: Funk soul
From and recorded in: Memphis, TN

The instruments in this song were played by Memphis funk group The Bar-Kays, with guitarist Charles Pitts playing the wah-wah solo, and Otis Redding's backup band. Isaac Hayes wrote "Shaft" under the condition he'd be considered for the lead role in the movie of the same name. It never happened; he was never called for an audition. "The character Shaft was explained to me, a relentless character always on the prowl, always on the move. I had to create something to denote that. Drummer Al Jackson was doing some stuff on a hi-hat, and I thought if I sustained that kind of thing on a hi-hat, it would give a relentless, dramatic effect, and it worked."

Backup singers were Telma Hopkins and Joyce Wilson, with Hopkins' saying, "shut your mouth!" In two years, that duo would be backing Tony Orlando as Dawn, hitting #1 with "Tie a Yellow Ribbon Round the Ole Oak Tree."

—

Sly, Slick & Wicked "Confessin' a Feelin'" SSW/Bad Boys 1972

Style: Soul vocal group
Where from: Texas
Where recorded: Los Angeles, CA
Original version: Tony Owens 1969

Vocalist Sonny Daye, Eddy Stovall, Larry Lewis, Freddie D. Holiday and Donny "Doc" Everheart put together Sly, Slick & Wicked for a cover of New Orleans soul singer Tony Owens' "Confessin' A Feeling" on Soulin', then reissued on Cotillion. Sly Slick & Wicked's version was an underground low rider hit with seeming perpetual sales as also noted in "I Want You Back" by The Larks. "Confessin' A Feeling" charted on radio from Inglewood, CA, in '73 to El Centro, CA, in 1977. As "Confessin' A Feeling" was such a consistent seller during the 1970s, Sly, Slick & Wicked didn't get around to putting out their next song, "Tonight's the Nite," until 1981.

—

The Staple Singers "I'll Take You There" Stax March 1972

Style: Soul vocal group
Where from: Chicago, IL
Where recorded: Memphis, TN
Suggested pairings: Harry J All Stars "The Liquidator" 1969; Tony Scott "What Am I To Do" 1969

Pops Staples said that Stax label president "Al Bell wrote a poem, 'I'll Take You There,'" about taking you to heaven. Writer credit went to Alvertis Isbell. The rhythm was borrowed strictly from the influential reggae sound of Harry J All Stars' "The Liquidator" from 1969. "We stayed with Stax until they went busted out," said Pops.

—

Jimmy Castor Bunch "Troglodyte" RCA April 1972

Style: Funk soul
From and recorded in: New York

"We were wearing suede boots," said Jimmy Castor. "I had everybody singing. Took the records up to RCA, Buzzy Willis, who used to be in The Solitaires, had the black music department. He put me in the black department, used my voice. We needed another song, had been playing live all the time. He said, 'Just play that caveman record.' I studied anthropology, did that one take, we're in the black department, I'm thinking ahead, yesterday sounds like right now. We put this LP out, went to Canada. Radio stations WPGC and WOL were fighting over "Troglodyte.' The Schwartz Brothers are on this record. Went in the U-Haul, came from the ice, what we're going to do is go back, they were all scared, I was shaking them up. That's a million seller."

The flip side was "I Promise To Remember," which Castor recorded with his group The Juniors in 1956 and which was covered by Frankie Lymon & the Teenagers.

—

Tower of Power "You're Still a Young Man" Warner Brothers July 1972

Style: Funk soul
Where from: East Bay, CA
Where recorded: Hollywood, CA
Suggested pairings: The Impressions "My Woman's Love" 1968

In the summer of 1968, tenor saxophonist/vocalist Emilio Castillo teamed up with baritone saxophonist Stephen "Doc" Kupka. Then known as The Motowns, they worked various gigs around Oakland and Berkeley, their soul sound appealing to both minority and rebellious listeners. About to play Bill Graham's Fillmore Auditorium in San Francisco, the band became Tower of Power. Vocalist Lenny Williams; trumpet/arranger Greg Adams;first trumpet Mic Gillette; first saxophone Skip Mesquite; on bass Francis "Rocco" Prestia; on guitar Willie Fulton; and drummer David Garibaldi formed the core of this horn-heavy ensemble with percussionist/conga/ bongo player Brent Byars. This was the first song Tower of Power had co-written by sax players Krupka and Castillo, whose true life story was portrayed, in that he had a girlfriend six years older when he was 18. Because he was too young, she dropped him. That gave rise to the thought that as he was still young, he was hardly wasting his time.

—

Billy Paul "Me & Mrs. Jones" Philaldelphia International September 1972

Style: Soul
From and recorded in: Philadelphia, PA

Billy Paul had been recording with scant success since the early 1950s, when he came up with the silky vocal on this ballad, "Me & Mrs. Jones," about a faraway love affair between Muhammed Ali and a Kentucky woman, who lived some distance from him.

—

Curtis Mayfield "Superfly" Curtom October 1972

Style: Funk soul
From and recorded in: Chicago, IL

"The screenwriter brought the script to me at the Lincoln Center back in 1971," said Curtis Mayfield of "Superfly," referring to the title song he wrote for the movie. It was his first major hit as a single. "I was flabbergasted to receive such honors. After the concert they came in with the script and asked if I'd possibly be able to deal with it. I read that script that night. The next two or three days, I was at home writing 'Superfly.'" The script "had its flaws, it was a little bit heavy, even for those early years. However it was strong enough in character to show this priest, who of course was Superfly, was quite ambitious and even though he was dealing with illegal forms of life, he set out to make a goal and he did it."

—

Elton John "Crocodile Rock" MCA November 1972

Style: Retro rock
Where from: England
Where recorded: France
Suggested pairings: Bill Haley and his Comets "Rock Around The Clock" 1954; Bill Haley and his Comets "See You Later Alligator" 1956; The Diamonds "Little Darlin'" 1957; Danny & the Juniors "At The Hop" 1957; Neil Sedaka "Oh Carol"; Del Shannon "Cry Myself to Sleep" 1962; Chris Montez "Let's Dance; Pat Boone "Speedy Gonzales"

When sounds of classic rock still rang up sales registers and registered on pop charts, one of rock's most derivative, "Crocodile Rock," featured Elton John on Farfisa organ and all vocals, as well as falsetto backing vocals, with a vocal interchange very similar to "Speedy Gonzales" by Pat Boone. A 1974 lawsuit filed on behalf of the "Speedy Gonzales" composer resulted in an amicable settlement. Case dismissed.

—

Bloodstone "Natural High" London February 1973

Style: Soul vocal group
Where from: Kansas City, MO
Where recorded: Los Angeles, CA

First known as The Sinceres, the group arriving in Los Angeles became Bloodstone and went straight to the top with this anthem, "Natural High," taken to be an anti-drug theme. While on the charts, "Natural High" was bootlegged on three labels out of L.A., just in case an original couldn't be located, which was absurd as the 45 was wildly over-pressed. These days, gang experts call "Natural High" a Pirus gang fave, probably because of the blood part.

—

Marvin Gaye "Let's Get It On" Tamla June 1973

Style: Soul
Where from: Washington, DC
Where recorded: Detroit, MI
Suggested pairing: Ed Sheeran "Thinking Outloud" 2014.

It is said this was recorded with Bobby Keys on saxophone and a vital bass line by Funk Brothers' member James Jamerson reportedly played while on his back, caused either by illness or a drunken stupor, with a session member holding the sheet music in front of his face, take your pick. A bookend to Marvin Gaye's "What's Goin' On," this much slowed down vocal with percussion, "Let's Get It On" has been invoked by many a gangbanger out looking for trouble. A similar backbeat and melody line was used by Ed Sheeran "Thinking Outloud" in 2014.

—

Redbone "Come & Get Your Love" Epic December 1973

Style: Latin rock
Where from: Salinas, CA
Where recorded: Hollywood, CA

Redbone, a Cajun term for Indian, were Pat Vegas (real name: Pat Vasquez) bass; brother Lolly Vegas, guitar; Anthony "Tony" Bellamy, guitar and Peter DePoe, drums. In his teens, Pat Vegas "had to help mother raise my sisters, young kids, stayed home in Salinas. My brother Lolly went to L.A. to pursue music. I stayed there to help mom. I was there raising them. I was in The Symphonics; our keyboard player, Sir Earnhart, had a classical background, put rock and roll to it. We did classical, with rock. I exploited his classical roots."

Vegas continued, "A contest came to town, Talentsville USA, sponsored by Coca Cola, had big auditions in Salinas, went and we auditioned. We won the whole thing, went to San Jose, played for the finals and won. I won the contest singing 'Red Sails In The Sunset' in Salinas, then sang 'Dream Lover' in San Jose. They offered me a contract with RCA and $25,000. We took the money and ran, split the money with the band.

In 1960, Pat Vegas went to Los Angeles to work with Lolly. He found Lolly working at Sears. "I took him to Hollywood, Richard Podolor's American Recording Studios on Sunset and Argyle. They made us house musicians, worked with Podolor. 'I need you overdub bass on this.' Worked there for ten years for Don and Richie Podolor, we did 20 tracks for $5 apiece."

As a recording artist, Pat Vegas debuted with "I Wanna Be A Movie Star" as Pat Vagas on Lute. More than ten years later, the first Redbone 45, "Crazy Cajun Cakewalk Band," was on the band's Axis label. "Axis was our label; that was instrumental, got us a deal with Epic. Larry Cohn discovered us, he came and saw the group."

"Come & Get Your Love," featuring a prominent part for the electric sitar, and a key opening lyric, "hey hey," came together when Pat Vegas was going to bed. His phone rang, it was his brother Lolly who was working on a new song. Pat gave in and joined his brother to work on the song, which at over five minutes, was too long for release as a single. Hearing it at a show on the Sunset Strip, an Epic A&R man said, "If you can get it to under three minutes, I can make it a top ten." Pat Vegas edited it down and it charted nationally at #5. Several versions of "Come & Get Your Love" were issued in mono for radio play. One version omitted the repeat of the chorus and went right to the ending after the "come and get your love, come and get your love, come and get your love now" with double tracked lead vocals that have more reverb, not the "dry" sound of the common stereo single; the reason it sounded "different" on AM radio is because it was. This was perhaps one of the last mono hit singles; all stock copies were stereo versions.

Sampled: Cyndi Lauper "(Hey Now) Girls Just Want to Have Fun" 1994

—

The Hues Corporation "Rock the Boat" March 1974

Style: Disco
From and recorded in: Los Angeles, CA

"Songwriter Wally Holmes wrote "Rock the Boat" as an extension of "row, row, row your boat," said RCA's John Florenz. Holmes took the material to Florenz and Florenz suggested a rewrite: "Tom Sellers the arranger came up with new musicians, Jim Gordon and two Jazz Crusaders, Joe Sample and Wilton Felder, came in. They took it from a standard 4/4 to a mambo. From a backbeat to that tom tom thing. It became a dance record from a pop record, structuring it so it started with 'I'd like to know' instead of the verse, with instrumental 'ever since love began.'"

Upon release, "Rock the Boat" by The Hues Corporation did nothing, until "a nightclub in New Jersey flipped it, started playing it, somebody at WABC heard it," Florenz added, "went on it almost immediately. 'Rock the Boat' is huge, Wally Holmes came to me, 'You basically have a new co-producer, since I was right on R&B, I'm going to write the material for the whole group.' After the song hit, 'the big Rock the Boat party was on a vessel, The Hues Corporation was opening for the Fifth Dimension, but I wasn't invited."

—

William De Vaughn "Be Thankful For What You Got" Roxbury March 1974

Style: Soul
Where from: Washington, DC
Where recorded: Philadelphia, PA

Salaried government drafting technician and part-time singer, William DeVaughn wrote "A Cadillac Don't Come Easy," re-written as "Be Thankful for What You Got," in 1972. Spending $900 to record at Omega Sound, a Philadelphia production house, the record's producer, John Davis, a member of the MFSB studio session group, came up with a smooth arrangement he recorded at Sigma Sound Studios in Philadelphia, used by Philadelphia International Records. Studio owner and chief engineer Joe Tarsia recorded and mixed the session featuring members of the MFSB group: Davis, keyboards; Norman Harris and Bobby Eli, guitar; Earl Young and Larry Washington, drums and Vince Montana, vibes. Allan Felder developed the separate ad-lib back-up chorus with his sister Nadine's vocal group, Honey & the Bees. Executive producer and co-coordinator Frank Fioravanti secured a deal with Roxbury, a subsidiary of Chelsea Records, run by industry veteran Wes Farrell.

Sampled: N.W.A "Gangsta Gangsta" 1988; Ludacris "Diamond in the Back" 2003; Ice Cube "Stand Tall" 2008

—

Lynyrd Skynyrd "Sweet Home Alabama" MCA April 1974

Style: Rock
Where from: Jacksonville, FL
Where recorded: Muscle Shoals, AL
Answer: Neil Young "Southern Man" 1972

Ronnie Van Zant sang this pissed-off Lynyrd Skynyrd answer, "Sweet Home Alabama," to Neil Young's "Southern Man," and even Young loved it. "I'd rather play 'Sweet Home Alabama' than 'Southern Man' any time," Young said. The admiration was mutual: Van Zant wore a Young T-shirt on the cover of Skynyrd's final album, Street Survivors, and according to legend, he is buried in the shirt.

—

First Class "Beach Baby" UK June 1974

Style: Retro rock
From and recorded in: England

Vocals of the California sand and sun sound of "Beach Baby" by First Class were by Tony Burrows, who had also recorded as Edison Lighthouse on "Love Grows (Where My Rosemary Goes)," The Pipkins' on "Gimme Dat Ding," Brotherhood of Man on "United We Stand," and "My Baby Loves Loving" by White Plains, all in 1970.

—

Patti Smith "Hey Joe" Mer November 1974/Sire 1977

Style: Garage rock
Where from: Chicago, IL
Where recorded: New York
Suggested pairing: Jimi Hendrix "Hey Joe" 1966

With oratorical reading over Lenny Kaye's guitar backing, to wit, Patti says, "Lenny the way you play guitar, makes me feel so masochistic, the way you go down deep in the neck, I would do anything." Then she traveled on to the subject of currently missing

Patty Hearst, "you stand in Symbionese Liberty Army with your legs spread and now that you're on the run, what's in your mind. Do you know what your daddy said Patty, 60 days ago, she was such a lovely child, now there she is there with a gun in her hand."

—

Patti Smith "Piss Factory" Mer 1974/Sire 1977

Style: Garage rock
Where from: Chicago, IL
Where recorded: New York
Suggested pairings: The Isley Brothers "Shout"; Chubby Checker "The Twist"; The Rascals "Mustang Sally"

A B-side of "Hey Joe," "Piss Factory" is spoken word over piano backing, very provocative with lots of pop references to "Mustang Sally," to "Twist" and to "Shout" with a New York street attitude about working life.

—

Freddy Fender "Before the Next Teardrop Falls" Crazy Cajun/ABC-Dot January 1975

Style: Country and western
From and recorded in: Texas

After two regional hits, "Holy One" and "Wasted Days and Wasted Nights," in February 1975, Freddy Fender's first national #1 hit, "Before the Next Teardrop Falls," was a combination of styles, from country and western to Spanish language. "My mother used to tell me, I aimed at everything and hit nothing. If I'd have known Japanese or German, I'd have put it in. Maybe one of them would have hit. This time I was completely under the guidance of a producer. If it had been up to me, I'd have done something else. I was completely unaware of what they were trying to do. They just said, 'Sing it in Spanish and English, put a little Spanish in it, just enough to spice it up and keep it mainly in English.' They did the rest. When I recorded "Before the Next Teardrop Falls," Angelica Maria, a very famous singer out of Mexico, covered me within four days. She tried to take it away, but it didn't work.

Early Fender pressings had title typo, "Teardrdrop" instead of "Teardrop."

—

Sammy Johns "Chevy Van" General Recording Corporation January 1975

Style: Retro rock
Where from: North Carolina
Where recorded: Atlanta, GA and Los Angeles, CA
Suggested pairing: Joe South "Games People Play" 1968

With instrumental backing by Los Angeles-based session musicians from The Wrecking Crew, Sammy Johns relentlessly promoted his "Chevy Van" by radio station visits across the country in, appropriately, a "Chevy Van."

In late 1975, Michael Thevis, owner of the General Recording Corporation label, went to jail.

—

John Lennon "Slippin' and Slidin'" Apple June 2, 1975

Style: Retro rock
Where from: England
Where recorded: New York
Original version: Little Richard 1956

In 1969, when The Beatles hit with "Come Together," a case for infringement was put together by the publisher of "You Can't Catch Me" by Chuck Berry, in which the lyrics "here comes old flat top" originated. Negotiations to settle this lawsuit involved mob-related Roulette label owner Morris Levy. The deal was if John Lennon would record "You Can't Catch Me," then that would amount to a settlement. Lennon recorded the LP, Levy bootlegged rough mixes onto "Roots: John

Lennon Sings The Great Rock and Roll Hits," and made it available through television sale in the USA for three days in January 1975 before Lennon and Apple/EMI pulled it off the market. Apple then rush-released Lennon's "official" version in February 1975.

—

Pete Wingfield "Eighteen with a Bullet" Island July 1975

Style: Retro doo wop
From and recorded In: England

Put together by Mike Vernon who also played percussion, and fronted by singer George Chandler, The Olympic Runners with DeLisle Harper, bass and Glen LeFleur, drums backed Pete Wingfield on "Eighteen with a Bullet," a pastiche doo-wop word play on a hit record, namely a bullet meaning a song moving up the charts. In fact, it did hit #18, with a bullet, and peaked at #15 a week later. In the intervening years, it became the theme song of L.A.'s feared 18th Street gang.

—

War "Low Rider" United Artists August 1975

Style: Soul funk
Where from: Compton, CA, Long Beach, CA, and San Pedro, CA
Where recorded: Hollywood, CA

Lonnie Jordan of War recalled how "Low Rider" came about. "Charles was the one who was singing, inspired lyrically wise, came in with the attitude of the song, the low voice. He had a bottle of tequila and lemon, sat down on a bench at Crystal studios, began to sing with this low voice, we looked at each other, How much has he been drinking?" as War played cruising's best anthem, "Low Rider." The picture sleeve used an image of Miller's own low-rider car, " a 1949 Chevy or '47 Chevy, it was pretty low. The picture was taken at Far Out Studios where Guitar Center is on Sunset Blvd.

"Those were some great times. We started going outside of Compton filming low-rider rival clubs because we were influenced by the In Crowd Car Club, we took that film, and next thing I know the song had been influenced. We were trying to be film producers at the time, we took a Bolex camera and a Niagara sound system into E[ast] L.A. The car clubs were the Dukes and the Imperials. We filmed the different car clubs, took that film on the road with us and used that as a backdrop in England and Germany where people had never seen or heard of low riders."

Later, "Charles Miller was murdered. He had money on him, doing things he shouldn't have been with drugs, he caught a young lady, at least her side of the story, he woke up and she was stealing money, she panicked and started stabbing him."

Remake: Latin Alliance featuring War "Low Rider (On The Boulevard)" 1984

—

East L.A. Car Pool "Like They Say In L.A." General Recording Corporation August 2, 1975

Style: Cha cha
From and recorded in: Los Angeles, CA

Retired judge Jack Gold thought up this project that resulted in "Like They Say In L.A." by East L.A. Car Pool. "I had this idea, to take English and Spanish music. It wasn't disco, it was a cha cha. In that band, drummer and arranger was Mark Levine, a jazz teacher at Berkeley who had played with Cal Tjader; Ray Pizzi, sax player; Jerry Rush, trumpet; Hector Andrade, timbales; Ernie McDaniels, bass" and Gold on congas. "The vocalist was Brooks Honeycut, cute very cute. It was recorded at Wally Heider's on Cahuenga, down the street from Martoni's. I got a deal, they put it out. If it's Latin, it's East L.A., today half the population is Spanish," so it was the East L.A. Car Pool on "Like They Say In L.A."

Gold added, "We hired an indie promo guy, it was all over the place, getting calls all, all the charts. It got play on "A Little Bit Of Heaven" with BMR on KMET, Johnny Magnus, Eric Chase. I got an advance, there was supposed to be an album, had some tracks they were working on. Buzz Wilborn was prexy [label owner and president] of label and he cut me down to a single. Unfortunately, Michael Thevis, the owner of the GRC [General Recording Corporation] label, went to jail."

According to IMDB, "The beginning of the end for Thevis came in 1976, when he was convicted of conspiracy to commit arson, and distribution of obscene materials." After a 1978 jailbreak and recapture, in 1980, Thevis, the "Scarface of Porn," who had once made $100 million a year and owned nearly half of the hardcore porn industry, was convicted of murder while on the lam.

—

Captain & Tennille "The Way I Want To Touch You" Butterscotch Castle/Joyce/A&M 1975

Style: Pop
From and recorded in: Los Angeles, CA

Keyboard player Daryl Dragon and vocalist Toni Tennille were Captain & Tennille who debuted with "The Way I Want To Touch You" backed with "Disney Girls" on their private pressing, Butterscotch Castle. "That was the label they used to press themselves," said Wayne Valot, one-time Nehi Distributing vice president, who presided over the just-established Joyce label. "We had decided we were going to form a label, so many people would come to us, trying to get their record placed. When they went into record stores with finished masters, they were always directed to us.

Valot continued, "'The Way I Want To Touch You' on Butterscotch Castle was selling maybe 200 at Wallichs Music City already," out of purported 500 pressed. "At that point we signed the group to a contract. The act themselves signed it. We pressed about 15 to 20,000 copies" of "The Way I Want To Touch You" backed with "Disney Girls" on Joyce before A&M took over.

"We proved to most of the large record labels, located in the L.A. area, that we had a confirmed hit recording," said Toni. "We then could almost take our pick from varied recording offers that 'magically' came our way. CBS decided to pass, because they said they already had a blonde singer, Chi Coltrane."

"Terry Melcher and I got them a deal with RCA," said Beach Boys member Bruce Johnston, "but RCA backed out after seeing them live, saying they didn't realize they were an older lounge act." Daryl said, "We decided to go with A&M because they said I could produce the first album."

Toni added, "It was perfect. If it was a hit, Daryl could continue to produce all our music. If it failed, A&M would assign us a producer for the second album." A&M reissued "The Way I Want To Touch You" backed with "Disney Girls," but it failed to chart. Then came Captain and Tennille's #1 hit, "Love Will Keep Us Together." After the success of "Love Will Keep Us Together," in both English and in Spanish, Captain & Tennille finally hit with a reissue of their first, "The Way I Want To Touch You," which sold well, starting in Rochester, Oklahoma City, Denver and Philly.

—

Steve Miller "Rock'n Me" Capitol 1976

Style: Rock 'n' roll
Where from: Milwaukee, MI
Where recorded: San Francisco, CA
Suggested pairings: The Clovers "Lovey Dovey" 1954; The Beach Boys "California Girls" 1965; Free "All Right Now" 1970; The Eagles "Take It Easy" 1972

Steve Miller Band's leader Steve Miller acknowledged that elements of "Rock'n Me," particularly the intro, was a tip of the hat to British group Free's "All Right Now." He stated, "Yeah, it's a tack on the wall for Paul Kossoff. I did one concert in the two years that I was off the road. I went to London and played with Pink Floyd. It was a big, huge outdoor show so we needed a big rock and roll number that was really going to excite everybody. I just put it together and didn't think much about it."

Composed for that kind of pop and rock festival atmosphere, the lyrics and vocals of "Rock'n Me" have been labeled as having an 'every man' quality to them. It is sung from the point of view of someone frequently traveling while keeping a positive, upbeat attitude. Locations mentioned in the song include the major cities of Phoenix, Arizona; Tacoma, Washington; Philadelphia, Pennsylvania; Atlanta, Georgia; and Los Angeles, California.

—

Shalamar "Uptown Festival (Part 1/Part 2)" Soul Train March 1977

Style: Disco
Where recorded: Ike and Tina Turner Studios Los Angeles, CA

Session singer Pat Powdrill was one of the key vocalists on "Uptown Festival" by Shalamar. The song was recorded at Ike & Tina Turner's Bolic Sound Studio in East L.A. in the autumn of 1976 and, as a former Ikette and good friend of Ike & Tina's, Pat came to the studio and joined Andrea and Gary Mumford, the other uncredited vocalists, on this million-seller.

Songs excerpted were all Motown originals: "Going to a Go-Go";"I Can't Help Myself;"Uptight (Everything's Alright)";"Stop! In the Name of Love";"It's the Same Old Song";"The Tears of a Clown";"Love Is Like an Itching in My Heart";"This Old Heart of Mine (Is Weak for You)";"Baby Love";"He Was Really Saying Somethin'." Session singer Pat Powdrill did the vocals and recalled at the session, producer Simon Soussan "told us this was a demo for his home use." Soussan then shopped it to various labels, and it was picked up by the Dick Griffey and Don Cornelius label partnership Soul Train. It hit the L.A. R&B charts in spring 1977.

"Uptown Festival" was recorded before the group Shalamar was formed," said later Shalamar lead singer Howard Hewitt. "If the tune starts making some noise, then they'd put the group together. Shalamar was a botanical garden from the Far East."

Hewitt continued, "All this was happening when I was overseas, I got back going to auditions, then I started working with Jeffrey Bowen at Motown, he was dealing with Anita Pointer. We produced [The] Commodores and The Temptations. It started getting a little shaky, checks were shaky. I dropped my girlfriend off at work with Cornelius at Soul Train dance studios, I was at [a] meeting, the phone rings, it's Jeffrey Daniels from Shalamar which was in New York. Jeffrey told me the lead singer Gerald Brown got into a disagreement and left them in New York in the middle of promotional tour. I met Jeffrey at Maverick's Flat. Jeffrey knew my girl worked for Don, he called Don who asked, 'Where are you in the building?' '15th floor.' 'Dick Griffey's on the 9th floor waiting for you.'"

According to Hewitt, Dick made Hewett an offer, "Give me a chance to rectify this with the Motown people, I called the Motown people." Hewett told Griffey, "If you want to rectify this, call me tonight." Saturday, Hewett called Dick, went to his house, "watched a Shalamar video, had me sing him something, 'well Lord me and you.' I got through the first verse and half the hook, he goes upstairs and comes downstairs, brings out $500 cash, handed me [an] airline ticket. 'Catch the redeye and meet the group in New Jersey. You gotta learn to lip synch 'Take Me to the Bank' and do a TV show in Paterson NJ on Monday. I did the Milli Vanilli thing, I'm lip synching a song I didn't even do. Finished out the promotion tour. It was a fly-by-night disco group, musically, it was a synthetic time, you didn't know what was real."

—

Plastic Bertrand "Ca Plane Pour Moi" Sire 1977

Style: Punk rock
From and recorded in: Belgium
Cover: Elton Motello "Jet Boy Jet Girl" 1977

Performer Roger Jouret's, aka Plastic Bertrand's, "Ca Plane Pour Moi," roughly translates as "This Life's for Me." o-written and produced by producer/songwriter Lou Deprijck, who took Plastic Bertrand to a Brussels court saying that he wanted to be recognized as the performing artist as well. He allegedly performed the vocals on the hit because Plastic Bertrand didn't make it to the studio the day they were recording it. With little evidence in support of his claim, since Bertrand had a signed contract and his name on the record-label, the judge fined Deprijck for a "groundless and vexatious" suit.

However, in 2010, Jouret said Deprijck performed the vocals. "I don't mind saying it wasn't my voice," he said. "I wanted to sing but he wouldn't let me into the studio." Bertrand added Deprijck had asked him to "keep his mouth shut in exchange for a percentage of the royalties, promising that he'd let me use my voice on another version, which, of course, he never did. I'm the victim. I wanted to sing but he wouldn't let me into the studio. This is going to dog me till my dying days." Jouret's admission came a day after a linguist appointed by the court concluded Jouret's accent did not match the distinctive twang on the record.

—

Toby Beau "My Angel Baby" RCA March 1978

Style: Retro rock
From and recorded in: Texas

Formed by a group of teenagers from the Rio Grande Valley, Toby Beau—named for a shrimp boat in Port Isabel—moved to San Antonio in the mid- seventies. The group was a country-rock band in the mold of The Eagles, but was signed to RCA mostly because of the easy fifties sound of "My Angel Baby," written by guitarist Danny McKenna and singer Balde Silva.

—

X "We're Desperate" Dangerhouse April 1978

Style: Punk rock
From and recorded in: Los Angeles, CA

Vocalist Exene Cervenka, bassist John Doe, guitarist Billy Zoom and drummer D Bonebrake of the pioneer punk band X recorded "We're Desperate" backed with "Adult Books" on Dangerhouse, a label started by Dave Brown and named after a house on Carondelet Street near Beverly Blvd. in Los Angeles occupied by David Brown and his record collector brother Richard Gibson, who filled the house with vinyl. Dangerhouse came from quarrels between the brothers wanting each other's records and the local kids calling the place "dangerhouse."

In Breakmyface.com, David Brown said, "X provided that rare mix of songwriting, personal charisma and musical expertise. More than any other band, their personalities were evident in their music, and were never even slightly conventional or dull." Test pressings were issued on clear vinyl, creating a hard to find 45 with six known copies. With help from various bands like the Germs and others, this started the L.A. punk scene. X advanced to the Slash label.

—

The Cars "Just What I Needed" Elektra May 29, 1978

Style: Rock
Where from: Boston, MA
Where recorded: AIR Studios, London, England
Suggested pairing: Ohio Express "Yummy Yummy Yummy" 1969

"Ric Ocasek and Ben Orr, who was the original lead singer" of the Cars, said their one-time manager Bruce

Patch, "I did all kinds of recording with them, first although Ric wrote all the music, exact music they did for years nobody was interested in. Originally they were Roger & the Rabbits, worked around Boston, Elliott on guitar, David Robinson on drums and Greg Hawkes on keyboard, then to Cap'n Swing. The first masters they did were as the Cars. Ocasek believed in his music, wouldn't change it." The opening guitar riff of "Just What I Needed" was lifted from the Ohio Express bubblegum hit "Yummy Yummy Yummy," and also features a prominent keyboard riff performed by Greg Hawkes. Patch added, "Boston has always had a great live music scene, [the] largest college market in the U.S. More students than any other area. Even though 9th or 10th in population, it's the 6th largest record and stereo market, the reason for WBCN."

—

Funkadelic "One Nation Under a Groove" Warner Brothers July 1978

Style: Funk
Where from: Washington, DC
Where recorded: United Sound Studio, Detroit, MI
Suggested pairings: LaVern Baker "So High, So Low" 1959; The Temptations "Psychedelic Shack" 1969

A George Clinton production, "One Nation Under a Groove" by Funkadelic portrays dancing as a path to freedom, as opposed to a previous commitment to rock. The opening lyrics, "So low, you can't get under it. So high you can't get over it," echo a mainline gospel theme, as well as LaVern Baker's "So High, So Low" from 1959 and the Temptations' "Psychedelic Shack" from 1969

—

Tierra "Gonna Find Her" MCA/Tody February 2, 1979

Style: Latin soul
From and recorded in: Los Angeles, CA

Tierra was Steve Salas, trombone, percussion; Rudy Salas, guitar; David Torres and Joey Guerra, keyboards; Andre Baeza from El Chicano, percussion; Bobby Navarrete, reeds; Steve Falomir, bass and Philip Madayag, drums. To decipher the 45rpm release schedule of Tierra is to deal with a serpentine series of reissues, new B-sides and even A-sides, mix-and-match labels on the laid-back vocal released first as "Gonna Find Her" on MCA in 1979. "Before we sold it to Boardwalk, we did an MCA single on it," said Rudy Salas. "Then we hooked up with Tody, an indie label, a combination of the names of the guys who financed it, Rudy and Tosh, something like that."

—

The Knack "My Sharona" Capitol June 15, 1979

Style: Rock 'n' roll
From and recorded in: Los Angeles, CA
Suggested pairings: The Miracles "Going to a Go-Go" 1965; The Who "My Generation" 1965; The Spencer Davis Group "Gimme Some Loving" 1967

The Knack debuted with "My Sharona." Lead singer and guitarist of The Knack, Doug Fieger, used the band's other guitarist Berton Averre's riff with lyrics about his own girlfriend, Sharona Alperin, whom he met in Hollywood.

"My Sharona" was an inversion of the signature riff from "Gimme Some Loving" by the Spencer Davis Group. Fieger acknowledged that the tom-tom rhythm is "a rewrite of 'Going to a Go-Go' by Smokey Robinson and the Miracles" while the song's stuttering vocal effect is reminiscent of "My Generation" by The Who from 1965.

Satire: Weird Al "My Bologna" 1979

Rap and Retro

1980s

Rocky Burnette "Tired Of Toein' the Line" EMI February 19, 1980

Style: Retro rock
Where from: Memphis, TN
Where recorded: Hollywood, CA

Rockabilly legend Johnny Burnette's rocker son, Rocky Burnette (real name: Jonathan Burnette; b: Memphis, TN, June 12, 1953) hit big during the era of The Blasters and Stray Cats with this pounder "Tired Of Toein' the Line" as a WBCN, Boston and KORG-FM, Garden Grove pick.

—

War "Don't Let No One Get You Down" LAX June 1980

War keyboard player Lonnie Jordan recalled, "I wrote 'Don't Let No One Get You Down' as a ballad, a slow song, just a piano and vocal thing. I had to leave the house real fast, [this song was] written about me being on a downer, about my first marriage, just went in there and laid the track down, drummer Harold Brown set up the tempo, same chords, just made it faster. Now people come up to me and tell me that song is a big request song, thanks for 'Don't Let No One Get You Down,' someone is in jail or someone has died. I'm honored I can uplift people with that song from that downer."

War's "Don't Let No One Get You Down" was integral to the sound track of prison life and listening, a #1 oft-dedicated song on Art LaBoe's L.A.-based radio show and the cruising LaOnda Bajita, KPFA in Berkeley backed with the original hit side aimed at those who celebrated a major Mexican/American holiday, "Cinco De Mayo", on LAX (02120).

Art LaBoe had a business plan for prison-related material. As he explained it, for every prisoner in California, there are about 20 others who care for each them. That's a potential of about 20 million consumers in California alone, a very good and underserved demographic for advertisers.

—

The Blasters "I'm Shakin'" Slash/Warner Brothers 1982

Style: Retro rock
Where from: Downey, CA
Where recorded: Hollywood, CA
Original version: Little Willie John 1958

The Blasters, created around Downey, CA, vocalist Phil Alvin and his songwriting guitarist brother Dave Alvin, can best be described as roots rockers. They began their recording career with one album, American Music, for Rollin Rock, literally run out of the living room of a San Fernando Valley rockabilly fanatic Rockin' Ronnie Weiser from Italy, who at the same moment also published Rollin' Rock, a magazine that proved his absolute fanaticism.

In 1980, Slash the magazine folded; Slash the label began. "Slash Records was a spin-off. There was a Slash Magazine started by great man, frontier pioneer Claude Bessy Kick Boy Face, who began the label with Bob Biggs and the doorman from Rick's Blues Bar in Santa Monica and few silent partners," said Phil Alvin. The Blasters' first Slash release was a remake of a Little Willie John obscurity from 1958, "I'm Shakin,'" their sole Slash single prior to that label coming under the Warners umbrella. "They probably pressed a single pressing worth five or ten thousand. It's the most syncopated of the 'Fever'ish type songs," said Alvin, "probably the only song in that format that doesn't require you to sing 'Fever.'" "I made them an arm of

Warner Brothers; I made them believe that we couldn't go unless we took Slash. Independent record labels give you the same deal; only thing they do is rob you more blind. I cut the deal in my bedroom; they made a deal a month later. They said they can make me a big star then pay me fairly for my performance. You let them go. What they would invest in [original songs] they would not back. What they [really] invested in was Dave singing a Rudy Toombs song 'I'm Shakin.' 'Marie Marie' was [scheduled to be] the flip side of one of these things. It would've been a hit." In 1982 Slash incorporated into Warner Brothers, then was spun off, bought, sold and revived in about 2003.

—

Ice T "Coldest Rap" Saturn 1983

Style: Rap
Where from: Newark, NJ
Where recorded: Los Angeles, CA

Tracy Marrow arrived in Los Angeles at age 12. At Crenshaw High, he wrote lyrics about Crip gang life. A fan of ex-pimp and black exploitation writer Iceberg Slim, he took the stage name Ice T. With rap barely underway, in 1983, Ice T cut this funk single, "Coldest Rap," with his vocals over the funk B-side, "Cold Wind Madness" by Terry Lewis and Jimmy Jam on Willie Strong's Saturn label, pressed by Macola on Santa Monica Blvd., the former home of the Alco Research & Engineering Pressing Plant.

DJ Greg Mack went on-air at Los Angeles' AM radio, KDAY, in July 1983 to showcase the first live mixing shows on L.A. radio with the legendary Mixmasters at clubs like the Radio and Eve after Dark, with Ice-T, Kid Frost, the Spin Masters and Grandmaster Lonzos' famous World Class Wreckin Cru to dance "The Freak" to synthesized and vocoder uptempo beats and Uncle Jamm parties in the L.A. Sports Arena. Alco advertised on KDAY, offering to press and market 500 12-inch or 7-inch singles for $600, of which Macola's owner Don MacMillan sent several hundred to his distributors and radio stations, and gave about 300 to the acts to take back to the 'hood. "Saturn Records, thirty cheap Sony recorders making bootlegs reel to reel," recalled record distributor/salesman Darryl Stolper. "We'd manipulate record stores. If they'd report our records [sales to labels and makers of record popularity charts], we'd give them 10 free copies. All they had to do is report the records, then we'd buy them back."

—

Johnny "Guitar" Watson "Strike On Computers" Valley Vue 1984

Style: Funk
Suggested pairing: Michael Jackson "Man In the Mirror" (bass line) 1988

Riffing on Pac-Man, Johnny "Guitar" Watson predicted the use of drones ("there is a computer that's connected to the nose of a missile that will seek a target and blow it up anywhere"), unemployment ("regular jobs have become computerized") and a guitar that plays by itself, and called for a "Strike On Computers" backed with the instrumental bed on Valley Vue (769), charting nationally and on L.A. R&B radio.

The bass line was reflected in Michael Jackson's "Man In the Mirror"

—

Los Lobos "La Bamba" Slash June 1987

Style: Latin rock
From and recorded in: Los Angeles, CA
Original version: Ritchie Valens 1959

Los Lobos (The Wolves) was a bilingual Latino East L.A. rock band with guitarists and vocalists David Hidalgo, Louie Pérez and Cesar Rosas; Conrad Lozano, bass from the group Tierra; and Steve Berlin, keyboard. Their rock redo of The Drifters' "Under the Boardwalk" and a redo of The Premiers' hit, "Farmer John" were on [the] NV [label] in 1981. Tied to the movie of the same name, their redo of Ritchie Valens' "La Bamba" shot to #1.

"La Bamba" by Los Lobos was a full circle starting with an original folk song from the Mexican tradition first recorded in the 1940s or before up to the #1 rocking interpretation for the movie, "La Bamba" about Ritchie Valens, who was strongly identified with the song. By combining all of these elements, the folk roots, Valens and the updating in the 1980s, it created a punctuation mark on a rock and roll scene from the 50s to the 80s, which more or less ended the 45 singles era.

The 1980s was also the decade in which most radio stations stopped issuing Top 40 surveys of 45 rpm hits, which had been the tradition since the late 1950s.
In other words, it had to end somewhere, and this is a better place than most.

Index

Made in the USA
Las Vegas, NV
01 May 2024

89371794R10240